The Chinese and the Iron Road

St. Helena Library
1492 Library Lane
St. Helena, CA 94574
(707) 963-5244

ASIAN AMERICA

A series edited by Gordon H. Chang

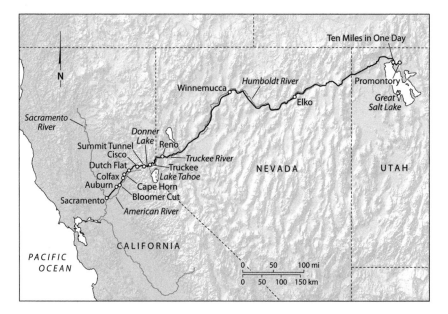

Central Pacific Railroad Line

The Chinese
and the Iron Road

BUILDING THE

TRANSCONTINENTAL

RAILROAD

EDITED BY

Gordon H. Chang and Shelley Fisher Fishkin,
with Hilton Obenzinger and Roland Hsu

STANFORD UNIVERSITY PRESS
STANFORD, CALIFORNIA

Stanford University Press
Stanford, California

Printed in the United States of America on acid-free, archival-quality paper

Library of Congress Cataloging-in-Publication Data
    Names: Chang, Gordon H., editor. | Fishkin, Shelley Fisher, editor. |
Obenzinger, Hilton, contributor. | Hsu, Roland, 1961- contributor.
    Title: The Chinese and the iron road : building the transcontinental
railroad / edited by Gordon H. Chang and Shelley Fisher Fishkin, with
Hilton Obenzinger and Roland Hsu.
    Other titles: Asian America.
    Description: Stanford, California : Stanford University Press, 2019. |
Series: Asian America | Includes bibliographical references and index.
    Identifiers: LCCN 2018037786 | ISBN 9781503608290 (cloth : alk.
paper) | ISBN 9781503609242 (pbk.) | ISBN 9781503609259 (epub)
    Subjects: LCSH: Railroad construction workers—West
(U.S.)—History—19th century. | Foreign workers, Chinese—West
(U.S.)—History—19th century. | Central Pacific Railroad Company—
Employees—History. | China—Emigration and immigration—History—
19th century. | Chinese—West (U.S.)—History—19th century. | West
(U.S.)—History—19th century.
    Classification: LCC HD8039.R3152 C49 2019 | DDC
331.6/251097509034—dc23 LC record available at https://lccn.loc.gov/
2018037786

Cover design: Susan Zucker
Cover photo: China Section Gang Promontory, J. B. Silvis. Denver Public
    Library.
Typeset by BookMatters in 11/14 Garamond Premier Pro

Contents

Maps, Figures, and Tables

Tables

Note on Romanization

It is a challenge to standardize the romanization of Chinese names. We have attempted to use the pinyin system throughout the book. In certain chapters, where appropriate, the names of persons, institutions, and places are romanized in the way that they most frequently appear in historical Western-language documents.

The Chinese and the Iron Road

Introduction

GORDON H. CHANG,

SHELLEY FISHER FISHKIN,

AND HILTON OBENZINGER

The Chinese railroad workers who built America's first transcontinental rail-road and then went on to help build scores of other railroads in North America have been largely invisible on both sides of the Pacific. In *The Chinese and the Iron Road*, scholars based in North America and Asia who are part of Stanford's Chinese Railroad Workers in North America Project deploy trans-national perspectives drawn from a wide range of disciplines to explore the many unanswered questions that we have: Who were these workers? Why did they come? What did they experience? How did they live? What were their spiritual beliefs? What did they do after the railroad was completed? What is their place in cultural memory? *The Chinese and the Iron Road* aims to recover this neglected chapter of the past more fully than ever before.

———

In 1862 with the passage of the Pacific Railway Act, the Central Pacific Rail-road Company (CPRR) was chartered to build the western portion of what became known as the first transcontinental railroad, east from Sacramento. Work began in the fall of 1863. The eastern portion of the line, built by the Union Pacific Railroad Company (UPRR), required laying tracks across vast flat expanses of prairie, but the western portion of the line required cutting through the Sierra Nevada—chipping and blasting deep rock cuts, dumping tons of rocks for fills, carving fifteen separate tunnels through long stretches of solid granite, and constructing trestles across deep canyons. At first, most of the workers on both lines were of European descent, especially Irish. But by the middle of 1864 white workers on the CPRR were abandoning the back-breaking work of railroad building in droves to seek their fortunes elsewhere, including the silver mines of the Comstock Lode. The Central Pacific's president, Leland Stanford, and his fellow owners—Collis Huntington, Charles Crocker, and Mark Hopkins (they called themselves the "Associates" but are often referred to as the Big Four)—faced a crisis: work had stalled with less than fifty miles of the railroad completed. Many at the time thought that the CPRR would not get through the Sierra Nevada, let alone out of California. The dire manpower shortage jeopardized the entire enterprise.

In early 1864 the Central Pacific had decided to try a few dozen Chinese workers from nearby mining communities. By late 1865 Chinese workers composed the vast majority of the labor force on the Central Pacific and numbered in the thousands. As Leland Stanford reported in a letter to US President Andrew Johnson that year, "Without them it would be impossible to complete the western portion of this great national enterprise, within the time required by the Acts of Congress."[1]

Despite their superlative efficiency, endurance, intelligence, and dependability, the Chinese worked longer hours for less pay than their white peers. Historians estimate that they cost the company between one-half and two-thirds of what white workers cost.[2] The line was completed on May 10, 1869, at Promontory Summit, Utah, when Stanford swung his mallet to drive the famous golden spike, setting off a message on the telegraph that went coast to coast: "DONE." The telegraph message launched festivities in cities throughout the country, making the railroad's completion the first national mass media event.[3]

The labor of Chinese workers, who eventually numbered between ten thousand and fifteen thousand at the highest point (and perhaps up to twenty thousand in total over time) made it possible to cross the country in a matter of days instead of months, paved the way for new waves of settlers to come out west, and provided a much less costly way to transport goods across the continent. Their work helped speed America's entry onto the world scene as a modern nation that connected the Atlantic and Pacific Oceans. Their labor also created vast wealth for the CPRR's four principals, including the fortune with which Leland Stanford would found Stanford University some two decades after the railroad's completion. But despite the importance of their work, the Chinese workers themselves are a shadowy presence in much of the written history of the transcontinental railroad.

That many Chinese workers labored on the rail line across the United States is part of American lore, but other than a sentence or paragraph or two in many accounts, little can be found about their actual experiences in either popular writing or academic scholarship. They are given no personality and are presented largely as interchangeable objects acted upon by forces beyond their control. They are not agents of history. The given interpretation of the construction and completion of the transcontinental line is therefore immensely deficient and one-sided. It is usually told as a story of national triumph and achievement, and as the culmination of "manifest destiny," linking the two coasts of North America. It is hailed as a great step in healing the divisive wounds of the Civil War. But the contributions of the Chinese railroad workers, if noted at all, tend to be overshadowed by attention to the Big Four, and are often omitted altogether. These lacunae are in large part a result of the long neglect of the historical role of racial minorities in American history. Yet they also reflect the fact that the recovery of the history of Chinese railroad workers is an immense challenge: there is no extant letter, diary, memoir, or even oral history that tells us something about their lived experience from their point of view. To this day, not one piece of textual evidence from them offering even a glimpse into their experiences has been located. With few exceptions, received histories carry not a single name of a Chinese railroad worker. Given historians' reliance on the written document, it is no wonder that the Chinese railroad workers have remained largely indistinct, a shadowy mass of figures hovering around the edges of our histories but never at the center of the story themselves.[4]

The Chinese Railroad Workers in North America Project at Stanford, from which this book originates, began in 2012 to address this void in historical understanding. It was the first comprehensive effort to recover and interpret the work of the Chinese railroad workers and became the largest effort to study any aspect of nineteenth-century Chinese American history generally. The project's objective was to try to recover as much as possible the history of the lived experience of the Chinese workers themselves. Eventually, more than one hundred scholars in North America and Asia from a wide variety of disciplines, including American studies, anthropology, archaeology, cultural and literary studies, heritage studies, and history, collaborated to locate and study as much primary material as possible. We hoped to locate new textual evidence, in English, Chinese, and other languages, but we understood early in the project that creative intellectual methodologies would be necessary to advance our understanding of the lives of these workers. Given that many other able and dedicated researchers had tried and failed for many decades before us to uncover a hidden cache of textual material, we could not assume that mighty efforts and good fortune would lead us to such a trove.

Doing the research has been challenging. Business records, including those from the Central Pacific archives, are incomplete, scattered in different locations, disorganized, and difficult to decipher. The fragmentary payroll sheets that are extant most often list only the "head men," or labor contractors who provided the actual workers, and not the names of the thousands of workers themselves; and the names that are present are in abbreviated form, not rendered fully or properly. Family oral histories are memories without textual documentation, though some families retain wonderful objects and occasional photographs handed down through the generations from their railroad ancestors.

The lack of textual evidence has been frustrating. Why is there nothing extant? Traditional explanations emphasize the illiteracy of the workers, but we now believe that many were literate, at least at a basic level, that many did send letters and remittances to China, and that many likely kept records and other documentation of their experiences. A writer in *Harper's Bazaar* in 1869 noted that "the Superintendent of the Central Pacific Railroad, after having employed thirteen thousand Chinese, said that he never heard of one who could not read and write in his own language." And in a letter to the Little Rock, Arkansas, *Morning Republican* in September 1869, another writer asserted, "The large number of Chinamen now in the Pacific states, who all or very nearly all read and write, have sent to China, in private letters, a vast amount of information concerning those states and the United States generally."[5]

So why do we not have a single letter from one of these workers? Violence and destruction, rather than their lack of schooling, may be better explanations for why we have nothing from them today: the home areas of the workers in China suffered extensive devastation due to social conflict and war in the nineteenth and twentieth centuries, and every Chinese community in America in the mid- to late nineteenth century suffered arson, looting, and other forms of obliteration. These factors are much more likely to be the reason for the lack of documentation. With the absence of reliable and abundant evidence, silence, myth, and lore have become attached to railroad history. The railroad, romanticized and demonized, elicits much emotion and controversy. We have made an effort to distinguish truth from fiction, even as we honor myth and storytelling as important to understanding the meaning of the Chinese railroad worker experience.

The Chinese Railroad Workers in North America Project has benefited from the digital revolution, which has greatly facilitated our research. An enormous amount of material, including hundreds of newspapers from the nineteenth century, has been digitized, giving us access to an array of sources that previous scholars did not have. Most importantly, the project's interdisciplinary, international, and collaborative approach involving dozens of scholars has produced results far beyond what previous individual efforts were able to yield. The ability to share images, text, comments, and questions electronically greatly facilitated collaboration. The project also benefited from a change in atmosphere: interest in and support for efforts to recover the history of marginalized people have grown significantly.

Archaeologists have over many years collected an enormous amount of material culture that Chinese railroad workers left behind. The Archaeology Network of the Chinese Railroad Workers in North America Project, under the leadership of Stanford archaeologist Barbara Voss, brought scores of scholars together to engage in unprecedented collaboration and in dialogue with scholars from other disciplines. They made fascinating, original contributions that add substantially to what we understand about the daily lives of the workers.

Scholars from other disciplines also made important contributions. Some in the project focused on the literary and cultural production about the workers over the years, visual images and representations, and the stories of workers' descendants in America and China as handed down through families. The project completed almost fifty oral histories with descendants to understand some of the legacies of the railroad workers and what their lives have meant for Chinese Americans. We continue to search for new evidence and materials.

Our effort, however, goes far beyond supplementing the existing narrative, as important as that is. Focusing on the Chinese workers raises basic new scholarly challenges. For one, placing the Chinese in the foreground of the narrative requires us to rethink important contexts and vantage points long dominant in the telling of American history, in particular of the American West. We have stretched the frame of investigation to consider new references, boundaries, and questions. The story of the Chinese railroad workers is necessarily a story of transpacific connections and of the intertwined social, economic, and political histories of nineteenth-century China and the United States. It is a story of the immense Chinese diaspora and of the overseas Chinese. It is also a story of ethnic America and a foundational experience in Asian American history. These different narratives and interpretive contexts all had to be considered to construct a fuller, richer, and more comprehensive understanding of the history. Consequently, our hope is that the project engages and speaks to many important bodies of knowledge beyond those of "the railroad" alone.

It is important to note that the history of these workers has been neglected not only in American scholarship but in Chinese-language historiography as well. Until recently Chinese scholars have not deeply engaged in what is called in the United States "social history." Their focus, rather, has been political history. Imperial and official documents form the vast majority of available currently collected archival material in China. The story of "overseas Chinese" occupied a largely marginal position in the national historical narrative. When told, the bitter experience of laborers who ventured overseas was offered mainly as further evidence of the oppression of the Chinese nation during the long "century of humiliation." Histories of the railroad workers, even those published most recently, draw almost exclusively on American sources used in English-language studies. Our effort has therefore been pioneering in bringing scholars together from the United States, Canada, and Asia to locate new materials and engage in scholarly conversation and collaboration.[6]

The volume in hand is the product of more than six years of concerted individual and collective efforts. Earlier versions of many of the essays included here were first presented in meetings held at Stanford University, Sun Yat-sen University in Guangzhou, and Academia Sinica in Taipei. In addition to this collection of essays, the project is producing digital publications, curricula, exhibitions for the general public, and an open-access digital materials repository hosted by Stanford University Libraries. Although our primary focus is the Chinese workers who built the Central Pacific Railroad, our research expanded to include late nineteenth-century rail lines built in the United States and Canada by the Chinese; in many cases, workers on these later lines were veterans of the Central Pacific.[7]

The following brief narrative of the Chinese railroad workers' experience is provided to help contextualize this volume's essays in temporal terms and highlight important issues and controversies in the existing scholarship.

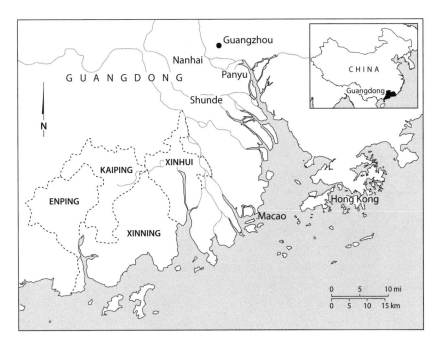

Map of China, Pearl River Delta Region

Laborers from the Pearl River Delta in the southern part of China began to leave the country in large numbers beginning in the 1830s due to the enormous social dislocation and human suffering caused by war, ethnic conflict, and economic privation. The principal home counties of the migrants were the Siyi, or the counties of Xinning (Taishan), Kaiping, Enping, and Xinhui, located near the city of Guangzhou (Canton). These were largely agricultural areas but with active commercial and urban cultures as well. The migrants who left home for work overseas were almost all males and thought of themselves as workers or fortune seekers who went abroad for temporary work with plans to return to their villages. Few thought of themselves as immigrants transplanting themselves permanently elsewhere. While they were overseas, many sent remittances to support their families, and they did return to a significant degree. Their connections to home were deep and abiding and transformed their home villages, even as their labor helped transform worlds far distant from their origins.

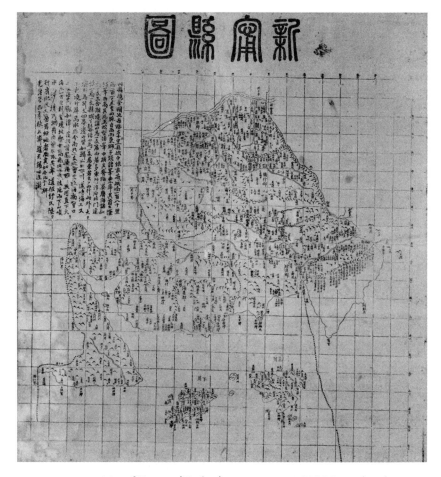

FIGURE 0.1   Map of Xinning (Taishan) region, ca. 1900. U.S. National Archives and Records Administration.

Many of those who traveled to South America and the Caribbean in the 1830s to the 1860s went as indentured labor, as part of the notoriously cruel "coolie trade" characterized by involuntary servitude and mistreatment. Most of those who ventured to North America arrived under different conditions, although they continued to suffer the stigma of being mistakenly seen as "coolies." California became a key destination for them after the discovery of gold in 1848, and Chinese men arrived by the thousands annually from the 1850s through the 1880s largely as free and independent labor, though often burdened by debt for loans used to pay for their travel. Before 1865 they labored principally as mine workers, but also as merchants, fishermen, farmers, laundrymen, and domestic workers. Females fared very differently. Though some arrived as independent migrants or as spouses, many were trafficked and enslaved as prostitutes.[8]

Chinese were involved in railroad construction before the first transcontinental railroad in the United States. For example, they worked in railroad construction in Cuba in the late 1840s and in Panama and then elsewhere in South America in the 1850s. They also were employed as railroad labor in California as early as 1858 in the Sacramento area and two years later in San Jose. The railroad also seems to have captured the imaginations of some Chinese early on, as it had for many others: one Chinese resident of the Sacramento area attracted public attention with his construction of a miniature steam locomotive, no more than twenty inches long, with a functioning furnace and pistons, that rode on a miniature track.[9]

The history of the Chinese who worked on building railroads in North America falls roughly into four periods:

1. 1862 TO MID-1865

In 1862 President Abraham Lincoln signed the Pacific Railway Act, authorizing the recently formed Central Pacific Railroad Company to construct the line eastward from Sacramento, California, and chartering the Union Pacific Railroad Company to build westward from Council Bluffs, Iowa, across the Missouri River from Omaha, Nebraska. The Union Pacific relied on European immigrant labor, especially Irish, Civil War veterans, a small number of African Americans, and a contingent of Mormons, as well as others from the eastern part of the country. In subsequent legislation, the federal government provided prodigious financial support to the two companies in the form of subsidies and land grants. Other funds came from personal investments, bonds, and the sale of stock. In January 1863 the president of the CPRR, Leland Stanford, who was also then governor of California, broke ground for the ambitious project at its starting point in Sacramento.

Because of financial, business, and construction problems, the company did not begin work in earnest until October 1863. The CPRR first tried to use Irish immigrants and other white workers, as Charles Crocker later testified to Congress: "[A]ll our people were prejudiced against Chinese labor.... [T]here was a disposition not to employ them." Nonetheless, in January 1864, as payroll records show, the Central Pacific hired a crew of twenty-one Chinese workers, and more later that year.[10]

In January 1865 James H. Strobridge, the CPRR construction supervisor, placed an advertisement in the *Sacramento Union* and distributed handbills to every post office in the state calling for "5,000 laborers for constant and permanent work; also experienced foremen."[11] Only a few hundred white workers answered the call, and as Charles Crocker recalled later, the workforce "never went much above 800 white laborers with the shovel and the pick." In Strobridge's estimation, the white workers were "unsteady men and unreliable. Some of them would stay a few days, and some would not go to work at all. Some would stay a few days, until pay-day, get a little money, get drunk, and clear out."[12]

The labor shortage compelled the company to turn to the hiring of Chinese. The idea itself may have come from Charles Crocker's brother, E. B. Crocker, a California Supreme Court justice and the CPRR's attorney. James Strobridge initially opposed the idea, believing that Chinese did not have the physical or intellectual capacity to do railroad work. He also feared that whites would not work alongside Chinese. But Crocker convinced him to experiment with a gang of fifty Chinese workers. He later testified, "We tried them on the light work, thinking they would not do for heavy work. Gradually we found that they worked well there, and...put them into the softer cuts, and finally into the rock cuts."[13] When they proved successful, the company added further numbers, assigning them increasingly difficult tasks. They drew workers first from Auburn and other Sierra Nevada mining towns, as well as from Sacramento and San Francisco. Many had worked and lived in California since the early 1850s. Fifty to sixty thousand Chinese lived in California at that time. In March 1865 the railroad began to arrange with Chinese merchants to recruit workers from China, initiating regular traffic in migrants for the railroad across the Pacific. Handbills from the company circulated around the Pearl River delta advertising the opportunities in California.[14]

By the end of July 1865, new migrants, seeking work on the railroad, began to arrive in San Francisco. The Chinese workforce became the mainstay of the CPRR labor force. As governor of California three years earlier, Leland Stanford had railed against the Chinese as undesirable and degraded, calling them "the dregs" of Asia and vowing to work to prevent their immigration.[15] But Stanford the businessman took a different view. As president of the CPRR he praised them in his report to President Johnson in 1865: "As a class they are quiet, peaceable, patient, industrious and economical. Ready and apt to learn all the different kinds of work required in railroad building, they soon become as efficient as white laborers. More prudent and economical, they are contented with less wages." He predicted that the company would soon have fifteen thousand Chinese on its rolls.[16]

Almost the entire CPRR construction workforce was Chinese. They were organized into gangs, led by a "headman" or contractor. Gangs lived together with their own cook and, in many cases, a medical practitioner who attended to illness and injury. Some became specialists in grading, in tunneling, in the use of explosives, in drayage, in masonry, in carpentry, or in track laying. Some brought distinctive labor skills from China; for example, the techniques of masonry they brought from China were used to construct many retaining walls along the railroad route. These structures became famous for their strength and longevity; indeed, many are still standing today. The kind of labor Chinese work crews performed, as well as their ethnic, clan, regional, and political identities, differentiated them.

Sharp ethnic divisions had produced bloody conflict in Guangdong and continued to fester in California. The Punti and Hakka peoples had long histories of animosity toward each other. Guangdong had also been the location of terrible fighting along political lines: some of the Chinese held anti-imperial sentiments, while others were fierce loyalists. But for most non-Chinese, they appeared to be remarkably cohesive and hardworking, ideal laborers for the railroad.[17]

The railroad's acting chief engineer, Samuel S. Montague, wrote the following in his annual report in 1865 about the Chinese:

> Some distrust was at first felt regarding capacity of this class for the service required, but the experiment has proved eminently successful. They are faithful and industrious, and under proper supervision, soon become skillful in the performance of their duties. Many of them are becoming very expert in drilling, blasting, and other departments of rock work.[18]

The Chinese workforce did make remarkable progress in laying the line. They reached Clipper Gap, forty-two miles from Sacramento, on June 10, 1865, and Illinoistown (later known as Colfax), fifty-four miles from Sacramento, on September 4, 1865.[19] In January 1866 Leland Stanford, along with E. H. Miller, the secretary of the CPRR, and Samuel Montague reported to the company's board of directors on the work of the past year. Although the report did not mention the Chinese workers by name, it described the enormous role they played and the conditions under which they labored. It must be appreciated, the officers wrote, that the completed work was nothing less than "the most difficult ever yet surmounted by any railroad in the United States, if not in Europe. It has been a herculean task." "Heavy rock excavations" that should have taken eighteen months to complete had "been pushed through in from four to five months" because of the "great vigor" of the effort.[20]

2. MID-1865 TO MID-1867

In the summer of 1865 construction began on a stretch called Cape Horn (named for the treacherous route through the waters around the tip of South America), which took a year to complete. The stretch had to negotiate "a precipitous, rocky bluff" about 1,200 feet high above the American River east of Colfax, California. The roadbed was to be a ledge that snaked around the rock and that required grading, leveling, and clearing of trees, stumps, rocks, and other obstructions along a slope of "about seventy-five degrees, or nearly perpendicular," as Chief Engineer Samuel Montague described the site.[21]

There are conflicting accounts of how the work was carried out. Some published reports describe Chinese workers hanging over sheer precipices in woven baskets to drill holes in the rock for explosives. Once a worker lit the fuse, he signaled to be drawn up to avoid the blast, knowing that he would lose his life if the basket was not drawn up quickly enough. The powerful image of Chinese laborers perilously hanging off cliffs in baskets to do such hazardous work has captured the imagination of writers and artists ever since.[22] Other sources, however, describe Chinese suspended by ropes tied around a worker's waist or by the use of bosun's chairs. Debate has been vigorous. New evidence located by the project supports the claim that Chinese workers used baskets in the construction effort (although not necessarily at Cape Horn).[23]

In the fall of 1865 Chinese workers embarked on the most daunting of all the challenging jobs they faced on the Central Pacific: the building of fifteen tunnels, most of them at high elevations, through the Sierra Nevada. The length of the tunnels totaled 6,213 feet (1,893 meters). The most difficult tunnel was No. 6, the Summit Tunnel, cut through solid granite, 1,695 feet (516 meters) long and 124 feet (38 meters) below the mountain's surface. Progress was agonizingly slow, with many kegs of black powder used each day. The recently developed explosive nitroglycerine was tremendously powerful but was highly unstable; too unstable to transport, it was mixed on-site by a chemist—but the risk of accidental explosions always remained high. In order to speed up construction, Chinese work gangs dug a vertical shaft seventy-three feet down into the projected center of the tunnel. Work could then proceed in four directions—at both external faces, and from inside out. Workers were let down into the tunnel and lifted out through the central shaft; debris and rock were hoisted out of the tunnel through the central shaft as well.[24]

The company experimented with workers from different backgrounds. At one point, at Summit Tunnel at Donner Pass, the CPRR tried Cornish miners from England, reportedly the best miners in the world. Crocker set up a competition between them and the Chinese, with the Chinese chipping away at the rock in one direction in the shaft and the Cornish miners working in the opposite direction. The Chinese always won. Crocker reported: "We measured the work every Sunday morning, and the Chinamen without fail always outmeasured the Cornish miners; that is to say, they would cut more rock in a week than the Cornish miners did, and there it was hard work, steady pounding on the rock, bone-labor."[25]

Work continued on the Summit and other tunnels through two of the worst winters on record. Chinese workers had to help construct miles of snow sheds and retaining walls to protect the line from the fierce winter storms. Snow from raging blizzards blocked tunnel entrances, and avalanches swept away camps of Chinese workers, carrying many to their deaths. Workers lived in caverns hollowed out below the surface in order to continue to work in the tunnels. When weather conditions inhibited construction work, many were furloughed and lived in towns such as Truckee until spring. When they lived along the construction line, they resided in camps and moved along with the work, leaving material evidence of their existence in the wilderness.

How many Chinese died in the construction of the CPRR? This too is a charged controversy, as the numbers estimated by writers range from a low of fifty to perhaps as many as two thousand. Newspapers occasionally ran articles reporting on deaths, but reports during the construction of the line were inconsistent and irregular. Long after the events took place, writers extrapolated the number of deaths by citing reports of the many thousands of pounds of human remains Chinese collected from around the West that were returned to China for final burial. These accounts, and manifests of ships sailing to China, are evidence that thousands, if not tens of thousands, of Chinese remains made it back to home villages, though the number killed during railroad construction work is impossible to calculate.

The deaths of Chinese railroad workers are most often associated with tragedies during the winter season, when snowslides took many lives. Louis M. Clement, one of the company's main engineers, recalled that "during the winter months there was constant danger from avalanches, and many laborers lost their lives." James Strobridge recounted that the workers had to live and work in tunnels beneath the surface of the immense snowdrifts in the winter. "In many instances," he recalled, "our camps were carried away by snowslides, and men were buried and many of them were not found until the snow melted the next summer." A. P. Partridge, who was on a bridge-building crew, also remembered the treacherous winters, and he too said about the Chinese workers that "a good many were frozen to death" in 1867.[26]

In June 1867 when the company hoped to make rapid progress to make up for lost work during the horrible winter, Chinese workers struck for higher wages and a shorter workday. On June 25 several thousand Chinese in the Sierra Nevada ceased work and stayed in their camps. When they were first hired in 1864, the company paid $26 a month for a six-day work week, with the Chinese paying for their own food, unlike white workers. Chinese workers were paid less than half the amount white workers were paid. In the spring of 1867, the company raised its wages from $31 to $35 a month to try to attract more workers. The striking workers, seeking parity with European American workers, demanded $40 a month, a work day reduced from eleven to ten hours, and shorter shifts digging in the cramped, dangerous tunnels.[27]

The strikers exhibited remarkable organization and discipline. The workers were spread out over several miles of the line in numerous camps, but they managed to communicate closely with one another and coordinate the work stoppage. It was the largest collective labor action in American history to that point. Over several days, strike discipline held firm. As Crocker would later recall, "If there had been that number of white laborers [on strike] . . . it would have been impossible to control them. But this strike of the Chinese was just like Sunday all along the work. These men stayed in their camps. That is, they would come out and walk around, but not a word was said. No violence was perpetrated along the whole line."[28]

Despite the workers' discipline and nonviolent approach, the strike posed a grave threat to Charles Crocker, Leland Stanford, and the other "Associates" who received government subsidies based on the miles of track laid. "The truth is they are getting smart," E. B. Crocker wrote, observing that the Chinese were aware of the scarcity of labor and therefore of their own leverage to bargain. E. B. Crocker and Mark Hopkins considered taking advantage of the newly created Freedmen's Bureau to hire recently freed slaves as strikebreakers. Hopkins reasoned, "A Negro labor force would tend to keep the Chinese steady, as the Chinese have kept the Irishmen quiet." The freedmen never arrived on the CPRR line.[29]

Several days into the strike, Charles Crocker cut off food and other supplies. He, Strobridge, the local sheriff, and a contingent of deputized white men confronted leaders of the workers, insisting that there would be no concessions to the strikers and threatening violence to anyone preventing workers from returning to the job. "I stopped the provisions on them," Crocker later boasted in his testimony to Congress, "stopped the butchers from butchering, and used such coercive measures." The workers split between those who wanted to continue and those who wanted to end the strike. The strike then ended, and although the company did not concede to the specific demands, they learned that the Chinese could not be taken for granted. Crocker also pledged not to dock the pay of the workers for their action. Work resumed, and pay appears to have improved for many of the Chinese workers over the following months.[30]

The company remained overall dependent on Chinese labor. A California newspaper's description of them revealed their value to the company and gave a glimpse into their camp life. The Chinese workers were

> competent and wonderfully effective because [they are] tireless and unremitting in their industry.... They work under the direction of an American foreman. The Chinese board themselves. One of their number is selected in each gang to receive all wages and buy all provisions. They usually pay an American clerk—$1 a month apiece is usual—to see that each gets all he earned and is charged no more than his share of the living expenses. They are paid from $30 to $35 in gold a month, out of which they board themselves. They are credited with having saved about $20 a month. Their workday is from sunrise to sunset, six days in the week. They spend Sunday washing and mending, gambling and smoking, and frequently, old timers will testify, in shrill-toned quarreling.[31]

Their work ranged from basic unskilled tasks, such as moving earth and snow, to highly skilled tasks, such as blacksmithing, carpentry, and drayage. They were cooks, medical practitioners, masons, and loggers. They cleared the roadbed, laid track, handled explosives, bored tunnels, and constructed retaining walls. Virtually all work was done by hand, with hand tools. No power tools or power-driven machinery was used in the construction work.

3. MID-1867 TO MAY 1869

After breaking through the Summit Tunnel in late 1867, construction pushed east of the Sierra Nevada. On May 1, 1868, the completed line ran from Truckee, California, near Lake Tahoe, to Reno, Nevada; a month later, a remaining gap between Cisco and Truckee was closed, and the line ran continuously from Sacramento to Reno. The first eastbound passenger train from Sacramento arrived in Reno on June 18, 1868.

As construction pressed farther eastward, the need for labor continued to be acute. Workers were still arriving directly from China to join their compatriots, who were pressed to lay track as fast as possible. In the summer of 1868, thousands of men worked in the desert, grading hundreds of miles far ahead of the end of the track. Water and ties had to be hauled by train to the end of the track and then by wagon teams across dry stretches of desert to the advance work gangs. Summer heat could reach 120 degrees Fahrenheit/48.9 degrees Celsius, and many workers collapsed. Water was essential, and out of desperation engineers discovered fresh water from springs inside mountains on the flanks of the railroad line, running pipes and building storage tanks along the route. Charles Crocker authorized a hot-season pay raise for all workers, including the Chinese. The railroad progressed through Nevada so rapidly that large campsites of up to five thousand men would have to move frequently to keep up with the pace of construction.[32]

The railroad ran to Winnemucca, 325 miles from Sacramento, on October 1, 1868, then to Elko on February 8, 1869. Both towns became centers of Chinese life and community in Nevada. In the spring observers could see masses of Chinese workers residing in three sprawling camp cities that together contained 275 tents.[33] As construction neared Promontory Summit, workers laid ten miles and fifty-six feet of track in one day on April 28, 1869. The accomplishment was in response to a $10,000 wager Charles Crocker made with Thomas Durant of the Union Pacific that his workers were capable of doing what seemed impossible. A squad of eight Irish rail handlers and an army of several thousand Chinese accomplished the feat. In the end 25,800 ties, 3,520 rails (averaging 560 pounds each), 55,080 spikes, 14,050 bolts, and other materials, weighing a total of 4,462,000 pounds, were laid down. The

San Francisco Bulletin called the effort "the greatest work in tracklaying ever accomplished or conceived by railroad men."[34]

On May 10, 1869, the Central Pacific Railroad met the Union Pacific Railroad at Promontory Summit, Utah, completing the Pacific Railway, as it was called, the key element in the first transcontinental railroad across the United States. A joyful ceremony was held with dignitaries from both companies, along with a military unit on its way to the San Francisco Presidio. Only four years earlier the country had been divided by a bloody civil war; the railroad that bound the East Coast to the West was hailed as an emblem of both unity and progress. At the same time, American Indian tribes were decimated, their lands stolen and cultures undermined, particularly during the construction of the Union Pacific Railroad through the Great Plains.

Thousands of Chinese had been central to the construction of the CPRR, but by the time of the ceremony that celebrated this construction accomplishment, almost all of the Chinese and other workers had been either dismissed or moved back west along the line to repair the work, leaving only a few to do the grading, laying of ties, and driving of the last spikes.

In Andrew Russell's iconic photo of the event at Promontory, *East and West Shaking Hands at Laying Last Rail*, it seems that Chinese do not appear in the crowd (see figure 12.10 in chapter 12). With locomotives from each railroad facing each other, their cowcatchers almost touching, men are lined up on each side to mark the moment as two engineers lean with bottles between the smokestacks for a toast. There may be one or two Chinese in baggy and patched work clothes worn by the workers laying the last track in the scene; yet, oddly, one worker has his back turned to the camera, although no one else stands with his back turned. Next to him there may be another man, similarly dressed, facing the camera, but a white man next to him has his arm extended holding up his hat. People had to hold their poses for a long time to take photos in those days, so it's odd that this man holds his hat very deliberately to hide the face of the person standing next to him. No one else is the target of a similar gesture or prank. Another photograph by Russell, less famous but most informative, taken minutes before his iconic one shows Chinese workers completing the final work to link the two lines. Eyewitness accounts confirm that it was the Chinese who laid the last rail of the transcontinental railroad.[35]

Although mostly absent from public recognition in 1869, however, Chinese workers were not entirely forgotten. One newspaper reported that, after the ceremonies, Strobridge "invited the Chinese who had been brought over from

Victory [a work camp] for that purpose, to dine at his boarding car. When they entered, all the guests and officers present cheered them as the chosen representatives of the race which have greatly helped to build the road...a tribute they well deserved and which evidently gave them much pleasure." And during the festivities in Sacramento, E. B. Crocker paid tribute specifically to the Chinese in his speech: "I wish to call to your minds that the early completion of this railroad we have built has been in large measure due to that poor, despised class of laborers called the Chinese, to the fidelity and industry they have shown."[36]

4. JUNE 1869 THROUGH 1889

After completion of the Central Pacific, some workers returned to China, where they eventually helped construct railroads there. Others went to work in agriculture, mining, and building levees along the rivers; or they entered domestic service or worked in manufacturing to produce cigars and other products. Some continued to work for the Central Pacific to upgrade the hasty, often makeshift construction, and later to work on maintaining the line. Others went to work on the Union Pacific. Chinese veterans of the Central Pacific, along with additional compatriots newly arrived from China, also helped build scores of other railroads throughout the United States and Canada during this period, a time in which the rail mileage of the country more than tripled. Their work continued well into the twentieth century.[37]

In 1869 the newly founded periodical *Scientific American*, along with dozens of other publications, ran one of the most striking appreciations of the Chinese in an article, "The Chinaman as a Railroad Builder." It reads in part:

> It is a significant fact...that at the laying of the last rail on the Pacific Railroad, John Chinaman occupied a prominent position. He it was who commenced, and he it was who finished the great work; and but for his skill and industry, the Central Pacific Railroad might not now have been carried eastward of the Sierras. The experience of this undertaking has proved that the Chinaman is an admirable railroad builder. His labor is cheap, his temper is good, his disposition is docile, his industry is unflagging, his strength and endurance are wonderful, and his mechanical skill is remarkable.
>
> The Chinaman is a born railroad builder, and as such he is destined to be most useful to California, and indeed, to the whole Pacific slope.[38]

After the completion of the line and the noise of the celebrations quieted, however, the erasure of the recognition of the Chinese work on the line in historical understanding began. Judge Nathaniel Bennett, the key speaker at the celebration in San Francisco, at great and ebullient length hailed the "Californians" who built the railroad. They were "composed of the right materials, [and] derived from proper origins," he said. "In the veins of our people flows the commingled blood of the four greatest nationalities of modern days. The impetuous daring and dash of the French, the philosophical and sturdy spirit of the German, the unflinching solidity of the English, and the light-hearted impetuosity of the Irish, have all contributed each its appropriate share."[39] The Irish, who composed the bulk of the workers of the UPRR and about 10 percent of those on the CPRR, managed to be part of this blend, but Chinese blood had not commingled in those metaphoric veins.

Journalist Samuel Bowles observed in 1869 in his book *Our New West* that although not all Americans might see the transcontinental railroad's "rails, or ride in its trains, they will feel its influence, and be more content and richer in their lives. It puts the great sections of the Nation into sympathy and unity; it marries the Atlantic and the Pacific; it destroys disunion.... It determines the future of America, as the first nation of the world, in commerce, in government, in intellectual and moral supremacy." Praising the vision, capital, and engineering skills of the leaders who "built" the transcontinental railroad, Bowles averred that the railroad was a distinctively American achievement, one that was "daring in conception" and "bold in execution beyond any other nation." Calling the transcontinental railroad "a triumph of the American people," Bowles declared that "no other people than ours" could have done it.[40]

While many had praised the Chinese for their work ethic and contributions to the country, others attacked the Chinese as racial inferiors and a competitive threat to white working people. Long stigmatized and persecuted in the American West, the Chinese faced even more threats after the completion of the line. A violent, virulent campaign arose to expel them from the country and culminated in 1882 with the passage of the first of many Chinese restriction, and then exclusion, acts that aimed to deny them the possibility of citizenship and even entry into the country. They were deemed social and political undesirables and suffered extreme racist violence, and they were pushed to the margins of public memory and historical scholarship.

On May 10, 1969, US Transportation Secretary John Volpe delivered the major oration at the centennial commemoration of the joining of the Central Pacific and the Union Pacific at the Golden Spike ceremony at Promontory Summit. In tones that echoed the comments of Judge Bennett and Samuel Bowles a hundred years earlier, he omitted any mention of the Chinese. As a *San Francisco Chronicle* reporter wrote:

> Secretary Volpe, the principal orator, succeeded in infuriating the Chinese delegation from San Francisco by wholly ignoring the 12,000 Chinese who helped build the Central Pacific over the Sierra to Promontory.
>
> "Who else but Americans could drill ten tunnels in mountains 30 feet deep in snow?," asked Volpe, speaking in a flat, nasal Bostonian accent.
>
> "Who else but Americans could chisel through miles of solid granite? Who else but Americans could have laid ten miles of track in 12 hours?"
>
> Sitting in angry silence at the rear of the bunting-draped platform were Philip P. Choy, chairman of the Chinese Historical Society of America, and his colleague from San Francisco, Thomas W. Chinn, founder and executive director of the society,... [who] were well aware that none of the Chinese railroad workers were Americans. In fact, foreign-born Chinese were barred for years from becoming Americans.[41]

The Chinese and the Iron Road seeks to ensure that the Chinese role in building the transcontinental railroad is never again forgotten or diminished but understood as a major episode in the history of the modern world.[42]

Essays in This Volume

The chapters that compose this volume of scholarship are the product of several years of collaboration, including conferences where preliminary versions were presented. They address many, but certainly not all, major questions and controversies in the history of Chinese railroad workers in North America, especially on the first transcontinental line, that have confronted scholars and the interested public for many years. They reflect the project's early recognition that recovering this history required taking international and multidisciplinary methodological approaches. We believe that the chapters taken as a collection reveal the rich potential of collaborative and innovative research that goes beyond traditional disciplinary boundaries. We also acknowledge that much more work needs to be done and that important questions about the Chinese workers, such as their relationship with the Irish, the business and economic implications of their work, their social organization and work systems, and the legacies of their experiences on the line, remain to be addressed more fully.

The volume begins in part 1 with chapter 1 from Gordon H. Chang and chapter 2 from Evelyn Hu-Dehart that place Chinese railroad workers' history in global and transnational perspectives. The workers' experiences were never bounded by nation but were inextricably linked to the histories of a score of countries and regions. Moreover, the significance of these experiences goes far beyond what is usually included in a national narrative, whether it be that of the United States or China. The railroad workers were part and parcel of an immense diasporic movement out of southern China, and their experience is intimately linked to questions of ancestral homeland, social identity, and international systems of labor migration. A comparative, transnational approach also helps address the basic and elusive challenge of identifying those who came to work on the railroad and their social backgrounds.

In part 2 we explore the social, cultural, family, and economic ties that bound the workers closely to their ancestral villages and shaped their behavior in a myriad of ways. Through their return migration and remittances, the workers also dramatically influenced the physical and social realities of their villages in profound and lasting ways. The southern China villages from which the workers came are still known today as "railroad villages." Essays by scholars from China—chapter 3 by Zhang Guoxiong, chapter 4 by Yuan Ding, and chapter 5 by Liu Jin—examine the cultural and economic dimensions of these home village ties. Working with a far from robust evidentiary base, each scholar creatively examines rare evidence to identify specific features of these ties and considers their significance from regional and national perspectives. Few Chinese females were among the railroad workers in North America, but the women's strong familial and spousal ties to the men who traveled overseas are an integral part of the story, as these chapters demonstrate.

The study of the material culture, and even physical remains, of the railroad workers has provided substantial insights into the workers' lived experience and is the subject of part 3. Although we have no texts from their own hands, the railroad workers left behind tens of thousands of objects that are invaluable sources of information. Barbara Voss, the director of the Archaeology Network of the project, explicates the methodologies of archaeology in the context of our project and the meanings archaeologists are gleaning from the found material. Until now, historical accounts of the railroad workers have not considered the evidence located and interpreted by archaeologists.[43] Chapters 6 and 7 by Voss, chapter 8 by Kelly J. Dixon, and chapter 9 by J. Ryan Kennedy, Sarah Heffner, Virginia Popper, Ryan P. Harrod, and John J. Crandall provide fascinating insight into the lives of the workers as actually lived based on the material culture that has been assembled from their work sites and camps along railroad lines in North America. These chapters help us understand their relationship to their physical environments, the textures and patterns of daily existence, their foodways and health maintenance, their leisure activities, their death and burial customs, and more.

Kathryn Gin Lum in chapter 10 and Hsinya Huang in chapter 11 consider other important dimensions of lived experience. Lum studies the religious, or spiritual, dimension that occupied a preeminent place in Chinese life, as well as how non-Chinese in America viewed Chinese practices. The Chinese held closely to their traditional beliefs, being far from home in a fraught environment. The Chinese also encountered Native Americans, groups often linked to them in the minds of many Americans as similar nonwhite, heathen others. Huang explores actual connections between the Chinese and the Native peoples they encountered, an important social interaction that earlier scholarship also neglected.

Denise Khor in chapter 12 and Greg Robinson in chapter 13 explore contemporaneous representations of railroad workers in photography and travelogue in fresh ways. Khor studies the rich yet elusive history of photographic imagery of the railroad and the Chinese both in and out of the frame. She deepens our understanding of these images and what they can say, but also what they omit. Though the Chinese were never the principal subjects of any of the photography, the images nevertheless provide intriguing visual perspective on the people under study and their work environment. Robinson examines previously ignored European eyewitness descriptions of the Pacific Railway and Chinese work on the line. From a vantage point uninflected by American historical and racial sensibilities, these visitors sometimes saw the Chinese in ways that were surprisingly different from those of the whites here. Robinson opens new avenues for future investigation into European sources on the railroad.

In part 4, chapter 14 by William Gow, chapter 15 by Yuan Shu, and chapter 16 by Pin-chia Feng examine writings beyond traditional railroad accounts to consider the ways that important reading audiences have interpreted the experience of the Chinese railroad worker. Gow studies the ways this history has been presented in American history school textbooks and reveals that the telling of the history has been inextricably connected to key issues in American history beyond the railroad itself. The Chinese railroad worker as historical figure was never stable. Shu's study of the Chinese railroad workers in Chinese histories and literatures also reveals that the history has been equally unstable, or even more unstable, in China since the Chinese Revolution in 1949. What has distinguished accounts published in China has not been the evidentiary base—Chinese writers have relied almost entirely on English-language sources—but rather the interpretive framework and conclusions, which have shifted through different political contexts. Pin-chia Feng highlights the perspectives on the railroad workers that emerge in the work of two prominent Chinese Americans writers, Laurence Yep and Frank Chin, who, along with Maxine Hong Kingston, have helped make the history of Chinese railroad workers known to the general public, characterizing them as central to Chinese American cultural and social identity.[44]

In part 5, chapter 17 by Shelley Fisher Fishkin, chapter 18 by Zhongping Chen, chapter 19 by Sue Fawn Chung, and chapter 20 by Beth Lew-Williams move the focus beyond the work on the first transcontinental railroad. Promontory Summit was in many ways just the beginning of the story for many of the railroad workers and other Chinese associated with them. Thousands of them continued to work on rail lines throughout the United States during the two decades that followed. The existence of these workers has been largely ignored in other historical accounts. Fishkin's richly documented essay opens up a new dimension of the Chinese contribution to building America's infrastructure as well as their lived experiences far beyond the West. Many of the workers also went north to labor on the Canadian transcontinental railroad—the Chinese experience there being better known and honored by Canadians than that in the United States. Chen's detailed account of the construction experience in Canada provides a valuable comparative perspective on labor organization, politics, and community life, and points the way for similar studies of Chinese communities in the United States.

Chung studies two important but long overlooked Chinese communities in Nevada, Winnemucca and Elko, and Lew-Williams presents a thoughtful treatment of Chin Gee Hee, a onetime railroad worker in the Pacific Northwest and one of the most famous nineteenth-century Chinese Americans. These two accounts expand our understanding of the world of Chinese railroad workers temporally as well as spatially. For some Chinese, railroad work remained their life's activity, while for others, it was a moment in time, but indelible. Chung's study of Chinese railroad workers and their Nevada communities shows them as deeply embedded in the landscape of the American West. Lew-Williams's essay on Chin provides a view of the lived experience of one of the few Chinese of the nineteenth century whose life we can document with some detail.

Gordon H. Chang's concluding chapter 21 provides a double frame, so to speak, to end the book: the fraught relationship of the Chinese to Leland Stanford, president of the CPRR, is a telling dimension of railroad history but is also emblematic of the place of the Chinese in nineteenth-century American history more broadly.

PART ONE

Global Perspectives

Chinese Railroad Workers and the US Transcontinental Railroad in Global Perspective

GORDON H. CHANG

Historical recovery is a matter of scholarly judgment and choice. Subject and interpretation, obviously, but also time and periodization, context, scale, and scope are all the historian's decision and not given by any divinity. The received history of the construction of the first transcontinental railroad across North America is a result of a writer's prerogative.

In the United States, the story of the transcontinental railroad is usually rendered within the parameters of the grand rise of the American nation. That has been the context chosen by the great majority of historians of the railroad. Begun in 1862 and completed in 1869, the first transcontinental line is cele-brated in mainstream American life as well as in scholarship as one of the sig-nal episodes of national life, elevated by some even to the level of importance of the Declaration of Independence. The railroad is honored as a "marvel" of *American* engineering and energy, as a "work of giants." It is presented as a physical and metaphoric bind that united the nation politically, economically, and socially. Linked to the recent end of the Civil War, the completion of the first transcontinental railroad is presented as a heroic contribution in over-coming the bloody division and in healing national wounds.[1]

Much is omitted from, or underplayed in, this grand narrative, and there are historians who are critical of the triumphal and celebratory account. They emphasize the terrible toll on the construction workers of all backgrounds, the invasion and violent subjugation of native peoples, and the corrupt business practices of the railroad magnates in obtaining public funds to finance the project to enrich themselves at the expense of the civic good. But even these critiques are contained by narratives of national history.[2]

These accounts have been so powerfully resonant with prevailing attitudes and perspectives that they have overshadowed, even displaced, the immense international dimensions of the line. Appreciating these dimensions can lead to a vast broadening of the interpretive vision, and the railroad story can take on a very different light.

What are some of these international dimensions?

There are many: flows of international capital helped finance the construction of the line, and workers with origins in Ireland, continental Europe, Asia, and Africa contributed their blood and sweat. These people had rich histories of labor rhythms, diverse cultures, and unique skills that need to be understood and appreciated.[3]

The massive construction project also captured the imaginations of people around the world at the time. Journalists and writers traveled from Europe to witness this gigantic construction effort with their own eyes. Their published accounts in different languages helped change the way that millions of people thought about the very world itself.

Expansive thinkers in faraway settings assessed the impact of the anticipated rail line. Karl Marx considered the international implications of forming the rail connection and industrializing the New World.[4] Jules Verne produced one of the most influential pieces of literature inspired by the completion of the transcontinental railroad. The idea for his classic novel *Around the World in Eighty Days,* which was published in 1873 and made into a Hollywood movie in 1956, originated in a Paris café when Verne read about the completion, in the same year, of the rail line and the Suez Canal that connected the Mediterranean Sea and Red Sea.

Verne understood the transformative possibilities these construction projects offered for travel and the human imagination. In Verne's captivating story, an Englishman shows that the globe could be circumnavigated in less than three months, an astonishing feat at the time and one made possible especially by the two grand construction projects. Verne's story is one of the first explicit expressions of a global vision of travel, a view that offered the world for the first time within the reach of an unexceptional person (at least a bourgeois Westerner), and not just a daring explorer or ambitious official.[5]

The development of the steam locomotive and the spread of rail lines, first in the 1830s in England, then in continental Europe and the United States, fundamentally altered the human relationship with space and time, and thus human life itself. Geography was compressed, which enormously expanded the proximate for the traveler, the businessman and merchant, and the geopolitical strategist. With the advent of the speed and power of mechanical travel using the powerful steam engine, the sense of time, the ordering of life, and the possibilities of human reach quickened and expanded in previously unimaginable ways. The US Pacific Railway, which is what the eighteen-hundred-mile western portion of the transcontinental line was called, was the first truly large-scale rail construction project. Its scale and completion astonished the world, and, as contemporary announcements of the completion of the railroad declared, the transcontinental railroad "revolutionized" the "travel and traffic of the world."[6] The Reverend John Todd, who delivered the dedication prayer at the completion ceremony at Promontory Summit, Utah, later proclaimed, "China is our neighbor now. The East and the West embrace; nay, we hardly know which is East or which is West. This one road has turned the world round."[7]

=====

Two features establish the first transcontinental railroad's indelible and fundamental link with China. The first is the place of China in the ambition that inspired the very idea of the line itself. The line reflected an early global, not just continental, American vision of commercial and civilizational connection with China, and more generally with the Pacific. The second is that mass labor migration from China was essential to the construction of the line and other railroad projects geographically and temporally far beyond the transcontinental line. The physical presence and productive efforts of Chinese laborers connected America and Asia in a web of mental, emotional, and physical strands.

The transcontinental railroad was the realization of a long-standing vision that appeared in 1840s America. More than a national or even continental business venture, the inspiration for the building of the line was trans-Pacific. Take, for example, the ideas of the most prominent early promoter of the building of the transcontinental railroad, Asa Whitney, a relative of Eli Whitney of cotton gin fame. Asa Whitney lived in China in the 1840s and enriched himself in the lucrative China trade. After he returned to the United States, and for much of the rest of his life, he campaigned for the construction of a rail line that would cross the three-thousand-mile-wide continent. His most powerful argument in favor of the huge project drew not from accounting calculations but from a dramatic historical imagination that bordered on the millennialist.

In 1849 Whitney argued for the project with language such as this:

> The change of the route for the commerce with Asia has, since before the time of Solomon even, changed the destinies of Empires and States. It has, and does to this day control the world. Its march has always been westward, and can never go back to its old routes.... Through us [the United States] must be the route to Asia, and the change to our continent will be the last, the final change.[8]

America, Whitney declared, would be the literal, physical link of the West (the United States and Europe) to the East (China and Asia). The realization of America's providential destiny as a great nation, he maintained, required the building of this line. Whitney won thousands of prominent supporters across the country for his project, and for years they pressed Congress to back the visionary idea. It is said that a young Leland Stanford, later the president of the Central Pacific Railroad (CPRR) that constructed the western half of the transcontinental line, heard Whitney expound on his vision to Stanford's father.[9]

One of Whitney's supporters was John C. Frémont, famed explorer, merchant, and the first presidential candidate of the newly formed Republican Party. In 1854 Frémont declared, echoing Whitney, that "America will be between Asia and Europe—the golden vein which runs through the history of the world will follow the track to San Francisco, and the Asiatic trade will finally fall into its last and permanent road."[10]

The engraving on the legendary Golden Spike (or Last Spike), which ceremonially completed the line when the Central Pacific and Union Pacific Railroad Companies met head to head at Promontory Summit, Utah, captures this interplay between the national and international contexts. On May 10, 1869, Leland Stanford, presiding over a gathering of some three thousand dignitaries, railroad officials, workers, and hangers-on, tapped an eighteen-carat gold spike into the last tie. After he was done with his light labor, Chinese workers, who had laid the actual last rails to the meeting site, replaced the ceremonial spike with a regular iron one. Inscribed on the gold one is "May God continue the unity of our Country." Following these frequently quoted words that highlight the national story are others that point to the grander vision. The engraving continues, "The Railroad unites the two great Oceans of the world."

Celebratory speeches repeatedly emphasized how the line connected the West with the Far East.

Railroad supporters boasted that the transcontinental line, in the "advance of civilization," ranked "with the landing of the Pilgrims" or the "voyage of Columbus."[11] The well-known economist Henry George wondered whether the transcontinental railroad would one day elevate San Francisco to the level of the "first city," not just of the continent but of the entire world. It would surpass the importance of the great cities of Europe, of Constantinople, and of New York City, he grandly predicted. These characterizations proved to be hyperbole and widely off the mark, but they nevertheless reflected the extraordinary enthusiasm for the project and its perceived global importance.[12] Leland Stanford himself referenced the then-popular cultural phenomenon of the "Siamese twins" to declare that the transcontinental line, along with a steamship system that linked North America to Asia, formed the "ligament" "that binds the Eastern Eng and Western Chang together."[13] Stanford's close business partner, Collis P. Huntington, once suggested that California would be all the better if a half million more Chinese came over and entered the state in 1868. Newspapers reported that at the very moment of the driving of the last spike, a shipment of tea from China started eastward on the line, inaugurating the hoped-for global trade for America. That had been the animating dream, not just the opening of the resources of the US West that inspired the building of the transcontinental railroad.[14]

Another keen observer of the construction of the railroad and its international implications was Daniel Cleveland, a young attorney who had recently arrived in California from the East. He later settled in San Diego, where he made his name and fortune and is honored today as one of the city's early leaders. In 1869 the significant presence of Chinese in Northern California so fascinated him that he was moved to share what he was witnessing with others in the country. Cleveland confidentially sent his thoughts to Washington officials and also completed a four-hundred-page study on the Chinese in California meant for the general public. Although it was never published, it contains unique firsthand observations on the Chinese and includes an entire chapter on Chinese railroad workers. Completed sometime in early 1869, it is the earliest known extended report on the Chinese involved in railroad construction. Cleveland describes the Chinese as workers, their ways of life, habits, appearance, and enormous contributions to California's economy. He saluted their presence in California in most enthusiastic terms.

Cleveland himself explicitly placed the transcontinental railroad in a global context:

> It is a singular circumstance, that the Chinese...should be constructing one half of the great trans-continental railroad, one of the most wonderful of the progressive achievements of this marvelous age. The two races of workmen on this road are rapidly approaching each other from the two great oceans, and will soon meet and connect [their] work. China and the United States will then strike hands, and feel more nearly drawn together in sympathy and interest than ever before. It is very appropriate that the people of the two mightiest nations of their respective continents should unite in the construction of this world's highway. May it draw and keep them close together, not only in commerce and interest, but in kindly sympathy and good offices.[15]

A New York newspaper expressed similar sentiments in its report on the laying of the last rail: "At Promontory Point, the Asiatic with his pick confronted the European with his, and the two civilizations looked into each other's eyes. There they met hand to hand. The one could point to all the Eastern half of the United States and all of Europe...the other had behind him the great wall of China."[16]

Soon after the transcontinental railroad was completed, a group of wealthy Bostonians traveled cross-country to San Francisco by train. According to a news report, they gathered in a solemn ceremony at the Golden Gate, where San Francisco Bay meets the Pacific. There they opened a bottle of water from the Atlantic that they had brought with them. They poured half of it into the cold surf. They then filled it back up, mixing the Atlantic water with that from the Pacific. Great cheering and celebration broke out, and reportedly some were amazed that the two waters mixed easily without problem—there was no clouding or violent chemical reaction. Then the group broke out in a rousing rendition of the song "America." The next day a young girl in the party was baptized with the mixed water, making her what one might call perhaps the first "global soul," anointed with the waters of the two great oceans of the world.[17] The story, taken quite seriously at the time, reminds us of how the railroad helped change fundamentally the way people thought about the world and themselves, and how the Chinese workers, thousands of miles away from their own homes, facilitated the transformation.

═══

Resources that originated far from the construction sites in the Sierra Nevada and the western deserts were required to complete the railroad. Most importantly, for the western half of the line the essential resource was the labor of thousands of workers from distant China. Their physical presence was the most dramatic manifestation of the globalized nature of the railroad construction project. Western expansion into Asia and Africa, European and American industrialization, and the explosive growth of market economies in the nineteenth century produced human movement unprecedented in scale, pace, and scope. Humans have always been migrant and mobile, but mechanized land and water transportation enabled large numbers of people to move relatively quickly and easily to destinations near and far.

Beginning in early 1864 and continuing until the laying of the last rail in May 1869, the CPRR employed directly, and indirectly through contractors, thousands of Chinese workers, up to ten thousand to twelve thousand at the high point. Some estimates place the total number of Chinese who worked on the line at more than twenty thousand due to turnover.[18] The workers formed what was likely the single largest workforce in a private enterprise in the United States until the late nineteenth century. Contemporary observers frequently expressed amazement at their sheer numbers. Hundreds labored simultaneously at different sites. Only a handful of the Chinese were citizens of the United States because federal law denied them naturalized citizenship. This alien workforce helped make possible a project celebrated as a national accomplishment.

The CPRR first hired Chinese who were already in California, having arrived in significant numbers in the early 1850s for work in mining and other sectors throughout the American West. The company later turned to recruiting labor directly from China. It advertised in newspapers and sent agents to China.[19] But Chinese had actually begun working on railroads in the New World as early as 1854, when the New York–based Panama Railway Company brought a thousand laborers from southern China to Panama to construct a trans-isthmus line. When the project failed because of ghastly working conditions—50 percent of the Chinese died from accidents, disease, and suicide—the railroad company sent the survivors to Jamaica and possibly some to California.[20] Those who were moved may have joined compatriots who were working on rail lines in the 1850s and early 1860s near Sacramento and San Jose. Chinese also joined the effort to construct the San Jose–San Francisco line, today the oldest continuously operated route in the West.[21]

These railroad workers formed part of a larger stream of a globalized workers from China. From the 1830s through the early twentieth century, hundreds of thousands of Chinese left their homeland and joined construction, mining, and plantation projects throughout Southeast Asia, the Pacific, North and South America, and the Caribbean. They formed part of one of the greatest human migrations in modern history.[22] Their migration to the United States and elsewhere was a "revolution," according to a British observer, who said that its importance to world history will be greater than the "intrigues and machinations of crowned heads of wily politicians."[23]

Although many who went to Cuba and Peru endured the semislave, "coolie" trade—a system of coerced, indentured labor—the Chinese workers who came to the United States were largely free and voluntary laborers, as many observers at the time repeatedly verified. US officials in Hong Kong reportedly confirmed the voluntary nature of the contracts signed by the Chinese and determined they were consistent with federal anticoolie legislation. In contrast, many Chinese women, if they did not arrive as the wives of merchants, came into the country as bound prostitutes.[24]

Almost all the migrants were male. Most came from the Pearl River delta in southern China, where the colonies of Portuguese Macao and British Hong Kong were located. This massive migration transformed the entire region and linked it to the rest of the world. The early commercial and social histories and identities of Macao and Hong Kong as transit, processing, and embarkation sites are rooted in this system of out-migration and transpacific trade.[25]

The Chinese were differentiated by class and work responsibilities: they were unskilled and skilled workers, cooks, doctors, and contractors/business agents. Many, if not most, appear to have received some education, perhaps through village and foreign missionary schools in the Guangzhou region. They were connected to other Chinese around the American West and in China who acted as provisioners, farmers and suppliers of food, and agents of various sorts. They formed part of a well-organized network of fellow Chinese involved with the recruitment, transport, and well-being of the workers. Non-Chinese observers at the time noted this well-organized transpacific network and its economic significance.

The Chinese workers ate food that was familiar, with many ingredients imported from their home origins. They practiced traditional customs and rituals, and engaged in distinctive leisure and nonwork activities. They and those who had come before them from China brought crop seeds and introduced new plants to America. One journalist at the time observed that, in addition to trying to cultivate silkworms, rice, and other staples common in southern China, the Chinese "introduced many of the vegetables which they cultivate at home." These they cultivated right alongside the rail line.[26] They may have even brought with them seeds of the now popular fruit known as the goji berry. Just a few years ago, hunters in Utah accidentally stumbled across wild goji plants. DNA analysis placed the plants as having originated in China, and it is believed that Chinese introduced them to the area. The plants were found near what had been one of the largest encampments of Chinese who worked on the transcontinental railroad.[27]

The Chinese workers internationalized the everyday commodities and objects they used in the US West. They used Vietnamese coins as tokens or chips in their games. They smoked opium grown in Turkey or in India and processed in Hong Kong. They wore clothing made from cotton, likely grown in South Asia. They ate rice grown in southern China from bowls made in kilns located near their homes. They consumed dried seafood from the South China Sea. They used medicinals, Chinese herbs, and ointments to maintain their health and help heal their injuries. They enjoyed Chinese gaming activities that became commonplace in the West. Their presence contributed to making the region one of the most diverse places in the world, which is another way of saying that they helped interconnect the American West with the rest of the world.[28]

In recent decades American archaeologists have located and collected an immense amount of refuse left by the Chinese along the route of the transcontinental railroad and other lines. This material evidence in the form of ceramics, food containers, cooking utensils, gaming pieces, tools, clothes, liquor bottles, and pipes displays what appears to be an uncharacteristic departure from frugality. This detritus was discarded on the ground where even the casual explorer can find it today. Did some Chinese mean to leave this garbage, this material graffiti, as markers of their presence 150 years ago?

Daniel Cleveland offered a vivid description of these worker camps:

> [The Chinese] live in little villages of cloth tents, containing from 50 to 500 inhabitants. As the work progresses, they fold up and remove their tents and establish their villages at other points along the line of the road. What yesterday was a noisy Chinese town is today but a barren waste, with only rubbish and debris to mark that it was once a settlement. It is to be regretted that gamblers, lottery dealers, and opium sellers always accompany them and

open their shops in every Chinese camp to absorb much of the earnings of the industrious laborers.[29]

Cleveland offers an image that inspires our imaginations today. He tells us that "at night these tents are illuminated with candles, and groups of Chinese can be seen gambling, smoking opium, visiting or engaging in household labor."[30]

The Chinese workers did not just import items from Asia to the American West; they in turn sent gold and silver mined in the Americas to their families in China. This specie, especially Mexican silver dollars, formed a significant portion of the southern China economy and mightily contributed to building countless numbers of homes, schools, temples, village halls, and towers throughout the region, giving it a distinctive identity. Because of the horrible opium trade, however, much of this precious metal wound up not going to their families in China but into the coffers of the British aristocracy and mercantile and banking elite. Much of the silver in these people's opulent homes likely came from the Americas to pay for the opium brought to China by the British.

The workers sent remittances back home to support their families, and this practice itself helped establish transpacific commercial life. The early history of American banks and transport companies such as Wells Fargo & Company and the Pacific Mail Steamship Company have early connections to this remittance business. Chinese store owners and merchants too gained valuable experience and connections through facilitating the labor and remittance traffic, helping them become astute businessmen in the United States and around the world.

After the completion of the first transcontinental line, Chinese became professional railroad workers. Throughout the rest of the nineteenth century, they joined railroad construction projects across the United States, including in the East, South, Southwest, and Northwest. More than ten thousand of them worked on the northern transcontinental line; thousands worked on the southern transcontinental route; thousands also later worked on the trans-Canada rail line. They worked on railroads in northern Mexico, beginning in 1864, and on lines to transport sugarcane in Hawaii. Thousands worked in the Andes building railroads in Peru. By the early 1880s, they were working in railroad construction in French West Africa.[31] Some workers and contractors, because of their wealth and experience, returned to China and played prominent roles in the first railroad projects there. Ten thousand Chinese workers later helped complete the trans-Siberian railroad in Russia. These tens of thousands of Chinese railroad workers occupy a central position in the development of a modern laboring class that emerged around the world in the mid- and late nineteenth century.

The American entrepreneur Henry Meiggs, who led the effort to build Peruvian railroads, considered bringing Chinese labor from California for his workforce. "For railway work they are the best men we can get," Meiggs declared in 1870. Thousands of laborers were brought from China, though the number from California is not known.[32] Chinese returned to China to build railroads in their homeland.[33] In 1869 the new journal *Scientific American* declared that the "Chinaman" was a "born railroad builder" and was destined for work not just in California but in the "whole Pacific slope."[34]

The Chinese maintained ties with their wives, families, and home villages long after their departures, in many instances for multiple generations. They established patterns of migration where the males left their homes, lived most of their lives overseas, returned to father families, and then had sons who again out-migrated. Along with the workers themselves came other linkages that tied them to their compatriots who went elsewhere. They corresponded with one another and remained linked through family and district associations. They were mobile and often traveled across many boundaries: they went back and forth from Hawaii, Canada, Mexico, the United States, the Caribbean and South America, and Southeast Asia.[35] They helped make the Guangzhou region one of the most globally connected in all of China. We wonder what important political leaders and thinkers such as Yung Wing (Rong Hong), Sun Yat-sen (Sun Zhongshan), and Liang Qichao heard from the railroad workers. These and other important figures in China's modern history were natives of the Guangzhou region and spent much time among the Chinese overseas, including in the towns and cities of the American West where many Chinese railroad workers and contractors settled. What role might any of the old railroad workers have played in stimulating Sun Yat-sen's famous passion about building railroads in China to elevate the country? Yung Wing's last effort to contribute to modernizing China was to try to build a rail line in northern China.[36]

Unfortunately, we do not know what the workers themselves said about their experiences in North America. We have no texts, besides signatures on payroll records and remittance receipts, from their hands. But we can speculate, or just imagine, what they might have said and how their experiences affected those back home. Their experiences shared from afar, or in person when they returned after their life in North America, brought new ideas and subjectivity into southern China.

Consider this: There was no mechanical travel in southern China until the latter part of the nineteenth century. Labor was almost all agricultural, conducted manually without mechanization, by families on small farms. The climate in southern China was semitropical; few Chinese railroad workers had seen snow before they arrived in the Sierra Nevada. The experience of working with thousands of other *tang ren* ("people of Tang," who because of the many ethnic divisions in southern China could be almost as unfamiliar to one another as people from other countries), as well as with whites, blacks, and Native Americans, who spoke completely unfamiliar tongues, must have been bewildering. They worked for wages and in large, organized groups. They engaged in collective action to struggle for improved living and working conditions. They encountered new technologies for travel, construction, transportation, and communication. They encountered new foods, ways of daily living, and spiritual beliefs. They dealt with the unforgiving demands of business competition and construction engineering, and these demands, not the seasons and the agricultural calendar, regulated their lives. They encountered examples of private wealth and consumption unimaginable in rural southern China. Aside from some who had previously been exposed to aspects of Western life through Christian missionary schools in China, they learned for the first time about Western ways of life. Living and working in the towering Sierra Nevada in California, and in the blazing-hot deserts of Nevada and Utah, must have been a formidable, and previously unimaginable, physical, emotional, and mental challenge.

The suffering and predicaments of the Chinese deeply moved the contemporary writer Daniel Cleveland. His sympathy for them is palpable. In one section of his manuscript, Cleveland includes a harrowing report on Chinese disembarking in San Francisco and their transport into the Sierra Nevada. Cleveland invites us to imagine what the Chinese experienced.

Cleveland estimated that in the late 1860s one hundred to two hundred Chinese were on *every* steamship arriving in San Francisco, after weeks of strenuous ocean travel. Upon arrival, white labor agents and scores of assistants and strong arms interrogated them, usually on board ships, separating out those whose contracts the agents held. The contracts, which were completed in Hong Kong or China, indebted the workers for a period of time to repay the cost of their transportation. This was the so-called credit ticket system in action. The scenes Cleveland describes were chaotic, with physical violence used at times against the Chinese:

> [I] once saw a mulatto man, a petty officer on one of these boats, who had perhaps been a slave himself, taking advantage of his little brief authority to lord it over the poor Chinese. He maltreated them with a rough tyranny and keen relish as though it afforded him intense satisfaction to find human beings helpless enough to submit to his domination. The Chinese as helpless as a flock of sheep, look the picture of misery and despair, as they are huddled together upon the deck of the tug-boat listless and aimless, impotent against the force which keeps them in confinement. A small squad of resolute white men, armed with heavy bludgeons, which they are not slow to use, keep vigilant watch over the Chinese to prevent their escape.[37]

Taken by small boat directly from San Francisco Bay to Sacramento, the beginning point of the Central Pacific, the Chinese were forced by white overseers into railroad boxcars, whose doors were closed and then locked to prevent escape. "If they were culprits who had committed some heinous crime," Cleveland noted, "they would not be more closely guarded and harshly treated." During the ride, he says, some did succeed in opening the doors and tried to escape, but they died when they hit the ground. Cleveland estimated that about half of the Chinese would escape en route if such draconian measures were not taken. As it was, he estimated that 5 percent did manage to escape.

Of all the occupations that employed the Chinese in California, Cleveland claimed, none was more frightening to them than toil on the Central Pacific. As the line snaked eastward through the Sierra, the Chinese became even more averse to the work, as they feared the construction would unleash powerful, evil natural forces. "They do not understand railroads and fear them," he said.

> They are utterly unknown in China and are regarded by the Chinese in America with suspicion and dread. They have a firm belief that a huge serpent of gigantic proportions is lurking in the Rocky Mountains and that someday he will dart out upon the laborers, as they work near his lair, and devour all within his reach. Americans can have no adequate conception of the terror, which this superstition inspires. Many of the Chinese in San Francisco declare and believe that terrible misfortunes will befall their countrymen who have the temerity to aid in the construction of this road.[38]

Cleveland was largely ignorant about Chinese ways and could certainly have dramatized his account for audiences on the East Coast. But we do know that the Chinese had firm beliefs in a cosmology that understood the human world as inextricably connected to supremely powerful natural forces. As late as the end of the nineteenth century, many Chinese believed railroads desecrated their natural world—the notorious antiforeign Boxer rebels in northern China targeted railroads for destruction during their uprising. Mountains, water, and trees had special meanings for the Chinese—we can wonder what they thought about what tunneling, blasting, massive tree cutting, and track laying meant for their cosmological universe, even if not being done in their native land. Accounts by whites invariably describe the many temples, worshipped gods, and spiritual practices of the Chinese wherever they went. Oh, the stories the Chinese must have told back home about the practices of the Westerners!

Even in death, these workers stimulated trade and monetary circulation: one of the most lucrative exports from the United States in the mid- to late nineteenth century was the cleaned and prepared physical remains of Chinese who had died in the United States and were returned to China for final burial. American steamship companies carried tens of thousands of containers of these remains across the Pacific. In the offensive words of an American official, sending "dead Chinamen" back to China was one of the most profitable commercial activities for Americans in the late nineteenth century.[39]

There is one more element that we might consider in thinking about the railroad and the globalized world in the 1860s and 1870s, and that is the white backlash to the growing American interconnection with Asia. Reactive chauvinism and national exclusivity countered global moves and openings. Following the completion of the transcontinental railroad, white workers, both immigrant and native-born, raised an increasingly violent and chauvinist campaign to rid the country of the Chinese workforce. Anti-Chinese labor activists highlighted the danger the transcontinental line posed even before its completion. With a rail line across the country, a Chicago periodical warned, "Chinamen will begin to swarm through the [R]ocky [M]ountains like devouring locusts and spread out over the country this side."[40] In the fall of 1871, a white mob attacked the Los Angeles Chinatown and killed nineteen Chinese residents. Former railroad workers were likely among those lynched and shot.[41]

By 1882 white hostility had forced tens of thousands of Chinese to leave the United States and had fueled a national political movement that resulted in the passage of Chinese restriction and then exclusion acts that had far-reaching international repercussions. The Chinese were deemed to be a dangerous threat to white supremacy, and they had to be excluded to protect the nation. The Chinese "race" question and immigration became festering sore points in international relations well into the mid-twentieth century.

The history of the transcontinental railroad has always been global; it has awaited us to appreciate it as such. But we can ask, Why does the story play upon our personal and public imaginations? We are now in a new globalizing moment, marked especially by the rise of China. We are prompted to think back in time and reflect on the earlier years of relations between the United States and China. Chinese President Xi Jinping during his state visit to the United States in 2015 repeatedly invoked the memory of the Chinese railroad workers and their important contributions to the building of the American West. President Barack Obama likewise paid tribute to their contributions.[42] The leaders of China and America today hail the Chinese workers as an important, constructive early tie between the peoples of the two countries.

Historical recovery is intimately linked to our current condition. Our attitudes and viewpoints today influence the way we think about the past. We students of the past are ourselves part of a historical continuum of the railroad's global story. We have come a long way out of ignorance and neglect, but we still have a long way to go to understand the Chinese railroad workers and establish the respect they are due.

CHAPTER 2

Chinese Labor Migrants to the Americas in the Nineteenth Century

An Inquiry into Who They Were
and the World They Left Behind

EVELYN HU-DEHART

The second half of the nineteenth century, from about the end of the first Opium War in 1842 to enactment of the US Chinese Restriction Act in 1882, was a time of large-scale labor migration from China to the Americas, notably to the United States West (California and the Mountain West), the Caribbean (Spanish and British), Peru in South America, and the Pacific coast of Canada. It appears that, whatever the destination, most migrants left home from the same places in South China, overwhelmingly from the Pearl River delta of Guangdong Province. They were pushed to migrate by bloody internecine wars (the Taiping Rebellion, the Punti-Hakka Clan Wars) and other peasant uprisings (the Nien Rebellion, the Red Turban Rebellion). And they left because of overpopulation, crop failures and famine, and the destruction of local industries, such as textiles, by foreign imports. They were recruited by countries that were without local sources of cheap, docile, and disciplined (if not necessarily highly skilled) labor, including independent countries (the United States, Peru, and Australia) and European colonies (Cuba, Jamaica, Trinidad, and Guyana) to fill the voids in the labor-intensive industries of capitalist development, notably gold mining, plantation export or cash crop agriculture, and large-scale infrastructure construction, such as the transcontinental railroad of the United States.

This chapter examines who these labor migrants were, collectively speaking, and what the local environment in which they lived and worked was like before migration. I pay special attention to the labor migrants recruited to work on the sugar plantations of Cuba, which is the subject of my own research. This migration was contemporaneous with the movement to California to build the Central Pacific Railroad. Information on the California workers, especially on the early generations in the 1850s and 1860s, is elusive, as no letters have emerged and few proper names in complete written Chinese were recorded, let alone the workers' hometown villages and occupations prior to migration. In other words, even though we know they came mainly from the Pearl River delta counties of Sanyi and Siyi, we have practically no information about the actual names of the tens of thousands of workers recruited to California to work on the railroads, or the actual names of their home villages. We also do not know their premigration occupations, even though we suspect that most of them were villagers or peasants, with or without land.

By contrast, we know quite a bit about the migrants who were recruited in that era to work in the sugar plantations of Cuba and toiled alongside African slaves in this last of the colonies in the once magnificent Spanish empire in America. Of the more than 140,000 migrants who boarded ships to Cuba, almost 125,000 arrived alive in Havana. Their eight-year contracts were sold to Cuban (Spanish) bosses, mostly sugar plantation owners but also other employers, such as those engaged in tobacco cultivation and road construction, as well those hiring for domestic service. We have the exact names, in Chinese, of thousands of these "coolies."[1] These names are derived, first, from the contracts the workers signed before embarking on ships for the long voyage to Cuba, many of which have been preserved, and, second, from the recontracts, residency and naturalization documents, and identification cards issued by the Qing government's representative in Havana.

In short, we have considerably more concrete information on the Chinese laborers who ended up in Cuba than we have on those who ended up in California during the same period. And since the recruitment took place in the same places in South China, we can assume that, but for luck of the draw, some ended up in Cuba while others landed in California. In other words, in the absence of better information on those who went to California, we can present a fairly detailed portrait of those who went to Cuba as, very possibly, representative of the California railroad workers as well. Admittedly, this is a bit speculative about the migrants to California, but I do not believe it requires a leap of faith.

Social and Economic Conditions in the Pearl River Delta

The Pearl River delta was highly developed socially, and people from all walks of life were well networked within an intricate web of relationships that was both horizontally spread out and vertically ranked. Interclass interactions were the norm, and translocal mobility was common. People of the Pearl River delta of every social class, both men and women, were not isolated individuals who were unaware of their immediate social environment and shielded from the world beyond. At the same time, for most of those near the bottom of the social order, life had become increasingly difficult, especially regarding ownership of or access to sufficient cultivable land for family subsistence. Many were making the transition from peasant to proletarian, but opportunities in wage labor were insufficient to absorb all those who needed a job. Nevertheless, the movement from subsistence survival to market existence was in full swing. In making this transition, villagers would make full use of their familiarity with the larger social environment and contact with other social players.

Being highly commercialized meant that this countryside, which was organized around market towns, was also highly monetized; business transactions, taxes, and rents were paid in cash.[2] With proximity to Guangzhou and its longtime international trade with the West and Japan, as well as its trade in luxury goods carried down by Fujian merchants coming from the north, one impact of trade was the "spread of silver dollars."[3] In lineage villages a variation of rotating credit was the *yinhui*, or money club, which met in ancestral halls and allowed for the pooling of resources for capitalization among members bound together by trust.[4] Thus, experience with buying and selling was strengthened in the market by familiarity with cash transactions, credit institutions for capitalization, and monetization.

By the end of the eighteenth century, the Pearl River delta was prosperous and definitely moving in the direction of capitalist development.[5] Social inequality was also growing as the local gentry, aided and abetted by local administrators who profited, and other venal landlords and merchants squeezed the peasant households over land ever more tightly as capitalist enterprises spread. It was in the market towns that dispossessed peasants first looked for alternative or supplementary income as hired hands, working as shop assistants, artisans and craftsmen, and service providers. It was also probably in these towns that labor recruiters from the Americas came looking for prospects. Here the destitute, unemployed, ambitious workingman—or simply someone who got himself into gambling debt or a loan that could not be paid back, or maybe someone addicted to opium—might bump into the hundreds of crimps, who were agents contracted by big brokers to scour the towns and countryside for recruits willing to ship overseas.[6]

Life for peasants and the emerging urban proletariat became more precarious by the mid-nineteenth century because of social upheaval, and though these were major push factors, as historian Yong Chen cautions, their significance should not be so exaggerated as to indicate that the delta was distinctively impoverished and its people the most immiserated in China, even if cultivable land was becoming insufficient to provide food for a growing population.[7] To understand the delta region, it is more important to note the significance of the long-standing market-oriented economy, especially in the Sanyi region of Nanhai, Panyu, and Shunde close to Guangzhou, where flourishing fisheries and the silk industry made it more prosperous than the neighboring Siyi region.[8]

Europeans and Americans (from the United States and Latin America) had become experts in the business of exporting Chinese labor. Chinese labor was a commodity to be "produced" (recruited), exported, and marketed, and they knew in detail the regional origins of the Chinese who went overseas (as cargoes or voluntarily). After acquiring Hong Kong, the British made the colony the main staging point for this business of labor trafficking. Even if the shipping of contract laborers or coolies to Cuba and Peru was shifted to Macau (also spelled *Macao*), in fact the agents who contracted ships for this increasingly notorious human trade—such as the Dutchman Cornelius Koopmanschap and his British partner, Charles Bosman—actually operated from their offices in Hong Kong.[9]

Scholars have pursued the question of why so many more people from these areas left China during the nineteenth century than people from other regions of the country, or even from other parts of these same provinces. Assertions that the people there were simply destitute and desperate, that their home regions were devastated by social upheaval and turmoil, that the population was growing too fast, and that they had to deal with famines and natural disasters are not enough by way of explanation, because other parts of China shared these characteristics. The delta was a generally prosperous region with long-standing market orientation, as well as a population transitioning from being land-dependent peasants to wage earners on estates and in towns, actively engaged in commerce and a cash economy. When times became difficult in midcentury due to civil wars and social turmoil, multitudes of people were ready and capable of going abroad to capitalize on opportunities.

Another reason that people migrated from these areas was the propitious locations of these sending regions of southern China. Whether Cantonese, Teochiu, Hokkien, or Hakka, these people all lived in or near the coast with its many ports, big and small. These included Guangzhou and Xiamen (Amoy); the lesser-known but still actively engaged ports of Shantou (Swatow) and environs (e.g., Songkou in the Hakka county of Meixian); as well as Macau, controlled by the Portuguese from the mid-sixteenth century on, and Hong Kong, controlled by the British after the first Opium War, both located at the mouth of the Pearl River. Invariably, the local people in these parts of China were described as agricultural and seafaring, or at least familiar with maritime travel and trade. They had also come in contact with foreigners—including many merchants and agents of foreign firms, travelers, occasional government officials, and a growing number of missionaries—since the Ming dynasty.[10] Since the sixteenth century they had come in regular contact with Portuguese and Spaniards, especially in the city of Manila on Luzon Island in the Philippines, which was colonized by Mexicans as an extension of Spain's New World American empire. (The name for Manila in Chinese, Lüsong [from Luzon], became the generic name for all Spanish-speaking places in the world, such as Mexico and Cuba.)

When foreigners came knocking on their doors looking to recruit them to work overseas, the residents of Guangdong, Fujian, Shantou, and Meixian, of all the peoples in China, were least likely to be totally bewildered or intimidated. That is not to say that they did not encounter deception, fraud, violence, and all sorts of abuse at the hands of coethnic local recruiters and foreign company agents who handled the labor-contracting business and shipping matters, but it does suggest that, in some measure, they were more likely than others to be mentally prepared to go overseas and work.

Occupational Profile of Labor Migrants to Cuba

We can discern a profile of the labor migrants to Cuba during this period, based on labor contracts and information supplied by the nearly three thousand workers who provided personal information to the Qing government commissioners sent to investigate conditions on the sugar plantations of Cuba in 1873.

The first shipments of Chinese workers left Xiamen for Havana in 1849 on the British ship *Duke of Argyle* and the Spanish brig *Oquendo*, having boarded 412 and 220 men, respectively; only 571 of these landed alive. Trade resumed after a short hiatus of three years. From 1852 to 1856 ships to Havana mainly sailed from the ports of Shantou and Macau, with one departing Xiamen in 1853, one from Canton/Whampoa in 1854, and one from Shanghai in 1854. From 1857 to the end of the coolie trade in 1874, ships departed exclusively from Portuguese Macau, usually passing first through Hong Kong, where labor agents such as the Dutchman Koopmanschap were stationed.[11]

Beginning in 1852 Shantou in Guangdong Province took the lead over Xiamen in the shipping of labor recruits or coolies. Although the Chinese were not officially allowed to trade with foreigners until 1860, opium went informally through Shantou, handled by two great British houses, Dent & Co. and Jardine, Matheson & Co. The proximity of Shantou and Xiamen to each other and their vast hinterland made them natural regions for coolie recruiting and trafficking, resulting in large numbers of Hokkien, Teochiu, and Hakka speakers going to Cuba in the early days. When the trade to Cuba was moved exclusively to Portuguese Macau, recruiting from the Pearl River delta region became predominant, although members of the other speech groups were also recruited and sent down to the Macau barracoons to await ships, such as the *Forest Eagle* in 1861.

The Cuban Commission Report, issued in English and French in 1874, contains all 1,176 oral testimonies (transcribed and translated by scribes from the spoken Chinese, in the dialects spoken by the coolies), with their correct and complete Chinese names in written form. Since these depositions were given voluntarily when the commissioners visited many sugar plantations and invited coolies to come forward with responses to fifty specific questions (or submit written petitions if they could not appear before the commissioners in person),[12] they do not constitute a scientific survey sample by today's social science standards. Moreover, the sample cannot be said to be large: it includes just 1,176 out of the approximately 124,000 Chinese who had been brought to Cuba by the time of the commissioners' visit in 1873.[13] Nevertheless, the depositions provide rich data that are not available in such detail, in Chinese, for any other group of migrants to the Americas in the nineteenth century.

A few scholars have pored over the Cuban Commission Report, and none so meticulously as Lisa Yun.[14] She found that 89 percent of the deponents named Guangdong as their *qiaoxiang* (hometown), but the remainder named at least fourteen other provinces, coastal and inland. In descending order of frequency, these workers hailed from the provinces of Guangdong, Fujian, Hunan, Jiangxi, Zhejiang, Guangxi, Jiangsu, Jiangnan, Anhui, Sichuan, Tianjin, Henan, Hebei, and Shanxi. Among them were Hakkas from various places. In addition, the workers included Vietnamese, Filipinos, and Manchu bannermen. Bai Yongfa pointed proudly to his "red border banner Manchu" status and named another worker surnamed Huang, who belonged to the "white border banner Manchu" group.[15]

An 1887 Chinese travelogue of Cuba by Tan Qianchu, believed to be the first of its kind in Chinese and published in China, gives an account of the Chinese population in Cuba at the time of his visit in the 1880s and includes the workers' hometowns. The account corroborates the diversity reported in the Cuban Commission Report issued ten years earlier.[16] Tan's list was copied by an 1889 travelogue on Cuba by Fu Yunlong, also in Chinese and published in China. The list follows, sorted here according to the historical source and following a geographic logic, from south to north and from coast to interior:

Guangdong: 38,234	Hunan: 176
Guangxi: 341	Hubei, Shandong: 3 each
Fujian: 3,733	Shanxi, Gansu: 2 each
Zhejiang: 105	Sichuan: 5
Jiangnan: 78	Yunnan: 1
Zhili: 115	Guizhou: 2
Jiangsu: 63	Annan (Vietnam) ethnic Chinese:
Jiangxi: 167	149
Anhui, Henan: 8 each	Born in Cuba: 196[17]

Equally significant and contrary to conventional wisdom was what these lists reveal about the occupations these men had before leaving China. In Yun's careful parsing of the more than one thousand testimonies, she discovered that 17.4 percent listed their occupations as "farmers or sellers of farming goods."[18] The vast majority of workers identified an impressive and fascinating array of small businesses, crafts, and occupations. These lines of work confirm what June Mei has suggested about men from southern China having had to move away from working family plots and into wage earning, and Yong Chen's observation about the advanced development of local market-oriented economies.[19]

Some of the Chinese who ended up working on Cuban sugar plantations alongside black slaves were owners of shops that sold a variety of merchandise: afterlife and funeral paper, bowls, chairs, cloth, coal, dyes, firewood, groceries, herbs, incense, jewelry, oil and wine, paper, paper fans, rice, shoes, silver, tea, and tofu; they also owned pawnshops and restaurants.

Some of the Chinese made and sold these products: baskets, buckets, candy, canvas, chicken, coal, crystal sugar, eggs, fences, fish, fruit, gold thread, groceries, hats, herbs, lamps, leather, milk, oil, opium, pastries, pork and mutton, pottery, salt, salt fish, sausages, vegetables, wood, machines, mirrors, silk, tobacco, and thread.

Some of the Chinese were service providers and skilled artisans: actors, blacksmiths, butchers, boat polers and boat rovers, animal drivers, carpenters, bamboo draftsmen, bricklayers, cloth weavers, cooks, copper forgers, cotton fluffers, court officials, doctors, craftsmen, engravers, farmers, fishermen, flax weavers, gardeners, glassblowers, government workers, haircutters, herders, jade shapers, japanners, painters, palanquin lifters, silversmiths, students, tailors, teachers, theater managers, translators, water mill operators, wine brewers, wine steamers, woodcutters, bookstore workers, dye shop workers, and workers in many types of shops that sold groceries, wine, jade, paper, silk, and tea. They were also general laborers, workers in the famous Tong Ren Tang herbalist, military and naval officers and soldiers, and even aristocrats.

Some of the Chinese claimed to be owners of small businesses in currency exchange, firecrackers, hemp/flax/jute, ships and boats, suitcases, general stores, and general business.[20]

In addition to the Manchu bannermen discussed earlier, there were even a few members of the gentry with imperial examination titles, leading Yun to describe them as "scholars" and "aristocrats." Again, this was not a scientific sample but one derived from testimonies and petitions voluntarily submitted by self-selected Chinese who approached the visiting commissioners at their work sites. We might surmise that landless peasants and others at the bottom of the social order in China might have been less motivated to give testimony than those who had some property or a decent job to lose when they were enticed to try their luck overseas.

What can we make of this revealing information about Chinese labor migrants to Cuba during the same period as others who went to California, especially those who helped build the Central Pacific Railroad in the 1860s? Despite the preponderance of Chinese from the Pearl River delta counties of

Guangdong Province in California, we can also surmise that Chinese from other provinces in China—both those along the coast, such as Fujian, and farther inland and farther north—were also found in California during this time. These workers were probably already in southern China, in cosmopolitan port cities, ripe for the ruthless recruiters' picking, whether to go to Cuba or to California. Hakka people from Fujian, and especially Guangdong, were well represented in Cuba and California, as Punti-Hakka (Bendi-Kejia) hostilities broke out in Cuba and likely in California as well.[21]

As long as we are speculating about these two contemporaneous labor migrations, here is another thought worth pondering. California railroad entrepreneurs were recruiting for workers at a time when the country was engaged in a civil war to resolve the loaded question of slavery, which was about to end at the time railroad construction began. So the railroad tycoons did not seriously contemplate the option of using indentured workers with fixed time contracts, shying away from any labor system that smacked of slavery.[22] In this regard, we might speculate that the railroad workers probably went to California as voluntary or free migrants, although certainly not free from tremendous pressure to pay back loans incurred under the credit-ticket system for their transpacific passage.

By contrast, countries in the Americas that introduced a formal system of indentured servitude—Cuba and the British West Indies—were colonies of imperial powers, Spain and Great Britain. Furthermore, in the case of Cuba, the practice was more firmly entrenched and protected by powerful metropolitan forces, as well as by the planters themselves. Planters in colonial regimes were not politically or morally restrained in introducing a form of coercive labor that many then and later would condemn as akin to slavery. Word spread around the world and into the inner circles of the Qing government that their people were being subjected to a terribly abusive system in Cuba.

Since the inception of the coolie trade, American officials in Guangdong and Fujian Provinces had been deeply concerned about American vessels being involved, and they vociferously debated the legality and morality of this human trafficking enterprise. On January 7, 1856, C. D. Mugford, an American official in Hong Kong, reported to Peter Parker, US commissioner and minister plenipotentiary to China, that coolies shipped to Cuba, Peru, and the British West Indies were being swindled and deceived by crimps to sign up and were going "against their will," while also noting that it was against the law in China to emigrate.[23] He and many other Americans readily compared the coolie trade to the slave trade, which was then under widespread condemnation around the world.[24]

Mugford and others did make occasional comments, but only cursory ones, on the Chinese laborers who went to California. Mugford noted that those Chinese who "embarked in...ships" owned by his "friends" "came from the country freely and of their own accord, as those do who have gone to Australia and San Francisco." Commissioner Parker himself wrote a brief memo to Secretary of State Daniel Webster from Canton on January 27, 1852, in which he said that "the favorable reports of those who have returned to China, having been fortunate at the Gold Mountain, seem to have imparted a new impetus to the tide of emigration" and predicted that five thousand Chinese would sail to California in the next month.[25] The high-minded Parker—who was also a medical missionary—followed up with another missive to Secretary Webster on March 27, 1852, to make the grandiose claim that those Chinese who had returned from California became enlightened and civilized because they

> have acquired new ideas of human rights and human existence even. This influence beginning to be rife in China, must inevitably, according to the established law of mind disenthralled from tyranny, work out important results to the Manchoo [sic] dynasty. Yet the character of this new element will depend materially upon the influence that shall be exerted upon these emigrants during their residence in the land of gold, and, what is still more valuable, the land of freedom.[26]

Sufficiently embarrassed by 1873 by the treatment its citizens were receiving, the Qing government's recently established Zongli Yamen (equivalent to a ministry of foreign affairs) sent a high-level commission to investigate the situation on the ground, discussed at length earlier. All over southern China, the word on Cuba was to avoid getting caught in the recruiters' dragnet at all costs. Under these circumstances, we can surmise that only the most desperate and destitute voluntarily signed up to go to Cuba by the 1860s and 1870s; the majority of those deposed in 1873 claimed to have been decoyed, deceived, and forced to sign contracts in the Macau barracoons. While those who went to Cuba and those who went to California most likely shared similar origins, California probably attracted more voluntary migrants than Cuba did.

One final observation: While the coolie trade to Cuba, Peru, and the British West Indies ended in the 1870s, the immigration of Chinese laborers to the West Coast of the United States and the Pacific Northwest, including the Seattle–Vancouver transborder region, continued unabated. This human trafficking in the last decades of the nineteenth century and into the first years of the twentieth century was primarily handled, managed, and controlled by highly adept and astute Chinese labor contractors, Siyi men such as Yip Sang of Vancouver and Chin Gee Hee (Chen Yixi) of Seattle. They recruited tens of thousands of fellow delta men and managed their mobility among many work sites on both sides of the US–Canada border. In this coethnic labor-contracting arrangement, migration was likely voluntary and the workers were probably well informed about their destinations.

Early on, enterprising Chinese in Hong Kong also seized opportunities in the "frontier" environment of Hong Kong to become involved in emigrant-related businesses. A good example is Tam Achoy of Kaiping (a Siyi county), who became a part owner of the first Chinese-owned ship to transport Cantonese labor migrants to San Francisco in 1853.[27] In my research on the coolie trade to Cuba, I have not found any Chinese involvement on the recruitment end in China comparable to that of Tam. We might conjecture that Chinese entrepreneurs like Tam, while definitely exploiting his coethnics, would have taken greater care to properly inform and secure the consent of those he recruited to California, thereby contributing to the speculation that those Chinese laborers who went to California were more aware of their destination and went more willingly than their likely more hapless counterparts who went to Cuba.

PART TWO

Ties to China

CHAPTER 3

The View from Home

Dreams of Chinese Railroad Workers across the Pacific

ZHANG GUOXIONG,

WITH ROLAND HSU

Scholars in the United States have long studied the Chinese workers who made a historic contribution to building the transcontinental railway. Both Chinese and American researchers have extensively referenced documents and popular materials available in US public and private collections. In Guangdong Province, we have pursued an important parallel path, uncovering and interpreting Chinese government documents and original materials of popular culture from the hometowns, or *qiaoxiang*, of the Chinese migrant laborers from the era.

In addition to using new sources, this chapter reveals new insights into the impact of the Chinese railroad workers upon their return to their home villages. Working alongside colleagues in the Chinese Railroad Workers in North America Project at Stanford University, we take this opportunity to "reverse the gaze" of subject and observer and view the Pacific passage of labor migrants to North America as it looks from the well-traveled coast of southern China.[1]

In this essay we develop an argument in two parts. First, the Pacific passage for those who went to build the Central Pacific Railroad mirrors the travel of those who migrated in search of gold in the United States. Second, the Chinese railway workers who returned home profoundly influenced their hometowns in ways that we can still detect today.

The Aspirations of Chinese Railroad Workers

Since the Song dynasty (960–1279), the coastal area of southeastern China had been the region historically associated with large-scale international labor migration to Southeast Asia. But in the late 1840s and early 1850s, news of the discovery of gold in the Americas and Australia, along with conditions at home of rapid population growth and poor agricultural harvests, led increasing numbers of individuals to engage in the complex and costly planning needed to leave home in search of work across the Pacific.[2]

In Guangdong Province, multiple sources conveyed a narrative from abroad that the hills of western North America were lined with productive gold mines.[3] For our study of the setting for the Chinese railroad labor migration, we draw on existing research on these narratives that flowed back home, including collections of letters sent by Chinese in California, reports by those who returned from overseas, and rumors spread by shipping companies about the fortunes that could be found—much like the proverbial pot of gold at the end of the rainbow—at the end of their shipping routes.[4]

In the Wuyi *qiaoxiang*, these narratives were soon followed by shipping agents, who were sent to spread the news that laborers were needed in America. Such narratives encouraged people who had hoped to go overseas to cast their sights on the other side of the Pacific. North America displaced Southeast Asia as the most desirable destination, and the oversell of the region led many to commit to financing travel aboard the fleet of steamers headed there. The saying "Going to Havana to drive poverty away, coming to Gold Mountain for a better way" even today is a well-known refrain in the villages in the Wuyi region.[5]

Sailing Overseas to Work on the Central Pacific Railroad

The Central Pacific Railroad Company, in concert with the Pacific Mail Steamship Company, actively recruited in southern China and Hong Kong. For each recruited laborer, the construction and transport companies did not advance the fee for the journey or other expenses. Each Chinese laborer signed a promissory note for $75 that was guaranteed by his relatives in China and that was to be repaid within seven months in installments deducted from his monthly wage of $35. If and when the loan was repaid, the Chinese laborer could be cleared by the construction and transportation companies to pay for passage to return home.[6]

Sources describe the additional expenses and debt incurred by Chinese migrant laborers during their transpacific voyage. According to a trade industry report, "The merchant and creditor at [the] same time advances the migrant fifty dollars for the travel expense and twenty dollars for other expenses on the condition that he will get back two hundred dollars."[7] In sum, the Chinese migrant laborers typically, and not by accident, incurred significant debt before they could begin to seek employment abroad.

Once at work in the United States, the Chinese miners earned an income that was not stable. Evidence indicates in many cases that Chinese railroad construction work earned less than that which could be earned mining gold. Miners earned on average $35 per month, while the monthly wage of the Chinese railroad construction workers was only $30. Besides servicing their transpacific passage debt, these monthly wages would barely be sufficient for the basic costs of living and taxation.[8] After covering these costs, if the miner had not become addicted to such costly habits as gambling and the use of opium, he could put away small amounts of savings. In view of these meager wages, the expectations of a prospective migrant seems especially poignant:

> Most of the travelers accepted any arrangement to enable them to board a ship bound for the Gold Mountain, without recognizing the heavy burden of the debt for passage. They hoped to earn two or three hundred dollars and then to come back to China. This sum of money was attractive enough for those who could earn in China barely one-tenth of this sum annually. In light of such a potential great reward it might not be considered foolhardy to risk incurring such debt.[9]

In Pursuit of a Dream

The migration of laborers from Taishan is described in several historical sources. In the *Memoir of Zhang Yinhuan on Matters of the Chinese Laborers in America*, dated July 14, 1886, the author writes:

> The western states of America are sparsely populated for such a large land area.... Through opening mines, exploiting wastelands, and constructing railways, cities have been gradually formed, of which the city of San Francisco

is especially prosperous. All the former work was dependent on recruiting Chinese laborers and by this opportunity Chinese people could earn their living, thus more and more people have been coming here.[10]

The same situation of "more and more people going overseas" emerged in the adjacent Kaiping County.[11] For the households listed in the *Kaiping County Annals* during the reign of Xuantong (1908–1912), more detail was recorded about the generations of Chinese laborers who had gone overseas: "The father carries his son, the elder brother takes the younger brother along, almost every family has persons gone overseas, and one family had more than ten persons go."[12]

For insight into the emotional impact of the decision to migrate, we turn to evocative sources from popular culture. The *wuyi muyudiao* (ballads accompanied by a wooden knocker) describe the emotive state of the Chinese laborers at the beginning of their journey overseas.

POEM 1

Verse 1

My Dear Neighbors,
Never get discouraged!
The right moment brings good fortune,
Your life that you have right now may not be the one that you are meant to
    have.
When the time comes,
It is easy to go from poverty to wealth.
One enjoys a family reunion, bringing home a fortune,
Which brings happiness and smiles.

Verse 2

Having toiled since childhood,
I had porridge for three meals a day,
I had too many stories of hunger and coldness to tell.
But now the time has come that was foretold,
I became prosperous overnight,
I can purchase land and build houses.
I give thanks to Heaven that knows my suffering,
And blesses me with longevity and happiness in my later years.

Verse 3

It is difficult to eke out a living at present,
My destiny has not yet been fulfilled.
I do not believe this is the way it will be until I am old.
This is only momentary bad luck.
When good luck comes,
All good things will follow,
One becomes rich and prosperous within a few years
I will then run my business and build my western-style mansions.[13]

In such *qiaoxiang* ballads we find popular descriptions of the feelings and hopes of those who migrated abroad. Protagonists are uniformly from impoverished families, they are not discouraged, and they believe that things will change for the better by going overseas and that they will return home wealthy.

The Economic Reality of Contract Labor

Most of the Chinese gold miners and railroad workers were obliged to pay for the expense of travel through loans from the company that recruited them. Some documents show how prospective migrants raised money by becoming indebted to extended family members. We see the weight of these loans in the following examples. The following text documents the agreement in a dispute over the amount to be repaid for a loan for passage to the United States:

In February 1852 (2nd year of Xianfeng's reign), Yantian lent Yanfeng 60 liang [1 liang equals approximately 50 grams] of silver for him to go to perform Gold Mountain business. Yanzhuo lent Yanbin 60 liang of silver for him to go to Gold Mountain. When they returned in August 1853, Yanbin paid back Ting Zhuo 65 liang of silver, and Yanfeng paid back Yanzhuo 40 liang of silver. Because the principal is not fully repaid, and the interest is small, Yanzhuo and Yantian suspect that Yanfeng and Yanbin have reserved some of their own funds. The dispute about the sum of money between them needs to be settled, so all have met at the house of the eldest clan member and reached the agreement that Yanbin further pays 2.2 liang of silver to Yanzhuo, and Yanfeng further pays 5.6 liang of silver for Yanzhuo and Yantian to share equally. The negotiation is noted by an independent witness and is agreed to by both parties. Under the terms of the agreement, all parties should avoid discussing the situation of the families of Yanfeng and Yanbin. Yantian and Yanzhuo should forfeit claim to any additional unpaid principal or interest, and their heirs are bound by the terms of the agreement. The agreement is written for posterity, and Yanfeng and Yanbin should thereby be satisfied with the terms of their repayment. No party is permitted to discuss the matter, and thereby the agreement should ensure the brothers' fraternal harmony. Yanzhao and Chaoying

The writer of the agreement: Yantian
December, 3rd year reign of Xianfeng [1853][14]

In this debt resolution agreement, the creditors of Yanzhuo and Yantian were not satisfied with the sum they received, suspecting that Yanfeng and Yanbin earned more money in America. The loan for the cost of transpacific passage was mostly from brothers of the same clan; the fact that Yanbin and Yanfeng were able to return home after only eighteen months indicates that the signatories found reliable the assumption that one was likely to earn considerable sums over and above the considerable cost of the transpacific transit.

The following is a receipt for a loan between the rural Xilong Association and the Chinese laborer Huang Guanyi for the purchase of a ship ticket:

Huang Guanyi, the borrower of the silver, hereby testifies that having gone to Gold Mountain with the purpose of earning money, he requests that the aged and honorable Mr. Huang Yuhan, Mr. Deng, and the executive clerks of Huang Huihui, Huang Dade, and Guan Ruijie of Xilong Association hereby issue a loan of 18 liang of silver for the ship ticket fee. The agreed upon terms of the loan are the span of one year, with annual interest of 0.5 liang of silver for 1 liang of the capital. The capital and the interest will be paid back at the specified date. In the event that the principal is not paid back, additional interest will accrue at the rate of 1.5 liang per year. If the monthly payments are absent or late, then the sum total of all remittances sent to the family at home must be exchanged according to the exchange rate at the time by the executive clerks of Xilong Association. The [a]ssociation will at that time collect all the owed principal and interest. Any funds in addition to that owed to the association remain with the family. In the event of an unforeseen circumstance during his oceanic passage, or at Gold Mountain, the contract would no longer have bearing on either party. If the borrower uses the money to pay business expenses other than repaying this loan, then this contract hereby binds his father and other family members to repay the debt. Hereby the receipt is written with the number of silver on the paper. This receipt is handed over for the executive clerk to keep. The 18 liang of silver is noted as received.

The whole family guarantees

Father: Huang Yuansheng
The person who receives the silver: Huang Guanyi
2nd of January, 6th year reign of Xianfeng [1856][15]

In the detail of the heavy obligation on the extended family to service a loan in default, we see the scale of anticipated earnings and the weight of family obligation.

The following assignment contract establishes the credit for a travel loan for a Chinese gold miner and is an example of a lender raising cash by transferring a portion of his loan to be repaid to another party. (In this sense, this is an antecedent to lenders selling loans in our modern era.)

> Yisuo enters into this contract to stipulate that in the event that the lender has an urgent need for repayment but there is no source from whom to collect the silver, after discussing with my father, it is our will that we assign our creditors' right to other parties. The sum of 40 liang of silver was lent to Zhenpei by me and Yichen in the seventh year of the reign of Xianfeng [1857] for Zhenpei to go to Gold Mountain to mine for gold. The contract clearly said that the principal with interest of 120 liang of silver would be paid back when due, and if there was no money to reimburse, additional interest would be calculated as 14 liang of silver and accumulate each month. Yisuo's part is half of the total principal with interest. In this contract, Yisuo wishes to assign the rights to Zhenneng for 40 liang of silver, and Zhenneng promises to accept the assignment. Thereby Yisuo willingly assigns the creditor's right to Zhenpei's debt to Zhenneng, at such time that he receives the 40 liang of silver from Zhenneng. By consequence, the interest that Zhenpei will reimburse will not be due to Yisuo, and will be shared equally between Zhenneng and Yichen. It is hereby noted that the earnings from gold mining that Zhenpei sent as remittances are claimed by Yisuo as the interest which Zhenneng should not be responsible for. The assignment contract is hereby written for posterity.
>
> Handwritten by Zhenyi the nephew
> Yisuo the contractor on 29th October, 1st year reign of Tongzhi [1861][16]

In these loan documents for Chinese gold miners, we note three points. First, these documents were written in the 1850s and 1860s during the period when migrants from the same home region came to work the mines and the railroad construction. Second, these documents provide details of private financial relationships that cannot easily be traced in official government archives. For example, the clan brothers and organizations are the main sources of loans for people to go abroad, so the relationship between the creditor and debtor mainly existed in the clan, which is valuable for the analysis of debt cost between the members of the clan. Third, the Chinese laborers leveraged multiple sources for credit to cover the cost to travel to North America. Some used personal funds (including selling family possessions), others borrowed on credit from an agent of the railroad company, which would subsequently be deducted from wages, while others borrowed money from extended family.

We also find in the contracts that debts were to be paid off in relatively short lengths of time. In the above mediation agreement (1853), the loan was due within eighteen months. In the above receipt for a loan (1856), the loan period was only twelve months. The documents indicate that at least at the time of signing, the Chinese prospective migrant and his creditor entered into contracts that spoke of confidence in the earning potential of work in North America.

Returning Home: Wealth and Marriage

As opposed to those who migrated to Southeast Asia, most of the Chinese gold miners and railroad construction workers were unmarried, and most hoped to return to their hometowns. Many of them sent remittances immediately after they earned their pay each week. A small number even returned home having amassed some relative wealth.

Benefiting from the new wealth, their home villages began the process of social transformation during the 1860s. Popular culture materials, including songs and ballads, are rich sources of evidence for the changes. Folk ballads include refrains that evoke images of Chinese laborers returning with fortunes and with the satisfaction that they will have a profound impact on their hometowns.

> In my past I used to be destitute,
> Then suddenly I became rich and famous.
> And it was no longer difficult to have a grand home and prosperous family,
> I recall my poverty as a whim of fate.
> But when good luck came,

Gold and silver was at my disposal,
Out of misfortune comes the bliss of wealth,
I would enjoy a glorious homecoming.
Turning my head toward the sun,
Toward the direction of my hometown,
Heading back to China with my newfound wealth,
via Yokohama to Hong Kong.
Seizing the splendor of spring,
Inviting friends to return together,
Compatriots return home for family reunions,
Which brings happiness and comfort to our parents.[17]

Along these lines, a ballad in Taishan conveys the social impact of new wealth:

In the spring, plum trees bloom, sisters-in-law are showing off:
My son's father went abroad to seek his fortune.
Every month money is sent home.
My husband will return by the year-end.
He'll ask the matchmaker to find a man for his sister.[18]

We see the narrative trope recurring in many ballads, poems, and popular refrains. The protagonist goes overseas with empty hands and returns flush with cash. He promptly purchases farmland and builds a new home. All the risk, hardship, and humiliation he had experienced signifies that his good fortune was richly deserved.

The ballads that we still hear today in the villages of Wuyi *qiaoxiang* dwell on the notion of the migrant laborer returning specifically from Gold Mountain with wealth:

Those Gold Mountain guests in San Francisco
Earn 800 to 1,000 dollars;
The venerable uncles who went to Southeast Asia,
Have their purses
Filled with gold coins
The young guys in Hong Kong
Can only earn and spend money locally.
After winter in November,
Comes the New Year in December,
Father, send money back from Gold Mountain more often;
Everyone here is getting new outfits made for the New Year holiday.
The family buys a fat goose to usher in a prosperous new year.[19]

People in Wuyi *qiaoxiang* still know to call those Chinese laborers who earned money in the United States their *"jinshan* [Gold Mountain] uncles," *"jinshan ke* [Gold Mountain guests]," or *"jinshan* men." The women who remained behind or who were married to the returning migrant workers are still termed *"jinshan* wives," and their sons and daughters are described as *"jinshan* sons" and *"jinshan* daughters."[20]

In the Wuyi *qiaoxiang* the family lineages of the repatriated workers are commemorated and celebrated. Ballads describe the honor that is bestowed on a family when it marries daughters to *jinshan* uncles:

> Don't marry your daughter to a scholar,
> Who would isolate himself to sleep alone;
> Don't marry your daughter to a baker,
> Who would not have enough time for sleep;
> Don't marry your daughter to a farmer,
> Whose earthy smell would be repellent;
> Marry your daughter to a Gold Mountain guest,
> He would come back home with glory and wealth.[21]

The contrast between the overseas Chinese laborer and the scholar, baker, and farmer underscores the social capital that the migrant laborer accrued along with wealth ("He would come back home with glory and wealth"). Another ballad describes the desire of a family with a daughter to have their daughter married to a Gold Mountain guest: "He left his hometown very young, coming back to China at around thirty; matchmakers are hurriedly running to and fro, the mother of the daughter was joyful, and she cannot keep from asking for an engagement."[22]

In these refrains, buying land, building houses, and getting married are the three wishes of all the Chinese gold miners and railroad workers. The concept of returning to their hometowns and carrying on the family line is deeply rooted in the popular narratives.

> Mr. Li Junqian, who goes by the name of Li Zuzhan, the second son of Mr. Li Zhinai, lives at Fengyi village of Michong, Taishan. He is hardworking, thrifty, modest, kind, and adventurous. He used to sail across the Pacific [to earn his living]. His footprints covered [such] places as New Gold Mountain, Sydney, Australia, and towns in North America, where he went back and forth several times. He bought land and built a house. He often says that the man is rooted in hardship and that without experiencing hardship a man

cannot become mature, and a man's success is achieved by no other way but [by] being hardworking and thrifty. What he says, though not sophisticated, are words [that] contain the truth.[23]

These words are on a porcelain tablet made by an individual named Li Yijun. The words narrate the fortunes of his grandparents, Li Junqian and Lady Zhang. The tablet is a rare relic of a Chinese laborer preserved in *qiaoxiang*.

Qiaoxiang *Transformed: Material Prosperity*

In the memoirs of some Qing officials, we find testimony that would seem to support the stories in the ballads and poems. In the memoir of Zhang Zhidong, the governor of Guangdong and Guangxi Provinces, and Zhang Yinhuan, an emissary to the United States (1886), we learn that, "according to many foreigners we have consulted, the annual service revenue earned by Chinese laborers, with their daily cost deducted, is remitted home to provide for their families; the total sum amounts to several million liang of silver."[24] In the memoir of Xue Fucheng (1890), who was in charge of establishing Chinese consulates in Southeast Asia, a similar record was found: "[A]ccording to the inspection in America of the San Francisco Bank's general ledger of exchange bills, the annual remittance to China from the overseas Chinese amounts to the sum of about eight million liang of silver."[25]

Chinese overseas laborers, through their remittances to their families, influenced the patterns of consumption and the standards of living in their hometowns. The following source documents a marked shift:

In Kaiping County, before the reign of Emperor Guangxu [1871–1908], the objects of daily life and provisions that were prominent in Wuyi were mostly produced locally, but subsequent to remittances from America the market grew for imported goods.

Since the foreign influence came, there have been five customs out of the six that have been changed. For example, in dressing and meals, people like to dress and eat in [W]estern style; in courtesy, they prefer free love to traditional marriage and bowing to kowtow; calendars do not contain the leap year and month; home lots are flat and houses are built with tall towers; is flat without surrounding walls and the house built high with towers around; the devices for plotting the land are no longer the plow with yoke, and the process of grinding hulled rice is improved; only the dialect is not greatly changed, but its change will happen soon; such [words] as English *no* instead of Chinese *fou* and English *yes* instead of Chinese *shi* come from the lips of the returned overseas.[26]

Even today, among families whose ancestors were *jinshan* uncles, their households retain objects that were brought back from overseas work on railroads. At Long'anli, Shuilouxiang, Dajiang Town, Taishan County, in the houses of Li Jiancong and Lijiangui, great-grandsons of Li Youqin, who worked as a labor-recruiting agent for the Union Pacific Railroad, one finds objects such as the "*jinahan* box"—perhaps referring to a travel trunk—and a kerosene packing case, along with four British Tower brand pots and basins that remain in use. Even after 150 years, the families still express pride of ownership of the well-made items.

Beginning in the 1860s, Chinese laborers who returned from North America brought altered designs for family home architecture. Researchers have been able to trace a number of examples of new multifamily clan homes that were built at the time alongside the older design. In some instances, there is evidence that multiple returning workers combined resources to buy land and extend the architectural footprint. The layout and model of the new houses blend traditional forms with Western influences, such as consistent layout of rooms and built-in ventilation, including windows. These family homes also use modern construction materials, such as concrete, and the tradition of the three-room, two-corridor low house, or *lu*, began to give way to a new style of building with two or more stories.

In the rural areas of Taishan and Kaiping, on the lintels of the Western-style buildings, architects infused wall paintings and ornamental designs with motifs from railroad lines, equipment, and Western scenery.

New Wealth and New Culture

Along with material wealth, home communities absorbed social and cultural markers of the migrants' lives abroad. We have noted evidence of changes in the *qiaoxiang* dialect, such as the introduction of the words *yes* and *no*; other changes are the habit of saying "hello" as a greeting and "bye-bye" when departing, along with the use of random words such as *chocolate, taffy, cracker, ball, stamp, cap, mark, face, sorry,* and other terms that in popular parlance have tended to replace the corresponding Chinese words. In *qiaoxiang* vernacular speech, speakers combine English and Chinese to form hybrid expressions. For example, *becoming naked* is expressed as *tuozhe blank*, which combines the Taishan dialect word *tuozhe* (to undress) and the English word *blank*. Another example is the hybrid word for the color scarlet, *hong blood*, which combines the Taishan dialect word *hong* (red) and the English word *blood* to characterize that type of red.

In terms of social roles, the absence of men while working overseas led some *jinshan* wives to become the primary wage earners in their families:

> Since the mid-reign of Emperor Guangxu, most of the men have gone overseas, and the women have been engaged in the tillage.... Women are wet with mud all over the body, doing hard labor in fields. In the [n]orthern provinces such scenes cannot be seen. When a person comes from the north he will feel strange [seeing] the women with naked feet and even naked to the part above the knees. Now such scenes can be seen only in the fields.[27]

Qiaoxiang women in this way began to play a role in the social transformation of the home villages that marked the influence of the laboring men in absentia.

Dreams Not Realized

Of course, not all the Gold Mountain dreams became reality. In *qiaoxiang* documents there are many records that testify to disappointment. Popular songs narrate the depression and pessimism of unsuccessful Chinese laborers who incurred the cost of travel abroad but returned with little or nothing to show for their efforts.

> The crescent moon is shining over China,
> Some people feel happy while others are distressed.
> Some return home after making a fortune,
> Others end up drifting abroad.
> Sojourners in a strange land,
> Still burdened with debt.
> I am not able to soothe my sorrow,
> Especially when I am thinking of my aging parents.
> I would wish to return,
> Yet without money to afford the journey;
> Having strived hard to migrate overseas for a better life,
> I still meet with hardship and discord.
> Born under an unlucky star,
> Achieving nothing in the comings and goings of life;

Even after going abroad,
I have gained nothing while journeying east and west;
Yin and Yang are misaligned,
Being away from home leads to solitude and destitution,
Moving around the world,
I cannot live in peace and walk with happiness.[28]

In 1992 a graveyard with 387 graves of destitute overseas Chinese was found in Huangkeng, Xinhui County.[29] Those interred there died abroad without leaving funds or biographical records. Philanthropic efforts during the 1880s and 1890s transported these remains to China, and the graveyard bears sad witness to their sacrifices. According to the custom in Wuyi *qiaoxiang*, the procedure for repatriating remains included unearthing, cleaning, and arranging the bones; gathering all the remains for shipment at the port of San Francisco; and sending the remains to China in batches. Of the 387 distinct bodily remains at the Xinhui graveyard, there are a number of individuals who may be identified with reasonable certainty to be former gold miners and railroad construction laborers in North America. This graveyard has thus far been preserved and is an important site for further research.

Songs of mourning from the era include refrains that echo the graveyard of the destitute:

A Letter to My Son

Furious at the mention of Gold Mountain,
My heart beaks at the thought of you my beloved son.
You promised with certainty when you departed,
You would be back in two or three years.
Exhorted by your mother,
Entreating you repeatedly.
We secretly wiped away tears when you departed,
It was because of poverty that you had to leave home.
Once you left your native land, how could you
Completely forget your hometown?
People say that a son in America will
Make his family rich and noble,
How could we have expected once you left home
That the money you sent back could not even pay for a cigarette.

Although poverty is determined by Heaven,
Gambling and whoring is your own failing.

As time passes, you have not found the gold that you sought,
You'd better turn around and come back home soon.
Since the outlook in the alien land is good,
Over ten years have passed already.

When will you pay back your parents' toil and care?
In order to avoid being ungrateful and in disrepute.
When will you see your brothers again?
To avoid more separation from your siblings
Who will be able to take care of your wife on your behalf?
To avoid leaving your wife in an empty house, sad and lonely.

"Charting your career path before the age of thirty," as the old saying goes,
You are almost thirty now.
Having no children of your own,
Your wife is drowning in tears all day long.
Your mother is becoming old and weak,
Me, your father, I am growing gaunt and weak
No longer able to step out of the house
Tired and without appetite for food or drink,
Often spending the day lying on a mat or sleeping in bed.

Today's world is full of disappointment,
Neither reason nor sympathy prevails.
People gossip about the absence of a son,
Saying that I do not have a son to attend to me when I may be dying leaves
    me feeling alone and helpless.
Hearing what people are saying makes me choke with tears,
Crying silently all the time.
If you want to see your parents, turn around now
Come back home without delay.
If you return home too late,
We may only meet in the afterworld.
However rich you may be at that time,
You will be facing our tombs alone and with only your sobs.
This letter is too short for me to express my feelings,
It's all up to your heart whether you will listen to me.[30]

This letter/ballad, to be sung in the manner of rhythmic *wuyi muyudiao*, relates the fate of many of the Chinese laborers who went overseas and never returned:

The Good Wife Anticipates the Return of Her Husband

In the evening, with watery eyes, I recall the time my husband left.
I said to you that we were married for only a half year.
At leisure I look to the distance with worry; from low to high I have vacant
    eyes.
Soon at New Year's I went out in the neighborhood,
    wondering when my husband would return.
At the lunar January lantern show it is crowded;
    men and women are watching the show eagerly.
But I just stay in my boudoir alone, alone in the room.
People are joyful at the lantern festival,
But I'm gloomy with untold complaints.
Thinking long and hard I cannot be relieved,
    with tears and a desolate mood.
One day if I become shameless,
I will shyly peek at a handsome man.[31]

The sentiments of wives and women who mourned the loss of those who
never returned from North America are heard in multiple popular ballads,
such as this representative sample:

This man of talent is right for me,
And the feeling between us is mutual.
Suddenly you are departing for America,
Leaving me your young girl of around ten years old.
How could you bear parting with me?
Standing tall and going forward to a foreign land.
Sailing across the Pacific Ocean,
Leaving me alone, cold, and inconsolable on my pillow.
I am young and afraid to sleep alone,
Why should you go and stay abroad?
Yet you still travelled to America,
I regret that we are separated by thousands of miles.
Let me ask you,
How long can one's youthful beauty last?
Even if you become rich and famous in America,
You will still make this beautiful woman frown with sadness.
Time flies,
And we can never retrieve it.

I lose my youthful looks with each passing day,
And I seek to seize the moment and live life to the fullest!
Sigh,
My husband is in Gold Mountain,
No matter how much money is brought back home,
You cannot buy back our youth.[32]

Absence stirred grief that led to special rituals of healing. Communities of the Wuyi *qiaoxiang* possess a heritage of reconstructing family lineages for those whose male line was interrupted by a migrant to North America who never returned. In the *qiaoxiang* tradition, these families were known to purchase a son so as to formalize the continuity of the male lineage of the absent migrant. In some cases the deceased migrant's parents found for their absent son a wife: the new bride was to hold a rooster in place of the husband during the wedding ceremony. With her marriage symbolically consummated, the daughter-in-law was thereby able to move into the now multigenerational family home. These special *jinshan* wives knew their symbolic husbands only from the evidence of a photo or from testimony from one of their former acquaintances that the husbands had indeed been *jinshan* uncles. Such special *jinshan* wives are known in some circles as "virgin widows."

Researchers from the Guangdong Qiaoxiang Culture Research Center met with such a family in Long'anli, Shuilouxiang, Dajiang Town, Taishan County. We express our appreciation to Li Zhuohao, who served as cultural informant and who himself is a descendant of the family. His grandfather was a Chinese railroad laborer who worked in the United States and subsequently moved to Canada. According to the family history, the grandfather continued to send remittances but never returned home and eventually died in Canada. The grandmother of Li Zhuohao was known as a virgin widow, and she was married into the family in a ceremony in which she held a rooster to stand in for the absent groom. She subsequently obtained a son from Enping County, and this boy grew to become the father of Li Zhuohao.

———

Based on the reference materials in the *qiaoxiang*, we have endeavored to reverse the perspective and to render the aspirations and realities of the gold miners and railroad laborers who made the passage to North America, as well as some who were able to return to their home villages. Evidence of Chinese laborers in North America may be found in official documents, but in the *qiaoxiang* the government records offer little in the way of personal stories. Popular and private sources are, as we demonstrate, indispensable for research on the Chinese laborers from the perspective of *qiaoxiang*. Indeed, we plan to continue to seek and interpret such relics, oral testimonies, and materials of popular culture.

Appendix

POEM 1

Verse 1

敬告诸梓里,
莫短英雄气,
发财终需遇时期,
独係眼前条命否。
运一至,
转贫为富易,
十万腰缠回家里,
天伦叙乐笑微微

Verse 2

自小真劳碌,
三餐共碗粥,
每受饥寒难尽录,

今幸时来唔驰卜。
发达速,
买田兼起屋,
感谢皇天撑开目,
赐我寿长享晚福。

Verse 3

目下难糊口,
造化睇未透,
唔信这样到白头,
祇因眼前命不偶。
运气凑,
世界还在后,
转过几年富且厚,
恁时置业起洋楼。

POEM 2

当年穷过鬼,
霎时富且贵,
唔难屋润又家肥,
回忆囊空因命水。
运气凑,
黄白从心遂,
杯极泰来财积累,
腰缠十万锦衣归。

挥首太阳望,
还家向甲方,
霎时富足就回唐,
顺经横滨到香港。
趁春光,
约友齐同往,
十万腰缠归乡党,
天伦叙乐慰高堂。

POEM 3

金山客,
冇一千有八百;
南洋伯,

银袋包,
大伯大伯;
香港仔,
香港赚钱香港使。

十一月冬,
十二月年,
阿爸金山多寄钱,
新年人人做新衣,
买个肥鹅过肥年。

POEM 4

有女毋嫁读书君，
自己闩门自己睇；
有女毋嫁做饼郎，
三年不睇倒半年床；

有女毋嫁耕田人，
时时泥气鬱败人；

有女要嫁金山客，
打转船头百算百。

POEM 5

月亮弯弯过九洲，
有人快乐有人忧，
有人发财还乡井，
有人离家外漂流。
逗留羁旅邸，
依旧满身债，
毫无振作暗伤怀，
每念高堂年纪迈。
欲归计，
囊中冇文解，

发愤图强来他徙，
仍然屯蹇事无谐。
一生条命薄，
来去都冇作，
纵使离乡转外国，
东走西奔无所获。
阴阳错，
出更门落索，
转过天涯四个角，
居弗安兮行不乐。

POEM 6 《寄子书》 A *letter to my son*

提起金山怒冲天，
忆着你们更凄惨。
来往该时讲口响，
三年两载转回乡。
你母叮呤言至嘱，
言来至嘱万千千。
临行暗拭离情泪，
缘贫无奈别家庭。
岂知一往离乡井，
忘却故园这一边。
人话有儿到美境，
穷根可断振家声。
讵知自别庭帏后，
付来未够买烟钱。
虽则贫穷天注定，
好嫖好赌怎能胜
日久黄金唔遂愿，
早宜拨马转回程。

既係他乡风景好
算来不觉十余年。
问你劬劳何时报，
忘恩背义非人形。
问你雁行何日叙
分离手足独茕茕。
问你妻房谁代养，
空帏岑寂自悲伤。
古语云创业前三十
,你今三十尚余零，
膝下未添男和女，
妻房终日泪涟涟。
你母近今年衰老，
风前之烛春水冰。
我今身瘦和血弱，
不曾移步出庭前。
茶饭不思精神疲，
时就身蓆在床眠。

况今世界三欺两，
道理唔通不念情。
人话有儿当作冇，
送终无子寡伶仃。
侧耳听闻喉哽咽，
暗垂珠泪落无停。
如欲见亲须速转，

即刻回家莫流连。
倘若迟来难见面，
相逢只恐在幽冥。
异日纵然千百万，
空对灵前哭几声。
纸短情长难尽述，
听乎否也问心田。

POEM 7

才郎合妹意，
正是两情痴，
忽然又话往花旗，
奴况青春年十几。
忍割舍，
挺生飘异地，
帆驾太平洋万里，
丢侬孤枕冷凄其。
青春怕独寝，
君何出外羁，
虽然游历到花旗，
恨隔程途千万里。

试问汝，
韶华曾有几?
纵使富贵留欧美，
空教红粉锁双眉。

光阴如急板，
得去不得返,,
催奴日日减朱颜，
行乐及时唔可慢。
一声叹，
夫婿在金山，
纵使腰缠归十万，
也唔能买青春还。

CHAPTER 4

Overseas Remittances of Chinese Laborers in North America

YUAN DING, WITH ROLAND HSU

The term *qiaohui*, or overseas remittance, refers to the money transferred by expatriate Chinese back to China through a variety of public and private organizations and individuals in foreign and Chinese currencies. In modern Chinese history, overseas remittances constituted a major source of foreign exchange and played an important role in regional economic development.

Bank draft remittances came mainly from the Americas and Southeast Asia. Remittance operations in North America consisted of a variety of institutions and developed into relatively complex enterprises. The earliest merchandise traders gave way to more sophisticated remittance businesses, which began to appear in North America, Hong Kong, Guangzhou, and the Pearl River delta in China in the form of what came to be known as Gold Mountain trading firms. With these firms, overseas Chinese initiated the method of remittance via what were by all intents and purposes bank drafts, and by these instruments they protected their families' interests.

In this chapter we explore how these remittance mechanisms developed and operated on both sides of the Pacific Ocean. Our sources of evidence in the banking sector date from periods somewhat later in the twentieth century.[1] We examine the development of remittance institutions in this later period and extrapolate to the origins in the period of the Chinese railroad workers and the construction of the Central Pacific Railroad.

In the late nineteenth and early twentieth centuries, approximately 80 percent of foreign remittances were sent to Guangdong Province.[2] Modern Guangdong remittances were directed to four clustered regions: the Pearl

River delta, the Chaoshan area, Xinmei, and the Hainan area. Due to differences between the regions' geographical conditions, historical traditions, economic development, social life, dialect, and distribution of overseas Chinese, remittance enterprises varied from place to place. The Pearl River delta area, with its Cantonese dialect, encompassed Taishan, Xinhui, Kaiping, and the Four Counties of Enping, as well as Guangzhou, Dongguan, the South China Sea, Panyu, Shunde, Zhongshan, Jiangmen, Heshan, and other cities and counties. It was where a major component of the overseas Chinese population came from, and it contained an abundance of foreign remittance exchange offices. Evidence from the twentieth century demonstrates that in addition to the public sector (post offices and state-owned banks), the private overseas remittance businesses (Gold Mountain trading firms, silver currency banks, China Information Bureau, and merchandise traders) operated in parallel economies.

From the 1850s on, a large number of Chinese laborers went to the United States for gold mining, setting off a wave of Chinese immigration to North America. The earliest migrants who returned to China carried back with them any money that they may have accumulated, or entrusted such funds to family or clan relatives. There was no specific agency dedicated to the remittance business, and the random and personal way that money transfers were handled did not guarantee delivery.

After 1854 the number of Chinese laborers in America rapidly increased, as did the market demand for the number and value of remittances. Chinese laborers in North America regularly sent money to their families in China to maintain family ties and sustain relatives. In response to this growing demand, some merchandise traders recognized the opportunity to launch remittance operations within their regular commerce. Based on their status as compatriots and their reputations as reliable merchants, these traders began to carry letters and money back to China for the laborers in the United States. As part of their exchange of goods and remittances, these traders also played a role in the informal recruiting of new migrant laborers, and as their operations grew, they began charging a fee for their remittance service. They also often wrote letters for illiterate laborers and their families, performed currency exchanges, and delivered letters and money to remote areas in China. This was the beginning of what was to become a large-scale and notably privately capitalized overseas remittance business.

As the market for such remittance business grew in North America, Hong

Kong, Guangzhou, and the Pearl River delta, the merchandise traders formed what came to be known as Gold Mountain trading firms. Many factors played a role in the development of these firms. By the end of 1850, because of the Taiping Rebellion in Guangdong and Guangxi, a large number of mainland and overseas Chinese had settled in Hong Kong. Many of them were well-off businessmen who opened a variety of stores and trading firms in Hong Kong.

In 1854 Li Sheng, from Guangdong, founded Li Hing Gold Mountain, one of the most famous of such firms. Li Hing Gold Mountain sold various goods from the Americas as well as Chinese native specialties while simultaneously operating as a remittance and currency exchange center. Later, Li Sheng turned his venture into a family business that he named He Hing Hong Gold Mountain. He became the leader of one of the earliest Chinese commercial enterprises and also one of the three wealthiest Chinese men in Hong Kong at that time.

The Gold Mountain trading firms in Hong Kong, which also operated subsidiary branches in the United States, specialized in import-export markets. In mainland China, Gold Mountain firms purchased silk, tea, porcelain, bristles, tung oil, handicrafts, and other goods. They sold these to the United States and exported flour and manufactured goods from the United States to China. These companies also found the remittance business profitable, so they entered that field as well, creating a new way for remittances to flow across borders.

The rise of the Gold Mountain remittance industry was not accidental. As the first model of a United States–China import–export business enterprise, the firms maximized earnings by capitalizing on margins on both exports and imports. At the time, many overseas Chinese, particularly the laborers in the United States, faced a dilemma: where to store their savings. Because many of them lived in simple communal accommodations with roommates, safeguarding money was not convenient or reliable. As a result, laborers often saved their incomes at a local Chinese grocery store through a familiar Chinese businessman whom they trusted. They sought to regularly transfer their money back to their hometowns in China. Thus, Chinese grocery stores were becoming in effect the laborers' safety deposit boxes. These shops leveraged the laborers' assets as a form of interest-free liquidity, thereby expanding their operating funds and facilitating their business operations.

The stores were willing to undertake custody of the laborers' money, then collaborate with Gold Mountain trading firms to transport remittances to

China. On the one hand, the firms could borrow money from the laborers; on the other hand, they could earn an additional fee from transporting that money for the laborers. Large importers and exporters cooperated with their counterparts in Hong Kong and mainland China to collect remittance funds and transport these funds back to the laborers' homes in China via regular shipping routes. They shared a cut of the profits from the fees. According to statistical surveys, by the 1920s the number of Hong Kong trading firms had grown to more than 380, and many major local companies also operated in North America to transfer remittances.

Because they specialized in the import-export economy, these firms in North America or China did not transfer cash directly but rather bought goods in America with overseas remittances and exported the goods to China together with other goods. In the process of buying goods for sale, they paid with remittances, which in turn expanded their own assets and earned them more profits. This was one of the reasons that official Chinese agencies (post offices and state-owned banks) could not compete with them. In addition, the Gold Mountain trading firms and grocery stores usually ran a variety of businesses besides remittances, such as selling travel tickets and hotel bookings, bringing them more profits. In addition, the Gold Mountain trading firms and various small shops often provided letter-writing services for overseas Chinese and their families that enabled transpacific communication. Moreover, as China's legal currency devalued compared to foreign assets, Gold Mountain trading firms, with their flexible exchange rates and payment modes, competed directly with government-run agencies that were tied to fixed exchange rates. In so doing, they won the majority of overseas Chinese customers based on reliability and competitive pricing.

Laborers from the Guangdong Pearl River delta who were working overseas in North America developed a unique way of sending remittances back home via bank drafts. This method emerged in the early twentieth century and continued into the 1950s. Given the proximity to our period of interest, it is worth investigating the remittance process with this available evidence and with an eye toward extrapolating its nineteenth-century origins.

The Chinese overseas laborers who purchased money orders in US currency or Hong Kong foreign drafts did so directly from banks, then mailed the money orders or drafts in the form of registered letters to their relatives in China. The money order was also known as the *zezhi* (bank draft) because it was mainly issued by three US banks (Bank of Manhattan Company,

American Express Company, and City Bank of New York). The bank draft could be resold to a third party after the payee in the destination country had received and endorsed it.[3]

It is noteworthy that the bank draft was not purchased from an American bank's foreign currency department but rather from the domestic unit of that bank. In other words, the bank draft was not a foreign exchange bill but rather a domestic remittance method that made it all the way through the flow of remittances in foreign financial markets.[4] The bank draft had two characteristics: first, the amount was denominated in US dollars; second, the place of payment was in the United States. Thus, the circulation of a bank draft began with purchasing it from an American bank and sending it to China, especially the area around Guangfu Township, then selling it from one town to another, then collecting the bank draft in Guangzhou and Hong Kong. The bank draft was finally redeemed in the United States by the importer-exporter or others who needed to purchase goods in North America. The reason that overseas Chinese did not like to buy their bank drafts in Chinese currency is because it would then need to be converted using unfavorable official exchange rates.

Thus, the bank draft was a smart way for overseas Chinese to maintain the value of their remittances by turning a US domestic bill into an international financial instrument. Overseas purchases of Hong Kong drafts can be described in the same way: they also fulfilled the purpose of maintaining and increasing the value of the remittances. The following text was published in the 1915 *Sunning* (Xinning) *Journal* of Taishan in Guangdong as an advertisement:

Remittances

WAI YICK MONEY BROKERS
SUN CHONG CITY
Sun Ning District
Canton China

Our firm is located on Xinchang Xiangfa Street, and we have specialized in the gold and silver exchange business for several years. We are very grateful for everyone's support and consistent trust, which has made our business stable and successful. All kinds of currencies, as well as gold and silver, from three counties, including En Ping, Kai Ping, and Xinhui, can go through our firm. If overseas laborers wish to send silver to their hometowns, they can use our store for guaranteed payment and send us their letters with their red papers, [and] we will exchange according to the current market price. We will deliver letters with the silver to your home quickly and safely. In case there is an accident on the way, we will pay you the full amount as reparations, and we will keep our promise. We will deliver your letter based on the address on the envelope and you will receive it without problem. To protect from loss, you can attach an additional letter to your red paper to show that your red paper is from a Hong Kong Bank account, so that we can keep track of your registered letter and avoid having it captured by others.

Contact persons: Chengzhen Tan, Wenfeng Tan

In four years of Ming Guo Xinchang XiangFa Street Hui Yi Silver. Yours.[5]

The ad is a clear indication that the company's mode of operation is to exchange bank draft paper remittances for payment.

In some cases, remittances from North America occurred through national postal transfer, and the process did not involve foreign exchange trading. In much of the early modern period the foreign exchange currency held by overseas laborers' relatives was legal tender. Thus, even though the national government discovered that the main way of escaping official remittance channels for overseas Chinese in North America was to purchase the US bank draft, it was unable to impose restrictions or to capture this market.

The Pearl River delta saw a large number of people moving to North America beginning in 1848 after the discovery of gold in California. The remittance industry benefited from the fact that relatives of overseas Chinese in the Pearl River delta lived in concentrated areas. This is related to the immigration history and the different characteristics of two regions: Meixian and Shantou, in Guangdong and southern Fujian. Beginning with the Ming dynasty, the history of those who emigrated from Meixian and Shantou in Guangdong and the southern region of Fujian to Southeast Asia spanned nearly six hundred years. Through the centuries, the process continued of waves of migrations following established routes and diaspora communities. Out of these population centers, emigration spread to most towns in the region. As the bank draft became the predominant instrument for sending North American remittances, the Guangdong Postal Authority Bureau began to pay more attention to postal management in the Pearl River delta, especially in the Siyi region, where a preponderance of overseas Chinese remittances were sent. In order to improve the delivery speed of imported mail for the Siyi region, in 1948 a postal service inspector, Liang Jun Chen, from Guangdong's Postal Service Management Bureau, personally visited Jiangmen, Xinhui, Xinchang, Changsha, and other post offices, inspecting postal routes, couriers, postal waiting times, and other aspects before giving detailed instructions on improvements and how to effectively implement them for each office.[6] In addition to improving the speed of mail delivery, postal administrations strengthened the security of Guangdong's international mail, and they uncovered cases in which overseas Chinese letters with bank draft remittances had been stolen and subject to fraud. For example, between August 1946 and January 1947, the postal administration arrested two men, Jie Lu and Guanxion Lu, who were the sons of a former Xinhui post office chief. They had stolen many letters containing remittances.[7] As a result, such remittances became more trusted by the overseas Chinese.

While the Chinese postal service sought to secure its operations, North American Gold Mountain trading firms expanded their market shares by delivering to a wider range of areas not covered by the postal service. Based on the Domestic Address Survey of 1948, conducted by the Postal Authority of Guangdong, we can establish that among the relatives of overseas Chinese in the Pearl River delta, many mailing addresses consisted of a town, a firm, or a business referred by a firm.[8] As overseas Chinese in North America increasingly sent bank drafts to deliver remittances, the firms captured more of the transfer, exchange, and delivery market. In Kaiping, Taishan, Xinhui, and other areas, the North American remittances transfer business occurred concurrently within the regular business of silver currency banks, pharmacies, grocery stores, and other import-export markets in local areas.[9]

The institution of the "City Running Horse," or postal courier service, also played an important role in the business of transferring remittances. The courier service operated in various urban and rural locales in the Pearl River delta and specialized in transferring letters to relatives.[10] Due to the efficiency of the service, remittance firms could trust that their bank drafts would be delivered, and the accompanying order for merchandise would be filled, often by the end of the same day.[11]

For those areas where there was no postal service, North American overseas Chinese could also send their bank drafts to relatives in Hong Kong or Guangzhou and use the family network to have the remittance forwarded to their mainland relatives. Overseas Chinese in North America chose this method because most had relatives who had settled in Hong Kong or Guangzhou. This characteristic of the Guangzhou population was another reason why the method of remittances differed between the Pearl River delta region and the Shantou/Meixian southern region.

Because of Hong Kong's geographical and political significance, it played a special role in the remittance business as a transit hub and as a key site for legally converting remittances from foreign currency into Chinese currency. It is worth noting that private overseas remittance firms were not the only ones to use Hong Kong as a hub. Even Chinese government organizations such as the Bank of China, agricultural institutions, and the Postal Remittance Bureau transacted currency exchange and transit through Hong Kong.

While China's economy continued to be unstable, most of the private overseas remittance firms transited their exchange business through Hong Kong and subsequently used private market exchanges to convert foreign currency into the Chinese national currency before mailing the remittances to inland Guangdong Province. Because Hong Kong was southern China's major port, there was great demand and a ready market to conduct transactions in Hong Kong dollars, which could be held as a hedge against the devaluing mainland currency. Particularly in Hong Kong, the British authorities permitted an open market for the sale of foreign currency and its conversion into Chinese currency. Most of the private firms that specialized in overseas remittances established a branch or agency in Hong Kong in order to retain a foothold in the profitable market. These private remittance establishments remitted funds to Hong Kong, then used black market exchange rates to sell the foreign currency in Hong Kong or Guangdong. They then converted the money into Chinese legal tender or gold yuan to pay the hometown recipients.

In San Francisco, for example, after Gold Mountain trading firms charged overseas Chinese workers in US dollars, the firms could hand over dollars to their Hong Kong branches through a Chinese or foreign bank or purchase Hong Kong currency from a Chinese or foreign bank before sending the money to the Hong Kong branch. The Hong Kong branch could sell the money locally.

The firms also had a variety of ways to convert Chinese currency into Hong Kong dollars. For example, for payment in Taishan, when the Hong Kong branch acquired the Hong Kong currency, agents could send it directly to their Taishan associates; the latter would exchange it for Chinese currency before paying it to the overseas Chinese relatives in Taishan. In practice, Taishan's overseas remittance operations had an ample supply of currency in savings. As soon as the San Francisco branch of the remittance business sent a number of overseas remittances for immediate payment, the Taishan branch did not have to wait for the funds from San Francisco to come into port. Because the supply of foreign currency might be sold out whenever the market reached a higher exchange rate, there was often a lag time between when the funds were sent and when they were paid out. The firm could place high-interest deposits and continue its advance distributions.[12]

Some large overseas offices also used a so-called reverse expenditure, or what may be called an inverted remittance process. That is, whenever the Gold Mountain firm transferred remittances from San Francisco to Hong Kong, the Taishan branch could write a money order that could be paid via Hong Kong dollars and sell it locally. The Hong Kong branch could subsequently write a money order payable to the firm that needed to withdraw money from the San Francisco branch, so that the three branches were connected in order to clear the transaction.

In the money order business, firms maintained a number of direct contacts with Shanghai firms to transfer funds from Shanghai to Hong Kong through Guangdong without leaving a trace. The money order business was very simple and flexible, since a piece of paper could suffice to complete relatively large monetary transactions. The flow of remittances through private businesses thus amounted to a form of corporate foreign currency smuggling.

There were many creative ways of conducting the private remittances business in Hong Kong. They included the development of the overseas remittances business as part of a franchise, in which the main import and export business concurrently ran an overseas remittances business. Similarly, transit businesses, hotels, general merchandise stores, currency exchange businesses, and gold and silver jewelry businesses could also run overseas remittances businesses alongside their import-export commerce.[13]

Table 4.1—an excerpt of a survey of Hong Kong firms—documents this mode of operation.

In the discussion of how North American remittances were transported, we cannot ignore the impact of the black market in the Pearl River delta area. Because the bank draft had a broad market demand, relatives could obtain the maximum redemption value from them. Therefore, once remittances entered the black market, extensive arbitrage took place that facilitated forms of evasion. The expansion of the remittance supply market contributed to the expansion of the black market for remittances. The number of remittances from North America in the Pearl River delta far exceeded the number from Southeast Asia in Shantou, Meixian, and the southern Fujian region. Also, the North American remittances in the Pearl River delta were dispersed to various relatives, mostly in the form of Hong Kong dollars and other currency instruments. By contrast,

TABLE 4.1 Hong Kong Gold Mountain Statistics (1956)

Firm Name	Business Scope	Remittance Methods	Remittance Regions	Monthly Remittances
Hang Xin Long	Chinese herbal medicine store, export trade, overseas remittance	Bank of China	Taishan: US, Canada	10,000 RMB
Zhou Yi-Tong	Overseas remittance	Domestic and overseas associates, Bank of China	Kaiping: US, Canada	5,000 to 10,000 RMB
Pan Baixiang	Import and export trade, overseas remittance	Mainland associates, Bank of China	Kaiping: South America, US, Canada	10,000 RMB
Liyuan Village	Overseas remittance	Mainland associates, Chiyu Bank	Xinhui: US, Canada	HK$100,000
Nanchang Goldsmith	Gold, money exchange, overseas remittance	Mainland associates, Guangdong Bank	Taishan: US	500,000 to 600,000 RMB
Li Heng Bank	Gold, money exchange, overseas remittance	Domestic and overseas associates, Bank of China, Commercial Bank of China	Taishan: North, Central, and South America	HK$600,000
Hengxing Chang	Overseas remittance	Mainland associates, Chiyu Bank	Taishan: North, Central, and South America, Burma, Singapore, Malaya	HK$400,000
Yongchang	Passengers, overseas remittance	Domestic and overseas associates, OCBC Bank, Dao Heng Bank, Hang Seng Bank	Zhongshan: US, Latin America, Canada	40,000 RMB
Wing Tai Company	Trade, overseas remittance	Mainland associates	Kaiping: US, Canada	10,000 RMB
Victory Village	Import-export, overseas remittance	Domestic and overseas associates, Bank of China	Taishan: Canada, US	10,000 RMB
Andrew Lo	Import-export, overseas remittance	Domestic and overseas associates, Bank of China	Kaiping: Singapore, Malaya, US, Canada	8,000 to 9,000 RMB

(continued)

TABLE 4.1 *(continued)*

Firm Name	Business Scope	Remittance Methods	Remittance Regions	Monthly Remittances
East Asia Trading	Import-export, overseas remittance	Mainland associates, Bank of China	Taishan: US, Canada, Australia	50,000 RMB
Liu Fen Kee	Overseas remittance	Mainland associates, Bank of China	Taishan: US, Canada, Australia	110,000 to 120,000 RMB
Hing Kee	Import-export, overseas remittance	Domestic and overseas associates, Salt Surplus Tax	Taishan, Guangzhou: US, Canada, Mexico	400,000 RMB
Da Hua Silver	Currency exchange, gold, overseas remittance	Overseas associates, Ka Wah Bank, Overseas Bank	Kaiping, Guangzhou: US, Canada	Unknown
Tak Kee	Meat company, overseas remittance	Domestic and overseas associates, Bank of China	Taishan: US, Canada	7,000 to 8,000 RMB
Ankang Ning	Food and drug department stores, overseas remittance	Mainland associates, Guangdong Bank	Taishan: US, Canada, Cuba	50,000 RMB
Prosperous Goldsmith	Real estate, overseas remittance	Mainland associates, Bank of China	Taishan: US, Canada	50,000 RMB
Njan Kee	Travel, overseas remittance	Mainland associates, Bank of China	Taishan: US, Canada	20,000 RMB

SOURCE: Guangdong Archives Bureau, Department of Government and Party Archives, collection 3; "Guangdong CCP Committee and Provincial Government and Departments, South China Bureau, South-Central Bureau of the CCP Central Committee." See: http://digitalassets.lib.berkeley.edu/ieas/CRM_045.pdf

the Southeast Asian remittances in Shantou, Meixian, and the southern Fujian region were mostly in the form of foreign currency that was controlled by the Overseas Remittance Bureau for resale in Hong Kong. Thus, the black market for remittances in the Pearl River delta was far larger than the one in Shantou, Meixian, and the southern Fujian region. Originally, the real demand for foreign currency and foreign exchange funds came from importers and others seeking to evade financial regulations through capital flight. However, many middlemen and speculators appeared to connect overseas relatives and the importers and evaders. These middlemen, speculators, importers, and evaders drove the formation of a huge black market in remittances. They played a key role in the market for North American remittances in the Pearl River delta.

In terms of the importers' role in the black market, all imported goods, whether they were purchased from foreign countries, Hong Kong and Macau, or Guangzhou's Jardine, Matheson & Co., needed to be paid for using foreign currency or Hong Kong dollars.[14] Those who fell under the category of importers included the businessmen who directly imported goods from foreign ports as well as those who purchased goods in the secondary market. Such foreign goods were popular and in demand in Cantonese-speaking regions; therefore, there were many foreign goods importers in these urban and rural areas. To conduct their transactions, the importers needed a large quantity of Hong Kong dollars and foreign currency. In order to obtain this sum, many of them leveraged their business of remittances. In some cases, the Hong Kong dollars and foreign currency they accrued may not have been able to meet their needs, or they themselves did not necessarily operate using Hong Kong dollars and foreign currency, so they had to ask for additional help from other Gold Mountain trading firms that operated their businesses using Hong Kong dollars and foreign currency.[15] This in turn promoted the Gold Mountain trading firms' connections to the foreign currency traders.[16]

To avoid government regulation, importers generally did not carry cash but rather bank drafts because drafts were easier to conceal.[17] This made the price of Hong Kong drafts rise to the level where they were sometimes more expensive than Hong Kong currency. In this situation, US dollars could also be worth less than the Hong Kong drafts. As an example from a later period, from 1946 to 1949, in order to align the Hong Kong currency with the United States currency, the British introduced a foreign exchange control policy in Hong Kong, limiting the supply of US currency.[18] This further prompted importers to increase the price they were willing to pay to purchase US currency in the

Pearl River delta area. Thus, the demand that grew from the origins with Chinese migrant laborers for foreign currency and financial instruments from importers caused American remittances to fall into the hands of importers in the form of money orders mailed by overseas Chinese. In the Pearl River delta, the middlemen and speculators from underground trading firms played a special role in the remittances black market. They were the link between suppliers and customers. That is, they were the most immediate customers and importers of the foreign currency remittances of overseas relatives as well as the most direct suppliers of fugitive capital for foreign currency remittances. As a result, their position in the remittances black market was critical, and their impact was direct.

From 1946 to 1947, although the Chinese national government banned the circulation of foreign currency, the expansion of the foreign currency remittances market allowed underground trading firms to thrive. Around 1946 there were forty firms registered with the government in Shiqi town of Zhongshan County.[19] To cloak their operations, these banks advertised other commodities, often under disguised names. Because of these firms' underground operations and secrecy, economic historians are unable to verify the precise number of firms in a given year. The black market for remittances in the Pearl River delta region thus evolved somewhat organically, with links in a network with Shanghai, Hong Kong, and other financial centers, and also with each overseas relative through firms in their home villages, towns, and counties. In this network trading firms in the nearby cities and towns were eager to conduct trade in the morning because the final price for Hong Kong and US bank drafts tended to rise throughout the day.[20] The larger currency-trading firms would buy the Hong Kong and US bank drafts from each village firm and subsequently bring them to Guangzhou for market-price liquidation. The selling price of these foreign drafts differed between the rural villages and the city of Guangzhou. For example, in Xinchang, a firm stated that "the black market foreign exchange rate here is based on Guangzhou's rate but usually ten to twenty or forty to fifty yuan lower per thousand than in Guangzhou."[21] This difference became their profit margin. In order to raise cash to buy Hong Kong and US bank drafts, these firms also carried remittances between local areas and Guangzhou and charged a premium for the service. According to the Xinchang branch of Bank of China's report: "As for remittances in Guangzhou Jiangmen, there are so many trading firms here. They absorb cash and charge a premium to purchase Hong Kong bank drafts and US bank drafts, the highest premium is seventy-six yuan per hundred, usually one to two yuan per hundred. There is no way for our bank to compete with them, so the remittances in the province are lost to us."[22]

Through the acquisition of Hong Kong and US bank drafts from firms in counties, towns, and villages, most of the foreign currency remittances in the Pearl River delta area were finally concentrated in the profits of Guangzhou black market firms. These firms became the main suppliers of imported goods and the principal source for those seeking capital flight by using bank drafts.

In order to capitalize on the market trends, the larger Guangzhou firms opened branch offices in other cities.[23] Many of these larger firms in the Guangzhou area established their own dedicated sales networks. For example, Guangzhou YouAn Silver Bank had branch offices in Jiangmen, Shunde, Xinchang, Foshan, Rongqi, Shiqiao, Shiqi, and Daliang, as well as other places. The Eu Yan Sang firm operated in Xinchang, Taishan, Zhongshan, Dongguan, Huizhou, Panyu, Xinyi, Shunde, Qingyuan, Heshan, Sanshui, Huaxian County, Gaozhou, Gaoyao, Zengcheng, Nanhai, and Xinhui, for a total of seventeen locations.[24] Although their practices were widespread, the operational details of underground firms for foreign currency remittances remained a guarded secret. Within each private network, they broadcast private radio news of black market rates. Their system was so sophisticated and lucrative that even the Bank of China's Xinchang branch wanted to negotiate with them to supply proprietary information on financial market rates.[25]

The operation of the remittances black market, as described above, was of course open to variation. A number of local underground firms could directly sell Hong Kong and US bank drafts in Guangzhou. Also, firms in towns and counties could directly bring Hong Kong and US bank drafts to Hong Kong in order to sell them more profitably. Furthermore, in addition to the simplicity of a single exchange using Hong Kong and US bank drafts, a number of black market firms may have found other ways to maximize profits. For example, extending our analysis to the mid-twentieth century and to the beginning of China's currency reform, Taishan underground firms acquired Hong Kong currency and bought gold in Hong Kong, then resold it at the public resale price set by China's national government in order to reap huge profits.[26]

The large-scale remittances black market operated by trading firms and importers thus enabled the evasion of regulations that characterized North American remittances, but it also served to prevent losses for individual overseas Chinese and their relatives.

CHAPTER 5

Chinese Railroad Workers' Remittance Networks

Insights Based on Qiaoxiang *Documents*

LIU JIN, WITH ROLAND HSU

The most significant flow of Chinese railroad workers in North America originated from the Pearl River delta region in Guangdong Province, especially from the four counties of the Siyi region—Taishan, Kaiping, Xinhui, and Enping. In this chapter we develop historical detail on the flow of remittances that the workers sent to China and on the impact of these remittances on home villages, based on recently discovered *qiaoxiang* (hometown) documents, including work and travel contracts to cross the Pacific Ocean during the period from the discovery of gold in North America to the US Chinese Restriction Act (1848–1882).[1]

In terms of the personal experience of the Chinese who migrated to work on the railroad, existing research has drawn on indirect accounts written by descendants. In *The Historical Record of the First Family Reunion Assembly of Ning Yeung People from Taishan in the U.S.*, first published in 1928, we find the following account from a descendant of a Chinese railroad worker who came to North America:

> During the reign of Emperors Xiangfeng and Tongzhi [1851–1875] in the
> Qing Dynasty, my hometown folks from Xinning (Taishan), pressured by
> the difficulty of earning a livelihood at home, went overseas to seek fortunes
> from colonial development. They traveled across the Pacific Ocean and settled
> down in the New World. Starting from scratch and carving out new routes,
> they built railroads and exploited gold mines. Every construction project was
> the product of our Xinning people's toil and sweat.[2]

This description conveys the factors that drove migration, as well as the poignant qualities of the narrative that have compelled historians to search for primary testimonies. In spite of extensive searches, as noted elsewhere in this definitive volume, there are no personal writings to be found in the remittance documentation, and the reasons are manifold.

During the 1850s and 1860s, the Chinese imperial and departmental governments lacked the ability to strictly regulate migration out of the territory. This may explain the incomplete nature of state archives from the era and why no specialized records have yet to be found, and in fact may not exist in the Chinese government archives. In addition, work on the railroad entailed exhausting menial labor. Available evidence indicates that the Chinese who traveled, in particular to the West Coast of North America, to work on the construction of the Central Pacific Railroad (CPRR) cherished a dream of making a fortune in what had recently become known as "Gold Mountain." Their journey, their sacrifice, and their flow of remittances were, they hoped, to be a story of accumulated wealth and glory. They were living an experience that was part of a narrative to migrate to this region of North America, choose their work, and transform themselves into wealthy businessmen. However, in reality the history of the Chinese contract railroad workers is replete with unskilled and underpaid manual labor, discriminatory employment practices, and an overall achievement that was uncelebrated in the railroad company's publicity, all of which seems hidden from the records that we are able to unearth from workers' remittance correspondence.

Finally, conditions in this era did not favor the preservation of paper documents. The overseas Chinese began to build *diaolou* (multistory defensive village houses) and Western-style mansions on a large scale only after the 1890s, especially during the period from the early twentieth century to the outbreak of the Sino-Japanese War in 1937. Our research has found that because *diaolou* and Western-style mansions were solid and durable, they were more weatherproof than the previous style of bungalows and proved to be ideal places for preserving paper *qiaoxiang* documents. For this reason, perhaps more than all others, we mostly find *qiaoxiang* documents dated from after 1900. The *qiaoxiang* documents dating from the years of the construction of the CPRR, to the extent that they were created and transferred to the workers' home villages, are thus most likely lost to the effects of time and circumstance.

Research by the Wuyi Overseas Chinese Museum

In the past fifteen years, during the process of conferring the status of a UNESCO World Heritage site to the Kaiping *diaolou* and the construction of the Wuyi Overseas Chinese Museum in Jiangmen, China, a great number of *huaqiao* (overseas Chinese) documents dating from around the start of the twentieth century have been discovered. These materials have been found by residents in the former hometowns of Chinese workers who traveled from the Wuyi region to build the CPRR.

Among the *qiaoxiang* documents, researchers have found *huaqiao* letters dating from the late Qing and early Republican eras (1880–1920), and we may be able to construct connections between the later evidence and the earlier history. Given that the CPRR was completed in 1869 and that most Chinese railroad workers employed on it were about eighteen to forty years old at the time, these same workers who returned to their home villages would have been sixty-one to eight-three years old at the time of the founding of the Republic of China in 1912. In this later era, when conditions were more favorable for preserving documents, the records of families would possibly include materials from veteran workers from the railroad construction in North America.

Chinese workers from the era of the construction of the CPRR, whether they built their wealth and returned home having worked on the rail line or in mining or other occupations, mainly came from the Pearl River delta, especially the Siyi region of Jiangsu Province, China. They spoke the same dialects and shared the same dietary customs and traditions of worship. They were compelled to seek work abroad by similar economic conditions in the home region and used the same network of remittances as a means of communicating with their hometowns. In this chapter we explore the Chinese railroad workers' interactions with their hometowns based on *qiaoxiang* documents dating from years after their work on the railroad construction.

Qiaoxiang documents provide special insight into the economic trajectories that led Chinese workers abroad, in particular to North America during the building of the CPRR. The path abroad up to the late 1870s may be traced through the transit of the Pacific steamships, especially the US Pacific Mail Steamship Company line. A memorial porcelain tablet made in Guangzhou in 1923 in honor of Mr. and Mrs. Li Junqian recorded that Li Junqian was born in Taishan County of Guangdong in 1831. The inscription on the tablet described Li Junqian: "He is industrious, thrifty, modest, kind and adventurous. He went across the Pacific to earn his living on a sailing boat in his boyhood. He had been to many port cities, including Sydney in Australia and Auckland, New Zealand and North America. He went back and forth among these places and finally bought a few plots of land and houses."[3] According to the inscription, Li Junqian earned a living overseas during the periods of the gold rush and the construction of North American railroads, but whether he had taken part in the construction of the railroads is not documented. Many folk songs circulating at the time in Siyi *qiaoxiang* evoked these Chinese laborers' experiences of going overseas by boat. The following is one poignant account:

> In the second reign year of Haamfung (Xianfeng [c. 1832]),
> a trip to Gold Mountain was made.
> With a pillow on my shoulder, I began my perilous Journey:
> Sailing a boat with bamboo poles across the seas,
> Leaving behind wife and sisters in search of money,
> No longer lingering with the woman in the bedroom,
> No longer paying respect to parents at home.[4]

The descendants of Li Junqian commemorated the arduous nature of the path and experience of overseas migrant labor:

> Men are born to suffer.
> No suffering, no growth.
> Everything is illusory,
> Only thrift is lasting wealth.[5]

The words *suffer* and *thrift* recur in numerous songs and poems about the experience of the Chinese who migrated to work in North America.

Research shows that most of the Chinese workers who went to European colonies in the New World were employed under coercive conditions by labor brokers. Records from colonial enterprises in such locations as the Spanish Caribbean, as well as Peru and Mexico, indicate that Chinese workers were predominantly indentured.[6] However, in the case of the Chinese in North America and especially along the Pacific Coast, new research using *qiaoxiang* documents indicates that Chinese workers took their own initiative to obtain loans to venture abroad to pursue gold and silver mining and railroad construction in the realm of Gold Mountain.

Here we analyze in depth three such overseas work loan contracts. The earliest existing deed related to gold mining was established by Ting Zhuo and Ting Zao during the third reign year of Xianfeng, in December 1853. The purpose of establishing this deed was to resolve disagreements arising from the repayments of the loan made to two family members, Ting Feng and Ting Bin, who borrowed the money to go to Gold Mountain for gold mining in the second reign year of Xianfeng, in February 1852. The deed was intended to "avoid conflict in the future and prevent discord in the family."[7] From the deed, it can be seen that neither Ting Feng nor Ting Bin made money at Gold Mountain, and Ting Feng could not repay the money that he had borrowed. The journey was not profitable, and he was fortunate to return home alive.

The second contract is a transfer deed (*rangtie*) established by Yi Suo during the first reign year of Tong Zhi, dated October 29, 1862. According to this deed, Yi Suo and Yi Chen lent forty taels of silver to Zhen Pei, who would "go to the Gold Mountain to dig for gold." In urgent need of money, Yi Chen and his father agreed to transfer the rights and interests of the deed to Zhen Neng. In the original deed signed in 1857, it was agreed that "120 taels" of silver should be repaid within one year, the loan and interest included.[8] "If the sum is not paid in time, an interest of 3 percent per month will be added to the total."[9] In 1862 Zhen Pei was still away from home, so the deed was transferred to a third party.

The third document is a loan receipt with Guan Ruyu as the borrower, who took out a usurious loan in order to travel to America. The agreement delineates the terms of contractual obligation:

> I, now in Hong Kong, draw three hundred and twelve dollars from the draft provided by Guan Guosong. The use of the sum is restricted to purchasing, through City Bank, ship's passage to the city of the City Bank Incorporation to the city of San Francisco. The sum of money should be remitted to Guan Guosong in Hong Kong within ten days after landing without delay. If the sum is not paid or if only part of the sum is paid, an interest of three dollars per one hundred will be added to the sum or the remaining sum. The money should be collected from the guarantor that should not decline the responsibility. I write this receipt as proof.[10]

On the paper loan receipt, the main items are preprinted, with blanks to be filled in to name the borrower and list the sum of the loan, the guarantor, and the date of the loan. In this we see that borrowing money to go abroad was a sufficiently common practice to warrant the printing of receipt forms. There was no signature of the guarantor on the receipt for a loan by Guan Ruyu. It is possible that he had a sort of kindred relationship with the loan provider, Guan Guosong, thereby making him a trustworthy person among

Guan Guosong's circle of contacts. Because Guan Ruyu reimbursed the lender more than half a year behind schedule, he may have paid interest in addition to the principal borrowed. In these three original loan deeds, we see evidence of the contracts that governed some Chinese who traveled to Gold Mountain during the era of free immigration to the United States from 1848 to 1882.

It was a common practice at that time to borrow money from relatives and friends to go abroad. Family members often offered help to one another for free out of a sense of obligation, but distant relatives and village folks offered only usury. This phenomenon can often be found in the *huaqiao* letters dated from the period of the late Qing dynasty [1850–1912] and the early Republican era [1912 and following] after the construction of the CPRR. In 1888 Guan Dekuan, from Kaiping County in Guangdong, wrote a letter from San Francisco to Guan Tingjie:

> My dear brother,
>
> Thank goodness! I have arrived at San Francisco safely. You may feel reassured...I hereby send you 65 *daying yuan* [Mexican dollars]. Please check your account for that, and return the money I have borrowed from Cong Zhen on my behalf. Please get back the deed and keep it for me. If there is any money left, you may use it on household management or keep the money yourself. As for the money I owe you, I will remit it one month later.[11]

In the letter from Guan Dekuan, we see that this was not the first time that he had gone abroad; he knew to collect money promptly from others to repay the loan as soon as he arrived in America. As we compare this letter with other historical sources, we find that this was a notably experienced migrant worker because in many cases it was difficult if not prohibitive for people to begin to send remittances immediately upon arrival. Migrant workers' feelings are vividly conveyed in their poems, such as

> In poverty I worried about daily meals,
> with a loan I came to the Gold Mountain.[12]

We learn in these materials that Chinese workers in North America prioritized accumulating wealth and returning home in glory.[13] Their correspondence with their families consisted mostly of money sent back home. Remittances (*yin*) combined with family letters (*xin*) were called *yinxin* (remittance letters) in the areas where the Cantonese dialects were spoken. It is especially intriguing for historians to uncover the methods of sending overseas remittances.

Yao Zengyin and other scholars have found, in a survey on overseas Chinese remittances in Guangdong *qiaoxiang* in 1938, that workers used a system of mail transfers. According to their research, mail transfer services were handled by Chinese-run firms based in San Francisco and Honolulu. They point to the well-studied "Six Companies" from San Francisco that handled many details of employment contracts and financial services, along with arbitration, and leveraged their contacts with US shipping companies to transmit remittances.[14] This early study provided the outlines for the transpacific money transfers; in what follows I look more closely at newly discovered *huaqiao* letters and account books.

One fully intact *huaqiao* letter that we have for study was sent from North America by Guan Renzi to Kaiping County, Guangdong Province, in 1883. The author mentions that he had been away from his brother Guan Tingjie for more than ten years. It can be inferred that he went overseas around 1873. The letter also documents that he "had sent 5 yuan this time" and "asked Yu A'you to take back 10 yuan" in November of the year before.[15] In this letter, Guan Renzi mentions that he had sent home two sums of money for household management, and that the 10 yuan he sent to his family in November the year before was "entrusted to Yu A'you." These two remittances and one more remittance were mentioned in Guan Renzi's letter to Guan Tingjie dated the fourteenth day of the seventh lunar month in the same year:

> I sent back 10 yuan in the middle of last November, which I asked Yu Fuzhang of the Yu Village to bring back. This year, I requested Li Bingxiang of San Bao Tong, Gou Pai Chong to take back 5 yuan for me. I wonder if you have received the money. Now I will entrust Guan A'qiang of Chuan Shan She with the task of taking back 5 yuan to you.[16]

The three sums of money were all entrusted to acquaintances who would return home. During the 1870s and continuing for some time thereafter it was common for overseas Chinese to take money back in person or entrust others to act as their couriers. Jiangmen Customs maintains records of this method, including this example from 1904:

> Inflow and outflow of money. Some money has been brought in by overseas Chinese in person, so the number was not recorded in the Customs account book. Numerous residents from the counties to the north and west of the Customs often go back and forth between their hometowns and foreign ports, such as San Francisco and Singapore. Vast amounts of money must

have been imported without being declared to the Customs, but it was hard to know how much money had been brought back. However, it goes without saying the place is affluent.[17]

Chinese Remittance Enterprises

Additional evidence indicates the emergence of a network of businesses around the Pacific Rim, including the places of *huaqiao* residences in North America, Hong Kong, and *qiaoxiang*. The network played an important role in delivering Chinese workers' *yinxin*, with Hong Kong as the hub. For additional details on the remittance industry, see the chapter in this volume by Yuan Ding.

Guang Tingjie, a man from Kaiping County in Guangdong, received a letter on the second day of the fourth lunar month in 1883 from Chao Chang of Baohua Business Establishment in Hong Kong:

Respected Tingjie,

Not long ago, a letter arrived, which said that Brother Renzi had sent a yinxin through Yong Tong'an. I have been sent to confirm it.[18]

Yong Tong'an may be a business establishment in Hong Kong. The early overseas remittances were first given to Chinese establishments that handled the *yinxin* courier services and delivered by regular international ferry service to a business run by Hong Kong affiliates. The remittances were subsequently deposited with a familiar business establishment in the *qiaoxiang*. Finally, the money was delivered to the dependents of overseas Chinese. Such a *yinxin* network formed among the acquaintances' circle was closely interwoven with a Chinese business network, which can be illustrated by *yinxin* account books from the era.

At the time Hong Kong was the commercial and financial center of South China; thus, most of the overseas Chinese savings deposits were kept in the financial institutions of this city. To suit the needs of trading with and sending remittances to the mainland, a number of so-called Gold Mountain firms and banking houses emerged that managed the remittances. In the collection of the Jiangmen Wuyi Overseas Chinese Museum, a book from 1901 titled *Records of the Sums of Remittances from Abroad*, includes the registration of numerous *yinxin* sent by steamship from North America and other points of

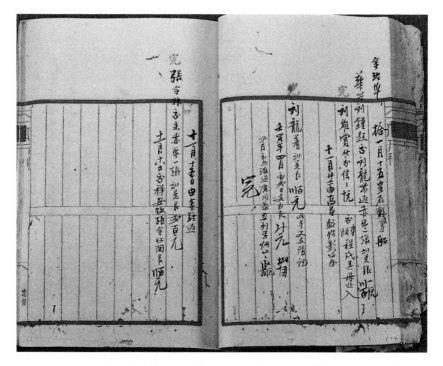

FIGURE 5.1   *Records of the Sums of Remittances from Abroad* (in Chinese, 1901),
containing items related to overseas Chinese remittances. In the collection of the
Jiangmen Wuyi Overseas Chinese Museum.

origin abroad (figure 5.1). This is a singular example and without publication
information beyond this example held in the museum collection.

Records of the Sums of Remittances from Abroad provides valuable information about the transmission and delivery of remittances. In case after case
we can trace the path of remittances from Gold Mountain firms or banking
houses, sent by passenger and cargo ships to Hong Kong, then transferred to
inland banking houses, and finally delivered to the families of the overseas
Chinese.

Impact of Remittances

The earliest Chinese gold rush pioneers, followed by thousands of railroad
workers, sent a flow of remittances that had a demonstrable impact on their

home villages. The remittances and letters convey the sense of responsibility that migrant workers carried with them on their contract labor journey. After covering costs of a family's food and clothing, most remittances were spent on the purchase of land, the building of houses, and payments for marriage of the overseas workers' descendants.

During the 1850s and 1860s, the Chinese economy was weakened by a number of endogenous and exogenous factors, and many from the Wuyi area left home to seek their fortunes abroad. By the late 1860s, records indicate that some migrants had returned to buy fields and build houses with their accumulated earnings. The Xinning County magistrate in the Qing dynasty, Li Pingshu, noted that "[l]ife had been bitter in Xinning, and thrift was popular then. As more and more people went abroad and took their earnings home, they began to build houses and renewed everything."[19]

The inflow of overseas remittances contributed an economic impetus for residential housing construction in the Wuyi area's home villages. Records indicate that some workers who returned from overseas bought land and built houses, not merely in their village but also in Jiangmen, in their county seat, and even in the provincial capital. The *Decade Report of Jiangmen Customs* (1904–1911) includes the record that "in the eastern part of the city there are newer and larger houses owned by returned overseas Chinese. The lighting conditions are greatly improved for bedrooms and the toilets are well constructed and managed, but the drainage is not good enough."[20]

This close reading of newly revealed documents at the Wuyi Overseas Chinese Museum provides new detail about the work contracts, overseas passage, remittance transfers, and relative accumulation of wealth. These details, along with the ongoing project at the museum and Wuyi University to discover additional documents, indicate directions for further study of the potentially rich treasure of testimony from the history of the Chinese railroad workers in the era of the building of the Central Pacific Railroad.

PART THREE

Life on the Line

CHAPTER 6

Archaeological Contributions to Research on Chinese Railroad Workers in North America

BARBARA L. VOSS

Historical archaeology investigates landscapes, sites, artifacts, and residues in order to trace material flows and spatial patterns that were central to the emergence of the modern and postmodern world. Because of its focus on material remains, historical archaeology can help recover the experiences of people who are underrepresented in documentary archives. Chinese railroad workers are a good example: to date, no personal writings, letters, or diaries of Chinese railroad workers on the first transcontinental railroad have been found. With notable exceptions,[1] the Central Pacific Railroad did not even record the names of most individual Chinese workers, instead "working and paying them by the wholesale."[2] Although newspaper journalists wrote extensively about Chinese railroad workers, the journalists generally interviewed white supervisors, not the Chinese workers themselves.

Archaeological landscapes, sites, and deposits form through human transformations of the landscape. At a typical railroad worker camp, workers smoothed patches of ground to create level sites for tents and cabins. They gathered stones to build foundations and cooking hearths and to anchor the edges of canvas tents. They broke dishes, discarded bottles and food scraps, lost buttons, and dropped small personal items. These material remains accumulated and, under favorable conditions, survived to the present day, providing a material archive of Chinese railroad workers' daily lives.

By studying cultural practices (what people do), alongside social discourse (what people say), archaeology reveals the choices that people made under circumstances of historical interest, including their relationship to the environment, their movements across time and space, and their participation in production and consumption.

Part 3 includes four chapters on the archaeology of Chinese railroad workers. This chapter presents a history and summary of archaeological investigations of Chinese railroad worker sites. My chapter 7 summarizes what archaeologists have learned about the material worlds of Chinese railroad workers. Chapter 8 by Kelly J. Dixon, with contributions by Gary Weisz, Christopher Merritt, Robert Weaver, and James Bard, considers how laborers from southern China coped with environments that were drastically different from their subtropical homelands. Chapter 9, by J. Ryan Kennedy, Sarah Heffner, Virginia Popper, Ryan P. Harrod, and John J. Crandall, examines how workers cared for their bodies and each other through diet and medicine.

The Archaeology Network of the Chinese Railroad Workers in North America Project

At the beginning of the Chinese Railroad Workers in North America Project at Stanford University, codirectors Gordon H. Chang and Shelley Fisher Fishkin expressed a hope that archaeology could provide an "inside-out perspective" on Chinese railroad workers' lives: What was daily existence like? Was it the same or different on particular segments of the railroad? What did the workers eat, and how did they cook their food? What was their housing like? How did they manage sanitation? What health challenges did they face? What leisure activities did they enjoy? What was the social organization of the work camps? What was the relationship between the Chinese laborers and the non-Chinese laborers? What supplies were brought from China? Did Chinese railroad workers participate in local and regional economies? Did they produce their own objects from local materials and eat food gathered from the local environment?

These research priorities are all questions that archaeology is well positioned to address. Yet we faced several challenges. Archaeological research is place based, with each study focused on specific sites, such as work camps, rather than the entire railroad. However, railroad workers were constantly moving across vast landscapes throughout the US West. Compounding this problem, it is difficult to access the results of archaeological research. Most archaeological studies of railroad work camps are reported in "gray literature": site records, cultural resource management reports, technical reports, and unpublished theses. Most of these documents are stored in government archives, with restricted circulation to protect archaeological sites from looting and vandalism. Finally, archaeologists use specialized language and reporting practices that are not easily understood by those outside the field. The practice of thinking with places and objects is unfamiliar to those who are trained to analyze texts and images. For the project, bridging these disciplinary differences required sustained communication between archaeologists and nonarchaeologists.

To address these challenges, Chang, Fishkin, and I established the project's Archaeology Network to facilitate communication about the archaeology of Chinese railroad workers. To date, this network has grown to more than one hundred members. Our first face-to-face meeting occurred in March 2013 at the annual meeting of the Society of California Archaeology; this has been followed by many other meetings and symposia at subsequent conferences of the Society of California Archaeology, the Society for Historical Archaeology, the Society for American Archaeology, the American Anthropological Association, the Northwest Anthropological Conference, and the Association of Asian American Studies.

To foster dialogue between archaeologists and nonarchaeologists, the Stanford Archaeology Center hosted a three-day workshop in October 2013. More than sixty-five people attended: roughly forty archaeologists representing diverse government, cultural resource management, museum, and academic affiliations; about twenty other scholars representing history, literature, visual studies, cultural studies, urban studies, geography, American studies, Asian American studies, and digital humanities; and several descendants of Chinese railroad workers.

To make archaeological research on Chinese railroad workers more accessible to other scholars and to the public, members of the Archaeology Network are contributing sources to the project's digital archive. In partnership with the Society for Historical Archaeology, we also produced a thematic issue of the journal *Historical Archaeology* ("The Archaeology of Chinese Railroad Workers in North America"[3]) and an interpretive book, *Finding Hidden Voices of the Chinese Railroad Workers: An Archaeological and Historical Journey*.[4] We also developed and collaborated on the four chapters on historical archaeology in this book.

An Overview of Archaeological Research on Chinese Railroad
Workers in North America

The first professional archaeological research on a Chinese railroad worker site was undertaken in 1969, almost one hundred years after the Central Pacific and Union Pacific Railroads were joined in the famous golden spike ceremony on May 10, 1869. Paul Chace and Bill Evans surveyed Summit Camp at Donner Pass, California, one of the largest and longest-lived residential bases for Chinese railroad workers in North America.[5] Summit Camp has continued to be a focus of archaeological research,[6] and evidence from these studies has been an important source of information for the archeology chapters in this section of part 3.

Promontory Summit, near Ogden, Utah, has also been extensively studied by archaeologists; the area was first designated as the Golden Spike National Historic Site in 1957 and has been subject to multiple historic and archaeological surveys since the 1960s. At least nineteen construction camps were identified, four of which were clearly occupied by Chinese workers during the bitterly cold winter of 1868–1869. The work camp sites near Promontory Summit are notable for the variety of architectural remains represented, including dugouts, pit structures, leveled platforms, and masonry foundations.[7]

Less is known about those segments of the first transcontinental railroad where railroad construction proceeded quickly, with workers moving camp every few days. A railroad grade survey in the Tahoe National Forest yielded evidence of two medium-term Chinese worker camps, Windmill Tree and China Kitchen, both containing artifacts similar to those found at Summit Camp, as well as several diffuse artifact scatters that may represent ephemeral tent camps.[8] Archaeologists studying the Fenelon, Nevada, railroad grade identified sparsely distributed Chinese ceramic fragments that were interpreted as possible evidence of 1860s tent camps.[9]

After completion of the first transcontinental railroad, many Chinese workers were hired as section hands to repair and maintain the lines. Notably, the Union Pacific, which did not hire Chinese workers during construction, quickly engaged Chinese veterans of the Central Pacific to support railroad operations in the eastern division. Anan Raymond and Richard Fike conducted surface studies of twenty-five Utah branch stations, six of which showed evidence of substantial Chinese habitation from the 1870s to the 1910s.[10] The Utah State Office of Historic Preservation, in partnership with the National

Park Service, is currently sponsoring new archaeological surveys of sidings and station camps on other segments of the first transcontinental railroad in Utah.[11] Dudley Gardner and colleagues have studied Chinese workers at the Aspen and Hampton Union Pacific station camps in Wyoming.[12]

Construction of the second US transcontinental railroad, the Southern Pacific Railroad (SPRR) (1873–1883), relied heavily on the labor of veteran Chinese workers from the first transcontinental railroad. Alton Briggs investigated the Langtry Camp, which housed Chinese workers at the Pecos River crossing.[13] The camp consisted of stone-lined tent platforms associated with double-hearth features. Artifacts were primarily residential and included a much higher percentage of European- and American-produced goods than is typically found at Chinese construction camps on the first transcontinental railroad.

Lyle Stone and Scott Fedick also surveyed a hundred-foot-wide (thirty-meter-wide) corridor along twenty-two miles of the historic SPRR alignment near Phoenix, Arizona.[14] Out of seven sites associated with railroad construction and maintenance, one contained an abundance of Chinese-associated artifacts, such as porcelain tableware and opium cans. Chronologically sensitive artifacts indicate that the site was more likely related to maintenance and repair of the railroad, pointing to the important role that Chinese employees played in the operation of the SPRR.

The Northern Pacific Railroad (NPRR) (1870–1883) similarly employed Chinese construction workers who were veterans of the first transcontinental railroad. Gary Weisz and colleagues have identified and recorded nine line camps on the NPRR alignment through the Clark Fork River valley in western Montana.[15] A tenth line camp site, the NPRR front town known as Cabinet Landing, was investigated by Keith Landreth and colleagues.[16] Comparative analysis of the ten sites shows several general similarities: they are oblong, linear camps along river valleys, and they all have tools representing the labor of railroad construction, along with horseshoes and other hardware from draft animal tack.[17] Spatial analysis shows clear segregation with distinct separate areas for Chinese workers, often with natural topography creating a spatial buffer between the Chinese workers and the white workers. Chinese encampments were invariably located in uneven, mosquito-infested areas, indicating that camp geography reinforced ethnic hierarchies among workers. Additional work to document Chinese work camps along the NPRR is currently under way in Bonner County, Idaho, through the University of Idaho.[18]

Along with the transcontinental railroads, railroad companies soon built "thousands of rail lines—large and small gauge—leaving extensive dendritic networks of railroad grades, trestles, and tunnels throughout the West."[19] From the 1860s to the 1890s, Chinese workers were central to the construction and operation of many of these railroads. David Wrobleski conducted a pedestrian survey of a six-mile section of the Virginia and Truckee (V&T) Railroad grade in Nevada and excavated three Chinese construction worker sites, which yielded evidence of tent platforms, hearth features, and dense distributions of artifacts related to food, alcohol, and opium consumption.[20] A fourth V&T Railroad work camp, the Lakeview Camp, was recorded and excavated in the late 1990s.[21] Also in Nevada, Charlotte Sunseri's research on the Bodie and Benton Railway's Mono Mills site is notable for documenting the co-residence of Chinese railroad workers with local Native American Paiutes.[22] Sunseri's investigations revealed material evidence of transcultural interactions and cooperation among members of these two subjugated worker populations.

In Utah archaeologists recorded a small itinerant Chinese railroad encampment associated with the Utah and Pleasant Valley Railway, completed in 1879, and identified rock structures likely representing Chinese work camps on the Denver and Rio Grande Western Railroad, completed in 1883.[23] In Mesa County, Colorado, Carl Conner and Nicole Darnell identified a distinct concentration of Chinese artifacts at the Excelsior train station site on the Denver and Rio Grande Western Railroad.[24] In Roundup, Montana, Timothy Urbaniak and Kelly Dixon have studied rock inscriptions likely carved by Chinese workers employed to mine coal for the Milwaukee Road.[25] In San Diego County, California, research at a late 1910s construction camp on the San Diego and Arizona Eastern Railway revealed evidence of a diverse multiethnic workforce including Chinese, Mexicans, European Americans, Native Americans, Indians, Pakistanis, Greeks, and Swedes.[26]

These archaeological studies reveal tantalizing glimpses of the historical experience of Chinese railroad workers in the US West. The rich descriptive accounts of work camp locations, archaeological features, and artifacts provide a robust body of evidence for comparative analysis. Since the 1970s archaeologists have drawn on these reports of artifacts found at Chinese railroad workers' camps to develop taxonomic and chronological guides to the material culture of Chinese immigrants in North America.[27] Researchers have also used evidence from Chinese railroad workers' camps as a point of comparison with daily life in historic urban Chinatowns.[28]

Attention to social identity—especially race, ethnicity, and nationality—also circulates throughout archaeological research on Chinese railroad workers. Emergent capitalist enterprises throughout the nineteenth-century US West recruited their workforces from diverse local, regional, national, and international populations. Workers were commonly organized into ethnically distinct work groups, often to deliberately divide workers from one another and suppress labor organizing. The Central Pacific Railroad's approach to staffing the construction of the first transcontinental railroad was particularly significant in forging and codifying this ethnic contract labor system during the early stages of industrial development in the US West. Alton Briggs and James MacNaughton note that this capitalist practice provides an opportunity for comparative archaeological research on ethnicity and consumption, because the archaeological record of railroad labor contains spatially discrete sites occupied by working-class men of different ethnic and racial groups.[29]

The archaeology of Chinese railroad workers is also beginning to expand beyond the work camps themselves.[30] Although workers' wages purchased the foods and objects that are found in archaeological deposits on work camp sites, many workers also saved as much as they could to pay off debts, send remittances to families in China, and develop capital for future investments and businesses. Even though few Chinese railroad workers became wealthy, this opportunity to earn and invest wages, however small, is another significant material aspect of Chinese railroad laborers' historical experience. The business districts of towns and cities throughout the US West were transformed by expanding Chinatowns which were fueled by Chinese-owned businesses providing workers and supplies to the railroad construction projects, as well as by other new businesses started by former railroad workers. In China remittances from railroad workers and other migrants transformed the landscape of Guangdong Province in the nineteenth century, sponsoring public works such as schools, orphanages, hospitals, assembly halls, roads, bridges, and even railroads.

The workers who built the railroads constructed far more than a new means of commercial transportation. The identities and communities they formed reshaped the fabric of social life in North America and China, and the wealth generated by their labor continues to influence commerce, education, and philanthropy today. Through the study of the material objects, residues, and places that the railroad workers left behind, archaeology provides a tangible point of entry into these dense webs of political machinations, economic relations, cultural meanings, and historical experiences.

CHAPTER 7

Living between Misery and Triumph

The Material Practices of Chinese Railroad Workers in North America

BARBARA L. VOSS

In 1979 archaeologists found a Chinese ceramic liquor bottle (figure 7.1) on a small ledge on Monument Peak, a mountain near Promontory Summit in Utah that overlooks the historic Central Pacific Railroad (CPRR) grade and the Great Salt Lake. The bottle rested on the surface of Native American archaeological deposits dating back three thousand years. This discovery was unusual: most archaeological evidence of Chinese railroad workers comes from collective deposits, especially the remains of work camps where groups of laborers lived, ate, and slept when they were not working on the grade.[1]

Researchers today will never know exactly why this liquor bottle was left on this hill for archaeologists to find over one hundred years later. Perhaps one evening a Chinese railroad worker left the work camp to explore the nearby mountains. He brought a liquor bottle with him, perhaps with its original potent *ng ga pei* (rice liquor with herb infusions) contents, or perhaps it was a reused bottle filled with water or tea. Maybe he climbed the mountain to look at the view and meditate on nature's beauty. Maybe he was a shy person, fed up with the noisy work camp, and wanted time alone. Or maybe he invited some friends, and they spent the evening sitting on the ledge, talking and drinking, watching the starlight sparkle off the Great Salt Lake.

Railroad companies often treated Chinese workers as interchangeable laborers, often not even bothering to record the workers' names. But archaeological discoveries like the liquor bottle recovered from Monument Peak remind us that each person who worked on the railroad had individual preferences and dispositions. He had family and friends, hopes and desires, and

FIGURE 7.1   Chinese brown-glazed liquor bottle, similar to that found on the Monument Peak ledge overlooking the Central Pacific Railroad grade in Utah. Photo courtesy of the Market Street Chinatown Archaeology Project, Stanford University.

sorrows and frustrations. These "small things forgotten,"[2] which are scattered along every railroad alignment throughout the US West, provide a material line of evidence into workers' daily lives.

Material Practices as Historical Evidence

In popular culture, historical sources, and literary representations, Chinese railroad workers are often portrayed through paired tropes of abject misery (suffering from exploitative work conditions and environmental stresses) and noble triumph (accomplishing the impossible under these same conditions). While these paired tropes speak powerfully to the structural conditions under which railroad workers labored, they reveal little about their embodied, lived experiences. The material practices that archaeologists study are especially useful in reconstructing these experiences. Social life, hobbies, self-care, and the necessities of existence are all represented in the small fragments that workers left behind.

One of the first general conclusions that can be made from archaeological research is that many of the artifacts found at nineteenth-century Chinese railroad workers' camps are very similar to those found in other Chinese diaspora communities, not only in the US West but also throughout the rest of the Americas, Australia, and New Zealand. Nearly all Chinese diaspora archaeological sites share a distinctive assemblage of material culture and other goods imported from China. These global similarities are evidence of a well-developed mercantile network that procured bulk commodities from southern China and exported them for sale to Chinese diaspora communities throughout the world.[3] Additionally, the same companies that shipped and distributed Chinese-manufactured household goods were involved in recruiting and contracting Chinese laborers. For example, in 1870 Sisson, Wallace & Co. advertised in the *Railroad Gazetteer* as "GENERAL AGENTS FOR CHINESE LABOR, Wholesale and Retail Dealers in CHINESE GOODS."[4]

Nineteenth-century Chinese immigrants, including railroad workers, thus entered into a social and economic environment that was in many ways a material extension of their prior lives in China. Preliminary archaeological reconnaissance in southern China has confirmed that many artifacts found at Chinese railroad workers' campsites were also used in Guangzhou and workers' home villages in the Pearl River delta.[5] Familiar household objects, clothing, foods, and other goods from China were readily available in nearly every Chinese immigrant settlement, including railroad work camps, allowing some measure of continuity in the habits of daily life.

However, Chinese immigrant sites throughout the world also have artifacts that show that residents were actively participating in economic networks outside of those orchestrated by powerful import-export companies and distributors. Local Chinese immigrant merchants blended Chinese-, European-, and American-produced goods in their stock-in-trade. Chinese immigrants also shopped in non-Chinese-owned stores and traded with non-Chinese for goods and services. The artifacts produced outside China show considerable variation from settlement to settlement. These goods thus not only provide evidence of Chinese railroad workers' participation in local economies but also suggest situations in which Chinese immigrants may have shared material practices with their non-Chinese neighbors.

Railroad companies, including the CPRR, were able to hire and mobilize such a large number of workers from China only because of preexisting business relationships between business houses in Hong Kong and Guangzhou and those in the emerging cities of the US West. Archaeological evidence from Chinese workers' camps shows that railroad construction projects extended and intensified these existing material distribution networks of Chinese-produced commodities. Additionally, the co-occurrence of goods produced outside China at workers' camps indicates that Chinese railroad workers were not wholly dependent on supplies from Guangzhou and Hong Kong; they also participated in local economies that distributed goods produced throughout the United States and Europe and obtained foods and raw materials from local resources. In summary, every artifact found at a railroad workers' campsite is evidence not only of the presence of the workers themselves but of the complex nineteenth-century commodity chains that connected manufacturers around the globe with consumers in even the most remote locations.

Residing on the Landscape

Summit Camp, located on Donner Summit, California, is a dispersed settlement of multiple housing clusters where Chinese construction workers lived during four long years while they blasted tunnels and grades through the Sierra Nevada. It was the longest-occupied and likely the largest residential base for Chinese railroad workers in North America and has been extensively studied by archaeologists since the late 1960s.[6] The work hazards and environmental exposures faced by railroad workers living at Summit Camp have been remarked on in nearly every history of the CPRR. Shelter was essential to survival, and today this stunning landscape, with breathtaking views of Donner Lake and the Sierra Nevada peaks, still bears traces of the stone foundations that supported wooden cabins that housed Chinese railroad workers during long, brutal winters and windy, blistering summers (figure 7.2).

Both documentary and archaeological evidence indicates that Chinese railroad workers primarily lived in segregated camps, separate from non-Chinese workers.[7] Chinese workers' housing was provided in part by the railroad companies and also augmented by the workers themselves.[8] Company-issued canvas tents were the most common shelters, as they allowed work crews to quickly strike old camps and set up new ones with each advancement down the line. Each camp required transformation of the landscape as railroad workers cleared away vegetation and debris, prepared level surfaces, cut large branches or small saplings for tent stakes, and collected rocks to anchor tent edges. Work tool artifacts commonly found at railroad campsites, such as shovel blades, sledgehammers, mauls, chisels, wedges, files, and railroad spikes, were

FIGURE 7.2   Summit Camp, Donner Pass, California. Archaeologist William "Bill" S. Evans standing next to the rough stone foundation walls of an eight-by-twelve-foot room below Donner Summit. Photo courtesy of Paul G. Chace, 1967.

likely used in setting up and maintaining camps. Canvas tents in particular require constant mending and patching to repair rips and punctures, so tent maintenance was unquestionably a routine aspect of many railroad workers' daily lives.

Today, shallow-level depressions, surrounded by alignments of rocks, survive as traces of tent encampments at some Chinese workers' campsites along the Central Pacific and other railroads. Tents were typically clustered closely together and varied in size. At the Langtry Camp of the Southern Pacific Railroad (SPRR) in Val Verde County, Texas, Alton Briggs identified four standard sizes: 9 by 9 feet, 9.5 by 12 feet, 9.5 by 14 feet, and 12 by 12 feet (2.7 by 2.7 meters, 2.9 by 3.7 meters, 2.9 by 4.3 meters, 3.7 by 3.7 meters).[9] Briggs estimates that the smallest tents likely housed a minimum of four people, with the largest tent holding as many as twelve. Tents afford minimal insulation, and sleeping closely together conserved body warmth, especially in cold climates.

At long-term work camps like the CPRR's Summit Camp, Chinese railroad workers typically sheltered in wooden structures built on stone foundations.

Wooden buildings were often larger than the tents and may have either housed more people in each building or afforded more personal space per occupant.[10] Whether these wooden structures were provided by the railroad companies or built by the workers themselves is unknown. Regardless, constructing such permanent structures required considerable investment of materials and labor. Other accommodations at Chinese railroad workers' campsites include corrugated iron buildings, platform tents, stone masonry blocks for rooms, circular pit structures, lean-tos, and rock shelters.[11]

Areas for food preparation are often clearly visible at Chinese railroad workers' campsites. The most common cooking features are U-shaped stone hearths, suitable for holding a large wok while allowing the cook to tend the fire from below. Sometimes, two U-shaped hearths were paired, sharing a central support. This configuration was also commonly used in kitchens in southern China in the nineteenth century, with one hearth used to prepare boiled foods such as rice, noodles, and tea, and the other used for wok-fried meats and vegetables.[12]

David Wrobleski and Lynn Furnis and Mary Maniery found that work camps on the Virginia and Truckee (V&T) line were divided into discrete activity areas, with sleeping areas separated from places used for eating, cooking, and socializing.[13] On the Northern Pacific and Southern Pacific lines, camps show integrated activity patterns in which sleeping tents were grouped in clusters, with each tent cluster sharing a central hearth and socializing area.[14] Neither residential pattern has yet been consistently documented on campsites associated with the CPRR. Indeed, overall, the work camps on the Central Pacific line show incredible variety in housing types and spatial organization, which often appeared quite haphazard. This is especially evident in camps identified in the Golden Spike National Historic Site, the area of the "meeting of the rails" at Promontory Summit, where campsites ranged from 0.1 acre (0.04 hectare) to more than 24 acres (9.7 hectares) in size.[15] The hectic construction schedule of the Central Pacific may have required constant improvisation as workers moved rapidly through different environments.

Although there was considerable variety in workers' housing and in camp layout, one commonality emerges: in the midst of the "wide open spaces" of the nineteenth-century US West, daily life in Chinese railroad workers' camps typically occurred in close quarters. In these crowded conditions, hygiene needed careful management. Chinese railroad workers appear to have followed good waste management practices: typically, archaeologists find only small fragments of artifacts in and around residences and hearths. Larger debris was disposed of away from the activities of daily life. No material evidence has yet been found that indicates how Chinese railroad workers managed personal sanitation. Privy pits, common at long-term lumber and mining work camps as well as in urban Chinatowns, have not yet been identified at Chinese railroad work camps. Perhaps it was not worthwhile to invest in constructing formal toilet facilities when workers knew that they would be moved down the line in a few days or weeks.

Work camp residents also would have needed to develop social conventions to manage the predictable conflicts that arise in close living. For most Chinese railroad workers, this would not be the first time they shared tight living quarters. Homes in rural villages in the Pearl River delta where most railroad workers originated were typically modest, with family members sharing a single sleeping loft above a common room. Ship travel from China to the United States also occurred under crowded conditions. Chinese railroad workers were thus able to draw on social conventions from village life and ship travel, along with interpersonal connections developed through clan organizations and district associations, in adapting to the new contexts experienced in the work camps. Having tentmates (and cabinmates, dugoutmates, etc.) also afforded opportunities for sociality and friendship, perhaps mitigating some of the loneliness that workers likely felt from being far from family and childhood friends.

Provisioning the Laboring Body

The most common artifacts found at Chinese railroad workers' camps are fragments of food storage containers. Chinese railroad workers, who were responsible for their own board, organized themselves into groups of twelve to twenty, with each group hiring its own cook and designating a headman who handled accounts.[16] Railroad construction thus depended not only on commodity chains that stretched around the globe but also on specialists who procured and prepared those commodities.

Discarded durable supply containers—ceramic, glass, and metal—remain on the landscape long after their contents are consumed. Chinese brown-glazed stoneware jars are the most plentiful. These have been produced for hundreds of years in Guangdong Province and continue to be made to the

FIGURE 7.3   Glass bottle finishes from Summit Camp, Donner Pass, California. Photo courtesy of Paul G. Chace, 1967.

present day. The waterproof glaze on the exterior protects the jars' contents from moisture, and the jars can be made airtight with corks and wax seals. These multipurpose vessels are found in a variety of forms, ranging in capacity from 8 to 6,000 fluid ounces (0.25 to 175 liters). Vessels with narrow openings typically contained liquids: soy sauce, fish sauce, oils, vinegars, condiments, wine, and liquor. Vessels with wide-mouthed openings were used for packing grains, beans, spices, pastes, preserved fruits and vegetables, and dried fish and meat.[17] Once the original contents were consumed, Chinese brown-glazed stoneware jars were commonly repurposed for serving tea and food, for storage of other goods, and for wash basins.

Glass bottles are also ubiquitous at Chinese railroad workers' campsites (figure 7.3). Liquor bottles are the ones most commonly found. Whiskey and wine bottles are found at nearly every Chinese railroad workers' campsite. Beer bottles are less common but have been identified at Promontory Summit[18] and at several work camps along the Montana segment of the Northern Pacific Railroad (NPRR).[19] At the time of the CPRR's construction, eyewitness accounts often praised Chinese railroad workers for their sobriety.[20] However, the archaeological evidence conclusively shows that alcohol consumption was a common aspect of camp life.

Glass bottles also contained nonalcoholic beverages such as soda and mineral water, along with foodstuffs. Lea & Perrins Worcestershire Sauce bottles have been found at many Chinese railroad workers' camps; other, less commonly found, food bottles contained mustard, pickles, salad dressing, and bouillon. Embossed labels allow archaeologists to identify the locations of food manufacturers: Chinese railroad workers were consuming bottled sauces and preserves from US companies located in Minnesota, New Jersey, Pennsylvania, and New York, and from European producers in Ireland, England, and France.[21] Glass bottles also contained medicines, including Chinese herbal medicines and European and American bitters, ointments, liniments, homeopathic tinctures, and patent medicines.

Metal canisters were first produced in Western Europe in 1810 and entered widespread use in the United States and China during the nineteenth century. Because iron and steel corrode when exposed to the elements, metal canisters do not always preserve well on archaeological sites. When they are present, archaeologists can study the canister size, shape, openings, embossing, and lithography to assess what kinds of goods were likely contained. These attributes show that Chinese railroad workers were consuming canned goods from both the United States and China. Canned goods produced in the United States included processed beef, fish, sardines, lard, beans, tomatoes, fruit, evaporated milk, and baking powder. Cans that contained goods produced in China included large rectangular tea containers, small rectangular spice containers, cylindrical cooking oil cans, and small rectangular brass boxes used to ship opium paste. Opium paste box lids often have impressed cartouches bearing the names of Hong Kong distributors. The Li Yun (Beautiful Origin) brand is especially common at railroad work camps.

Containers, once emptied of their original contents, also became readily available raw materials. Archaeological studies at the V&T Lakeview Camp recovered an impressive collection of handmade objects made from reused metal canisters, including funnels, a charcoal brazier, carrying containers, strainers, bean sprout germinators, and more than five dozen flattened metal rectangles of unknown function.[22] Improvised funnels and strainers have been found at other Chinese railroad workers' camps, including Summit Camp and camps near Truckee and Folsom on the CPRR line.[23] Handmade gaming tokens, cut from flattened opium cans and from sheets of copper and iron, have also been recovered from Summit Camp and from camps on the Northern Pacific line.[24]

These improvised objects may be evidence of frugality: railroad workers may not have wanted to spend their hard-earned wages on a manufactured object when they could fashion an acceptable substitute with free materials. These modified containers may also point to gaps in commodity chains, indicating situations where available supplies were not adequate to meet workers' requirements. Additionally, making improvised objects provided an opportunity for Chinese railroad workers to express their creativity: living in remote areas, with few opportunities for formal entertainment, Chinese railroad workers may have modified used containers as a mode of self-expression and as a diversion from the mundane routines of camp life.

Dining and Commensality

Shards from white-bodied, blue-decorated ceramic porcelain rice bowls are found at almost every Chinese railroad camp (figure 7.4). These bowls represent one of the primary reasons why young men left southern China: economic need. In the nineteenth century, war, natural disasters, political turmoil, and exploitative taxes and land tenure caused widespread poverty in the Pearl River delta. Bioarchaeological research has demonstrated that at least some Chinese railroad workers were undernourished as children and benefited from an improved diet after immigrating to the United States.[25] Sending sons overseas to earn wages was an economic survival strategy for many families, and "filling the rice bowl" became a common metaphor for working abroad.[26]

Ceramic tablewares provide useful information about how meals were prepared and served. Because of the social importance of meals, tableware ceramics are often elaborately decorated, introducing symbolic and didactic content into the visual field of each meal. Ceramic tablewares also provide evidence of the commodity chains involved in bringing supplies to remote work camps.

Archaeological evidence shows that Chinese railroad workers used a combination of Chinese- and British-produced ceramics. The Chinese-produced vessels were the inexpensive folk porcelains produced by pottery guilds in

FIGURE 7.4   Double Happiness rice bowl from Summit Camp, Donner Pass, California. Photo courtesy of Paul G. Chace, 1967.

southern China.[27] Rice bowls and other Chinese tableware dishes used at railroad work camps appeared delicate to European American observers, whose table settings used comparatively thicker earthenware vessels. But Chinese users would have readily recognized these bowls, plates, cups, and spoons as the type of robust, durable ceramics used in everyday meals.

In southern China in the nineteenth century, a wide variety of porcelain tablewares were produced, but four decorative patterns dominate assemblages at Chinese diaspora settlements, including Chinese railroad camps: Double Happiness, Bamboo, Four Season Flowers, and Winter Green. Double Happiness and Bamboo patterns are *qinghua* (blue-on-white) decorations and appear only on rice bowls. Double Happiness bowls feature three calligraphy motifs (喜喜: *shuangxi*, commonly translated as "double happiness" or "double joy") surrounded by swirls representing vines. These are the most common rice bowls used in the Central Pacific and other railroad work camps until the 1870s. After the 1870s Bamboo rice bowls became more common in Chinese diaspora settlements. Bamboo rice bowls present a landscape vignette: plum tree with blossoms, rock, and bamboo grove. On the other side of the bowl, a stylized figure, possibly a *ling qi* (*Ganoderma* fungus), floats in midair next to three circles. The three circles are interpreted as representing the "three friends" of the winter season: plum, bamboo, and pine or evergreen.

Four Season Flowers and Winter Green tablewares come in a wide variety of forms, including rice bowls, soup bowls, serving bowls, condiment dishes, plates, medium cups (used for tea), small cups (used for liquor), and spoons. As the name implies, Four Season Flowers vessels include floral elements representing the four seasons: spring (peony), summer (lotus), fall (chrysanthemum), and winter (plum). These floral elements surround a longevity peach, and the base of the vessel often includes an endless knot, representing infinity. The elements together create a pattern that is often interpreted as expressing values of nature and the repetitive cycles of life. In contrast, Winter Green vessels are plain in appearance, their sole decorative feature being a light bluish-green glaze. Green glazes were first developed in China about 800 CE and have a long aesthetic history as an expression of values associated with nature, sky, heaven, and jade.

Larry Felton and colleagues have observed that in comparison to urban Chinatowns, CPRR work camps contain more Double Happiness and Bamboo rice bowls and fewer Winter Green and Four Season Flowers vessels.[28] They interpret this finding as an indication that railroad workers had less economic purchasing power, since the blue-on-white patterns generally cost less than green-glazed or polychrome vessels. The difference in tableware ceramics between railroad work camps and Chinatowns may also reflect Chinese workers' unique dining arrangements. If documentary sources are correct in describing railroad workers as being organized into groups of twelve to twenty, with each group hiring a cook, then the ratio of personal rice bowls to serving vessels at work camps would have been significantly higher than on family dinner tables in urban Chinatowns.

Chinese railroad workers also used British-produced refined earthenware vessels in their meals. In some camps, British refined earthenwares are common; in others, they are rare or absent. At Summit Camp on the CPRR, British refined earthenwares include oval serving dishes (John Molenda, personal communication, June 22, 2016). At Lakeview Camp on the V&T line in Nevada, British refined earthenwares include plates and bowls with scalloped rim designs.[29] SPRR workers living at the Langtry Camp in Texas used plain British refined earthenware plates along with Chinese porcelains.[30] At the NPRR Cabinet Landing camp in Montana, residents used thick-bodied white earthenware bowls and Chinese rice bowls.[31] In comparison, none of the nine other Chinese railroad workers' camps recorded on the Montana segment of the Northern Pacific line contained any British refined earthenware.[32] Overall, the archaeological evidence indicates that Chinese railroad workers used British refined earthenwares to supplement Chinese porcelain dishes. By and large, railroad workers ate their meals from dishes that were very similar, and at times identical, to those they had previously used in their home villages.

Making It Personal

From time to time archaeologists working on Chinese railroad work camps find ceramic sherds that bear peck marks—Chinese characters or abstract symbols that have been pecked through the vessel's glaze, permanently marking the vessel. Likely accomplished with a metal awl, marking a ceramic in this way requires precision and skill: enough force must be applied to break away a small dot of the brittle glaze, but the pressure also has to be light enough to avoid cracking the entire vessel.

Peck marking was a common practice in the Pearl River delta region of southern China, and includes characters that foster good luck or blessings, personal names, and abstract symbols. Among Chinese immigrants, peck-marked vessels became a hybrid art form that adapted traditions from China to the crowded living conditions common to urban Chinatowns and work camps.[33] In these new contexts, "marking a bowl suggests individuality: 'I was here' or 'It is mine.'"[34]

Like peck-marked vessels, other personal possessions found on campsites provide tangible links to workers' personal lives. Some of the most evocative are objects used in personal grooming, such as metal straight razors, bone-handled toothbrushes, and clothing fasteners. Clothing artifacts found at Chinese railroad workers' camps are typical of those used for Western-style work garments: metal suspender clasps and belt buckles; fragments of leather and rubberized work boots; metal trouser buttons and pressed-glass Prosser shirt buttons; and small metal rivets used to reinforce stress points on workpants, shirts, and jackets. However, some distinctive ball-shaped Chinese buttons have been found at work camps associated with the NPRR in Montana.[35] Curiously, luggage parts are not commonly found at sites associated with the CPRR, although they are frequently present on other railroad work camps.[36]

Asian coins found on Chinese railroad workers' campsites—predominantly Chinese *wén*, Vietnamese *dong*, and Japanese *mon*—had no monetary value but instead were used as gaming tokens, in feng shui practices, in folk medicine, and for other talismanic purposes.[37] Coins are often found in association with glass *zhu* (small black or white tokens) and carved bone dice. With these simple materials, workers could play fan-tan (spreading out), *sanliu baozi* (three-six dice), and *weiqi* (go). The ubiquity of these artifacts on Chinese railroad workers' campsites points to the importance of games to workers' leisure time and sociality. Games were likely accompanied by drinking and smoking, as evidenced by the high frequency of both Chinese and North American liquor bottles, along with clay tobacco pipes. Fragments of ceramic opium pipe bowls are also a frequent archaeological find on sites, along with brass fasteners, opium spoons, and opium lamps.[38] Opium smoking was undoubtedly a social activity, but it also had medicinal qualities, soothing the aches and pains caused by hard labor.

Archaeologists sometimes find fragments of small ceramic incense burners, oil lamp stands, and oil lamp dishes at camps. These artifacts, common in urban Chinatowns of the same period, are used in home altars to make offerings to ancestors and deities. More bulky than small gaming tokens or personal grooming artifacts and more fragile than tableware dishes, these objects would have required special packing and care during transport from camp to camp. That these religious objects are found as part of workers' personal effects points to the importance of home-based spiritual practices amid the canvas tents, dugouts, and shanties in work camps.

Together, these small objects—peck-marked dishes, personal grooming items, clothing, talismanic charms, gaming pieces, smoking pipes, and altar furniture—provide intimate glimpses into the routine material practices of Chinese railroad workers. In the morning, buttoning up work shirts and belting canvas trousers, and maybe tucking a special good-luck coin in the pocket to ward against the hazards of the day; in the evening, playing familiar games and sharing a drink and a smoke after a hard day's work; at night, carefully lighting oil and burning incense to honor the ancestors; on an afternoon off, taking time to carefully peck a blessing or name into a rice bowl: these routines, repeated in camp after camp, offered stability and familiarity in the midst of a life otherwise characterized by movement and novelty.

Living between Misery and Triumph

The Chinese laborers who constructed the Central Pacific line entered cultural and natural environments that were beyond anything they could have imagined from their childhoods in the Pearl River delta. While some had lived in the United States for several years before being recruited for railroad work, the vast majority were new immigrants, transported directly to railroad work camps after their ships docked in San Francisco. Today they are commemorated both as victims of Gilded Age labor practices and as heroes who accomplished previously unthinkable feats of civil engineering.

The artifacts found at railroad work camps afford opportunities to focus on the everyday experiences of the workers themselves, exploring the middle space of daily life between the paired tropes of misery and triumph that characterize many historical and present-day accounts. One of the most significant findings of this archaeological review is that there was substantial continuity in certain material practices across Chinese railroad workers' camps and among other settlements, including the workers' home villages in Guangdong and other types of Chinese diaspora settlements. By and large, macro-level material practices, such as architecture and camp organization, varied significantly from place to place, using local materials to address local conditions. In contrast, the portable objects that residents used are remarkably similar. At the broadest level, this consistency is evidence of strong, centralized networks of commodity distribution. While the commodity chains evidenced at Chinese railroad workers' camps were undoubtedly motivated primarily by profit, those who operated these exchange networks also provided a valuable service by provisioning workers in remote locations. As Elizabeth Sinn describes, these Hong Kong and Guangzhou business houses often operated in spaces of both "power and charity."[39]

Maintaining familiar domestic routines across a wide variety of work and living contexts may have helped Chinese railroad workers adapt quickly to new environments and situations. Eating familiar food from familiar dishes, relaxing with workmates by playing a game learned in childhood, marking one's name on the bottom of a rice bowl—all of these practices may have ameliorated some of the stress and culture shock of constant relocation.

Wherever they labored, Chinese railroad workers engaged actively with local economic networks. They acquired and used packaged foods, liquors, medicines, tableware ceramics, clothing, and personal items that were manufactured in Europe and throughout the United States. They also modified other goods to personalize them or to fashion new tools and objects. Today, these objects provide a powerful tangible link to individual railroad workers: Did the owner of this rice bowl peck-mark his name on it because he was tired of his tentmate "borrowing" it? Whose hands shook these small bone dice, hoping for a small win that might signal good luck for the coming day? What frustrated cook, tired of losing his perfectly cooked noodles in the fire, hammered holes into a flattened metal canister to create a makeshift strainer? Researchers may never recover the lost voices of nineteenth-century Chinese railroad workers who labored to build the first industrial transportation network of the US West, but these material traces provide a glimpse of what life was like in the camps, places where Chinese immigrants created domestic routines and social lives in these spaces between misery and triumph.

CHAPTER 8

Landscapes of Change

Culture, Nature, and the Archaeological Heritage of Transcontinental Railroads in the North American West

KELLY J. DIXON WITH

CONTRIBUTIONS BY GARY WEISZ,

CHRISTOPHER MERRITT, ROBERT

WEAVER, AND JAMES BARD

Southern China has a humid, subtropical climate. The average temperatures in the summer range from 30 to 34 degrees Celsius (87 to 93 degrees Fahrenheit), and the winter temperatures are around 18 to 22 degrees Celsius (65 to 70 degrees Fahrenheit).[1] From the 1850s to 1870s, temperatures in southern China were slightly cooler and wetter than they are today, representing one of many global repercussions of the Little Ice Age (1300 to 1850 CE).[2] Even so, the region was still not as cold as the craggy Sierra Nevada in California. Moreover, in North America the Little Ice Age caused colder, harsher winters, which manifested in extreme snowfall in the northern Sierra Nevada—a region known for heavy snow and severe winter conditions.

The Sierra Nevada range is made up of granitic bedrock steps that reach as high as 4,418 meters (14,495 feet); the mountains have been scoured and polished by glacial activity and are known to reflect sunlight with such clarity that they have been referred to as the "Range of Light."[3] Although the summer months in the Sierra Nevada are dry, with relatively little precipitation, the region is renowned for substantial snowfall in the winter and is often documented as one of the coldest and snowiest places in the United States. Temperatures can drop below zero, wind gusts often reach 160 kilometers (100 miles) per hour, and snowfall can be over 10 meters (33 feet) in a year.[4]

The Central Pacific Railroad (CPRR) started recording weather patterns, including precipitation and snowfall, in 1870 in the area around Donner Pass at the crest of the Sierra Nevada west of Truckee, California.[5] These records of historical weather events—as well as ominous tales told by nineteenth-century travelers to the region[6]—can help connect us with the railroad laborers from southern China, calling to mind the environmental extremes people faced while building transcontinental railroads that traversed North America's rugged mountain ranges. And the CPRR workers were individuals who had moved from a subtropical homeland to an unfamiliar and drastically different environment on the Donner Summit crest of the Sierra Nevada, where snow still clings to north-facing slopes and upper elevations well into the summertime.[7]

Without doubt, completing the monumental work at Donner Summit (altitude 2,151 meters [7,057 feet]) required bravery, and the laborers there successfully excavated seven tunnels through granite rock within 3.22 kilometers (2.0 miles) of the summit. During the winter of 1866–1867, at least forty-four storms left 13.4 meters (44 feet) of snow on Donner Summit. Just one of those storms dumped 3 meters (120 inches) on CPRR laborers working near Donner Summit. This was the same winter that an infamous avalanche took out a CPRR work camp on the summit, burying the laborers while they still clutched tools in their hands; their bodies could not be recovered until the following spring.[8] A second avalanche that winter killed at least twenty other CPRR laborers who were working on Tunnel 9 near Donner Summit.[9]

These extreme environmental conditions, in tandem with the hazardous work setting and situations, meant that daily life at Summit Camp called for the utmost courage and endurance. As one of the earliest examples of a Chinese labor camp in the United States, Summit Camp had a reputation that certainly fueled awe and admiration for those living and working there.[10] Summit Camp was unique among the more common ephemeral construction camps because it took "four long years of hard labor, often with more than 40 feet [12 meters] of snow on the ground. As a result, what would have been a temporary labor camp developed into what was essentially a small town, known as Summit Camp."[11] Today, archaeological traces of this internationally significant site are scattered across Donner Summit's windswept granite benches and boulders.

After the camp fell into disuse, artifacts and cabin foundations lay exposed on the granite surface. The artifacts have been easy targets for travelers along several corridors: a highway, the Pacific Crest Trail (a hiking and equestrian trail), a petroleum pipeline, a fiber-optic cable line, utility lines, and a railroad grade that is now used by off-road vehicles, bicyclists, and hikers. Users of these transportation corridors, and others intentionally targeting the site, collected many large and nearly intact artifacts without the permission of the current landowner, the US Forest Service.[12] As a result, today the physical remains of the camp are subtle and fragmented. Still, analyses of the material collected in the mid-twentieth century from the site helped establish precedents for working with Chinese cultural consultants and for understanding that there were distinct archaeological signatures of Chinese-inhabited sites in North America.[13] And even though the archaeological remains at Summit Camp have been disturbed, they still represent a "hallmark for archaeological studies of Chinese American sites."[14]

The archaeological remains of work camp sites at Donner Summit have been documented and investigated since the 1960s.[15] Archaeological signatures of adaptation to the cold winter months are evident in the physical remains of cabins, as well as in historic photos such as figure 8.1, which shows wooden cabins in the Summit Camp within sight of one of the iconic tunnels in the area.[16]

Although the wooden remains of the cabins are long gone, the celebrated tunnels created by their inhabitants are still visible. The most recent fieldwork indicates that there is still a collection of stones delineating at least one deteriorated cabin foundation (see figure 7.2 in the essay by Barbara Voss in this volume, "Living between Misery and Triumph"), along with the remains of a stone hearth the residents used for heating and cooking. Another collapsed hearth was observed outside the cabin foundation, likely representing an outdoor wok stove area;[17] these wok stoves, situated outside the tent or cabin areas and constructed of locally available stone, have been observed at other Chinese work camps in the region.[18] As archaeology crews continued to examine the subtle remains of the camp, they found another, larger collection of stones that appears to have been used as a roasting hearth—and then they found yet another cabin foundation, "at either end of which were a pair of wok stoves."[19]

In the vicinity of the stone shelter foundations and cooking and heating features, archaeologists observed artifacts such as window glass and nails, which provide evidence of the long-term nature of this camp, setting it aside from the more typical transient railroad construction camps made up of tents with more ephemeral archaeological signatures—and fewer opportunities for such amenities as glass windows. They also found other artifacts, including gaming pieces; Chinese coins; cast-iron wok fragments; tableware fragments, such as Chinese Double Happiness and Bamboo bowls, as well as broken pieces of wintergreen vessels; tableware fragments, such as those

FIGURE 8.1   A portion of Summit Camp, with wooden cabins nestled along the rugged, granite backdrop at the east portal of Tunnel No. 6, documented as "Hart's East Portal of Summit Tunnel #199." Photo by Alfred A. Hart, Library of Congress.

from a European American "hotelware" cup; food storage containers made of Chinese brown-glazed stoneware; olive green glass beer/ale bottle fragments, as well as aqua-colored glass bottle fragments; broken ceramic opium bowls; and brass opium or spice can fragments.[20]

These objects, together with the remains of shelters and hearths, evoke images of the human condition in a transcontinental railroad construction camp. The CPRR laborers who lived in this camp legendarily wrought drastic changes to a landscape that had been previously viewed as a hostile and unfamiliar environment to settlers and newcomers to the region.[21] Such transformations were among the consequences of transcontinental railroads, underscoring the significance of the laborers' role in changing the ways in which North America's Indigenous peoples, as well as people throughout the world, perceived and accessed the landscapes of the North American West.

Archaeological Signatures of Railroad Workers' Camps

By the early 1880s, North America's transcontinental railroads had penetrated the Intermountain West: river valleys in the Rocky Mountain region of western Montana. The archaeological remains of a selection of early 1880s Chinese labor camps associated with the construction of the Northern Pacific Railroad (NPRR) in western Montana provide evidence that complements the stories generated by archaeological investigations of Summit Camp. Whether the Rocky Mountains or the Sierra Nevada, the mountainous landscape influenced the nature of railroad construction, putting laborers in arduous and unfamiliar settings where they met and adapted to challenges.

In addition to using the archaeological remains of Summit Camp to better understand the experiences and landscapes of railroad workers on the CPRR, this chapter explores the landscape and archaeological remains of ephemeral Chinese railroad construction camps that were active during the 1882–1883 construction of the NPRR through the Rocky Mountain region of western Montana. The majority of these work camps were far more short-lived than Summit Camp. As presented here, most of the NPRR railroad construction camps were transient, consisting mainly of tents and other temporary shelters that were relatively portable and/or that involved the use of local resources.[22]

The archaeological remains of NPRR Chinese railroad workers' camps discussed here were observed along the Clark Fork River and Flathead River valleys in the Rocky Mountains.[23] In order to navigate rugged mountain ranges, the NPRR construction crews needed to follow the rivers, which provided natural travel corridors for the region's Indigenous people since time immemorial.[24] By late February 1883, the NPRR track arrived in Paradise, Montana, where construction crews faced winter conditions and the challenge of a large amount of rockwork to lay grade between the base of the mountains and banks of the Clark Fork River (figure 8.2).[25] Modern average annual snowfall for the area is 0.81 meter (32 inches), and average winter temperatures are 0 degrees Celsius (32 degrees Fahrenheit), although it would have been colder working along the river. A large construction

FIGURE 8.2 An example of the landscape in northwestern Montana where NPRR laborers had to lay grade in the narrow areas at the base of steep mountain slopes and along the banks of rivers such as the Clark Fork River. Illustration by Kelli Casias.

camp known as the Last Chance camp (Site No. 24SA0596; figure 8.3) was situated on the floodplain downstream from the confluence of the Clark Fork and Flathead Rivers. The *Last Chance* camp name is among those that have historical documentation. Last Chance, which purportedly housed nearly eight thousand railroad workers, at least four thousand of whom were Chinese, got its name from its location as the last place that alcohol could be legally purchased before crossing the nearby western boundary of the Flathead Indian Reservation, where liquor sales were prohibited.[26] By the spring of 1883, the Last Chance camp area was all but abandoned, as crews had moved along the line to new camps, and the remains were mostly underwater as a result of seasonal snowmelt from mountains causing high water on the floodplain. Every year, the remnants of Last Chance camp have become more fragmented as seasonal flooding continues and because the site has also served as part of a ranch.

Among the last archaeological traces of Last Chance's Chinese line camp are rock piles that appear to be remnants of rock hearths, along with scattered fragments of brownware vessels, Bamboo-style bowls, and bottle glass. The

FIGURE 8.3   The type of camp where thousands of Chinese laborers worked and lived while constructing transcontinental railways throughout the American West. Few historical images of such camps are known, and this artistic rendition was created by integrating historical records and archaeological evidence to present a snapshot of work and life in the Last Chance Northern Pacific Railroad line camp along the Clark Fork River in northwestern Montana. Artwork by Eric Carlson.

archaeological remains of the Chinese camp at Donner Summit have similar, subtle material signatures, including rock hearths, but the hearths are in better states of preservation than those observed at these sites along river valleys in Montana, as the latter have been affected by more than a century of snowmelt and associated spring floodplain dynamics.[27] In the 1980s Gary Weisz reported finding a rock drill in situ, driven into the ground at an oblique angle to the surface of the ground at one corner of a tent platform at the Chinese encampment of the NPRR's Last Chance camp.[28] Weisz noted that a large bridge or trestle bolt about 2 feet (61 centimeters) long was driven into the opposing corner, giving the impression that the rock drill and industrial bolt, necessary tools for railroad construction, were adapted for use as tent stakes in the camp.

Another NPRR railroad construction camp is situated 2.6 kilometers (1.6

miles) southeast of the Last Chance camp along the railroad grade, on a peninsula that extends from a geologic rock outcrop along the Flathead River. The tremendous amount of rockwork mentioned above was necessary to complete the railroad bed between Last Chance and this point. The peninsula represents one of the few flat locations for a camp along this narrow stretch of the Flathead River valley. The camp, identified as Site No. 24SA0597, along with Site No. 24SA0598, which represents the next NPRR construction camp southeast along the railroad grade and river, appear to have artifacts traditionally associated with Chinese labor camps elsewhere. The historic names of these camps remain unknown and have yet to be located in NPRR archival sources, assuming that such details exist in those sources at all.

In the 1980s Weisz observed at least twenty tent platforms at Site No. 24SA0597. Although subtle, these archaeological remains signify the ways in which inequality pervaded the lives of Chinese laborers in North America. At other NPRR camps elsewhere in the Rocky Mountain region, European American railroad workers had the option of partaking of the room and board offered by contractors; in contrast, the NPRR provided canvas tents to the Chinese workers.[29] In addition to the tent platforms, other archaeological remains present a picture of the material world of the railroad construction camps occupied by Chinese laborers. Weisz's report indicates that the associated artifacts include rice bowl fragments with a Bamboo design, Chinese utilitarian brown stoneware fragments, Asian coins, tools (including evidence of blacksmithing), ammunition, lanterns, and opium-smoking paraphernalia.[30] The site appeared to be one of the more intact Chinese railroad sites in the region, as its remote location and controlled access have limited the exposure to looters. In addition, since most of the site is situated on a forested peninsula above the Flathead River's floodplain, its location on slightly higher elevation provided more protection from erosion and flood damage than the Last Chance (24SA0596) camp.

During the summer of 2014, the tent platforms were hardly visible to a small team walking along the riverbank at 24SA0597 due to extensive vegetation growth. A dugout feature was observed, however (figure 8.4). During discussions at the Sun Yat-sen University International Symposium on the North America Chinese Laborers and the Guangdong Qiaoxiang Society on September 8–10, 2014, in Guangzhou, Sue Fawn Chung noted that her book *Chinese in the Woods* discusses dugouts at Chinese labor camps in the Lake Tahoe basin of the Sierra Nevada.[31] Chung observed that the dugouts

FIGURE 8.4   A dugout feature discovered by Gary Weisz
in the 1980s. He also discovered at least twenty tent platforms at
Site 24SA0597 along the Flathead River. Photo by Kelly J. Dixon.

appear to be communal dining and gathering areas amid camps that comprised
mainly tents.

The dugouts were created by excavating rectangular-shaped pits in the
ground; they served as windbreaks and insulation to shelter the occupants
from the cold and snowy falls, winters, springs, and sometimes summers in
this region.[32] Chung's observations not only provide another archaeological
signature of Chinese labor camps but also suggest that the dugout found, the
only one at 24SA0597, may represent a communal structure that provided

NPRR railroad workers with shelter from inclement weather during the winter along the Flathead River. This is just one example of the ways in which the stories of railroad labor can still be viewed amid the backdrop of the natural environment.

During the summer of 2015, Weisz led a team of archaeologists, including Robert Weaver, James Bard, and myself, to locate another one of several NPRR construction camps dating from about 1882–1883 near Plains, Montana. We observed a surface scatter of Chinese ceramic fragments, bottle glass shards, footwear fragments, insulator fragments, and possible collapsed rock hearth features. These items were dispersed in a relatively narrow area between the NPRR grade and a slough that is situated on private and state land along the east bank of the Clark Fork River; while there is a larger floodplain on the other side of the grade, we did not observe any immediate surface archaeological traces of a railroad construction camp there. It is possible that seasonal flood cyles have disturbed or destroyed the site in that area—or, for some reason, the laborers chose to set up camp along the edge of the slough instead. Given the likelihood of the winter shelter and camp adaptations observed elsewhere, perhaps this area provided more windbreak from cold winter conditions along this river valley in the Rocky Mountains. Additional research at this recently discovered site, including research into the region's climate and weather history, is necessary to make more informed interpretations and to determine if the site might have been situated atop the slough if it froze over during the winter of 1883, when the NPRR was being constructed in this area. While private landowners have given enthusiastic permission to conduct more research at the site, the current owner of the adjacent railroad grade and right-of-way, Montana Rail Link (MRL), denied our permit for a noninvasive, surface survey of their property, noting that "MRL would not be able to ensure the safety of [our] crew" there, although they did encourage our team to reapply to work at another site in the future.[33]

Cultural Perseverance, Environmental Transformation

The physical remains of these labor camps involve scarcely visible cultural features, such as collapsed rock hearths, remnant stone foundations from shelters, tent pads, and sparse, often disturbed, artifact scatters. Though meager, the archaeological evidence reflects activities associated with food, health, shelter, leisure, and labor, offering glimpses of life in these temporary work camps and providing a tangible connection to the places associated with remarkable achievements of humanity. The similarities in artifacts and archaeological features (e.g., rock hearths) on the Sierra Nevada CPRR sites and the Rocky Mountain NPRR sites provide additional evidence of the fact that "the uniformity of material culture shipped to overseas Chinese communities represented a familiar but restricted material repertoire."[34]

The archaeological information about Chinese labor camps can be used as a springboard for interpreting archaeological evidence through multiple scales of analysis, connecting sites across regional, national, transnational, and global contexts to understand the adaptability and resilience of laborers when faced with extreme and unfamiliar environmental conditions.[35] Inspired by Barbara Voss's call for a transpacific overseas Chinese perspective, we can view these remote and nearly lost nineteenth-century work camps as part of a long-term series of "internal and external Chinese migration" that began in the 1400s, coinciding with the repercussions of the Little Ice Age and impacts of climate change on the economy of late-imperial China.[36]

The extreme winters the Chinese railroad laborers experienced while working in the Sierra Nevada and the Rocky Mountain regions help explain the presence of archaeological features such as dugouts and hearths as likely adaptations for shelter, heat, cooking, and community—material relics that are even more ephemeral than broken rice bowls and tea cups. Though subtle, these archaeological traces help reconstruct experiences of Chinese laborers in railroad construction camps across multiple scales, connecting sites across the North American West. The winter context of the examples presented here is also noteworthy due to the transnational lens that underscores the tremendous differences in climate and landscape between subtropical southern China and the North American West's wintry mountain ranges.

As reflected by observations of professional archaeologists over the course of several decades, Summit Camp's archaeological integrity has been severely compromised. Even so, it is still possible to go to the site location and experience the awe-inspiring landscape of Donner Summit that the railroad workers would have witnessed. Moreover, the extant transcontinental tunnels through solid granite represent a permanent signature and the reason for the work camp's position there in the first place.

The archaeological sites representing Chinese line camps along the NPRR's route through the Rocky Mountain region of northwestern Montana were initially documented in the 1980s. When first documented, the sites had visible tent platforms and artifacts on the surface. While there are still some surface artifacts that provide a tangible connection with the people living and working in those camps, the tent platforms have nearly vanished as annual spring flooding caused by rain and snowmelt from the mountains, erosion, and vegetation have gradually reclaimed the physical traces of these locations. Thus, partnerships with the current owners of the transcontinental railroad's right-of-way are essential for permission to conduct large-scale surveys of the region's historic railroad grades.

Although we can learn much from a single site or landscape within a continental-scale network, we will attain the potential of historical and archaeological contributions by collectively investigating the various types of archaeological and historical evidence representing that network. This work, which requires embracing the challenging issue of scale, will provide a platform that will help contextualize these places beyond the level of individual sites.[37] Collaborations with colleagues in other fields, such as the researchers involved in the Shaping of the West project of the Stanford Spatial History Project (SSHP), will greatly benefit the development of such large-scale endeavors.[38]

At past Chinese Railroad Workers in North America Project gatherings, I drew attention to the value of SSHP maps, showing how it was possible to add layers of environmental data, such as annual rainfall and major rivers, to existing SSHP maps with transcontinental railroad routes.[39] Given the natural resource data available via publicly accessible natural resource information systems (e.g., see the natural resource information available for Montana: http://nris.mt.gov/gis/), we can examine the complex ways in which the rivers and railroads created large-scale "industrial ecosystems."[40] The railroad lines and line camps frequently followed river corridors, providing collective evidence that can help explore the ways in which forest and river ecology influenced—and were in turn influenced by—the labor that made transcontinental railroads possible.

While research like this can help democratize the history of laborers for whom there are few written records and relatively meager archaeological signatures,[41] there are also historical ecological narratives interlaced with the development of railroads. Working from the assumption that human actions have a history of dramatically altering "the functioning of ecosystems of which humans are a part,"[42] archaeological investigations of the interface between culture and nature at these railroad camps along the rivers have the potential to yield data relevant for land managers, researchers, decision makers, and the general public interested in the ways in which humans have influenced and adapted to landscape transformations in the region over time.[43]

A scene from 1882 from the NPRR construction corridor along the rugged Clark Fork River valley of northwestern Montana illustrates the rapid, drastic scale of environmental transformation associated with the creation of railroad landscapes in the Rocky Mountain region:

> For more than 20 miles workmen are seen digging, chopping, lifting, blasting, cursing, and shouting. Trees are crashing down, earth is flying from countless shovels and huge rocks are being riven and scattered from all sides.... [M]en, hundreds in a gang, proceed to mow down the forest. The trees are felled with surprising rapidity... and a broad swath, 200 feet wide, is opened up through the forest.... [A]nd now come... thousands of [Chinese laborers]... to level the earth.[44]

This quote poignantly presents the pace of change and sheer number of workers involved in such a monumental undertaking. Given the fact that Chinese immigrants recruited to work in railroad construction composed a vast majority of the transcontinental workforce, a continental-scale analysis of the extant feats of their work and the traces of their work camps will have powerful interpretive value for projects dedicated to the broad geographic span of Chinese and Chinese American history, transcontinental railroad history, and transnational cultural heritage in general.[45] We have a long road ahead considering the time and effort it will take to document, protect, and preserve the archaeological sites that have the potential to help all of us better understand the cultural heritage and human condition of railroad workers who profoundly transformed the landscapes of western North America. Future researchers still have much work to do on this front. As more is learned about this transnational narrative of tenacity and adaptability, mainstream histories of this region will be able to underscore the region's multicultural, shared history.

CHAPTER 9

The Health and Well-Being of Chinese Railroad Workers

J. RYAN KENNEDY, SARAH HEFFNER,

VIRGINIA POPPER, RYAN P. HARROD,

AND JOHN J. CRANDALL

On a daily basis Chinese railroad workers on the Central Pacific Railroad (CPRR) and smaller lines dealt with the harsh conditions of life on the line; they experienced extreme environments, cave-ins and explosions, disease and malnutrition, and the ever-present risk of personal violence. Unlike their American and European counterparts, Chinese workers typically paid for their own room and board,[1] and they were not supplied with medical care directly by the railroad companies. Instead, they bought and prepared their own food and relied on one another for medical care using a variety of creative and effective strategies. This chapter explores what archaeological and historical data can tell us about the health and well-being of the Chinese workers who constructed many of the railroad lines in western North America.

While Western popular thought often dichotomizes the body and mind, medical anthropologists have shown that the two concepts are instead inextricably linked through the embodiment of lived experience.[2] Rather than focusing solely on the physical health of Chinese railroad workers, we find it more productive to view well-being holistically by taking into account its intersection with "physical health, satisfaction, and happiness."[3] This definition provides room to consider contributing activities, including medicine, food practices, and living and working conditions, and it situates well-being as a "state of mind that can help in coping with destabilizing factors such as violence in the home, racism, and economic deprivation."[4] For Chinese railroad workers, maintaining a sense of well-being likely involved treating both physical impacts to the body, from disease and injuries, and mental impacts, from racism, discrimination, and homesickness.

In this chapter we use a combination of data sets to understand the health and well-being of Chinese railroad workers. First, we incorporate information from historical accounts to explore workers' common health concerns and the toolkit of health-related strategies they brought with them from China. Second, we present bioarchaeological data collected from skeletal remains of Chinese railroad workers to serve as the starting point for our archaeological inquiry into health and well-being. Third, we discuss the concepts of health and well-being, and we argue that not only did Chinese railroad workers creatively use a wide array of techniques and approaches to treat their ailments, they also maintained their mental and social health through strong community bonds created by shared practices. Fourth, we explore medicine-related artifacts and archaeological plant and animal remains from campsites that provide insight into the medicinal and culinary practices of these railroad workers.

Historical Background

Contemporary newspaper accounts described a number of deadly railroad construction incidents resulting from severe and unpredictable weather, explosions and other accidents, cave-ins, and disease. In January 1868, for example, near Emigrant Gap, California, a Chinese employee of the CPRR was killed in a snowslide when he was swept in front of an oncoming locomotive.[5] In another incident, recorded by John R. Gillis, "some fifteen to twenty Chinamen" were killed in a single landslide.[6] Other environmental risks along the railroad included violent sandstorms in desert conditions, such as at Brown's Station near present-day Lovelock, Nevada, that could flatten tents, sweep belongings away, and make it impossible to see.[7] While these incidents would have been trying under any circumstances, the fact that most Chinese railroad workers were from Guangdong, a subtropical locale generally devoid of snowstorms and sandstorms, potentially made adjusting to these events even more difficult.

Beyond contending with the natural environment, Chinese railroad workers were subject to dangerous accidents, workplace violence, and the effects of disease. The *Sacramento Daily Union* recorded the 1866 deaths of three

Chinese railroad workers due to a premature explosion in Placer County, California, as well as six more deaths caused by a cave-in in a railroad tunnel near Dutch Flat, California.[8] Chinese railroad workers were also subject to injury and death from violence. For example, a group of thirty to forty Chinese workers employed by the McCloud River Railroad in Sisson, California, were attacked by a mob of mostly unemployed white laborers.[9] Many workers perished from diseases such as smallpox, which spread rapidly in the close quarters of the camps.[10] The exact number of Chinese injured or killed while working on the railroads is unknown, as newspaper accounts variably underreported or exaggerated accidents and deaths from construction. For example, on June 30, 1870, the *Sacramento Reporter* published an article on the transportation by train of the bones of 1,200 Chinese to be reburied in China.[11] This same shipment was reported on by the *Sacramento Daily Union* as consisting of the bones of 50 Chinese who had died while working on the construction of the CPRR, to be interred in a private cemetery, "as had been already the bones of about one hundred others similarly deceased."[12]

Bioarchaeological Data on Chinese Railroad Workers

By assessing patterns of nutrition, activity, illness, and traumatic injury, we can get some insight into the historical contexts behind the stories of these immigrants. This understanding is especially important given the sparseness of the written history and material record. Limitations associated with bioarchaeological analyses, however, include the small number of Chinese railroad workers' remains that are available for analysis and the fact that individuals often lived beyond the years that they were working for the railroad, and obtained a range of social and occupational positions in numerous communities. Yet the "situated analysis of skeletal data sheds light on the dynamic relationship that human health plays with the environment, both social and natural."[13] In this section we will look at traumatic injuries and pathological conditions present on the skeletal remains of thirteen men who at one point in their lives were identified as immigrant Chinese laborers, to attempt to determine if the injuries and pathological diseases they sustained were a consequence of social inequality and discrimination or occupational hazards other railroad workers would have faced. Skeletal remains provide a wealth of information about the health and well-being of these immigrants and the injuries and pathologies their bodies accrued while engaged in hazardous activities while working on the railroad.[14]

The town of Carlin in northeastern Nevada was founded in the 1860s around a terminus point of the CPRR.[15] Thirteen sets of human remains were recovered from private land that was several blocks from the town's cemetery and was being impacted during a construction project. The individuals were interred in the cemetery between 1885 and 1923,[16] a period that began less than two decades after the CPRR connected to the Union Pacific Railroad (UPRR) at Promontory Point, Utah.[17] The reason they were interred in the local cemetery rather than being shipped back to China—which was a common practice due to the "traditional belief expressed in the popular Cantonese saying, Falling leaves return to their roots (*luo ye gui gen*)"—is unclear. Possible reasons include financial difficulties and emerging global political issues, such as the Sino-Japanese War (1937–1945), that prevented the shipping of the remains back to China.[18] The remains from Carlin have been analyzed by a number of researchers interested in understanding the lives of Chinese immigrant laborers.[19]

Overall, the individuals appear to have worked hard during their lives (high rates of activity-induced changes), been victims of hazardous conditions or violent interactions (antemortem and perimortem traumatic injuries), and lived in conditions at one point in their lives that put them at risk of infection and disease (presence of pathological conditions). Among the individuals recovered from Carlin, all had some form of traumatic injury, two had suffered lethal trauma, and only four showed no sign of having some sort of pathological condition. The remains of Yee Hong Shing (Burial 10) had a fractured skull and numerous other broken bones that, based on differential diagnosis and different stages of healing, appear to be the result of violent encounters. Sue Fawn Chung and colleagues found that coroner homicide files describing Shing's death matched the osteological evidence left on the bones.[20] These records and the injuries present on the skeletal remains clearly indicate that at least some Chinese workers faced the prospect of periodic interpersonal violence during their time on the railroad or at other times of their lives, and this violence could have originated from other Chinese laborers, and particularly from other ethnic groups present at railroad camps.[21]

Aside from revealing the hardships these people suffered, the bodies also shed light on how these men took measures to enhance their health and well-being. Several individuals had healed fractures, but the individual identified as Burial 4 (an adult of fifty-plus years of age) had a severe leg trauma that involved the complete fracture of both the left tibia and fibula. When this man died, these bones had completely healed and, though noticeably displaced, the two halves of the broken long bones had been reunited, suggesting some sort of treatment (splint, anti-inflammatory herbal medicine, opiates for pain, etc.). While cranial and facial injuries found on the individual identified as Burial 8 (an adult thirty to forty years of age) indicate that he was exposed to violence, the three healed rib fractures and healed fractures of the hands and feet likely indicate that he was treated for his injuries. While healed trauma indicates that a person survived the injury, it does not necessarily mean that he received care from other members of the community. However, nineteenth-century Chinese immigration to the United States was driven by family and village networks, and these connections, as well as other social groups like district associations, provided much of the foundation for support in Chinese immigrant communities.[22] It is likely, given these strong community bonds, that a system of care developed that included both informal medical treatment within social groups and the services of the growing number of Chinese doctors and herbalists serving urban and rural communities.[23]

Other evidence of possible medical treatment found on the remains from Carlin, Nevada, is the presence of staining on the teeth of all individuals, which may have been the result of smoking tobacco and opium.[24] Though these two substances are often associated with recreational use, they were also used for medicinal purposes.[25] In China opium was used as a general analgesic among manual laborers (Yi-Li Wu, personal communication, December 15, 2015), and it was commonly used to treat a variety of conditions, including diarrhea, dysentery, and coughing.[26] Carol Benedict notes that "tobacco's continued inclusion in various materia medica throughout the Qing period [1644–1912] indicates that it was never completely regarded as a recreational drug," and that it was often considered to have antifebrile qualities.[27]

Concepts of Health and Well-Being in Chinese Culture

The historic record suggests, and bioarchaeological data confirm, that Chinese railroad workers were subject to injury, death, and illness from a variety of sources. However, Chinese workers relied on an extensive toolkit of strategies designed to preserve their overall health and well-being; these included traditional medicinal practices, consumption of food to maintain general health and treat specific ailments, and family and kin ties they could draw on for emotional support. Each played an important role in railroad worker health and well-being, and in this section we describe common nineteenth-century Chinese beliefs about each. Primary principles in Chinese medicine include yin/yang, *qi*, blood, meridians, and the Five Elements (or Phases) theory, also known as *wu xing*. Yin (female) and yang (male) are two opposite but complementary forces interacting within the human body. Meridians are channels that carry energy, or *qi*, and blood through the body and serve to guide physicians in the application of external treatments, such as acupuncture and moxibustion (heat therapy). Moxibustion treats chronic diseases by applying burning mugwort (*Artemisia chinensis* or *Artemisia vulgaris*) to the skin.[28] The Five Elements/Phases (Wood, Fire, Earth, Metal, Water) are used to interpret the relationship between seasonal changes and the organs of the body and their various functions.

There are two primary methods of applying treatments in Chinese medicine: internal and external. Internal treatments are ingested in the form of teas, soups, pills, powders, medicinal oils, and tonic wines, and they are often made from a combination of plant, mineral, and animal parts. External treatments include plasters, poultices, acupuncture, moxibustion, scraping (*gua sha*), massage, and cupping. Acupuncture involves the insertion of needles of various lengths and widths into specific points, or meridians, on the surface of the body. Scraping is done using a coin, soup spoon, or specialized scraping tool made from polished bone, wood, or stone.[29] Massage in Chinese medicine targets the meridians in an attempt to stimulate circulation of the blood, balance yin/yang elements in the body, strengthen muscles, and relieve cramps.[30] Cupping involves the application of heated cups to the surface of the body for a period of approximately ten to fifteen minutes, and is used to treat arthritis, rheumatism, dampness, stomach pain, bruises, and abscesses, among other ailments.

While very little documentary information exists on Chinese railroad worker health care practices, an understanding of contemporary medical practice and knowledge in China can aid in developing a more complete understanding of Chinese medical practices in the nineteenth century. During the Qing period, there were no restrictions on who could provide healing services. Sick patients relied on themselves and their families as the first recourse for diagnosis and treatment, and many households kept popular household almanacs that provided advice on a range of topics, including maintaining good health and well-being.[31] Haiming Liu has argued that this "widespread knowledge of herbal medicine in China challenges the stereotypical image of early Chinese immigrants as poverty-stricken and illiterate individuals."[32] Likewise, familiarity with household almanacs and herbal medicine further suggests that Chinese immigrants would have employed similar health care strategies in the United States.

Chinese railroad workers would have also brought with them an understanding of Chinese culinary practices and their relationship to health. This knowledge would have included an understanding of both balance between different attributes of foods and the use of specific ingredients and preparations to achieve desired health outcomes.[33] Balancing foods in the diet to promote good health related to specific medicinal properties pertaining to flavor (e.g., sour, bitter, pungent), thermal characteristics (warming, cooling), organ groups (spleen, stomach, kidney, etc.), and direction of movement (upward, downward, floating, falling).[34] Of these, the thermal properties of food were perhaps the most important, with hot foods being used to treat cool conditions, such as chills, anemia, and tuberculosis, and cool foods being used to treat warm conditions, such as sore throat, dry skin, and rashes.[35] Additionally, individual ingredients and preparations were used to alleviate acute symptoms, and they include a plethora of plant and animal ingredients often consumed in teas and soups. The prevalence of herb shops and Chinese doctors who relied on food-based medicines in nineteenth-century North America demonstrates the popularity and understanding of these kinds of medicinal treatments among Chinese immigrants.

Nineteenth-century Chinese cuisine also sought to balance *fan* (rice and other starches) and *cai* (vegetables and meat side dishes), with *fan* forming the base of most meals and *cai* serving as an accompaniment to add flavor and nutrition.[36] Proper balance of *fan* and *cai* promoted general good health, and was also seen as preventing wastefulness. The frequent importation of rice for use within Chinese immigrant meals supports the notion that rice was valued for nostalgic reasons and also played a key role in the construction of meals within the *fan* and *cai* dichotomy. Although no known nineteenth-century English-language sources directly address the importance of balance within Chinese immigrant cookery, more recent cookbooks describing San Francisco's

Cantonese cuisine detail the role of rice in these relationships,[37] and it is reasonable to suggest that similar beliefs were held by Chinese immigrants who came to the United States in the nineteenth century.

Finally, the importance of community support in the maintenance of Chinese railroad workers' well-being cannot be overstated. In particular, the Chinese Consolidated Benevolent Association (also known as the Six Chinese Companies) and other community associations played important roles in providing support, resources, and protection to Chinese immigrants.[38] Further, as will be discussed below, many Chinese health care practices such as massage were reciprocal in nature and facilitated interaction between workers, as did the group consumption of food and meals; these shared experiences would have further strengthened community bonds among workers.[39]

Health Care Practices of Chinese Railroad Workers

Chinese workers living in isolated railroad construction and maintenance camps could not readily access either Chinese doctors or Chinese medicines that were sold at the herb stores that had been established in Chinatowns across the American West by the mid-nineteenth century. Chinese doctors may have been hired by the railroad to treat workers in the case of serious ailments such as smallpox. One example is Dr. Fong Dun Shing, who was hired by the CPRR to treat sick workers. Following completion of the CPRR, Dr. Fong opened an herb store, Kwon Tsui Chang (Success Peacefully), on I Street in Sacramento.[40] Analysis of medicinal artifacts dating from 1865 to 1910 recovered from railroad sites in California, Idaho, Montana, Nevada, Texas, and Utah suggest that railroad workers maintained their health and well-being through a combination of traditional/familiar practices (diet, herbal medicine, strict hygiene) and nontraditional treatments (European American patent medicines, homeopathy). Health care–related artifacts recovered from these sites include patent medicine bottles, homeopathic medicine vials, Chinese medicine vials, opium-smoking paraphernalia, and Chinese liquor bottles and liquor cups.[41] Additional artifacts not typically thought of as having medicinal uses but possibly used for such purposes include soup spoons, coins, and teacups. Faunal and floral materials associated with health care treatments and the maintenance of good health are discussed later in this essay.

European American patent medicine bottles have been recovered from several Chinese railroad sites. Patent medicines typically contained large amounts of alcohol combined with bitter-tasting herbs and water, and examples found at Chinese railroad sites include bitters, sarsaparillas, extracts, liniments, tonics, and veterinary medicines. Bitters were used to treat stomach complaints, malaria, fever, and chills.[42] Sarsaparillas were a popular nineteenth- and early-twentieth-century cure for syphilis. Liniments were commonly used to treat bruises, muscle aches, and headaches and could also be applied to the chest to treat lung ailments. Archaeologists identified a bottle of Ballard Snow Liniment at the Cabinet Landing site, an 1882 Northern Pacific Railroad camp in Bonner County, Idaho. Ballard Snow Liniment claimed to cure rheumatism, nervous disorders, and lower back pain, leaving one "as spry as a colt."[43] Veterinary medicine, such as The Celebrated H.H.H. Horse Medicine, a bottle of which was found at the site of a Southern Pacific Railroad labor camp in Val Verde County, Texas, was introduced by Daniel D. Tomlinson in 1868 and marketed for use by both man and horse.[44] Similar to liniments, veterinary medicines could be used to treat headaches and sore joints and muscles. The preparation of herbal medicines often involved chopping, grinding, soaking in wine, and boiling, which would require a stove, pot, and other tools that might not be available in a camp setting, whereas patent medicines provided a convenient way to self-medicate.

Homeopathic medicine vials have been recovered from the Cabinet Landing site in Bonner County, Idaho. Homeopathy involved administering tiny doses of medicine made from a mixture of herbs and minerals whose chemical properties produced symptoms similar to the disease being treated.[45] Homeopathic medicines were sold as individual vials or in kits for home use with instructions for proper administration, and they were a popular way to self-medicate in the nineteenth century.

Chinese medicine had its own version of patent medicines in the form of small, single-dosage medicine vials. These medicines were mass produced and did not require a written prescription from a doctor. A Chinese medicine vial with a paper label identified at the Terrace Site, a maintenance and repair headquarters along the Salt Lake Division (Wells, Nevada, to Ogden, Utah) of the transcontinental railroad,[46] contained peppermint oil, which was taken orally to treat digestive disorders, upper respiratory infections, and gallbladder disease, or applied externally to treat muscle pain and headaches.[47]

Artifacts associated with opium smoking, including opium cans, lamps, and pipe bowls, are ubiquitous in railroad camps, as well as in other Chinese archaeological sites in North America. Opium was smoked while lying down, using a pipe with a bamboo stem and a bowl attached to the far end of the stem. As mentioned earlier, although most commonly associated with recreational use, opium may have been used for medicinal purposes, including to relieve aches and pains from performing hours of backbreaking, repetitive work and to treat diarrhea and coughing.

Fragments of Chinese liquor bottles containing rice wine or tonic wine have been found on several railroad sites. Tonic wines contained herbal ingredients distilled in liquor and were considered to have restorative powers. They could increase one's energy flow, or *qi*, enhance blood circulation, strengthen the kidneys, and treat rheumatism. Wine was often served in tiny porcelain cups decorated in patterns such as the Four Season Flowers (a polychromatic pattern painted with flowers representing each of the four seasons), and fragments of these porcelain liquor cups have been found at several Chinese railroad camps in the American West.

Railroad workers may have used porcelain soup spoons and coins in the application of *gua sha*, or scraping. Fragments of porcelain soup spoons and brass and zinc Asian coins have been found at many railroad worker–related sites. Soup spoons, as well as rounded stones or pottery sherds, warmed in the palms of the hands, may have been used in massage.[48] Frontier Chinese doctor Ing Hay of John Day, Oregon, used a coin or coinlike disk to treat meningitis and to revivify the nerves.[49] Dr. Ing Hay also ran an herbal medicine business and general store in the Kam Wah Chung Company Building in John Day, Oregon, from 1887 to 1940, and he specialized in the treatment of blood poisoning, meningitis, and other infectious diseases.[50] Chemical analyses of a brass Kangxi coin (1662–1722) from the Kam Wah Chung Museum showed that the coin contained traces of human skin and therefore was likely used by Ing Hay to perform *gua sha*.[51]

Drinking tea was, and still is, one of the most popular means of ingesting herbal medicine. Herbal teas do not contain tea leaves but instead are made from the flowers, berries, seeds, roots, peels, and leaves of various medicinal plants. Boiling water for tea helped reduce the risk of contracting a waterborne illness, such as giardia or dysentery. As a result, Chinese railroad workers had lower rates of dysentery than European American railroad workers. Fragments of Chinese teacups and teapots have been found at several Chinese railroad sites, highlighting the importance of this practice.

Food and Diet of Chinese Railroad Workers

By necessity, Chinese railroad workers would have made compromises and adaptations to both the procurement and preparation of food in railroad contexts, and they would have had to contend with the elements and challenges associated with cooking outdoors. However, documentary evidence suggests that many Chinese railroad workers ate more varied and nutritious food than did their European and American counterparts, although this came at the cost of having to purchase their own food rather than having it provided to them, as was the case for non-Chinese workers.[52] For workers on the Central Pacific Railroad, food was supplied and sold to Chinese laborers from rail cars stocked by labor contractors with a variety of difficult-to-obtain foods that enabled Chinese railroad workers to maintain a semblance of Chinese food practices even in the most rural railroad campsites.[53] This was likely the case on smaller rail lines as well, and Charles Nordhoff provides an example of such a setup in his description of the foods available for sale to Chinese workers in the early 1870s on the Merced Railroad:

> dried oysters, dried cuttle-fish, dried fish, sweet rice crackers, dried bamboo sprouts, salted cabbage, Chinese sugar (which tastes to me very much like sorghum sugar), four kinds of dried fruits, five kinds of desiccated vegetables, vermicelli, dried sea-weed, Chinese bacon cut up into salt cutlets, dried meat of the abalone shell, pea-nut oil, dried mushrooms, tea, and rice. They also buy pork of the butcher, and on holidays they eat poultry.[54]

For workers on the Southern Pacific Railroad, Alton Briggs reports a "ration table per day for each [Chinese] man—Rice 2 lbs.; tea, ⅓ oz.; fish, beef, or pork, 1 lb.; vegetables ⅓ oz.; lard or oil in small quantities,"[55] suggesting that at least in some cases Chinese railroad workers were supplied a standard food ration by the railroad. Additionally, Chinese railroad workers were observed fishing for suckers, chubs, and lake trout in the Clark Fork River while working at the Noxon Line Camp in Montana,[56] and it is possible they collected other wild animals and plants as well. Finally, while some workers would have prepared and cooked their own meals, others pooled their resources to hire cooks and pay for communal food supplies.[57]

ARCHAEOLOGICAL EVIDENCE OF CHINESE RAILROAD WORKERS' MEAT DIET

While documentary evidence records that workers consumed pork, beef, and fish, zooarchaeology, the study of animal remains from archaeological sites, has the potential to provide a much more detailed understanding of the meat diet of Chinese railroad workers. To date, however, only scant faunal data exist from Chinese railroad campsites, and much of our understanding of the diet of workers comes from railroad-related sites, such as lumber camps, and the Chinatowns where workers spent time between jobs.[58] Still, data from two small faunal assemblages collected from camps used by Chinese workers in the early 1870s along the Virginia and Truckee (V&T) Railroad in Nevada corroborate the documentary record. David Wrobleski identified two V&T Chinese sites that had small numbers of both pork and beef bones,[59] and C. Lynn Rogers provides data from a slightly larger assemblage (ninety-four bones), which included unidentified mammal remains and a small number of bones from trout- or chub-size fish.[60] Additionally, Keith Landreth and colleagues provide data from 170 bones collected from the Cabinet Landing site in Bonner County, Idaho, an 1882 railroad camp for the Northern Pacific Railroad, which housed both Chinese and non-Chinese workers.[61] While these faunal remains cannot be solely linked to either group, they include pork, beef, sheep, deer, and sucker bones, and minimally suggest that Chinese workers' food practices contributed some portion of this collection. Beyond these railroad campsites, a collection of 368 faunal remains from Mono Mills, a lumber and mining town with strong railroad connections in California, provides further evidence of Chinese railroad workers' diet.[62] At Mono Mills Chinese residents consumed pork, beef, sheep or goat, and chicken, and they supplemented these meats with a variety of wild animals, including turkeys, deer, jackrabbits, ducks, and fish. While the range of species represented at Mono Mills is greater than that in either of the V&T assemblages, it is significantly less diverse than that found in faunal collections from the small Chinese communities and large, urban Chinatowns in which railroad workers would have spent time between jobs.[63]

Faunal data from the Aspen Section Camp, a circa 1869 to 1890 railroad maintenance camp in southwestern Wyoming, provide the most extensive evidence of Chinese railroad workers' meat diet to date. Used by Chinese workers formerly employed by the CPRR, the Aspen Section Camp was one of many maintenance and repair camps along the Union Pacific grades of the transcontinental railroad. As at other railroad section camps, the Aspen Section Camp's Chinese workers were responsible not only for basic rail maintenance but also for clearing and repairing tracks damaged by snow, erosion, and other natural phenomena. Following his excavations at the site, A. Dudley Gardner has argued that the Aspen Section Camp was a peripheral Chinese site in relation to a larger core Chinese community in nearby Evanston, Wyoming, and the section camp's residents likely received food both from Evanston and directly from shipments along the rail line.[64]

The Aspen Section Camp faunal assemblage contains 3,914 bones from a wide range of taxa, including both domestic and wild animals (table 9.1). These data were collected by the lead author of this chapter and are presented here using two standard zooarchaeological measures: the total number of identified specimens per taxon (NISP, designated as N in the text) and the percentage of the total assemblage by weight. While these measures relate specifically to the bones recovered and identified, they can be taken as representative of the relative importance of individual animal taxa in the diet of Chinese railroad workers.

Pig bones dominate the assemblage in terms of both measures ($N = 183$, 34.4 percent of weight), and the medium mammal fragments, which are likely from heavily fragmented pig bones, account for another 16.4 percent of total assemblage weight. If the assumption that these are pig bones is correct, then pig remains represent roughly half the assemblage by weight, indicating that pork provided a significant portion of the meat and protein consumed at the Aspen Section Camp. Pork was supplemented with moderate amounts of domestic chicken ($N = 85$, 3.6 percent of weight) and wild rabbit (both *Lepus* sp. and Leporidae, $N = 84$, 3.8 percent of weight), both of which were commonly consumed in nineteenth-century southern China.[65] The remains of both chickens and rabbits at the Aspen Section Camp show butchery marks indicative of being chopped into small pieces with a cleaver, a pattern typical of traditional Chinese butchery but not usually found in European American cuisine. Both chickens and rabbits could have been prepared stir-fried in a wok, braised, or cooked in a soup or stew. A number of bird eggshell fragments were also identified in the assemblage, as were chicken long bones with medullary bone present. Medullary bone is a spongelike calcium deposit found in

TABLE 9.1   Faunal Remains from the Aspen Section Camp

Common Name	Taxonomic Name	NISP	% of total NISP	MNI	% of total MNI	Wt (g)	% of total Wt (g)
Mammals							
Pig	*Sus scrofa*	183	8.6	2	5.26	421.04	34.4
Cow	*Bos taurus*	1	0.0	1	2.63	5.00	0.4
cf. Deer	cf. *Odocoileus* sp.	1	0.0	—	—	4.31	0.4
Jackrabbit	*Lepus* sp.	61	2.9	5	13.16	41.79	3.4
Rabbit, unspecified	Leporidae	23	1.1	—	—	4.94	0.4
Porcupine	*Erethizon dorsatum*	1	0.0	1	2.63	1.73	0.1
Badger	*Taxidea taxus*	1	0.0	1	2.63	2.38	0.2
Domestic cat	*Felis catus*	2	0.1	1	2.63	2.01	0.2
Small mammal		34	1.6	—	—	9.22	0.8
Medium artio-dactyl (not pig)		1	0.0	—	—	7.10	0.6
Medium mammal		150	7.0	—	—	201.40	16.4
Large mammal		2	0.1	—	—	18.95	1.5
Mammal, unspecified		672	31.6	—	—	341.28	27.9
Packrat	*Neotoma* sp.	1	0.0	1	2.63	0.02	0.0
Rat	Murinae	1	0.0	1	2.63	0.10	0.0
Mouse	Murinae	5	0.2	1	2.63	0.06	0.0
Birds							
Chicken	*Gallus gallus*	85	4.0	7	18.42	43.69	3.6
Bird, probable galliform	Galliformes	8	0.4	—	—	4.03	0.3
Duck, unspecified	Anatidae	4	0.2	1	2.63	1.51	0.1
Bird, unspecified		241	11.3	—	—	36.06	2.9
Bird, chicken-sized		63	3.0	—	—	14.98	1.2

Common Name	Taxonomic Name	NISP	% of total NISP	MNI	% of total MNI	Wt (g)	% of total Wt (g)
Local Fish							
Carps and minnows	Cyprinidae	45	2.1	3	7.89	4.02	0.3
Pikeminnow	*Ptychocheilus* sp.	20	0.9	1	2.63	4.00	0.3
Suckers	Catostomidae	10	0.5	1	2.63	1.22	0.1
Carp or sucker	Cypriniformes	2	0.1	—	—	0.11	0.0
Trout or salmon	Salmonidae	2	0.1	1	2.63	0.26	0.0
Imported Fish							
Sacramento perch	*Archoplites interruptus*	4	0.2	1	2.63	0.22	0.0
Sacramento blackfish	*Orthodon microlepidotus*	1	0.0	1	2.63	0.04	0.0
Tilefish	*Caulolatilus* sp.	2	0.1	1	2.63	0.56	0.0
Rockfish	*Sebastes* sp.	16	0.8	1	2.63	5.25	0.4
Scorpionfish	Scorpaenidae	3	0.1	—	—	0.26	0.0
California sheephead	*Semicossyphus pulcher*	28	1.3	2	5.26	12.64	1.0
Starry flounder	*Platichthys stellatus*	5	0.2	1	2.63	0.76	0.1
Pacific sanddab	*Citharichthys sordidus*	1	0.0	1	2.63	0.03	0.0
Flatfish, unspecified	Pleuronectiformes	1	0.0	—	—	0.02	0.0
Yellow croaker	*Larimichthys crocea*	1	0.0	1	2.63	0.28	0.0
Cod family	Gadidae	1	0.0	1	2.63	0.04	0.0
Fish, unspecified		447	21.0	—	—	34.02	2.8
Unspecified vertebrate		1785	—	—	—	154.05	—
TOTAL		3914	100.0	38	100.00	1379.38	100.0

NOTE: NISP = number of identified specimens; MNI = minimum number of individuals; Wt (g) = weight in grams; cf. denotes specimens that compare favorably with the indicated taxon; sp. denotes specimens that can be definitively identified as to the genus but not the species level.

the long bones of egg-laying female birds, and its presence alongside eggshell fragments suggests that the Aspen Section Camp's Chinese residents were not only eating fresh chicken meat but also raising chickens on site and likely eating some of their eggs. The few bones identified from beef, porcupine, badger, domestic cat, duck, and a possible deer all showed definitive signs of butchery, and their low numbers suggest that these taxa played only a minor role in the meat diet of the Aspen Section Camp's Chinese residents. While some of these animals, such as the badger and porcupine, may have had medicinal uses, they may also simply have been taken opportunistically to add meat and variety to the diet. Finally, a wide range of local and imported fish was present in the Aspen Section Camp assemblage. Local fish included carps and minnows (N = 45), pikeminnow (N = 20), suckers (N = 10), and trout (N = 2), while imports included the Sacramento perch (N = 4), Sacramento blackfish (N = 1), tilefish (N = 2), rockfish and scorpionfish (N = 19), California sheephead (N = 28), starry flounder (N = 5), Pacific sanddab (N = 1), and yellow croaker (N = 1). All of the imported fish are native to California waters except the yellow croaker, which is found in the South China Sea. The unspecified cod (N = 1) could not be identified as to species, and it could have originated from either Pacific or Atlantic Ocean cod populations. All the fish imported to the Aspen Section Camp would have arrived as dried or salted fish, a common ingredient in nineteenth-century southern Chinese cuisine.

Taken as a whole, the documentary and faunal evidence suggests several broad patterns in Chinese railroad workers' meat diet. Chinese railroad workers typically had access to a variety of animal foods, including pork, beef, chicken, and dried fish. Although these would have all been familiar foods from home, archaeological and historical evidence reveals that Chinese railroad workers consumed significantly more meat and a wider range of animals than were typically eaten in the home villages of Chinese immigrants.[66] Additionally, Chinese workers took the time to supplement their diet with local, fresh-caught fish and, as shown in the Aspen Section Camp assemblage, wild game, including deer, porcupines, and badgers. While turning to wild game could be seen as a sign of desperation or need, the faunal remains from the Aspen Section Camp do not carry the signature of a starvation diet (i.e., extreme processing of bone to render every last bit of nutrition from the bones).[67] Instead, fish and wild game seem to be the result of Chinese railroad workers pursuing the freshest food possible as well a diversity of ingredients.[68]

ARCHAEOLOGICAL EVIDENCE OF CHINESE RAILROAD WORKERS'
PLANT DIET

Documentary sources, the presence of food containers recovered from railroad workers' campsites, and our understanding of Chinese cuisine indicate that plant foods also played an important role in the diet of Chinese railroad workers. Soups were made with dried mushrooms and vegetables, and most meals consisted of rice with a side dish, which included vegetables and seasonings. Such well-balanced meals provided the carbohydrates and vitamins for a nutritious diet that promoted good health. However, published direct evidence of this plant use from archaeological sites is rare. To a large degree this stems from the low potential that plant remains would preserve in short-term ephemeral sites, but few projects report a systematic attempt to collect this material.

Plant remains from three railroad worker sites and one supply town suggest that fresh fruits and vegetables and possibly wild greens and other wild resources (table 9.2) supplemented the purchased rice, noodles, dried fruits, and dried vegetables recorded by Charles Nordhoff and Alton Briggs.[69] Hearths at Donner Summit Camp contained a rice grain, an elderberry seed, and seeds from a variety of other potentially useful locally available wild herbs that could have been collected by Chinese railroad workers: manzanita has edible fruits, and some wild legumes have edible leafy greens.[70] Food remains collected from the Cabinet Landing Site included squash seeds, peach pits, and possibly apricot pits.[71] While the association of these items with the Chinese occupation at the site is not clear, cucurbits and stone fruits were among the most common items recovered from trash pits at Market Street Chinatown in San Jose, California, indicating their importance in Chinese cuisine.[72] The site also contained pottery used for shipping and storing Chinese foods.[73] One unit in a trash area of the Aspen Section Camp was sampled for plant remains.[74] The only clear food was a blackberry/raspberry seed fragment, although the presence of goosefoot seeds could indicate that Chinese railroad workers collected wild goosefoot leaves as edible greens.

The town of Evanston, Wyoming, twenty-four miles (thirty-nine kilometers) north of the Aspen Section Camp, had a Chinatown that served as a center for the Chinese railroad workers in the area.[75] Linda Scott Cummings and colleagues analyzed the pollen and macrobotanical remains from an outhouse pit dating to the 1920s, which provided evidence of a wide range of foods.[76]

TABLE 9.2 Food and Potential Medicinal Plants Recovered from Chinese Railroad Workers' Sites

Common Name	Scientific Name	Plant Part Recovered	Energy	Examples of Medicinal Uses
Blackberry/raspberry	*Rubus* sp.	Seed	Warm	Improves vision, kidney tonic
Cereal flour, cf. wheat	Cerealia	Pollen		
Cherry/plum/peach/ apricot	*Prunus* sp.	Pollen		
Chile pepper	*Capsicum* sp.	Seed	Warm	Stimulates digestion, treats rheumatism
Currant	*Ribes* sp.	Pollen		
Elderberry	*Sambucus* sp.	Seed	Warming	Treats dropsy, ague, skin diseases
Fig	*Ficus* sp.	Seed	Neutral	Stomachic, treats piles
Goosefoot	*Chenopodium* sp.	Seed		Anthelminthic, treats insect bites and sunburn
Grape	*Vitis* sp.	Seed	Neutral	Diuretic, treats dropsy and vomiting
Hawthorn	*Crataegus* sp.	Seed	Warm	Laxative, treats lumbago
Knotweed	*Polygonum* sp.	Seed	Neutral	Stops itching, disinfects
Legume family	Fabaceae	Seed		
Manzanita	*Arctostaphylos* sp.	Seed		
Olive	*Olea europaea*	Seed	Neutral	
Peach	*Prunus persica*	Pit	Warm	Laxative, treats burns
Possible apricot	*Prunus armeniaca* cf.	Pit	Warm	Treats coughs and bronchitis, laxative
Possible eggplant	*Solanum melongena* cf.	Seed	Cooling	Treats abscesses and piles
Rice	*Oryza sativa*	Grain	Neutral	Energy and spleen tonic
Squash	*Cucurbita* sp.	Seed		
Strawberry	*Fragaria* sp.	Seed	Cooling	Laxative, liver tonic
Tomato	*Solanum lycopersicum*	Seed	Cooling	Treats poor appetite and hypertension

NOTE: cf. indicates specimens that compare favorably with the indicated taxon; sp. denotes specimens that can be definitely identified as to the genus but not the species level.
SOURCES: Shih-Chen Li, F. Porter Smith, and G. A. Stuart, *Chinese Medicinal Herbs: A Modern Edition of a Classic Sixteenth-Century Manual* (Mineola, NY: Dover Publications, 1973); Daniel P. Reid, *Chinese Herbal Medicine* (Boston: Shambhala, 1993); Henry C. Lu, *Chinese Natural Cures: Traditional Methods for Remedies and Prevention* (New York: Black Dog & Leventhal, 1994); Carl-Hermann Hempen and Toni Fischer, *A Materia Medica for Chinese Medicine: Plants, Minerals and Animal Products* (Edinburgh: Churchill Livingstone, 2009); Tong Kwee Lim, *Edible Medicinal and Non-Medicinal Plants,* vol. 1, *Fruits* (New York: Springer, 2012).

Seeds of fig, strawberry, blackberry/raspberry, grape, and hawthorn provide evidence of fruit consumption, while those of chile pepper, tomato, squash, olive, and possibly eggplant show the variety of vegetables in the diet. Pollen data add the use of flour (possibly wheat), currants, and *Prunus* fruit, such as cherry, plum, peach, and apricot, to the cuisine. It seems likely that many of these foods would have been available to the railroad workers at Aspen Section Camp either from visits to Evanston or as supplies purchased through the railroad.

The recovered plant foods from these archaeological sites provided a mix of warming, cooling, and neutral elements necessary to the well-balanced Chinese diet (see table 9.2). In addition, some of these foods had specific medicinal properties. For example, traditional Chinese medicine uses the dried fruits, seeds, and leaves of raspberry and blackberry to cure a variety of ailments related to vision and the kidneys. Chinese railroad workers also may have collected wild plants growing in the area to use as medicine. For example, knotweed was found in the Aspen Section Camp samples; in China many parts of these plants are used medicinally, and some are steeped to prepare *liangcha* (cooling tea), an herbal drink used in the summer to promote good health.

═══

Life on the railroad was difficult, and historical and archaeological evidence— as seen in the bones of the men from Carlin, Nevada—demonstrates that Chinese railroad workers experienced injury, disease, and death as a direct result of their working and living conditions. Chinese railroad workers were also affected by racism in the form of discrimination. This included receiving lower wages than white workers, being provided with few or no housing amenities, and having to work more dangerous and labor-intensive jobs than their white counterparts. Chinese railroad workers were also always under the threat of violence, such as the attacks that occurred on the McCloud River Railroad and to the man referred to as Burial 10 in Carlin. While it is tempting to cast Chinese railroad workers as helpless victims, archaeological data present a different picture entirely, one of Chinese railroad workers creatively managing their health and well-being through a combination of medicinal treatments, culinary practices, and community support that combined traditional practice with the realities of life on the railroad.

To address their health and well-being, Chinese railroad workers drew on a complex combination of traditional treatments and new and novel solutions. They maintained their physical health with European and Chinese medicines, and they also may have employed medicinal practices, such as massage and *gua sha*. Likewise, they consumed a generally healthy diet centered on balancing rice with a wide range of domesticated and wild plant and animal ingredients, some of which no doubt had specific medicinal uses. Simultaneously, Chinese workers directly supported one another when they performed massage and other treatments, and they bonded together over shared meals. These activities would have served as the basis for community and belonging, which themselves would have greatly enhanced the mental health of Chinese railroad workers. None of this would have been possible without the ability to fully use the resources at hand, namely goods obtained via rail and materials collected from the immediate environment surrounding their work camps. As effective as these strategies were, however, it is important to note that they were necessary in large part due to the racially driven power dynamics implicit in railroad labor. Thus, the ability of Chinese railroad workers to maintain their health and well-being is not just a story of making do in a difficult environment; it is one of success and survival in the face of intense discrimination.

While historical and archaeological data provide tremendous insight into the health and well-being of Chinese railroad workers, there is much we still do not know. Although there is much left to do to fully understand the health conditions present in railroad workers' daily lives, the data presented here serve as a testament to the creativity and perseverance of Chinese railroad workers in the face of daunting adversity and hardship.

CHAPTER 10

Religion on the Road

How Chinese Migrants Adapted Popular Religion
to an American Context

KATHRYN GIN LUM

In this chapter I seek to reconstruct the religious atmosphere in which the Chinese railroad workers lived and labored by surveying the popular religious milieu in which they would have participated in China, the written evidence of white observers, and the material evidence of the temples in which they might have worshipped in the United States. I have attempted to piece together, on the basis of these varied sources, a portrait of a people determined and largely able to continue and adapt popular Chinese religious practices to an often-hostile environment, and of a small but significant few who found meaning in the teachings of missionaries.

Popular Religion in Chinese Villages

While some Chinese railroad workers in the United States had been gold miners before they turned to the tracks, most came directly from China, brought over by labor contractors working for the railroad companies. The religious lives of these sojourners were rooted in China. As Madeline Hsu has argued in *Dreaming of Gold, Dreaming of Home*, "Even as they became immersed in work overseas and were able to return to Taishan [Toishan] only infrequently, if at all, many Taishanese men remained bound to life in Taishan, primarily by commitments to close relatives such as wives, parents, children, and siblings." Their goals remained "very much local in scope," as they sought to provide for their families and maintain their obligations to ancestors.[1]

In the southern Chinese provinces from which the railroad workers came, villagers' day-to-day lives were punctuated by cycles of festivals and observances that made up the ritual calendar of Chinese popular religion, an amalgam of Buddhism, Daoism, Confucianism, and folk tradition. Seasonal festivals included the Lunar New Year, the Qingming Festival (held in the spring), and the Mid-Autumn Festival. The New Year was a time of joyous celebration when family members who had left the villages returned (if they could) to be with loved ones.[2] The Qingming Festival saw villagers sweeping the graves of ancestors and bringing offerings of food and drink to the deceased, while enjoying the awakening beauty of the season. Confucian rituals (*li*) coincided with these seasonal celebrations and were guided by *lisheng*, or ritual masters, working in conjunction with Buddhist monks and Daoist priests. Confucian rituals focused on "lineage building, the establishment of community compacts, and the development of local temple networks."[3] The *lisheng*, monks, and priests were particularly important in the observance of "life-cycle ceremonies," marking births, weddings, and deaths; ancestral rites, such as the presentation of offerings and incense, whether at family shrines or in ancestral halls and temples during the New Year, Qingming, and Mid-Autumn festivals; and rituals for the gods, who "like ancestors...are in need of care from the living," including food and incense offerings and theatrical performances meant to "entertain the gods" as well as the villagers.[4]

In addition to the temporal rhythms of calendrical rituals, villagers' lives were shaped spatially by practices of feng shui, or geomancy. Feng shui (wind water), growing out of Daoist beliefs about natural harmony and energy (*qi*), sought to determine auspicious locations for everything from dwelling places to temples to gravesites. As Wendy Rouse puts it, "Hills and mountains provided a barrier to dangerous winds that might carry evil spirits while allowing beneficial winds to pass. Water balanced the *yang* influence of the mountains and carried along *yin* energy with it."[5] Grave locations were particularly important, for the site of a grave could influence the happiness of the deceased, their susceptibility to evil spirits and negative energy, and the likelihood of blessings or curses on the living from the dead. As we will see later, the significance of space and place would be deeply felt by migrants who sought to interact with their natural surroundings and bury their dead according to feng shui principles, but who did not always have the expertise of professional geomancers to assist their efforts.

Villagers believed in the duality of the soul, with the spiritual, intellectual component (the *hun*) "ascend[ing] to the realm of immortal beings" at death, and the physical action component (the *po*) "remain[ing] with the body." Relatives of the deceased needed to appease the *po* with regular offerings, for "if the *po* soul remained comfortable in the grave, the living would reap the blessings of their contented ancestor." If it did not, the "discontented ancestor [could] return to earth in the form of a *gui* (*kuei*, demon or ghost)."[6] In Guangdong some villagers viewed the flesh of the dead as dangerous and their bones as powerful, and they practiced "secondary burial," in which the dead were first buried in a shallow grave, exhumed after a few years so that the decomposing flesh could be removed, and then the bones reburied in an auspicious location.

This brief overview of popular religious beliefs and practices in Chinese villages suggests the challenges railroad workers faced in trying to maintain their religious lives overseas. Unlike the Protestant Christianity that dominated the United States, which was seen as an interiorized and individualized form of worship that could be abstracted from one's environment and relationships, Chinese popular religion was intimately connected to both the land and kinship networks. The natural environment vibrated with energy and spirits both good and ill; ritual experts helped ordinary people navigate the complexities of an enchanted world. In the United States, the landscape was both unfamiliar and under the control of often hostile European Americans who dictated where the railroad would go and where the Chinese could be buried, often outside "white cemeteries." Ritual experts were fewer and farther between than in China and were prohibited from coming to the country under Chinese Exclusion, when they were redefined as "laborers" instead of religious leaders.[7]

Coming to Gold Mountain

Nevertheless, the gods came with the migrants. On the long voyage to the United States, the railroad workers might have turned to several deities for assistance in the almost all-male environment in which they found themselves and in the turbulent ocean crossing. One of these deities was Guan Di, or Guan Gong, the god of war and brotherhood. He originated as a deified human named Guan Yunchang, or Guan Yu (ca. 162–220 CE), who was renowned for his honesty, bravery, and dedication. Guan Di became a favorite of businessmen, policemen, and soldiers, and was also an object of Confucian worship, since he exemplified "loyalty to the Han royal house... and loyalty (*zhong*) is one of the most important Confucian virtues."[8] Since most nineteenth-century Chinese migrants were men, it is not surprising that Guan Di would have been as popular in America as he was among fraternal organizations back in China. He served as an example of "right action," "social stability, and peace," as well as "protector from all forms of evil," helping the railroad workers endure the hardships of migration, close quarters, hard labor, and racism.[9]

Tian Hou, the Empress of Heaven and goddess of the sea, also known as Mazu (Great Mother), was another deity popular among the migrants. She was loosely based on a historical figure, Lin Moniang, "who was born in the first year of the Song dynasty and died at the age of twenty-seven, unmarried, in Meizhou, on the coast of Fujian province." Lin became famous for her "spiritual powers: she was able to help fishermen, including her father and brothers, to survive storms at sea." After her early death, and over time, her special powers came to be seen as applicable beyond sailors—she was able to "come to the aid of anyone who was in need of her help."[10] For Fujianese migrants, she came to be seen as "an ancestral god (*zufu*) of Fujian people, even though she had no children." They were more likely to refer to her by the familial title of Mazu than by the imperial name of Tian Hou.[11] Since Fujian and Guangdong were the two provinces from which most migrants came and which neighbored each other on the southern coast of China, it would not be surprising that the sojourners who came to work on the railroad from Guangdong considered her a patron deity as well.

In Chinese popular religion, Tian Hou/Mazu was sometimes seen as an incarnation of Guanyin, the bodhisattva of mercy and compassion, who became popular during the Song dynasty (960–1279) with the spread of the *Lotus Sūtra* in China. Originally a male bodhisattva known as Avalokiteśvara in India, Guanyin's transformation to female in China "began around the tenth century and took several hundred years." In the *Lotus Sūtra*, "Sakyamuni praises Guanyin as one who will grant immediate salvation to anyone who is suffering."[12] Both Guanyin and Mazu combine feminine and masculine qualities, including "fierce, war-like attributes capable of powerful defence of territories," as well as virginal virtue and self-sacrifice.[13] As a bodhisattva, Guanyin had forsaken nirvana for the time being in order to help other humans become enlightened. She and other bodhisattvas were amalgamated with local Chinese gods as Buddhism spread throughout China, becoming objects of worship in Mahayana Buddhism and in popular Daoist practice. Like Tian Hou, Guanyin was sometimes seen as a patron of seafarers, as well as of the sick and disabled, the poor, and the desperate. Since the largely male migrants came without mothers, wives, and daughters, the mercy and compassion offered by these popular female deities may have been particularly welcome, even though both were also seen as the special protectors of women and of fertility.

Indeed, one of the oldest Daoist temples in the United States, Tin How Temple in San Francisco's Chinatown, was established in 1852 in honor of Tian Hou/Mazu by the Chinese who had come to mine for gold. The railroad workers could benefit from the temples and associations the earlier adventurers had already constructed, whether the "joss houses" in San Francisco or the temples that dotted gold country. Recently landed migrants could come to pay their respects and give thanks for a safe ocean crossing, as well as seek fortune papers that might divine what their future in Gold Mountain might be. Migrants also used San Francisco temples as social gathering places and temporary dwelling places. Here they were targeted by missionaries who thought that the arrival of the Chinese in America provided a providential opportunity for their conversion to Christianity.

The observations of white onlookers can provide us with a window into the religious experiences of the Chinese railroad workers just before they embarked on their journeys into the interior. In the late 1860s, Daniel Cleveland, a San Francisco lawyer, penned a lengthy but never-published manuscript, "The Chinese in California," which he based on his firsthand observations and research. In a handwritten chapter on missionary work with the Chinese, he told of visiting a temple in San Francisco "shortly after the arrival of a large bod number of immigrants, about one hundred of whom were quartered there" (edits in the original). Cleveland described "the temple proper" as "filled with hideous idols, banners, standards, censers, and other things used in idol worship. Incense [^sticks] were burning before the huge idol. The floor was covered with Chinese, lying upon their small mats, reading, talking and smoking. Occasionally one of them would kneel and bow before the idol, mutter a prayer, and burn a few incense sticks, but and would then rejoin his companions."[14]

Into the room stepped "Chu Shing Chong," a Christian convert and missionary colporteur, who "took a seat near the idol and commenced talking to his countrymen. He had a bundle of tracts in his hand, which he offered them. Nearly every person took one, though a few refused to do so. He remained about half an hour, and then he left." Cleveland continued,

> [A] number of the Chinese read the tracts, some of them reading aloud, in their peculiar singing tone. I saw them again in the afternoon of the same day, when they were about [to] depart for the P̶a̶ line of the Central Pacific R.R. upon which they were engaged as laborers, carefully pack[ing] up these tracts in their bundles and boxes. Yet the probability is t̶h̶a̶t̶ notwithstanding their apparent care in preserving these tracts, and interest in reading them, that not a single heart was touched, or mind in any way influenced by their truths. They were valuable to them simply because they were something to read, and they could not destroy them, because, with their reverence for p̶r̶i̶n̶t̶ written or printed characters, it would be a sin to do so.[15]

Cleveland saw the Chinese as a "most conservative" people whose hearts and minds it would be very difficult to change. Confident in their own "heathen empire," which Cleveland himself dubbed the "greatest of modern times," the Chinese were respectful toward Americans but satisfied with their own ways.[16]

Following on the heels of the Chinese "helper" with his tracts came a white missionary. According to Cleveland, the Chinese treated him in much the same way as they had treated the tracts. The missionary

> seated himself so he could touch some of the idolatrous paraphernalia, and in the idol temple, a̶n̶d̶ and in the presence of its worship, talked to the heathens about him of the one True God. They answered his questions, and asked some themselves, but did not manifest any interest in his subject. T̶h̶e̶y̶ ̶d̶i̶d̶ ̶n̶o̶t̶ Though not specially disrespectful, they continued to lie and lounge about the floor, as [^previous]b̶e̶f̶o̶r̶e̶ his entrance.[17]

Cleveland, who would go on to become a railroad man himself,[18] supported Chinese immigration, and his discussions of Chinese religion lacked the vitriol and disgust that dripped from some other accounts. His description of the temple scene allows us to see both how missionaries reacted to Chinese material religion, touching the "idols" to try to show that they had no sacred power, and how some Chinese reacted to American Protestant emissaries—coolly, but with respect. Cleveland's description also shows us how nineteenth-century Chinese popular religion was largely misunderstood by those who sought to convert them. The Chinese mingled the social with the sacred in both their temples and their homes, so the missionary's attempt to defuse the power of the "idols" by sitting next to them and touching them in a nonceremonial way was not effective. The migrants were themselves lounging on the ground and chatting in the presence of the gods, and small shrines to ancestors and deities often sat in kitchens as well as temples.

Though we have no direct evidence that any of the railroad workers themselves converted to Christianity, we do know that they were aware of and sometimes evangelized by Chinese Christians like Chu Shing Chong.[19] Some Chinese converts had been educated in mission schools in China before coming to the United States. Another path to conversion was through the tracts distributed by missionaries and colporteurs. Often, tracts included times and dates of chapel services and English classes, drawing in potential converts through social services. Chen Chung, a colporteur in California who had converted in Australia, became interested in Christianity after reading missionary tracts left at a temple he and his countrymen had built there. In an 1870 article written for *The Occident*, he explained:

> I went to the little temple to worship the idol which we had placed there, and to pray for good luck in mining; and on the altar before the god we found some small books in the Chinese language, of which each of us took some, and carried them home to our cabins. I read with care those I had taken, and afterwards re-read them, and that many times. I soon became anxious to know more about the doctrines taught in these books.[20]

Chen actively sought out "two strangers who had been to our camp distributing books" who could teach him more. Though Cleveland had dismissed the possibility that any migrants might be swayed by the tracts that colporteurs offered, Chen's case suggests that some did find their curiosity piqued and sought to learn more. It would certainly not be impossible for some of the railroad workers to read the tracts they were offered and to seek out missionaries and Chinese churches upon returning from the interior.

That Chinese converts often assisted the missionaries in tract distribution and colportage work also suggests that they treated their conversions with seriousness and were actively committed to spreading Christianity among their peers. White missionaries employed Chinese colporteurs to "improve opportunities of conversing with the people of their nation respecting the Christian doctrines, and explaining the Scriptures, and reading and explaining the tracts to such as might not be able to read themselves."[21] One such colporteur, Sit Ah

Moon, wrote a letter back from the southern mines in the Sierra Nevada, in which he explained that his work was met with "great satisfaction and delight." He had even found himself evangelizing the American population alongside the Chinese: "Of the Americans there appeared to be few, very few, who were followers of Jesus," he noted. "On the Sabbath...[f]orty or fifty Chinese assembled, and afterwards as many more of the people of the village (Americans) came to see what we were doing. I told them of the Son of God who came from Heaven to save us." After the southern mines, he planned to travel to Sonora, Columbia, and Jamestown, California. Other colporteurs focused on San Francisco and its surroundings, likely encountering railroad workers on their way to the interior. Some converts achieved a modicum of fame, like Jee Gam, who became a Congregationalist minister and wrote a series of articles for the *American Missionary*, and Ng Poon Chew, who also became an ordained minister and established a Chinese-language daily newspaper (*Zhongxi ribao*, or China West Daily). These prominent converts used their positions to argue against exclusion, even while telling their countrymen that "[i]t is Christianity which China needs."[22] In the midst of harangues against the "heathen Chinee," missionaries held up Chinese converts like Jee and Ng as evidence that the Chinese could convert and become a part of American society.

But most American observers were more interested in what they saw as the "heathen" rites and festivals that the Chinese celebrated on Gold Mountain. Temples held "bomb day festivals," with roots in southern China, in which large firecrackers dropped "bamboo rings or sticks ('wands') high in the air" that observers would run and try to catch. Those who caught a ring or wand and ran with it to the temple "might receive various rewards: community-wide prestige, a framed painting, an image of the deity involved, or in some cases, the right to collect temple revenues." Non-Chinese often came to "watch and perhaps to buy souvenirs," and some temples opened for outsiders on these celebratory occasions.[23]

Temples also opened to non-Chinese visitors for the Lunar New Year, which American observers found particularly fascinating, seeing the Chinese festivities as strange, fantastic, colorful, smelly, foolish, and titillating. Reading between the lines of one such account allows us to see how the Chinese did not abandon their ritual calendars when they crossed the Pacific, but adapted their celebrations to new surroundings. In a March 2, 1870, piece for the *Boston Traveler*, Russell Conwell described "The Chinese in San Francisco.—Their

Celebration of New Year.—The Idols and Ceremonies of Worship." Conwell at the time was a young journalist who had made his mark reporting on the Civil War battlefields and who would later become famous for his gospel of wealth lecture, "Acres of Diamonds." He had come to San Francisco not long before. He explained how the Chinese had spent "weeks…making preparation for their New Year," making and purchasing new clothing, preparing food for consumption, and readying firecrackers and food for sacrifices.[24]

Conwell's bewildered gaze—he labeled the Chinese preparations "as interesting as they are strange"—suggests how Western observers approached Chinese migrants through an Orientalist lens that rendered everything they did exotic and inexplicable. Yet even through that lens we can see how Chinese migrants were able to modify their religious practices for a new environment. Conwell wrote: "Everyone offers a sacrifice to his household gods and to his dead ancestors, by placing vegetables on a table and lighting a candle near them, and by bowing several times in front of odd-looking pictures, crudely drawn on paper, to represent their household gods and ancestors." Conwell's description shows how the Chinese continued their traditions of paying respect to loved ones and deities far from their ancestral homes and villages. In bowing to these rough, portable images, they were not worshipping the actual pieces of paper, as white observers sometimes accused, but rather making do, paying respects to representations of real spiritual forces, and also bringing to themselves, and to the American landscape, the power that those forces held. "One of the former they burn up after bowing before him and offering him vegetables," Conwell continued, "and they say that he then goes up to heaven to give an account of the family proceedings for the past year."[25] Burning ritual objects wafted them to the gods and spirits, whether incense, food, paper money, paper clothes, or in the case Conwell describes, an ancestor or deity whose representation oversaw the migrants during the year and could now be sent to the spirit realm to report on their doings in this strange new land.

Into the Interior

The railroad workers likely brought portable objects of devotion with them as they journeyed into the interior. We have photographic evidence, for instance, of a figure of Guan Yu, from Alfred A. Hart's *Stereoscopic Views of the Central Pacific Railroad.* The statuette may well "have been installed in the corner of one of the construction train cars.... The small cups visible at the figure's feet probably contained wine or tea as a drink offering."[26] Daniel Cleveland likewise explained how, not only the railroad cars, but also "[e]very house, camp, or other place in which Chinese reside in our Pacific states and territories with rare exceptions, has some kind of tablet, or idol which is worshipped." Though they could not clean the graves of their ancestors in China, it is possible that they celebrated occurrences like the Qingming Festival by burning paper money and incense and by providing offerings of food to the ancestral representations that they may have tucked into their knapsacks. They could have restocked their supply of devotional materials at Chinese stores they came across along the way. As Cleveland noted, "Almost every Chinese store, shop, and place of business" kept "as a part of its stock, incense sticks, mock-money, tapers, and other articles used in idol worship, and their sale constitutes no small proportion of the business done." Cleveland claimed that the Chinese spent "not less than 300,000 [dollars] per annum" on objects of worship, from inexpensive pieces of paper to fine furniture imported from France for their temples. He and other white Christian observers saw this as a colossal waste of money and a reason for the Chinese people's lack of innovation (in their eyes): rather than invest in technology and science, the Chinese spent money on the past, revering dead ancestors instead of investing in the future.[27] Of course, they failed to see that the Chinese people's reverence for ancestors was a way of investing in their future, since ancestors rightly treated had the power to assist and protect the living. By viewing Chinese religious practices as benighted heathenism, Western observers refused to grant them legitimacy or rationality, instead seeing them as ignorant delusions that needed to be eradicated.

Without fully understanding how the Chinese could bring their religious worldviews and practices with them, missionary supporters of Chinese immigration believed that they might easily convert them in America, where they were thousands of miles away from their ancestors, village and city temples, and priests. The missionaries hoped that the Chinese might become even more unmoored from their traditions as they left San Francisco for work on the railroad. Though missionaries may not have followed the Chinese as they laid track and dynamited mountains (at least in any records I have come across), the fact that they disbursed tracts to them beforehand suggests that they hoped the Chinese might read the tracts and ponder the Christian message in their camps at night.

Missionary William Speer thought that laboring on the most cutting-edge technology the nineteenth century could offer might teach the Chinese to forsake their own traditions

> as they learn to look for help and safety not to a dumb wooden idol, but to a mighty power which surpasses all they have ever imagined. It has limbs of iron, heart of fire, lungs of steam, ravenous appetite and thirst, with the strength of a thousand horses, and yet tractable to the touch of a man's finger. What a teacher is the steam-engine, in all its thousand applications in this country, to the strangers whose nation never till recently possessed one!

Speer criticized Chinese religion for being supernaturalistic rather than scientific. Protestant Christianity, he suggested, had enabled Americans to rightly understand natural forces (rather than attributing them to supernatural powers) and to harness them in the service of technological innovation. The railroad would teach the Chinese to understand the same:

> They commence work upon one of our railroads. In what a domain of wonders do they live! The thundering locomotive and cars, instead of the train of weary coolies—the sweep of the road, setting at defiance all the superstitions as to winds and waters and hills—the punctual and daily requisitions, without respect to stars, or gods, or luck.... They had lived in abject terror of the gods of lightning, with bodies like leopards or like birds of prey; now they learn that this mysterious power is seized and compelled to carry our verbal messages of business or of affection thousands of miles, in an instant of time, over mountains, rivers, continents and oceans.[28]

Speer foresaw the migrants bringing their knowledge back to China and introducing the railroad there, "though these will be much interfered with by the superstitions in regard to the *fung-shwui*, or powers of nature, fear of disturbing the tombs of the dead, and apprehensions of opium-smuggling and foreign violence and crime."[29]

Like Speer, Cleveland pointed to Chinese "superstitions" as a reason for their supposed reluctance to innovate. The similarities between Speer's and Cleveland's perspectives again suggest how widespread was the notion that the Chinese were heathens engaging in "besotted idolatry"; it was not simply missionaries who advanced this view.[30] "How singular it is," Cleveland mused, "that the Chinese, the most conservative a people in the world, should be constructing one half of the great trans-continental railroad, one of the most ~~advanced movements~~ [wonderful progressive achievements] of this ~~age~~ marvelous age." He explained how

[t]hey are more reluctant to work upon this road than in any other employment and as it extends westward, this increases. The reason for this is their
superstitious nature. They do not yet fairly understand [the] railroad[s] as
yet. They are unknown in China, and are regarded with suspicion and dread.
They have a superstitious belief that a huge serpent of gigantic proportions is
lurking in the Rocky Mountains, and that some day he will dart out upon the
Chinese laborers as they approach his lair, and devour all within his reach.
Americans can have no adequate idea of the terror which this superstition
inspires.[31]

Speer's comment about "*fung-shwui* superstitions" and Cleveland's description of the serpent, though less than neutral, nevertheless point to the close
relationship that many people of non-Christian faiths have had to the land, in
contrast to the extractive, property-based attitude more typical of Christian
communities who believed that they had a God-given right to dominate
the natural environment. If we set aside the European American assumption
that belief in the sacredness of the land and its spirits is primitive, we can
acknowledge, without value-laden judgment, that non-Christian peoples have
historically been more reluctant to parcel out the land and excavate its contents.[32] For the Chinese railroad workers, dynamiting mountains and cutting
the land risked "terrible misfortune," as Cleveland put it.[33] We might surmise
that among the things they propitiated their ancestors and deities for was
protection from such disaster.

Serpent aside, the Chinese were right to fear railroad work, given the
risk of accident and death. According to the Chinese Railroad Workers in
North America Project, some "historians estimate from engineering reports,
newspaper articles and other sources that between 50 [and] 150 Chinese
were killed as a result of snow slides, landslides, explosions, falls and other
accidents." The number could also be much higher, and scholars continue
to assess and uncover evidence to help us better understand the hazards the
migrants faced. Smallpox and disease were also factors in the laborers' camps,
though the extent to which they factored into the death rate remains a matter
of speculation. Reports from the period on the death rate ranged from 50 to
1,200 Chinese; railroad magnate "Charles Crocker, testifying before Congress
after the line was completed, acknowledged that a great many men were lost
during construction—and most of those workers were Chinese."[34]

Chinese preparations for death garnered a great deal of attention from
white observers. Most of these observations focused on the Chinese in settled

communities, where they had more time and resources to send off the dead with rich ceremonies, but these descriptions are nonetheless significant for understanding what the railroad workers might have hoped for and how they might have pared down such ceremonies for the exigencies of camp life. In an 1869 article titled "Chinese 'Funeral Baked Meats,'" the missionary Augustus Ward Loomis focused on Chinese death rites, which "the residents of California have had opportunities of observing," though "the exact meaning of many of these funeral ceremonies may not be generally understood."[35] Descriptions of Chinese funerals are not rare in publications like *Overland Monthly*; funerals were public affairs that engaged the senses with the sounds of wailing and "weird music," the smells of food, burning incense and paper money, and the sight of white-robed mourners and bodies covered in white cloth. Loomis purported to provide readers with the "exact meaning" of these ceremonies. He explained that although the Chinese reverence for their dead might seem to be "pleasing" and even "commendable," there is in fact "much idolatry... mixed with it." "When... we become acquainted with some of their superstitions respecting the dead," he wrote, "and when we know that they not only presume that the souls of those who have left the world need to be fed and clothed and amused the same as while in the body, but that they also fear their wrath or seek their aid, and therefore worship them with religious rites and address petitions to them, our admiration changes to pity."[36]

Loomis provided a cursory overview of what was then known about Chinese popular religion. He explained that Chinese attitudes toward the dead represented an amalgam "of the Buddhist doctrine, of purgatory, and of the transmigration of souls," and "of the Tauists' [*sic*] notions respecting spirits—their agency and interference in human affairs, and the methods of dealing with them." In addition to these, said Loomis, was "ancestral worship, which is older than the religions of Buddha and Tau.... It is very seldom indeed we may meet with a Chinaman who has not his head full of the superstitions of all the three."[37]

Perhaps the greatest fear of the migrants was dying in the United States and not having enough money to have their bodies shipped back to China, where their bones could rest with their ancestors and be properly cared for and worshipped by their families. Chinese migrants expended a great deal of money, Loomis explained, not only to ship the bodies of the dead back to China, but also "to lure home the spirit." Migrants paid the Six Companies, mutual benevolent organizations, to ensure that their bones were sent back to China, to hire mourners, and to provide food and paper goods to burn at their funerals. Loomis decried these beliefs as corporeal instead of spiritual, illusory instead of everlasting: "[M]uch as we ourselves might relish a savory dish of pig and chicken, none of us, we think, would be willing to exchange the anticipations of a paradise in which hunger, thirst, and carnal desires may never more torment us, for a heaven of tinsel money, tallow candles, paper garments, boiled rice, and samshu." And yet he affirmed that "[t]here is room for them all in that place where 'the many mansions be,' and there is a power which is able to fit them for companionship with prophets and apostles." In other words, Loomis saw the migrants as convertible. He described them as earnest but deluded, in contrast to contemporaneous anti-Chinese demagogues, who focused on the willful trickery and heathenness of the Chinese.[38]

Reading between the lines of Loomis's descriptions, which as we saw with other white observers, filtered everything through an Orientalist lens of exoticism and heathen error, what we see is a picture of Chinese migrants who were motivated, not crippled, by the support of family and ancestors. Though Loomis saw their practices as silly and pitiable, we can see in his descriptions the ability of the migrants to make space in the United States for their death ways. They claimed aural and olfactory space, as they unabashedly paraded down streets with music and mourners and burned fragrant incense and paper goods. They claimed space in the ground for the flesh of their dead. And they claimed space on roads and transit vehicles to ship the bones of their dead from the interior back to San Francisco, and from San Francisco back to China. As Wendy Rouse explains, "The practice of secondary burial took on a new meaning to overseas Chinese," as their "belief in the dangers of the flesh," combined with their "desire to rest in native soil," led to the regular exhumation of bodies after the flesh had had a chance to decay. In the ideal situation, exhumers would scrape the flesh off the bones carefully and make sure that "not a piece of bone is allowed to escape."[39] But the ideal situation was not always achieved, and when laborers were on the move to build the railroad, sources allude to burials that were hastier than that and probably identified with rough markers. Graves were shallow, which made sense when on the move, but also made for easier exhumation at a later date. There may not have been as much time to carefully sort through bones or rebury the flesh. As Rouse notes, "In 1862, the grand jury of Butte County reported that in Oroville, 'they divest the bones of flesh, and leave the latter, with their grave clothes, in all stages of decomposition, scattered on the ground, creating a stench and endangering the health of the adjacent inhabitants.'" As the quotation suggests, white observers described the shallow graves with disgust and viewed decomposing flesh as a sign of "heathen" disrespect for both the living and the dead. But in fact, sources like these show how committed the Chinese remained to repatriating the bones of their countrymen, even when circumstances made it difficult.[40]

After the Railroads

When their labor on the railroads was complete, some Chinese migrants decided to stay in the United States, making their way to cities throughout the western states, to mining towns, fishing and lumber camps on the coast, and even to Napa and Sonoma to help establish the wine industry in California. As noted earlier, some of the places where they settled already had Chinese populations established during the gold rush, with Chinese-run businesses and temples. The temple in Oroville, California, which dates to the 1860s, stands as a testament to the connections between the gold rush migrants and the Chinese railroad workers.[41] One of the original patrons of the temple was Chun Kong You (also rendered "Yuo," and also known as Fong Lee), from Wong Toon Village in the Taishan District of Guangdong. For 140 years, his family believed that he had come "from China directly to Oroville," where he set up a successful store, the Fong Lee Co. (Big Profit Company), and invested in local real estate, agriculture, and other enterprises. But they discovered that he had actually first come to work on the railroads, giving that work up because it was too "strenuous." He instead "sold merchandise to his fellow laborers by carrying items on a bamboo pole upon his shoulder," then invested those earnings in his store.[42] By the time Chun, or Fong, came to Oroville, two wooden temples constructed by the earlier gold miners had already burned down, so he and some other local Chinese men erected a new structure: "They ordered the altar from Shanghai and hired a priest from China.... The emperor donated a second heavily enameled teak altar with carvings depicting his day—cooks, musicians, scholars—and appointed Chun Kong You to collect taxes from the Chinese immigrants and send them back to China."[43] This anecdote illustrates the direct connections some railroad workers made to temples founded in the gold rush; but even where such direct evidence is lacking, we can surmise that the reason some temples survived is because former railroad workers kept the

Chinese populations of their towns high enough in numbers to sustain them into the twentieth century.

That said, many temples disappeared. The 1906 earthquake in San Francisco "destroyed the religious heart of Chinese America," while "natural disasters, population movements, urban development, and racial and religious prejudice" devastated the hundreds of others that dotted the western United States.[44] The Chinese temples in the gold-mining towns of Weaverville, Oroville, and Marysville, and in the fishing and farming village of Mendocino, persisted in the face of these odds, largely intact in both exterior appearance and interior artifacts.[45] Scholars have seen them as "complete and authentic" windows into the nineteenth-century Chinese popular religion shared by gold rush era and railroad migrants, as well as by the people in the Chinese villages from which they came. Indeed, research suggests that these temples might even tell us more about nineteenth-century Chinese popular religion than many of the temples in China, Hong Kong, and Taiwan, which were either destroyed in the Cultural Revolution or modernized in the twentieth century with the addition of "LEDs, neon, or concrete altars."[46]

But the surviving temples are not just Chinese structures plopped down in the United States without regard for the surroundings. They also reflect the ways in which Chinese migrants sacralized their new environs by shaping their buildings according to the landscapes in which they found themselves. In Weaverville, California, for instance, the exterior of the Won Lim (Cloud Forest) Temple, dedicated in April 1874, is painted a celestial blue, indicating its proximity to heaven (and its altitude, 2,051 feet [625 meters] above sea level). The temple's name also reflects its surroundings at the foot of the Trinity Alps Wilderness, in a forested region.[47] The temple features a doorframe with a high floorboard, over which one must carefully step, and a permanently sealed interior door just inside the entrance, around which one must navigate to reach the inner sanctum (figure 10.1).

According to the temple's docent, these structures were intended as obstacles to keep out demons and evil spirits.[48] Such "spirit screens" were common in Chinese buildings, and some scholars have argued that they served primarily "for privacy, not spirit deflection."[49] Either way, the sealed doors may indicate the desire of the temple's builders to keep someone or something out, whether hostile spirits or the prying eyes of neighboring non-Chinese.

By contrast, the Temple of Kwan Tai in Mendocino, dating to 1854,[50] features a brightly painted red staircase as wide as the temple itself, leading up to a

FIGURE 10.1   Won Lim Temple, Weaverville, California. Left: A doorframe across which one must step to enter the temple. Right: A sealed interior door structure. Photos by Kathryn Gin Lum.

broad porch and a green door that, when open, provides unobstructed entrance to the interior altar. Loretta Hee-Chorley, the great-granddaughter of one of the temple's original founders, explains the difference as a result of location and landscape. The Temple of Kwan Tai is situated on a south-facing hill, in accordance with feng shui principles, with an unobstructed view of Mendocino Bay. In the nineteenth century, it would have looked out on a bustling Chinatown in the lowlands. Its fortuitous situation looking down on the ocean meant that it could be designed with an architecture that seems to welcome rather than shut out, whereas the temple in Weaverville, in a region often subject to forest fires and dramatic climatic variation (from temperatures of above 100 degrees Fahrenheit to below freezing), needed more structural resistance against evil influences.[51] Indeed, the currently standing Weaverville temple was not the first; there may have been a temple in Weaverville as early as 1855, and the historical record indicates that the predecessor to the Won Lim Temple stood from at least 1861 to 1873, when it "burned down…due to a fire started by a drunken miner in a nearby cabin."[52] Another reason for the difference is that the Weaverville temple was more richly financed than the Temple of Kwan Tai; hence, its builders could afford an ornate and gilded spirit screen. The former is more like a city temple in China, supported by wealthy merchants and businessmen, whereas the latter is closer to a simple rural village temple, like the kind ordinary migrants might have worshipped in before they left for Gold Mountain.[53]

The nineteenth-century Chinese temples also featured elements drawn from the very surroundings in which migrants found themselves. The Temple of Kwan Tai was constructed from "virgin redwood" and its altar "crafted of locally milled tongue-and-grove and plain boards with simple cornice features."[54] Meanwhile, the very deities in the Won Lim Temple were crafted from local soil. After fires burned down earlier incarnations of the Weaverville site, including the original gods that the migrants had brought from China, the worshippers turned to indigenous sources. In 1873 a missionary described how he "came upon three big Chinese gods sitting on the sidewalk and sunning themselves. An old Chinaman was just putting on the finishing touches to their features and here they were in the sun to become hardened and fixed." The locals had arranged for the elderly artist to come from San Francisco, and "he had gone to the side of a hill nearby and taken his pick of the clay of the soil of this Christian land of ours and made it into three big Chinese gods and now here they were almost ready to be worshipped, baking hard in that bright morning sun of our Christian land."[55] As the quotation's repetition of "our Christian land" suggests, local whites looked with disfavor on the transformation of American soil into "heathen" deities. They assumed that the California clay was—or at least should be—Christian, and thus saw the use of it to create "idols" as the very height of damnable incongruity.

The Oroville temple, in particular, highlights the ways in which migrants brought the amalgamated Confucianism, Daoism, and Buddhism of Chinese popular religion to the United States. The temple includes a main space dedicated to Daoist worship (the Liet Sheng Kong, or Temple of Many Gods), and two smaller, separate spaces dedicated to Confucian rites (the Temple of Suijing Bo, also known as the Chan Room) and Buddhist worship (the Moon Room, or Buddha Temple). The Chan Room was built for the ancestral worship of Suijing Bo, a Chan clan member known as the "Pacifying Duke." It is likely the oldest Suijing Bo temple in the United States.[56] The Moon Room is similarly the oldest Buddhist place of worship in North America.[57] Most other temples did not have separate spaces for Confucian and Buddhist rites; rather, the deities sat together in one main room. Among the most common figures worshipped in American Chinese temples were the popular Guan Di (Kwan Tai), to whom the Mendocino temple is dedicated, and Tian Hou, as we have seen. These deities also appear in the Oroville, Marysville, and Weaverville temples, alongside others like Hua Tuo, the god of medicine; Cai Shen, the god of wealth; and Bei Di, the god of the north, with power over fire and floods.[58]

In addition to housing the deities, these temples offered censers for burning paper and incense to the gods and ancestors, divination papers that migrants could use to ascertain their fortunes, and community-building festivities such as bomb day festivals, once held in Idaho City, Salt Lake City, and Evanston, Wyoming, as well as in San Francisco, Grass Valley–Nevada City, Pacific Grove, Oroville, Weaverville, and Marysville.[59] The temples also sponsored New Year festivities that could be elaborate affairs involving the entire town. To this day, some of the surviving temples continue to offer New Year celebrations and parades, and bomb day festivals are still held annually at Marysville.

At the time that the Chinese railroad workers were coming to the United States, some European Americans were becoming increasingly interested in East Asian religious traditions, especially in Buddhism. However, they tended to draw a distinction between "pure" and ancient scriptures, and the living people who had supposedly corrupted them. They devoted much energy and attention to translating and publishing Eastern texts, seeing in East Asian traditions an ancient path of dissent against the dominant Protestant Christian culture,[60] but they tended to gawk at and condemn the actual practices and beliefs of the flesh-and-blood people who came to the United States.

This attitude, coupled with the lack of firsthand sources written by the Chinese railroad workers, means that the religious lives of the workers can be pieced together only through disparate sources. It is no small thing that several temples have survived through the years, but these too are in danger due to a contemporary lack of popular interest in their funding and preservation. As Chuimei Ho and Bennet Bronson put it:

> Simple racial prejudice may have gone underground but is still alive.... The feeling that Chinese temples are unsavory places continues to surface from time to time.
>
> Religious hostility may add to that feeling. In America, Taoist and Buddhist temples have been seen as "pagan" by Christians, and some of the most intolerant Christians are ethnic Chinese.... Even more unfortunately,

modern Buddhist and Taoist sects can be equally hostile.... Followers disdain many aspects of traditional Chinese worship, including grassroots temples, as outdated superstition.[61]

On the other hand, tourists from Asia, especially Taiwan, where temples proliferate and popular religion has been preserved to a greater extent than on the mainland, are becoming increasingly interested in these historic temples. They are sometimes surprised to find such well-preserved artifacts of a shared past standing amid the towering redwoods of the California interior or on the dramatic Pacific Coast. Meanwhile, those involved in the temples' upkeep have traveled to Asia to learn from scholars and practitioners about the living meanings and significance of the historic objects in their preserve.[62] Future interest in and collaboration between scholars and community members in China, Hong Kong, Taiwan, and the United States, such as on the Chinese Railroad Workers of North America Project, will hopefully deepen our understanding of the religious lives and labors of the railroad workers and contribute to the upkeep of the temples at which they may have worshipped.

CHAPTER 11

Tracking Memory

Encounters between Chinese Railroad Workers and Native Americans

HSINYA HUANG

This chapter examines the encounters and relationships between the Native Americans and Chinese railroad workers who built the Central Pacific Railroad in the United States. It investigates how European American modernity and US territorial sovereignty were built on the management of racialized labor. As a part of that dynamic, it examines how Chinese laborers became liminal figures that mediated the relationship between white settlers and Native Americans.

Much has been written about the confrontations and conflicts between Chinese workers and Native Americans during the construction of the transcontinental railroad; most of this scholarship replicates the stereotypical image of Native Americans as murderous savages.[1] The construction of the railroad and the white settlement that followed spelled increasing conflict between whites and Native Americans. Instead of introducing threat or savagery, Native Americans became the victims of a huge loss of life, much as the Chinese laborers did who sacrificed for the railway construction. This chapter recounts a hidden history of interconnectedness between Chinese railroad workers and Native Americans.

Despite numerous photographs, drawings, and testimonies about Chinese railroad workers, we know little about their firsthand experiences or any interactions with their coworkers or other ethnic groups as they lived and worked on Native American lands during or after the construction. In light of the lack of documents authored by the Chinese workers themselves, I aim to explore the alliance between these two ethnic groups by delving into Native American tribal archives related to these Chinese laborers during and after construction of the railway. Interpretations of oral histories from tribal archives move beyond available documentation surrounding Chinese labor and trace the interactive experiences of these workers with native peoples as they entered new environments and indigenous landscapes. The Chinese and Native Americans suffered similar plights while they provided labor for the United States to move forward into modernity, and in their plights they indeed constitute mirror images of each other.

Railroad and Transethnic Relationship

The railroad was identified as a national success and technological wonder that revolutionized transportation and propelled America into a golden age of economic prosperity, but it meant something else for ethnic minorities. Ethnic minorities were segregated and denied recognition. The railroad gave the nation new life, yet it destroyed old life. The painting *The First Train*, by Herman Schuyler, depicts three Native Americans looking past their encampment at a train in the far distance (figure 11.1). The railroad brought increasing numbers of European Americans west, resulting in the forced removal and subsequent dispersal and diaspora of Native Americans. The result was a cultural chasm that could hardly be bridged. On May 29, 1869, *Harper's Weekly* featured a double-page cartoon that celebrated the completion of the first transcontinental railroad that connected two oceans (the Atlantic and the Pacific) and two continents (Asia and Europe) through the new link across North America (figure 11.2).

The image, however, is ambivalent. Ostensibly, the railroad bridges the gap between the railroad workers on the left and the Native Americans on the right. The two groups nevertheless are separated pictorially and symbolically by a river chasm: the Chinese workers cheer the arrival of the train, while the natives watch in silence, ready to turn away and depart their land.[2] The railroad was a national icon of progress and modernity. Yet far from binding the nation, the railroad and the culture surrounding it have been the root cause of separation and division.

As the transcontinental railroad stretched across the West, between ten thousand and fifteen thousand Chinese were employed, introduced into areas in which they had had no previous presence. The railroad had to cut through

FIGURE 11.1 *The First Train* (ca. 1880) by Herman Schuyler. Robert B. Honeyman, Jr. Collection of Early Californian and Western American Pictorial Material, BANC PIC 1963.002:1378-FR. Courtesy of the Bancroft Library, University of California, Berkeley.

FIGURE 11.2 *Completion of the Pacific Railroad, Harper's Weekly*, May 29, 1869. Reproduced with permission from the Center for Digital Research in the Humanities, University of Nebraska–Lincoln.

many Native American lands, where native peoples were hired to assist in the construction as well.[3] According to David Roediger and Elizabeth Esch, the Central Pacific management offered a particularly revealing rationale for lumping Chinese and Native Americans in one category (as racialized labor) in paying wages: Chinese workers could not receive individual wage payments because they had "such incomprehensible names and so looked alike," and "this pattern also applied where the Central Pacific used American Indian labor."[4] This loss of individuality allowed management to practice exploitation of both groups.

Interconnected and close relationships developed between Chinese laborers and indigenous people. The railroads that Chinese workers helped to construct ran through indigenous communities. The intersection of these communities as a result of intermarriage is a key area for understanding the experiences of transethnic contact.[5] Intermarriage between Chinese railroad workers and Native Americans (Paiute and Shoshone) produced Chinese ancestry in Native American families.[6] In their everyday lives, they intermingled, living in proximity, so sometimes "it was impossible to tell Chinese apart (they were just like Indians)";[7] "Indians sold fish to Chinese working in railroad construction camps";[8] in the face of illness, "there were some similarities between Chinese and Native American herbal medicines";[9] "some of the Chinese men of Island Mountain married the Shoshone women...with the chief's permission and... the women praised the good treatment that they received from their Chinese husbands."[10] Kate B. Carter recorded that a Chinese worker of the Central Pacific Railroad, Wong Sing, spoke the Ute language and displayed knowledge of and respect for Native American culture and could "tell from memory the different things that [had] happened" in the indigenous community.[11] When Wong Sing passed away, he was memorialized as part of the community by sixty Paiute men assembled at the office of the Indian agency.[12]

The Paiute and Shoshone were hired as railroad laborers and worked side by side with Chinese as the railroads went through their territory.[13] Kerry Brinkerhoff observes that Chinese workers and Native Americans both called the railroad the "Iron Road" and that the only women recorded as working on the Central Pacific Railroad were Native Americans.[14] Brinkerhoff relates a number of stories of Chinese being adopted into Native American tribes. Yong Luu Sing, for instance, was orphaned and adopted into the Shoshone tribe and became known as "Sharp Eyes"; Lee Yik-Gim was captured and became part of a tribe, living with them for two years and becoming a minor chief.[15]

Examples of these direct encounters between Chinese workers and Native Americans help reveal intimate kinship relations. Archaeological scholarship provides additional examples of positive interactions between Chinese railroad workers and Native Americans, demonstrating "alliance strategies in the racialized railroad economies of the American West."[16] For instance, Charlotte Sunseri examines how Chinese and Native Americans shared work in the development and maintenance of the railroad as part of a transethnic community:

> The Paiute used their knowledge of the Mono Basin [in California] landscape to scout and plan the railroad location and maintain the line. The Chinese provided numerous trained laborers for the railroad, mill, and service industries. Chinese men were also assisted in their growing culinary reputations as boardinghouse cooks by their new community partners, the Mono Lake Paiute, who knew the local culinary resources of the region and could procure new foods for the cooks.[17]

As Sunseri's research shows, Chinese and Native Americans not only had direct encounters or contacts but also engaged in "trafficking of artifacts, objects, food, and foodways."[18] Such exchanges of everyday items suggest how closely the groups may have lived together and shared a common material culture.

History of Intimacy

As early as 1852, a few years after gold was discovered in California, European American newspapers began to report on contact and interaction between Chinese and Native Americans.[19] These contacts and interactions were based more on the status of both groups at the bottom of the hierarchy than on any shared privilege or benefit. In other words, these alliances were established on a foundation of similar social standing, roles as laborers, and shared need to survive in the European American–dominated world, as Sunseri contends.[20] When thinking about archaeological evidence (and some archival evidence), archaeologists have touched on direct encounters, involving face-to-face, interpersonal interactions. They consider indirect encounters as well, involving spatial or material interactions: for instance, Chinese immigrants established work camps or Chinatowns on top of abandoned Native American village sites or campsites; Native Americans and Chinese immigrants used the same locations for seasonal campsites and temporary work camps, but not at the same time; and Native Americans collected abandoned objects from former Chinese workers' camps, and vice versa.[21]

Unlike archaeologists, I adopt a framework of a shared history or a history of intimacies between Chinese workers and Native Americans that stresses the significance of emotions. Intimate feelings of one group for the other as mediated through stories and narratives that spread along the lines of the railroad have been held on to and passed down as common memories of the two ethnic groups. As the oral stories of the indigenous tribes show, their emotional sense of connection to Chinese railroad workers revolved around their shared experiences of survival in the face of common threats by engaging in specific, life-preserving actions.

My interest here is in the communication and transmission of feelings among those living, working, and surviving together at the bottom of the social hierarchy in the Americas—a history generally buried in the colonial archive, an archive that is replete, as Lisa Lowe notes, with colonial administrators' injunctions that "different groups must be divided and boundaries kept distinct."[22] Despite "the colonial need to prevent these unspoken 'intimacies' among the colonized,"[23] these intimacies happened nonetheless, as two groups of racialized workers survived alongside one another.

Contextualizing Intimacies

Modern-day writers such as Maxine Hong Kingston and Paul Yee represent the dynamics between Chinese laborers and Native Americans as related to connected histories. For example, in *China Men* Kingston notes that the railroad's management required the Chinese and the Native Americans to compete against each other: "The demon" who managed the Central Pacific "invented games for working faster.... Day shifts raced against night shifts, China Men against Welshmen, China Men against Irishmen, *China Men against Indians.*"[24]

Yee's novel *A Superior Man* evokes a different kind of relationship.[25] Told from the viewpoint of Yang Hok, a former railway worker (referred to as a "coolie"), the novel details Hok's journey to find the mother of his son, a Native American woman with whom he had a relationship three years earlier.

In his quest Hok enlists the assistance of a mixed-blood Chinese–Native American man, Sam Bing Lew, as a guide. Set ten to fifteen years after the completion of the Central Pacific Railroad, the story retrieves a "third space," to use Homi Bhabha's terminology,[26] inhabited by children of Chinese workers and Native Americans, a space where Chinese is spoken and the Chinese–Native American mixed blood leads the way for a child to return to his "Native mother."[27] The narrative is interspersed with flashbacks to Hok's time as a coolie—the injuries he endured, the abhorrent living conditions, the constant threat of violence, and the deaths of his fellow workers: "Redbeards [whites] loudly disdained the Chinese as being one and the same as Native people."[28]

It is not only in novels like Yee's, however, that traces of intimacies can be found. Although many Native American communities disappeared after the completion of the transcontinental railroad, some remain to this day. My assistant, Anna Szücs, and I got in touch with some of these tribes, contacting the staffs of tribal museums, councils, or archives and soliciting materials that have become significant in our endeavor to construct a shared history of intimacies between Native Americans and Chinese workers. We identified two sets of culturally sensitive materials that are significant in retelling the encounter stories between the two groups. They include oral history excerpts pertaining to Chinese railroad laborers from the Cultural Resources Protection Program of the Confederated Tribes of the Umatilla Indian Reservation, and oral tales and interviews from the Walker River Paiute Tribe.

Such traces from the neighboring indigenous communities along the railways may help to reconstruct the history that has long been lost. Through the materials we have acquired from the aforementioned tribes, we speculate that the Chinese workers who were recorded in their tribal oral histories may have overlapped or had connections with those who built the first transcontinental railroad.

The following fragments from Native American tribal archives, therefore, suggest traces of history that have not been included in contemporary scholarship on Chinese railroad labor. These fragments are crucially important in understanding how Native Americans subverted the strategy of white management of manipulating racial stereotypes and segregating Native Americans from Chinese railroad workers. They yield a critical paradigm about racialized labor and the connected histories of ethnic minorities in the process of railroad and nation building. How do discourses of race and labor, the diasporic and indigenous subjects, intersect?

Evidence from the Walker River Paiute Tribe

The Walker River Paiute reservation is located in Schurz, Nevada, northeast of Sacramento and southeast of Reno, approximately one hundred miles from Lake Tahoe and also about the same distance from the Central Pacific Railroad tracks to the south. The railroad that went through the reservation was the Carson & Colorado Railroad, which was later bought by the Southern Pacific. It is an extension of the Virginia and Truckee Railroad that was meant to open up the south-central part of Nevada to mining. According to Misty Benner, the cultural resources specialist of the Walker River Paiute Tribe, Chinese workers were brought to the area from elsewhere, possibly after the completion of the Central Pacific Railroad. As Walter, a member of the Walker River Paiute Tribe, said in an interview, "There were lots of Chinese laborers that were brought in from San Francisco to build the railroad."[29] Since these workers arrived at the Walker River reservation in the 1860s and 1870s, the tribal historians speculate that they had previously helped build the Central Pacific Railroad. This has been suggested by archaeological research as well. According to Sunseri, "Many Chinese workers in Virginia City and the Comstock may have ended up there by happenstance after losing their employment on the Central Pacific Railroad (CPRR) as the railroad reached Reno"; she also says that "[b]ecause labor unions used leverage to bid against Chinese employment in mining companies, many skilled Chinese crews opted for work on the nearby Virginia & Truckee Railroad (V&TRR) line from Reno to Carson City and Virginia City."[30] The connections between the Walker River Paiute and Chinese workers on the Central Pacific are obvious.[31]

The construction of the transcontinental railroad is a story of intense racial competition. The railway construction was made possible by managing diasporic/migrant people against indigenous ones. Racialized labor was used to complete projects of huge scale and great danger, at the same time that white settlers were brutally displacing indigenous peoples.[32] The land grants to railroad companies eradicated Native American claims to land along the tracks. The attempts to eliminate Native American resistance never stopped, while white settlers formed alliances with friendly tribes and used Native American labor for construction.[33] Yet in Native American sources, in the stories from the Walker River Paiute, the Chinese pass as native through intimate interactions with the indigenous people.

Many family stories relate how a number of tribal members were descended from the Chinese railroad workers. There are also newspaper articles and reports by Indian agents regarding the interactive intimacies between tribal members and the Chinese.[34] For example, according to Misty Benner, there is an Indian agent's report regarding John Hoy, a Chinese railroad worker, who married a Paiute woman from Walker River and had a son. The agent wrote asking Hoy to pay child support to the mother of his child. Hoy was later allotted land as "head of household." Land Allotment No. 49, retrieved from the tribal archives, shows that "John Hoy was a Chinese R. R. worker who married a Paiute woman from Walker River. He was allotted land as 'Head of Household' in the 1906 Indian Lands Allotment" (personal communication, Misty Benner, December 11, 2015).

This diasporic Chinese worker became indigenized through marriage and performed his duty as "head of household" to support his child. A similar story informs the family history of Sandy Lee, a third-generation Chinese Native American, whose great-grandfather, a railroad worker, was captured and later adopted by a Native American chief who had just lost his son; as Lee says, "he actually became a minor chief."[35] Sue Fawn Chung relates that Chinese laborers (mostly gold miners and lumberjacks) had intimate relationships with Paiutes and Shoshones through intermarriage and daily interactions.[36]

This contact makes us reconsider the stories of Chinese workers leaving jobs in Native American areas that were not yet controlled by white settlers, including the accounts that the Native American snake myth scared Chinese away from working on the Central Pacific Railroad.[37] The Central Pacific hired Northern Paiute, Washoe, and members of other tribes living in the Great Basin to maintain and improve the rail line. In 1868 railroad executive Charles Crocker reported to C. P. Huntington that one thousand Chinese workers ran away through fear of Native Americans in the desert.[38] Stephen E. Ambrose, Daniel Liestman, and George Kraus, among others, recount a similar story of Paiute scaring Chinese workers away by telling them tales of big snakes in the desert that were "large enough that they could swallow a Chinaman easily."[39] Hearing these stories, Chinese fled en masse to Sacramento, and Central Pacific officials had to pursue the fleeing Chinese and persuade them to return to their work, "after discounting the serpentine tales."[40]

The snake story, as directly or indirectly cited in newspapers in June and July 1868, could be part of a Paiute strategy to chase away strangers, not just the Chinese. Also, as newcomers to the land of Native Americans, both whites and immigrant railroad workers may have misinterpreted the myth.

The Paiute of the Great Basin, a region located between the Rocky Mountains and the Sierra Nevada, face one of the harshest desert environments in the world, and stories of snakes, common in this region, are part of their tribal cultural memories and still exist in their everyday experiences: there are snake women, snake people, a snake river, and so on, in the tribal storytelling tradition.[41] Renowned Native American writer Leslie Marmon Silko, for instance, identifies the archetypal snake as the source of water and life, a creature that tends to bring a certain cultural homogeneity to the American indigenous traditions. Silko mentions how tribal snake myths inspired her writings in her "Notes on *Almanac of the Dead.*" The Pueblo Indians always had plentiful rumors to spread about the snake, which, as Silko says, "emerges out of a rainstorm and [is] surrounded by flowers, birds, and other creatures."[42] Her novel *Gardens in the Dunes* pivots on heat and drought as forms of Native American catastrophe and begins with the disappearance of a giant snake. All desert springs have resident snakes: "If people kill the snakes, the precious water would disappear."[43] In this way, she re-creates the tribal snake myth to resist colonial usurpation and exploitation of tribal lands, to which the lives of the mythic serpents are closely connected.

If snakes were associated with sacredness, life, and spiritual power and were often looked upon with both fear and awe, the Paiute circulated stories about snakes as part of their everyday common experience, and the region that snakes appeared in was culturally significant, imbued with divinity and power of water, where life is made possible. In this sense, the rumors about the snakes, which scared away Chinese laborers who first arrived in the tribal lands to build the rail line, can be read as an episode of Chinese workers' cultural shock upon their first contact with the indigenous people of North America. They exemplify the interracial and transethnic contact during the construction of the railway and the misunderstanding that commonly occurs when two different cultures meet.

The newcomers and natives developed mutual understanding, however, through their sharing of daily practices, despite disapproval from their "white boss." Among the oral history project interviews conducted with the elders of the Walker River Paiute in the 1970s, one conducted by Edward Johnson with Edna Jones provides evidence of how the first contact between the two groups inspired something new and motivated the indigenous peoples to evolve in terms of their food culture. The Chinese culinary practices and ingredients they employed inspired the natives to do something new. The interactive intimacy was mediated through food. Native Americans welcomed the strangers and appreciated their food culture, and the Chinese reciprocated the hospitality and became the community partners to them as the Chinese introduced a new vegetable, cabbage, to feed the indigenous body:

> EDWARD JOHNSON, INTERVIEWER: Do you remember your mother telling you about the railroad?
> EDNA JONES: Yes, she told me about the railroad.... They used to follow [the Chinese] because they were nice.... [The Chinese] always used to give them something to eat, like cabbage, and... they didn't know what cabbage was.... [My mother]... used to go and borrow from Chinamen, too.... She used to be one of them to go and get the food from the Chinese.
>
> JOHNSON: They worked on the railroad?
> JONES: Yes, they cook for them, that is, working on the railroad. She said they follow them up to the white mountain up there. That is where they go, follow them.[44]

Cabbage connects the indigenous people and the diasporic people from belly to belly, and for the Plains Indians and Pueblo Indians, the belly is also the body organ that stores and preserves stories.[45] There were other ways for the native people to relate to the Chinese people. A newspaper report focused on the newly built work camps and a "well-regulated Chinese store," where the supplies for these railroad workers were unloaded and distributed:

> Following the line of [the] road from this point to the reservation, [C]hinese camps were [e]ncountered every half mile containing forty to fifty [C]hinamen, graders, working with picks and shovels, each gang [headed] by a white foreman. One mile this side of the reservation house is a well-regulated [C]hinese store, where the supplies for all the [C]hinamen along the line are unloaded and distributed.[46]
>
> Old Hon Ess, [a] Chinaman who came here in the [e]arly days of Hawthorne, keeps a restaurant in Chinatown, which is probably the only one of its kind in the United States. His building is not very elegant, nor is his table adorned with silverware and butter knives, but he seems to satisfy his patrons, who are Paiutes.[47]

A copy of the 1861 Nevada statutes, which is maintained in the archives of the Walker River Paiute Tribe, shows how the law segregated different races and ethnic groups. Specifically, the Act to Prohibit Marriages and Cohabitation of Whites with Indians, Chinese, Mulattoes and Negroes is worthy of quotation to disclose the odds Chinese railroad workers faced as they tried to survive in the indigenous land of America:

> Section 1. If any white man or woman intermarry with any black, mulatto, Indian, or Chinese, the parties to such marriage shall be deemed guilty of misdemeanor, and, on conviction thereof, be imprisoned in the territorial prison, for a term not less than one year, nor more than two years....

> Section 3. That, if any white person shall live and cohabit together with any black person, mulatto, Indian, or Chinese, in a state of fornication, such person so offending shall, on conviction thereof, be fined in any sum not exceeding five hundred, and not less than one hundred dollars, or be [i]mprisoned in the county jail, not less than one, nor more than six months, or both such fine and imprisonment, as the court may order.[48]

The centrality of white law in the tribal archive cannot be overestimated as we consider how Native Americans and Chinese workers were bound together through their common trauma. The tribe preserves the evidence of racial segregation imposed by white supremacy, in which black, mulatto, Indian, and Chinese are lumped together as one category at the bottom of the social ladder. The alliances were thus established on a foundation of similar social standing and mutual survival. Besides, intermarriage between the Chinese workers and Paiute women was not uncommon; hence, the interlocking genealogies between the natives and the foreigners, both of whom provided labor to build the railroad and open up the West to the European American frontier settlers. One incident, titled "Bought a Chinese Girl" as reported in the *Lyon County Times,* for instance, relates the story of the purchase of a "5-year-old halfbreed girl, paying for her the sum of $400 in gold."[49] The purchaser was an old Chinese merchant, Fat Sam, who for many years ran a laundry in Dayton, Nevada. The girl was the progeny of a Chinese worker named Leon and a Paiute woman.

Oral History of the Confederated Tribes of the Umatilla Indian Reservation

The Umatilla Indian Reservation is located in northeastern Oregon, where the Oregon Railway and Navigation Company built a railroad as far back as 1860, the route of which eventually became the backbone of the Union Pacific

Railroad's main line from Utah to the Pacific Northwest. Geographically, the Umatilla Reservation is close to the Central Pacific Railroad, and veterans of the Central Pacific Railroad workforce were employed to repair, rebuild, and extend the lines after 1869. Tribal archives show that Chinese railroad workers were either present in the natives' daily lives, sharing food and living spaces, or buried in a separate area on the tribe's land, on which Native Americans would not trespass.

The oral histories archived by the Cultural Resources Protection Program of the Confederated Tribes of the Umatilla Indian Reservation can be read as supplementary texts to the Paiute people's testimonies. The elders' histories describe a division into two areas in the tribal village, with the Chinese railroad workers inhabiting a part of the tribal space as ghosts rather than living humans. The workers' cemetery, located next to where native people lived their daily lives, became a forbidden realm, yet the emotional communion is implicit in the testimonies of the native people. The elders speak of the Chinese with sympathy. In the following two excerpts, the native informant identifies the persecutors as "they" and names the abusive labor management that caused numerous deaths of Chinese people: "instead of paying them, they killed them."

> INFORMANT: Then when they built the railroad, you know, they shipped in thousands of Chinese. And a lot of them died, you know, just working them to death. And one guy was telling me that there's a lot of 'em that are buried up there where [redacted] lives, under that hill.[50]

> INFORMANT: We used to go digging up there and we only could dig on one side because they said that there was Chinese buried on the other side.

> INFORMANT: They were trying to build a railroad and instead of paying them, they killed them. So they buried them on the side; the Chinese men.[51]

The Chinese are often present in native stories. One informant starts with "my grandma told me a story" of the time when the Chinese used to work there. He describes how the tribe had to feed the Chinese workers during the time when the railroad was built, and the Chinese would always give something in return:

> INFORMANT: And I think, like, when the railroad came through they had to feed the Chinese laborers.... And they would get something in return and I don't remember what that was. But it was always they just had to. [redacted]

It was just something they were providing something for somebody else. And it was non-Indian; it was railroad workers.[52]

Native American–Chinese connectedness is materially visible. By feeding the Chinese laborers, Native Americans demonstrated responsiveness, responsibility, hospitality, and generosity toward the strangers/foreigners. This constitutes a counterpart to the story from the Walker River Paiute, where the Chinese fill the indigenous belly with nutrition and stories. The two exchanges of food run in opposite directions yet make up an integrated whole of how the indigenous and the diasporic subject intersect. Setting up Chinese railroad workers as the other/non-Indian, Umatilla peoples claim the identity of the self as the host. They exercise, as Jacques Derrida puts it, their "sovereignty as host."[53] Hospitality toward Chinese laborers thus involves indigenous claims to the land as well as the desire to establish a form of self-identity. This encounter, however, is based on reciprocal connectedness that "they would get something in return." It bespeaks intersubjective relations—relations of reciprocity between the indigenous and diasporic subject.

Tribal stories of the encounters between Chinese workers and Native Americans can help compensate for the lack of such accounts of transethnic connections in the official history of building the railroad and the nation. This chapter presents culturally sensitive materials from the tribal communities of the Umatilla and the Paiute and explores the complex relationship of affect between Native Americans and Chinese workers during and after the time of railroad building. It reconstructs a shared memory and common labor history of Chinese and Native American agency. Crisscrossing the landscape with permanent railroad tracks, depleting trees for railroad ties and bridges, and decimating herds of bison transformed the indigenous home-place into an everlasting foreign space called the "frontier."[54] If, as Maxine Hong Kingston puts it so eloquently, Chinese railroad workers are "the binding and building ancestors" of the Americas,[55] the indigenous people worked and survived with them to share a common history of intimate connections and mixed genealogy. Testimonies and stories from Native Americans who encountered the Chinese on the railroads counter forgetting with narratives of connection and presence. Like other researchers, I struggle to comprehend the absence in the record of the intimacy between indigenous people and Chinese laborers who came from afar to build the railways. Like archaeologists with whom I work as part of the Chinese Railroad Workers in North America Project initiated by Stanford University, I dig out the matters and materials—otherwise absent, entangled, and unavailable—from the tribal archives. The indigenous tribal historians and archivists actively acknowledged the significance of this project and volunteered to help retrieve the loss to the present. Together we try to imagine what could have been and in this way counteract the violence of forgetting and erasure and ensure that this violence is not reproduced in our discourse, historicity, and practices.

CHAPTER 12

Railroad Frames

Landscapes and the Chinese Railroad Worker in Photography, 1865–1869

DENISE KHOR

Shortly before the transcontinental railroad was completed, a photographer took a picture of a railroad workers' camp next to the tracks as a train passed by. The velocity of the moving train is signaled by the steam billowing from the engine's locomotive. Several workers stand at the foot of the tracks, their gaze on the speeding train. Dozens of tents, along with clotheslines and workers' provisions, are spread out on the arid landscape. In taking the photograph, the photographer was elevated and stationed at a distance to gain a bird's-eye view. The entire scene is set against dry shrubs, rocks, and a towering foothill. The photograph, titled *Chinese Camp, at End of Track* (figure 12.1), was taken by Alfred A. Hart. The image shows the power of the train to traverse space, to rapidly move into and through a natural landscape. Along with the speeding locomotive, the workers and their camp represent the incursion of men and machines into that landscape. The once-barren land appears on the cusp of transformation, the static and unchanging landscape having been interrupted by technology and industrial progress. Significantly, the Chinese workers are stationed on the ground, looking toward the train with a sense of reverence and awe.

Chinese Camp, at End of Track was one in a sequence of photographs taken by Hart as he traveled along the construction route of the Central Pacific Railroad (CPRR). Hart photographed many scenes as the workers built rail lines from Sacramento and across the Sierra Nevada. As the workers approached the end of the line at Promontory Summit, Utah, the landscape became flat and desolate. In addition to *Chinese Camp*, Hart took other photographs, which

FIGURE 12.1   *Chinese Camp, at End of Track*, by Alfred Hart. Alfred A. Hart 12-2. Photograph Collection, 1862–1869, Stanford University Digital Repository.

he titled as a series, Advance of Civilization. These photographs registered similar scenes of a brutal desert landscape intercut with the signs of railroad technology and human labor and settlement. In taking these photographs, Hart prefigured some of the dominant narratives and imagery that would later emerge after the transcontinental railroad's completion in May 1869.

The railroad symbolized modernity itself, not only in transforming the frontier but also in ushering in new scales of mobility and perception. Transcontinental rail travel shortened distances between places, synchronized time standards, and introduced new ways to experience time and space.[1] *Chinese Camp* portrays the prowess of technology and its ability to "civilize" the natural landscape. Moreover, the image features the Chinese railroad laborer as both worker and witness. With his camp settled into the landscape, the Chinese railroad worker stands as observer, the still figure against the momentum of the speeding train. This depiction of the transcontinental railroad, the landscape, and the Chinese worker would be reproduced in the nation's leading newspapers and periodicals throughout the 1870s. The pictorial newspaper *Frank Leslie's Illustrated Newspaper* published a series called "Across the Continent" that included illustrations by Joseph Becker. These images, according to scholar Deirdre Murphy, situated the Chinese laborer at the periphery of the saga of the transcontinental railroad. "Like sentinels of industrial change posted between the locomotive and the natural landscape, the Chinese workers witness and react to the mechanical velocity of the railroad, even as it leaves them behind."[2]

At the start of the transcontinental railroad's construction, photographers were the eyes of the railroad company, furnishing visual records for officials eager to placate the public and their investors. As such, the Chinese were visually documented as workers in unprecedented ways. The photographers included Alfred A. Hart, Charles Savage, Andrew Russell, J. B. Silvis, and the famed landscape photographer Carleton Watkins. In my research I have identified all existing photographs of Chinese railroad workers taken during the period of the transcontinental railroad's construction, roughly between the years 1865 and 1869. These images have been collected and preserved in various institutional archives and collections, reproduced in countless publications and print materials, and widely circulated on the internet and in digital media. The entire collection of photographs will be made available by Stanford University's Chinese Railroad Workers in North America Project digital archive.[3]

These photographs function as a material record of the labor of the thousands of Chinese who built the transcontinental railroad. As photographic objects, the images circulated in the railroad companies' archives and were reproduced for popular consumption to promote railway travel and the expansion of the western frontier. Most of these photographs were taken as the rail route extended eastward from Sacramento. The Chinese were captured in the photographic frame while laboring in the Sierra Nevada and in the canyons, mountains, and valleys traversed by the overland route. While their working conditions and subjection to racial violence were muted in these photographic productions, their presence in the photographic frame underscored the power of the railroad to transform the natural landscape. The railroad photographs offered much of the nation its first glimpse of a West that would soon attract many settlers from other regions. They formed a significant part of the canon of western landscape photography.

The photographs of Chinese railroad workers, moreover, contributed to the emerging national debate over the status of Chinese workers as "free" or "unfree" in the post–Civil War era and help shape our understanding of the place of the Chinese and the railroad in historical memory and representation today.

In the fall of 1853, John C. Frémont led an expedition to explore the possibilities of a railroad route along the thirty-eighth parallel. Frémont was a former major in the US Army during the Mexican-American War, and in the years afterward, he led numerous explorations of the US West, significantly advancing western expansion and settlement of the region. His journey in the fall of 1853 was his fifth expedition. He and his party set off from Missouri and made their way through the San Luis Valley in Colorado, crossed into Utah, came up through the Sierra Nevada, and arrived at the port city of San Francisco, California. His published account of this expedition was submitted to the US Congress in 1854 as members deliberated over the feasibility of a "central railroad route to the Pacific." In Frémont's recounting, the pathways across the Rocky Mountains and the rugged topography of the proposed route were both knowable and exploitable. His numerous expeditions in the region, he noted, "enable me to speak of it with the confidence of intimate knowl-edge." He detailed his observations of the land: "Numerous well-watered and fertile valleys, broad and level, open up among the mountains, which present themselves in detached blocks [outliers], gradually closing in around the heads of streams, but leaving open approaches to the central ridges." His was a survey of the land, a subjection of the topography to knowability and the needs of western progress. In describing the mountain ranges between the Colorado River valley and the Great Basin, he opined, "they are what are called fertile mountains, abundant in water, wood, and grass, and fertile valleys, offering inducements to settlement and for making a road." "These mountains," he continued, "are a great storehouse of materials—timber, iron, coal—which would be of indispensable use." While vast and grand, the valleys and moun-tains along the proposed route of the railroad were ripe for development, their natural resources abundant and available for commodification. Topography and climate conditions were certainly potential challenges in the proposed railroad route, but Frémont was surprised to learn that in December the Sierra Blanca mountain range was free of snow. His party had taken "Daguerre views [*sic*]…[to] show the grass entirely uncovered in the passes." In fact, along this route the expedition determined the land elevation by taking a "barometrical observation" and "a series of Daguerreotype views." These instruments allowed for Frémont and his expedition to, as he put it, "give a thoroughly correct impression."[4]

Frémont's account reframed a view of the western landscape. The land was not only knowable but also visible—distances could be measured, snowfall predicted, and natural resources identified. Frémont's survey offered a way to see the land anew and envision it as a repository of raw materials awaiting the future builders of the transcontinental railroad. The daguerreotype was an instrument in this endeavor, a technology, not unlike the railroad itself, that could transform the space, break it into measurable units, and make it available for western settlement and progress. When the federal government sponsored expeditions to survey the West, photographers were among the corps of explorers. The photographic image purportedly provided a scientific view, a means to map the landscape and to visualize a view by which lands could be measured, divided, and parceled out. As art historian Shawn Michelle Smith suggests, photographers provided the means to transform the landscape into geographic space, to visually map and systematize the land. In doing so, photographers preceded western settlers.[5] Indeed, photographers paved the way for western developers and speculators, providing a lens to reenvision the landscape as a frontier for industry and development.

With the start of the construction of the transcontinental line, both the Central Pacific Railroad and the Union Pacific Railroad (UPRR) encouraged photographers, along with journalists, travel writers, and artists, to follow the construction routes in an effort to publicize and win public support for their endeavors. In 1862 Congress passed the Pacific Railway Act, which authorized government bonds and granted land to the railroad companies. Railroad officials were eager to placate their largest investors. Photography was a part of the railroad companies' efforts to bolster their image, offering a form of visual evidence to track the railroad's construction progress and to generate public enthusiasm for the rail line's completion.

The vast majority of photographs of Chinese railroad workers were taken by a single photographer, Alfred A. Hart. He was the primary photographer for the Central Pacific Railroad Company, which built the western portion of the transcontinental line. By some estimates, four men in every five hired after 1865 by the Central Pacific were Chinese. Because of his role as the principal photographer for the Central Pacific, Hart consequently took more photographs of Chinese workers than any other photographer. In total, he produced over 400 negatives of the railroad, 364 of which were purchased by the railroad company. Other railroad photographs were sold to the stereo-publishing firm Lawrence & Houseworth, which was based in San Francisco and owned by George S. Lawrence and Thomas Houseworth. The photography firm produced stereoscopic images that were popular for parlor viewing.

Not much is known of Hart's time in California prior to his work for the Central Pacific, and he left no written records of his time doing the photographic work. As the company's primary photographer, Hart photographed the scenes of the transcontinental railroad over the five years of its construction. He followed the routes of the workers, stopping trains and work crews to set up his camera.[6] While many photographers would return to the sites along the transcontinental railroad route after its completion, none could duplicate the timeliness of his photographs of the work in progress.[7]

Hart's stereographs for the Central Pacific were dramatic portrayals of the railroad in the wilderness. His views convey the magnificence of the natural landscape and the mastery of technology to tame and subdue it. According to art historian Glenn Willumson, whose book *Iron Muse: Photographing the Transcontinental Railroad* is perhaps the most comprehensive and critical work on the photographs of the transcontinental railroad, Alfred Hart brought a compositional control and clarity to his photographs. He had a sense of narrative in his images, a focus on and reverence for the railroad itself as it cut through the Sierra Nevada and transformed the landscape.[8] All of Hart's photographs for the Central Pacific were stereographs, which were immensely popular from the 1850s until well into the twentieth century. Stereoscopic photography was one of the early forms of photography to be produced and commercialized as an industrial commodity. Unlike the nonreproducible daguerreotype, the stereograph was a reproducible photograph printed on paper that was small, inexpensive to print, and easily transportable. To view, the user placed a card with two photos of the same image from slightly different angles in the handheld stereoscope. When the stereoscope was held up to the eyes, the two images merged to produce a three-dimensional view. Hart's photographs in the stereographic format, according to Ginette Verstraete, "added to the spectacular distance, depth, and magnitude of both America's sublime landscape and, most important, the even more sublime transcontinental railroad conquering it."[9]

Indeed, Hart's images, the majestic views of the landscape, and the immense power of the machine to tame and conquer the wilderness, evoked the "technological sublime." As Leo Marx notes, the railroad had long been figured in

FIGURE 12.2   *Bank and Cut at Sailor's Spur*, by Alfred Hart. Alfred A. Hart
Photograph Collection, 1862–1869, Stanford University Digital Repository.

American art as a representation of modernity itself, symbolizing a heightened
sense of change and progress. Moreover, these ideas and images of the railroad
imagined the expansionary project of western settlement and the inevitable
and divinely ordained promise of America's manifest destiny.[10] Photographers
like Hart celebrated this view of technology as the machine as it triumphed
over nature and "civilized" the wilderness. Chinese workers in Hart's photographs were not the agents of this providential progress. Their presence in the
field of vision was often subsumed in relation to nature and the machine.

In the stereograph *Blasting at Chalk Buffs above Alta. Cut 60 Feet Deep*, the
panoramic view offers a dramatic perspective of railroad construction in
the Sierra Nevada. The blasting by the workers has literally bisected the landscape with the towering mountain on one side and the deep forest on the
other. The photograph underscores the immensity of the feat of building
across the Sierra Nevada. The Chinese workers in this image, however, are
barely visible; they are dwarfed by the vastness of the mountains and forests.

FIGURE 12.3   *Laborers and Rocks, Near Opening of the Summit Tunnel,* by Alfred Hart. Alfred A. Hart Photograph Collection, 1862–1869, Stanford University Digital Repository.

Bank and Cut at Sailor's Spur (figure 12.2) also captures the vastness of the wilderness in a stunning panorama of the construction as it pushes through the towering forests. The workers in this scene are completely engulfed in the landscape as the sight line of the camera disappears into the wilderness.

Indeed, Hart emphasized the construction process, the techniques of clearing the land, cutting the granite, and building the railroad. In *Building Bank across the Canyon Creek*, the Chinese workers are pictured in the right of the frame. The scene shows horse-pulled carts, piles of cut lumber, and a built tunnel. As the title indicates, the primary subject of the image is the building process itself. The Chinese workers in this scene seem to almost disappear into the canyon's bank.

Other Hart stereographs bring the gangs of Chinese laborers into closer view and center them in the frame. *Laborers and Rocks, Near Opening of the Summit Tunnel* (figure 12.3) displays a scene of men at work amid the impenetrable granite. This image is taken at a closer distance than the images at the

Alta, and the workers are acknowledged in the title of this view. However, no other discerning details are indicated. Neither the workers' names nor their ethnicities are acknowledged: they are largely anonymous. Furthermore, the blunt titling of the stereograph, *Laborers and Rocks*, indicates that the image is as much about the rocks as it is about the laborers.

The appearance of Chinese workers in Hart's stereographs as anonymous and unnamed is not surprising. Indeed, they remain largely unnamed even in the payroll records of the Central Pacific. Although the company's payrolls are subdivided by occupation, number of days worked, and rate of pay, with a few exceptions Chinese workers are not identified by their actual names. Rather, workers are documented and acknowledged as units within crews or their assignments to headmen or contractors (whose names are also rendered only approximately, as in "Ah Sing"—the equivalent of "Mr. Sing"). The nameless-ness of workers, their legibility as labor time and work units, reproduces the logic of the capitalist mode of production. Hart's photographs similarly situate the Chinese workers as alienated labor. As *Laborers and Rocks* suggests, they are aligned with the "rocks," the raw materials harnessed by the railroads into use value.

There were a few photographs in which Chinese workers were referenced not by individual names, but by "Chinaman" or "John Chinaman." Hart pho-tographed three Chinese workers atop a train heading through Bloomer Cut, in California. Though their faces appear barely visible, the three laborers are foregrounded in the frame. The foreman stands behind the workers, and the sight line of the camera follows the train down the deep corridor. In the distant background another set of workers appears. Hart's photograph was acquired by Lawrence & Houseworth and titled *Wood Train and Chinamen in Bloomer Cut* (figure 12.4). In another photograph Chinese workers are captured on a railroad handcar. The white foreman sits to the left in the frame. The workers are foregrounded in this image, and their faces are clearly visible as they direct their gaze at the camera. The photograph was titled *John Chinaman on the Rail Road* (figure 12.5). Although the photographer is unknown, the image was acquired and likely titled by E. & H. T. Anthony, a photography firm based in New York. In both photographs workers are the primary subjects of the image. While the white foremen are pictured, they are not acknowledged in either title. The subjects of the photographs are identified as either "Chi-namen" or "John Chinaman." In *John Chinaman on the Rail Road*, the posed workers and the foreman, centered in the frame, cast their gazes ahead and into

FIGURE 12.4   *Wood Train and Chinamen in Bloomer Cut*, by Alfred Hart. Society of California Pioneers Photography Collection. Courtesy of the Society of California Pioneers, San Francisco, Gift of Florence V. Flinn.

the camera's view. Their assemblage aboard the railroad handcar conveys not a scene of work but rather a portrait of workers. Hart, however, did not take the photograph. In fact, the Central Pacific photographer chose to take very few photographic portraits despite his background in commercial portraiture. Unlike his contemporary, Andrew Russell, Hart took almost no portraits of the railroad officials, the engineers, or the workers.

The etymology and popular usage of "Chinaman" emerged in part out of the context of the transcontinental railroad. The phrase "Chinaman's chance" developed as an idiomatic American expression, meaning "little or no chance," from the context of the dangerous and at times deadly work performed by Chinese workers on the railroad. The name "John" is also noteworthy.

FIGURE 12.5   *John Chinaman on the Rail Road: Union Pacific Rail Road*,
photographer unknown. BANC PIC 1995.012—STER. Courtesy of The Bancroft
Library, University of California, Berkeley.

According to historian John Tchen, Chinese men commonly adopted the
English name "John." Between 1855 and 1870, the number of Chinese men
with the name "John" rose from half the population to two-thirds. It is unclear
whether missionaries or ship captains designated this name or whether it was
a Christian name of choice among the Chinese themselves.[11] By the time
the transcontinental railroad was completed, the figure of "John Chinaman"
had emerged as a stock racial stereotype, appearing in the satirical writings of
Bret Harte and Mark Twain, the pro-Chinese cartoons of Thomas Nast, and

in varying anti-Chinese expressions, from American popular songs to major newspapers and illustrated weeklies.

The namelessness of Chinese workers, as well as their designation as "Chinamen" or "John Chinamen," underscores their perceived status as unfree and un-American laborers. In the post–Civil War era, the subject of Chinese workers often appeared in national debates between capital and labor. Wage work supplanted autonomous craft production, leaving fewer individuals in control of their own means of production. The notion of "free labor" represented the right to sell one's own labor for wages. Despite the fact that the majority of Chinese were not contract workers and their work arrangements were essentially aligned with wage workers, their labor purportedly undermined white labor and the ability of European American workers to gain security, demand higher wages, and organize and unionize their labor.[12] This racialization of labor, the frequent association of Chinese workers with the abject conditions of "unfree labor," can be read in the characterization of the Chinese railroad workers as "Crocker's pets," a reference to Charles Crocker, one of the founders of the CPRR.[13]

Instead of photographic portraits, which attend to the individual and the perception of self-representation, Hart's stereographs conveyed scenes of men at work. His photographs functioned as public documents and as corporate records for the Central Pacific. His images of Chinese workers, however, were also aesthetic productions. They had a market among the commercial products intended for tourism and advertising. His majestic views of the American West, its mountains, valleys, and rivers, aestheticized the landscape for commerce and consumption. In 1870 Hart published *The Traveler's Own Book*, a travel guide intended to promote tourism for the transcontinental railroad. The book contained wood engravings based on his original stereographs, hand-drawn maps of the overland routes, and hotel listings and other tourism-related details.[14] Hart's publication and commercial photography firms presented his photographs to the public audience to tap a growing market for the tourism and travel made available by the transcontinental railroad.

Hart's photograph *Coldstream, Eastern Slope of Western Summit* (figure 12.6) circulated as a part of these efforts to promote scenic views of the western landscape. The image appeared in the Central Pacific archive and as a part of the Central Pacific Railroad, California, Scenes in the Sierra Nevada Mountains series presented by the Golden State Photographic Gallery. It is a striking image. The photograph depicts a single Chinese laborer standing at the edge of

FIGURE 12.6 *Coldstream, Eastern Slope of Western Summit,* by Alfred Hart. Alfred A. Hart Photograph Collection, 1862–1869, Stanford University Digital Repository.

a stream. He balances water buckets on a shoulder pole. Two other onlookers appear in the frame. The photograph is distinctive because, of all the Central Pacific photographs of Chinese workers, only this one captures a worker in a contemplative and reflective moment; the laborers and the onlookers appear harmonious with the natural landscape even as they perform the labor to transform it.

The photograph *Heading of East Portal, Tunnel No. 8, from Donner Lake Railroad, Western Summit* shares a similar composition. Both images appear in the Scenes in the Sierra series, and both depict a single Chinese worker. The worker balances tea canteens on a shoulder pole, but in this photograph, the scene takes place against a hulking granite mountain. The railroad or machinery is nowhere pictured; instead, the photograph conveys a sense of the frailty of the human body in the wilderness. The scene seems quiet, even serene in contrast to the loud explosions and frenetic work schedules that characterized the massive construction effort of building tunnels through the Sierra Nevada.[15]

The winter season in the northern Sierra Nevada was brutal for the Central Pacific laborers. While workers were laboring on the stretch from Cape Horn to Cisco, the first snow fell there. The 1866–1867 winter was the worst on record as fierce blizzards and snowstorms, forty-four in total, devastated the Sierra. With freezing temperatures and damp and heavy snow accumulating on the slopes, work in the mountains was grueling. Central Pacific workers excavated the tunnels and built thirty-seven miles (sixty kilometers) of snow sheds to stymie the massive buildup of snow. They also hand built seventy-five-foot-high (twenty-three-meter-high) retaining walls, so-called Chinese walls, to reinforce the railroad grade between the tunnels. The ruthless blizzards and snowstorms proved deadly for the Chinese workers. Accounts vary, but countless laborers were killed in landslides and in collapsing sheds and barns. The campsites were buried in avalanches, while some workers simply froze to death.

In his photographs Hart documents the snowfall and the railroad work in the winter season. His images, however, capture not the workers' struggles—their subjection to the brute force of nature—but rather the use of machines to triumph over the harsh weather conditions. *Constructing Snow Cover, Scene Near the Summit* showcases the massive construction feat. A Chinese worker poses in the foreground while a number of other workers mount the top of the snow cover, revealing the size and scale of the structure. In *Snow Plow, at Cisco* (figure 12.7), two workers are depicted in the photograph, yet it is captioned *Snow Plow*, with no reference to the workers. Similar to the photograph of the snow cover, the appearance of the Chinese worker in the foreground merely illustrates the size and scale of the machine. Hart's focus was the machine, not the man.

In each and every photograph, Hart concealed the colossal impact of the winter on the Central Pacific's progress in the Sierra Nevada, emphasizing the railroad's ability to control nature. As Willumson notes, the snowfall was a subject in his photographs that railroad officials deliberately censored in order to convey a favorable image of the railroad's progress.[16] While Hart captured the might of machines, he took no photographs that conveyed the workers' struggles, their plight in the perilous winters, or the pitiless toil required to continue building through the Sierra. In focusing on the machinery and the

FIGURE 12.7   *Snow Plow, at Cisco*, by Alfred Hart. Alfred A. Hart Photograph Collection, 1862–1869, Stanford University Digital Repository.

technology of the railroad, his photographs obscured the physical labor, the corporeality of the railroad's progress.

Hart was not the only photographer who captured the work of Chinese laborers on the transcontinental railroad. The Mormon photographer Charles Savage took two photographs of Chinese workers constructing the line at Weber Canyon in Utah. In both images the work appears halted as the laborers turn to face the camera. In *Mouth of Tunnel No. 3*, Chinese workers and a white foreman stand on a handcar at the mouth of a tunnel. Two other foremen are perched against the entrance of the tunnel. The workers are the central subjects of the photograph, positioned down the middle of the frame. *One Thousand Mile Tree* (figure 12.8) was a pine tree that represented a significant geographical point in the construction of the transcontinental railroad. It marked the 1,000 miles (1,609 kilometers) of track from Omaha, Nebraska/Council Bluffs, Iowa, the eastern terminus of the transcontinental line. The site was photographed by a number of photographers and artists,

FIGURE 12.8   *One Thousand Mile Tree*, by Charles Savage. *One Thousand Mile Tree,*
1869, Charles R. Savage, photographer, Charles R. Savage Photographs, Church History
Library.

including Andrew Russell and Edward Muybridge. In the Savage view, the tree
appears in the background, while the Chinese workers and railroad track are
foregrounded. In both photographs by Savage, the camera is positioned at eye
level and seemingly placed at the same distance.

Like Hart, Savage photographed the scenes of the transcontinental railroad
in the stereo format, largely because stereographs were commercially viable.
Savage's images captured the railroad construction in Utah, specifically in
Weber and Echo Canyons. Born in England in 1832, Savage became a member
of the Church of Jesus Christ of Latter-Day Saints at the age of fifteen, against
his parents' wishes. He worked as a missionary and immigrated to the United
States in 1855. In 1862 he established the photography firm Savage & Ottinger
in partnership with George Ottinger. Savage also developed a close working
relationship with photographer Andrew Russell. They both developed photographs for the Union Pacific Railroad Company. In fact, many of Savage's
photographs were taken within minutes of Russell's photographs, suggesting
that they worked in the field together and had a truly collaborative relationship, which was unusual for independent photographers of the era.[17]

The ceremony at Promontory Summit, Utah, on May 10, 1869, to com-
memorate the completion of the transcontinental railroad was an unparalleled
event for the nation. Three photographers, Alfred Hart, Charles Savage, and

Andrew Russell, were on-site with cameras and tripods. CPRR officials built a telegraph station to wire the news as soon as the final spike was placed in the rails. Across the nation public gatherings and ceremonies were orchestrated to begin when the official word was received. At Promontory Summit twenty-seven journalists were in attendance, along with hundreds of spectators. The ceremony there was, as a number of scholars have suggested, the nation's first great media event.[18] Because of the technology of the telegraph, citizens around the country were able to receive word of a spectacular event as it happened. Audiences from New York to San Francisco celebrated with a sense of immediacy and simultaneity as the two rail lines met to complete the nation's first transcontinental railroad.

Photographer Alfred Hart accompanied CPRR president Leland Stanford on a train bound for Promontory Summit. Along with Hart and Stanford, this delegation included railroad commissioners, newspaper publishers, a chief justice from California, and several governors, as well as a number of prominent citizens. Dr. J. D. B. Stillman was among the latter, and he published an account of his journey in *Overland Monthly* the following month. "The car was arranged with a kitchen, dining [area], bedroom, and parlor, with sleeping accommodation for ten persons," and considerable amenities. There was excitement in the air as the excursionists left Sacramento. As Stillman recalled, "Stretching myself out on a sumptuous lounge, I looked out on the brimming, turbid river and breathed the morning air.... [T]he town was on tip-toe of expectation, and gushing with the enthusiasm of triumph."[19]

As preparations for the celebration continued, the delegation with Stanford departed on sightseeing expeditions. They traveled to the Wasatch Range to take in the dramatic views and then on to see the Great Salt Lake. Hart accompanied the excursionists, and, according to Stillman, "the Central Pacific artist took some fine views of the mountain from the railway overlooking the town of Ogden."[20]

When the day of the ceremony arrived, Hart remained with the Stanford delegation. He took a number of photographs of the locomotives as they met on the track, and of crowds of onlookers and the procession led by Stanford. The Central Pacific documenter, who had taken more images of Chinese railroad workers than any other photographer, took no pictures of the Chinese at Promontory Summit.

According to J. H. Strobridge, the superintendent of the Central Pacific's workers, in his unpublished biography, Chinese work crews arrived in the

FIGURE 12.9   *Chinese Laying the Last Rail,* by Andrew Russell. Oakland Museum of California.

morning to begin "the final grading for the last two rails, the laying of the ties and rails, the driving of the spikes, and the bolting of the fishplates of the west rail."[21] The work was captured in a photograph, not by Hart but by the Union Pacific photographer Andrew Russell. Titled *Chinese Laying the Last Rail* (figure 12.9), the photograph shows two Chinese workers adjusting the last rails as the assembled crowd looks on. In the background the telegraph wires and the Central Pacific locomotive are pictured. Of the approximately thirty-five photographs taken by Hart, Savage, and Russell on the day of the ceremony, this is the singular photograph of the Chinese railroad workers.

Born in 1829 in New Hampshire and raised in New York State, Andrew Russell became the Union Pacific Railroad's primary photographer. He learned of photography while a soldier in the Civil War. He began taking photographs of the Union Pacific's construction in 1868. According to Willumson, Russell was much more concerned with laborers in his photographs than was Central Pacific photographer Hart. His views depict a variety of the Union Pacific's workers and center on the story of the individuals responsible for the railroad's completion. Unlike Hart, he tended to stay with the work crews for months at a time.[22] The photograph *Chinese Laying the Last Rail* is a work scene, an

FIGURE 12.10   *East and West Shaking Hands at Laying Last Rail,* by Andrew Russell. Oakland Museum of California.

image of laborers at work on the railroad, not uncharacteristic of Russell's photographs for the Union Pacific.

At Promontory Summit Russell took the most celebrated photograph of the day. *East and West Shaking Hands at Laying Last Rail* (figure 12.10) depicts the two locomotives meeting on the railroad tracks. With the large crowd surrounding the engines, the Central Pacific engineer Samuel Montague and Union Pacific engineer Grenville Dodge stand before their respective locomotives and shake hands while surrounded by workers and onlookers. The joining of the rails captured by Russell was not immediately visible to the nation but would become the defining symbol of the moment. Depicting the two rail lines coming together, the two rival railroad companies meeting on the track, the photograph conveyed a message of the nation itself being drawn closer together by the completion of the transcontinental railroad. The photographs taken by Russell would be reproduced in the nation's leading newspapers. *Frank Leslie's Illustrated Newspaper* and *Harper's Weekly* published illustrations based on Russell's photographs, each conveying similar themes of national unification.

The absence of Chinese workers in the publicly circulated and celebrated Promontory Summit photographs has prompted larger questions about the representation of Chinese labor in the history of the transcontinental railroad. Some accounts diminish or leave out the contributions of Chinese workers, while other accounts incorporate the Chinese into the narratives of national redemption.[23] One article in the *Daily Alta California* described the monumental moment in the following passage:

> The day was clear and beautiful, and the little gathering of less than one thousand people, representing all classes of our people, from the humblest citizen to the highest civil and military authorities... met to enact the last scene in a mighty drama of peace.... The Occident and the Orient, North and South, Saxon, Celt, and Mongolian, each clad in his peculiar costume, mingled on common ground. All personal and sectional animosities, all distinctions of class, all prejudices of race and nationality were forgotten for the moment in the all absorbing interest of the grand event of history and civilization about to take place.[24]

The article conveys a theme of national unity, as the regional divides that split the country during the Civil War were now mended in the triumphant completion of the transcontinental railroad. In particular, the article includes the Chinese worker in the theme of national unity, suggesting that the railroad itself was an arbiter of racial harmony. Later in the article, the journalist takes note of a celebratory dinner hosted by J. H. Strobridge. While Stanford and others crowded before the cameras, Strobridge entertained dignitaries, toasting the achievement of Chinese laborers.

> With the other guests arose from the table, Mr. Strobridge introduced his Chinese foreman and leader who had been with him so long, and took the head of the table. The manly and honorable proceeding was hailed with three rousing cheers by the Caucasian guests, military and civilians, who crowded around Strobridge to congratulate and assure him of their sympathy.[25]

We might read this passage, not as a firsthand account of the event, or as evidence of whether or not the railroad officials included or excluded the Chinese, but rather as a representation of Chinese railroad workers within—as inextricably a part of—the narrative of national unity. In the coming decades, there would be the driving-out campaigns, the cries of Denis Kearney and American labor that the "Chinese Must Go," and the culmination of these movements in the seemingly inevitable passage of the 1882 Chinese

FIGURE 12.11   *China Section Gang Promontory*, by J. B. Silvis. Denver Public Library, Western History Collection, X-22221.

Exclusion Act. However, I want to note the passage from the *Daily Alta*— its description of Promontory Summit as a place of "common ground"— alongside Russell's *Chinese Laying the Last Rail* to highlight how in 1869, as the nation celebrated the completion of the transcontinental railroad, the place of Chinese labor in the United States had yet to become clear. The photographic archive marks this moment as the Chinese railroad worker shifts in and out of the camera's view.

After the May 1869 celebratory events had long waned, J. B. Silvis, an itinerant photographer, staged a photograph of Chinese workers at Promontory Summit. Titled *China Section Gang Promontory* (figure 12.11), the photograph depicts a crew of Chinese workers at the railroad track. Each worker strikes a pose. Most notable, however, is the roving photographic studio, pictured in the background, with visible inscriptions: "J. B. Silvis," "Stereoscopic and Landscape Views," "Notable Points." Built in a Union Pacific Railroad car, the mobile studio set up by photographer Silvis featured living quarters, a dark room, and a portrait studio. He adapted the roving studio car for the "nomadic" life of a photographer on the road, working the newly settled territories made available by the transcontinental railroad.[26]

China Section Gang Promontory not only features Chinese railroad workers but also calls attention to the act of photography itself. The placement of the photographic studio car directly in the frame highlights the production and constructedness of the image. Moreover, the Chinese workers appear so obviously posed. The photograph was a work of pure artifice, as the Chinese were mostly not Union Pacific workers. Silvis's photograph was neither an evidentiary record for railroad officials nor a scenic view for commercial markets. Moreover, his views were not technically sublime. Rather, his photograph offers illuminating contrasts to the sweeping and majestic vistas portrayed by photographers like Alfred Hart. The deliberate staging of the Chinese workers at Promontory Summit also serves as a lingering reminder of their relative absence in the photographs taken by Russell, Savage, and Hart.

Silvis was not the only person to reproduce the historic scene. Thomas Hill, who was associated with the Hudson River school of art, produced a mammoth painting entitled *The Last Spike*. The painting (which is currently on display at the California State Railroad Museum in Sacramento) was commissioned by Leland Stanford and completed in 1881. While Hill used the Promontory Summit photographs as points of reference, his painting further revised the scene by highlighting the role of the Central Pacific while obscuring the rival Union Pacific. The painting placed Stanford and the cadre of CPRR officials at the center of the saga of the transcontinental railroad.[27] Because their appearance represented the Central Pacific, Chinese workers were acknowledged in Hill's painting. While the Chinese workers were absent in the iconic photograph *East and West Shaking Hands at Laying Last Rail* by Union Pacific photographer Russell, they were present in Hill's famous painting, a revisionist portrait initiated by Stanford himself.[28] This presence, however, was merely ornamental, an acknowledgment not of the workers but of the company they worked for. With the two workers kneeling before Stanford, the image situates the Chinese as witnesses to the grandeur of the railroad, a depiction circulated in the aforementioned pictorial publications such as *Frank Leslie's Illustrated Newspaper*.

Photographers continued to work along the overland route after the completion of the transcontinental line in 1869. They followed the workers who remained to maintain and repair the newly built rail line. Perhaps the most popular and frequently reproduced image of the Chinese railroad workers is *Filling in Secret Town Trestle, C.P.R.R.* (figure 12.12) by famed landscape photographer Carleton Watkins. The photograph was taken around 1876 and foregrounds Chinese workers moving rocks and filling in a ravine. The view shows a curving trestle and bridge constructed through the Sierra Nevada.

FIGURE 12.12   *Filling in Secret Town Trestle, C.P.R.R.*, by Carleton Watkins. Collection of Photographs by Carleton Watkins, ca. 1874–1890. Phoebe Hearst Museum of Anthropology, University of California Berkeley.

After his San Francisco studio was forced to close due to financial woes, Watkins began taking photographs for the CPRR and received support from the Big Four railroad baron Collis P. Huntington.[29] *Filling in Secret Town Trestle, C.P.R.R.* in 1876 was a part of what he called his "New Series of Pacific Coast Views." Although he also made stereographs (like Hart and Savage), Watkins experimented with large-format outdoor photography. The wide angle of the camera takes in the vastness of the landscape. Chinese workers are also pictured in the frame, their presence set against the immensity of the land and the railroad structures. As a historical document, the photograph indicates that the story of the Chinese and the transcontinental railroad continued well after Promontory Summit.

Railroad companies hired photographers to capture the pace and scale of their construction efforts. As such, Chinese workers—their bodily form and their labor—appeared before the camera's lens. This appearance in the photographic frame functioned as evidentiary record for the railroad companies. The worker appears nameless as he was, for the most part, in other official records such as payrolls, contracts, and land surveys. He is a witness to the sublime technology of the transcontinental railroad moving through space and paving the way for development and progress. Because of the mandate for documentation, the railroad companies amassed an incomparable archive of photographs depicting Chinese workers and their efforts at building the nation's first transcontinental railroad. The photographs taken by Hart, Russell, Savage, Watkins, and others that gave the public their first look at the landscapes traversed by the completion of the transcontinental railroad had considerable afterlives. Artists reproduced the photographs in wood engravings for illustrated periodicals, in travelogues, for public lectures, and for a circuit of commercial exchange—all of which contributed to the vision of the transcontinental railroad as a symbol of modernity and the nation's future.

CHAPTER 13

Les fils du Ciel

European Travelers' Accounts
of Chinese Railroad Workers

GREG ROBINSON

A long-obscured aspect of the history of the transcontinental railroad is the work of the more than ten thousand Chinese immigrants who were employed by the Central Pacific Railroad (CPRR) to build the western portion of the route and who made up the large majority of the CPRR's labor force.

Despite their indispensable contribution in blood and toil, the surviving record on the daily living and work experience of the Chinese railroad workers remains scarce. There is, however, a useful and still largely untapped source for scholars seeking to recover this story: during the period that the Chinese immigrants were employed in railroad construction in the United States, their presence and labor were attested to by a host of foreign witnesses, especially French people, who passed through the Pacific West. The letters, diaries, and travel narratives that these visitors assembled, the majority of which were originally published in French, provide vital information about the Chinese workers. What is more, these travel narratives offer a novel perspective on the unfolding debate in American circles over Chinese immigration and clearly suggest the international resonance of these issues.

The authors varied widely in their expressed views of the Chinese laborers, ranging from sympathy to admiration to disdain to outright racist caricature. Still, they all inevitably saw the railroad workers from a different standpoint than that of the ethnic Chinese themselves or of their white American coworkers or bosses. Foreigners themselves, and not in direct competition with Chinese workers, these writers tended to be more objective and less crudely nativist than the Americans (especially in California) who addressed the subject, and their views were in many cases further informed by their travels or sojourns in Asia.

The View from Europe

How did such interaction between foreign witnesses and Chinese workers come about, and how did these authors come to write about it? Visiting the United States and then writing travel narratives mixed with social and political commentary was something of a cottage industry among Europeans in the nineteenth century.[1] Diverse English visitors such as Frances Trollope, Charles Dickens, and Harriet Martineau wrote accounts of their American travels, as did notable travelers from the continent such as Michel Chevalier, Alexis de Tocqueville, and Friedrich Ratzel.[2] Countless Europeans, like their American counterparts, became enchanted by the mythology of the "Wild West" and stories of cowboys and Indians (beginning in the mid-1870s, German novelist Karl May—who did not visit the United States until the end of his life— published a series of novels set in the West that made him one of Europe's best-selling authors). The transcontinental railway itself became a subject of great popular attention. In the wake of Jules Verne's 1873 novel, *Le tour du monde en quatre-vingts jours* (Around the World in Eighty Days), which features its protagonist, Phileas Fogg, rushing across the North American continent by train, a number of authors were inspired to recount their real-life adventures in the American West.[3]

Finally, the labor and social status of the Chinese immigrants were matters of considerable interest to Europeans. Throughout the nineteenth century, the problem of race relations in the United States occupied a particular place in the works of such European-born analysts as Tocqueville, Gustave de Beaumont, and Friedrich Kapp. In addition, discussions of Chinese immigrants in America by European writers, particularly the French, reflected their widespread interest in China and in Asia generally. The culture of China, with its exotic character and ancient roots, exercised an irresistible attraction on French thinkers and artists from Voltaire to Victor Hugo, Pierre Loti to Paul Claudel. In more practical terms, at a time when France was increasing its commercial and missionary activities in China in the wake of the Taiping Rebellion and was assuming imperial control over southern Indochina, the matter of Asian labor and emigration assumed a particular importance for European readers.

At the same time, European visitors to California—like other outsiders—were fascinated by the racial difference of the Chinese immigrants and the "exotic" nature of their communities. The German-born photographer Arnold Genthe was an indefatigable chronicler of San Francisco's Chinatown, and travel narratives of San Francisco included extended sections on visits there.[4] The sections of travel narratives that dealt with the Chinese railroad workers were influenced by all these preoccupations.

Analysis of Texts

My purpose here is to offer translated extracts from works by a selection of authors with distinct occupations and itineraries. These writings—based in most cases on eyewitness testimony—provide direct evidence of the Chinese railroad workers' experience.[5] A note on the translations: Even as the Europeans differed in their attitudes, their language varied widely—for instance, they spoke of the workers alternately as "Chinese," as "coolies," "celestials," and sometimes as "yellows" (the word *jaune* is particularly loaded, as it means not only "yellow" but also "strikebreaker"). One favored term was the slightly poetic *les fils du Ciel* (sons of heaven). Jacques Siegfried and Count Ludovic de Beauvoir, authors in their early twenties who were writing for a popular audience, used colloquial language. Conversely, the engineer Émile Malézieux, writing a semiofficial report, was less colorful in his descriptions.

JACQUES SIEGFRIED

Jacques Siegfried (1840–1909) was an Alsatian-born French banker/merchant and educational reformer who in 1861 founded the company Siegfried Frères, a cotton-importing business. In 1866–1867 Siegfried took a round-the-world trip, in the course of which he visited Egypt, India, Indochina, China, and Japan, before sailing to San Francisco and crossing the United States (one of his stops was Salt Lake City, where he met with Brigham Young). In his memoir of his trip, *Seize mois autour du monde 1867–1869* (Sixteen Months around the World, 1867–1869), Siegfried described his twenty-six-day voyage across the Pacific from Yokohama, Japan, to San Francisco, during which he interacted with Chinese immigrants arriving for work on the railroads:

We had aboard 400 or 500 Chinese who were seeking their fortune in the Golden Land. A portion of them were there to engage in various small trades in which they excel, such as the jobs of tailor, cobbler or laundryman; most had signed up in advance for road work on the [Central] Pacific Railway; all were probably already thinking of when they would return. For love of country is so strong in these people that when circumstances do not allow them to return there during their lifetimes, they always commission their friends to return their coffins, so that they can be buried with their ancestors.[6]

Although Siegfried clearly saw the Chinese workers as sojourners whose "love of country" would keep them from settling permanently on the other side of the ocean, he was nonetheless respectful about their potential as workers and scathing about the white union members who unfairly restricted their entry: "They are already 40,000 in California, and this number would surely be even higher if white workers' unions, fearing the prospect of labor competition from such persevering and thrifty workers, had not tried to discourage their entry by all kinds of harassment, and had even gotten the State of California to enact numerous laws against them."[7] One interesting feature of Siegfried's account is that he refers to the United States as "the Golden Land." In the wake of the 1849 California Gold Rush, America became known as "Gold Mountain" to the Chinese, and San Francisco is still referred to as Old Gold Mountain (旧金山).

LUDOVIC DE BEAUVOIR

Count Ludovic de Beauvoir (1846–1929) was born in Belgium to an aristocratic family. He was just nineteen years old in 1865 when he set out on a round-the-world tour that lasted for more than two years, in the course of which he stopped in Australia, the Dutch East Indies, Hong Kong, Macao (Macau), Peking (Beijing), and Tokyo. During his voyage Beauvoir wrote daily notes as well as letters to his parents, including his observations. Upon his return home, he then transformed his material into two volumes, *Voyage autour du monde: Australie* (Voyage Around the World: Australia) and *Java, Siam, Canton* (1869). Beauvoir's memoirs caused a sensation and gained such a large audience that an English translation was soon published. After serving in the Franco-Prussian War in 1870–1871, for which he was awarded the Legion of Honor, in 1872 Beauvoir published a third volume, *Pékin, Yeddo, San Francisco*, in which he related his adventures in Beijing, Tokyo, and the

Les Fils du Ciel ont laissé les pioches plantées dans le sable et se promènent les bras croisés avec une insolence vraiment occidentale. (*Voir p. 859.*)

FIGURE 13.1 "The Sons of Heaven left their spades in the sand and walk around with arms folded with a truly occidental insolence." Comte Ludovic de Beauvoir, *Voyage autour du monde* (1878), p. 858.

United States, accompanied by illustrations. The following year, Beauvoir's memoirs were produced as a set, along with illustrations (see figure 13.1), under the title *Voyage autour du monde* (Voyage around the World). A new revised edition followed in 1878.[8]

In *Voyage autour du monde,* Beauvoir describes his arrival in San Francisco in 1867, on the home stretch of his voyage, and his decision to take passage on the unfinished railroad east; even before the transcontinental connection was completed, it was already possible (and desirable) to travel over the already completed stretches of track and to bridge the distance by stagecoach or other means. By a stroke of fortune, Beauvoir happened to be passing through the Sierra Nevada just at the time that the Chinese railroad workers went out on strike to protest unequal treatment and wages—a brave but ultimately unsuccessful action. He took advantage of the work stoppage to spend time in the Chinese camp. As far as is known, his account represents the sole eyewitness testimony of the strike:

Nevada, June 30, 1867

From Cisco to the summit of the [Sierra Nevada] chain is 27 kilometers [17 miles], along which the tracks rise a further two thousand feet. There we see 5,000 Chinese railroad workers; without them, the construction of the California tracks would have been very difficult and expensive to accomplish.... But in this foreign soil they quickly took up the worst part of Anglo-Saxon civilization, and their first order of business was to go out on strike. Each railroad worker was earning up to 34 dollars a month. Today they demand 40 dollars a month. As the company had not the least wish to give in, the Sons of Heaven have left their pickaxes buried in the sand, and walk around with arms crossed with a truly occidental insolence.

We stayed a few hours in the middle of the Chinese camp, our minds taken up completely by thoughts that brought to mind both our recent memories of the Middle Kingdom, frozen for centuries in its own backward mold, and the sight of these Chinese who were brought in to accomplish the greatest endeavor ever undertaken by modern civilization.[9]

What is particularly interesting is the distinction that Beauvoir makes between Chinese in China, whom he considered as inevitably backward, and those working in railroad construction in the United States. These workers he saw as modern—even adopting the "curse" of labor organizing and conducting their protest with Western-style effrontery.[10]

EDMOND COTTEAU AND GUILLAUME DEPPING

Edmond Cotteau (1833–1896) was a journalist/photographer and globe-trotting reporter for the journals *Le Temps* and *Autour du monde*. He made an extended trip to North and South America in 1876–1877, visited India in 1878–1879, and toured Japan, China, and Indochina in 1881–1882. In 1884 he circled the world by sea. In his American travel diary (whose title, *Six mille lieues en soixante jours* [Six Thousand Leagues in Sixty Days] referenced the titles of two of Jules Verne's popular novels), Cotteau reported on his observations regarding the construction of the railroad during his trip to the United States:

21 September. During the night we have climbed the steep slopes of the Sierra Nevada.... We cross deep valleys on trestle bridges whose fragile appearance is hardly reassuring. It is true that whenever we cross on these trembling viaducts, the train slows its progress. One of these bridges was really scary: Just

as we passed over the bridge, an army of Chinese workers was busy reinforcing it and, from the platform of the train car, at regular intervals between each crossing, I saw at an enormous depth under our feet, a swarm of bustling men.

Soon the descent is slowing; we pass several Chinese camps. John (the nickname that Californians give any man of the Yellow Race) is not demanding. To avoid expense, he builds in a clearing, near a stream, a hut made out of branches. As for food, he is satisfied with a handful of rice and a cup of tea without sugar—thus he has neither rent nor restaurateur to pay, and can save almost his entire salary.[11]

Although this passage describes the privations in diet and living conditions that the Chinese underwent (doubtless with some truth) as a voluntary action by the workers to save money, it also clearly reflects the lack of support offered by the Central Pacific in terms of feeding its labor force, as well as the difficulties that workers in such remote areas faced in procuring supplies.

Cotteau's description of the hardships faced by the Chinese workers was echoed by Guillaume Depping (1829–1901), a travel writer who visited the United States during the 1860s and who later became known for a travel book on Japan, entitled *Le Japon* (Japan, 1884), which went through multiple editions. In an article that appeared in a Paris newspaper in the 1870s, Depping described the extreme conditions under which the Chinese railroad workers were forced to labor, including work done standing in rushing streams:

[Passing on a bridge in Utah at the 1,000-mile mark west of Omaha,] [w]e just had to slow down the pace of the train, the storm of the previous Thursday having washed away some of the land and damaged the track. While passing, we heard the waters of the Weber River jumping up and frothing at the bottom of the precipice. Chinese laborers, immersed in water up to belt level, finished off the repair work, so that the train did not have to stop; [the engineer] only slowed his pace, for the first time on our trip, then once beyond this point, returned to its rapid running.[12]

HEMMANN HOFFMANN

Born in Basel, Switzerland, Hemmann Hoffmann (1844?–?) attended the Polytechnique in Zurich. In a published memoir of his experiences, *Californien, Nevada und Mexico: Wanderungen eines Polytechnikers* (California, Nevada and Mexico: Travels of a Polytechnician), he described how in the mid-1860s, at about age twenty, he was invited by a cousin to come work as an engineer in California. He was employed successively as a chemical engineer in Nevada, a railway foreman for the Central Pacific Railroad, and a boss at a hacienda in Mexico.

Hoffmann described at length in his memoir the months he worked for the Central Pacific in the Sierra Nevada as the foreman of a Chinese construction crew. Hoffmann clearly delineates the racial hierarchy in the railroad camp, explaining that white workers dwelled in substantial cabins in individual dormitories, while the Chinese workers were warehoused in stacked bunks in low huts, with no tables or other furniture. Similarly, the white workers ate beefsteak prepared by cooks, while the Chinese were given inferior meat (or, seemingly, cast-offs from the whites' kitchens) and cooked their own rice:

> Alongside the [t]racks there were 22 camps, each one holding more than a hundred workers. A work section had been assigned to every camp. It was meant to defy the chaotic (looking) terrain and overcome it by the beauty of marvel....
>
> Engineers, foremen, and workers of all nations dwelled there. Most of the latter were Chinese. Every camp was divided into two sections, one for the whites, the other for the Chinese. The former consisted of various log cabins and booths. One of them served as church and dining hall, another as forge and workshop, a third served as a stall for about eighty horses, a forth as dormitory and bathroom for the foremen, and a fifth as a dormitory for the workers. There the bunks were stacked up, manger-like, along the walls, like on ships. The camp of the Chinese, on the other hand, consisted of many small individual huts, in which an ordinary man could hardly stand erect. Their dining hall was a simple platform, on which they squatted with folded legs.[13]

Hoffmann states that he was assigned to Camp No. 9, where he commanded a section of some thirty Chinese. Their work started in the early morning and lasted all day:

> Bells rang at 5 o'clock each morning to announce the beginning of the day.... After taking care of watering the horses and setting up the tipcarts, everyone had breakfast together. There was a hearty piece of beefsteak, potatoes, fresh bread, and coffee [for the whites]. The Chinese had their rice, their meat, and their tea.
>
> Starting at 6 o'clock all the workers gathered for a roll call. After that, horses were harnessed, tools were handed out, and then all started walking across the dirt roads, often wading through knee-deep feces, to our worksite about a mile away [from the camp]....

One evening at 6 o'clock we packed up our gear and marched back to the camp. As soon as worktime was over, it appeared as if we were all back in kindergarten. With fatuous jumping and childish screaming these braided men, among them old fellows, ran to their huts. In the white section [of the camp] people thought it was important to look after the horses first, and then to change clothes. Then came a really hearty supper that helped refresh everyone. Since I was tired from constantly walking up and down near the workers, from the stress of relentlessly motivating them, and getting up early the next morning, I hit the sack early, and passed right out.[14]

Much of Hoffmann's text in regard to his time as a foreman is given over to rants against the Chinese laborers who worked under him: "[W]ith none of these thirty sons from the heavenly kingdom did I ever become closely acquainted. All of them revealed themselves to be devious, deceitful, and indifferent concerning work."[15] He states that the Chinese were "feeble" and indifferent workers, able to accomplish the work only because of their large numbers, though he grudgingly admits that it was the cheap labor of the Chinese that made the building of the railroad possible. Yet his reference to the threat of Chinese immigration (he alludes to the story of the sorcerer's apprentice, which would later be popularized by Paul Dukas and Walt Disney) suggests that he was unable to picture Chinese as human beings:

Still, the work of the Chinese as a whole is highly significant for California, particularly in two ways: on the one hand, because of the current increase in work force, on the other, essentially, because of the wage reduction they triggered, as wages used to be phenomenally high. The [w]hite man gradually had to force himself to be content at first with a third, then half, and eventually a quarter of their initial wages [*sic*]. It was this wage reduction that first made the quick construction and expansion of big cities and structurally designed roads, and ultimately the whole Pacific Railroad possible. The individual white worker's loss was a gain to society at large.

However, Californians should remember the story of Goethe's sorcerer's apprentice and not forget the formula which can be used to send these servile ghosts/spirits back to where they came from, once the white population has increased some more, in order that this Chinese tribe does not become rooted in this country.[16]

Throughout his text, the cruel viciousness of Hoffmann's language and his disdainful, mocking tone suggest that his opposition to the Chinese workers was based more on racial prejudice than on their actual performance. For example, Hoffmann complains that the workers did not understand English, yet he admits that he made no effort to learn their "absurd jargon" (the reader can only wonder what Hoffmann's American hosts thought of *his* Swiss-German jargon):

> My Chinese subjects bothered me a lot and often stirred up my anger.... First, the Chinese are weaker in build than whites. Also, they have something child-ish and trifling in themselves that does not leave them even in old age. They are unbearably loquacious. They prattle incessantly in their absurd jargon, so strident and loud, and top this off with such ugly grimaces and ridiculous gestures that in their company one feels constantly as if among half-insane people. At all times of the day they stop work, sneak over to their keg of tea, which is constantly surrounded by Chinese, and take a sip of tea. Soon, against orders, they light a pipe that holds only a pinch of tobacco. If then one of them faces even the slightest difficulty (at work), he makes a big deal out of it; everyone jumps in, curious, and raises hell. While only a few of them under-stand English, everyone understands powerful cussing, which brings order back to work for a while: because they are submissive, repulsively submissive.[17]

ÉMILE MALÉZIEUX

Émile Malézieux (1822–1885) was born in Saint-Quentin in northern France. After studying at the École Polytechnique, he enrolled at the École des Ponts et Chaussées (Bridge and Roadbuilding School). In June 1870, at the twilight of the Second Empire, Malézieux led a delegation of French officials to study American public works projects. He turned the notes taken during his Ameri-can visit into a trio of books: a set of recollections of his visit, an official report on public works (which also included a section on the Brooklyn Bridge, then at the outset of its construction), and a study of American meteorology.[18]

In the section of Malézieux's official report that deals with railroads, there is an extract from a long conversation he had with an (unnamed) white American engineer who worked on the construction of the Pacific Railway (then just completed). Like Hemmann Hoffmann, this engineer considered the Chinese laborers to be docile and willing to work for lower pay. Unlike the Swiss writer, though, he considered these positive attributes, and indeed spoke with enthusiasm of the devotion, skill, and intelligence of the immigrants:

There are nine tunnels on the eastern slope of the mountain and five on the western, not to mention the one at the summit, which is the longest [at 516 meters, 0.3 mile]. Their total length is 1,900 meters [1.2 miles].... All laborers employed in this hardship work, except foremen, were Chinese. Their docility, their zeal, their dexterity and finally their intelligence were all the more appreciated in that they hardly received a dollar and a half for a day's labor, instead of the three or four we had to give to US workers.[19]

Malézieux took from the conversation the same conclusion as Hoffmann—that the Chinese workers' work on the railroad would bring pressure for mass immigration of a kind that whites, and particularly unions, would find difficult to accept:

> We understand just from this one example what self-interest the mine owners and public works contractors have in encouraging Chinese immigration, which the workers of the country oppose. But when you see three hundred million men suffocating for lack of space on one shore of the Pacific Ocean, while there on the other there is a wealth of uncultivated land and untapped riches, it seems very unlikely that the most violent demonstrations in Boston and New York will long have the effect of limiting to eight or ten thousand the number of Chinese who land annually in San Francisco.[20]

LE PETIT JOURNAL

One of the most picturesque articles on the role of the Chinese immigrants in building the railroad, contributed by an anonymous author, was published in the popular Paris newspaper *Le Petit Journal* on the first anniversary of the driving of the Golden Spike. As the article's title, "Sixteen Kilometers in a Day," would indicate, the author spent most of the article describing the activities during the final workday before the meeting at Promontory Summit, when the Central Pacific workers managed the astounding feat of laying ten miles (sixteen kilometers) of track and thereby covering the last part of the effective distance to the meeting place. One noteworthy aspect of the article is the detailed description of the operations of the various teams of laborers to lay down the tracks:

> [Everything was prepared for April 27,] but the derailment of a locomotive forced [Charles Crocker] to hold up until the next day. On April 28, at four in the morning, all the workers, an army of around ten thousand, were in

position, ready for the glorious struggle. The signal given, the heavy wagons advanced, loaded with rails that, with the aid of an ingenious mechanism, they slid onto the tracks prepared for this purpose by Chinese coolies. Workers held on to each side of the track, then seized and laid down the long iron bands over which the cars would then immediately pass, with the workers restarting the same operation at the end. Meanwhile, behind the car the rails were fixed onto their pads and securely bolted by elite workers.

Finally, the road workers, who are still more Chinese, completed the ballasting. All this was done under the active supervision of the department heads; the engineers on horseback galloped all up and down the line to watch over the construction. Director Crocker, riding in an open carriage and with a spyglass in hand, preceded [them], watching over and encouraging all parts of this valiant army.[21]

Perhaps even more striking than the narrative of tracklaying is the author's description of the interracial camaraderie between the different teams of workers. First, the various Yankee, Irish, German, and Chinese workers collaborated and encouraged one another to work: "Everyone seemed sustained by the same energy; not a worker spoke of rest; all, on the contrary, excited each other; we could hear only these words: 'Courage, boys…let's go on…forward!' and in fact the movement of the mass of men who performed this work, is almost like that of a man taking a casual stroll."[22] Then, after the morning's work, they take their noontime meal together—presumably the reference to love and goodwill (*agape*) refers to their sitting down together at the table of brotherhood to eat their food:

> At noon, more than ten kilometers of track were already laid down, and there was no doubt of the final victory. The train-hotel then came up, bringing in the solid meal that had been so well earned by the Yankees, Irish, Germans and Chinese. All attacked their food with the same ardor, and thus for a moment there is a truly fraternal sense of *agape* in the desert, but it promptly came to an end. It is useful to remember that it was necessary to transport to the worksite all the provisions necessary to feed such an agglomeration of men.[23]

The descriptions here of the daily life and relations of the Chinese workers with the others stand diametrically opposed to those offered by Hemmann Hoffmann, who had described the Chinese workers as segregated from the whites, obliged to prepare their own food (using leftovers from the whites), and the target of resentment from other workers for allegedly bringing down wages. It is unclear what explains the difference in customs and attitudes. Was it that the railroad found it too inefficient to separate out Chinese laborers? Did the immigrants turn to eating Western food when they were in Utah, where they could not count on obtaining Asian food products? Or did they shift their food tastes as part of a process of assimilation?[24] Similarly, is the interracial camaraderie that the *Le Petit Journal* article describes a product of increased contact (and understanding) between workers after the experience in the Sierra Nevada? Or could it be that one or both of the authors were guilty of falsehood or exaggeration in their portraits?

RUDOLF LINDAU

The final author to be considered is Rudolf (or Rodolphe) Lindau (1829–1910), a German diplomat and author.[25] The following extract was taken from a series of travel articles that Lindau wrote for the popular French magazine *Revue des Deux Mondes*.[26] Lindau describes how, while sojourning in San Francisco on his way home from Japan, he and his friends learned that the railway was being completed and took passage on the first through train: "Since I was in California at such an auspicious moment, I promised myself that I would attend an event whose importance in political, commercial and civilizational terms dwarfed even the calculus of American exaggeration."

Lindau's text implies that the author was personally present at the completion of the transcontinental link and the driving of the golden spike. While this cannot be verified, it is obvious that he was in communication with those who were, as his account includes a mass of detail regarding the proceedings. In any case, like the article from *Le Petit Journal*,[27] Lindau's account places the Chinese workers at Promontory Summit and reveals their collaboration in the climactic stages of the work, underlining the skill of the workers and the respect that they earned from other workers and from spectators:

> The preparations for the solemn placing of the last rails were quickly made. An empty space of about 100 feet had been left between the edges of the ties. Two squadrons, composed of white men on the Union Pacific side and Chinese on the Central Pacific side, advanced in proper workman's attire to fill this gap. In both camps the best workers had been chosen, and it was a pleasure to see how they took up the work in such lively fashion. The Chinese especially, serious, silent, alert, ably helped one another, and were the object of general admiration and approval. "They work like magicians," said one eyewitness.[28]

Taken together, these narratives provide unique firsthand information as to the work and social lives of the Chinese workers, as well as picturesque accounts of such events as the construction of tunnels in the Sierra Nevada and the driving of the golden spike. Beyond their interest as testimony to the work and daily lives of the Chinese workers, they expand and reshape our sense of the debates provoked by their presence. While the mass of Europeans expressed respect or even admiration for the skill of the Chinese railroad workers, they also betrayed unease, and sometimes downright hostility, toward the idea of any permanent settlement of Chinese immigrants. In a widely read text, the Austrian diplomat Baron Alexander Hübner, using considerable exaggeration, exposed the conflict as a question of basic economic survival, albeit couched in racial terms:

> In the mines, white workers receive daily, in addition to food, three, three and a half, or four dollars. The Chinese worker is not fed and must be satisfied with seventy-five cents, one dollar, at most a dollar and a half. The same is true for other industries. In cities, the Chinese works as a domestic or as a launderer and cook; in the countryside, he excels as a farmer, and especially as a gardener. The roadwork being done now in different parts of the Sierra Nevada is being executed by the Chinese. They are the best workers. Without their help, the Pacific line could not be completed in so little time. On board the large steamers, sailors (bad sailors in fact) and boys assigned to passenger service are all Chinese. In the factories, they replace more and more whites. Everywhere their competition is great. Bosses, foremen, all those who need hands seek them out because they do roughly the same jobs as whites for less than half the salary.... This is their crime, expiated by acts of brutality against them leading up to murder, by laws which are the shame of legislators, by jury verdicts as contrary to common sense as to justice. And yet they hold fast, and nothing seems to stop them.[29]

These foreign-language texts help remind scholars of American studies and ethnic studies of the importance of looking beyond the United States and the English language in their researches.

PART FOUR

Chinese Railroad Workers in Cultural Memory

CHAPTER 14

The Chinese Railroad Worker in United States History Textbooks

A Historical Genealogy, 1849–1965

WILLIAM GOW

In 1911 David Saville Muzzey published *An American History*, propelling himself into the forefront of the burgeoning market in high school text-books.[1] As one of the best-selling textbook authors of the twentieth century, Muzzey exercised an influence matched by few others in shaping the way that American high school students understood the nation's history. In a foot-note accompanying his text on the administration of President Rutherford B. Hayes, Muzzey included a one-paragraph description of nineteenth-century Chinese immigrant laborers. By the beginning of the twentieth century, many high school history textbooks discussed Chinese laborers to some degree. But whereas actual nineteenth-century immigrants from China occupied a range of professions—from miners to farmworkers to laundrymen—Muzzey and most other textbook authors of his day turned increasingly to one figure, the railroad worker, to represent all Chinese labor.

Today the employment of Chinese laborers on the Central Pacific Railroad has firmly entrenched itself in the nation's historical imagination. Alongside the US government's incarceration of Japanese Americans during World War II, and to a lesser extent the arrival of Southeast Asian refugees after the Viet-nam War, the story of nineteenth-century Chinese railroad workers in high school history textbooks plays a definitive role in constructing the way Asian Americans are understood in relationship to this nation's past. Despite the cur-rent prominence of the Chinese railroad worker in the historical imagination, scholars have done little research on when or why this figure began to appear in the nation's textbooks.

This chapter places the emergence of the Chinese railroad worker in American history textbooks in the Progressive Era. The Chinese railroad worker became a staple of the nation's textbooks during a moment when large-scale immigration from Southern and Eastern Europe, the growth of the American empire in the Pacific and the Caribbean, and an increasingly multiethnic urban population challenged the vision many Americans had of the nation's global relationships. This was a period when the nation redefined its relationship to immigration and immigrants. Between the passage of the 1882 Chinese Exclusion Act and the 1924 Immigration Act, the Progressive ideology of "social betterment" became linked with notions of whiteness and civilization, creating an immigration policy rooted in quotas and exclusion. As a result, the nation's immigration policy was infused with the white supremacist logic of eugenics and social Darwinism. This chapter argues that the cultural contradictions inherent in the figure of the Chinese railroad worker allowed that figure to simultaneously represent the hopes and the anxieties that many US-born whites had about immigration in general during the Progressive Era.

The Emergence of Chinese Immigrant Laborers in American History Textbooks

American history textbooks have their own history. The form that these textbooks took, their use in classes, and the nature of knowledge they contained all changed dramatically over the course of the nineteenth and twentieth centuries. Understanding this history is pertinent to contextualizing the first representations of Chinese immigrants in the nation's history textbooks. Scattered representations of Chinese immigrants began to appear in American history textbooks shortly after the arrival of the first wave of Chinese to California in the 1850s, and yet a confluence of historical factors would ensure that Chinese immigrants did not become a significant part of the nation's history curriculum until after the passage of the 1882 Chinese Restriction Act.

In the first three decades following the arrival of large numbers of Chinese immigrants to the West Coast, Chinese Americans appeared only occasionally in the nation's school textbooks. Shortly after the arrival of the first wave of Chinese immigrants to California following the gold rush of 1849, textbooks began including the first fleeting references to Chinese people in the American West.[2] These early representations often portrayed Chinese immigrants as a symbol of a cosmopolitan gold rush attracting immigrants from around the world. Then in the 1870s, following the Civil War, the country witnessed the nationalizing of the so-called Chinese question. Following the economic panic of 1872, the Chinese question became a national focus, but somewhat surprisingly this heightened awareness of Chinese immigration did not lead to an increased discussion of the issue of China and Chinese people in the nation's textbooks.[3]

In the 1880s textbooks began representing immigration as one of the institutional building blocks of the nation. During this period, immigration increasingly began to appear in the thematic headings of texts and as a separate category in indexes even while textbook references to immigration during the 1880s were far from standardized. Textbook authors began to include discussions of the Chinese as part of a larger emphasis on immigration in general. No longer were the Chinese simply a cosmopolitan backdrop in the story of the California Gold Rush. Instead, the Chinese became a central part of the nation's historical narrative around immigration. Mary Thalheimer's 1880 textbook, *An Eclectic History of the United States*, exemplifies the trend, by including a section entitled "The Chinese Question."[4] Published one year before the passage of the Chinese Restriction Act, *An Eclectic History of the United States* presents a conflicted portrayal of Chinese immigrants. Simultaneously portraying the Chinese as tools of American capital and law-abiding immigrants, Thalheimer's textbook embodied the paradox in representation that many racialized immigrants of the period faced.

Of course, not all textbook authors portrayed the Chinese with the same ambiguity. Alexander Johnston's 1885 textbook discusses "Chinese immigrants" in a separate section, arguing that because the Chinese could "work at lower wages than the white laborers," the US government decided to stop Chinese immigration.[5] John Bach McMaster's 1897 text also discusses the "Anti-Chinese Movement" as a prelude to discussing legislative attempts to stop Chinese immigration.[6] Regardless of how they were portrayed in textbooks of the 1880s and 1890s, by the final decade of the nineteenth century Chinese immigrants were no longer used primarily as a symbol of cosmopolitanism but rather an example of the broader complexities of immigration.

Even as the nation's textbooks increasingly addressed the Chinese as part of a larger discussion of immigration, the railroad worker was not the dominant representation of Chinese labor in textbooks of the late nineteenth century. Numerous textbooks mentioned Chinese immigrant laborers, yet few of these textbooks provided examples of the types of employment in which the Chinese engaged. When these textbooks did give examples, they often included railroad workers as part of a series of examples of Chinese labor. For example, Horace Scudder's 1884 textbook states that the Chinese "have helped to build railroads, work the mines and to do many kinds of household labor but they have rarely become citizens."[7]

By the beginning of the twentieth century, though, the railroad worker was increasingly becoming the only representation of Chinese immigrant labor in the high school history curriculum. Representations of Chinese railroad workers did at times occur alongside other examples of Chinese labor such as domestic service and mining, but between 1900 and 1924 it was rare to find a textbook that provided an example of Chinese immigrant labor that did not mention railroad work. Textbooks by Charles Adams and William Trent (1903), Edward Eggleston (1904), and many others portrayed railroad work as the only example of immigrant Chinese labor.[8] At the turn of the century, the emergence of the railroad worker as the primary symbol of Chinese immigrant labor reflected the figure's ability to speak simultaneously to many of the hopes and anxieties that US-born whites held about immigration during the Progressive Era.

The Cultural Contradictions of the Chinese Railroad Worker

Unlike the Chinese laundryman or migrant farm laborer, the figure of the Chinese railroad worker maintained a type of cultural ambiguity that allowed it to embody both the hopes and fears that US-born whites felt toward the Eastern and Southern Europeans then entering the nation in large numbers. At a time when the racial status of these European immigrants was far from settled, the Chinese railroad worker could simultaneously represent widely divergent ideas about race, immigration, and nation to different people. On the one hand, the figure's association with the coolie allowed the Chinese railroad worker to represent the worst excesses of American capitalism and racialized labor. On the other hand, the figure's association with the railroad allowed the railroad worker to embody ideas of American modernity and progress. Miners, agricultural workers, and laundrymen may have had equal claims to representation in textbooks on historical grounds, but these and other nineteenth-century Chinese laborer professions did not have the same symbolic value as the railroad worker.

Furthermore, the appearance of the Chinese railroad worker as the primary representation of Chinese labor in school curricula had little to do with the scholarly literature on Chinese immigration from the period. The most respected scholar on the topic of Chinese immigration at the beginning of the twentieth century was the sociologist Mary Coolidge. In many ways Coolidge's 1909 book, *Chinese Immigration*, marked the beginning of the scholarly field of Chinese American history. Over 530 pages in length, the text presents Coolidge's analysis of the roots of the anti-Chinese movement. Coolidge devotes only four total pages to the topic of Chinese railroad workers, a surprisingly small amount of space, especially when one considers that she devotes six pages to Chinese boot makers and five pages to Chinese cigar rollers.[9]

Rather than looking toward the historical or scholarly record to explain the increasing representations of Chinese railroad workers in textbooks during the Progressive era, I would argue that the presence of Chinese railroad workers in history textbooks was the result in part of the fundamental changes in the way American society understood racial and ethnic difference. By the beginning of the twentieth century, disciplines such as eugenics, rooted in philosophies of white supremacy, had supplanted older ideas of race rooted in biblical notions of difference. During this period, notions of progress and modernity were often linked with notions of whiteness and purity. Popular and scientific literature increasingly represented many of these new immigrants from Southern and Eastern Europe, along with "degenerates," and "social misfits," as a threat to the racial stock of the nation. Of course, Chinese immigrants were also represented as a threat, but the perceived threat of the Chinese had essentially been mitigated by exclusion.

Given this historical context, the increasing presence of the Chinese railroad worker in the nation's textbooks at the beginning of the twentieth century was almost certainly not a result of fears of increased Chinese labor. If white fears of Chinese laborers alone had driven textbook representations, textbook representations of Chinese immigrants would logically have reached their height in the 1870s and 1880s when anti-Chinese rhetoric was at its height. Instead, the Chinese railroad worker became the dominant representation of Chinese laborers in the early twentieth century after the passage and renewal of the Chinese Restriction Act. I would argue that the figure of the Chinese railroad worker became dominant in textbooks during this period because the figure could symbolize simultaneously a complex assemblage of fears and hopes then circulating in US society. More so than the Chinese miner or farm-worker, the Chinese railroad worker was able to embody the increasing racial anxieties of many US-born whites regarding racialized European immigrants then arriving from countries such as Russia, Greece, and Italy. At the same time, the figure came to represent the hope these same whites had that these newly arrived immigrants might one day make meaningful contributions to American society. This dialectic of hope and fear was embodied in the figure's association with the transcontinental railroad. The railroad was a contradic-tory symbol that represented the possibilities of American modernity, the risks of American corporate capitalism, and fears of racialized immigrant labor. This symbolic ambiguity is what accounts for the figure's longstanding place in the nation's textbooks.

The origin of the railroad worker as the representative of all nineteenth-century Chinese labor lies in the complex relationship between the figure of the Chinese coolie and the place of the railroad in the national imagination. Despite the fact that relatively few, if any, coolies ever arrived in the United States, the figure of the Chinese coolie played an important role in defining the way Americans thought about a range of topics, from race to labor to freedom itself.[10] Coolies were popularly believed to be Asian contract laborers who were coerced or forced into work in the nineteenth century. As historian Moon Ho Jung has pointed out in his study of Chinese labor in postbellum Louisiana, the figure of the coolie "was a conglomeration of racial imaginings that emerged worldwide in the era of the slave emancipation, a product of the imaginer rather than the imagined."[11] According to Jung, the coolie rep-resented a contradictory site at the intersections of free and slave labor, and black and white labor. This allowed the coolie to take on different meanings in different moments of the nineteenth century. The Chinese railroad worker, unlike the Chinese migrant farmworker or Chinese cigar roller, embodied many of the attributes of the coolie while also simultaneously embodying many of the characteristics of the railroad as a symbol of American modernity and progress.

Like the coolie, the railroad occupied a complex, contradictory place within the nineteenth-century American imagination. Not only was railroad work one of the first highly visible forms of wage labor that the Chinese engaged in, but the railroad companies were often seen as the embodiment of corporate capital by the nineteenth-century anti-Chinese movement. Groups such as the Workingmen's Party of California often saw themselves as caught between the corporate power of the railroads and what they viewed as the debased standard of labor provided by the Chinese contract worker. Yet while the Chinese railroad worker came to embody many of the fears latent in popular descriptions of the coolie, the Chinese railroad worker also came to embody a separate set of possibilities tied into the notion of the railroad itself. The railroad was not only a representation of corporate capital, it was also simultaneously a representation of movement, modernity, and progress deeply tied to the notions of whiteness, civilization, and manifest destiny. As such, the Chinese railroad worker became the perfect figure on which white Anglo-Saxons could project not only their fears but also the hopes for the immigrants then arriving in large numbers from Southern and Eastern Europe.

The Chinese Railroad Worker and the Textbooks of David Muzzey

The complex role that the figure of the Chinese railroad worker occupied in American history textbooks during the Progressive Era is embodied in the work of David Muzzey. The author of at least five separate American history textbooks, each published in multiple editions, Muzzey may have exerted a greater influence over the way the nation's schoolchildren understood their collective past than any other single textbook writer from the period. Even after his death in 1965, his textbooks remained in circulation into the 1970s.[12] Over the span of decades, Muzzey's textbooks often reproduced the exact same wording about Chinese immigrant laborers despite the new titles under which his books were published.

In his 1911 textbook, Muzzey introduces the issue of Chinese immigrant labor as part of his discussion of Hayes's administration. Muzzey writes in a footnote, "Between 1850 and 1860 the Chinese immigrants to our shores had increased from 10,000 to 40,000. The work on the western end of the Union Pacific Railroad [*sic*] attracted tens of thousands more in the next decade." Having begun the paragraph by describing the Chinese as immigrants, Muzzey goes on a few sentences later to call them coolies: "Mobs in California and Oregon organized to 'run out of town' the Chinese coolies, in spite of the fact that our government, by the Burlingame Treaty, had guaranteed the Chinese visiting our shores protection in trade, religion, and free travel." He then tells his reader that the Chinese, who "lived on a few cents a day and were content with dirty quarters and poor food," were "a menace to the American laborer of the Pacific coast, who demanded 'four dollars a day and roast beef.'"[13]

Muzzey's 1911 textbook simultaneously portrays Chinese railroad workers as immigrants and as coolie laborers. As coolies, Muzzey argues, they drove down wages, yet as immigrants, he argues, they were victims left unprotected from white workers despite the passage of the Burlingame Treaty. The contradictory nature of the figure of the Chinese railroad worker is further complicated by Muzzey's representation of the railroad itself as a site of contradiction. In another passage in the text, Muzzey describes the transcontinental railroad this way: "But even this greatest feat of American engineering (with the exception of the construction of the Panama Canal) was performed under the shadow of widespread corruption."[14]

By portraying the Chinese railroad worker as immigrant and coolie and by portraying the railroad itself as an engineering feat and a source of corruption, Muzzey imbues the figure of the Chinese railroad worker with a symbolic ambiguity. Scholars such as Robert G. Lee have noted how representation of Chinese immigrant laborers as coolies in the late nineteenth and early twentieth centuries allowed the European immigrant working class to construct itself as white.[15] Yet the symbolic ambiguity that the Chinese railroad worker poses in the 1911 textbook complicates the ability of this figure to play the role of Orientalist foil against which both whites and the West define themselves.

Rather than portraying Chinese immigrants in opposition to Southern Europeans, Muzzey represents both Chinese and Southern Europeans as examples of immigrants who are racially different from white Anglo-Saxons. He argues that this new wave of European immigration was the part of a "race problem" that included US colonial subjects in the Philippines and African Americans in the US South.[16] He ends his discussion of Southern European immigrants by asking if it will ever be possible for these new immigrants to assimilate into American society. In this way, Muzzey makes clear in his 1911 textbook that he sees Southern European immigrants as more similar to the Chinese immigrants than to Anglo-Saxons. In his 1911 textbook, the Chinese railroad worker is the perfect representative of broader fears of the immigrant Other.

Influenced by shifts in immigration policy, Muzzey's representation of Chinese immigrants began to change in the 1920s. The 1924 Immigration Act introduced a series of national quotas that reduced the numbers of immigrants from Southern and Eastern Europe and explicitly excluded nearly all immigration from Asia by denying entry to aliens ineligible for citizenship.[17] The passage of the 1924 Immigration Act eliminated the perceived social and cultural threat that many white Anglo-Saxons saw in immigrants from Eastern and Southern Europe, while hastening the transformation of all European immigrants into white Americans.

At the same time, in the 1920s the nation's history textbook authors and publishers found themselves at the center of a national debate over how the country would portray its immigrant past. During this period authors like Muzzey came under attack from two factions. One group, composed of conservatives, wanted a return to the textbooks of the nineteenth century that celebrated the actions of a clearly defined group of national heroes and villains. Conservative critics saw Muzzey's textbooks as an attack on American patriotism. A second group wanted a more inclusive history that reflected the country's increasing ethnic diversity. They saw in works of authors like Muzzey a "cult of Anglo-Saxonism" that attempted to link the United States culturally and racially to Great Britain in ways they found offensive.[18] The textbook debates of the 1920s, coupled with the changes in immigration policy in 1924, led to a transformation in the way textbooks dealt with the topic of immigration.

For the next three decades, Muzzey would portray Chinese immigrant laborers in his textbooks only as coolies, eliminating the symbolic ambiguity of earlier editions. Muzzey would repeat the same treatment of Chinese laborers in his discussion of exclusion nearly verbatim in different textbooks and editions published in 1927, 1934, 1936, and 1945.[19] In the 1930s Muzzey began describing the presence of "gangs of coolies imported from China [who] labored on the Central Pacific" in his section on the transcontinental railroad.[20] In the textbook *Our Country's History*, published in 1957, Muzzey's text, which was found in a footnote in many earlier editions, was moved to the main body of the book.[21] As a result, Muzzey's 1957 textbook contained references to Chinese coolies in the sections on Chinese exclusion and on construction of the railroads. In both of these sections, Chinese had become a racialized Other against which whites, both immigrant and US-born, could define themselves.

In the 1960s, as the nation began to rethink its understanding of immigrants and immigration, the representations of Chinese railroad workers in Muzzy's textbooks shifted again. In his 1963 textbook, *Our American Republic*, coauthored with Arthur Link, Muzzey stopped using the term *coolie* in references to Chinese labor. The updated wording in the section on the transcontinental railroad is worth quoting at length:

> There were plenty of sensible people who insisted that the task was impossible. To lay iron bands across eighteen hundred miles, from Missouri to the Pacific, through deserts and country inhabited by hostile Indians, and over yawning chasms seemed utterly fantastic.... From 1866 on, however, arduous work progressed rapidly. It gave employment on the eastern end to countless immigrants and to thousands of soldiers returning from war. Many Chinese workers were brought over to labor on the Central Pacific. The tracks met at Promontory near Ogden, Utah, on May 10, 1869.[22]

Here the figure of the Chinese railroad worker had begun to take on a new role. Muzzey paints a picture of the railroad as a symbol of manifest destiny that pits the ostensibly civilizing influences of the United States against a seemingly untamed American wilderness. Within this narrative, the figure of the Chinese railroad worker is positioned in ways that not only buttress claims of the United States as a tolerant, accepting nation of immigrants but also are meant to demonstrate the role that Chinese laborers played in the processes of manifest destiny. By contrasting the Chinese worker against the "hostile Indians," Chinese Americans are rhetorically wrapped into the logic of American modernity, accepted as part of the immigrant nation, and put to symbolic work rationalizing settler colonialism.

Where their racial difference had been used in Muzzey's textbook since 1927 as a symbol against which European immigrants could be constructed as white, in 1963 this same difference was beginning to be used to construct a multicultural narrative of manifest destiny wherein Chinese workers too could be portrayed as settlers on the side of American civilization taming an ostensibly savage wilderness. While the process was not complete in that the textbook still described the Chinese as "brought over to labor," the broader shift had begun toward the inclusion of the figure of the Chinese railroad worker as a symbol of America as a tolerant nation of immigrants—and simultaneously as a representation of the US settler colonial project.

Since the early twentieth century, the contradictions inherent in the Chinese railroad worker have given this figure a place in the nation's history textbooks. For most of this period, the figure's presence was not the result of a robust scholarship on Chinese railroad work or of specific fears about

Chinese immigrants per se. Rather, the Chinese railroad worker became a type of cipher onto which different audiences and authors projected their own feelings and opinions. In part because of this cultural ambiguity, the figure of the Chinese railroad worker has remained a site of contestation over the meaning of race, immigration, and national belonging in US history textbooks for more than a century.

CHAPTER 15

Representing Chinese Railroad Workers in North America

Chinese Historiography and Literature, 1949–2015

YUAN SHU

The study of the Chinese railroad workers in North America as an independent research project was not launched until the turn of the twenty-first century in the People's Republic of China. Because of the limited opportunity to conduct research at US archives, museums, libraries, and historical sites, and also because of wars and social and political turmoil in China during the twentieth century—ranging from the war of resistance to the Japanese invasion (1937–1945)[1] to the so-called Great Proletarian Cultural Revolution (1966–1976)—Chinese historians and social scientists today find little material culture to sustain any new understanding of what Michel de Certeau calls "the practice of everyday life" of these railroad workers, who were mostly living and working in the four (now expanded to five) counties of Guangdong Province before they left for North America in the 1860s.[2] The tremendous interest in the subject today in the media, publishing industry, and academic world reflects China's increasing willingness to participate in global affairs and a desire to improve United States–China relations. However, for the most part, Chinese scholars' study of these railroad workers has continued to depend on the primary research conducted by US-based historians and social scientists of material culture from the late nineteenth century to the present, research that historical documents unearthed in China have corroborated and supplemented. The significance of Chinese historiography on the subject lies more or less in the ways in which the Chinese historians and social scientists frame and reframe the narrative of the railroad workers; these framings reflect the ethos of specific cultural and historical junctures in contemporary China.

In this chapter I divide Chinese historiography of the Chinese railroad workers in North America into three periods since the founding of the People's Republic of China in 1949: the anti-colonialist and anti-imperialist period from 1949 to 1978, the reform and opening period from 1978 to 2000, and the rise of China period from 2000 to the present. I begin by surveying the relevant chapters and sections in history texts of the 1950s on China's encounter with the United States, highlighting their focus on US military and economic interventions in China and the exclusion of Chinese from North America. I then investigate journal articles, book chapters, and translations of US histories on the workers that were in studies of overseas Chinese, as well as Chinese American experiences in the 1980s and 1990s. Finally, I explore why and how the experience of the railroad workers has been expanded and given a higher profile in the Chinese media and academic circles. In this respect the heightened profile of the railroad workers should be understood in terms of what Paul Kennedy calls "the rise and fall of great powers" and also in relation to the changes in the relationship in the twenty-first century between the United States and China.[3]

The Anti-colonialist and Anti-imperialist Period: Nationalism and Global Third Worldism, 1949–1978

The anti-colonialist and anti-imperialist period in the Chinese academic world was ushered in not only by the founding of the People's Republic of China in 1949 but also by the previous two decades of theoretical interests and social movements. Since the 1930s Chinese historians had experimented with Western theories, from Marxism to Freudian psychoanalysis—theories that challenged traditional Chinese historiography, which was based on chronologies of dynasties. While some historians redirected their attention to antiquity or the history of everyday life,[4] others applied Western concepts and methodologies, particularly Marxism, to refashion Chinese historiography with new perspectives and terminologies such as totems, feudalism, and class struggle.

These leftist and liberal orientations and interests prepared for the first turning point in Chinese historiography in the 1950s; in this turn, history writing adopted a Marxist approach with a Leninist emphasis on violent revolution and a strong critique of imperialism. Such an approach to historical studies recast modern Chinese history as part of the nation-building process for the newly established regime. Using the Marxist framework of capitalist exploitation and expansion on a global scale, Chinese historians represented the Chinese railroad workers in North America as the exploited victims of US colonialism and imperialism, and of Chinese feudalism. Because most of these historians were trained in the United States and often had access to the primary sources in both the US government archives and the Chinese Qing dynasty archives, they substantiated their claims by using evidence from the exchanges between Chinese and US officials on such issues as labor shortages in the United States and the recruiting practices of US companies.

Anti-US sentiment defined the historiography of the early 1950s, and that sentiment was also fueled by the ongoing Korean War (1950–1953). By the mid- to late 1950s, there was renewed interest in China in developing a transnational and global coalition against Western colonialism and imperialism among the newly independent nation-states in Asia, Africa, and Latin America. This interest and coalition culminated in the Bandung Conference in 1955,[5] and it popularized the fundamentals of China's burgeoning foreign policy on the five principles of peaceful coexistence.[6]

In *A History of US Aggression against China* (1951; reissued 1954),[7] Liu Danian, a leading Chinese Communist historian in US history, defines "US aggression against China" as evolutionary. The US aggression begins by following the lead of the European powers, continues by struggling for hegemony, and culminates with intervening directly in China. Starting with a focus on the unequal Treaty of Wanghia (Wangxia) between the US and Qing governments in 1844 and concluding with a chapter on the Korean War, Liu interprets the founding of the People's Republic of China and the signing of the Korean armistice agreement as the grand finale of the Chinese people's struggle against colonialist and imperialist interventions in China. Because his focus is exclusively on US intervention in China, Liu considers the Chinese Exclusion Act of 1882 as part of the US imperialist and institutional violence against the Chinese. He devotes extensive treatment to the Chinese laborers and railroad workers in California; he characterizes the workers as persecuted under federal and local laws and ordinances, and as brutally assaulted and murdered by white mobs and hoodlums.[8] The book was questioned for its accuracy and overstatement,[9] and Liu himself admitted in the preface of the second edition that he would need more evidence to back up his claims;[10] nonetheless, his work continued to have impact, and it was translated into Russian and circulated widely in the socialist camp of the Soviet Communist bloc during the 1950s. Liu's work in that sense served as the first officially endorsed history book on modern China's encounter with the United States.

Also in 1951, *A History of US Imperialist Exclusion of the Chinese* was published.[11] Its author, Zhang Renyu, announces from the outset that his work is exclusively based on the work of US historians and the accounts given by US officials and diplomats, and that readers may consider these sources as confessions if they are not comfortable with US viewpoints. He divides the history of the exclusion into three periods: beginning period, 1852–1880; escalating period, 1880–1924; and completion period, 1924–1950. The railroad workers fall into the beginning period, in which he argues that they came to the United States to fill a labor shortage and build the transcontinental railroad under the Burlingame-Seward Treaty of 1868. Like other Chinese historians of the beginning period, he emphasizes that exclusion of the workers started as soon as the transcontinental railroad was completed in the United States in 1869 and in Canada in 1885.[12] But unlike other historians, who highlighted the harsh working conditions for these workers, Zhang considers their experience as an interlude in the exclusion drama and an exception to the harsh treatment of the Chinese workers during the peak of exclusion. In comparing the United States with Britain, France, and Japan, which resorted to trade, missionary work, and brutal violence and aggression as their distinctive modes of engagement with China, he argues that US imperialism demonstrated an exceptionalism, which had been defined by its gesture to acknowledge China's sovereignty, territorial integrity, and mutual trade benefits.

In 1952 Ding Zemin published *A History of US Exclusion of the Chinese*.[13] He interprets the Burlingame-Seward Treaty as an official gesture to legitimize the trafficking of Chinese laborers to North America so that they would embark on the daunting task of clearing land and building the transcontinental railroad for the emergence and expansion of the new US empire. Extending the basic Marxist model of extracting surplus value in capitalist exploitation, he reads the process of recruiting Chinese labor, often through both coaxing and capturing, as a strategy to make up for America's labor shortage and maximize surplus value in the development of the American West. In his view Chinese laborers in the United States were a mixture of free and indentured. He also critiques the exclusion of the Chinese as the capitalist strategy of scapegoating and replacing class struggle with racial conflict. Based mostly on Mary Roberts Coolidge's *Chinese Immigration* and Hubert Howe Bancroft's *History of California*,[14] Ding's work does not provide any detail on the everyday life practice of the railroad workers but attempts to develop the interpretive framework of labor shortage and class struggle to contextualize their experience.[15]

In 1952 another major history text, *A History of US Aggression against China*,[16] was released. With training and working experience in the United States and research conducted at both US and Chinese national archives,[17] Qing Ruji offers what one Chinese American historian describes as "a leading Sino-American diplomatic history in the Chinese language."[18] He devotes a whole section to the Chinese laborers in the American West and refers specifically to the Chinese railroad workers and their contribution under the sensational title "Criminal Exploitation of Several Hundred Thousand Chinese Workers in Their Slavery Working Condition." The transcontinental railroad, according to Qing Ruji, served as the prelude to the opening and development of the American West and became a major means of transportation for the products exported to China from the East Coast. The Burlingame-Seward Treaty was designed specifically to bring in Chinese labor to finish the construction of the railroad. He focuses on the fact that the Central Pacific Railroad (CPRR) could not find enough white laborers and had to turn to Chinese labor, and he also notes that Leland Stanford himself acknowledged the indispensable contribution of the Chinese workers to the railroad's completion. Even though these Chinese workers created tremendous surplus value for the capitalists and contributed disproportionately to the revenues of the state of California, Qing Ruji laments, they were harshly treated and unfairly targeted, just like their compatriots who worked in mining and agriculture after the completion of the railroad.[19]

Zhu Shijia's *Historical Materials Concerning US Persecution of Chinese Laborers*,[20] which was published in 1958, quickly became recognized by Chinese and Chinese American historians as one of the monumental works on Chinese immigration to the United States during that period.[21] Zhu structures the book around four themes:[22] "US Criminal Acts of Kidnapping and Defrauding Chinese Laborers," "US Crime of Persecuting Chinese Laborers," "The Attitude of the Qing Government toward US Persecution of Chinese Laborers," and "The Chinese People's Efforts to Boycott US Products." What has direct bearing on the railroad workers is the material in the first two sections, which had been collected from the US National Archives and the Library of Congress and also from the Qing dynasty's Zhongli Yamen Archives in Beijing. In the first part, Zhu suggests that the US government had been aware of the activities of the kidnapping and coaxing of Chinese laborers to go to the Americas, railroad workers included. He titles one section "The Crime of American Consul in Amoy [which is now Xiamen] Charles W. Le Gendre in Coaxing Chinese Laborers to Go Overseas" and another section "The Crime of American Companies in Coaxing Chinese Laborers to Go Overseas"; the latter section documents the involvement of US merchants in the shipping business as well as diplomats, such as the American consul in Canton (Guangzhou), Charles P. Lincoln.

To highlight his discovery, Zhu incorporates the correspondence between John E. Ward (the US ambassador to China under President James Buchanan) and Secretary of State Lewis Cass in 1860, in which the US ambassador explains in graphic detail how a Chinese man had been tortured repeatedly by his captors to get him to pronounce that he would be willing to emigrate to the United States and board a US ship as a free laborer rather than as a coerced coolie.[23] In focusing on such details in the exchanges among US officials, Zhu concludes that there was no fundamental difference between Portuguese/Spanish and British/American ways of recruiting Chinese labor, even though the latter officially declared that their vessels would not be allowed to engage in the coolie trade. He also maintains that the US government had been well informed of the nature and practice of "free emigration" specified in the Burlingame-Seward Treaty. Similarly, in his introduction to the second part, Zhu discusses how the completion of the railroad and the Long Depression in the late nineteenth century led to the anti-Chinese exclusion laws. He mentions Denis Kearney, the California labor leader, as a crucial player in the anti-Chinese farce and as a speculative loser serving the interests of the US capitalist class, who instigated and organized the anti-Chinese movement. These activities would finally lead to the laws of Chinese exclusion in the western states. To Zhu, these were not the prime examples of government-sanctioned racism but instances of how the US capitalist class had sought to replace class conflict with racial conflict.

If Chinese historiography in the early 1950s on the railroad workers reflected a nation-building effort by criticizing US foreign policies and military intervention in East Asia and by presenting China as a victim of US colonialism and imperialism, then Ah Ying's work, *A Literary Anthology on Resistance to the US Exclusion of Chinese Laborers* marked a subtle paradigm shift that started the reconsideration of Chinese laborers, railroad workers included, in light of Third World anti-colonialist and anti-imperialist movements on a global scale.[24] This volume was part of his book series Literary Anthologies of Modern China's Resistance to Foreign Aggressions, which focuses on the two Opium Wars with Britain, the Sino-French War, the First Sino-Japanese War in 1894, and the Boxer Rebellion, as well as the Chinese exclusion movement in the United States. Because Chinese historians could not find any detail or description of the actual functioning of the transpacific coolie trade, they often resorted to literature and quoted specifically from A Ying's volume, which includes in full the novel *Bitter Society*,[25] based on the oral history of a few surviving laborers as explained in the novel's preface.

A Ying worked on the volume in Shanghai during the savage bombing and invasion of the Japanese Imperial Army in 1937 and expanded it at the Sun Yat-sen Library of Guangdong Province in Guangzhou in the late 1950s. He collected an array of poems, plays, novels, and travel writing that represent the conditions and experiences of Chinese workers coming to the United States and the Americas, including that of the railroad workers. Following the consensus of the Chinese historians in the early 1950s, A Ying dated the first officially recorded arrival of the Chinese workers in North America back to 1847 and framed their experiences in terms of the shortage of labor in California and the western states, with allusion to the construction of the transcontinental railroad. Inspired by the Bandung Conference in 1955, he underscored the connection between the Chinese and other people of color in the Third World and articulated the Chinese experience in the United States as an interaction between the global movement of Western capital and Third World labor. Specifically, A Ying located the connection between the Chinese coolie trafficking and the African slave trade and called attention to similarly brutal treatment of these laborers in the recruitment/capture process and the Middle Passage. In that sense, he categorized all Chinese laborers to the United States and the Americas, railroad workers in North America included, as coerced labor, without exception or differentiation.

In the introduction to *A Literary Anthology*, A Ying quotes sections from chapter 29 of the novel *Bitter Society*, which graphically describes the experiences of the workers, who were unable to move their legs upon arrival after months in chains and captivity and had been severely brutalized by the impatient sailors and the ship's captain. The details include how the captain and sailors kicked bodies on the dark and humid bottom deck of the ship but found more than eighty dead bodies mixed with dried blood, urine, and a repugnant smell. A Ying authenticates this scene as an accurate representation of the middle passage of the Chinese laborers coming to the Americas, even though he acknowledges that the latter part of the novel focuses on the experiences of Chinese laborers in Peru.[26]

Because of the connection he makes between Africans and Chinese as victims of Western capitalist exploitation and expansion, A Ying questions Liang Qichao's work *Travel Writing on the New Continent* (1904) for Liang's condescending attitude toward other people of color, and he construes the author's failure to understand the nature of Chinese exclusion in racial terms as a symptom of a national inferiority complex in China's encounter with the Western powers.[27] As a gesture to remedy these problems, A Ying includes in the volume several chapters from Lin Shu's translation of Harriet Beecher Stowe's *Uncle Tom's Cabin* and underscores the similarities between the transatlantic African slave trade and the transpacific Chinese coolie trade in the nineteenth century.[28]

A Ying devotes a full page in the volume to the experience of the Chinese railroad workers and emphasizes the harsh conditions under which they lived and worked, enduring the severe winter snows of the Sierra Nevada that could be up to forty feet (twelve meters) deep, and battling summer heat as high as 120 degrees Fahrenheit (49 degrees Celsius) in the Nevada desert.[29] He echoes the sentiment of the Chinese historians of the early 1950s that these workers were dismissed as soon as the railroad was completed, without being given the chance to work for the CPRR as members of operations staff or maintenance personnel.[30]

The Reform and Open-Door Period: A Revived Interest in Western Learning, 1978–2000

If the first turning point in Chinese historiography in the 1950s was to embrace Marxism in its Soviet style, then the second one in the 1980s was an ironic reversal of that trend and an intense passion for new Western theories and methodologies. This enthusiasm came mostly from the younger generations of Chinese scholars, who had been deprived of the higher education opportunity during the Cultural Revolution and who would develop what cultural historians today call "a culture fever" of the 1980s, a passion for Western learning in theory and methodology.[31]

What captured the zeitgeist of the period was the production of the galvanizing television documentary series *River Elegy*.[32] The series, which premiered in 1988, questioned the stagnation of Chinese civilization, on the one hand, and embraced Western civilization wholeheartedly, on the other hand, with an implicit allusion to Arnold Toynbee's theory and practice in understanding world civilizations.[33] One historian calls the *River Elegy* series "a barometer of the intellectual climate during the culture fever movement."[34] What the "culture fever movement" entailed was, first, translation of masterpieces in Western historiography and philosophy, and, second, promotion of new theories and methods in Chinese academic training. As the younger generation of scholars themselves lacked proper training in Western history and philosophy, the older generation of historians and scholars suddenly became academically active again, particularly those who had gone through formal training in the United States and Western European countries in history and philosophy.

Zhang Zhilian, a historian trained in France and teaching at Peking University, introduced the Annales school to the Chinese academic community and brought its leading practitioners, such as Fernand Braudel, to China for lectures and seminars, exposing Chinese historians to concepts such as *longue durée*.[35] Ding Zemin, author of *A History of US Exclusion of the Chinese* (1952), called attention to Frederick Jackson Turner's "frontier thesis" and studied its impact on US foreign policy in the twentieth century, particularly in relation to the US expansion in the Asia Pacific and Latin America.[36] The most important venue for the movement was the publication of many book series, including both the translation of Western masterpieces in historiography and philosophy and monographs written by Chinese scholars on cultural issues. The best-known book series were Walking toward the World[37] and Walking toward the Future,[38] which prioritized the history of Chinese encounters with the West and the prospect of embracing the US-centered global powers. However, two lesser-known book series, Collections of Historical Documents on Chinese Workers Going Overseas[39] and History of Overseas Chinese around the Globe,[40] were the main ones that would have a direct bearing on research related to the Chinese railroad workers in North America.

The first book series, Collections of Historical Documents on Chinese Workers Going Overseas, is by far the most comprehensive and authoritative collection of historical documents on Chinese workers living and working overseas. The series was produced under the supervision of Chen Han Sheng, a prominent historian at Peking University, who had been trained in the United States and Germany. The book series contains a total of ten volumes and several subvolumes, and features the railroad workers in its seventh volume, *Chinese Workers in the US and Canada,* which was released in 1984. Taking a Marxist approach, in the general introduction Chen interprets the experiences of Chinese laborers in North America as examples of the global labor movement in the history of Western capitalist expansion. He also questions US historiography in differentiating between the Portuguese/Spanish and the British/US modes of recruiting Chinese workers as indentured labor versus free labor. He divides Chinese labor into four categories and explores the meaning of "free labor" promoted by the US government. He argues that the Burlingame-Seward Treaty was specifically geared toward meeting the needs of the CPRR's labor shortage, but the company dismissed the workers as soon as the railroad was completed, and the US government never deescalated the anti-Chinese movement.[41] Chen also invokes the transatlantic slave trade as a reference framework and describes the ships transporting the Chinese laborers to the Americas as "floating hell on the sea," which accounted for 15.2 percent of the deaths among laborers heading for Cuba and 30 percent of all deaths of laborers going to Peru. He quotes a British newspaper article's comment that the fate of these indentured laborers was worse than that of African slaves because the slave owners in the Americas would at least treat slaves as their own private "properties."[42] Above all, Chen construes the Chinese laborers in North America, railroad workers and miners particularly, as pioneers of the Chinese working class and represents their experiences as the first encounter of the Chinese people with the institutions and practices of Western industrial capitalism.[43]

In their selection of historical material for the seventh volume, subtitled *Chinese Laborers in the US and Canada,*[44] its executive editors, Lu Wendi, Peng Jiali, and Chen Zexian, privileged the work of US historians and devoted substantial space to the Chinese railroad workers in North America. Their work contextualizes the socioeconomic background in southern China from which Chinese laborers emigrated for North America, and the changing receptions of Chinese laborers in California. They translate a chapter from George F. Seward's book *Chinese Immigration in Its Social and Economic Aspects,*[45] and comment on the author's favorable assessment of the role of Chinese laborers in the development of the western states, including their work in constructing the transcontinental and local rail lines. They also translate chapters from Gunther Barth's *Bitter Strength: A History of the Chinese in the United States, 1850–1870,*[46] which analyze the social and historical background of the railroad workers in Guangdong Province and their work in railroad building and plantation agriculture in the American South after the completion of the Central Pacific line.

The editors treat the transcontinental railroad as the most tangible accomplishment of the Chinese laborers in North America and thus include texts that detail the experiences of the Chinese railroad workers. They translate several chapters from Mary Roberts Coolidge's *Chinese Immigration*,[47] focusing on her argument that the Chinese laborers were not coolies and that the introduction of the railroad workers intensified the misunderstanding of Chinese workers as indentured laborers. They also translated Alexander Saxton's well-known essay "The Army of Canton in the High Sierra," in *Pacific Historical Review*,[48] which incorporates not only details of the life of these workers but also assessments of their accomplishments from historical figures. The article describes E. B. Crocker, legal counsel to the CPRR and former justice of California, who offered a toast to "the greatest monument of human labor" on the day of the celebration ceremony in Sacramento and made this famous statement: "I wish to call to your minds that the early completion of this railroad we have built has been in large measure due to that poor, despised class of laborers called the Chinese—to the fidelity and industry they have shown."[49]

The editors also selected another essay of Chan Koonchung's, "A Brief Bloody History of Overseas Chinese in America," from the Hong Kong magazine *Ming Pao Monthly*,[50] which dramatizes the ceremony at Promontory Summit, Utah, fictionalizing the occasion when Leland Stanford, the president of the CPRR, could not find a proper tie to drive in the golden spike but was saved by the appearance of four Chinese workers carrying a tie to complete the ceremony.

Since the publication of these volumes, all of these translated book chapters and articles from US historians and officials, Chinese language materials produced in Hong Kong and overseas, and official documents collected from China's First Historical Archives in Beijing and National Library of China in Beijing have now become the standard primary sources for the researchers in China working on the Chinese railroad workers in North America. Every newspaper and magazine article on the subject in China without exception incorporates the dramatic moment of the golden spike ceremony in 1869 and the one-sentence statement from E. B. Crocker, even though these journalists, historians, and scholars often mistake him for his brother, Charles Crocker, one of the Big Four of the CPRR.[51]

The second book series was History of Overseas Chinese around the Globe, edited by Zhu Jieqin, former chair of the history department and director of the Institute of Overseas Chinese Studies at Jinan University in Guangzhou. In his general introduction to the book series, he cautions his colleagues and fellow historians in overseas Chinese studies to beware of Western misrepresentation of the Chinese and to avoid the pitfall of Sinocentrism. The volume *A History of Overseas Chinese in the United States,*[52] coauthored by Yang Guobiao, Liu Hanbiao, and Yang Anyao, is an attempt to synthesize all the available sources in US historiography and give a comprehensive introduction to the Chinese railroad workers in North America. Their work notes historical background for the construction of the transcontinental railroad, including the effort to connect the East and West Coasts, the congressional approval process, and the labor shortage that the Central Pacific faced when it came to the railroad construction. There is a detailed section on the hardships and accomplishments of the Chinese railroad workers, which covers Cape Horn, the Summit Tunnel, and the extreme weather conditions in the Sierra Nevada.

In 1990 another major work, *A History of Overseas Chinese and Chinese Americans in the Americas,* was published by the East Press.[53] As its editors, Li Chunhui and Yang Shengmao, synthesize the available sources on overseas Chinese and prioritize the experiences of Chinese Americans in North America, they devote much space to the railroad workers to underscore the sacrifices they made. They argue that if the death toll for the Irish workers was one for every mile, then a larger number should logically and definitely apply to the Chinese railroad workers, quoting a report from the *Sacramento Reporter* on the remains of 1,200 Chinese laborers and estimating the death toll at more than 10 percent.[54] The historians also call attention to the competition between the Chinese and Irish railroad workers, with the latter accepting the new tracklaying record set by the Chinese. Finally, they discuss how the Chinese workers continued to work on other lines, such as the Northern Pacific Railway and the Southern Pacific Railroad, quoting Oswald Garrison Villard's praise of the Chinese railroad workers in his essay "Justice for the Chinese," published in 1943, as a summary of their contribution to US development and prosperity.[55]

During this period there were also several journal articles that explored Chinese labor, and specifically railroad workers on the West Coast. Zhu Jieqin, editor in chief of the book series History of Overseas Chinese around the Globe, published the essay "The Role and Predicament of Chinese Laborers in the Late

Nineteenth-Century US Development,"[56] which foregrounds the contribution of Chinese labor to the development of the American West. Though still resorting to the Marxist model of class struggle, Zhu draws extensively from US historiography and official documents in support of the contribution of Chinese labor to the United States. He quotes the communication and exchange on the Chinese labor issue between Senator Oliver P. Morton and Ambassador Frederick F. Low and also lists other strong witnesses, such as the adviser and president of the Tide Land Reclamation Company, Solomon Heydenfeldt, and George D. Roberts. Zhu explores in depth the acts of racism perpetrated against the Chinese laborers, dividing the US working class into progressives and reactionaries. While the former were more aware of capitalist exploitation than racial differences, the latter blamed racial minorities for their class oppression. He lists Denis Kearney and his Workingmen's Party and Terence Vincent Powderly and his leadership in the Knights of Labor as both speculators and opportunists who discriminated against and assaulted the Chinese laborers as scapegoats for US economic crises and labor conflict. Zhu concludes that the Chinese laborers played an indispensable role in US economic prosperity but never received fair treatment or proper recognition during their lifetimes.

In 1990 Ding Zemin, after introducing Turner's "frontier thesis" to Chinese historians, wrote the first major essay about the Chinese railroad workers in North America, "Construction of the American Central Pacific Railroad and the Tremendous Contribution of Chinese Workers."[57] Beginning with the vision and effort of Theodore Judah, the central figure in the design of the first transcontinental railroad, Ding reiterates some basic facts concerning the construction of the line. He argues that the building of the transcontinental railroad, which combined US technology and Chinese and Irish labor, not only reinforced the unification of the young nation-state politically and geographically but also connected the East and West Coasts economically and culturally, which would contribute significantly to the rise of the United States as a global power at the turn of the twentieth century.

The Rise of China Period: Global Power Shifts and United States–China Relations, 2000–2015

With China's continuing economic expansion, the Chinese academic world was optimistic about China's place in the world. Historians and social scientists generated what critics call "the discourse of the rise and fall of the great powers,"[58] which culminated in another television documentary series, *The Rise of the Great Powers*,[59] produced and released by China Central Television network in Beijing in November 2006. Following a similar format and pathos of *River Elegy* in 1988, the new television series created another fever among Chinese intelligentsia and the general public, who sought to understand this new moment of economic prosperity and cultural confidence in light of China's own historical mission and in reference to the history of Western civilization. Unlike *River Elegy*, which revealed a sense of the Chinese intelligentsia's inferiority complex in their recent encounter with the technologically advanced and economically developed Western societies and cultures, the new television series demonstrated a sense of eagerness and confidence to meet the West on an equal footing. The producers not only selected the nine great historical world powers—Portugal, Spain, the Netherlands, Britain, France, Germany, Japan, Russia/the Soviet Union, and the United States—but also interviewed leading political scientists and historians, such as Joseph Nye and Paul Kennedy, and politicians, such as former French president Valéry Giscard d'Estaing and former US national security advisor Zbigniew Brzezinski.

With new attention to the US experience, there has been growing interest in rereading the contribution of the Chinese railroad workers to the United States. If the earlier focus was on class exploitation and the economic contribution of the railroad workers in relation to the development and prosperity of California and the American West generally, the focus shifted to how the railroad contributed to the emergence of the United States as a global power spanning the continent from the Atlantic to the Pacific. It is in this sense that I want to introduce the work of Huang Annian, who not only authored important work in American history and American studies in the late 1990s, such as *The Rise of the United States*[60] and *The Socioeconomic History of the United States*[61] but also developed a special interest in the Chinese railroad workers by writing a series of articles and publishing a number of books on the subject.

In 1999 Huang published his groundbreaking essay, "The Completion of the Central Pacific Railroad and the Contribution of Chinese Workers in the United States."[62] Unlike the previous work in Chinese historiography on the railroad workers, which focused on the issues of social class and racial discrimination, Huang inserts the story into the grand narrative of the rise of the United States as a global power and identifies the construction of the transcontinental railroad as a key moment in the process of US empire building. By retelling the narrative of the Chinese railroad workers in this new framework, he gives higher value to the official documents of the US government from national archives and substantiates his argument by quoting from US congressional reports, testimonies, and investigations, and by using statements, speeches, and the correspondence of federal, state, and local officials. He makes claims based on his rereading of these documents. First, whether for or against Chinese labor, US politicians and historians on both sides of the political spectrum recognized that the transcontinental railroad would not have been completed on time had it not been for Chinese laborers. Second, both sides also recognized that these Chinese workers had constructed the most difficult sections of the railroad and in the process sacrificed tremendously for its completion. Third, both sides equally acknowledged that these workers' hard work and low compensation had paradoxically been the source of both their praise and exclusion. Fourth, both sides understood that the governments and the railroad companies inadequately compensated the Chinese laborers in comparison with the white laborers. He emphasizes the Chinese laborers' indispensable contribution to the emergence and maintenance of US economic power, and critiques the injustice of US immigration policy.

In a shorter essay, "The Construction of the Central Pacific Railroad by Chinese Workers and the Rise of the United States,"[63] published in 2007, Huang reiterates the connection between the completion of the railroad and the rise of the United States as an economic empire and engages the prevailing discourse in China on the rise and fall of the great powers. In another short essay, "In Search of the Historical Footprints of the Chinese Workers Building the Central Pacific Railroad,"[64] in 2015, Huang reprises his early points but suggests that the railroad workers from Guangdong Province were members of the first generation of what the Chinese today call "migrant workers," implicitly comparing and contrasting the similarities and differences between the two groups in terms of unfair treatment and economic exploitation across time and space.

In 2010 Huang published another book, *Spikes, No Longer Silent: To the Chinese Workers Constructing the North American Railroads*,[65] as a supplement to his previous pictorial history book; the book republished the previous book's general and section introductions, his published journal articles, blog posts reflective of his random thoughts, and even a few book reviews of his pictorial book. Sharing the story of how he collected photos from archives and museums without support from either Chinese government agencies or private foundations, Huang boasts of single-handedly undertaking the daunting task of communicating with different US agencies and organizations, and selecting thousands of photos and book illustrations for their authenticity for the pictorial book. To further his efforts, he even created an account on China's ScienceNet.cn and periodically updates news on his new projects. As of September 18, 2017, Huang's 18,521 blog posts had been visited by almost 41.95 million Chinese readers and netizens from around the globe.[66]

In 2015 Huang and Li Ju, an amateur photographer in China, collaborated on another pictorial book, *The Footprints of the Silent Spikes—In Memory of the Chinese Workers Who Constructed the American Railroads.*[67] The book contains some six hundred photos, which were taken during Li's four trips tracing the routes of the Chinese railroad workers, particularly one following photographer William Henry Jackson's photographic journey in the 1860s, and it contains some photos that were paired with Alfred Hart's photos from the 1860s. The pictorial book offers another version of this history and gives the growing number of Chinese tourists something to think about when they tour North America. Divided into four parts, "Reasons for the Railroad Construction," "Pioneers in the Railroad Construction," "In Search of the Footprints of the Railroad Workers," and "In Memory of the Spike," this book blurs the boundaries between traditional history and popular culture, professional history and popular history.

Even though a few master's theses related to the construction of the American transcontinental railroad have been written since the 1980s,[68] the only book-length study of the Chinese railroad workers in North America remains Sheng Jianhong's work *The Chinese Workers in the Construction of the United States' Central Pacific Railroad,*[69] which was based on her dissertation and research trips to the United States. Like the recent Chinese scholarship and historiography on the railroad workers generally, Sheng describes the purpose of her project as strengthening the friendship between the Chinese and American peoples, and she represents the railroad construction as an instance of Chinese contribution to US economic prosperity. This book emphasizes the political and economic necessity to construct a transcontinental railroad, the socioeconomic background of the Chinese laborers in Guangdong Province, the hardships and sacrifices involved in constructing the railroad, Chinese workers' contributions to the US economy, and the whereabouts of the workers after the completion of the railroad and during the exclusion era. Unlike older generations of Chinese historians, whose work mostly depended on US historiography and scholarship, Sheng not only visited the historical sites in person but also interviewed many descendants of the railroad workers in the United States and developed questionnaires to gather information. In that sense, the uniqueness of her work lies in her interest in social science methodology and her employment of oral history practice.

———

The narrative of the Chinese railroad workers has been widely circulating in China and overseas Chinese communities. When President Hu Jintao visited the United States in 2011, he mentioned specifically the Chinese railroad workers' contribution to US prosperity and development.[70] Similarly, in his state visit to the United States in 2015, President Xi Jinping delivered a speech in Seattle and invoked the railroad workers as a trope for collaboration and friendship between China and the United States. He stated, "We must foster friendly sentiments among our peoples. People-to-people relations underpin state-to-state relations. Though geographically far apart, our peoples boast a long history of friendly exchanges.... Some 150 years ago, tens of thousands of Chinese workers joined their American counterparts in building the transcontinental Pacific Railway."[71] At the moment when China wanted to cultivate a new type of relationship between the two global powers, the Chinese president implicitly expressed the hope of avoiding the Western model of the zero-sum game and conveyed the wish for a new model of coexistence and coprosperity. In this light, the construction of the Central Pacific Railroad in the nineteenth century has achieved new significance in United States–China relations.

CHAPTER 16

History Lessons

Remembering Chinese Railroad Workers in Dragon's Gate *and* Donald Duk

PIN-CHIA FENG

To respond to the persisting racialized practice of Asian *alien*ation, and to make present the contributions of nineteenth-century Chinese railroad workers in the United States, Chinese American writers have long engaged in various writing projects to right this wrong. "The Grandfather of the Sierra Nevada Mountains" section of Maxine Hong Kingston's *China Men* presents an imagined biography that retraces the footsteps of Ah Goong, Kingston's grandfather, in the United States as a railroad laborer.[1] Shawn Wong, in his autobiographical novel *Homebase*, imagines how, in 1866, the protagonist's great-grandfather struggled with, and survived, loneliness and harsh natural elements while working on the railroad in Nevada.[2] The reference to a mysterious night train carrying the spirits of all the Chinamen who died on the railroad is a nod to what may be an apocryphal legend of the Iron Moonhunter that appears in Frank Chin's play *The Chickencoop Chinaman* and Kathleen Chang's illustrated bilingual children's book *The Iron Moonhunter*.[3] Together, the imagined stories of the great-grandfather and the Iron Moonhunter become part of the "legends with spirit" that Wong created in the process of his mythmaking.[4] In *The Dance and the Railroad,* David Henry Hwang offers a theater piece in which he dramatizes, via the dialogues of two characters, the hardships and dreams of Chinese railroaders against the background of the strike in June 1867.[5]

While most of these literary representations attempt to reconstruct the lives of Chinese railroad workers from an adult's perspective, we must not forget that many of the workers were likely still in their teens when they joined the construction workforce. This chapter focuses on the plots of two Chinese American novels featuring teenage characters: Laurence Yep's *Dragon's Gate* (1993) and Frank Chin's *Donald Duk* (1991).[6] In *Dragon's Gate*, Yep realistically portrays, through the first-person narrative voice of the adolescent Otter, the hardships and heroism of Chinese railroad workers who blast their way through the mountains of the frozen Sierra Nevada. In the process of digging railroad tunnels, Otter grows from a spoiled teenager into a competent railroad worker with evolutionary vision. While resisting the imposition of racial alienation, at the same time he is able to overcome his sense of inferiority as a "stranger," or a *hakka*, and an adopted orphan.

Frank Chin, on the other hand, mixes realism with fantasy by allowing his twelve-year-old protagonist, the eponymous Donald Duk, to travel back in time to revisit the famous record-making Ten Miles Day, April 28, 1869, through a series of dream sequences. The marvelous achievement of the Chinese railroad workers and their absence in official history prompt the white-identified Donald to finally recognize and embrace his neglected Chinese heritage. Narrating stories of formation about different generations of Chinese America and in different narrative modes—realistic for *Dragon's Gate* and fantastic for *Donald Duk*—these two novels clearly present a common desire to make up for the absence of the Chinese railroad labor force in the American national imagination.

In addition to sharing a desire for recovering Chinese American history, these two novels have some similar thematic features. Both Otter and Donald identify with adult workers as their role models—Otter's Uncle Foxfire and Donald's foreman, Kwan—which follows the traditional pedagogical and formative pattern of the *Bildung*.[7] At the same time, the young protagonists are forced to witness the setbacks and frustrations of their models before gaining any insight into the racialized nature of American society. Moreover, both novels create interracial homosocial bonding for their Chinese American protagonists, with the white counterparts functioning as supporters and sympathizers for the Chinese American protagonists, an emplotment that significantly reverses the convention of Asian sidekicks for the Caucasian heroes, thereby offering a renewed vision of interracial cooperation and communication.[8]

Although *Dragon's Gate* and *Donald Duk* are often classified as young adult literature, the vivid portrayals of adolescent insecurity resonate for readers of all races and ages. Most important, the growing pains of the protagonists effectively shed light on the treacherous routes of constructing Chinese American subjectivity, specifically the difficult task of achieving manhood in a culture permeated with racial violence and exclusionist practices.

The Education of a "Stranger" in Dragon's Gate

The protagonist of *Dragon's Gate,* Otter, speaks about his journey to America, Gold Mountain, as having "been 'educational'—to say the least."[9] What Otter learns from this journey to the West, in addition to the experience of working on the railroad, are the meanings of being a stranger, or guest, both in China and in the United States.

Dragon's Gate is the third volume of Laurence Yep's *Golden Mountain Chronicles,* a series of ten novels about a Chinese American family, the Youngs from Three Willows Village in Guangdong Province, and their stories on both sides of the Pacific between 1835 and 2011.[10] The novel begins in June 1865 with the fourteen-year-old Otter leading a privileged life at Three Willows because members of his family have "gone overseas to *America* to become guests of the Land of the Gold Mountain."[11] His pampered life is nevertheless overshadowed by the tragic memory of losing his birth mother to interethnic conflicts and his own identity as a "stranger," which means he belongs to an ethnic minority group of Han people who are regarded as "guests," even in China.[12] Otter's adopted family, the Youngs, "have been rebels and trouble-makers for seven generations" and have dedicated themselves to overthrowing the Manchu rulers.[13] When his adoptive father and Uncle Foxfire return temporarily to the village and talk about American modern wonders, such as the "fire wagon," the railroad, and democratic freedom, Otter is eager to leave to contribute to "the Great Work" of saving China from its ruinous state.[14] Eventually Otter's dream of joining his father and uncle in the Gold Mountain comes true, yet at a price beyond his wildest imagining.

By becoming a *jinshan ke*, or Gold Mountain guest, Otter finds himself suffering from multiple levels of estrangement since in addition to his Hakka identity and physical features—he is of exceptional height among his fellow teenage workers[15]—he is a stranger/guest in a new country, where he faces a demanding physical environment and a racialized social hierarchy that are unaccommodating and even downright hostile. By representing the effect of the estrangement experienced by his young protagonist, Yep offers an analysis of one of the "racial feelings," in Jeffrey Santa Ana's term, of Asian Americans.[16]

Otter's feeling of alienation is strongest in the American West, where he is exploited by ruthless capitalist institutions and forced to do hard labor. Whereas in China having Gold Mountain guests in the family entitles Otter to enjoy social and economic privileges, he discovers the harsh reality confronting a "guest" on the other shore of the Pacific. As a member of a Chinese railroad crew, he is required to undertake dangerous tasks and suffers violent suppression. His worship of Uncle Foxfire as a legendary figure comes to an abrupt end when he witnesses how Foxfire submits to unfair demands from Strobridge, the chief engineer, and Kilroy, the overseer. Foxfire tries to explain the different class hierarchies and the imminent danger of resistance to his disappointed nephew: "In the Middle Kingdom, you and I were on the top of the heap, but here we're on the bottom. Question the bosses or talk back, and they'll kill you in a dozen different ways."[17] In China Foxfire had tried to preach to his nephew in pidgin English his own understanding of American exceptionalism: "Everybody there, they free. Everybody, they equal."[18] Otter is shocked by the sharp contrast between his uncle's rosy picture and the racist reality in America. Thus, when Otter learns that he is stuck in the railroad camp, he angrily accuses Foxfire of being "a humbug" who has tricked him into believing in a phantom vision of American democracy.[19]

What Otter fails to understand is that once Foxfire and his brother-in-law, Otter's father, signed up for the railroad work, they lost their autonomy as free laborers. While as miners they could come and go at will, the construction workers are not allowed to leave the railroad site even though they are extremely dissatisfied with the dangerous nature of their work and the unreasonable working hours and wages. What Foxfire and his fellow workers experience, in fact, exemplifies the changing status of *jinshan ke* in the second half of the nineteenth century, as Chinese immigrants were transformed "from entrepreneurs to wage earners, from independent prospectors with their own claims to workers dependent on capitalists for their livelihood. Increasingly, their employers were white."[20] They are absorbed by an early model of corporate capitalism that lies behind the enterprise of railroad construction, becoming its racialized labor force, and in the process gradually lose their individual personhood.

When the uncle and nephew risk their lives in vain to save the work camp from being buried by snow, Foxfire tries to explain to his young companion how "guesting" has given him "a double set of eyes."[21] "You can never go home now," he tells Otter. "When you go to Three Willows, you'll see things with

[W]estern eyes."[22] Yet when Foxfire is in America, he sees things with Chinese eyes. Otter comes to understand that his uncle has been changed by the Gold Mountain, becoming "a halfling,"[23] and begins to "realize all the loneliness that lay behind the legend."[24] When Foxfire sacrifices his life to save Otter, the young man finally learns to once again appreciate his uncle's futurist vision and his patriotic investment in the Great Work.

In the novel Yep provides the reader with all kinds of embodied experiences suffered by the Chinese workers in railroad construction sites. Otter's father is blinded in a tunnel accident, and the teenage worker himself is whipped by Kilroy for wanting to leave. Otter bitterly reflects on his own lesson in enslavement after the violent punishment: "What are the white demons going to teach us?...How to make a wasteland? How to turn people into slaves?"[25] Through Otter's lacerated body, Yep attempts to present "corporeal" evidence of the violence against the Chinese workers.[26] Otter is also physically marked with a scar on his cheek when a new type of explosive, nitroglycerine, is used.

One of the cruelest ironies in the novel is the "double tragedy" of his teammate Doggy.[27] After Otter manages to convince members of his team to contribute their hard-earned money to replace Doggy's stolen moon guitar so that they can enjoy his music, a music that promises to assuage their nostalgic longing for home, Doggy loses two fingers to frostbite and can never play again. Otter's excitement over how the crew members have cooperated for the first time because of their love for Doggy's music turns to a bitter awareness of their physical and spiritual entrapment in the hellish Sierra: "This mountain...kills singing. It kills laughing. It kills everything. Every day we're here, we die a little."[28]

Trapped in the mountain with a crew of outcasts, Otter chooses to cultivate a forbidden friendship with Kilroy's son, Sean—"It didn't matter where we were from, or who we had been. On the mountain, he and I were in a secret conspiracy against the world. It didn't matter what our fathers thought."[29] The way in which Yep portrays the interracial bonding between the two boys is almost utopian: "On the mountain, we had founded our own country with just two citizens; and it didn't matter what the [W]esterners or T'ang [Chinese] people thought."[30] Sean is the one white person who expresses indignation over the exclusion of the Chinese workers from the golden spike ceremony. This unlikely interracial friendship is important to Otter in that it provides him with a temporary reprieve from the hellish construction work; it also offers a hopeful vision of the ability of people of different races to go beyond xenophobic distrust and antagonism. Moreover, Sean is the one who supplies Otter with information about the difference between the wages and working hours for the Chinese workers and those for the Caucasian workers, which eventually leads to the 1867 strike and the completion of Otter's education.

The title of the novel, *Dragon's Gate*, alludes to a Chinese legend "that if a fish can make the long, difficult swim upstream and through the gate, it will change into a dragon."[31] In the novel Otter is undergoing a metaphorical transformation from "a young country gentleman" in a Chinese village to a bona fide Gold Mountain guest;[32] the Snow Tiger mountain in the Sierra is where he has to perform the needed rite of passage. A conversation with Foxfire on how to modernize China helps him realize that he has been made heir to all of his uncle's dreams during the climb to the top of the mountain.[33]

A Pedagogy of the Mind in Donald Duk

In the third dream sequence of *Donald Duk*, King Duk takes Donald to see an herbalist, for he suspects that his son is not well. Donald's "symptom," as King describes it, is his stealing and lying and treating "Chinese like dirt."[34] King exclaims, "I can't believe I have raised a little white racist. He doesn't think Chinatown is America."[35] This "little white racist," unfortunately, has a name pronounced exactly like the Disney animation character Donald Duck, even though he is actually named after his father's Cantonese opera master; he also secretly aspires to become a tap dancer like Fred Astaire.

Born and raised in San Francisco's Chinatown, Donald, for reasons unexplained, is sent to a private school "where the Chinese are comfortable hating Chinese."[36] His school education, as represented by the lessons from his history teacher, Mr. Meanwright, imposes on this prepubescent boy stereotypical images of Chinese Americans as being "made passive and nonassertive by centuries of Confucian thought and Zen mysticism,"[37] or, as translated by Donald into a colloquial lingo for his white friend, Arnold, "Chinese are artsy, cutesy and chickendick."[38] Obviously, Donald is one of the victims of internal colonization who have introjected mainstream (white) values and learned to despise their own ethnic cultures.

As the scholar Wenying Xu observes, Donald's school education embodies what Frantz Fanon labeled "cultural estrangement," and the boy's character "reveals what Fanon names 'the colonized personality.'"[39] To be extracted from racist acculturation and brainwashing, Donald needs to undergo a pedagogy of the mind. The key to the project of "decolonizing of the mind" in the novel is the memory of his great-great-grandfather, who worked on the Central Pacific Railroad when he was Donald's age.[40] Hence, Donald's mental decolonization is dependent upon the retrieval of the history of Chinese railroad laborers, and the narrative focus rests on the process through which Donald gets in touch with his ancestral past. Whereas in *Dragon's Gate* Yep chronicles the *Bildung* of Otter among a group of adult workers, Chin peoples his railroad scenes with young Chinese of Donald's age. Chin also links the Chinese workers with the legendary figures from classical Chinese romances—Kwan Kung from the *Romance of the Three Kingdoms* and the 108 outlaws from *The Water Margin*—to create his own mythopoetics.[41]

Unlike Otter, who personally experiences the life of a railroad worker, as a fifth-generation Chinese American of the late twentieth century, Donald can "directly" access the history of his Chinese American ancestor only via the mechanism of dreams. The novel in fact can be read as an extended dream in which the dream world interpenetrates the "real" world, and dreaming leads to recovering repressed memories of the historical past. Thus, the omniscient narrator reports, "Donald Duk dreams he's sleeping at night and wakes up dreaming, and wakes up from that dream into another, and wakes up into the real."[42]

In a sense, Donald's affective responses to his dreams are similar to those of one who is experiencing the return of repressed memories. The dreams enable him to travel in time and to physically experience the suppressed history. Donald initially reacts to these mysterious dreams with fear. We are told that even before his dreams have been recorded in the text he has "bad" dreams about the "old railroad" and "about Chinese he does not understand."[43] Despite his fear of the bad dreams, Donald wills himself into dreaming about his great-great-grandfather, when Uncle Donald Duk reveals a family secret: that his family surname is Lee, not Duk. In the first dream sequence, in which Donald assumes the identity of his great-great-grandfather, "the first Lee of the family in America,"[44] he is fascinated by the scene he witnesses—the challenging work by teenage Chinese workers on the railroad; the food wagons that traveled alongside the Chinese work team; Doong, the kung fu brew peddler, and his twin children—and feels reluctant to wake up, yet at the same time he is released by the return to the mundane reality of Chinatown: "He wants to stay asleep and dream he is a powder boy, taking to prying iron and spiking rail across Nevada, and never wake up. That's why he wakes up fast, and is happy to hear the double-stringed fiddle singing throaty and shrill out in the street, in the real world. Even if that real world is nothing but Chinatown."[45] As in a typical time travel narrative, in his dreams Donald is fully conscious of his own identity as someone from a different temporal space. What is intriguing here is that he is not an intruder but simultaneously Lee, the boy worker on the Central Pacific *and* Donald Duk from San Francisco.[46] This double identity, along with his contradictory feelings about his nightly visits to the past, evidences Donald's split identity and consciousness.

The novel is, in fact, full of doubles and doubled identities. Scholar David L. Eng points out that Chin presents "a vertiginous doubling, deformation, and expansion of the proper name" and "a series of 'body doubles' in the form of female twins."[47] The extravagance of doubleness can be read as a deliberate gesture to create a sense of the carnivalesque that fits the Chinese New Year setting and the comedic mode of the novel. On the dark side, however, the excessive doubling metaphorically embodies Donald's split psyche as he is caught between different cultures and different versions of histories.

The third dream sequence presents Donald with another role model, Kwan, the foreman, whose name apparently alludes to Kwan Kung, a figure from Chinese history who is honored as the god of war and literature.[48] By linking Kwan with Kwan Kung, Chin presents the Chinese foreman as a demigod figure; he also reinscribes King Duk, who is an expert in performing Kwan Kung, as a heroic figure despite his seemingly effeminate profession as a cook. Kwan first appears in Donald's second dream as a powerful and uncompromising masculine character. He openly contradicts Crocker, one of the Big Four of the Central Pacific, by asserting his own autonomy: "I build a railroad, Ah-Mist. Crocker. You do no own nutting me";[49] then he takes away Crocker's horse, fires his six-gun, and jokes about eating Crocker's white horse.[50] Kwan's series of extravagant cowboy moves at once express defiance against the white capitalist authority and show off his masculine prowess. In the third dream sequence, it is also Kwan—not Crocker, the white boss, or Strobridge, the superintendent—who acts as the driving force behind the railroad construction project; he makes speeches and leads the four hundred Chinese workers "moving the railroad forward, eastward" to set a world record for laying track.[51]

Donald is mentally and physically affected by what he witnesses of the tracklaying competition. In contrast to his boast about his mental superiority

and all-Americanness just moments before, Donald feels weak and insignif-
icant among the boys of his own age when he is told to do a lion dance: "He
can't dance. He can't lift rail or drive spike. He feels too small, and it's an odd
feeling, for he sees all the Chinese. Even the biggest look hardly larger or
older than him."[52] When in the fourth dream sequence the work gang has
successfully set the world record of laying down "[t]en miles, twelve hundred
feet" within a ten-hour workday,[53] legendary Chinese heroes suddenly appear
on the horizon, along with the thunder from the Sierra Nevada:

> The thunder does not stop; it is the gallop of 108 horses out of the west, over
> the track. Clouds roll and boil ahead of the galloping horses and riders, clearly
> visible now, over the track. Ahead of the 108, Kwan Kung gallops his horse
> Red Rabbit up to the end of track, twirling his halberd. He reins Red Rabbit
> up, opens his mouth to a thunderclap and gallops on as the thunder of the 108
> horses and riders rolls close.[54]

With the appearance of all the legendary characters from the Chinese heroic
tradition, Chin is orchestrating a belated celebration for the achievement of
the Chinese labor force and incorporating the workers into the grandiose military tradition that Chin and his fellow *Aiiieeeee!* editors propagate. In Chin's
personal mythopoetics, Chinese railroad workers, with Kwan as their representative, are recognized as a part of a heroic continuum that can be traced as
far back as third-century China. The charismatic Kwan guides Donald to place
and reroot himself in Chinese and Chinese American historical discourse.[55]

One should see in these details that Chin has deliberately selected a prepubescent boy protagonist who may be starting to feel interested in heterosexual
relations but who remains much more attached to homosocial bonding. With
their rhyming names, Donald and Arnold, the two boys build a friendship
that crosses racial and class boundaries. We are told that in a mysterious way
Arnold even shares Donald's dreams,[56] although he is never part of the dream
content. In fact, Arnold seems to be more enthusiastic about Chinese American culture and Chinatown than is Donald, and his wealthy parents happily
leave him in Chinatown to experience the two-week-long Chinese New Year
celebration. Their friendship is temporally breached when Donald unleashes
his anger on Arnold for his frustrations over the destruction of the last laurel
crosstie, signed by the Chinese workers.[57] Nevertheless, when Donald objects
to Mr. Meanwright's lecture in which the history teacher again repeats how
Chinese railroad workers were subject to "exploitation and victimization"

because of their "passive philosophy and noncompetitive nature,"[58] Arnold stands by his friend.

Although ironically Donald seems to need white support and sympathy to complete his history lesson, it is even more significant that Chin allows Donald to visualize his diasporic identity as an American of Chinese ancestry by creating a paper plane that has "the face of Walt Disney's Donald Duck on the underside of the cowl and the arms and chest of Lee Kuey, the Black Tornado, on the wings and belly."[59] The hybridized coexistence of the American pop culture icon with the ultramasculine Chinese legendary outlaw on the model plane signals Donald's acceptance of dual identification with both sides of his cultural identity and the completion of his education of decolonizing his mind.

Please Remember

At the end of *Dragon's Gate*, Otter is writing in Chinese with his heel on the ground after the golden spike ceremony. Upon Sean's query, Otter explains that it is a phrase that promises "I won't forget."[60] In a way, Otter is responding to the plea of his crewmate, Shaky. Shaky used to work as a basketman, like Kingston's grandfather, and in the narrative present is a shell-shocked survivor of the demolition operation at Cape Horn. In his only lucid moment in the novel, Shaky describes how fresh-off-the-boat Chinese workers have been singled out to perform the dangerous work. Unlike Ah Goong, who releases his loneliness and anxiety while riding the basket by "fucking the world,"[61] Shaky loses his sanity. At the end of his fleeting moment of clarity, Shaky plaintively pleads, "Remember. Someone please remember."[62]

Shaky's description of how all his crew members lost their lives in their struggles with the granite cliff and the many explosions is enough to raise the specter of historical haunting, just like the dreams that haunt Donald Duk and make him fearful of nightly visits to episodes on the railroad. As Donald confesses, "I dream I'm laying track with them when I sleep, and nobody knows what we did. Nobody, just me. And I don't want to be the only one who knows, and it makes me mad to be the only one who knows, and everything I dream makes me mad at white people and hate them. They lie about us all the time."[63]

Both Yep's realistic and Chin's fantastic reconstructions of the stories of Chinese railroad workers who built the Central Pacific Railroad present a desire to remember. Theirs and other literary representations of Chinese railroad workers imagine an important segment of Chinese American historical memory, and they contribute to efforts to effectively amend historical accounts and achieve "a transformative recognition" of the past.

PART FIVE

Chinese Railroad Workers after Promontory

CHAPTER 17

The Chinese as Railroad Builders
after Promontory

SHELLEY FISHER FISHKIN

In 1869, in the weeks after the meeting of the Central Pacific and the Union Pacific at Promontory Summit, accolades for the Chinese railroad workers appeared frequently in the nation's press and around the globe. While these pieces often cited among the Chinese workers' virtues their ability to live economically and accept lower pay than Caucasian workers required, they generally lauded, as well, the Chinese laborers' intelligence, work ethic, steadiness, dependability, personal discipline, strength, endurance, precision, and skill.[1] "As an artist with shovel or drill, wheelbarrow and cart," one widely circulated article asserted, the Chinese railroad worker "has proved himself unsurpassed."[2]

By far the most frequently reprinted commentary was a lengthy piece entitled "The Chinaman as Railroad Builder," which ran in dozens of newspapers in every region of the country, as well as in *American Railroad Journal* and *Scientific American* between May and September 1869.[3] The author of the glowing encomium wrote that without the "skill and industry" of the Chinese railroad worker, "the Central Pacific Railroad might not now have been carried eastward of the Sierras." The Chinese worker's "industry is unflagging, his strength and endurance are wonderful, and his mechanical skill is remarkable," he wrote. But his insistence on the superlative qualities of the Chinese railroad workers went even further:

> There are Chinamen in the employ of the Central Pacific Company who are more clever in aligning roads than many white men who have been educated

to the business, and these Mongols will strike a truer line for a longer distance with the unassisted eye than most white men can with the aid of instruments. A great deal of nonsense has been talked about the Chinaman's want of strength and capacity for work. The Central Railroad has pretty thoroughly settled that point; for numerous experiments have been made during its construction, with a view to test the respective capabilities of the two races. On one occasion a party of Irishmen and a party of Chinamen were pitted against each other in blasting a hard rock for a tunnel. Bets were freely made that the white men would come out winners; but at the end of the day, when the work of each party was measured, it was found out that John Chinaman had burrowed farther into the rock than his antagonist, and was moreover less fatigued.

"The bands of Chinamen now organized by the Central Company," the writer concluded, "are as fine railroad builders as can be found anywhere."

In the years that followed, Chinese railroad workers *could* be "found anywhere," building railroads in every part of the nation, including in some rather unexpected places. During the two decades after the laying of the golden spike at Promontory Summit, Utah, the railway mileage of the country more than tripled. There were close to 47,000 miles in 1869; by 1889 there were over 161,000 miles.[4] The boom in rail lines during this period had a transformative impact on the nation's economy and social fabric. The Chinese played a key role in this frenzy of railroad construction not only in the West, the Northwest, and the Southwest (as well as Canada), but also in the South, the Midwest, and even the Northeast. During this period they were building and rebuilding railroads in Alabama, Arizona, California, Colorado, Georgia, Idaho, Louisiana, Maryland, Minnesota, Montana, Nevada, New Jersey, New Mexico, New York, North Dakota, Ohio, Oregon, South Dakota, Tennessee, Texas, Virginia, Washington, Wisconsin, and Wyoming.[5] Thousands of Chinese railroad workers went on to build scores of cross-country lines, intercity and local lines, standard-gauge and narrow-gauge lines—trains that transported people, produce, wood, coal, and anything else you can imagine. We don't have even a preliminary inventory of which railroads they built, rebuilt, and kept in good repair, let alone the obstacles and challenges they faced and their responses. This essay is a first effort to consolidate our knowledge on these topics.

We begin with an overview of railroad lines that Chinese workers built or rebuilt during the two decades after Promontory, when they did this work, and why the lines mattered.[6] We then discuss what their contracts entitled them to and what they did when those terms were violated, what hazardous conditions they were exposed to, what forms of hostility they encountered, and what feats they accomplished. A number of these workers clearly were veterans of the Central Pacific, but many other workers for whom we don't have such documentation probably were as well.[7]

The Central Pacific and the Union Pacific may have been nominally "completed" when the two lines met on May 10, 1869, but both employed Chinese workers after that date to repair, rebuild, and extend portions of the lines as needed.[8] The Union Pacific employed men like Chin Lin Sou (who had worked as a labor contractor for the Central Pacific) to supervise efforts to bring its line up to the standards required by the US government in Utah, Wyoming, and Colorado.[9] Another Chinese labor contractor who worked on the Union Pacific and became an assistant foreman of a track-building gang there was Leo Quoon, who "contracted several thousand Leos from his village for the work."[10] By June 1, 1870, the Union Pacific in Ogden, Utah, had 225 Chinese track hands on its payroll.[11] Ten days later 150 Chinese workers passed through Corinne, Utah, to work on "the Utah division of the Union Pacific Railroad."[12] In June and July 1870 newspapers around the country noted that Chinese workers were being "extensively introduced" on the Union Pacific, particularly west of Cheyenne, Wyoming, repairing the line, as well as working in the railroad's coal mining operations, a fact that was prompting indignation and threats on the part of displaced white workers.[13] On the Central Pacific, too, Chinese veterans of the railroad's initial construction continued to do maintenance work on the line—including replacing the ties every five to ten years, a necessity given the rate at which they deteriorated.[14]

In addition to working on the Central Pacific and Union Pacific during the two decades after the lines met at Promontory, Chinese workers helped build and maintain seventy-one other rail lines (and railroad depots) in the United States for which there is a paper trail (and probably more as well).[15] These include, in alphabetical order, the Alabama and Chattanooga Railroad; Bodie and Benton Railroad; California and Oregon Railroad; California Central Narrow Gauge Railroad; California Pacific Railroad; California Southern Railroad (Atchison, Topeka & Santa Fe); Carson and Colorado Railroad; Carson Tahoe Railroad; Celilo and Wallula Railroad; Cincinnati, Hamilton, and Dayton Railroad; Clear Lake and San Francisco Railroad; Coronado Railroad; Cuyamaca and Eastern Railroad (also known as the San Diego,

Cuyamaca, and Eastern); Denver and Rio Grande Western Railroad; Denver Pacific Railroad; East Side Railroad; Echo and Park City Railroad; Eureka and Palisade Railroad; Fremont, Elkhorn, and Missouri Valley Railroad; Galveston, Harrisburg, and San Antonio Railroad; Great Northern Railway; Houston and Texas Central Railroad; Lake Valley Railroad; Loma Prieta Railroad; Long Island Railroad; Los Angeles and Independence Railroad; Memphis and Selma Railroad; Mendocino Railroad; Midland Railroad; Monterey and Salinas Valley Railroad; Napa and Lake Railroad; Napa Valley Railroad; Nevada–California–Oregon Railway; Nevada County Narrow Gauge Railroad; New Orleans, Mobile, and Texas Railroad; North Pacific Coast Railroad; Northern Pacific Railway; Ohio and Mississippi Rail Road; Oregon and California Railroad; Oregon Central Railroad; Oregon Pacific Railroad (formerly Corvallis and Yaquina Railroad); Oregon Railway and Navigation Company; Pacific Coast Railway; Puyallup Railroad; Rutherford and Clear Lake Railroad; San Diego and San Bernardino Railroad; San Francisco and North Pacific Railroad; San Luis Obispo and Santa Maria Valley Railroad; San Rafael and San Quentin Railroad; Santa Clara Valley Railroad; Santa Cruz Railroad; San Luis Railroad; Santa Cruz and Felton Railroad; Seattle and Walla Walla Railroad; Selma and Gulf Railroad; Selma, Rome, and Dalton Railroad; Shenandoah Railroad; Sierra Valley and Mohawk Railroad; South Pacific Coast Railroad; Southern Pacific Railroad; Stockton and Copperopolis Railroad; Texas and Pacific Railway; Thurston County Railroad; Utah and Pleasant Valley Railroad; Utah, Idaho, and Montana Railroad; Utah Northern Railroad; Virginia and Truckee Railroad; Walla Walla and Columbia River Railroad; West Side Railroad; Western Pacific Railroad; and Yosemite Mountain Sugar Pine Railroad.[16] Chinese workers could be found building eleven of these railroads during the second half of 1869, after Promontory. During the 1870s they worked on thirty-six additional lines, and in the 1880s they worked on twenty-four more.[17]

Many of the lines they built during these two decades were tremendously important. For example, the Denver Pacific Railroad, a north–south line built by Chinese workers in 1870 under the supervision of Chin Lin Sou (who brought the project in under budget), connected Denver and the state of Colorado with the transcontinental trunk line in Cheyenne, Wyoming. It was widely credited with having revived Denver's flagging economy, positioning Denver to become a dynamic center of commerce, banking, and tourism and a leading city in the West.[18] The Virginia and Truckee Railroad,[19] completed in 1872 by Chinese who had worked on the Central Pacific, helped transform Reno, Nevada, from a sleepy backwater town into a dynamic commercial hub for the vast silver fortunes of the Comstock Lode. The Thurston County Railroad in Washington State, which the Chinese worked on starting in 1873, saved Olympia "from economic oblivion" and preserved it as the state's capital.[20] The almost completely Chinese workforce that extended the Southern Pacific Railroad across Texas in the early 1880s, connecting Texas directly to California and other points west, helped Texas become a leading producer of both cattle and cotton in the years that followed.[21] By 1883 the Northern Pacific, built by fifteen thousand Chinese workers (many of them veterans of the Central Pacific), made it possible to transport minerals, cattle, lumber, wheat, and other farm products from the Pacific Northwest to the rest of the country and played a huge role in opening the region both to settlement and commercial development.[22] In California the more than two dozen railroads the Chinese built during these decades had an enormous impact on the state: they connected Sacramento and San Francisco (via Oakland, where a ferry transported people and goods across the bay); they linked Northern and Southern California; they promoted settlement in Southern California; they made it possible to transport lumber, agricultural products, and silver-lead ore to national and regional transportation hubs; and they helped vacationers reach the state's scenic beaches.[23]

Even in the Northeast, where the initial development of railroads predated the first transcontinental line, the Chinese played important roles during the two decades after 1869 when railroads faced difficult construction challenges or needed careful and meticulous work done expeditiously. Chinese workers played key roles in railroad projects in New Jersey and New York in the 1870s.

In the fall of 1870 New Jersey became the first East Coast destination for Chinese railroad workers. One hundred fifty Chinese, the first installment of a gang of five hundred, arrived in Jersey City in Passaic County, furnished by labor broker Cornelius Koopmanschap under contract to S. P. Simpson & Co., to construct a portion of New Jersey's Midland Railroad that ran through a hard "rocky and uncultivated" region between Pompton and Newton.[24] The portion of the railroad that was involved was described as "one of the most difficult of construction of any on the line, there being many deep cuts and heavy grades."[25] The white workers who had been hired on the line had not worked out. "When the work was heavy and difficult," the *New York Times* reported, they would "desert their ranks." The reporter added, "The reports coming from the Pacific relating to the qualities of the Chinese as railroad laborers, led to the opening of negotiations with Koopmanschap for a large force."[26]

In 1876 executives of New York's Long Island Railroad faced a serious problem that required that the tracks at the Rockaway branch be completely rebuilt within a short time frame. Rockaway was a popular beach destination on Long Island Sound. But the previous summer, the poor condition of the tracks and the roadbed had led to two accidents involving nine fatalities, and the railroad came to be known as a "death trap." The stellar reputation of the Chinese as railroad builders led the railroad's owners to import more than one hundred of them to get the job done.[27] After they completed the work, beachgoers began using the railroad again with confidence that summer.

Just as white workers on New Jersey's Midland Railroad tended to "desert their ranks" when the work became "heavy and difficult," white workers on California's South Pacific Coast Railroad failed to show up when the work became grueling and unpleasant. Caucasian workers had started building the narrow-gauge line, but they were daunted by the prospect of laying "nearly three miles of new grade" in the wetlands of Dumbarton Point, in Alameda County, on San Francisco Bay. As Bruce MacGregor describes it, "The tide crested twice a day, saturating the earth fill, flooding the cord grass with dark water, and disguising sink holes that waited for a misstep of man or horse.... With the mud, tide, and brackish water came the rank smell of decaying detritus. Morale among the graders went steadily downhill," and the "crew soon took to strong drink." On "any given Monday morning in the spring of 1875," as the *Santa Cruz Sentinel* reported, "only a quarter of the track crew were fit for work. The rest, more than one hundred men, were either 'drunk or sobering,'" with only seven men fit for work. By November 1877 the South Pacific Coast Railroad was being built by an all-Chinese workforce. Soon Chinese gangs "as large as five hundred men at a time" were doing the grading. By 1878 there were nine hundred Chinese working on the line.[28]

Even in the Midwest, where other ethnic groups had previously dominated railroad construction, the Chinese were recruited as the ideal workforce during this period. In July 1873 a *Cincinnati Enquirer* reporter found that a number of Chinese laborers in Morristown, Ohio, employed by the Cincinnati, Hamilton, and Dayton Railroad were hard at work in the railroad's gravel pits. When the reporter asked the contractor in charge whether any of the men working for him had worked on railroads before, he replied that all of them had worked on the Central Pacific. The contractor noted how much more dependable they were than white workers.[29]

While the white workers would quit work a half day early "if a picnic or show" came to town, the only thing that could get the Chinese workers to depart from their usual pace of work was a reporter visiting their workplace. Aware of the fact that they'd be the subject of his story, they did even more work than usual in order to impress him.[30]

The Chinese honored their own contractual obligations and expected their employers to do the same. Their wages during these decades ranged from a low of $16 a month (or about $0.61 a day) on the Alabama and Chattanooga in 1870 to nearly $36 a month (or $1.38 a day) on the Northern Pacific in 1882.[31] Generally, their wages hovered between $20 and $30 a month, with their board taken out of their wages and twenty-six days counting as a month. The Chinese usually (but not always) boarded themselves; sometimes the workers furnished their own food but had the contractors pay the cook. On the East Coast, they could generally earn significantly more in other industries. Chinese working in the Belleville, New Jersey, steam laundry in 1880, for example, earned between $40 and $48 a month, while Chinese cooks in New York boardinghouses earned from $30 to $50 a month and house servants, from $18 to $30 a month. Chinese house servants and cigar workers in New York could command higher wages than German and Irish workers in these fields could.[32] This may help explain why, when Chinese workers were sent to New York and New Jersey to build railroads, they tended to disappear as railroad workers after the work was done, presumably having moved into other, higher-paying jobs in the region. (In the West, the Chinese in other industries, such as cigar manufacturing, continued to earn less than white workers during this period.[33])

The Chinese railroad workers' employers sometimes reneged on even the most paltry wages. In 1871 Koopmanschap abandoned without pay about 350 Chinese workers whom he had sent to Tuscaloosa to work on the Alabama and Chattanooga Railroad; when he visited them, he found them living "on blackberries and crawfish." He left them in that situation and made no effort to help them.[34]

The contracts that Chinese workers signed when they went to work on these rail lines sometimes specified, in addition to the wages they would earn, the hours they would work and the items with which they would be supplied.

For example, contracts for work on the Selma and Gulf Railroad in 1870 stipulated that in addition to getting "sixteen dollars in gold monthly," each worker was to receive "free board, lodging, water and fuel." Furthermore, the contract promised that "the working hours shall be 10 hours per day, six days in the week; that there shall be five cooks; that a sufficient quantity of rice, pork, fish, beef and vegetables shall be furnished; that when a man falls sick he shall receive no wages, but provisions, and guarantees free return to San Francisco after the term of service."[35]

As San Francisco labor contractor B. J. Dorsey noted in a circular reprinted in the *Railroad Gazette* in 1870, the daily rations for Chinese workers contractually agreed upon were "rice, 2 lbs.; tea, ⅓ oz.; fish, beef or pork, 1 lb.; vegetables, ⅓ lb.; lard or oil in small quantities."[36] The Chinese furnished their own bedding, and the contractor furnished "comfortable and weather proof quarters," as well as "all tools and implements" and "medicines and medical attendance."[37] The South Pacific Coast Railroad contracted to furnish Chinese workers with wood and water.[38]

One California labor contractor who claimed that he "had business relations with not less than twenty-five thousand" Chinese workers was quoted in October 1869 as having "never known a single case where a Chinaman has broken his contract."[39] If Chinese railroad workers were famous for abiding by the terms of their contracts, they were equally known for demanding that their employers abide by them as well. Collis P. Huntington, as president of the Chesapeake and Ohio (C&O) Railroad in 1870, noted that the Chinese workers he planned to hire on the C&O required that he supply them with "certain quantities and kinds of food at stipulated rates, not to be changed during the continuance of the contract, no matter whether the market prices rise or fall." The Chinese, he said, "are very particular and minute in making these bargains."[40]

On July 28, 1870, the *New-York Daily Tribune* ran the headline "Chinese in West Virginia. Tunneling for the Chesapeake and Ohio Railroad." Construction on the line had stopped at a particularly challenging tunnel. Huntington bragged to the press that "his agents know to pick out particular men who have had abundant experience in the kind of work to be done, and he thinks he can get together a lot of the best tunnel hands in the world."[41] Despite press reports all that summer about the imminent arrival of Huntington's Chinese workers, they never came.[42] The fact that they would require contracts that would mandate that he pay for their transportation to and from West Virginia and employ them for a full year (when the hard tunneling would not take that long to complete) made the cost of importing this "cheap labor" to West Virginia prohibitive. Huntington decided to use local black convict labor instead.[43] (The Lewis Tunnel, on the West Virginia stretch of the Chesapeake and Ohio, where Huntington had planned to use expert Chinese "tunnel hands" from the Central Pacific, was not just any tunnel: it would become the most famous tunnel in the nation. As Scott Reynolds Nelson argues persuasively, it was there in the Lewis Tunnel that a short, black nineteen-year-old from New Jersey would become the stuff of legend: having been convicted of shoplifting from a general store while visiting Virginia, the teenager ended up in the Virginia Penitentiary, where he was leased out, under the convict lease system, to Huntington's railroad.[44] In the Lewis Tunnel he would test his strength and endurance against the steam-powered machine that was his rival. If Huntington had not changed his mind, it might have been a Chinese veteran of the Central Pacific, rather than John Henry, who competed with the steam drill.)

The Houston and Texas Central Railroad agreed by contract to establish a Chinese store stocked with $3,000 worth of particular goods of specific quality near where the Chinese railroad laborers worked.[45] The list of goods that would be supplied included

[n]arrow leaves, 500 pounds; bamboo brushes, 5 dozen; foo chuck or bean curd sticks, 10 boxes, or 400 pounds; 10 boxes vermicelli, 500 pounds; 200 pounds of ginger root; 50 pounds orange peel; 200 pounds cuttle fish; 10 boxes of soy; 10 jars ketchup; 20 reams Chinese writing paper; 200 Chinese pencils; 10 daily account books; 5,000 Chinese visiting card papers; 5 pieces paper (for lights); 300 pounds California abalones; 40 pounds red melon seed; two dozen frying-pan shovels; four dozen copper spoons (large);...
50 pounds sugar candy; 50 pounds red dates; six counting boards; 1 pound Chinese ink; 100 Chinese pens; 10 paper boxes pills; 10 bottles medicine powder; 10 boxes (100 gallons) China nut oil; 10 jars or 700 pounds salt turnip; 40 sets bowls; 40 sets chopsticks; 1 dozen knives; 2,000 pounds salt shrimps; 15 bags or 1,950 pounds salt fish; 200 bags fungus; 50 Chinese pass books; 50 Chinese general ledger books; 5 boxes or 50,000 firecrackers; 2 boxes firecrackers; jos[s] paper; [joss] sticks; one box or 55 pounds dried oysters; five mats or 250 pounds black peas; two mats or 100 pounds red peas; 18 large kettles; 16 small kettles; two boxes or 120 pairs Chinese common shoes; 20 Chinese purses; 10 buckskin purses. Additional goods for Chinese new year.[46]

Journalist Charles Nordhoff described a store "kept in several cars near the end of the track" at a camp of Chinese railroad workers along the San Joaquin River near Merced in the early 1870s. Food sold to Chinese workmen included "[d]ried oysters, dried cuttle-fish, dried fish, sweet rice crackers, dried bamboo sprouts, salted cabbage, Chinese sugar (which tasted to me very much like sorghum sugar), four kinds of dried fruits, five kinds of desiccated vegetables, vermicelli, dried sea-weed, Chinese bacon cut up into salt cutlets, dried meat of the abelona [sic] shell, pea-nut oil, dried mushrooms, tea, and rice. They buy also pork of the butcher, and on holidays they eat poultry.... At this railroad store they also sold pipes, bowls, chop-sticks, large shallow cast-iron bowls for cooking rice, lamps, joss paper, Chinese writing-paper, pencils and India ink."[47] On some lines all of the provisioning was handled by Chinese labor contractors, who made as much money from selling food and other goods to the workers as they made from procuring the workers for the railroad company. This was the case with Chinese labor contractor Ah Quin, who secured workers for the California Southern Railroad in the early 1880s and whose income was generated in large part from provisions that he sold to the hundreds of Chinese workers he hired to build the line.[48]

Chinese railroad workers generally contracted to work for two to three years.[49] They often traveled to jobs with interpreters as well as headmen who negotiated on their behalf when their contracts were violated. The workers typically lived in tents or dugouts, in temporary work camps near the tracks,[50] or, in some cases (in Rockaway, Long Island, for example), in empty train cars brought in as temporary sleeping quarters.[51] The workers would often construct double hearths for cooking ("one was used for steaming rice and the other for frying meats and vegetables").[52] When their workday was done, in railroad camps across the country, they usually took sponge baths with hot water, a practice largely unheard of among Caucasian railroad workers. The gambling pieces that archaeologists have found at multiple sites where Chinese worked between 1869 and 1889 (made from Chinese coins or fashioned out of copper or tin) suggest that they often relaxed by playing games of chance. And the occasional fragments of opium pipes that archaeologists have found suggest that smoking opium was also a form of relaxation (it was legal to smoke opium in most of the United States during this period).[53] Although Chinese workers on railroad lines after Promontory were celebrated for their sobriety compared to Caucasian workers, on one occasion in 1883, as the *Nevada State Journal* (Reno) reported, two Chinese section hands in

Lerdo, California, "took a hand car without leave, ran to Sumner, and went on a raging drunk."[54] This behavior was clearly the exception; drunkenness was rare among the Chinese workers (although bottles of beer or Chinese brandy have been found at Chinese campsites).[55] The annals of exceptional behavior by Chinese railroad workers after 1869 would not be complete without the report of a group of Chinese workers employed by the Central Pacific in 1872 "to shovel gravel from a pit near Chico." Something unexpected caught their eye as they did their work; the observant workers staked a mining claim on the pit and managed to develop "an excellent gold mine."[56]

The writing supplies that the Houston and Texas Central Railroad was obligated to provide for Chinese workers in 1869 and that the Central Pacific stocked for the Chinese workers near Merced in 1870 (in the latter case, one pound of Chinese ink and one hundred Chinese pens) suggest that the workers may have also spent some of their leisure writing letters home. Observers of Chinese railroad workers during this period often noted that they could read and write in Chinese.[57] *Harper's Bazaar* reported in October 1869: "We have seen it stated that the Superintendent of the Central Pacific Railroad, after having employed some thirteen thousand Chinese, that he never heard of one who could not read and write in his own language."[58] Indeed, a correspondent for the *New York Evening Post* in June 1869, discussing the "Chinese who came to California to work on the Central Pacific Railroad," noted that they "have nearly all been educated to read and write"; he further stated that "[t]he large number of Chinamen now in the Pacific states who all, or very nearly all, can read and write, have sent to China, in private letters, a vast amount of information concerning those states and the United States generally."[59] Contractors on later lines, such as California Southern labor contractor Ah Quin, who left a detailed diary, and Northern Pacific labor contractor Chin Gee Hee, who left correspondence and an account and letter book, were literate in both English and Chinese.

Despite the popular belief at the time that that the Chinese didn't strike,[60] Chinese workers on these later lines often did strike. Some of them mounted strikes to demand shorter hours, and on occasion they met with success. On August 31, 1869, a report said that "about a fortnight ago the Chinamen on the San Rafael railroad [numbering] about sixty, who had been working eleven hours a day, struck for ten hours." The workers reportedly "laid off under the trees and smoked opium [and] drank tea. The overseers urged them to go to work, and they laughed at them; they scolded and the Chinamen scowled.

At last a herald was dispatched to San Francisco, and a Chinaman who works in Wells Fargo & Co.'s office went up. After consultation the men agreed to work eleven hours per day for one month longer, and after that the days will be reduced one hour."[61] In April 1873 a contract grader supervising work at the difficult Collins Summit on the North Pacific Coast narrow-gauge railroad found himself under pressure to get the work done more quickly. He issued an order for "mandatory overtime for his Chinese crews, an increase in the length of the work day from ten to eleven hours. Infuriated, seventy-five of [his] Chinese workers went on strike the next day, forcing the contractor to recant."[62]

Sometimes strikes occurred to object to pay delays or to protest working conditions or contract violations. In August 1869 Chinese workers on the Western Pacific reportedly went on strike because their bosses failed to pay them promptly enough, delaying work for one or two days.[63] In 1870 all the Chinese employed on the Houston and Texas Central went on strike and filed suit against the company for "wages and a failure of compliance with contract."[64] In 1871 forty or fifty Chinese workers engaged on a Union Pacific work train near Medicine Bow, Wyoming, "struck on account of the cold."[65] In 1875 Chinese workers on the Southern Pacific at Calistoga went on strike when poll taxes were taken out of their pay, and three thousand Chinese workers at Tehachapi struck "on account of some dissatisfaction with the overseers of the work."[66] In May 1881 Chinese workers on the Northern Pacific struck "because tolls on rice were increased."[67] Although we don't always know the outcome of these strikes, sometimes we do. The *Los Angeles Herald* reported on July 19, 1887, that in Siskiyou "[t]en Chinese gangs numbering about 300 men employed by Sisson & Crocker struck to-day, the railroad fare of $4 having been taken from each man's wages. They claim that their contracts called for free transportation."[68] Less than a week later the *San Bernardino Daily Courier* reported that "[t]he striking Chinese section hands at Siskiyou, Oregon, resumed work Thursday, their claims having been paid in full."[69] Sometimes these strikes were broken in a manner similar to that used by the Central Pacific owners to break the 1867 strike.[70] In June 1875 the nearly five hundred workers on the Eureka and Palisade Railroad staged a strike. Management broke it by withholding their drinking water.[71]

The passage of the Chinese Restriction Act in 1882 reduced the supply of available Chinese workers, and by 1883 the shortage seems to have emboldened a number of Chinese railroad workers across the country to strike for higher wages.[72] In 1889 Southern Pacific Railroad officials received word that

"Chinese section hands are demanding higher wages than have ever been paid before, wages about equal to those received by white men."[73]

Much as their work on the Central Pacific had, work on these later rail lines exposed Chinese laborers to physical hazards. In 1875 a Chinese worker was killed in one of the railroad cuts in the Tehachapi Pass when he was ordered to check why one of several charges that had been set had failed to go off.[74] Also that year a report said that several Chinese workers on "the Southern Pacific Railroad grade, near the Colorado Desert, have died from the intense heat prevailing in that region," where "[i]t is a common thing for the thermometer to mark 120 in the shade, when shade can be found, and yet the work has proceeded without interruption."[75] Heat and sun could be a hazard in more northern construction sites as well. In August 1870 the *Weekly Oregon Statesman* reported, "Another Chinamen [*sic*] working on the railroad had died from sunstroke."[76] In 1879 a gas leak in Tunnel 3 on the narrow-gauge South Pacific Coast Railroad from San Jose to Santa Cruz caused a series of huge explosions in which some thirty Chinese workers were killed.[77] In March 1881 two Chinese workers were killed and two dangerously injured by an explosion that occurred when they were "thawing giant powder near the Grange City railroad cut" in Washington Territory.[78] In January 1882 eight Chinese workers were buried alive in a snowslide while cutting timber on the Pacific Coast Railway when "half a mile of mountain snow" slid down on them; ten more barely escaped with their lives.[79] In December 1882 four Chinese workers "were blown to pieces and four badly hurt by an explosion in an Oregon and California Railroad tunnel near Riddle, Oregon, when they accidentally drilled into a charge of giant powder."[80] In 1885 "a Chinese grader on the California Southern Railroad, working in the Temecula canyon, was instantly killed…by a rock weighing over 2000 pounds rolling over him."[81]

In addition to the physical hazards of their construction work, Chinese workers often had to deal with the hostility of white workers and supervisors. In September 1869 some 350 white miners destroyed the huts of Chinese workers on the Virginia and Truckee (V&T) Railroad and drove the workers out of the construction camp. Work on the railroad could continue only after a V&T official promised that Chinese workers would never be allowed to work in the mines.[82] In August 1870 two Chinese workers were shot by the section boss on the Union Pacific at Table Rock, Wyoming.[83] In November 1870 the *Sacramento Daily Union* quoted a correspondent from Alabama who reported that "[s]till another Chinaman has been killed by a blow from a brutal and reckless white overseer."[84]

In 1871, under pressure from white workers, the Nevada legislature began granting railroad charters only to companies that promised not to employ Chinese in the construction or operation of the railroad.[85] In August 1873 a camp of Chinese working on a narrow-gauge railroad near Benicia, California, was attacked by drunken white men, who tore down their tents and stoned and clubbed them.[86] In June 1876 Chinese workers at the V&T roundhouse in Carson City, Nevada, who had been working on a gravel train were driven off by hostile whites, who forced them to gather everything they owned and flee to the next county.[87] In December 1876 a number of Chinese laborers were driven off from their work on the Eureka and Palisade Railroad.[88] As a result of anti-Chinese feelings harbored by the white population on the Comstock Lode in Nevada, during the summer of 1880 the five hundred Chinese workers building the Carson and Colorado Railroad had to be transported to their work site by a roundabout route that avoided the V&T—ironically, a rail line that the Chinese had built.[89] In January 1882 eleven Chinese railroad workers who were killed at Eagle Springs, Texas, near El Paso, were reported to have been massacred by Apache;[90] it was later learned that "the deed was committed by disguised white men recently employed on the railroad."[91]

In late September 1885 in Cheyenne, Wyoming, where the Chinese had been employed as Union Pacific section hands for fifteen years, Chinese workers woke up one morning to find printed notices posted on the doors of their houses warning that "[a]ll Chinamen found in the city of Cheyenne after October 1st will be subjected to a coat of tar and feathers and ridden from the city on a rail."[92] That same month, in Rock Springs, Wyoming, where the Union Pacific employed large numbers of Chinese workers in a company coal mine, about 150 white miners marched into Chinatown, ordered the Chinese Union Pacific workers to leave, fired on them with shotguns, and burned the fifty houses owned by the railroad company and fifty owned by the Chinese.[93] More than five hundred Chinese workers fled; some twenty-eight were killed outright, many more were wounded, and it was said that "several who were feeble and helpless from disease perished in the flames."[94]

Many white railroad officials simply did not place high value on Chinese lives. As a child growing up in Box Elder County, Utah, Wallace Clay had genuine affection for the Chinese railroad workers who had befriended him and given him "Chinese candy and firecrackers."[95] Clay had many vivid memories of the Chinese section hands who, missing their own children back in China, fondly took him in "as a sort of pet." But he recalled what little value railroad officials ascribed to their lives: "It wasn't considered murder to kill a Chinaman," he told an interviewer years later:

> WALLACE CLAY. Ya know, it was just like killing a jack rabbit, or something that way, so there was a number of Chinamen that were killed by white people because they had a grudge against them for some reason or other.
>
> INTERVIEWER. And, nothing was ever done?
> CLAY. No, nothing was ever done.
>
> INTERVIEWER. They [the killers] were never brought to the law?
> CLAY. No, they were never brought to justice or trial, or anything that way.[96]

H. K. Wong, in his book *Gum Sahn Yum—Gold Mountain Men,* notes a similar comment recorded by community historian William Hoy, founder of the California Chinese Pioneer Historical Society and later associate editor of the California Chinese Press. Hoy's notes included stories passed down from a Southern Pacific Railroad worker to his grandson, Sing Lum. Sing Lum remembered hearing his grandfather talk about "'doin' the Southern Pacific railroad goin' down the San Joaquin Valley into the Tehachapis.'"[97] When Sing Lum was six years old, his grandfather, Lum Kai Kun, who "used to live with us and tell me a lot of stories about the railroad," mentioned that "the white man—the boss man—if they didn't like you, they'd just put a bullet through your head. Real tough times. Every day some killing going on."[98]

During the two decades after Promontory—despite the punishing physical hazards they faced on a daily basis and despite violence they met at the hands of white supervisors and white workers—Chinese railroad workers in the United States accomplished wonders. Building the Western Pacific Railroad required grading that was described by the *Sacramento Daily Union* as being "very heavy, mostly cuts through slate rock."[99] Building the Livermore Pass (later known as the Altamont Pass), the northernmost pass between San Francisco and the mines of the Mother Lode, required blasting and digging an 1,182-foot-long tunnel, as well as a cut that was 1,400 feet deep.[100] (In addition, a reporter observed, "the number of rattlesnakes seen" in the area was "somewhat astonishing."[101]) Building the Loma Prieta Railroad in central California, as Sue Fawn Chung notes, required that Chinese workers contend with a final section of 1.3 miles that had "a grueling grade of 108 feet, or 2 percent grade, which has been regarded as a great construction feat even by today's standard."[102] Building the Southern Pacific required that the workforce, which was dominated by the Chinese, construct the Tehachapi Loop, a roadbed that spiraled through eighteen tunnels up the Tehachapi Mountains in south-central California, gaining 77 feet of elevation at a steady grade of 2.2 percent—an achievement that has been named "one of the railroad wonders of the world."[103]

An 1882 article in the *Philadelphia Times* by a special correspondent "on the Southern Pacific Railroad" conveys the daunting challenges that the six thousand Chinese workers met as they completed what the correspondent called a "marvel of modern railway construction":

> Even along the Rio Grande, where canyons were created a thousand feet deep, mountains tunneled a mile through and rocky ridges miles in extent leveled and graded, these Mongolians moved forward a mile every twenty-four hours. I passed along the line for the first time last summer and it was a source of never-failing wonder to note the rapidity and precision with which the work was accomplished. A hill of solid rock one hundred yards long had to be cut down to the depth of thirty feet. A thousand Chinamen would swoop down upon it with drills and sledges. In six hours a blast would be ready. Tons of powder would be poured into the innumerable holes made in the rock by Ah Sin [a generic name for a Chinese worker]. Fuses would be prepared, an electric battery attached, the engineer would press the little button, and by the time the smoke from the explosion cleared away, the track-laying outfit would be back at work placing ties in position and spiking down rails.[104]

The 1,000 Chinese workers in the 1,500-man force that bored the 6,975-foot-long San Fernando Tunnel through the San Gabriel mountains deep in the "bowels of the earth hundreds of feet below the surface" had to deal with "stifling heat and dampness" that "made it almost impossible to work."

> Workers stripped to the waist, perspiration pouring from every pore. The air was so foul that candles burnt but dimly. Laborers passed out with monotonous regularity; cave-ins and accidents took a fearful toll. But the men kept on working. By July 1876 the tunnel had become a reality and on September 5, 1876, Los Angeles was connected to San Francisco by rail, giving a tremendous boost to the development of the San Joaquin Valley and the Los Angeles area.[105]

The challenges posed by the rugged terrain of the Northern Pacific Railway were equally daunting. As one newspaper observed, in places the mountain "rises like a wall" from the water's edge, "presenting no break or crevice for a foothold," thus posing an "insurmountable barrier." The reporter went on to explain how the Chinese created footholds where none existed:

> By and by, cable ropes holding a plank staging go down the precipitous side of the mountain. Down rope ladders to this staging clamber Chinamen armed with drills, and soon the rock sides are filled with giant powder. Then they clamber up, the blast is fired, and the foothold made by the explosive soon swarms with Celestials; the "can't be done" has been done, and man's skill, energy, and perseverance have triumphed.[106]

The weather they had to contend with was as difficult as the terrain, with "the thermometer registering on an average ten and twelve degrees below zero, abetted by razor-like winds."[107] As Robert Swartout Jr. notes, "the special skills, dedication, and perseverance of the Chinese workers were critical in overcoming these tremendous obstacles."[108]

In circumstances that were difficult at best, and unbearable at worst, Chinese railroad builders after Promontory accomplished a series of truly remarkable feats. Whenever a hopelessly steep, rough, rock-solid mountain range needed to be blasted through—the Tehachapi Mountains, the North Cascade Mountains, the Cuesta Grade, the Siskiyou Mountains—the Chinese were put on the job. They performed herculean feats of endurance and strength while being treated with gratuitous disrespect and hostility. During the two decades after the Central Pacific and Union Pacific met at Promontory, Chinese railroad workers triumphed over some of the most punishing landscapes America had to offer, playing a major role in building the rail infrastructure of the nation.

CHAPTER 18

The Construction of the Canadian Pacific Railway and the Transpacific Chinese Diaspora, 1880–1885

ZHONGPING CHEN

This chapter uses sources related to the Canadian Pacific Railway (CPR) to examine how the railroad's Chinese labor contractors led the large-scale laborer migration from China to Canada in the early 1880s despite the racist attempts to halt Asian immigration.[1] It also explores how both Chinese labor contractors and laborers for the CPR created organizations to develop new transpacific relations with their homeland, with mainstream Canadian society, and with their compatriots throughout North America. Thus, this study distinguishes itself from previous scholarship on the subject by taking a broad focus on the contributions of these railroad builders to the transpacific Chinese diaspora.[2]

Chinese Labor Contractors and Laborer Immigrants for the Canadian Pacific Railway

After the completion of the first transcontinental rail line in the United States in 1869, British Columbia joined the Canadian Confederation as a province in 1871. The American railroad had a primary influence on the union, which was based partly on the agreement to build the British Columbia section of a trans-Canada line. However, the railroad project was delayed for nearly a decade because of partisan struggles in Ottawa and the economic depression of the 1870s. British Columbia even threatened to secede from the Canadian Confederation because of the delay. However, in 1878 its legislature still enacted a bill to prohibit the employment of Chinese laborers in public works, including road construction. In the next year, the Confederation delegate and a former lieutenant governor (1871–1876) of British Columbia, J. W. Trutch, advised the federal government in Ottawa that white workers in the province could provide less than one-tenth of the workforce needed for railroad construction. He warned that the prohibition of Chinese employment in the CPR's construction would significantly increase the cost of the work.[3]

In 1880 an American engineer, Andrew Onderdonk, purchased all four contracts for building the rail line across the rugged canyons of the Fraser and Thompson Rivers, totaling 127 miles, even though the tendered price from the original contractors was more than $1.5 million (currency in Canadian dollars throughout this chapter) lower than his own previous bid. He also had to pay an additional $215,000 to the successful bidders. His budget, therefore, was $1.715 million less (19 percent less) than his original calculation for building the most difficult section of the CPR in British Columbia,[4] in the "sea of mountains"[5] (figure 18.1).

Moreover, the federal census of Canada in early 1881 recorded only 49,459 residents in British Columbia, including 4,350 Chinese.[6] Because Onderdonk planned to recruit about 10,000 male adults as railroad builders by August 1882,[7] his company had to look for a cheap and abundant workforce through Chinese labor contractors.

The main labor contractors of the CPR included Lee Tin Poy (Li Tianpei), Lee Yau Kain (Li Youqin), Lee Yick Tack (Li Yide), and Lee Tin Shat (Li Tianshi).[8] Evidence confirms that all of them were clansmen from the Lee (Li) lineage of Shuilou Township of Taishan County, Guangdong Province.[9] Previous studies have claimed that the four men partnered in the Lun Chung (Lianchang) & Company based in Victoria and Hong Kong and used it to recruit laborers for the CPR. This company or its major owner, Lee Tin Poy, has even been identified with the Lee Chuck Company that appeared in Canadian newspapers as the CPR's labor contractor.[10] However, available data suggest that the four men used their different companies in Hong Kong, San Francisco, and Victoria to recruit Chinese laborers for the CPR. In particular, Lee Tin Poy also used Kwong On Wo (Guang'anhe) & Co. to manage laborers on the CPR line.[11]

According to newspaper accounts, the "passage money" for the railroad workers "was $40 [per person for the trip from China to Canada], but they have to pay the Chinese companies $80."[12] The Chinese contractors usually

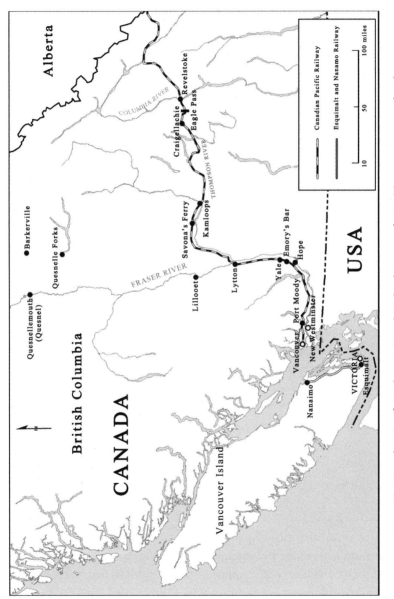

FIGURE 18.1 The Canadian Pacific Railway in British Columbia, around 1885. The map was created with cartographic help from Professor Li Zhijun, Xiamen University, Xiamen, China.

advanced passage money for the labor immigrants from China, but the latter had to work on the railroad until the amount of passage money was deducted from their wages.[13] Onderdonk was reported to "have an interest in vessels" that profited from shipping Chinese laborers for the CPR.[14]

Lee Tin Poy and the three other men from his lineage in Shuilou Township of Taishan County were not merely responsible for recruiting and transferring a large number of Chinese labor migrants for the CPR through their respective companies in Hong Kong, San Francisco, and Victoria, as well as Yale and other inland cities and towns of British Columbia. They also developed close relations with Onderdonk and shipping agents, including Thomas Lett Stahlschmidt, British Columbia's agent-general in England,[15] used the institutions and facilities of these white associates to organize large-scale transpacific Chinese immigration, and even received political help from them in battles against anti-Chinese racism in Canada, especially in British Columbia.

The anti-Chinese activists, organizations, and politicians in British Columbia intensified their call for prohibiting Chinese employment on the CPR just before its construction started in mid-1880.[16] At a meeting with the delegation of the Anti-Chinese Association in Victoria in April 1880, Onderdonk promised to give "white labor the preference" in the CPR construction and to "engage Indians and Chinese" only as the last option.[17] However, he soon found it hard to hire enough satisfactory white workers, and those "from San Francisco were the worst useless lot of broken down gamblers, barkeepers, etc." In contrast, the first groups of Chinese laborers, from the Northern Pacific Railway in Oregon and the Southern Pacific Railroad in California, proved to be "trained gangs of rockmen."[18] Lee Tin Poy's Kwang On Wo & Co., together with Onderdonk, consigned the steamship *Victoria* to transport seventy-four Chinese, a portion of the first group of Chinese laborers, from San Francisco to Victoria as early as May 30 to June 1, 1880.[19]

Onderdonk came to rely mainly on Lee Tin Poy and his clansmen's companies for recruiting larger numbers of Chinese laborers, and his agent, D. Henshaw Ward, went to Hong Kong for the same task in November 1881.[20] The labor contractors from the Lee lineage also organized a large-scale migration from China to Canada with the support of Onderdonk and other white associates. While the American government passed the Chinese Restriction Act of 1882, the anti-Chinese movement in British Columbia also peaked during the federal election of that year.[21] In the same year, the firm of Stahlschmidt & Ward alone shipped "between 5,000 and 6,000 Chinese" from Hong Kong to Canada for the CPR.[22]

In Febuary 1885 the provincial legislature of British Columbia enacted a Chinese exclusion act, which was similar to a previous one of 1884 that had been disallowed by the federal government as being unconstitutional. Instantly, Onderdonk informed the president of the Canadian Pacific Railway Co., George Stephen, of the still urgent need for more Chinese laborers. In turn, Stephen warned Prime Minister John A. Macdonald of the issue twice in two weeks. In March of 1885, this exclusion act was again disallowed by Ottawa. Large-scale immigration from China to Canada, including that for the CPR, continued until mid-1885, just before the Canadian government was ready to impose a head tax on all Chinese immigrants at the end of the CPR's construction in British Columbia.[23]

Victoria's Custom House recorded the arrival of a total of 17,007 Chinese immigrants between January 1881 and October 1884,[24] but this figure has been misused as the rough number of Chinese builders of the CPR by some scholarly and popular publications.[25] In fact, the Custom House of Victoria reported a total of 17,428 Chinese immigrants from January 1881 to December 1884.[26] Moreover, local newspapers in Victoria reported at least 710 Chinese arrivals from May to December 1880, and 1,199 from January to June 1885.[27] The newspapers in New Westminster reported 187 Chinese arrivals in May 1880 and in May and August of 1881.[28] Thus, the Chinese immigrants to British Columbia during the CPR's construction from May 1880 to September 1885 numbered at least 19,524, but more likely over 20,000. Although only 7,413 of these arrivals were confirmed by newspapers as the CPR-hired laborers, the total number of Chinese railroad workers, including those who arrived before or after May 1880 for other businesses but joined the CPR's construction later on, evidently reached more than 10,000.[29] Whatever the specific number, the mass migration of Chinese during the CPR-building era not only provided sufficient laborers for the CPR's construction but also prompted the development of the Chinese community in Canada, despite the racist attempts at exclusion.

Relatively reliable data on the CPR's workforce, especially the Chinese builders, were provided by newspaper reporters at the construction sites, by Andrew Onderdonk and his office, and by other technical authorities related to the railroad project, as given in the following discussion.[30] They refute the assumption that "white labor usually outnumbered the Chinese" except in the section between Yale and Port Moody.[31] These figures also reflect the rises and falls in the numbers of railroad workers from China and other ethnic origins during the CPR construction.

When the CPR construction started in May 1880, the numbers of Chinese and white workers began at 101 and 330, respectively. However, the former rose steadily to 1,100 and further to 1,500 from May to December of 1881, while the latter fluctuated between 1,500 and 1,600 during the same period. About 150 indigenous people also engaged in the CPR's construction from the beginning, and their figures remained at about 100 by mid-1881.[32] From mid-1882 to late 1883, the figure for Chinese workers first skyrocketed to 4,050, then peaked at about 6,500, while the number of white workers slowly reached 2,000 to 3,000, then declined to 1,500.[33] More indigenous people joined the railroad construction around mid-1882, when one newspaper reported "a little over 2,500 Chinamen, with a white foreman to every 30, and about 350 Indians" on the lower section of the railroad between Yale and Port Moody.[34] In late 1884 the figures for Chinese and white workers decreased to 4,000 and 1,000, respectively, although more Chinese may have been hired to build the last section of the CPR toward the Eagle Pass in early 1885.[35] Thus, the Chinese laborers and workers of Caucasian and indigenous origins together accomplished the feat of building the CPR in British Columbia, as did Onderdonk and the Chinese labor contractors, who helped organize the laborers.

Because as many as 6,500 Chinese laborers worked and lived on the CPR line at the peak of the railroad construction, their working units and other organizations were naturally more diverse than the thirty-men gangs that have been frequently mentioned in previous studies.[36] Moreover, the CPR's labor contractors from the Lee lineage not only led the transpacific migration through their various networks but also engaged directly in the organization of Chinese laborers for the CPR construction. Such organizations brought new institutional relations among Chinese builders of the CPR and their diaspora in Canada and beyond.

Organizations of Chinese Labor Contractors and Laborers for the CPR

Chinese labor contractors, together with their white counterparts such as Onderdonk, used both their companies and the working units of railroad workers to manage the laborers from China. They also initiated the earliest community-wide Chinese organization as a benevolent association on the CPR line. Meanwhile, the Chinese railroad laborers formed fraternal organizations for self-protection and mutual assistance. These organizations expanded and transformed the Chinese diaspora in Canada, but none of them have received close examination, and most have been ignored by previous studies.[37]

The construction of the CPR in British Columbia started with "the first shot at No. 1 tunnel, at 9 a.m., May 15th, [1880]. The location is just out of Yale." About 110 Chinese laborers started work under two white foremen, and they probably worked in two gangs and lived in separate camps of roughly 55 men each. On the construction site there was a wayside or makeshift store, which was obviously operated by Lee Chuck Company's agents there.[38] The Chinese laborers cleared the way for the railroad, cut timbers for making ties, graded for laying ties and rails, used drills and hammers to cut rocks, and engaged in the most dangerous work of all: blasting rocks and opening tunnels.[39] From Emory to Yale and northward,

> Fraser River is bordered with rugged mountains of solid granite from 6,000 to 8,000 feet high. In the first 17 miles there are 13 tunnels—4 in one mile and 6 in another 2 miles.... [F]rom Emory to Kamloops Lake, a distance of 127 miles,... [t]he total number of tunnels is 27, and the longest is 1,500 feet.... On the division above Emory there are no less than 600 trestles and bridges, and in the last 85 miles more than 100.... For miles the road is literally hewn out of the sides of the cliffs.... It required 18 months to build the first two miles, working in tunnels night and day.[40]

In the first stage of railroad work, on the most challenging section, Chinese workers were often killed by rolling rocks, flying stones, and other accidents after explosions. They sometimes refused to work because of the frequent accidents.[41] Chinese contractors engaged directly in the management of the workforce, as a reporter witnessed in August 1880:

> As the wagon ascends a hill a distinguished-looking Chinaman, well mounted on a powerful horse with a large umbrella protecting his head from the rays of the sun, and followed at a respectful distance by a Chinese servant, is passed. He is described to us as the "chief" of all the Chinese working on the river—a sort of commissioner, who passes up and down the line to ascertain their grievances and settle disputes between them and their employers.[42]

Under such Chinese labor contractors, other Chinese superintendents worked as "bookmen," or bookkeepers, among the Chinese gangs of laborers. For instance, Yip Sang, also known as Ye Chuntian, was hired by Lee Tin Poy's Kwong On Wo & Co. as a "book-keeper, time-keeper, and paymaster." He would become the richest Chinese merchant in Vancouver, which later replaced Port Moody as the terminal of the CPR.[43] Although previous studies have often assumed that each of the Chinese bookkeepers worked with a white foreman to manage a working gang of thirty Chinese laborers with its cooks, their working and living units were more diverse organizations.

In May 1881 the Canadian census takers in the Yale district recorded quite a few large "households" with more than twenty Chinese laborers each. Among the eleven households from No. 176 to No. 186, each of them normally included a Chinese "bookman" and a cook, with the rest laborers, except for No. 180, which had no cook. The number of residents in each "household" ranged from twenty-three to thirty-two men. In contrast, No. 14 had twenty-eight laborers and three cooks of Chinese origin, and the two Chinese storekeepers at the neighboring No. 15 probably served as bookkeepers for them. Similarly, No. 26 had 144 residents, including 2 washermen, 3 cooks, and 139 laborers of Chinese origin, or nearly five regular gangs. Two Chinese storekeepers living in the same building were recorded as a different household, but they evidently held concurrent positions as bookkeepers. There is no record of either a Chinese bookman or storekeeper for No. 29, 31, 32, 33, 63, or 120, but each of them had Chinese laborers, from twenty to fifty-seven persons (nearly two regular gangs), including one to three cooks in some cases. Of these surveyed households, No. 14, 26, 33, and 120 also included white workers, and in other cases two or three Chinese laborers lived in households with dozens and even over one hundred white workers (e.g., No. 22, 28, 30, 34, 54, 63, 92, and 114).[44] Such households brought many Chinese laborers into daily contact with white workers.

Among these diverse work units, many Chinese units did not meet the standard of thirty laborers per gang, most likely a result of losses due to accidents, desertion, disease, and other causes. After Chinese railroad laborers began to build the relatively easy section of the ninety miles between Yale and Port Moody in mid-1882, the first dozens of miles of the CPR line were still in the lower canyon of the Fraser River, and the construction involved the dangerous work of blasting rock and opening tunnels with explosives. Occasionally, Chinese laborers would attack their white foreman after the latter's carelessness caused deaths from explosions.[45] Even in the relatively smooth terrain around Maple Ridge east to Port Moody, two landslides occurred in February 1883 and another one in May of that year, and each of the three accidents killed two or three Chinese railroad workers.[46]

The mistreatment of Chinese laborers by Onderdonk's company and its white foremen caused desertions among railroad workers. On October 3, 1882, about five hundred Chinese laborers and twenty white foremen were relocated from the Harrison River to Port Moody, but their number was nearly one hundred fewer than the number in twenty standard gangs. These white foremen did not announce that the relocation was to take place until the end of work on the previous evening. They also forced all the Chinese laborers to move their tools, tents, provisions, and railroad company facilities to a ship under heavy rain, which poured from 7:00 a.m. to noon that day. After the ship reached Port Moody at 11:00 p.m., the Chinese laborers had to disembark in heavy rain and total darkness:

> [T]he men were punched and hammered off the boat by sticks in the hands of [o]fficers as well as the bull-dozing crew.... [W]hen about one half of them were off the crew commenced to play the hose on the remainder from the [e]ngine room, wetting the men, their bedding and goods; this was resorted to in order to drive them off quicker; the men being so thickly crowded could not jump over each other's heads, and were therefore compelled to stand the full force of the hose. The boat was all cleared at 1 a.m.; during all this time the men had not one mouthful to eat.[47]

Moreover, the Chinese laborers did not receive payment for the normally paid "half day" off for the relocation.[48] In the face of similar mistreatment, gangs of Chinese laborers left their CPR work in the late autumn of 1882 because "their white bosses refused to let them have fires on the grade to heat their big teapots and toast their fingers."[49]

Because the winter of late 1882 to early 1883 was "one of the severest ever known in Canada,"[50] the cold weather and subsequent scurvy caused many deaths among the Chinese laborers, who came from the tropical area of Guangdong Province. One Chinese labor gang was relocated to Port Moody in late 1882, and at least thirteen of its members had died by January 1883.[51] In the same month, a half-dozen deaths occurred in a Chinese camp near Yale and seven more in another camp. Shockingly, the "Onderdonk Accident Hospital," as it was called by a local newspaper, refused to admit these Chinese patients for medical care.[52] A few miles south of Emory, a gang of twenty-eight Chinese laborers lost ten members by late February 1883. At a meeting of Chinese merchants in Victoria in June 1883, claims were made that about two thousand Chinese had died on the CPR line in the previous year alone.[53] Reports of the high mortality of Chinese laborers appeared in the English-language newspapers of Yale, New Westminster, and Victoria in early March 1883. But these reports mainly blamed Lee Chuck Company's agent on the CPR line, Lee Soon, for his refusal to pay for doctors' bills or medicine.[54]

In fact, Yale's Chinese merchants, evidently including Lee Soon, had already formed a "benevolent society" by February 1883 and planned to open a hospital for the medical care of Chinese patients and those injured in railroad accidents. A hospital was indeed established at Yale's Chinatown thereafter, and six Chinese doctors were hired on the CPR line later on, although scurvy continually wreaked havoc among the Chinese laborers as late as March 1883.[55] The appearance of this benevolent association was a collective response of the merchant leaders in Yale's Chinatown to the medical discrimination against the Chinese laborers on the CPR. The association spearheaded the future efforts of Chinese merchants, especially the Chinese labor contractors of the CPR, to launch a similar organization in Victoria.

In addition to this benevolent association under merchant leadership, Chinese railroad laborers formed their own organizations as branches of a well-known "secret society," the Hong Fraternal Society (Hongmen). But both Chinese organizations on the CPR line have been neglected by previous studies. The origins of the Hong Fraternal Society in China and North America are still under debate by scholars,[56] but the available evidence suggests that it had spawned lodges in San Francisco and Sacramento as early as 1854.[57] By the 1870s such lodges had also appeared in Victoria and in at least one gold-mining town of British Columbia, Quesnel Mouth, in the northern Cariboo Region in the province. The early branches of the Hong Fraternal Society in North America seem to have adopted their name, the Hongshun *tong* (Society of Hong Obedience), directly from China.[58] However, an American-born branch, the Chee Kong Tong (CKT, Zhigongtang, Active Justice Society), had also appeared in San Francisco by 1879. The CKT gained fame in English-language newspapers as the "Chinese Freemasons," and it would become a dominant organization in many North American Chinatowns.[59]

The expansion of the CKT from California to British Columbia was clearly related to the Chinese construction work on the CPR. According to a newspaper report from the CPR line in August 1883, "a Chinese Freemasons Lodge, a branch of the Victoria and San Francisco organizations," had existed in Yale for "some years." It bought a lot and building from On Lee, a local Chinese merchant, which were used as its premises. On the afternoon of August 25, 1883,

> a fine flagstaff, 63 feet in height, painted red, with a turned ornamental top painted blue, was raised in front of the [h]all. Soon after an attractive flag, red with white border, width at staff 21 feet tapering to the end, length 27 feet, containing some Chinese characters, was run up; and two yellow streamers 28 feet long float[ed] in the breeze.... [T]he lodge numbers here over sixty members and are governed by a charitable and protective policy toward all belonging to the craft especially. The [o]fficers of the [l]odge here at present are Chung Gim, Chung Yoy and Ming Tehe, popular members of the organization.[60]

This lodge was probably founded when, in 1880, the construction of the CPR began around Yale and Chinese railroad workers arrived from California. It not only claimed to be a branch of similar organizations in Victoria and San Francisco but also named itself Gee Kung Tong,[61] namely the aforementioned CKT. The lodge in Yale owned a joss house,[62] and the opening ceremony of the religious building in April 1883 was attended by "a number of visitors from Victoria and New Westminster and a band of music."[63] Around 1882 another joss house also appeared in the Chinese quarter of Lytton, which was at the junction of CPR lines along the Fraser and Thompson Rivers. This religious building, like its counterpart in Yale, clearly indicated the existence of a CKT lodge there. Moreover, in April 1884 a newspaper reported the death of a CKT member near Spences Bridge, north of Lytton.[64]

A self-publication of the Chinese Freemasons in Canada in 1989 also indicates the existence of a few of its early lodges along the CPR line in British Columbia by 1885, including those at Lytton, Boston Bar, Yale, and New Westminster.[65] These CKT lodges were probably involved in most, if not all, of the large-scale collective actions undertaken by Chinese railroad builders because these collective actions often demonstrated organizational features and strength. The collective actions targeted the mistreatment of Chinese laborers by white foremen, Onderdonk's company, Chinese labor contractors, and local authorities.

A strike of Chinese railroad builders in May 1881 received attention in contemporary newspapers and recent works, but its organizational characteristics have been neglected.[66] Nearly two thousand Chinese railroad workers around Yale started a general strike on May 10, 1881, not only because their wages had been cut 2 percent as a commission by Lee Chuck Company's agents, but also because they had to accept supplies that were deficient in weight and quality from Lee's store inside Onderdonk's warehouse. In the early afternoon of May 14, more than two hundred of these laborers marched into Yale with picks, shovels, crowbars, and other tools demanding the 2 percent wage back from Lee Chuck's agent, Lee Soon, in the store. However, one staff member from Onderdonk's warehouse shut most of them out, then fired three shots from a pistol through a window. The enraged Chinese protesters then threw stones and rocks in retaliation, destroying the door and windows of the warehouse. When two police officers arrested one of the protest leaders, a large number of Chinese laborers followed them all the way to the local jail, threw stones at them, and eventually grappled with the officers in an unsuccessful attempt to rescue the prisoner.[67]

The strike lasted for nearly ten days, until May 19, 1881; it was finally settled through negotiation with the Chinese laborers. Two of their leaders went to trial in Yale's county court, and the case was dismissed.[68] However, they were still convicted by the grand jury in the court of assizes on July 26 because its judge claimed that the Chinese workers had "such an habitual aptitude for organization, so complete, so effective yet so secret in its character that the prospect of their collective action in a wrong direction must inspire proportionate caution and firmness in dealing with them." The attorney general of British Columbia also warned the grand jury that "a Chinese riot suddenly carried out under an apparently organized system...could command the attendance of men and take them away from their work at a moment's notice from camps along the road, some of them being 15 miles away." He pushed for the conviction of the two Chinese labor leaders as a warning "against similar outbreaks in the future,"[69] and one of them eventually received a sentence of eighteen months' imprisonment.[70]

Nonetheless, Chinese laborers continued their collective action, and they even launched a protest against the provincial government of British Columbia. On July 2, 1881, a tax collector in Victoria tried to levy a $3 school tax on the Chinese arrivals on the steamship *Quinta*, even though the annual tax was for local residents and not due until January 2 of the next year. After the Chinese rejected his demand, the tax collector seized their personal property, triggering physical attacks on him and his assistant. Ten days later, a police officer was sent to Yale to collect the same tax from Chinese railroad builders, but he also met a threat of physical attack and had to abandon the attempt. An agent of the provincial government in Yale then pressed Lee Soon to pay the school tax, and Lee had to pay a $500 penalty for his failure to collect the tax from Chinese laborers in mid-July 1881.[71]

At both the county court and the Supreme Court in Victoria, some Chinese immigrants successfully proved that they had nonresident status at the time of their arrival and thus won their lawsuits against the collector of the school tax by mid-August 1881.[72] However, in October 1881 a provincial superintendent of police from Victoria, together with six special constables around Yale, was still dispatched to collect the tax from the Chinese railroad workers. The constables were "all well-armed with first-class revolvers, in battle array," but their demand for the tax payment still met with collective resistance. Starting from Yale and moving up to Spences Bridge, the police seized each Chinese camp, threw their blankets and other personal property outside, and collected the tax with brute force. Nonetheless, at one camp a gang of Chinese laborers still refused to pay the tax. After its bookkeeper made the payment under pressure, the police had to face three hundred angry Chinese laborers "screaming from all sides above on the hill, below and in front."[73] Probably due to the mobilization of the CKT, the Chinese laborers soon started a strike "with a wonderful degree of unanimity," and many of them left various construction sites as soon as they could.[74]

The clashes between Chinese railroad workers with their white foremen at Maple Ridge in February 1883 escalated into a large-scale confrontation with the police. After a foreman was allegedly attacked by two Chinese laborers and called a constable to arrest them, another gang of Chinese laborers "began talking loudly and demonstratively" and forced a police officer to take his two prisoners into a store. Large numbers of Chinese laborers then encircled the store with axes, shovels, and other tools in their hands and threatened to tear the store to pieces unless the prisoners were released. The police officer had to accede to their demand, and the two Chinese were successfully set free, but they were later recaptured by the local magistrate.[75] It is hard to imagine that such a large number of Chinese laborers would have joined in the collective rescue of two coworkers without the coordination of an organization like the CKT.

In another collective action, the Chinese railroad workers received not only support from the CKT but also sympathy from their labor contractors. In May 1883 the white foreman of a Chinese gang at Lytton dismissed two laborers, but its Chinese bookkeeper objected, and their quarrel escalated into a scuffle between more white foremen and all of the Chinese gang members. A white teamster struck some Chinese workers with a pick handle and injured a few of them. At 10:00 p.m. on May 8, about twenty white men stormed the camp of the Chinese gang, struck the residents inside with sticks, and set fire to their log houses. As a result, six Chinese laborers were seriously wounded, and one of them later died. Because all the wounded Chinese were brought into the joss house operated by the CKT in Lytton for treatment, it is clear that this fraternal organization provided organizational strength in the initial scuffle and medical treatment and other assistance for the injured victims of the riot.[76] After the British Columbia government offered a $500 reward for information about the suspects, Lee Tin Poy's Lun Chung & Co. and Lee Yick Tack's Tai Yuen (Taiyuan) & Co. at Victoria, as well as a Chinese shop in Lytton, provided an additional $500 for the same purpose. However, four suspects were later acquitted by two courts in Victoria on June 12 and September 3, 1883.[77]

Anti-Chinese riots, such as the one in Lytton, rarely happened on the CPR line, and even clashes between Chinese gangs and their white foremen were relatively rare among the nearly four hundred work gangs.[78] In Yale, the early center of the construction, the organizations of both Chinese merchants and railroad laborers even made attempts to form close relations with the Caucasians in the local society. After a fire in Yale in late 1883, the CKT lodge, together with six Chinese merchant companies, donated $140 to the local fire brigade for street improvement, maintenance, and other public works. Won Alexander Cumyow (Wen Jinyou), the first Canadian-born Chinese and the branch manager for Kwong Lee (Guangli) & Co. in Yale, together with two white residents, formed a special committee to "carry out the intentions of the donators."[79] Around the time of the Chinese New Year in January 1884, this Chinese company "gave a grand entertainment" to a large number of local residents and dignitaries, most of whom were undoubtedly CPR officers and staff. As a result, "the popularity of the famous firm of Kwong Lee & Co., and especially the polite [m]anager here, Mr. [Won] Cumyow, largely increased."[80] Thus, the development of Chinese merchant and labor organizations along the CPR line laid a solid foundation for the improvement of relations of the Chinese diaspora within and beyond Pacific Canada.

Toward the Completion of the CPR and the Consolidation of the Chinese Diaspora

In 1883, halfway to the completion of the CPR, Onderdonk's company encountered a serious financial crisis. It survived partly by discharging a large number of Chinese railroad workers.[81] Many discharged Chinese laborers were left destitute and desperate in the severe winter of 1883–1884. This caused widespread panic among white residents, who were concerned about the social disturbances in British Columbia, and the movement to stop immigration from China intensified. Meanwhile, Chinese community leaders were alarmed at both the rising racism and the anticipated discharge of all the Chinese railroad workers after the CPR's completion. In particular, Chinese labor contractors for the CPR led a collective effort to establish a community organization to fight against racial discrimination and deal with the imminent crisis for Chinese laborers.

The employment of Chinese laborers for the CPR construction reduced its costs by 25 percent, as mentioned by the governor-general of Canada, the Marquis of Lorne, in a letter to Prime Minister Macdonald on October 24, 1882. The lower labor costs helped Onderdonk avoid bankruptcy and saved his company $3 million to $5 million over the period 1880 to 1884. Nonetheless, he had still lost $2.5 million on the railroad work by March 1883.[82] In the summer of that year, many Chinese laborers were sent north to Spences Bridge to work on the section of the railroad line around Savona's Ferry. However, they were kept idle there, without work. In December 1883 about three thousand Chinese were discharged from railroad work above Yale.[83]

The dire situation facing the Chinese workers on the CPR in 1882, together with the surplus of laborers in the job market of British Columbia, alarmed the merchant leaders of Victoria's Chinatown. In the early summer of 1883, they held a special meeting to discuss the issue and sent a dispatch to companies in China, urging them to discourage further migration into Canada.[84] After Onderdonk's company discharged large numbers of workers in the winter of 1883–1884, the Chinese merchants in Yale also expressed indignation and worked hard with sympathetic white residents to contribute to the "charity of their countrymen."[85]

The reports of the mass dismissals and the resulting distress of so many Chinese laborers also caused anxiety among the white population, who were concerned about the threat to law and order. This issue became a major subject of debate at the provincial legislature in early December 1883. One legislator claimed that the unemployed Chinese could only "gain a subsistence by stealing or murdering."[86] The provincial government pushed Ottawa repeatedly for immediate restrictions on immigration from China and also dispatched a police superintendent to investigate the issue along the CPR line.[87] After the initial investigation of the line from Yale up to Lytton, the police report showed that Chinese laborers living in the log shanties along the CPR line had been kept idle without work since the previous summer, and they were compelled to use their own money, or to receive rice on credit, to survive. Newspaper reports from Yale confirmed the suffering of the discharged railroad workers, but they also noted that "Chinese merchants and others are contributing to the cause of charity," and "no tendency to crime, however, has been noticed."[88]

On the CPR line beyond the section between Yale and Lytton, the police superintendent reported that about 2,700 Chinese were encamped near Spences Bridge and were well provided for, except for those who "left the camps."[89] In fact, many of the Chinese laborers had left the railroad during the idle time and thus had lost their share of four hundred pounds of rice each gang was given at the time the work was entirely stopped. About four hundred to six hundred of the unemployed laborers had to move northward into the colder Cariboo Region and seek survival by working on the abandoned gold mines in the dead of Canada's winter.[90] A resident from Lillooet in the southern Cariboo Region reported in March 1884: "I have lived here for twenty years, and this is the longest spell of cold weather we ever had.... Flour is $10 a hundred [pounds], and the settlers have none for sale." The resident went on to say that many Chinese could not get flour, even if they could pay for it.[91] From December 1883 to February 1884, a large number of Chinese laborers suffered destitution and starvation in Lytton, Yale, Port Moody, and New Westminster during the severe winter, although they had helped the CPR construction move so fast that trains were ready to run between Port Moody and Lytton during that period.[92]

Although the Chinese labor contractors for the CPR had been collaborating with Onderdonk's company in managing and even exploiting the railroad workers from China, they became the major leaders in a joint battle with these workers and other Chinese immigrants against the discriminatory bills of the British Columbia legislature. In particular, because of the urgency to help the poor labor immigrants from China, including those on the CPR line, three of the four labor contractors from the Lee lineage—Lee Yau Kain, Lee Tin Poy, and Lee Yick Tack—led a joint effort to establish the Chinese Consolidated Benevolent Association (CCBA, *Zhonghua huiguan*) for the battle.[93]

On April 10, 1884, a circular was issued to all the Chinese in British Columbia by twenty leaders of the newly formed CCBA, including one of its two copresidents (*zongli*), Lee Yau Kain; two of its six vice presidents (*fuzhongli*), Lee Tin Poy and Lee Yick Tack; and twelve directors (*zhishi*). The CCBA promised in its circular that it would not only lead the legal battle against the anti-Chinese bills of the British Columbia government but also manage all internal and external affairs for the Chinese community, especially charitable care for poor, sick, and homeless immigrants from China.[94] This circular was further distributed in the names of the twenty CCBA leaders throughout the Chinatowns in British Columbia, together with a list of eighty fund-raising directors (*quanjuan zhishi*), a set of the CCBA's rules, and more than forty names of the earliest signers for large donations, especially the three major labor contractors of the CPR, Lee Tin Poy, Lee Yau Kain, and Lee Yick Tack, as well as their companies.[95]

More importantly, the three Lees actively used their own business networks to help the fund-raising campaign. Lee Yau Kain had Kwong On Lung & Co. in Victoria and its branch in New Westminster.[96] Lee Tin Poy's Lun Chung & Co. operated in Victoria and Ladner; his Kwong On Wo & Co. had at least four branches, in Yale, Lytton, Savona's Ferry, and Kamloops, along the CPR line by the mid-1880s. All of these companies run by the Lees, including Lee Yick Tack' s Tai Yuen & Co. at Victoria, helped collect donations from Chinese immigrants in the province, especially those on the CPR line.[97]

Meanwhile, newspapers in British Columbia pointed out that the scheme of the Canadian government was to postpone restricting Chinese immigration by conducting the royal commission's investigation of the issue. This delay would allow Onderdonk's company to continue to use Chinese laborers to complete the CPR without interruption for another year.[98] Indeed, by October 1884 Onderdonk had secured the contract for building the last "easy section" of the CPR line east to Savona's Ferry and fully expected its completion one year later. However, the superintendent of his company, Michael J. Haney, still predicted that 9,000 laborers, including 7,500 Chinese, would be needed by November 1 of that year.[99] By early the following year, this plan for labor recruitment was still not fulfilled. After the British Columbia legislature again passed a bill against Chinese immigration in February 1885, Onderdonk reacted strongly and pressed President George Stephen of the Canadian Pacific Railway Company to have Prime Minister Macdonald disallow the provincial bill again.[100]

The repeated enactment and disallowance of this bill reflected the conflicting attitudes of both the white politicians and the people of Canada toward

Chinese laborers on the CPR line. In Port Moody, originally the designated terminus of the CPR, the local newspaper in early 1884 criticized a provincial representative in Parliament for his anti-Chinese speech in Ottawa: "[W]hen a man knows that we cannot put them [Chinese] out until the railway is finished he ought to hold his tongue."[101] However, after the Canadian Pacific Railway Company relocated the terminus from Port Moody nine miles west to Coal Harbor, the future Vancouver, in late 1884,[102] the provincial government still forced the company to refrain from hiring any Chinese to work on the extended railroad line, even though the prohibition could "delay the completion of the work for about a twelvemonth."[103] On or near the CPR line, the city councils of New Westminster and Maple Ridge successively banned Chinese from employment in public works in April 1884.[104]

The CCBA soon faced a new but long-anticipated challenge. On September 26, 1885, Onderdonk's company made the following announcement: "The last spike notice! As our last rail from the Pacific has been laid in Eagle Pass today,...[a]ll employees will be discharged on the evening of September thirtieth."[105] In fact, from late August to early September 1885, 2,000 to 3,000 Chinese and white workers had already been laid off. As many as an additional 1,900 Chinese workers were discharged at the end of that month. However, Onderdonk's company provided them transportation only to Yale and then to Port Hammond, near Maple Ridge;[106] it totally shirked its responsibility for their survival in Canada or return to China.

According to the careful calculations of Huang Sic Chen (Huang Xiquan), an attaché to the Chinese general consulate in San Francisco who visited Victoria in July 1884, the average Chinese laborer on the CPR received only $25 a month at the rate of $1 per working day, or $225 a year excluding the three months of winter. After paying for tax, rent, provisions, and other expenses, the yearly balance was only $43. In other words, each of these Chinese laborers had to work for nearly two years to pay off the $80 passage money advanced by the Chinese labor contractors. Because most of them came in 1882 or 1883, and their wage was reduced from $1 a day to as low as 50 cents a day in some cases in 1884, they could barely accumulate enough money for a return ticket at $70 in late 1885, as Huang had indicated one year before.[107]

Worst of all, an economic recession hit North America in mid-1885,[108] and the Chinese in British Columbia, especially the workers discharged from the CPR, faced discriminatory mistreatment from both white trade unions in the tight job market and the government at local, provincial, and federal levels.

In Victoria a local representative in Parliament founded a "labor association" around the end of the CPR construction in September 1885. Its objective was "to provide white labor for all the manufacturers and contractors in the province" by harassing and forcing employers to discharge their Chinese workers.[109] In late November 1885 the provincial government of British Columbia reported to Ottawa that thousands of discharged Chinese laborers had been "in a starving condition" and might face "every prospect of their perishing during the winter." The report blamed the federal government for its use of these Chinese workers for the construction of the CPR and placed on its shoulders "the duty of providing relief for these starving people."[110] In February 1886 Secretary of State J. A. Chapleau's report to the Privy Council fended off the provincial government of British Columbia. He downplayed the issue as merely a "momentary inconvenience, which has, perhaps, become intensified as the result of the local legislation or regulation, [and] should be borne by the local authorities."[111]

Consequently, the CCBA's leaders, especially the Chinese labor contractors for the CPR, provided urgent assistance for the unemployed Chinese laborers. In late 1885 they consigned steamships to send large numbers of unemployed railroad laborers back to China. At the beginning of 1886, they further responded to the appeal of the Chinese general consulate in San Francisco and worked with the CCBA's leaders there to provide subsidies to engage four steamships to repatriate Chinese laborers by charging only $2.50 for the trip from Victoria to San Francisco, and $25 for the trip from there to Hong Kong.[112] Moreover, these merchant leaders had donated 15,800 pounds of rice and $240 cash for destitute laborers in Victoria by late January 1886. They also promised to erect a soup kitchen to feed about three hundred people for two months starting immediately.[113] An extant list of donors to Victoria's CCBA in March 1886 shows that about twenty Chinese business establishments, including Lee Tin Poy's Lung Chung & Co., Lee Yau Kain's Kwong On Lung & Co., and Lee Yick Tack's Tai Yuen & Co., all contributed to the "relief funds" (*zhenji jiaoyin*).[114]

Evidently, under the leadership of these CPR's labor contractors from the Lee lineage, the CCBA not only rallied Chinese railroad laborers in their joint battle against racial discrimination but also helped the railroad workers survive the unemployment crisis after the completion of the transcontinental railroad. Its formative process and organizational activities brought the Chinese labor contractors, railroad laborers, and other Chinese immigrants in

British Columbia together in a united front, though they had been divided by class differentiation and even class clashes during the railroad construction. The CCBA typically reflected the institutional consolidation of the Chinese diaspora in Canada during the CPR-building era.

———

This examination of the Chinese construction of the CPR from a diasporic perspective advances our understanding of the development of the Chinese diaspora both in Canada and in the transpacific arena during the railroad construction years of 1880–1885. Such a development in the diaspora also had long-term historical significance beyond the CPR-building era. During the CPR-building era, the formation of the CKT's lodges among Chinese railroad workers and the establishment of the CCBA by the merchant leaders, especially the labor contractors from the Lee lineage, enabled the diaspora to expand its new institutional networks across and beyond Canada. The American-born CKT, or the Chinese Freemasons, spread across Canada from the early 1880s, evidently because many of its members moved northward from California and joined the Chinese builders of the CPR. The Canadian CKT would later join its counterparts in the United States as a major force in the political movements of the Chinese diaspora in the early twentieth century, especially in Sun Yat-sen's 1911 Republican Revolution, which greatly strengthened the long-lasting links between the Chinese diaspora and its homeland.[115]

CHAPTER 19

Beyond Railroad Work

Chinese Contributions to the Development
of Winnemucca and Elko, Nevada

SUE FAWN CHUNG

The important role of the Chinese railroad workers in contributing to the development of railroad towns in the American West is exemplified in two Nevada towns: Winnemucca and Elko. Winnemucca was established as a trading post in the 1830s and a small settlement in the early 1860s. In 1868 the town changed its name from French's to Winnemucca and prospered as a railroad town, transportation and commercial center, and mining community. Elko became a railroad town in late 1868. Unlike many ephemeral rail line settlements, both have endured and remain important towns along the first transcontinental route between Sacramento and Salt Lake City.

The towns offered slightly different lifestyles and experiences: the older transportation center of Winnemucca had more Chinese families, while the new train town of Elko was a predominantly male Chinese community. Both towns had Chinese American organizations and leaders who promoted the preservation of traditions and ties to the homeland (*qiaoxiang*, "ties to ancestral village/county, kinship/lineage, province, and/or country"), organizations such as the *huiguan* (district/regional associations), *gongsi* (clan associations), guilds (*gongsuo*), and secret societies or fraternal brotherhoods (*dang*, meaning association or meeting hall; in Cantonese *tong*) that had no birthplace or clan requirements. Some Chinese sent letters and money home and exchanged photographs in order to maintain ties. Those who returned to visit their birthplaces, especially if they had their own families, sometimes became more firmly rooted in tradition, while others, who regarded China as economically and socially backward, identified more with their new American

TABLE 19.1   Chinese Population by Nevada Counties, 1870–1920

County	Date Established	1870	1880	1890	1900	1910	1920
Churchill	1864	16	32	30	7	9	17
Douglas	1864	23	159	56	19	14	17
Elko	1869	439	613	311	191	151	93
Esmeralda	1864	56	242	277	115	64	8
Eureka	1873	—	633	284	101	30	14
Humboldt	1861	220	529	377	225	162	78
Lander	1862	218	387	87	71	24	13
Lincoln	1866	23	100	34	72	32	18
Lyon	1861	116	390	86	39	24	15
Nye	1864	6	66	23	7	59	44
Ormsby	1861	769	988	760	152	118	73
Storey	1850	749	639	245	76	44	13
Washoe	1861	221	526	217	246	155	155
White Pine	1869	292	107	46	31	25	32

NOTE: Roop (1859, merged with Washoe by 1890), Mineral (1911), and Clark (1909) Counties are not included.
SOURCE: Bureau of the Census, *Compendium of the Eleventh Census: 1890,* Table 14, Chinese Population by Counties, 1870, 1880, 1890, p. 520, and *Fourteenth Census: 1920,* vol. 3, Population by States. The figures differ slightly from one table to another in the census records. Tuscarora, Elko County, had the largest Chinese population due to its prosperity as a center of mining and the railroad industry.

environment. Some adopted Western customs, including language, foods, dress, and holidays.

According to the 1870 and 1880 United States census manuscripts, the majority of railroad workers in the Central Pacific Railroad (CPRR) towns, including Winnemucca and Elko, were Chinese (table 19.1). Most of the European Americans working for the railroad held skilled and supervisory positions. A few even lived with the Chinese in the 1870s and 1880s.[1] The Chinese population declined primarily as a result of restrictive anti-Chinese laws. In 1882 Congress passed the Chinese Restriction Act that prohibited Chinese laborers and their wives from immigrating; the restrictions and means of enforcement increased in the 1892 extension (known as the Geary Act), resulting in a shortage of Chinese workers.[2] Federal legislation passed in 1902, 1904, and 1924 essentially closed the door to the Chinese. Between the late 1870s and 1890 attorneys for both the CPRR and Southern Pacific Railroad (SPRR) became involved in some civil rights and other cases in support of railroad employees on behalf of the Chinese Consolidated Benevolent Association (CCBA) and other organizations, such as the Chinese Native Sons of the Golden State (in 1915 renamed the Chinese American Citizens Alliance).[3] The exclusion acts changed in fundamental ways Winnemucca and Elko, Nevada, where unskilled laborers were hard to locate for railroad work after 1892. Many of these former railroad workers changed their occupations to less strenuous work, and some still worked in support services for the railroads, doing such things as cooking, farming, coal mining, and woodcutting.

Winnemucca

The *Humboldt Register* showed that in May 1863 Chinese already lived in the agricultural and mining county of Humboldt, which was established in 1861. The CPRR reached Winnemucca on October 1, 1868. By late 1868 to early 1869 merchants had rushed in, hoping to establish businesses. Albert Sisson (1827–1888), William H. Wallace (d. 1882), and later Clark W. Crocker, a younger brother of Charles Crocker (1822–1888, one of the principals of the CPRR), operated a general merchandising store and freighting enterprise as Sisson, Wallace & Company or, after 1870, Sisson, [Clark] Crocker & Company, in addition to their Chinese labor recruitment activities. Several Chinese also opened merchandising stores, for example, Sing Fat Company of San Francisco. As in many western towns, the arrival of the railroad changed the nature of the town, and the CPRR played an important role in its economic development, physical layout, and growth of businesses.[4] In 1873 Winnemucca became the county seat of Humboldt County, much to the resentment of the residents of the former county seat, Unionville, some forty-five miles south of Winnemucca.[5] The new county seat attracted important businessmen and politicians. Because of its location, Winnemucca served as a natural commercial center for not only the equipment needed to complete the CPRR to Promontory Summit, Utah, but also later as a transportation hub for traffic to San Francisco to the west, Salt Lake City to the east, and Washington, Oregon, and Idaho to the north.

According to the 1870 United States census, the Chinese constituted 18 percent (54) of Winnemucca's total population of 289, and Chinese railroad laborers numbered 34 out of the total Chinese.[6] In that year the Winnemucca census also listed three European American conductors and five section foremen, as well as car repairmen, firemen, brakemen, yardmasters, a freight agent, switchmen, a Chinese cook, and a Chinese store clerk as railroad employees.[7] The Chinese worked as mechanics and section hands; helped to maintain the railroad shop, roundhouse, tracks, and trains that stopped at the station; cleaned engines and cars; cooked for passengers and crew members; and did odd jobs. Housing owned by the CPRR was provided near the tracks, and the pay for unskilled Chinese workers was 22.5 to 27.5 cents per hour.[8] Several European American railroad foremen lived next door or in the same residence as Chinese railroad workers.[9] Chinese living in nearby towns who were employed in railroad, mining, and service industries visited Winnemucca for supplies and recreation. In his reminiscences of his life in Winnemucca, James R. Chew (1901–1984), whose great-grandfather worked for the CPRR, recalled that in the late nineteenth century there were four hundred Chinese in or around town, almost all of them railroad workers. The group included four women, two fewer than in the 1870 census that listed a total of six women, all "prostitutes."[10] Census takers in the nineteenth century were seldom accurate in counting the Chinese, especially women and children, and many Chinese mentioned in the newspapers never appeared on any census list. Chew's reminiscences indicated that there were several married women with children living in the town, but none were included in the census figures.

The CPRR and its subsidiaries leased, rented, or sold buildings and land to the Chinese, transactions made legal by federal land grants made to the CPRR; in 1915 the Nevada State Legislature reaffirmed CPRR land transactions in Winnemucca, Elko, and other major Nevada railroad towns.[11] The CPRR had been responsible for the location of Chinatown on Bridge Street. In 1870 influential European American community leaders, who had formerly lived in nearby Unionville,[12] where they had expelled the Chinese from town in 1866, demanded the Chinese move out of Bridge Street, the center of Winnemucca, and relocate farther away to Baud Street (figure 19.1).

In the 1850s to 1880s, property was often transferred unofficially without deeds or contracts, but some buyers and sellers officially recorded their transactions. For example, in September 1883 Ape Lee paid D. H. Haskell $500 for three lots.[13] Eventually, Chinese men in Winnemucca were joined by women

FIGURE 19.1   Winnemucca's new Chinatown. Quong On Lung on the far left was originally a two-story building until a fire in 1900. The Zhigongtang building in center rear was on Baud Street. The buildings were built perpendicular to the lot lines because of feng shui (geomancy). Author's collection.

and families, owned homes and businesses, and were making their mark by the turn of the twentieth century. This was seen in the case of Low Sing Hee, owner of the general merchandising store Quong On Lung. European American patrons called him by his company's name, a common practice in the West. His wife and children remained in Winnemucca until the 1950s, when they moved to San Francisco and bought a home in the upscale "avenues," outside of San Francisco's Chinatown.[14]

Although Americans believed that the Chinese were "docile," in 1877 a gang of about forty Chinese railroad workers, who had been grading and laying side tracks near the Winnemucca depot for two or three months, rebelled against the railroad company's directive to move eastward to Carlin. Their headman, who said they had been working for the railroad company for two or three years, wanted to go westward in hopes of eventually returning to San Francisco or China.[15] Whether or not they were able to work on the westward line is unknown, but their protest contradicts the stereotypical image of Chinese as docile workers. Their actions inspired other Chinese railroad worker strikes, such as the wage dispute on the construction of the Tehachapi Railroad in 1876.

The ten cooks, one physician, and one laundryman listed in the 1870 census of Winnemucca were part of the support system for the railroad. Cooks worked in the hotels and restaurants that provided service for traveling passengers and crews, while the laundryman did the wash for the travelers, train crews, and community. Cooks from southern China were noted for being highly skilled due to their use of a variety of local ingredients and spices. They purchased produce and meats from Chinese farmers and ranchers. In some enterprises, such as mining and wood camps, Chinese cooks earned more than the average Chinese worker's pay per month, and sometimes more than their non-Chinese counterparts.[16] It was not unusual to find a Chinese chef or head cook making $40 to $60 per month in a hotel, private household, ranch, or wood camp.[17]

Winnemucca did not have an anti-Chinese club—often present in other western towns. The town's major newspaper, the *Silver State,* was located next to Chinatown, and therefore the Chinese were often "newsworthy." At the height of Nevada's anti-Chinese movements in the mid-1880s, the newspaper editor decided not to stir up the population against "cheap Chinese labor," as the earlier local newspaper, the *Humboldt Republican*, and many other western newspapers had done because of their support of white labor.[18] In Winnemucca, a town dependent upon the railroad, the growing railroad industry needed the Chinese workers, so the citizens were less hostile to the Chinese. The people also personally became acquainted with some of the Chinese, for example, members of the Jim Low family.

There were two well-known Chinese railroad workers who settled in Winnemucca: Wing Qui Chew and Jim Low. Little is known about Wing Qui Chew, but he was probably related to Jim Low's wife, Chew Fong Low. Chew was the father of Charley Chew Yee (d. 1922 in San Francisco), who was probably born in Winnemucca and lived as an adult, from around the early 1870s, in nearby Fort McDermitt. On November 3, 1894, Charley Chew Yee registered for his certificate of identity, as required by the Geary Act of 1892.[19] He and his wife, Mary, had eleven children, including William F. (Fook Hing) Chew, James F. (Fook Yuen) Chew, and Thomas (Fook Hong) Chew.[20] Because the family was so poor, they allowed Thomas to be adopted by Chinese friends, who took him to Carson City, Nevada. Eventually, Thomas ended up in China with another family. In 1920 William F. Chew went to China to search for Thomas and bring him back to San Francisco, where the family was then residing.[21] He was not successful, but another brother encountered Thomas during World War II in China.[22] Because of the absence of formal diplomatic relations with the People's Republic of China, Thomas

FIGURE 19.2   Drawing of Winnemucca's Chinatown by James Chew. This image shows half of a larger work by Chew. The Zhigongtang building is flying a Republic of China flag out front. The five-barred banner with five hues was used by the national government between 1912 and 1928. Throughout the scene, people are seen going about their daily business. A copy of the drawing was given to the author in 1997 by James Chew's nephew, the late William F. Chew.

had a difficult time obtaining a visa, despite his proven American birth, and the family reunion did not occur until 1981. On that occasion James Chew drew a picture of Winnemucca's Chinatown and wrote an essay based on his reminiscences of his early life in Winnemucca (figure 19.2).

In his memoir James Chew recalled that the family lived on Baud Street and that all of the buildings were wooden except for a single adobe house.[23] One of the most notable features of Chinatown was the Chinese vegetable garden (about two blocks long) located across the street from the Zhigongtang (Chinese Freemasons, in Cantonese Chee Kong Tong) building with its high staircase (center of drawing). Chew pointed out that Wong Git owned the Hi Loy Jan Store at 501 Baud Street, dealing in herbs and groceries. He portrayed everyday life in the memoir.

Another former CPRR worker who settled in Winnemucca was Jim Low (1846–1909, immigrated in 1849), who established a small trading post that became a significant merchandising store and raised a large family.[24] At first his customers included local Paiute, hunters, trappers, outlaws, and ranchers, but his business eventually spread to Oregon and northern California. He became a very prosperous merchant and by 1885 decided to go to San Francisco to find a bride through the well-known Occidental (or Presbyterian) Mission Home for Girls, later called Cameron House. He married Chew Fong (1869–1936), who was born in San Francisco. When her husband was away mining or delivering goods, Chew Fong Low managed the store and learned to speak Paiute (which she claimed was close to Cantonese) from her employees. In 1890 she worked with them to gather wool from sheep that had died during a terrible winter storm that year.[25] She also urged her relatives and her husband's relatives to move from San Francisco to Winnemucca. Consequently, there were several related Low and Chew families, an example of chain migration not only from Guangdong but also from San Francisco.

Other CPRR workers lived briefly in Winnemucca as well. The most famous among these was Chen Yixi (1844–1929, in Cantonese Chin Gee Hee, also called Ah Chin), who eventually became a labor contractor, railway entrepreneur, and merchant in Seattle. He spearheaded the project to build the first railroad in China, called the Xinning (Sunning) Railroad.[26] He had attended the 1911 rally in Winnemucca when Sun Yat-sen raised funds for his revolutionary cause.[27] Many Chinese Americans contributed to projects in their home counties or hometowns in Guangdong in an effort to share the prosperity they derived from their American enterprises.

Several former Chinese railroad workers who had rural backgrounds became farmers. One of the longtime Chinese residents was Lee Sam Melarkey (1827–1929), who moved to Winnemucca in the 1860s, adopted the last name of a public official/friend, and started a "Chinese garden."[28] Because the plots of land for growing produce were small, Chinese gardeners did not merit recognition as being farmers in the census. Lee Sam Melarkey was famous for his fresh vegetables, spices, and other foodstuffs, and advised other farmers about when and what to plant. He was regarded as the walking local farmers' almanac. The garden was irrigated by a waterwheel system reminiscent of the Guangdong agricultural irrigation systems. Nearby, but outside of the town proper, an area known as "Chinese Gardens" had terraced fields and waterwheels as a part of the irrigation system. The gardeners raised produce for Chinese cooks, the Chinese community, and, in all likelihood, railroad passengers and crew.[29]

While some of the former railroad workers observed the custom of having their bones sent back to their home villages in China after death, others were buried in a segregated cemetery with a fence around it.[30] European Americans often commented on how well their local cemetery was kept, but this was because of the "grave sweeping" in the spring and fall, an old Chinese tradition. An altar was built to provide for offerings to the spirits of the deceased. As in many cemeteries throughout the West, the bodies of some of the deceased residents who had paid for this service were exhumed and the bones cleaned, then sent back to Guangdong for a final burial.[31] Resistance to this practice occurred in 1888, when District Attorney M. S. Bonnifield, who had served as a senator in the Nevada legislature and later became a judge, tried to prevent the bones from being shipped to China.[32] Apparently he was not successful, because bones continued to be sent to places of birth in accordance with Chinese tradition as long as the individual belonged to a funerary organization or family association with burial provisions, or had an agreement with the labor contractor or employer for reburial. Some deceased remains were not disinterred until the cemetery was razed.

Elko

According to a popular legend, Charles Crocker, one of the Big Four and the general superintendent of construction for the CPRR, named Elko after a favorite animal and then added the *o* to its name.[33] From Winnemucca 124 miles to the west, the construction crew reached the desert environment of Elko, in Elko County, on December 24, 1868. It became the last major town before Salt Lake City, and served miners, ranchers, and travelers. From Elko, travelers could take the stagecoach to several new booming mining towns. The CPRR built a station, three large freight depots, and a hotel, and persuaded Wells Fargo to purchase a stagecoach line in order to bring goods to be shipped from its station.[34] Later the CPRR added hotels and restaurants to serve the traveling public. The Depot Hotel (previously called the Cosmopolitan, then the Chamberlain) was one of the most popular and featured a Chinese chef known as Gee.[35] From 1869 until 1930 Elko provided ice for the trains to keep perishable goods from spoiling.[36] Chinese railroad workers and Chinese merchants became a part of the community from Elko's early heyday and helped lay the foundation of its prosperity.[37]

In terms of the ties that the Chinese in Elko maintained to their place of birth, the adjustments they made to their new Nevada environment, the growth and maturity of the second and later generations, and their contributions to their new communities, the Chinese experience differed slightly from that in Winnemucca.

According to the 1870 United States census manuscript, 153 Chinese railroad workers had settled in Elko County, including 43 living in the town of Elko proper out of a total Chinese population in the state of 3,162.[38] This does not include the number of laborers who may have done supportive work for the railroad. Elko was also home to one European American CPRR conductor and six European American CPRR laborers. In 1871 Elko had a total population of approximately 1,000, with more than 120 businesses. In October 1871 a fire swept through part of the town and destroyed almost all of Chinatown, which was located in the center of town by the railroad tracks. The Chinese had no fire insurance, so rebuilding was financially difficult.[39] In the special state census of 1875 Elko County counted 179 Chinese males and 1 Chinese female in residence.[40] By 1880 many Chinese railroad workers had moved from Elko to nearby Carlin, a major railroad maintenance center, or other locations.

Elko had the largest Chinatown in the county and served as a place for recreation, socialization, medical care, and protection for workers in outlying areas. In 1870 Elko County Chinese railroad workers ranged in age from fourteen to forty-five (Sin Fook, the oldest, worked in Wells). The average age was thirty. Chinatown was also a refuge for seasonal workers because of the available boardinghouses and recreational facilities. According to the 1870 United States census manuscript, nine Chinese merchants, seven in the town of Elko, supplied the Chinese railroad workers with provisions and sold goods to the Chinese and the larger community.[41] These men were usually the leaders of the Chinese community, and had some basic knowledge of reading and writing Chinese and English.

Hop Sing (b. 1844, also known as Bow Shee, or "Fat Stuff," because of his rotund figure) was one of the two youngest merchants. The 1870 census listed him as having $300 in assets.[42] Like Ah Lung (b. 1847), he was probably sent by his family or clan to open the store, and they provided him with the merchandise through a network system that connected Hong Kong to San

Francisco or Sacramento and then on to frontier towns. He sold groceries, drugs, and general merchandise. Recognizing the importance of water in a desert community, especially for the "Chinese vegetable gardens," Hop Sing, under his store name of Hi Loy, invested in the construction of the first irrigation ditch, originally called the Elko Water Works. This system supplied water to Elko for several decades. The wooden flume originated in Kittridge Canyon, eight miles to the east, and ended in a small reservoir above China Ranch, where the Chinese farmed. Eventually the Osino Ditch, popularly known as the "China Ditch," added another mile by connecting to the Humboldt River. Le Hi served as the foreman of the Elko Water Works. This irrigation system resembled those in Guangdong. In the late twentieth century, the Hi Loy Water Tower was still visible from the western entrance to Elko.

Another Chinese merchant, community leader, and possible former railroad worker or agent was Yee Foo Jung (b. 1851), who headed Wha Lung and Company.[43] His two sons and several daughters were born in Elko. In 1879 Yee took his family back to Woo Bin Village, Taishan, Guangdong. Before departing he put his nephew, Yee Gow Jung, who had been working for him for four years, in charge of the business. In 1896 Yee Foo Jung and his two sons returned, and his sons took over the business. That year Yee Foo Jung moved to San Francisco and became an influential community leader and the president of the Hehetang (Hop Wo Association). After two trips to Woo Bin, in 1890 and 1892, Yee Gow Jung also relocated to San Francisco to work at Quong Wah Chung on Sacramento Street. In the 1900 Elko tax records, Wha Lung and Company was valued at $1,000, indicating that it was prosperous. This was an example of the connections or networking between merchants in South China and the American West.

According to the *Elko Daily Free Press*, several former railroad workers decided to establish a vegetable garden at China Ranch (present-day City Park).[44] Others established smaller gardens along the river near Seventh and Pine Streets. In Guangdong the Chinese had been farmers, so agricultural work in Elko was familiar. However, it was more challenging in Elko because of the desert environment with its dearth of water. Human-powered waterwheels, like those in China, irrigated the crops with water from the Humboldt River. Chinese gardeners provided fresh produce to Chinatown residents, Chinese cooks working for restaurants, and members of the European American community. Wah Sing was regarded as the best gardener in Elko and earned enough money to return to China.[45] Fresh produce enhanced the demand for Chinese cooks in restaurants and work camps.

The 1870 census counted seventeen Chinese cooks in Elko. The number dropped to twelve in 1880, with none of the names repeating, but some of the names may have been misspelled, so some individuals were probably the same. In 1902 the *Elko Free Press* reported that China Sing, known as "Gee," had cooked for the Depot Hotel (located near Chinatown and the railroad tracks) for the past twenty-eight years and had saved enough money to return to China.[46] The Nevada Historical Society has a photograph of Gee seated with a cigar in his hand with two European American friends flanking him. Gee was well known and well liked in the community. The hotel closed its doors in 1904, so he probably left Elko sometime during the intervening two years. He was not listed as a resident in the 1900 census and does not appear on the incomplete National Archives and Records Administration's immigrants list of departing Chinese persons for the period 1894 to 1912.

Another notable Elko cook was Quong Kee (1841–1938), who left his job as assistant cook in Virginia City to work as a cook for the CPRR. He attended the golden spike ceremony of 1869 as an observer. He commented to his biographer about the ceremony by saying, "Lailload men work plenty hard. In rain, snow, mud, but paydays they raise plenty hell."[47] Quong Kee continued cooking for railroad workers in Elko in the 1870s. His specialty was Irish stew, so he undoubtedly was not cooking for the Chinese workers. He adopted Western dress early.[48] He earned enough money to visit China several times and eventually settled in Tombstone, Arizona, where he opened the famous Can Can Restaurant that featured pheasant under glass served on white tablecloths with linen napkins. When he died in neighboring Bisbee, the people of Tombstone insisted on having him buried in the town with great fanfare (all the prominent men turned out). His grave in the Boothill Graveyard, next to the Zhigongtang leader of Tombstone, Mrs. Ah Lum, is clearly marked even today.

By June 1869 Elko had eight European American doctors, none of whom would provide medical care for the Chinese at either the six-bed public hospital or the "pest hospital" (for communicable diseases), so the Chinese asked their district association, family association, or labor contractor to provide medical care, which was a common request.[49] In 1870 three Chinese men, probably connected with railroad work, died from smallpox, but no one from any other ethnic group died from the disease that year.[50] In 1870 Dr. Ah Lee (b. 1838) served Elko's Chinese population in a similar role to Winnemucca's Chinese physician.[51] In 1873 Dr. Ken Fung, a graduate of the School of Medicine and Surgery in Guangzhou, served as the resident physician of the newly established two-ward Chinese-built hospital, which had open admission.[52] The hospital rivaled the small "whites-only hospital" built in 1869 in Elko and continued to offer its limited services to the general population for several years. As in many towns in the American West in the late nineteenth century, positive testimonials from non-Chinese patients brought customers of many ethnicities to Chinese physicians.

A few Chinese women and children lived in Elko and were included in the census. The 1870 census, for example, counted nine Chinese women, including three "keeping house," but in 1880 their numbers dropped to four, all young "prostitutes." Nevada census takers in the 1870s wanted to justify passage of the 1875 Page Act prohibiting Chinese prostitutes from entering the country. None of the names were repeated, and none match any of the names in newspaper accounts or marriage records. On November 25, 1873 the *Elko Independent* noted the marriage of Charlie Sue to Miss Tie Que (neither listed in the census) by Justice of the Peace Stafford.[53] In 1878 Ah Wing married Fanny Wing, and in 1879 Ah Young married Ah Few You.[54] Other marriages were announced infrequently in the newspaper, but neither the bride nor the groom was ever listed by that name in the census. When Chin On (b. 1859, immigrated 1890), a railroad laborer, died on January 20, 1917, his wife, Hon Shee, received his estate of $1,900 and an interest in the Cottage Hotel in Tuscarora.[55] Chin On's wife and three daughters were not listed in any of the United States census manuscripts. Chin On was probably regarded as a wealthy man and was another example of the financial success of a former railroad worker. No children were ever listed in the Elko census for 1870 to 1900, and only two Chinese women were listed in 1890.

Chinese children attended public school. In his reminiscences of Elko in 1890, Charles Keyser mentioned that Chinese children were given days off of school to attend Chinese New Year's celebrations at the "joss house" (the popular name for the Zhigongtang, which had an altar on the top floor of the building for religious purposes) and for funerals.[56] As in most towns, the Chinese cemetery was segregated and located on a hill north of the Presbyterian church at the end of Sixth Street, then later relocated to Eighth and Cedar. A bone house was built to preserve the bones of the deceased until they could be sent back to China for final burial.[57] In the mid-twentieth century, teenagers allegedly destroyed the wooden bone house and its contents. Unlike the cemetery in Winnemucca, Elko's cemetery did not garner any praise in the local newspapers, but because of the traditional Qingming, or Spring Festival, of cleaning the graves and remembering the ancestors, the Chinese section was fairly well maintained, and even today there are a few readable grave markers.

———

The Chinese contributed to the development of Winnemucca and Elko, Nevada, with their knowledge of irrigation and farming, of medical treatments, of logging and charcoal making, of road construction, of cooking, and of laundry services. They provided these services in support of the railroad industry and the European American community. Both towns had a Zhigongtang, and the members were dedicated to supporting the 1911 Republican Revolution and the new Republic of China. Both towns had a predominance of men—some married with wives in China, a few with wives in the American West, and others single. Some families did exist. Women like Chew Fong Low and Mrs. Dip Lee, both of Winnemucca, were not shy, retiring types but played a major role in their husbands' affairs and interacted with at least the Chinese community, if not the larger community. Mrs. Lee, as a midwife, probably helped in the birthing of Chinese, Native American, and even European American babies because of the shortage of western physicians. In both towns the Chinatowns were the centers of their recreational and social activities until the Chinese population began to decline after the 1890s. The Chinatowns also served the needs for recreational gambling, opium smoking, and prostitution that characterized many Chinatowns. Chain migration, as exemplified by former railroad workers Jim Low and Hop Sing, brought relatives into the towns. Wealth and prosperity were in the grasp of some former railroad workers.

As in many western rural communities, the first generation tried to maintain their cultural heritage by celebrating major traditional holidays like New Year's and Qingming and maintaining contact with their birth villages, but the children who were born in the United States and educated in the public school system became more Americanized. Minor Chinese holidays and festivals gradually ceased to be a part of their lives. Some younger members of the first generation registered their marriages with the county recorder's offices, which became more common with each passing decade. The second generation not only married in Christian churches but also married non-Chinese, which was not looked upon with favor by more conservative Chinese or many European Americans. Nevertheless, these practices were indicators of increasing Americanization as the "transplanted society" evolved. In both towns the former Chinese railroad workers and their American-born descendants had a significant impact on the development of the American West. Although they have often been overlooked or forgotten in the past, new research is helping to fill in the details about the lives and experiences of these early Chinese immigrants. Nevadans have striven to correct this. A monument erected in Sparks, Nevada, in 1981 commemorates the contributions of the Chinese railroad workers and others to Nevada.[58]

CHAPTER 20

The Remarkable Life of a Sometime Railroad Worker

Chin Gee Hee, 1844–1929

BETH LEW-WILLIAMS

A central problem in the history of Chinese railroad workers in North America is the lack of individual voices. Though thousands of Chinese migrants worked on the transcontinental railroads, too often this is a history of "nameless builders" and "silent spikes."[1] One glaring exception, however, is Chin Gee Hee (also known as Chen Yixi). After migrating in the 1860s, Chin began life in the United States as a domestic, miner, and railroad worker, seasonally grading roadbeds for the railways in Oregon and Nevada. Over the next several decades, he rose to become a labor contractor, provisions supplier, and ticket agent for railroads in Washington State. In the early twentieth century, he became a railroad financier and developer in China, raising over $4 million for his company that laid about 85 miles (137 kilometers) of track in Taishan (Toishan).[2] His tale is an exceptional one of upward mobility, and we know about him only because of his ascent. While most Chinese railroad workers left behind only enigmatic traces, Chin left behind immigration files, county court records, newspaper articles, diplomatic correspondence, appeals to the Chinese Consolidated Benevolent Association (known as the "Six Companies"), private letters, a personal account book, photographs, and family lore. As a result, scholars know more about Chin than we will ever know about ordinary Chinese railroad workers.

Chin's story cannot stand in for all Chinese railroad workers, even if he once was one, but his experiences do offer at least three avenues into deciphering their history. First, we can attend to the (limited) ways in which his life was typical of Chinese railroad workers. To the collective history of Chinese workers, Chin's well-documented story adds a vividness that cannot be captured in the aggregate. Second, we can consider the ways in which Chin, as well as his socioeconomic mobility, was atypical of Chinese railroad workers. By picturing Chin as a photonegative of the norm, we can see in his rise hints of what kept other workers down. Third, we can examine Chin's work as a labor contractor for what it can tell us about the workers in his employ. His efforts to protect, as well as exploit, his countrymen provide insight into the precarious existence of Chinese railroad workers.

Student/Migrant/Worker

Chin Gee Hee's life story has been partially shrouded in myth. Most written accounts claim he was born to an impoverished family in 1844 in Langmei Village in Guangdong Province. When Chin was a child, so the story goes, his father owned a soy sauce crockery business, and he grew up carrying the wares on a pole to market each day. One day a group of game-playing boys accidentally bumped into Chin as he walked along, causing his crocks to fall. As he gazed at his broken merchandise, Chin was approached by an old man, Kung-pei, who had just returned from America. "Young man, how would you like to go to the mountain of gold?" asked the man. Chin answered, "I [would] like to go, but there is no way that I can." Kung-pei smiled and said, "There is a way and don't worry! I will go with you!" According to Chin's biographers, it was this fateful meeting that sent an ordinary Chinese peasant to America.[3]

But this origin story may be apocryphal. Chin's great-grandson, Wingston Chan, disputes that the family was ever in the crockery business, locates Chin's hometown as Mei Tong Village, and suggests that he was a student from a farming family. "One day, while the young man was studying at home, pushed by his mother," Chan wrote of his great-grandfather, "a man outside his window, going [through] the street, r[a]ng the bell and [told] the people to join him to go to Gum Shan (San Francisco) to find gold and…[a] better life in America. Seeing there [was] no future for him in China,…[my great-grandfather] decided to try his luck in the Gold Rush." This account explains how Chin arrived in California already fully literate in Chinese, an unusual trait among Chinese migrants in the 1860s.[4]

Before departing, Chin hastily married a woman from nearby Luk Chuen but then left his young wife behind, as most migrants did. He boarded a junk that took him over the waterways of the Pearl River delta. When he reached Hong Kong, he either stayed in a dormitory provided by passage brokers or found a bed in the home of a friend or relative. If, like most migrants he could not afford the $40 or $50 one-way ticket to America, he would have used the credit-ticket system, signing away a portion of his future earnings to repay the price of his ticket.[5]

When the day for departure arrived, Chin and the other passengers lined up on deck for health inspection, then descended to their quarters below. It was there, in the dark space below deck, that they would spend most of the two-month journey. During the voyage Chin spent much of his time with the man who had recruited him, soaking up what he could of English, Christianity, and American ways. This also set him apart from the rest of the Chinese passengers and sped his adaptation to this new land. Before he even stepped foot on American soil, Chin's great-grandson recounts, "he [had] already equipped himself with [a] little spoken English, although still very little, but enough to impress the people he met."[6]

Chin disembarked in San Francisco around 1862. Although he left no record of his landing, the reminiscences of another Chinese migrant, Huie Kin, give a sense of the excitement of arrival. Kin recalled, "On a clear, crisp, September morning…the mists lifted, and we sighted land for the first time. We had left the shores of Kwangtung [Guangdong] over sixty days before. To be actually at the 'Golden Gate' of the land of our dreams!" Disembarking onto the crowded piers of San Francisco, Chinese migrants were greeted by a loud and confused scene. As Kin recalled, "Out of a general babble someone called out in our local dialect and like sheep recognizing the voice only, we blindly followed and soon were piling into one of the waiting wagons." Other Chinese migrants followed labor brokers on foot, walking single file with bamboo poles slung across their shoulders to the Chinese quarter of the city.[7]

Once they reached Chinatown, new arrivals like Chin spent their first night in America in the crowded dormitories of the Chinese companies that had arranged their passage and would likely contract out their labor. The Chinese quarters of the city felt familiar to the newcomers. According to Kin, "in the [1860s] San Francisco's Chinatown was made up of stores catering to the Chinese only.... Our people were all in their native costume, with queues down their backs, and kept their stores just as they would do in China, with the entire street front open and groceries and vegetables overflowing on the sidewalks."[8]

Chin did not stay long within this ethnic enclave surrounded by the trappings of home. Instead, within two weeks he journeyed out into the multiracial space of the rural US West. First he went to Long Bar and then San Juan, both tiny California mining towns on the edge of the Sierra Nevada. It appears he took on a series of jobs, perhaps shifting seasonally. He worked as a gold miner and a laborer for Bow Chew Tong, a firm that provisioned miners. He briefly worked as an unskilled railroad worker, most likely on the Central Pacific in Nevada.[9] He also spent several years as a domestic serving a white mining family.[10]

Chin's varied work life was typical of unskilled Chinese laborers, many of whom shifted in and out of railroad work. To be a railroad worker was not to have a fixed trade for life. Chinese railroad workers were also the men who mined for gold, felled trees, drained swamp lands, washed laundry, and cared for white children. And many Chinese migrants who never laid track still helped build the road by providing provisions, foodstuffs, lumber, and services for those who did. In other words, there is little that separates the history of Chinese railroad workers from the history of other Chinese in the West.

Chin's work as a domestic servant proved transformative. He was hired by John W. Brown, a miner, and his wife, H. Adeline Brown. Chin washed their clothes, cooked their meals, and helped to care for their two children. He later recalled his time with the Browns as "a pleasure." John was busy searching for gold (mostly in vain), but Adeline found the time to improve Chin's English and begin his education in reading and writing. This gave Chin the ability to record his business and life in two languages; few Chinese domestics were so fortunate.[11]

When Chin left the family a few years later to journey north, he took these invaluable skills with him. He moved to Washington Territory, following the small stream of miners and laborers who had heard of opportunities in the Pacific Northwest. To get there, he boarded a ship at San Francisco bound for Victoria, British Columbia, then made his way south to Port Townsend, Washington Territory.[12] From the wooden dock that jutted out into the harbor, Chin would have been able to see the neat little town, composed of small houses and muddy streets, surrounded on three sides by dense forests, and on the fourth by the water and the San Juan Islands beyond.

At the time Washington Territory and British Columbia formed an interlocked community. Cyclical migration blurred the line between "American" and "Canadian" workers, as people in both countries moved back and forth across the national boundary as opportunities arose.[13] The local indigenous people crossed the border seasonally, following the fish runs. Likewise, the Chinese community was in constant motion, circulating goods, people, and knowledge across the land and sea border. When Chin arrived in Washington, there were only a few hundred Chinese in the entire territory and even fewer in Canada, but soon that would change.[14]

With the help of a labor contractor, Chin began work at the Port Gamble Lumber Mill. Located fifteen miles (twenty-four kilometers) south of Port Townsend on Puget Sound, Port Gamble was a company town, designed and constructed to supply laborers for the huge mill. The mill work was grueling, the wages were low, and the atmosphere was unpleasant. A decade later a journalist described the giant mill with both admiration and horror. "The mill itself," he wrote, "was a deafening, blinding, terrifying storm of machinery: saws by dozens, upright, horizontal, circular, whirring and whizzing on all sides; great logs, sixty, a hundred feet long, being hauled up, dripping, out of the water, three at a time, by fierce clanking chains, slid into grooves, turned, hung, drawn and quartered, driven from one end of the building to the other like lightning."[15] Chin spent the better part of six years working in Port Gamble as a laborer, cook, and laundryman. Although Chinese workers like Chin labored alongside white workers, they were paid lower wages for the most grueling work. This too the journalist observed: "Literally it may be said that the Chinamen do the dirty work, whilst the more pleasant parts of the business are reserved for white men."[16] Along with gaining new skills in carpentry and factory work, no doubt Chin and his countrymen learned lessons at the mill about race and place.

Businessman/Employer/Friend

Although Chin Gee Hee's first decade in America mirrored the experience of other Chinese railroad workers, starting in the mid-1870s his trajectory diverged. In Port Gamble Chin encountered another sympathetic white woman, a Mrs. Thomas, who continued his education in Christianity, American customs, and English.[17] As his language skills improved, Chin began to make connections outside the Chinese community, befriending a white pioneer, Henry Yesler, who would become mayor of Seattle. After he began to amass some savings, Chin sent for his wife (known by the family as Madame

Wong) and found her a job as a cook for the mill hands. If his life as a Chinese man in a US territory was isolating, her experience had to be even more so. According to the 1880 US census, nearly a decade after she arrived, there were only twenty-five Chinese women in the territory among more than three thousand Chinese men. When Madame Wong gave birth to their first son in 1875, the infant was likely the first Chinese born in Washington Territory.[18]

By 1873, after six years of working at the lumber mill, two backbreaking seasons spent grading railroad beds in Oregon, and one year operating a laundry, Chin had acquired the monetary and social capital to go into business.[19] Chin and his wife moved to Seattle, where he connected with a merchant from his home village, Chin Ching Hock. With the help of borrowed money, Chin purchased 25 percent of Chin Ching Hock's business and became a junior partner of the Wa Chong Company, a tea and Chinese import business. When Chin Ching Hock created the company in 1862, it was the first Chinese-owned commercial establishment in Seattle and was located on the flatlands beside Seattle's first lumber mill. By the time Chin Gee Hee joined the company a decade later, Chin Ching Hock had a large storefront in the emerging Chinese neighborhood in Seattle complete with an upper-floor dormitory to house lodgers and itinerant laborers.[20]

Although Chin Ching Hock had focused primarily on commerce, Chin Gee Hee expanded into the lucrative business of labor contracting. He would travel around the territory to coal mines, railroads, farms, and private homes to find employers looking for workers. Then he would arrange for Chinese laborers, many of whom did not have the language skills or knowledge to seek their own work, to be supplied to the employers for a fee. Sometimes he acted as both passage broker and labor contractor, recruiting Chinese across the border in British Columbia to work in Washington Territory. Under Chin Gee Hee's guidance, Wa Chong Company thrived, and soon Seattle's Chinese community grew up around it. By 1880, census takers counted 200 Chinese in Seattle, 29 of whom lived in Chin's boardinghouse.[21]

As he prospered, Chin continued to study English with uncommon persistence and obvious brilliance, teaching himself a vast vocabulary, including highly specialized legal, technical, and business terms. He kept a 200-page business notebook with entries dating from 1880 to 1910. The book is a collection of notes, including Chinese-English translations, tallies of goods, business letters, lists of addresses and names, and copies of telegraphs. The translated words show his preoccupation with business: column after column of numbers, dates, locations, and the language of buying and selling. The tran-scribed letters speak to his varied and successful business interests: page upon page of missives from railroad company executives, coal miners, and wealthy individuals from all over the Puget Sound region asking for Chinese laborers. In addition to labor contracting, Chin traded rice, tea, soap, and opium—in the Puget Sound region and beyond. Addresses he recorded included contacts in Oregon, California, Montana, New York, British Columbia, Hong Kong, and England.

Chin's notebook reveals that he often had to worry about legal concerns. He needed to learn the terms *warrant, a bad case, interpreter,* and *treaty stip-ulations.* He needed to know the names of the sheriff, the governor, the local judge, US attorneys, and customs officials. He also kept close a list of members of the Chinese consulate in San Francisco and the Chinese delegation in Washington, DC. While many of the translated words and notated places have clear connections to his expanding business, the notebook is punctuated by words that are anomalous. Chin studied such words as *destroy, rascal, assas-sin, adultery,* and *rape.*[22] These isolated words, provocative and unexplained, remind us of the world of violence and danger in which Chin lived.

Armed with near-fluent English, Chin built connections to some of the most prominent white men in the territory as he provided workers for their businesses and servants for their wives. Observing Chin's extensive business network, historian Madeline Hsu argues, "Many of Seattle's leading business-men had welcomed and even embraced his presence in their city as a notable force in the growth of the local economy." For Hsu, this is a sign of camaraderie that transcended race, a "recognition that regardless of race or country of origin those who contributed most to the building of Seattle were almost all immigrants who by dint of hard work and determination overcame humble origins to become influential men of business."[23] Can we see in Chin's success and acceptance the power of a shared American dream? Perhaps, but we must not forget that these relationships were built upon the fickle flow of capital, and blossomed only when business prospered.

We can find a glimpse into Chin's relationships with white Americans through the letters he exchanged with the Brown family and then painstak-ingly copied into his notebook. In 1880 Chin wrote to Adeline Brown, the woman he used to serve in San Juan, California. "It has been seven years since I left your place," he wrote in flowing cursive. "I look back with a great deal of pleasure all time and would like to see you very much, but it is so far away that

[I] cannot go to see you at present." Chin reported on his growing family and business, seemingly eager to tell Brown of his success and thank her for past kindness.[24]

Adeline Brown responded enthusiastically: "We were very pleasantly surprised a few weeks ago by receiving a letter from you. I have often thought of you and wondered what had become of you. Thought you must have gone to China to live with your wife. We would like very much to see you again but you would find [us] greatly changed." She reminded Chin to "read your bible and talk to your wife and children about [J]esus," but then explained, in plaintive language, that their financial situation had weakened. "You would feel badly to see how hard we all have to work now," she continued. "Just think of us doing all the washing ironing & cooking for six of us, we have another little boy 4 years who looked just like Butu did & a little girl 20 months....Just think of Mr. Brown work[ing] for $2.50 per day to keep us all." Brown ended her unhappy tale with a request for aid. She noted that Chin's business must contract domestic servants and asked if he would send them one and "pay his board too." Chin's onetime employer was now requesting a substantial act of charity.[25]

"Dear friend," Chin began his response, then launched into more of his own good news. Despite Brown's awkward appeal, he did not attempt to hide his growing prosperity, reporting that he leased a three-story brick building in Seattle for his home and business, owned four acres that were good for farming, and had ambitions to build a railroad from Seattle to Walla Walla the following spring. He commented that America was a "very lively" country and that his family had grown to two wives and five children, all of whom were currently living in China. He concluded the letter with a simple refusal of Brown's request: "I think I cannot send any boy."[26] He may have been fond of the Browns, but his feelings had (financial) limits.

Smuggler/Advocate/Victim

Chin had been importing Chinese workers from British Columbia for almost a decade when the practice was declared illegal. In 1882 the Chinese Restriction Act barred new Chinese workers from entering the United States for ten years, and subsequent exclusion laws extended this policy until 1943. The laws did not halt the movement of Chinese migrants across the northern border, nor did they stop Chin's involvement with it.[27] They did, however, force Chinese workers to depend even more on men like Chin. By "running" Chinese workers across the border, Chin defied exclusion, but he also profited from it at minimal risk to himself.[28]

Little more than rumors tie Chin to the network of smuggling that flourished in the Chinese exclusion era. Chin took great care to leave behind few traces of his unlawful activities. Occasionally, federal officials caught wind of smuggling schemes, but still they struggled to stop them. In July 1883, for instance, Deputy Collector of Customs Arthur Blake apprehended a man named Ah Sin. "I had a long talk with him," Blake reported to his superiors, "and in my opinion, he is the man who is piloting the Chinese across. He speaks English very imperfectly, but as well as I could make out, he offered to pay me $2 per head on all Chinamen I would allow to come in." To keep the man talking, Blake played along: "I humored his fancy to learn all I could from him. He mentioned Wa Chong's name frequently, though I could not understand what he said about him." One of the many things Blake did not understand was that "Wa Chong" was the name of a company (not a man), and that company was owned and operated by Chin Gee Hee.[29]

Chin himself did not need the aid of a smuggler to cross the border; as a newly minted member of the merchant class, he was exempt from the Restriction Act and the exclusion laws that followed. He was not exempt, however, from the ritualized humiliation of border enforcement.[30] The demands of work and family sent him out of the United States at least twenty-seven times between 1885 and 1898. Each time he reentered the country, he could expect to be followed by the watchful eyes of customs officials, separated from white passengers for additional questioning, asked for papers to prove his identity, and (when he was unfortunate enough to encounter an official he did not know) subjected to extensive interrogation about his business, his family, and his entire life history.[31] Chin's unauthorized workers, of course, faced all of this, in addition to the prospect of detention, trial, and deportation.

America's gates never closed to men like Chin, but even merchants could not escape the shadow they cast. It is noteworthy, therefore, that when Chin was presented with an opportunity to denounce Chinese exclusion, he did not take it. In 1905, after Congress had indefinitely extended Chinese exclusion and abrogated its treaties with China, Chinese merchants launched a transnational boycott of American goods in protest. Spearheaded by merchants and intellectuals in Shanghai, the protest movement soon spread along China's coast and across the Pacific to Hawaii and San Francisco. Though brief, fractured, and denounced by both the US and Chinese governments, the boycott was a stunning act of transnational organizing against American racism. But at the time, Chin was more concerned by his plans to build a railway in China. Not only did he refuse to participate in the movement, but he also publicly urged Chinese merchants to drop the effort.[32]

In other matters, however, Chin could be a powerful and needed advocate for Chinese workers. Unlike in San Francisco, where the Chinese consulate and the Six Companies looked after the interests of the Chinese community, there were no Chinese political, social, or benevolent organizations in Washington until 1892.[33] Before then, Chinese merchant-contractors like Chin served as informal representatives, translators, and guides for the working class. When his workers were arrested at the border, Chin was the one to bail them out. When his workers were treated unfairly on the job, he was the one to lodge a protest. And when anti-Chinese violence came to Washington Territory in 1885, Chin was the one to negotiate with American officials, report to the Chinese consulate, and testify against the conspirators.[34]

In November 1885, when vigilantes expelled several hundred Chinese from nearby Tacoma, Chin monitored the news from Seattle with growing fear. Writing an urgent telegraph on November 4 to the Chinese consulate in San Francisco, he reported, "Chinese residents of Tacoma forcibly driven out yesterday, from two to three hundred Chinese now in Seattle. Imminent danger. Local authorities willing but not strong enough to protect us. We ask you to secure protection for us. Chin Gee-hee for Wa Chong Co."[35] No doubt Chin was anxious about his own welfare, but he was also concerned with the fate of Chinese workers in the territory, hundreds of whom he employed. If all Chinese workers were driven from Seattle, he would lose both his coethnic community and a significant portion of his livelihood.

When Chin sent this desperate appeal to the Chinese consulate in San Francisco, he did so as a prominent, wealthy merchant with connections. The consul general, Owyang Ming, took notice. Ming reported to the Chinese minister, Cheng Tsao Ju (Zheng Zaoru), in Washington, DC, that "outrages are still going on" in Washington Territory and "strong appeals for protection arrive here hourly." In turn, the Chinese minister wrote to the US secretary of state, Thomas F. Bayard, beseeching him to protect Chinese citizens from the violence.[36] The pleas of Chin and other Chinese merchants did not go unheard, but while diplomats were busy corresponding, the situation in Washington Territory continued to worsen. Before Chin could receive a response from the Chinese consulate, he was arrested.

A day after the Tacoma expulsion, US District Attorney J. T. Ronald had filed an indictment against Chin for the crime of "maintaining a public nuisance." The indictment alleged that Chin had maintained an acre of land next to his store where he was "slaughtering a great number of hogs and other animals and storing large quantities of decaying vegetable matter and filth." These "offensive substances" were "occasioning noxious exhalations, offensive smells and stenches" that were "injurious and dangerous" to the "entire community." Sheriff John McGraw, warrant in hand, arrested Chin on November 5, just as the anti-Chinese excitement in Seattle was coming to a head.[37] There is no evidence that this indictment ever resulted in a trial. In fact, Chin spent less than a day in jail. Apparently, the timing of the arrest was meant to intimidate him and to influence the outcome of a meeting that had been arranged for that afternoon. Chin was one of five prominent Chinese merchants who sat down with anti-Chinese leaders on November 5 to discuss the peaceable removal of Chinese from Seattle. The merchants were not official leaders of the Chinese community there, but the anti-Chinese vigilantes, and presumably the merchants themselves, believed that they could speak on behalf of the Chinese laborers.

According to the local papers, Chin and the other Chinese merchants agreed to send away Chinese laborers as fast as funds would permit, but they asked for more time for Chinese businessmen like themselves. Chin pointed out that Wa Chong Company held property in Seattle worth $135,000 and was owed some $30,000 by the city, so he and his partners could hardly be expected to leave overnight. The Chinese merchants asked for patience and a reasonable timetable for them to pack up, dispose of their property, and leave the city.[38] Even if such figures were exaggerated, it is clear that elite merchants like Chin ran sizable businesses. They had significant financial stakes in the community, and the community benefited from the revenue, goods, and labor they brought to the area. Although the anti-Chinese leaders left the meeting believing that Chinese merchants and laborers would soon leave voluntarily, it is unclear whether the Chinese merchants actually intended to leave the territory when it would mean incurring such a large financial loss.[39] With the heightened state of agitation in the city and Chin's suspicious arrest, they may have been more concerned with placating the vigilantes and buying time.

As promised, the merchants quickly began to send away Chinese workers;

within two days 150 of them left Seattle by train or boat.[40] As Chinese residents began to leave, the foundation of the Chinese community in Seattle started to come apart—shops and buildings stood empty, labor contracts were broken, and social networks crumbled. As departures mounted, reasons to stay dwindled. But this "voluntary exodus" of the Chinese ended suddenly when news of arson in Tacoma pushed the territorial government to oppose the growing climate of threatened and real violence. On November 7 the mayor of Seattle, Henry Yesler, issued a proclamation enjoining citizens to uphold the law, Sheriff McGraw organized a company of Home Guards to oppose the vigilantes, and Governor Watson Squire asked the president of the United States, Grover Cleveland, for permission to deploy federal troops to enforce the peace. Early the next morning, at 1:30 a.m., the remaining Chinese watched as 350 federal soldiers arrived in Seattle and abruptly defused the threat of expulsion. Seattle was so peaceful on November 8 that Lieutenant Colonel I. D. De Russey, the commanding officer, ordered half of the federal troops to return to their bases and divided the remaining soldiers between Seattle and Tacoma.[41]

Chin, however, continued to advocate on behalf of Chinese workers, most of whom did not have sufficient knowledge, resources, or connections to bring federal and international attention to the threat of expulsion in Seattle. He gathered together more than forty Chinese laborers who had been expelled from Coal Creek when "a mob of masked men" burned their buildings to the ground on September 11. He arranged to have all the laborers declare him their "lawful attorney" to recover from the US government indemnity for the losses they suffered. Each man swore to his individual monetary loss—ranging from $14 to $191—and Chin recorded his businesses' loss at more than $1,000. These claims, properly witnessed by a notary, were submitted to Consul General Ming in San Francisco. Chin also recorded in his notebook, in English and Chinese, a list of twenty-six Chinese labor camps that were destroyed during the anti-Chinese riots. On November 10 he again spoke out on behalf of the Seattle Chinese, testifying before a grand jury in a case against fourteen leaders of the agitation. The indictment alleged that the men had engaged in a conspiracy "to threaten, intimidate, harass and annoy" all Chinese in King County and all people who employed or protected the Chinese. The defense attorney cited the first amendment in their defense. In January 1886 the jury found all fourteen defendants not guilty.[42]

Vigilantes renewed their efforts in Seattle in February 1886. This time it was the mob, not the police, who came to Chin's boardinghouse, and their intent was forcible expulsion, not mere intimidation. It is unclear whether the mob found Chin at home that day, but it is certain that they found his first wife, Madame Wong, who was heavy with child. One of the vigilantes grabbed her by her hair, dragged her down the stairs, and pushed her out onto the street. In a matter of minutes, the vigilantes had violated all that Chin held dear: his business, his household, his wife, and his unborn child. In a complaint, he wrote to the Chinese consul, Chang Yen Hoon (Zhang Yinhuan), who later recounted the scene to Secretary of State Bayard. "The fright and bodily injuries received made [my wife] seriously ill," Chin wrote to the consul, "and three days afterwards she was prematurely delivered of a child." Chin's wife, after much time and pain, eventually regained her health. The child died.[43]

Even this did not drive Chin from Seattle. While others fled, he held his ground, and soon federal troops returned to Seattle. Within a few weeks, the soldiers managed to quell the unrest, but they remained in the city for several months longer. Not long enough, according to Chin. On May 6 Chin telegraphed the Chinese consulate: "United States troops ordered from Seattle. See President and have them retained two months." If the troops withdrew, Chin explained, "[the] Knights of Labor say they drive us out in thirty days." Nationally, the Knights promoted the cooperative ownership of industries, but locally the labor organization had become a recognized focal point for anti-Chinese violence. Chin's appeal was forwarded to Secretary Bayard, who quickly granted the request and ordered the troops to remain through late July.[44]

In a bid for redress, the Chinese consulate sent a delegation to investigate the events in Seattle. Chin was the first to file a claim. Leaving aside the physical and emotional toll on his family, he reported only his financial losses. After consulting a lawyer, he estimated that his business lost $67,000 "caused by the nontenancy of [his] houses, debts owed by Chinese uncollected & discontinuance of their labor-brokers business in several coal mines and other places." In addition, he had invested $85,000 in fifteen buildings that now remained unoccupied and $4,500 in eight farm lots that now lay fallow. In these personal claims of loss is an untold tale about the wider Chinese community in Seattle. Although Chin remained in the city, his laborers, his renters, his community had fled.[45]

As Chin waited to see if the US government would grant indemnity to China for the expulsion at Seattle and Tacoma, he continued to follow the fate of Chinese communities elsewhere in the West. In his notebook he saved a newspaper clipping on the expulsion in Napa, California, in 1886, and recorded the exact figure ($147,748.74) Congress granted in indemnity to China in 1887 for the Rock Springs massacre in Sweetwater County, Wyoming Territory, that took the lives of twenty-eight Chinese miners several years earlier. In 1888, when indemnity finally was granted for the expulsion at Seattle, Chin took the lead in contacting the Chinese consulate.[46] His telegraph was simple and formal:

> Representing large interests in the indemnity appropriation, we earnestly pray [to] Chinese government to make an early distribution as … the conditions of many sufferers is very distressing.
>
> Chin Gee-hee for Wa Chong Co.

The message was signed by eight other Chinese companies from Seattle.[47] Although Congress issued the funds to the Chinese government, there is no evidence that Seattle merchants saw their portion.[48]

Developer/Nationalist/Dreamer

While the violence threw others into a "distressing" condition, Chin seemed to rebound quickly. Within a few years, he formed his own company, Quong Tuck Co., and forged ties with a wealthy American patron, Thomas Burke, who served as general counsel for the Great Northern Railway, a system of railroads that eventually connected Saint Paul, Minnesota, to Seattle. At the behest of Burke, Chin supplied thousands of Chinese railroad workers and, in 1887, became a general agent for the railroad and its associated steamship lines. This meant steady access to Chinese migrants and Chinese goods, even as the Chinese exclusion laws continued to tighten the border. With the growth of his fortune, Chin saw the expansion of his family. By 1905 he supported three wives, six children, and houses on both sides of the Pacific (figures 20.1 and 20.2).[49]

Chin soon developed ambitions beyond Seattle. When the former territorial governor of Washington, Watson Squire, became a US senator, Chin wrote to him to try to get a post as a Chinese consul.[50] After nothing came of this plan, Chin decided to return to China and bring his knowledge of Western railroads to his home district of Taishan. In his mind's eye, the line would transform Jiangmen into a modern trade hub akin to Seattle,

FIGURE 20.1 *(above)* Chin Gee Hee, ca. 1904. Chin's bicultural identity is on dramatic display in these two portraits taken only a year apart. In this photo by A. Curtis, Chin is pictured in his office dressed in American business attire. University of Washington Libraries, Special Collections, Asahel Curtis, photographer, A. Curtis 01281.

FIGURE 20.2 *(left)* Chin Gee Hee, ca. 1905. In this studio portrait, Chin wears the black satin robe of a Chinese official. Courtesy of the Wing Luke Museum. 1991.200.111.

and its agricultural regions into something akin to the fertile hinterland of Washington State. To raise the necessary capital, Chin went on a lecture tour, titled "Expand Communications, Build Railroads," traveling across the United States and to Hong Kong. With the help of big and small overseas Chinese investors, he started a company in 1904 that would be entirely Chinese funded and Chinese built. At the time, foreign developers were dominating the railroads of China; by 1911 more than 90 percent of railroad lines in China were built by Westerners or based on Western loans. As railroads were becoming a powerful symbol of Western imperialism, Chin promoted his Xinning Railroad Company in the image of Chinese nationalism. Many overseas Chinese bought into his plan. Chin returned to Taishan in 1906 with 2.7 million yuan (approximately $140,000), two-thirds of which was from Chinese migrants in the United States. He personally helped to engineer and supervise the construction of the railroad.[51]

At first, the railroad appeared to be the culmination of Chin's dreams, a personal and national triumph. Two years into construction, Chin invited his American patron, Thomas Burke, to Taishan to see the progress. Together, they rode the brand-new rails from Gongyi to Taishan, gazed upon the marvel of Chin's engineering, and dreamed of Western modernity spreading into the Chinese interior. Xinning Railroad had already begun to bring prosperity to the region, as it put thousands of locals to work, and it seemed primed to bring further wealth. By 1920 the railroad's 85 miles (137 kilometers) of track connected Doushan, Taishan, Gongyi, and Jiangmen at a final cost of 9.7 million yuan, or $4.8 million.[52]

Ultimately, neither Chin nor his home district grew wealthy from the railroad. Xinning lacked much of what had made the Great Northern Railway a success: extensive federal support, local access to fuel, and bountiful natural resources in need of transport. Instead, Chin's railroad was kept afloat by passenger traffic and a flow of remittances from abroad. This stream of profit from overseas was susceptible to recessions in other countries, which meant it slowed to a trickle during the Great Depression of the 1930s. To make matters worse, the railroad became a popular target for theft by local bandits and extortion by local officials. In 1926 provincial authorities, eager to raise state revenues, seized the railroad from Chin's hands and, in 1927, they forced him into retirement. Deprived of his life's work, Chin fell into a state of depression and, a little over a year later, passed away at age eighty-five in the village of his birth.[53] Today, Taishan marks his life and his railroad with celebratory monuments, but at the time he died a humble death.

One cannot help but marvel at the remarkable life of this sometime railroad worker. There were moments when Chin's experience seemed utterly ordinary, but more often his life differed from that of other Chinese migrants, as he quickly learned English, found wealthy American patrons, amassed an army of workers, and battled for their right to stay in Seattle. As Chin's life diverged from that of most Chinese railroad workers, so too did his understanding of what the railroad symbolized. Many Chinese wished to forget the railroad. Ashamed of the drudgery of their labor, they spoke little about their time laying track. For Chin, the railroad was something to be celebrated, as his personal path to upward mobility and his dream for China's future.

Seven years before his passing, Chin gave a speech to the Seattle Chamber of Commerce. It was a moment of triumph, before his fortunes had turned, when he could stand before a crowd of wealthy white American men and feel their equal. He took the opportunity to reflect on how the railroad had run through his life. "I had all my railroad experience in Seattle, where I was once a track laborer, a contractor, and afterwards one of the contracting builders of the old Front Street cable line," he told the room. He had also been a passenger on "the principal railway lines of the country," an engineer in Taishan, and now the president of the Xinning Railroad Company. "Could I ever be what I am if it wasn't for Seattle men?" he asked the room. Their support was the "greatest gift," never to be "forgotten from [his] heart."[54]

All Chinese migrants in America dreamed of discovering riches abroad and sending them home to their countrymen. While most managed only to remit their meager wages, Chin's remittances were in the form of a steel road, a hulking machine, and a powerful vision of Chinese modernity.

CHAPTER 21

The Chinese and the Stanfords

Nineteenth-Century America's Fraught Relationship with the China Men

GORDON H. CHANG

A rhetorical question circulates among Chinese Americans: do you know why the tiles of the roofs of Stanford University are colored red?

The answer: because they are stained with the blood of Chinese railroad workers who died while constructing the transcontinental railroad for Leland Stanford.

Simultaneously expressing feelings of anger, of pride for contribution to the nation, and of unpaid debt of blood, the question-as-commentary expresses profound resentment toward the individual who most influenced the lives of Chinese immigrants in nineteenth-century America. More than anyone else, Leland Stanford is held responsible for the mistreatment and exploitation of thousands of Chinese workers in the United States—the enormous wealth he accumulated, in substantial part from their labor during the construction of the first transcontinental rail line, came from the hardship they endured. Stanford personifies the America that victimized them. To this day, there are Chinese Americans who refuse to set foot on the grounds of the university that carries the Stanford name.[1]

Other Chinese Americans hold Stanford in high regard: he is seen as a benefactor, a protector, and an advocate for the Chinese. He and his wife, Jane, it is said to this day, so loved a Chinese youngster in their employ that they sought to adopt him. When Leland Stanford died, many in America saw him and his wife as great friends to the Chinese.

How do we reconcile these very different views of the Stanfords and their relationship to Chinese in America?

346

We might conclude that the Stanfords were themselves emblematic of nineteenth-century America's own deeply conflicted and often contradictory attitude toward the Chinese who came here. The Stanfords, and America at the time, were neither consistently malevolent nor benevolent toward Chinese—tense, ambivalent, and complex are more appropriate ways to describe their stance toward the Chinese, with whom they engaged in a fraught and complicated relationship.

===

One of the first white merchants that Chinese immigrants in the 1850s might have encountered in California was Leland Stanford. He grew up in New York State, moved to California, and made his early money by selling dry goods to those who flocked to the gold rush. In 1852, the year that saw the first large influx of Chinese into California, Stanford set up shop in Placer County, a booming center of mining. His store appealed directly to the newcomers from Asia—a sign prominently displayed beneath the Stanford name advertised "This store always has Chinese goods (*bendian changyou tangshan zahuo*)."[2]

In late 1861, soon after the start of the Civil War, Stanford, a Republican, was elected governor of the state of California, and his first official speech in January 1862 is widely cited today as an ugly expression of the prevailing anti-Chinese sentiments of the time, and today these are still his most widely circulated comments on Chinese. Stanford began his short inaugural address by offering thoughts on ways to stimulate the growth of the state's population and then declared:

> While the settlement of our State is of the first importance, the character of those who shall become settlers is worthy of scarcely less consideration. To my mind it is clear, that the settlement among us of an inferior race is to be discouraged, by every legitimate means. Asia, with her numberless millions, sends to our shores the dregs of her population. Large numbers of this class are already here; and, unless we do something early to check their immigration, the question, which of the two tides of immigration, meeting upon the shores of the Pacific, shall be turned back, will be forced upon our consideration, when far more difficult than now of disposal. There can be no doubt but that the presence of numbers among us of a degraded and distinct people must exercise a deleterious influence upon the superior race, and, to a certain extent, repel desirable immigration. It will afford me great pleasure to

concur with the Legislature in any constitutional action, having for its object the repression of the immigration of the Asiatic races.[3]

Immediately following this declaration, Stanford called for the development of steamship connections with Asia, which would be critical, he said, for the state's economy and future as part of the Union. He would seek Washington's support for promoting transpacific trade, an ambition that Asa Whitney, the early promoter of the construction of a transcontinental rail line, regaled Stanford's father with when Stanford was a youngster. Stanford also called for attention to the urgent need to construct a transcontinental rail line, "the great work of the age," in his words, that would connect the state to the rest of the Union. He betrayed not a glimmer of awareness that closer commercial ties with Asia, China in particular, would inevitably result in more social interaction and further emigration of a "degraded race."

Stanford's anti-Chinese prejudice was rooted in the antislavery, "free soil" logic then popular among many Republicans. Early in his political career, he had declared his opposition to chattel slavery, which in his view hurt the interests of "free white men," whom he said he much preferred over any other people. "I believe," he said, that "the greatest good has been derived by having all the country settled by free white men."[4] White labor, he maintained, could not fairly compete against Africans in chains, and he extended that logic to his public hostility toward Chinese migrants.

At the same time, however, Leland and his wife, Jane, developed a very different personal relationship with Chinese, one that was remarkably close and affectionate and stood in sharp contrast to his public position. In the summer of 1861, before he was elected governor, Leland and Jane purchased a ramshackle mansion in downtown Sacramento and staffed it with a number of homeworkers, including a Chinese cook named Moy Jin Kee, who introduced his younger brother, Moy Jin Mun, to the couple. Jin Mun had recently arrived from China and began working for the Stanfords. According to several accounts, Jane Stanford, childless at the time, became especially fond of the youngster and sought to adopt him formally into the family. The older brother, Moy Jin Kee, opposed the idea because he and his brother were not orphans—the parents of the brothers were still alive in China—and because of the deep social and racial divide between them and the Stanfords. When Moy Jin Mun left the Stanfords' employment a few years later, in the mid-1860s, Jane gave him a gold ring with his name engraved on it for remembrance. He cherished the keepsake for his entire, long life, according to the biographical information provided by his son, and he proudly wore it for the next seventy years, until his death in 1936. According to the family history, Moy Jin Mun worked as a foreman for Chinese workers on the Central Pacific Railroad in the 1870s.[5]

Moy Jin Kee, for his part, also played a critical role in the life of the Stanford family. In 1862, the same year that Leland Stanford called for efforts to rid the state of Chinese, Jane Stanford developed a serious illness that threatened her life. When Western medical practices failed to improve her condition, Moy Jin Kee introduced her to Yee Fung Cheung, a Chinese traditional doctor who had arrived in California in 1850 and lived in Sacramento's Chinese quarter. Yee used Chinese remedies to treat Jane and restored her to full health. He later treated Chinese and white workers on the Central Pacific Railroad and became one of the most prominent Chinese medical practitioners in California.[6]

Also in 1862 Stanford assumed the presidency of the newly formed Central Pacific Railroad Company (CPRR), which the United States government soon selected to build, with the Union Pacific Railroad (UPRR), the rail line that would help span the continent. Heading the CPRR would enormously enrich Stanford and establish him as the individual who most influenced the destinies of Chinese in nineteenth-century America.

Stanford turned the first shovel of dirt in a Sacramento ceremony to start the work of the CPRR in January 1863, but because of funding issues and the difficulty in obtaining sufficient numbers of workers for the massive project, the company made very slow progress. It hired only whites at first, but far fewer than the number needed signed on to work. Stanford confessed to the federal government that "labor is scarce and dear in this State." Desperate, the company turned to hiring Chinese in early 1864.[7] Chinese in significant numbers had been living in the state since the early 1850s and had become an important labor force in mining and agriculture. They had also worked on local rail construction projects around the San Francisco Bay Area. Stanford himself and a close associate, E. B. Crocker, the older brother of Charles Crocker, one of the other directors of the company, might have first proposed the idea of employing Chinese on the construction project. Other accounts attribute the idea to Charles Crocker's capable manservant, Ah Ling, with Crocker then raising the idea to his business partners.[8] Whatever the details of the story, the controversial decision to employ Chinese was made at the highest levels of the Big Four—Stanford, Crocker, Mark Hopkins, and Collis P.

Huntington. They wondered whether Chinese were physically fit for railroad work and whether whites would agree to work with them.

The Chinese quickly proved themselves to be excellent workers, and the CPRR dramatically increased its Chinese workforce into the thousands. Stanford himself, in a July 1865 report to company stockholders, highlighted the crucial role Chinese were playing for the company. They were already "an important element of labor," Stanford stated, and they numbered about 2,000 out of a total of 2,500 workers. The number of Chinese on the CPRR would continue to grow. At their most numerous, they constituted 90 percent of the CPRR construction workforce and numbered more than 12,000 workers. Because of turnover, perhaps 20,000 Chinese actually worked on the CPRR, with thousands more working afterward on northern and southern transcontinental lines, trunk lines throughout the country, and the Canadian transcontinental railroad.[9]

In an October 1865 public report to President Andrew Johnson on the progress of the Central Pacific, Stanford expressed an opinion about Chinese that signified a dramatic change of heart:

> As a class they are quiet, peaceable, patient, industrious and economical. Ready and apt to learn all the different kinds of work required in railroad building, they soon become as efficient as white laborers. More prudent and economical, they are contented with less wages. We find them organized into societies for mutual aid and assistance. These societies can count their numbers by thousands, are conducted by shrewd intelligent business men who promptly advise their subordinates where employment can be found on most favorable terms. No system similar to slavery, serfdom or peonage prevails among these laborers.

Stanford noted that "a large majority of the white laboring class" preferred employment other than in railroad work, and thus the "greater portion" of the company's workers were Chinese. "Without them," Stanford bluntly stated, "it would be impossible to complete the western portion of this great national enterprise, within the time required by the Acts of Congress."[10]

Completely absent from Stanford's statement was his avowed preference for white workers over an allegedly inferior people. Instead, Stanford offered warm praise for the physical abilities and social qualities of the Chinese workers, and, as he noted at the end of his report, Chinese workers were a force "that could be increased to any extent required." He anticipated hiring far greater numbers of Chinese in the near future. His business partners were in full agreement: a few months later, in private correspondence with his partner in charge of labor recruitment, Charles Crocker, Stanford considered hiring fifteen thousand more Chinese workers for the project, a number that "leading Chinese merchants" could easily supply, he claimed.[11] In an even more expansive mood, Stanford's close railroad associates E. B. Crocker and Collis P. Huntington mused that California would greatly benefit if there were one hundred thousand, or, in Huntington's words, "a half million [Chinese]" in the state, a staggering number considering that the total population of the state in 1860 was under four hundred thousand.[12]

Reports from the field kept Stanford fully informed on the progress of construction and the company's reliance on Chinese labor. The workers completed the staggering task of cutting the line through the intimidating Sierra Nevada, across the burning Nevada deserts, and to the Great Salt Lake in Utah. On his regular tours of the line, Stanford personally witnessed thousands of Chinese tunneling, shoveling snow, building snow tunnels, and laying the roadbed and track. On May 10, 1869, at Promontory Summit, Utah Territory, more than nine hundred miles from where the CPRR began its work, the CPRR and UPRR held a grand ceremony to mark the completion of the transcontinental rail line. There, Stanford encountered Chinese workers laying the last rails, ties, and spikes. After Stanford and Thomas Durant, representing the Union Pacific, spoke and used ceremonial tools to symbolize the hard work, Chinese workers, dressed in "denim pantaloons and jackets," returned to replace the ceremonial spikes and ties with permanent pieces.[13]

Stanford had once referred to the then-popular cultural spectacle of the "Siamese twins" when he declared that the transcontinental line helped form the "ligament" "that binds the Eastern Eng and Western Chang together."[14] At Promontory Summit, however, he made no mention of Asians in his formal remarks, but journalists who recorded the historic event for posterity noted their central presence at the ceremony. "The Chinese really laid the last tie and drove the last spike," one journalist wrote. After the festivities concluded, the laborers gathered ceremonial material left behind by others. "The ever-watchful Chinamen then took up the remains, sawed [them] into small pieces and distributed it among them." James Strobridge, the construction boss, invited leaders of the Chinese to dine in his personal train car, and when they entered, the guests "cheered them as the chosen representatives of the race which have greatly helped to build the road—a tribute they well deserved, and which evidently gave them much pleasure."[15]

The Central Pacific made Stanford a very, very wealthy man, and in the years after Promontory he accumulated vast holdings of land throughout the state. In 1869 he began to purchase hundreds of acres in Alameda County for his wine-making ambition. Not satisfied, he eventually amassed 55,000 acres for his sprawling Vina Ranch in the northern Sacramento Valley, where he thought he could produce Bordeaux-quality wine. In 1874 he moved his residence from Sacramento to San Francisco's Nob Hill, where he built the largest private residence in the state, and in 1876 he started what became his Palo Alto stock farm of 8,800 acres. This "summer home" would become the site of Stanford University. A few years later, Stanford purchased 20,000 acres in Butte County, forming his Gridley Farm. He controlled tens of thousands more acres in California through his many companies. In all of these sites and projects, Stanford hired hundreds of Chinese workers, including an estimated four hundred to one thousand on his Vina Ranch, where they tended to the vineyards and built miles of irrigation works, dams, and canals. In his several palatial homes and estates, Chinese served as domestic workers and groundskeepers.[16] An estimated fifty Chinese were employed at his Palo Alto family residence alone. Many of them were former railroad workers.[17]

There was a China presence even in the most personal of spaces of the Stanford family. In 1876, when Leland, Jane, and their son, eight-year-old Leland Jr., attended the Centennial Exposition in Philadelphia, Stanford tried to purchase elaborate bedroom furniture featured at the China exhibition. Chinese officials refused to accept money for the pieces and instead offered them to the Stanfords as gifts, in the words of Jane's personal secretary and biographer, "in appreciation of his fair treatment and protection of the Chinese in California." The furniture and several rolls of the "finest silk brocade" later decorated what was called the "Chinese Room" in their opulent San Francisco residence.[18] Six years later, when Leland Jr. died of typhoid fever while touring Europe with his parents, a "trusted Chinese houseboy, who had been long in the family," accompanied his body on the long, sad train ride back across the country. He sat "throughout the nights by the side of the bier, broken-hearted," according to Jane's assistant. When the funeral was held at Grace Church, a towering tribute occupied a central position: a white cross of flowers stood in the central aisle and "reached up into the vaulted ceiling." It was from the Chinese gardeners at the Palo Alto residence who had transported it to the church. A card from them read, "For little Leland, from the Governor's Chinese boys." On Easter mornings afterward, Chinese gardeners placed a replica of it at the front of Leland Jr.'s tomb and trimmed it with white flowers they had grown.[19] Other Chinese employees left rice bowls and other food vessels next to the crypt for Leland Jr.'s use in the afterlife.[20]

———

Although Leland Stanford pandered to anti-Chinese public sentiment in his early political career, anti-Chinese extremists targeted him in the 1870s after the completion of the rail line when an economic depression hit the country. Agitators held Stanford, and other railroad barons, responsible for the presence of Chinese laborers who allegedly took work away from deserving whites. The Chinese were a thoroughly degraded and undesirable race in California, agitators declared, using words Stanford himself had employed earlier. The "Chinese must go" movement, identified with the demagogue Denis Kearney, sought to rid the state of the Chinese presence by whatever means necessary, including the possible use of violence. The transcontinental line, built in substantial part by Chinese, enabled thousands of whites to migrate to the West and settle, and newcomers, such as Kearney, who was himself an immigrant, believed their future well-being depended on the expulsion of Chinese. Stanford, "the millionaire, the banker and the land monopolist, the railroad king and the false politician," and his ilk, Kearney charged, used the Chinese against the white working man. Deadly anti-Chinese violence swept the West: in 1871 a mob in Los Angeles tortured and lynched eighteen Chinese. It was the largest mass lynching in American history.[21]

This anti-Chinese movement reached its height over several days in the summer and fall of 1877, when thousands of whites took to the streets in San Francisco to protest business monopoly and the Chinese. Extreme rhetoric escalated into open violence. Rioters threatened to torch the docks of the Pacific Mail Steamship Company, which brought Chinese to the port, and they destroyed Chinese businesses in the city. Even the Chinese Methodist Church was stoned. Kearney, who helped found the so-called Workingmen's Party, which had become influential in California, expressed typical anti-Chinese, anti-monopoly sentiment in an October 29, 1877, speech before several thousand at the top of Nob Hill, where the residences of Stanford and other elites stood.

"The Central Pacific Railroad men are thieves," Kearney declared, "and will soon feel the power of the workingmen." Kearney pledged to rid the city of corrupt officials and police and said he would give "the Central Pacific just three months to discharge their Chinamen." If they did not comply, "Stanford and his crowd will have to take the consequences."[22] Speakers denounced Stanford by name and threatened open violence if the Chinese remained. Stanford was so disturbed about the threats against him that he personally wrote to the chief of police of San Francisco requesting special protection for his Nob Hill mansion. "Chief Ellis," Stanford wrote, "I know the mobs have considered the question of burning my house," and "their threats may be serious. I would be glad to have you detail a proper guard." The forces of law and order soon suppressed the rioters, and left four dead and more than a dozen wounded.[23]

The next year Kearney took to the road to make his anti-Chinese, anticapitalist campaign a national crusade. In speeches throughout the East and Midwest he repeatedly vilified the "railroad robbers," Stanford being the most prominent, and Chinese. Kearney helped popularize the image of Stanford as a patron of the Chinese, and not the Sinophobe he was in earlier times.[24] In the East, Stanford was in fact viewed as a defender of Chinese against the threat of violence from the mob. A writer for the *New York Times* who traveled to the West described Stanford's position as one of "sturdy championship of the Chinese." Stanford was supposedly fearless "in demanding for them simple justice and humane consideration" and for employing them in his enterprises and in his homes. Stanford, from his own practical experience, the writer observed, appreciated the Chinese worker as "the most reliable and in the end the most efficient."[25]

Still, Stanford maintained connections with the anti-Chinese movement that continued to grow in the country. Newspaper articles reported that Kearney and Stanford held private discussions in 1878 during which they reportedly resolved differences and found common ground regarding Chinese labor. Kearney was said to have announced publicly that he found Stanford to be a "much smarter man than he had supposed" and believed that Stanford would even vote in favor of Kearney's Workingmen's Party in the next election. Stanford reportedly told Kearney that he had to hire cheaper Chinese labor because he had to accumulate funds to bribe Sacramento officials. But if "honest workingmen," like those Kearney said he represented, held office, then Stanford said there would be no need to pay the bribes and he could follow "the instincts of his great labor-loving heart." Stanford reportedly said that then "none but Caucasians would be employed in running and extending railways."[26]

Although Stanford's friends refuted what Kearney said to the press,

Stanford himself never disavowed the reports, and he continued to pander to racist grievances. In 1886, for example, white hostility to Stanford's use of Chinese workers at his sprawling Vina Ranch escalated, and the Citizens' Anti-Coolie League of Red Bluff demanded that he discharge all his Chinese workers. A provoked Stanford defended his hiring practices as a matter of principle, saying it was his "right" to handle his affairs as he saw fit for himself and his legitimate business interests, within the dictates of the law. But he also declared that as a matter of "my race prejudice," he was inclined to favor "my own people" and give them his "preference." He acknowledged that "a very large portion of the people of our State" opposed the employment of Chinese and therefore ordered his Vina foreman "to direct that the preference for white labor be carefully exerted," in response to the Anti-Coolie League and "in harmony with my own inclinations." The Vina Ranch steadily discharged hundreds of Chinese, and by 1890 all his Vina workers were whites except for a few Chinese, who did the work that "whites refuse to do," according to a local newspaper.[27]

In the mid-1880s Stanford turned from his business interests to pursue political ambitions once again. He successfully ran for the US Senate from California in 1885 and was reelected in 1891, and his name was openly circulated as a possible presidential contender. He publicly supported federal restrictions on Chinese immigration, endorsed the 1882 Chinese Restriction Act, and backed further legislation against Chinese immigration, unlike his former business partner Collis P. Huntington, who opposed anti-Chinese measures and endorsed further Chinese immigration. Stanford never advocated violence against Chinese, but his public political positions kept in step with the anti-Chinese vitriol in the country.[28]

Stanford carefully positioned himself in the debate about further restricting Chinese entry into the country. He recognized that Californians felt passionately about the issue, and he supported measures that he thought addressed their concerns. At the same time, he still acknowledged the important contributions Chinese had made to the state, including to his own business ventures. "The Chinamen," Stanford declared, "have played an important part in the development of that section of the country by the work they have done in the building up of railroads and in other improvements, as well as manufactures; but the limit of their usefulness has been reached." Therefore, no further Chinese should be allowed into the country, he announced, and those already here should gradually return to China. On other occasions, he accepted the legitimacy of anti-Chinese sentiments, while downplaying their urgency. Chinese, he observed, were neither troublesome nor "fecund," and, with federal controls on them, they would not become a serious problem. White workers should not fear the Chinese as labor competitors, he claimed, as opportunities were readily available to them all.[29]

Extremists, however, were unsatisfied, and they continued to accuse Stanford of being soft on Chinese immigration. Stanford fired back with a vigorous defense of his racial credentials and personal character as an advocate for the white working man. He reaffirmed his support for restriction of Chinese immigration, claiming he recognized that "our people on the Pacific Coast" opposed it and because the Chinese, for racial and religious reasons, could not "be absorbed by our own people." He then added a strangely worded thought that revealed frustration with the complexity of the "race" question in America: "I would be very glad if all colored people of the United States became white people. I think an unmixed race of white people is better than mixed ones."[30]

With the campaign for his reelection on the horizon, Stanford wanted nothing to be said that suggested he was weak on the Chinese question. In early 1889 Stanford reminded white voters that he had been among the first in California to oppose the immigration of Chinese into the state and that he had adamantly and consistently opposed the presence of Chinese in California soon after he had moved there. The Chinese, he reportedly declared, were a "most undesirable class," and he favored the "very much more desirable class of people," the "white population." Stanford adamantly maintained that he had "and always shall do all in his power to keep out of California an unhomogeneous class," by which he meant Chinese.[31] It was the most stridently anti-Chinese message since his gubernatorial inaugural address in 1862 and clearly contradicted his praise of Chinese workers as railroad workers, and his own personal ties with the hundreds of Chinese workers in his homes and estates. In the election of 1890, Stanford was reelected US senator, with his position on Chinese immigration winning him broad support among whites.[32] But his position would shift again one final time.

In early 1893, which would be the last year of Stanford's life, he inexplicably and dramatically altered his public position on the Chinese. A Chicago newspaper reported that Stanford, during a discussion of a variety of issues, offered an aside that surprised the reporter. Stanford reportedly expressed "rather a good opinion of the Chinese," such a view being "a strange thing in a

Californian." Stanford was said to have praised the work ethic of Chinese and maintained that there was no danger of "their trying to overrun the country, as eventually they all want to get back to their own."[33]

Then, in May, just weeks before he died, Leland Stanford offered his most extensive comments on Chinese in America. From a comfortable seat on the porch of his Palo Alto ranch on a lovely spring day, likely within earshot of the Chinese workers who were in his employ, Stanford condemned the recent federal legislation known as the Geary Act of 1892, which required all Chinese in the country to obtain and then carry on their body at all times an authorized certificate of residence in the United States. This was an unprecedented development in American history. The certificate included a photograph and a physical description of the resident. No other immigrant group in the country was required to carry anything similar, and a Chinese found without such a certificate faced deportation or a year of hard labor. Stanford condemned the act, named for his fellow Californian, Congressman Thomas H. Geary, and declared:

> There should never have been a restriction law passed in the first place, and the Geary law, which has followed, is an outrage. I did not oppose it, for it appeared that some of the people at any rate wanted it. I will admit that at one time I had some fears of the Chinese overrunning this country, but for some years I have had none.…
>
> Then there is another thing. We need the Chinese here to work in our fields, vineyards and orchards and gather our fruit and do the common labor of the country. I do not know what we would do without them, and I undertake to say that they are the most quiet, industrious and altogether commendable class of foreigners who come here. There is no other class so quick to learn and so faithful, and who can do the kind of work we have for them to do. I am persuaded, too, notwithstanding all that has been said about the majority of the people being opposed to the Chinese, that they are not opposed to them. It is only the few. Our intelligent businessmen are not opposed to them. Neither are the mechanics, because Chinese do not take up the trades. They do simply the commonest kind of work, and in doing so they do not really come into competition with white labor. The white men are, as a result, promoted to a better and more paying kind of labor.[34]

Stanford believed that the Geary Act was receiving "universal condemnation" and that Americans "will support the Chinese in defiance of the deportation provision." Ninety-six percent of the Chinese in the country themselves protested by not registering for the certificates by the government deadline. Stanford charged that the Geary Act and other insults against Chinese immigrants would damage vital American business interests in transpacific trade and in the development of the West. "The people of the ranches and contractors of railroad lines and other public improvements," he observed, "are always ready to employ the Chinese and without them they could be scarcely able to get along." Stanford also recalled his experience in leading the CPRR and argued that white workers, rather than being displaced by Chinese, benefited from their employment. The company early in the project hired "600 white men," he said, but they were unreliable and frequently ran off to pursue a speculative venture. The company was then forced to hire Chinese "in self-defense" and eventually had as many as 15,000. The company retained the 600 white men, who were then promoted to "positions of teamsters and bosses" and "had better wages" and then hired even more whites, increasing the number to 2,000, "all in superior places and all making more money than the Chinese."[35]

Remarkably, the abstemious Stanford provocatively and favorably compared Chinese as workers and residents of the country to whites in the state. "Who ever heard," he observed, "of a single Chinaman of all the 400,000,000 in China, being drunks. They are sober, hard-working, and in all respects admirable laborers." In contrast, Stanford continued, thousands of "white persons" were running bars and selling liquor rather than working productively in America. Stanford estimated that "there is $1,000,000,000 spent in America every year for drink. In some respects, therefore, we might emulate the Chinese." Driving home his point, Stanford suggested, "Do I put this too strong?"[36]

These would be Stanford's last words on the Chinese question, and they attracted widespread attention. The *San Francisco Chronicle* evinced surprise, while commentators on the East Coast again offered high, eloquent praise to the senator. The *Washington Post* called the anti-Chinese movement a product of "fanatics, demagogues, and schemers" and saluted Stanford for bravely exerting "his own exalted manhood and the dignity of this enlightened age in denouncing the contemplated outrage," referring to the expansion of exclusion efforts then in Congress. Stanford "deserves the thanks of every humane and patriotic and self-respecting citizen of the Republic" for his forthright comments. The paper called on all others "of high character and broad intelligence" to go on record as Stanford did. "The vicious, the ignorant, and the credulous should not be left to monopolize the controversy."[37]

Stanford died in June 1893 at his residence in Palo Alto. Chinese workers from what had become the university campus and from his personal home attended his funeral in full force and in their finest clothes. They contributed flowers and memorials, including a broken wheel and pillow of flowers, as expressions of their grief. As they had at Junior's death years before, Chinese gardeners brought a huge, elaborate flower arrangement to his mausoleum. In San Francisco the Chinese Six Companies, the association of the most important Chinese civic organizations, formally honored Stanford with the greatest respect. A local newspaper observed that they displayed their sorrow in a most conspicuous way: they flew the flag of China and their own organization banners at half-mast. The only other time they had done so "upon the death of a Caucasian" was for President James A. Garfield when he died from wounds from an assassination attempt in 1881. Garfield was known to be sympathetic to Chinese immigration.[38]

To be clear, Stanford's final praise of the Chinese focused on their utility as workers, as those whom he and others employed in the many enterprises that enriched them. As he once mused, hostility toward the Chinese was "not due to their vices, but to their virtues. They are cleanly and are willing to work seven days a week if permitted to. I have employed a great many Chinese. They are willing to work for less and longer hours than any other people." The Chinese had contributed to the greater good, Stanford indicated, and in that way, all Californians, including white workingmen, should appreciate the work of Chinese.[39]

Beyond his praise of Chinese as workers, Stanford rarely offered positive public comments about Chinese as people deserving of equal rights and respect. His praise for their sobriety was one of the exceptions. In contrast, he supported extending the right to vote for African Americans in the South after the Civil War (if for nothing else than to offset the political hostility of the defeated white population toward his Republican Party) and for women. He never expressed support for extending citizenship and the political franchise to Chinese immigrants, unlike political leaders such as Radical Republican Charles Sumner, and he never endorsed racial integration.[40]

=====

Many Chinese businessmen and homeworkers themselves developed remarkably genuine respect and affection for the Stanfords.

During his career in San Francisco and Sacramento, Stanford regularly appeared in public in friendly association with Chinese merchants and spoke on the same podium with them. In January 1867, for example, Stanford was one of the featured speakers at a large celebration of the inaugural voyage of the first ship of the newly formed Pacific Mail Steamship Company. Chinese merchants joined two hundred other business, military, and government leaders and heard Stanford declare that in San Francisco "the commerce of the Pacific [will] find its entrepôt." Following Stanford on the podium were several Chinese merchants who echoed his sentiments about the bright future in America-China relations. One of these was a man identified as Fung Tang, who said he represented the Chinese merchants of the city. He proudly declared that he looked forward to the time when San Francisco would become "one of the greatest cities of the world" and thanked the local business community. "They have always treated the Chinese merchants with great kindness," he said, saying that he had "a good many acquaintances among the first merchants and business men" of the city. Stanford maintained his ties with Chinese merchants through the following years.[41]

In Palo Alto the Stanfords conducted regular dealings with local Chinese farmers, leasing them land, purchasing their produce, and hiring them for many kinds of work. Hundreds of Chinese from the 1870s to the 1890s worked on the huge estate to build and maintain an infrastructure of canals and waterworks, tend to an extensive farm, staff the large stable and stock farm, cultivate gardens, and meet the many demands of their employers' home life and entertaining. The records are incomplete and unclear about the actual numbers of hired Chinese, but they were everywhere on the property for years. One of Stanford's bookkeepers responded to a private inquiry in 1884 about employment for a white job seeker, saying that "there [are] very few places at the ranch for white 'laborers.' As a rule all the plain laboring work is done by Chinese." But the Chinese could also be found in "skilled" work around the estate. They are listed in the family records as carpenters, painters, teamsters and drivers, horsemen, gardeners, vineyard tenders, and vegetable growers. Many lived in boardinghouses right on the property that now is the heart of the university campus.[42]

Stanford was part owner with Charles Crocker of the first true resort destination in the United States. Their Pacific Improvement Company constructed the Hotel Del Monte, which opened in 1880 in Monterey, to attract railroad passenger traffic from the East. A mostly Chinese workforce developed the extensive grounds, which included more than 125 acres of gardens, a racetrack, polo grounds, and a golf course, as well as the sumptuous hotel. They also worked the nearby 7,000-acre forest that became known as Pebble Beach, where they constructed the road now known as the famed 17-Mile Drive, which linked the resort to Carmel, and a twenty-five-mile-long pipeline and reservoir to supply water. Hotel managers and reporters regularly praised the Chinese, who numbered some 1,250 on the reservoir project alone, according to one report, for their low cost, hard work, and disciplined habits.[43]

In 1885 when the Stanfords began construction of the university, they employed large numbers of Chinese in the effort. The first university architect, Charles Hodges, recalled, "The Senator was a great advocate of Chinese labour." Hundreds of them were employed to help construct the early building foundations of the university. They built the early infrastructure of the university, including its famed Palm Drive, and planted its signature palm trees. As late as 1893, there were still more than one hundred Chinese employees at the university.[44]

The Stanfords also lived with "China" all around themselves, as was the case with many of California's elite. Chinese furniture, objets d'art, ceramics, and wall decorations filled their homes, including one in Washington, DC. There they selected for their residence a grand house that had previously served as the legation of China. Chinese decor remained on abundant display to visitors. The Stanfords planned on amassing Chinese art that would be displayed in the university museum.[45]

The couple ate food not only prepared by Chinese cooks but prepared in the Chinese style. One newspaper noted curiously that Jane Stanford, one of the richest women in the world, who brought four Chinese cooks with her when she and Leland moved to the capital, served bird's nest soup, a special Chinese dish reportedly "much talked of" among the Washington social and political crowd at her high-society dinners. She circulated the recipe for it to a reporter. During dinners, pet birds, such as doves and parrots, reportedly flew around freely through the entire house. One of her house workers was fond of birds, which were popular among Chinese hobbyists, and Jane appears to have been similarly captivated. Even Leland during his lunch was said to have doves "perched on either side of his chair." An aquarium with goldfish decorated the reception area, and songbirds enlivened the couple's bedroom. A column on Jane in the *Ladies' Home Journal* reported that "the Chinese have her sympathy and she considers them somewhat abused," and in turn it was said "her retinue of servants have the greatest affection for her."[46]

In addition to the special relationship with the Moys, as noted earlier, the

Stanfords developed other business and personal ties with Chinese in the Palo Alto area. Jim Mok Jew You, known as Ah Jim, contracted to work forty prime acres in the main area of the Stanford estate in the 1870s to 1890s. Ah Jim and his family lived on the property, and Jane Stanford became fond of his children, who were all born on the property. When a son came along in 1891, Jane nicknamed him "Palo Alto," and the Stanfords gave the family a silver mug, knife, fork, spoon, and gold-lined cup engraved with the child's name and birth information: "Mock Who Ham, Palo Alto, July 7, 1891."[47] A few years later Jane supplied a notarized affidavit confirming the American nativity of Ah Jim's children and the fact they "are citizens of the United States." The family needed the evidence to help them reenter the United States after they visited China. She served as the unimpeachable and necessary "white witness" for Ah Jim's family.[48] Jane remembered several Chinese workers in her last will and left them money.[49]

Among the most poignant evidence of the Chinese employees' affection for Jane Stanford and, to a lesser degree, Leland is testimonies and memoirs that expressed gratitude to the Stanfords not only for employment but for their solicitude, generosity, and even protection in a hostile environment.

In the late 1960s a longtime Chinese resident of Santa Clara County offered this story about the Stanfords:

> There is an old Chinese story of aid to the Chinese. A Mr. Milbra presented Mr. Leland Stanford, Sr. a document for his signature to oust the Chinese from the state of California. When Mr. Stanford was about to sign, Mrs. Stanford interposed and related to her husband that the Chinese people have been good to him. The Chinese had helped him in the building of the transcontinental railroad, in building the university, and in many other ways. Why should they force the Chinese to leave? Mr. Stanford then refused to sign and walked away. This proved the fact that Mrs. Stanford held a great love for the Chinese people.[50]

Connie Young Yu, one of the leading community historians of Chinese American history, recalls that her own father remembered the Stanfords with great affection. John Young told her that he recalled hearing stories from the old railroad workers who visited his San Jose store in the early twentieth century. The railroad workers told of the times when white gangs attacked them and Stanford hired guards to protect them. Connie's mother also heard about the Stanfords' providing employment to Chinese and protecting them. Connie's father was proud to have later graduated from the university and "always spoke of Leland Stanford and Mrs. Stanford with respect and reverence." Local Chinese close to the Stanfords honored Leland by calling him "Great Master [or Great Teacher] Stanford [*shidanfo dalaoshi*]."[51]

One of the most poignant testimonials about the Stanfords is a remarkable letter sent from China from one of Jane's devoted homeworkers. Ah Wing worked for the Stanfords for more than twenty years, beginning in the early 1880s. He had come from Taishan County, in Guangdong Province, and had worked as a cook for the Stanfords. After years of employment he became manager of the entire Chinese staff in the Stanford homes in San Francisco and Palo Alto. When US immigration officials prevented his reentry into the country after he visited China, despite his possession of a valid registration certificate as required by the 1892 Geary Act, he eventually was allowed back in because of his connections with the Stanfords. Jane named him in her will, bequeathing him $1,000 upon her death in March 1905.[52]

After the 1906 earthquake and the destruction of the Stanford mansion in San Francisco in the fire, Ah Wing returned to China for good. A few years later, he was asked to submit his recollection of the destruction of the city and the end of the Stanford mansion in San Francisco. In a long letter Ah Wing wrote sorrowfully of feeling the earthquake of April 18, 1906, and the ensuing firestorm that destroyed the Nob Hill mansions and much of the rest of the city. He told of watching the fire gather force as it came up from the waterfront area and consumed the heights where those of wealth resided. He watched the Stanford mansion burn and collapse. Despondent and bereft, he traveled back to the Palo Alto estate, where he worked for a few months in the university's museum. He sadly recalled that his beloved Stanford employers "were gone. Their house at San Francisco was completely burned. There was only one-half of the old house [in Palo Alto] left. All these were too great a blow to me. I could not stay here in this country any longer to entertain such awful truths." On the morning of his departure for China, he recalled that he brought a bouquet of flowers to Jane Stanford's tomb. Ah Wing cited Confucius when he thought of Jane: "Treat the deceased as if they were still living. This is the utmost state of filial piety." When Jane Stanford was elderly, he wrote, "[it was] natural for me to serve her as I would treat my own mother." He ended his letter expressing his sincere wish: "May the university be prosperous, the trustees be guided with wisdom and strength, that the name of Stanford may live forever throughout the world. May the Stanfords find everlasting pleasures and gladness in heaven."[53]

Today, long after the day when Ah Wing honored the Stanfords and the university, a score of Chinese American families can claim two and even three generations of proud alumni. Many express personal gratitude to the university for their educations and the opportunities they enjoyed because of their connection to the institution. Some current Chinese American employees at the university proudly trace their own roots back to the construction of the transcontinental railroad.

The name *Stanford* continues to hold a special power among many Chinese Americans, and not simply because of the university, with its elite status in the educational world today. *Stanford* occupies a unique and emotional place in their social history. Leland Stanford is reviled as a racist, exploitative robber baron, and political opportunist who used Chinese workers to enrich himself and get himself elected to office by pandering to public prejudices. But the Stanfords, especially Jane, are also remembered for their generosity and protection against a violent and hostile society. They were reliable employers and helped individual Chinese immigrants with personal and business matters.

Of course, the varying opinions of individual Chinese Americans toward the Stanfords can be explained by their relationships with the powerful and wealthy couple. Chinese who held favorable views often benefited from their connections. Crass ambition can account for Leland's racial comments, often made for a voting public or for fellow government officials. He was sensitive to public opinion as a prominent and controversial businessman and opportunistic politician. But even with these considerations, the historical record on the Stanfords and Chinese defies simple characterization.

The Stanfords' connection with the Chinese in America was a long and complicated one that was conflicted, even contradictory. This study of Leland and Jane's relationship with the Chinese does not speak to issues of the Stanfords' intelligence or personal integrity that occupy the attention of other scholars. These are not central concerns here, as considering the relationship of the Stanfords and Chinese actually opens up a much wider and more interesting discussion. The fraught relationship is emblematic of the general experience of the Chinese in nineteenth-century America as a place for them that was both "Gold Mountain" and a "land without ghosts," a soulless place of tragedy, humiliation, and cruelty.[54] The name *Stanford* will continue to evoke powerful feelings of anger and respect, of resentment as well as appreciation, just as America itself has very different meanings to the many Chinese who came here.

Acknowledgments

A book of this scope and depth of this one would not have been possible without the dedication and support of many individuals and institutions.

Hilton Obenzinger (Associate Director of the Chinese Railroad Workers in North America Project) brought energy, wisdom, and his enviable skills as a writer to his role as associate editor of this volume. Roland Hsu (Research Director of the project) fulfilled his role as managing editor of this volume with scholarly experience, tireless project, and meticulous attention to detail. We are grateful to both for the good humor and grace with which they helped a complex, multidisciplinary, multilingual, transnational research project produce a fresh and significant compendium of scholarship.

We give our special thanks to Project lead members. During our first few years, Dongfang Shao and Evelyn Hu-DeHart helped shape the project as coconveners, Research Director Denise Khor helped identify and gather important primary materials, Project Manager Gabriel Wolfenstein helped coordinate all things digital and keep the team on track, and core team researcher Teri Hessel mined archives for intriguing pieces of the puzzle. Archaeology Director Barbara Voss integrated archaeology fully into the project and assembled a national network of archaeologists who added immensely to our research. Yuan Ding and Zhang Guoxiong led research efforts in Guangdong (along with Selia Tan), Hsinya Huang coordinated an impressive team of contributors to the project in Taiwan, and Pin-chia Feng organized our first workshop in Asia at Academia Sinica in Taipei. Oral History Director Connie Young Yu, herself the descendant of a Central Pacific

Railroad worker, connected us with a broad range of other descendants, whose perspectives on their ancestors' experience enriched our scholarship. Barre Fong was instrumental in recording descendants' stories. Erik Steiner provided immense help with our digital projects. Kevin Hsu contributed his talents to help address our technical demands.

Without the early and enthusiastic support of Stanford President John L. Hennessy, Provost John W. Etchemendy, Dean of the School of Humanities Richard Saller, University Librarian Michael J. Keller, Vice Provost and Dean of Research Ann Arvin, and Associate Dean for the Humanities Debra Satz, the Chinese Railroad Workers Project in North America would not have gotten off the ground.

We gratefully acknowledge the support we received from Stanford's Office of the President and Office of the Provost; Office of the Vice Provost and Dean of Research; Office of the Vice Provost for Undergraduate Education; Bill Lane Center for the American West; Stanford University Libraries and Information Resources; American Studies Program; Center for East Asian Studies; Center for Spatial and Textual Analysis; Department of Anthropology; Lang Fund for Environmental Anthropology; Department of English; Department of History; Dean of Research; Stanford Global Studies; Stanford UPS Foundation Endowment Fund; Office of Community Engagement and Diversity; and Roberta Bowman Denning Fund for Humanities and Technology.

A number of individuals associated with these Stanford entities deserve our special thanks, as well: John Groschwitz, Kelley E. Cortright, and Kristen Kutella Boyd at the Center for East Asian Studies; Monica Moore and Rachel Meisels at the American Studies Program; Elaine Treharne, Zephyr Frank, Erik Steiner, Celena Allen, Amanda Bergado, Amita Kumar, and Rani Sharma at the Center for Spatial and Textual Analysis; Bruce Cain at the Bill Lane Center for the American West; Benjamin Stone, Timothy Noakes, Mary Munill, Mimi Calter, Qi Qiu, Zhaohui Xue, Jidong Yang, Michael Widner, and Jason Heppler at Stanford University Libraries and Information Services.

We deeply appreciate the support we have received from external funders who recognized the importance of our work: the American Council of Learned Societies; the Chiang Ching-kuo Foundation; the National Endowment for the Humanities; the Consulate General of the People's Republic of China in San Francisco; Duxiu Corporation; Guangxi Normal University Press (Group) Company, Ltd; the Madeleine Haas Russell Fund for Chinese Studies; and the Silicon Valley Community Foundation.

We express our deep gratitude to William K. Fung, whose munificent gift played a major role in allowing our work to proceed. We are also extremely grateful to Monica and Adrian Arima, Mr. and Mrs. Donald Atha, and Joseph and Lee Anne Ng, all of whom provided generous support.

Academic conferences, both at Stanford and in Asia, have been key to developing and sharing the scholarship reflected in this book. In addition to the external funders, individuals, and Stanford offices acknowledged above, the following provided support that helped make these conferences happen: Guangdong Qiaoxiang Cultural Research Center, Wuyi University, Jiangmen, China; Sun Yat-sen University, Guangzhou, China; Department of Foreign Languages and Literatures, National Chiao Tung University, Taiwan; Institute of European and American Studies at Academia Sinica, Taiwan; National Science Council/Ministry of Science, Taiwan; National Sun Yat-sen University, Taiwan; National Taiwan Normal University; and in the United States the Society of Historical Archaeology.

We are pleased to thank the following individuals for having shared their expertise, their suggestions, their personal libraries, and their research leads; for translating texts, assisting with field trips and conferences, and acting as interpreters during bilingual meetings; and for helping us explore ways of melding historical research and the arts: Barbara Armentrout, Jerry Blackwill, Peter Blodgett, Judith Bookbinder, Jindong Cai, Julie Cain, the late Philip Choy, Linda Clements, Lorraine Crouse, Ryan Dearinger, Sik Lee Denning, Xiaoya Du, Angela Duan, Amanda Felix, Daniel Hartwig, Katie Holley, Ingi House, Julia Huddleston, Elizabeth Huntington, David Kilton, Maxine Hong Kingston, Selina Lai-Henderson, Amy Lam, Sue Lee, Li Ju, Li Ling, John Molenda, Chaun Mortier, Eugene Moy, Anna Naruta-Moya, Jason Nou, William Oudeegest, Cara Randall, Bryanna M. Ryan, Philip Sexton, Roger Staab, Dale Stieber, Raina Sun, Laura Tennent, Greg Walz, Helen Wayland, Betsey Welland, Glenn Willumson, Lee Witten, Kasia Woroniecka, and Kyle Wyatt.

We thank scholars who participated in project conferences and meetings and contributed to our scholarly exchange. They include Rebecca Allen, James Bard, Kenneth Cannon, Paul Chace, Chiung-huei Chang, Mei-shu Chen, Shu-ching Chen, Yong Chen, Bo-wei Chiang, Lynn Furness, Annian Huang, Madeline Hsu, Wen Jin, Tsui-yu Lee, Jack Hang-tat Leong, Iping Liang, Haiming Liu, Brad Lomazzi, Mary Maniery, Christopher Merritt, Steve On, Jean Pfaelzer, Mike Polk, Adrian Praetzellis, Mary Praetzellis, Matthew

Sommer, Charlotte Sunseri, Kim Tong Tee, Robert Weaver, Gary Weisz, Rene Yung, and Xiao-huang Yin.

Research assistants at Stanford University and at universities affiliated with this project have shaped the Project in invaluable ways—mining archives, searching databases, developing visualizations and exhibits, and annotating and translating research materials: Natasha Avery, Griffin Bovée, Ellie Rose Bowen, Preston Carlson, Juliana Chang, Trenton Chang, Mark Flores, Krista Fryauff, Catherine Gao, Maria Greer, Keren He, Annaliese Heinz, Kim Phuong Huynh, Corey Johnson, Asher Kaye, Justin Lai, Lin Le, Kristen Lee, Qingcheng Li, Yue Li, Yvonne Lin, Christopher Lowman, Jenny Lu, Sharon Luk, Pearle Hsiao-Yueh Lun, Jill Madison, Monica Masiello, Sophie Louise McNulty, Maria McVarish, Calvin Miaw, Ian Miller, Laura Ng, Stephanie Linlin Niu, Cleo O'Brien, Debra Pacio, Jeongeun Park, Ben Pham, Ronald Pritipaul, Rachel Roberts, Sarah Sadlier, Emilia Schrier, Eve Simister, Christina Smith, Bojan Srbinovski, Chris Suh, Aoxue Tang, James Thieu, Niuniu Teo, Alexandra To, Bryce Tuttle, Alexander Veitch, Mai Wang, Nathan Weiser, Olivia Wong, Daniel Wu, Vivian Yan, Renren Yang, Lowry Yankwich, Hyejeong Yoon, Tian Yuan, Angela Zhang, Xiaolin Zhao, Bright Zhou, and Hau Zou.

A number of libraries and archives have played a key role in our work, and we are grateful for the research support we received from them. In addition to Stanford University Libraries, we acknowledge the importance to this project of the Bancroft Library, University of California at Berkeley; Becker Collection, Drawings of the American Civil War Era, Boston College Library; Brigham Young University Library Special Collections; California State Library, Sacramento; Huntington Library, San Marino, California; National Archives and Records Administration in San Bruno, California; Occidental College Library Special Collections, Los Angeles; United States Library of Congress, Prints and Photographs Division; University of Utah, J. Willard Marriott Library, Special Collections; and Utah Division of Archives and Special Services.

Historical societies, museums, research centers, and other institutions have also been helpful in our research. We appreciate the research support we received from the Alpine County Museum, Markleeville, California; California State Railroad Museum; Chinese Historical Society of America, San Francisco; Chinese Historical Society of Southern California; Colfax Heritage Museum, California; Donner Memorial Park and Immigrant Trail Museum,

California; Golden Spike National Historical Site, Utah; Guangdong Provincial Museum; Historical Society of Dayton Valley, Dayton, Nevada; Jiangmen Wuyi Museum of the Overseas Chinese; Ogden City Cemetery, Utah; Placer County Archive & Research Center, California; Placer-Sierra Railroad Heritage Society, California; Truckee-Donner Historical Society; Utah State Railroad Museum; and Virginia and Truckee Historical Society.

We are grateful to the many descendants of Chinese railroad workers and their families who agreed to be interviewed for our Project and who shared family photographs and papers with us. The list is too long to include everyone here, but we would particularly like to thank Gene O. Chan, Bill Chen, Raymond Chong, Willson Chow, Anthony Hom, Gary Hom, Montgomery Hom, Carolyn Kuhn, Grace Lee, Sandy Lee, Paulette Liang, Russell Low, Glen Robert Lym, Andrea Yee, and Vicki Tong Young.

We would like to thank Laura Daly for her painstaking copyediting. We thank Margo Irvin and Nora Spiegel of Stanford University Press for ably guiding this book to publication.

We owe our greatest debt to the contributors to this book for having devoted so many hours of their waking lives over the past few years to the challenge of recovering the history of Chinese railroad workers in North America.

Notes

Introduction

1. Leland Stanford, *Statement Made to the President of the United States, and Secretary of the Interior, of Progress of the Work* (Sacramento: H. S. Crocker & Co., 1865).

2. Alexander Saxton, "The Army of Canton in the High Sierra," *Pacific Historical Review* 35, no. 2 (May 1996): 149; David R. Roediger and Elizabeth D. Esch, *The Production of Difference: Race and the Management of Labor in U.S. History* (New York: Oxford University Press, 2014), 77.

3. The National Park Service has produced the most thorough study of the Golden Spike site and ceremony: Robert L. Spude, with the assistance of Todd Delyea, *Promontory Summit, May 10, 1869* (US National Park Service, Intermountain Region, Cultural Resources Management, 2005). See also J. N. Bowman, "Driving the Last Spike at Promontory 1869," *Utah Historical Quarterly* 37 (Winter 1969): 76.

4. Histories of building the first transcontinental line across the United States abound: Wesley Griswold, *A Work of Giants: Building the First Transcontinental Railroad* (New York: McGraw-Hill, 1962); George Kraus, *High Road to Promontory: Building the Central Pacific across the High Sierra* (Palo Alto, CA: American West, 1969); John Hoyt Williams, *A Great and Shining Road: The Epic Story of the Transcontinental Railroad* (Lincoln: University of Nebraska Press, 1988); David Haward Bain, *Empire Express: Building the First Transcontinental Railroad* (New York: Viking/Penguin, 1999); Stephen Ambrose, *Nothing Like It in the World: The Men Who Built the Transcontinental Railroad, 1863–1869* (New York: Simon & Schuster, 2000) are among the best known. There are accounts of the management of the railroad, such as the classic by Oscar Lewis, *The Big Four: The Story of Huntington, Stanford, Hopkins, and Crocker, and of the Building of the Central Pacific* (New York:

Knopf, 1938); of the economic effects of the transcontinental railroads, notably Richard White, *Railroaded: The Transcontinentals and the Making of Modern America* (New York: Norton, 2012); and of California history in William Deverell, *Railroad Crossing: Californians and the Railroad, 1850–1910* (Berkeley: University of California Press, 1994). Close attention was paid to the Chinese railroad workers in Thomas W. Chinn, H. Mark Lai, and Philip P. Choy, eds., *A History of the Chinese in California: A Syllabus* (San Francisco: Chinese Historical Society of America, 1969), 43–47; Alexander Saxton, *The Indispensable Enemy: Labor and the Anti-Chinese Movement in California* (Berkeley: University of California Press, 1975); and George Kraus, "Chinese Laborers and the Construction of the Central Pacific," *Utah Historical Quarterly* 37, no. 1 (1969): 41–57. Chinese American writers on the railroad worker experience include Lisa See, *On Gold Mountain: The One-Hundred-Year Odyssey of My Chinese American Family* (New York: St. Martin's, 1995); and Iris Chang, *The Chinese in America: A Narrative History* (New York: Penguin, 2004). An excellent work on the experience of Chinese railroad workers on the Central Pacific is William F. Chew, *Nameless Builders of the Transcontinental Railroad: The Chinese Workers of the Central Pacific Railroad* (Bloomington, IN: Trafford, 2003). Chinese American writers who have produced memoir, fiction, drama, and historical narrative on the railroad worker experience include Frank Chin, *Chinaman Pacific & Frisco RR Co.* (Minneapolis: Coffee House, 1988) and *Donald Duk* (Minneapolis: Coffee House, 1991); David Henry Hwang, *The Dance and the Railroad and Family Devotions: Two Plays* (New York: Dramatists Play Service, 1983); Maxine Hong Kingston, *China Men* (New York: Vintage, 1989); Shawn Wong, *Homebase* (New York: Plume, 1991); and Laurence Yep, *Dragon's Gate* (New York: Harper Trophy, 1993).

5. "Sayings and Doings," *Harper's Bazaar*, October 16, 1869, 663; "The Chinese Question," *Morning Republican* (Little Rock, AR), September 11, 1869.

6. Studies in China include Annian Huang, ed., *The Silent Spikes: Chinese Laborers and the Construction of North American Railroads*, trans. Zhang Juguo (Beijing: China Intercontinental Press, 2006); Annian Huang, "The Construction of the Central Pacific Railroad by Chinese Workers and the Rise of the United States," *Issues in History Teaching* 6 (2007): 39–41; Chen Hansheng 陈翰笙编, ed., *Huagong chuguo shiliao huibian* 华工出国史料汇编 [Collection of the Historical Materials about the Overseas Chinese Laborers], vol. 7 (Beijing: Zhonghua shuju 中华书局, 1984); and Sheng Jianhong, 美国中央太平洋铁路建设中的华工 [Chinese Builders of the US Central Pacific Railroad], 中西书局 (Shanghai: Zhong xi shu ju, 2015). These works rely almost exclusively on materials in the United States used by American writers.

7. In some cases, there are primary materials extant from workers on these later lines. See, for example, Andrew Griego, "Rebuilding the California Southern

Railroad: The Personal Account of a Chinese Labor Contractor, 1884," *San Diego Historical Society Quarterly* 25, no. 4 (Fall 1979), http://www.sandiegohistory.org/journal/1979/october/railroad/.

8. Judy Yung, *Unbound Feet: A Social History of Chinese Women in San Francisco* (Berkeley: University of California Press, 1995), 16–41; George Anthony Peffer, *"If They Don't Bring Their Women Here": Chinese Female Immigration before Exclusion* (Urbana: University of Illinois Press, 1999), 12–27.

9. "News of the Morning," *Sacramento Daily Union,* June 15, 1858; Barbara Voss, "The Historical Experience of Labor: Archaeological Contributions to Interdisciplinary Research on Chinese Railroad Workers," *Historical Archaeology* 49, no. 1 (2016): 4; "The City," *Sacramento Daily Union*, November 8, 1855.

10. Charles Crocker, testimony, *Report of the Joint Special Committee to Investigate Chinese Immigration,* February 27, 1877, 44th Congress, 2nd Session, Senate Report 689 (Washington, DC: US Government Printing Office, 1877), 666; CPRR Payroll Record, January 1864, California State Railroad Museum, Sacramento.

11. *Sacramento Daily Union*, January 7, 1865.

12. James H. Strobridge, testimony, *Report of the Joint Special Committee,* 723.

13. Crocker, testimony, *Report of the Joint Special Committee,* 667.

14. "The Chinese in California," *Sacramento Daily Union*, July 9, 1866; Crocker, testimony, *Report of the Joint Special Committee,* 667.

15. Leland Stanford, Inaugural Address, 1862, accessed October 27, 2017, http://governors.library.ca.gov/addresses/08-Stanford.html.

16. Leland Stanford, *Statement Made to the President of the United States*, 990.

17. "Second Dispatch," *Daily Alta California* (San Francisco), May 8, 1869, 1.

18. Samuel S. Montague, *Report of the Chief Engineer upon Recent Surveys, Progress of Construction, and Approximate Estimate of Receipts of the Central Pacific Railroad of California, October 8, 1864*, Engineer's Office, C.P.R.R., p. 17. In Pamphlets on California's Railroads, Bancroft Library, University of California, Berkeley.

19. John Debo Galloway, *The First Transcontinental Railroad* (New York: Dorset Press, 1950), 118–135, http://cprr.org/Museum/Galloway6.html; Kraus, *High Road to Promontory*, 308.

20. Leland Stanford, E. H. Miller Jr., and Samuel S. Montague to the Board of Directors of the Central Pacific Railroad Company, January 5, 1867, in *United States Pacific Railway Commission*, vol. 5 (Washington, DC: US Government Printing Office, 1887), 3050, 3051.

21. Montague, *Report of the Chief Engineer*, 13.

22. An early description of Chinese workers hanging in baskets at Cape Horn appears in Isabella Bird, *A Lady's Life in the Rocky Mountains* (New York: Putnam, 1879–1880), 5. Such a description also appears in *Nelson's Pictorial Guidebook: The Central Pacific Railroad: A Trip across the North American Continent from Ogden to*

San Francisco (New York: T. Nelson & Sons, 1870), 83. An anonymous eyewitness account published in 1868 and reprinted in 1869 in several newspapers around the country describes a dramatic incident involving "Chinamen who did the work" being "let down in baskets" to place explosive charges (the precise location of the scene described is not mentioned): "Wholesale Blasting," *Providence* (RI) *Evening Press*, December 14, 1868; *Weekly Union* (Manchester, NH), January 19, 1869; *Bangor* (ME) *Daily Whig and Courier,* February 11, 1869. In *China Men* Maxine Hong Kingston imagines a memorable scene in which her paternal grandfather, Ah Goong, is suspended from a cliff in a basket during his work on the Central Pacific Railroad. Kingston, *China Men*, 130. Visual representations of Chinese railroad workers in baskets (or buckets) include one that appears in Helen Hinckley Jones's *Rails from the West: A Biography of Theodore D. Judah* (San Marino, CA: Golden West Books, 1969), 184, captioned "Chinese laborers were let down in buckets to chisel away at the granite cliffs" at Cape Horn (identified as from the John Garmany Collection); however, the artist draws cliffs that are much steeper than those at Cape Horn. In one watercolor in a series commissioned by San Francisco restaurateur Johnny Kan in the 1960s, the renowned Chinese American artist Jake Lee depicts Chinese railroad workers hanging off cliffs in baskets. See *Finding Jake Lee: The Paintings at Kan's* (San Francisco: Chinese Historical Society of America, 2011), exhibition catalogue, 24. See also the painting of Chinese workers in baskets by artist Tyrus Wong in William Harland Boyd, *The Chinese of Kern County, 1857–1960* (Bakersfield, CA: Kern County Historical Society, 2002), 24.

23. Descriptions of workers hanging by ropes at Cape Horn appear in Wallace H. Atwell, *Great Trans-Continental Railroad Guide* (Chicago: G. A. Crofutt, 1869), 202; Henry Morford, *Morford's Scenery and Sensation Handbook of the Pacific Railroads and California* (New York: Chas. T. Dillingham, 1878), 163–165; William Mintern, *Travels West* (London: Samuel Tinsley, 1877), 277; and Anonymous, *Adams & Bishop's Illustrated Trans-Continental Guide: The Pacific Tourist* (New York: Adams & Bishop, 1884), 252. Although he does not deal with Chinese workers on the Central Pacific, Thomas Curtis Clarke, in *The American Railway: Its Construction, Development, Management, and Appliances* (New York: Scribner's, 1889), 53, provides a description of how ropes and bosun's chairs worked in railway construction on cliffs. Secondary sources also feature Chinese Central Pacific workers being lowered by ropes, including Edward L. Sabin, *Building the Pacific Railway* (Philadelphia: Lippincott, 1919), 114, 115; and Earle Heath, "From Trail to Rail," *Southern Pacific Bulletin,* May 1926, accessed October 27, 2017, http://cprr.org/Museum/Farrar/pictures/2005-03-09-02-02.html. See the discussion, for example, at http://cprr.org/Museum/Chinese.html#baskets. This controversy is explored in Gordon H. Chang, *Ghosts of Gold Mountain: The Epic Story of the Chinese Who Built the Transcontinental Railroad* (New York: Houghton Mifflin Harcourt, 2019).

24. John R. Gillis, "Tunnels of the Pacific Railroad," *Van Nostrand's Eclectic Engineering Magazine* 2 (January 5, 1870): 418–423.

25. Crocker, testimony, *Report of the Joint Special Committee*, 667.

26. Testimony of Lewis M. Clement, July 21, 1887, and James H. Strobridge, July 23, 1887, *United States Pacific Railway Commission*, vol. 5, 2577, 2580; Gillis, "Tunnels of the Pacific Railroad" (paper delivered before the American Society of Civil Engineers, January 5, 1870); "Reminiscences of A. P. Partridge," Lynn D. Farrar Collection, Central Pacific Railroad Photographic History Museum website, accessed May 30, 2017, http://cprr.org/Museum/Farrar/pictures/2005-03-09-01-08.html. These references are for the above three paragraphs.

27. *Sacramento Daily Union*, July 1, 3, 6; Crocker, testimony, *Report to the Joint Special Committee*, 669; Eric Arneson, *Encyclopedia of U.S. Labor and Working-Class History*, vol. 1 (Milton Park, Didcot, UK: Taylor & Francis, 2007), 242.

28. Crocker, testimony, *Report to the Joint Special Committee*, 669.

29. E. B. Crocker to Collis P. Huntington, June 27, 1867, and Mark Hopkins to Collis P. Huntington, June 27, 1867, Collis P. Huntington Papers, 1856–1904, microfilm, Stanford University Libraries.

30. Crocker, testimony, *Report to the Joint Special Committee,* 669.

31. *Alta California* (San Francisco), November 8, 1868.

32. Kraus, *High Road to Promontory*, 203, 310; Williams, *A Great and Shining Road*, 207, 208.

33. Williams, *A Great and Shining Road*, 241; George E. Crofutt, *Crofutt's Great Trans-Continental Tourist's Guide* (New York: G. A. Crofutt & Co., 1870), 143.

34. "Telegraphic Despatches: From the End of the Track," *San Francisco Bulletin*, April 29, 1869.

35. See Andrew J. Russell's photographs *East and West Shaking Hands at Laying Last Rail*, H69.459.2030, and *Chinese Laying the Last Rail*, H69.459.5426, Andrew J. Russell Collection, Oakland Museum of California; Spude, *Promontory Summit*, 43.

36. *San Francisco Newsletter*, May 15, 1869; *Sacramento Daily Union*, May 8, 1869.

37. While there were close to 47,000 miles in 1869, by 1889 there were over 161,000 miles. Donald B. Robertson, *Encyclopedia of Western Railroad History*, vol. 2, *The Mountain States* (Dallas, TX: Taylor Publishing Co., 1991), 37.

38. "The Chinaman as a Railroad Builder," *Scientific American*, July 31, 1869, 75; see also "The Chinaman as a Railroad Builder," *Idaho Statesman* (Boise), May 25, 1869, 3. The article ran in dozens of newspapers in every region of the country from May through September 1869.

39. "Completion of the Pacific Railroad," *San Francisco Bulletin*, May 8, 1869.

40. Samuel Bowles, *Our New West: Records of Travel between the Mississippi River and the Pacific Ocean, etc.* (Hartford, CT: Hartford Publishing Co., 1869), 73, 74.

41. Dale Champion, "The Forgotten Men at Gold Spike Ceremony," *San Francisco Chronicle*, reprinted in *Chinese Historical Society of America Bulletin* 4, no. 5–6 (May–June 1969): 6, 7.

42. Recent scholarship deepens our understanding of the Chinese role in this major episode. See, for example, the special issue of *Historical Archaeology*, "The Archaeology of Chinese Railroad Workers in North America," *Historical Archaeology* 49, no. 1 (2015); Barbara L. Voss, "Towards a Transpacific Archaeology of the Modern World," *International Journal of Historical Archaeology* 20, no. 1 (2015): 146–174; Denise Khor, "Archives, Photography, and Historical Memory: Tracking the Chinese Railroad Worker in North America," *Southern California Quarterly* 98, no. 4 (Winter 2016): 429–456; Hsinya Huang [黃心雅] 北美鐵路華工：歷史、文學與視覺再現 [Chinese Railroad Workers in North America: Recovery and Representation] (Taipei: Bookman, 2017); Shelley Fisher Fishkin, "Seeing Absence, Evoking Presence: History and the Art of Zhi Lin," in *Zhi Lin: In Search of the Lost History of Chinese Migrants and the Transcontinental Railroads* (Tacoma, WA: Tacoma Art Museum, 2017), 31–48.

43. Exceptions are the special issue of *Historical Archaeology*, "The Archaeology of Chinese Railroad Workers in North America," edited by Barbara Voss, that came out of a conference sponsored by the Chinese Railroad Workers in North America Project: *Historical Archaeology* 49, no. 1 (2015); and earlier works such as Priscilla Wegars, ed., *Hidden Heritage: Historical Archaeology of the Overseas Chinese* (London: Routledge, 2016), which includes several essays that discuss the railroad.

44. Maxine Hong Kingston's *China Men* (1980)—a pioneering blend of history, memoir, and fiction that won a National Book Award—played a seminal role in bringing attention to the experience of Chinese railroad workers in the United States. See Pin-chia Feng, "Remembering the Railroad Grandfather in *China Men*," Chinese Railroad Workers in North America Project at Stanford (forthcoming).

Chapter 1

Acknowledgments: Shelley Fisher Fishkin, Roland Hsu, Hilton Obenzinger, Gabriel Wolfenstein, Teri Hessel, and others in the Chinese Railroad Workers in North America Project at Stanford University offered very helpful comments on an earlier version of this essay. I thank them.

1. Wesley S. Griswold, *A Work of Giants: Building the First Transcontinental Railroad* (New York: McGraw-Hill, 1962); Stephen E. Ambrose, *Nothing Like It in the World: The Men Who Built the Transcontinental Railroad, 1863–1869* (New York: Simon & Schuster, 2001).

2. David Haward Bain, *Empire Express: Building the First Transcontinental Railroad* (New York: Penguin Books, 2000); Richard White, *Railroaded: The Transcontinentals and the Making of Modern America* (New York: W. W. Norton, 2012).

3. Ryan Dearinger, *The Filth of Progress: Immigrants, Americans, and the Building of Canals and in the West* (Berkeley: University of California Press, 2015).

4. See Greg Robinson's essay in this volume, "*Les fils du Ciel:* European Travelers' Accounts of Chinese Railroad Workers."

5. Although Jules Verne does not mention Chinese in the fictional account, he was well aware of their presence in California, which he reveals in "Tribulations of a Chinaman in China" (1879), a short story that he published later. In that work, the storyline revolves around financial connections between China and California.

6. See Wolfgang Schivelbusch, *Railway Journey: The Industrialization of Time and Space in the 19th Century* (New York: Urizen Books, 1979), foreword, 89, 90; Edgar B. Schieldrop, *The Railway: Conquest of Space and Time* (London: Hutchinson, 1939), 29, 228, 229; Union Pacific Railroad Company, *Around the World by Steam, via the Pacific Railroad* (London: Union Pacific Railroad Co., 1871), 4.

7. John Todd, *The Sunset Land; or, The Great Pacific Slope* (Boston: Lee & Shepard, 1870), 261.

8. Asa Whitney, *A Project for a Railroad to the Pacific* (New York: George W. Wood, 1849).

9. *Memorial Addresses on the Life and Character of Leland Stanford* (Washington, DC: US Government Printing Office, 1894), 11.

10. John C. Frémont, letter to the editor, *National Intelligencer,* June 15, 1854, cited in Hoyt Williams, *A Great and Shining Road: The Epic Story of the Transcontinental Railroad* (Lincoln: University of Nebraska Press, 1988), 17, 18. See also "China and the Indies—Our 'Manifest Destiny' in the East," *DeBow's Review* (December 1853): 541–571; and Sidney Dillon, "Historic Moments: Driving the Last Spike of the Union Pacific," *Scribner's* 12 (September 1892): 253–259.

11. The speeches, including the one made by Leland Stanford, and celebratory messages offered for the completion of the line highlight its global significance. See "Transcontinental Railroad Postscript," *San Francisco News Letter and California Advertiser,* May 15, 1869; and "Pacific Railroad Inauguration," *Sacramento Daily Union,* January 9, 1863.

12. Dillon, "Historic Moments"; Henry George, "What the Railroad Will Bring Us," *Overland Monthly* 1, no. 4 (October 1868): 297–306.

13. "The China Mail Line," *Sacramento Daily Union,* January 3, 1867.

14. Edwin L. Sabin, *Building the Pacific Railway* (Philadelphia: J. B. Lippincott, 1919), 228, 229; C. P. Huntington to E. B. Crocker, October 3, 1867, *Letters from Collis P. Huntington to Mark Hopkins, Leland Stanford, Charles Crocker, E. B. Crocker, Charles F. Crocker, and D. D. Colton from August 20, 1867 to March 31, 1876,* microfilm (Berkeley: University of California Photographic Services).

15. Daniel Cleveland, "The Chinese as Railroad Laborers," a chapter in his 1869 unpublished manuscript, "The Chinese in California," Daniel Cleveland

Manuscripts, 1868–1929, mss. HM 72175-72177, Huntington Library, San Marino, CA; see also in the same collection Daniel Cleveland to J. Ross Browne, US Minister to China, July 27, 1868. Cleveland had worked on the manuscript for a year and had arranged for its publication by Bancroft, the largest publisher in the West. It is not clear why the book was never issued. Cleveland to Benson J. Lossing, February 10, 1869, Bancroft Library, UC Berkeley, BANCMSS C-B-858.

16. "The Chinese," *Commercial Advertiser* (New York), July 6, 1869.

17. "Mixing the Waters of the Atlantic and Pacific," *Frank Leslie's Illustrated,* July 2, 1870, 245.

18. William F. Chew, *Nameless Builders of the Transcontinental Railway: The Chinese Workers of the Central Pacific Railroad* (Victoria, BC: Trafford, 2004), 40–45.

19. Russell H. Conway, *Why and How: Why the Chinese Emigrate, and the Means They Adopt for the Purpose of Reaching America* (Boston: Lee & Shepard, 1871); "Mass Laborers Hiring in San Francisco," *Feilong* (California *China Mail and Flying Dragon*), January 1, 1867.

20. Lucy M. Cohen, "The Chinese of the Panama Railroad: Preliminary Notes on the Migrants of 1854 Who 'Failed,'" *Ethnohistory* 18, no. 4 (Autumn 1971): 309–320; Lok C. D. Siu, *Memories of a Future Home: Diasporic Citizenship of Chinese in Panama* (Stanford, CA: Stanford University Press, 2005), 38, 39; *The Railroad Record,* May 26, 1859, 162; Minutes of the Meetings of the Board of Directors, June 28, 1854, Records of the Panama Canal Panama Railroad Company, National Archives, Washington, DC.

21. Gilbert Olsen and Richard Floyd, "The San Jose Railroad and Crocker's Pets," in *Chinese Argonauts: An Anthology of the Chinese Contributions to the Historical Development of Santa Clara County,* edited by Gloria Sun Hom (Los Altos Hills, CA: Foothill Community College District/California History Center, 1971), 132–142; *Report of the Joint Special Committee to Investigate Chinese Immigration,* Sen. Rpt. 689, 44th Cong., 2d sess. (Washington, DC: US Government Printing Office, 1877), 667.

22. Philip A. Kuhn, *Chinese among Others: Emigration in Modern Times* (Lanham, MD: Rowman & Littlefield, 2008). Eric Hobsbawm offers his own historical perspective on Chinese migration in *The Age of Capital: 1848–1875* (New York: Vintage, 1996), 63.

23. Special correspondent, "From the Pacific," *Standard* (London), November 17, 1869, 5.

24. "Chinamen as Free Immigrants," *Massachusetts Spy,* July 30, 1869, 2; Diana Lary, *Chinese Migrations: The Movement of People, Goods, and Ideas over Four Millennia* (Lanham, MD: Rowman & Littlefield, 2012), 91; Aristide R. Zolberg, "The Great Wall against China: Responses to the First Immigration Crisis, 1885–1925," in

Migration, Migration History, History: Old Paradigms and New Perspectives, ed. Jan Lucassen and Leo Lucassen (Bern, Switzerland: Peter Lang, 1999), 291–316.

25. Elizabeth Sinn, *Pacific Crossing: California Gold, Chinese Migration, and the Making of Hong Kong* (Hong Kong: Hong Kong University Press, 2013); Madeline Hsu, *Dreaming of Gold, Dreaming of Home: Transnationalism and Migration between the United States and South China, 1882–1943* (Stanford, CA: Stanford University Press: 2000).

26. "How Our Chinamen Are Employed," *Overland Monthly* 2, no. 3 (March 1869): 231. This long article records the wide variety in the types of work performed by the Chinese throughout the West.

27. Alexandra Kichenik DeVarenne, "Goji Farm USA Brings Superfruit to Sonoma County," *Edible* 29 (Spring 2016): 67–70.

28. See Patricia Nelson Limerick, *Legacy of Conquest: The Unbroken Past of the American West* (New York: Norton, 1987). See also J. Ryan Kennedy, Sarah Heffner, Virginia Popper, Ryan P. Harrod, and John J. Crandall's essay in this volume, "The Health and Well-Being of Chinese Railroad Workers."

29. Cleveland, "The Chinese as Railroad Laborers," in "The Chinese in California."

30. Other writers provided similar descriptions of the Chinese labor camps. See, for example, James Ross, *From Wisconsin to California and Return, as Reported for the "Wisconsin State Journal"* (Madison, WI: Ross, James, 1869), 33–35.

31. Raymond B. Craib, *Chinese Immigrants in Porfirian Mexico* (Albuquerque: University of New Mexico Press, 1996), 6; Jacques Meniaud, *Les pionniers du Soudan* (Paris: Société des Publications Modernes, 1931), 99, 100; Watt Stewart, *Chinese Bondage in Peru: A History of the Chinese Coolie in Peru, 1849–1874* (Durham, NC: Duke University Press, 1951), 75, 89; Watt Stewart, *Henry Meiggs: Yankee Pizarro* (Durham, NC: Duke University Press, 1946), 161–163; and Sophia V. Schweitzer and Bennet Hymer, *Big Island Journey* (Honolulu, HI: Mutual Publishing, 2009), 74.

32. Stewart, *Henry Meiggs*, 161–163. On the development of the modern worker in the mid-nineteenth century, see Hobsbawm, *Age of Capital*, 213–229.

33. See Beth Lew-Williams's essay in this volume, "The Remarkable Life of a Sometimes Railroad Worker: Chin Gee Hee, 1844–1929."

34. "The Chinaman as a Railroad Builder," *Scientific American* (July 31, 1869): 75.

35. "Chinamen as Free Immigrants," *Massachusetts Spy*, July 30, 1869. See also Hsu, *Dreaming of Gold*. See essays by Yuan Ding/Roland Hsu, Zhang Guoxiong/Roland Hsu, and Liu Jin/Roland Hsu in this volume.

36. Yung Wing, *My Life in China and America* (New York: Henry Holt, 1909), 237, 238.

37. Cleveland, "The Chinese as Railroad Laborers," in "The Chinese in California."

38. Cleveland, "The Chinese as Railroad Laborers," in "The Chinese in California."

39. Edwards Pierrepont, "Banquet to His Excellency Anson Burlingame," June 23, 1868. One estimate in 1870 put the number at 1,200 Chinese bodies sent back annually at a cost of $100 gold each. Todd, *The Sunset Land,* 280.

40. *Workingman's Advocate,* February 6, 1869, quoted in Liping Zhu, *The Road to Chinese Exclusion: The Denver Riot, 1880 Election, and Rise of the West* (Lawrence: University of Kansas Press, 2013), 17–20, 34, 35.

41. Scott Zesch, *The Chinatown War: Chinese Los Angeles and the Massacre of 1871* (New York: Oxford University Press, 2012), 6–14.

42. Acknowledgment of the importance of the railroad workers in United States–China relations by political leaders is not altogether new. The famous nineteenth-century Chinese diplomat Wu Tingfang acknowledged the importance of the workers in his *America through the Spectacles of an Oriental Diplomat* (New York: Frederick A. Stokes, 1914), 44, 45. American presidents did so in the nineteenth century when they opposed passage of anti-Chinese immigration acts. See Gordon H. Chang, *Fateful Ties: A History of America's Preoccupation with China* (Cambridge, MA: Harvard University Press, 2015), 78. Annelise Heinz, "Report on Chinese Immigration Pamphlets," Chinese Railroad Workers in North America Project (unpublished paper) which examines references to the railroad workers in the 1870s–1880s public debate over Chinese immigration restriction.

Chapter 2

1. The term *coolie* has origins in the Hindi "hill coolies" of India, but it has become widely but unsystematically applied, including by historians, to Chinese manual laborers of the lowest or basest order since the nineteenth century.

2. David Faure, *The Structure of Chinese Rural Society: Lineage and Village in the Eastern New Territories, Hong Kong* (Hong Kong: Oxford University Press, 1986), 156.

3. Faure, *The Structure of Chinese Rural Society,* 6, 233.

4. Faure, *The Structure of Chinese Rural Society,* 224–227.

5. Yong Chen, "The Internal Origins of Chinese Emigration to California Reconsidered," *Western Historical Quarterly* 28, no. 4 (Winter 1997): 532–535; Yong Chen, *Chinese San Francisco, 1850–1943* (Stanford, CA: Stanford University Press), 11–44.

6. Ching-Hwang Yen, "Chinese Coolie Emigration, 1845–74," in *Routledge Handbook of the Chinese Diaspora,* edited by Tan Chee-Beng (London: Routledge, 2013), 75.

7. Chen, *Chinese San Francisco,* 17.

8. Faure, *The Structure of Chinese Rural Society,* 233; Frederic Wakeman, *Stranger*

at the Gate: Social Disorder in South China, 1839–1861 (Berkeley: University of California Press, 1966), 14, 15.

9. Elizabeth Sinn, *Pacific Crossing: California Gold, Chinese Migration, and the Making of Hong Kong* (Hong Kong: Hong Kong University Press, 2013), 114–117.

10. Dolors Folch, "Crime and Punishment: Ming Criminal Justice as Seen in Sixteenth-Century Spanish Sources," paper presented at the World History Association Meeting, Beijing, July 9, 2011; Zhang Xie (张燮), *Dong Xi Yang Kao* (东西洋考) (1618; Taipei, 1962); Wakeman, *Stranger at the Gate;* Paul Van Dyke, *The Canton Trade: Life and Enterprise on the China Coast, 1700–1845* (Hong Kong: Hong Kong University Press, 2005); Paul Van Dyke, *Merchants of Canton and Macao* (Hong Kong: Hong Kong University Press, 2011).

11. In 1861 Cornelius Koopmanschap and Charles Bosman in Hong Kong contracted with a Captain Pillsbury of Rockland, Maine, to bring his clipper *Forest Eagle* to load five hundred Chinese migrants in Macau and deliver them to Havana. The contract between Koopmanschap and Pillsbury, dated January 2, 1861, is archived in the *Forest Eagle* file in the Penobscot Marine Museum, Searsport, Maine.

12. The lead commissioner was the Qing official Chen Lanbin (陈兰彬), who would become the first Chinese ambassador to the Americas in 1876, shortly after concluding the Cuba investigation; the other two were foreigners in the service of the Qing court: the Briton A. MacPherson, commissioner of customs at Hankou, and the Frenchman A. Huber, commissioner of customs at Tianjin, both treaty ports. The report was issued in 1876, in English and French versions, soon after the commissioners visited Cuba and many of the sugar plantations in 1873. No report in Chinese was issued at the time, but the Chinese text was partially published much later. The original is in the National Library of Beijing.

13. The year 1874 saw the last shipments of coolies, totaling 2,490.

14. Lisa Yun, *The Coolie Speaks: Chinese Indentured Laborers and African Slaves in Cuba* (Philadelphia: Temple University Press, 2008).

15. Yun, *The Coolie Speaks,* 70.

16. Tan Qianchu (谭乾初), *Guba Zazhi* (古巴杂记) (China, 1887).

17. Fu Yunlong (傅云龙), *Youli Guba tujing erjuan* (游历古巴图经二 卷) (China, 1889).

18. Yun, *The Coolie Speaks.*

19. June Mei, "Socioeconomic Origins of Emigration," *Modern China* 5, no. 4 (1979); Chen, "Internal Origins of Chinese Emigration"; Chen, *Chinese San Francisco.*

20. Yun, *The Coolie Speaks,* 67, 68.

21. Evelyn Hu-DeHart, "From Plantation to Chinatown: Hakka–Punti Relations in Cuba," paper presented at the Changing Hakka Culture and Society Workshop,

Hakka Research Department of Jiaying University, Meixian, Guangdong, China, May 7–9, 2014.

22. Moon-Ho Jung, *Coolies and Cane: Race, Labor, and Sugar in the Age of Emancipation* (Baltimore: Johns Hopkins University Press, 2006).

23. Jules David, ed., *American Diplomatic and Public Papers: The United States and China,* series 1, vol. 17, "The Coolie Trade and Chinese Emigration" (Wilmington, DE: Scholarly Resources, 1973), 14, 15.

24. One among many such comparisons of the coolie trade to the slave trade was given in the extensive report by H. P. Blanchard of Whampoa to Oliver Perry, US consul in Canton, dated April 27, 1859. David, *American Diplomatic and Public Papers,* 83–88.

25. David, *American Diplomatic and Public Papers,* 149.

26. David, *American Diplomatic and Public Papers,* 153.

27. Sinn, *Pacific Crossing,* 31.

Chapter 3

Note: Unless otherwise indicated, all translations are by the authors with assistance by Renren Yang and Gordon H. Chang.

1. The Guangdong Qiaoxiang Culture Research Center at Wuyi University has helped in the construction of the Jiangmen Wuyi Overseas Chinese Museum, Jiangmen Shi, Guangdong. Since 2001 the center has been focused on field research and the preservation and analysis of cultural relics.

2. Tan Biao 谭镖, ed., *Xinhui xiangtu zhi* 新会乡土志 [Xinhui Local Annals], vol. 9 (Guangzhou: Yuedong bianyi gongzi 粤东编译公司, 1908). See also "Hukou" 户口 [Households], in *Kaiping xian xiangtu zhi* 开平县乡土志 [Kaiping Local Records], edited by Zhang Qichen 张启琛 (Kaiping, 1909); "Jing zheng" 经政略 [Economics and Politics], in *Kaiping xian zhi* 开平县志 [Kaiping County Annals], vol. 13, edited by Kaiping shi difang zhi banggongshi 开平市地方志办公室 (Beijing: Zhonghua shuju 中华书局, 2002).

3. Chen Hansheng 陈翰笙编, ed., *Huagong chuguo shiliao huibian* 华工出国史料汇编 [Collection of the Historical Materials about the Overseas Chinese Laborers], vol. 1 (Beijing: Zhonghua shuju 中华书局, 1984), 1378.

4. Chen, *Huagong chuguo shiliao huibian,* vol. 7, 97; see also Liu Boji, *The History of Overseas Chinese in America* (Taipei: Dawn Cultural Enterprise, 1983), 12:

> Americans are extremely wealthy people. They need us Chinese to go and [they] sincerely welcome us. In America, pay is excellent, housing, food, and clothing are abundant and first rate. You may remit money and send letters to your relatives and friends any time as you please, and we may be trusted to deliver and cash your remittance and hand over your letters. It is a civilized country, and there are no Qing officials and soldiers. Everyone is equal there. It has no emperor and its people are great. Currently

there are many Chinese who are earning their [living] there, so it is not a foreign place. If you are to pray to the Chinese gods, we can do it for you. You need not feel fear, and you will have luck. If you are interested, please come to our company in Hong Kong or Guangzhou, and we will provide you with earnest guidance. Money is abundant in America. If you want to earn wages and guarantee your position, submit an application with us.

5. Chen, *Huagong chuguo shiliao huibian*, vol. 1, 1377, 1397.

6. Chen, *Huagong chuguo shiliao huibian*, vol. 7, 125, 171.

7. Chen, *Huagong chuguo shiliao huibian*, vol. 7, 97, 98.

8. Chen, *Huagong chuguo shiliao huibian*, vol. 7, 66.

9. Chen, *Huagong chuguo shiliao huibian*, vol. 7, 151.

10. Chen, *Huagong chuguo shiliao huibian*, vol. 7, 62.

11. Chen, *Huagong chuguo shiliao huibian*, vol. 1, 1351.

12. "Jing zheng."

13. Yu Baiyun 余白云, ed., *Jinshan geji* 金山歌集 [Ballads of Gold Mountain] (San Francisco: Daguang shulin yinhang 大光书林印行, n.d.). This collection was discovered while researching family clan materials at the mansion of Linlu at Qinglin Village of Majianglong, Kaiping City. The text is preserved in the Institute of Diaolou Culture of Kaiping City. It was printed by Daguang Library, and there is no date of publication. Judging by its design format, it appears to have been issued around the end of the Qing dynasty or the early years of the republic, circa 1875–1925.

14. Private collection, Li Jingyao, Jingmen, China.

15. Original manuscript, collection of the Jiangmen Wuyi Overseas Chinese Museum, Jiangmen Shi, Guangdong, China.

16. Rang tie 让贴 [Assignment Contract], October 29, 1862, Jiangmen wuyi huaqiao huaren bowuguam 江门五邑华侨华人博物馆, Jiangmen, China.

17. Yu, *Jinshan geji.*

18. Zhongguo minjian wenxue jicheng Guangdong juan Taishan xian ziliao ji 中国民间文学集成广东卷台山县资料集 [Guangdong Taishan Data Set of the Chinese Folklore Collections] (Taishan: Taishan xian minjian wenxue jicheng bianwei hui 台山县民间文学集成编委会, 1987), 276.

19. Zhongguo minjian wenxue jicheng Guangdong juan Taishan xian ziliao ji, 226.

20. Zhongguo minjian wenxue jicheng Guangdong juan Taishan xian ziliao ji, 275.

21. Zhongguo minjian wenxue jicheng Guangdong juan Taishan xian ziliao ji, 276.

22. Chen Yuanzhu 陈元柱编, ed., *Ttaishan geyao ji* 台山歌谣集 [Taishan Ballads] (Guangzhou: Guoli Zhongshan daxue yuyan lishixue yanjiusuo 国立中山大学言语历史学研究所, 1929), 30.

23. Porcelain tablet in the collection of Li Jingyao, Jiangmen, China.

24. Zhang Zhidong and Zhang Yinhuan, "Memoir of Zhang Zhidong, Governor of Guangdong and Guangxi Provinces, and Zhang Yinhuan, Commissioner to America, Sending Wang Ronghe and Yu Juan on an Inspection Visit to Towns of Southeast Asia Regarding the Situation of Chinese Laborers, and in preparation to Establish a Chinese Consulate, dated January 25, 1886, twelfth year in the reign of Guangxu," in Chen *Huagong chuguo shiliao huibian*, vol. 1, 267.

25. Xue Fucheng, "Memoir of Xue Fucheng, Commissioner, on Visits to England, France, Italy and Belgium, Charged with Preparing the Establishment of Chinese Consulates in the Islands of Southeast Asia to Protect Chinese Overseas, dated October 10, 1890, sixteenth year in the reign of Guangxu," in Chen, *Huangong chuguo shiliao huibian*.

26. *Kaiping xian zhi* [Kaiping County Annals].

27. *Kaiping xian zhi* [Kaiping County Annals].

28. Yu, *Jinshan geji*. For an alternative translation into English of the final eight lines, see Marlon K. Hom, *Songs of Gold Mountain: Cantonese Rhymes from San Francisco Chinatown* (Berkeley: University of California Press, 1987), 95.

29. Chen Hanzhong, "The Graves of the Overseas Chinese Destitute in Xinhui," in China County and Town Yearbook, Xinhua, China, 2004, section 7. The process of preparing and repatriating the remains of the overseas Chinese is described on the website for the Chinese in Northwest America Research Committee (CINARC), accessed October 26, 2015, http://www.cinarc.org/Death-2.html.

30. Yu, *Jinshan geji*.

31. *Jinshan po zi tan* 金山婆自叹 [The Sighs of Gold Mountain Wives] (Guang-zhou: Huaxing shuju 华兴书局, n.d.), 1. This manuscript was discovered during research for this essay in the family clan materials at Linlu Building of Qinglin Village, Majianglong Community, Kaiping City, China, and is now in the collection of the Diaolou Culture Institute of Kaiping City.

32. "Ballad of the Young Wife's Sentimental Farewell" and "Ballad of the Aged Unable to Recover Youth" in Yu, *Jinshan geji*, 36, 58.

Chapter 4

Note: Unless otherwise indicated, all translations are by the authors.
Acknowledgments: We express special appreciation for Chinese-to-English trans-lations by Mai Wang, Catherine Zhao, and Renren Yang.

1. For an introduction to the importance of overseas remittances to the history of the Chinese economy, see Cheong Kee Cheok, "Chinese Overseas Remittances to China: The Perspective from South-East Asia," *Journal of Contemporary Asia* 43, no. 1 (2013): 75–101.

2. Guangdong sheng yinhang ni zai haiwai ziyou xuanze qiaomin juju didian kaishe fen zhihang chu 1947 广东省银行拟在海外自由选择侨民聚居地点开设

分支行处 1947 年 [Kwangtung Provincial Bank to set up branches where overseas Chinese choose to reside], Guangdong sheng dang'an guancang 广东省档案馆藏 [Guangdong Provincial Archives], Guangdong sheng yinhang dang'an, ed. 41, cat. 3, vol. 284.

3. Yao Zengyin 姚曾荫, "Guangdong sheng de huaqiao huikuan" 广东省的华侨汇款 [Overseas Chinese Remittances in Guangdong Province], *The Commercial Press*, 1943, 3.

4. Guowai qiaobao ji guonei qiaojuan dizhi diaocha biao, jin chu kou qiao you tongji biao 国外侨胞及国内侨眷地址调查表、进出口侨邮统计表, 1948. [Overseas Compatriots and Addresses of their Chinese Relatives, Statistics on Inbound/Outbound Mail], Guangdong sheng dang'an cang you zheng ting dang'an 广东省档案馆藏邮政厅档案 [Guangdong Provincial Archives, Post Office Archive], ed. 29, cat. 2, vol. 372.

5. *Sunning Journal,* 1915.

6. Li Long 李龙, Meiguo de huaqiao huikuan 美国的华侨汇款 [Overseas Chinese Remittances in the United States] *Zhongmei zhoubao* 中美周报 [Chinese-American Weekly] 第 266 期, in Guangdong sheng dangan guancang Guangdong sheng yinhang dangan, ed. 41, cat. 3, vol. 289; Ben hang ni zai tanxiangshan sheli jigou de diaocha baogao 1947–1948 nian 本行拟在檀香山设立机构的调查报告 1947–1948 年 pp. 18–19 [Bank to set up office in Honolulu, Report on Investigation 1947–1948].

7. See Guangdong you qu po huo daoqie qiaobao jia xin, chai qie nei Zhuang ze zhi mao ling kuan xiang jig e zong an jian chu li jing guo qing xing wen shu 1949 nian 广东邮区破获盗窃侨胞家信、拆窃内装仄纸冒领款项及各宗案件处理经过情形文书 1949 年 [Guangdong Postal Area recovers theft of overseas Chinese letters, stolen and cashed checks that came with the letters, various cases (1949)], Guangdong sheng dang'an guancang youzheng ting dang'an 广东省档案馆藏邮政厅档案 [Guangdong Provincial Archives, Post Office Archives], no. 29, cat. 2, vol. 367; Guanyu ceh cha you meiguo ji jilongpo hui jiao Guangzhou shi huangyan'ai, quain jun guahao xin nei ze bi bei mao ling jingguo wneshu cailiao 1947–1949 nian 关于彻查由美国及吉隆坡汇交广州市黄雁爱、伍千均挂号信内仄币被冒领经过文书材料 1947–1949 年 [Documents about the investigation on the stolen and illegally cashed checks sent by registered mail from the United States and Kuala Lumpur to Huang Hui'ai and Wu Qianjun of Guangzhou City (1947–1949)], Guangdong sheng dang'an guancang youzheng ting dang'an 广东省档案馆藏邮政厅档案 [Guangdong Provincial Archives, Post Office Archives], no. 29, cat. 2, vol. 496; Guanyu zhuicha jianada qiaomin hu yunfa ji heshan xia cun jiaren shou hang xin neizhuang huipiao bei maoling jingguo qingkuang laiwang wenshu 1948–1949 nian 关于追查加拿大侨民胡运发寄鹤山夏村家人收航信内装汇票被冒领经过情况来往文书 1948–1949 年 [Documents about the investigation on the

stolen checks from airmail sent by Canadian resident Hu Yunfa to family in Xia Village of Heshan (1948–1949)], Guangdong sheng dang'an guancang youzheng ting dang'an 广东省档案馆藏邮政厅档案 [Guangdong Provincial Archives, Post Office Archives], no. 29, cat. no. 2, vol. 497.

8. Guowai qiaobao ji guonei qiaojuan dizhi diaocha biao, jin chu kou qiao you tongji biao 国外侨胞及国内侨眷地址调查表、进出口侨邮统计表 1948. [Overseas Compatriots and Addresses of their Chinese Relatives, Statistics on Inbound/Outbound Mail], Guangdong sheng dang'an cang you zheng ting dang'an 广东省档案馆藏邮政厅档案 [Guangdong Provincial Archives, Post Office Archive], ed. 29, cat. 2, vol. 372.

9. Yao Zengyin 姚曾荫, Guangdong sheng de huaqiao huikuan 广东省的华侨汇款, pp. 1–3.

10. Lin Jiajin et al. 林家劲等, Jindai guangdong qiao hui yan jiu 近代广东侨汇研究, p. 8; Shicha yuan chenliangjun shicha xinchang, Jiangmen deng youju guanyu gaijin ge he xia nei xiang cun youdi qingkuang de baogao, 1948 nian 视察员陈亮骏视察新昌、江门等邮局关于改进各核辖内乡村邮递情况的报告 1948 年 [Inspector Chen Lianjun inspected Xinchang, Jiangmeng etc. post offices to improve rural postal services, Report from 1948], Guangdong sheng dang'an guancang youzheng ting dang'an 广东省档案馆藏邮政厅档案, ed. 29, cat. 1, vol. 229, pp. 3–13.

11. Yi chu lai han (li jie qiao hui di ming biao lv fei ming xi biao, cha zong fu mei jin chu quan, cha xun hui kuan deng) 1946 nian 邑处来函（理解侨汇地名表旅费明细表、查总付美金储券、查询汇款等）1946 年 [Department Letter: Understanding the Remittance and Destination List, Travel Itinerary, Checking Total Payments of U.S. Dollars, Checking Remittances, etc. 1946], Guangdong sheng dang'an guan cang zhong guo yin hang dang'an 广东省档案馆藏中国银行档案 [Guangdong Provincial Archives, Bank of China Archive], ed. 43, cat. 1, vol. 305, p. 40; Zhong guo yin hang tai shan ban shi chu zhi guang zhi hang guan yu you di chi huan ke yi kao xun cheng ma dai song you jian de han jian 中国银行台山办事处致广支行关于邮递迟缓可依靠巡城马带送邮件的函件 1946 年7月 11日 [Document on Bank of China, Taishan Branch to Guangdong Branch, on the slow mail delivery that can be delivered by non-official postmen], July 11, 1946.

12. Guanyu jinzhi feifa baiyin wai yun ji maimai jin yin waibi de guizhang banfa laiwang wenshu, 1948–1949 nian 关于禁止非法白银外运及买卖金银外币得规章办法来往文书，1948–1949 年 [Documents about the prohibition of the use of illicit silver for foreign shipments and regulations on trading gold and silver foreign currencies, 1948–1949], Guangdong sheng dang'an guancang, caizheng ting dang'an 广东省档案馆藏，财政厅档案 [Guangdong Provincial Archives, Department of Finance Archive], ed. 4, cat. 2, vol. 23; Sheng zhengfu guanyu jinyuanquan, jin yin waibi chuli zhi sheng canyi hui de wenshu cailiao, 1948–1949 nian 省政府关于金圆券、金银外币处理致省参议会的文书材料，1948–1949 年 [Documents from

the provincial government, about the administration of the gold yuan note, gold and silver foreign currencies, to the provincial legislature, 1948–1949], Guangdong sheng dang'an guancang, caizheng ting dang'an 广东省档案馆藏，财政厅档案, ed. 4, cat. 5, vol. 36.

13. Guangdong sheng dang'an guancang, guangdong sheng zhongguo yinhang dang'an 广东省档案馆藏，广东省中国银行档案 [Guangdong Provincial Archives, Guangdong Bank of China Archives], vol. 186. The unit of currency is the renminbi (RMB). The study was conducted in 1956. At this time, Malaysia and Singapore were not yet independent states but were the colonies of British Malaya and British Singapore; Vietnam was also not a unified state.

14. Yao Zengyin 姚曾荫, Guangdong sheng de huaqiao huikuan 广东省的华侨汇款, p. 6.

15. Yao Zengyin 姚曾荫, Guangdong sheng de huaqiao huikuan 广东省的华侨汇款, p. 7.

16. Guangdong qu jing du chu tang shi dao feng pai si yi shicha chuli feifa waibi maimai raoluan jinrong wenti de laiwang wenshu 1948 nian [Guangdong, District Economic Supervision Department], 广州区经督处唐视导奉派四邑视察处理非法外币买卖扰乱金融问题的来往文书 1948 年 [Documents about the investigation where Director Tang of Guangzhou District Economic Supervisory Office was sent to Siyi to supervise and handle the problem of illegal foreign currency exchange that was disturbing the financial market], Guangdong sheng dang'an guancang caizhengting dang'an 广东省档案馆藏财政厅档案 [Guangdong Provincial Archives, Department of Finance Archives], ed. 4, cat. 2, vol. 25, pp. 71–74; Li shun luecheng siyi jinrong zhuangkuang baogao shu 李舜略呈四邑金融状况报告书 October 10, 1948 [Briefing of Siyi's financial situation by Li Shun].

17. Liu Zuoren 刘佐人, Zhengqu nanyang qiao hui wen ti 争取南洋侨汇问题 [Obtaining Nanyang Remittances], from Liu Zuoren: Jinrong yu qiaohui zonglun 金融与侨汇综论 [A Comprehensive Review of Finance and Overseas Chinese Remittances], pp. 67–68.

18. Ling Yu 凌羽, Xiang gang yu nan yang [Hong Kong and Nanyang], *Guangdong sheng yinhang yuekan* 广东省银行月刊 [Guangdong Banking Monthly], vol. 3, no. 56, p. 57.

19. Zhongshan xian you guan siying qianzhuang, ting fuye ji qudi bufa yin hao baogao yu caiting de laiwang wenshu diaocha biao, qingce 1947–1949 nian 中山县有关私营钱庄、停复业及取缔不法银号报告与财厅的来往文书调查表、清册 1947–1949 年 [Documents on Zhongshan County's private banks with the Department of Finance: closings and reopenings, and suppression of illegal banks], Guangdong sheng dang'an guancang caizheng dang'an 广东省档案馆藏财厅档案 [Guangdong Provincial Archives, Department of Finance Archives], ed. 4, cat. 2, vol. 74, p. 73; Zhongshan xian shiqi zhen xiancun sheli ge yin hao qingce 中山县石岐镇

现存设立各银号清册 [List of Current Banks in Shiqi Town, Zhongshan County], September 1946.

20. Yi chu lai han (li jie qiao hui di ming biao lv fei ming xi biao, cha zong fu mei jin chu quan, cha xun hui kuan deng) 1946 nian 邑处来函（理解侨汇地名表旅费明细表、查总付美金储券、查询汇款等）1946 年 [Department Letter: Understanding the Remittance and Destination List, Travel Itinerary, Checking Total Payments of US Dollars, Checking Remittances, etc., 1946], Guangdong sheng dang'an guan cang zhong guo yin hang dang'an 广东省档案馆藏中国银行档案 [Guangdong Provincial Archives, Bank of China Archive], ed. 43, cat. 1, vol. 301, pp. 179–180; Zhongguo yinhang taishan zhihang zhi ao hang chen bao dai gou gang bi hui piao qing kuang 中国银行台山支行致粤行陈报代购港币汇票情况 [Status of bank drafts, from Bank of China, Taishan Branch to Guangzhou Branch, purchasing Hong Kong Dollars], December 27, 1946.

21. Yue hang zi qu han (. . . wei jie qiaohui qingdan, meijin qiaohui hui lv, shougou meihui deng) 1947 nian 粤行字去函（. . . 未介侨汇清单、美金侨汇汇率、收购美汇等）1947 年 [Guangzhou Branch documents: unlisted remittances, U.S. dollar remittance exchange rate, purchases of American remittances, etc.] 1947, Guangdong sheng dang'an guan cang zhong guo yin hang dang'an 广东省档案馆藏中国银行档案 [Guangdong Provincial Archives, Bank of China Archive], ed. 43, cat. 1, vol. 1492, pp. 72–82; Chang chu sanshiqu nian du ye wu bao gao 昶处三十五年度业务报告 [Chang Chu 35th annual business reports].

22. Chang chu lai han (qiao hui deng) 1948 nian 昶处来函（侨汇等）1948 年 [Letter from Chang Chu office (on foreign remittance), 1948], Guangdong sheng dang'an guan cang zhong guo yin hang dang'an 广东省档案馆藏中国银行档案 [Guangdong Provincial Archives, Bank of China Archive], ed. 43, cat. 1, vol. 959, pp. 122–131; Chang chu ye qu tan hua ji lu 昶处业务谈话记录 [Document on business conversation by Chang Chu office], March 27, 1948.

23. Du Zhiying 杜之英, Zijin tao gang dui zhongguo jingji de yingxiang 资金逃港对中国经济的影响 [The effect of capital flight from Hong Kong on China's economy], *Guangdong Sheng Yinhang Yuekan* 广东省银行月刊 [Guangdong Province Banking Monthly], vol. 3, no. 9–10, p. 9.

24. Shunde, zhongshan, taishan, kaiping, enping, xinhui, sanshui, heshan, dongguan, sihui deng xian guanyu siying qianzhuang qingli, ting fuye ji quid feifa jingying deng wenti yu caizhengting de laiwang wenshu 1946–1949 nian顺德、中山、台山、开平、恩平、新会、三水、鹤山、东莞、四会等县关于私营钱庄清理、停复业及取缔非法经营等问题与财政厅的来往文书 1946–1949 年 [Shunde, Zhongshan, Taishan, Kaiping, Enping, Xinhui, Sanshui, Heshan, Dongguan, Sihui, etc. counties and the reorganization of private banks, suspension of business, suppression of illegal operations], Guangdong sheng dang'an guancang, caizheng ting dang'an 广东省档案馆藏，财政厅档案 [Guangdong Provincial

Archives, Department of Finance Archive], ed. 4, cat. 5, vol. 32, pp. 159–160; Guang-zhou jinrong guanli ju jiancha guangzhou tianxiang, youan, yiji san qianzhuang 广州金融管理局检查广州天祥、佑安、怡记三钱庄 [Guangzhou financial management department inspects three banks in Tianxiang, Youan, Yiji].

25. Zhongguo yinhang xin chang zhihang zhi wangzhengfang jingli guanyu yu dangdi mimi diantai shangqia gongji sui shi hang shi 中国银行新昌支行致王振芳经理关于与当地秘密电台商洽供给穗市行市 January 14, 1947 [Bank of China, Xinchang Branch to Wang Zhenfang, Manager, on talks with local underground radio to serve Guangzhou banking sector], Guangdong sheng dang'an guan cang zhong guo yin hang dang'an 广东省档案馆藏中国银行档案 [Guangdong Provincial Archives, Bank of China Archive], ed. 43, cat. 2, vol. 1205, p. 135.

26. Taishan xian zhengfu dian cheng taishan bi zhi gaige qingxing 台山县政府电呈台山币制改革情形 1948 [Telegram from Taishan County Government on currency reform], Guangdong sheng dang'an guancang, caizheng ting dang'an 广东省档案馆藏，财政厅档案 [Guangdong Provincial Archives, Department of Finance Archives], ed. 4, cat. 2, vol. 25, pp. 19–22.

Chapter 5

Note: Unless otherwise indicated, all translations are by the authors.

1. *Qiaoxiang* refers to the hometowns of the overseas Chinese; *qiaoxiang* documents refers to *huaqiao* letters, account books, coaching papers, and deeds related to overseas Chinese and their dependents that were inherited and preserved in *huaqiao* hometowns.

2. Zhu Zhongji 朱仲缉, "Xuyan san" 序言三 [Preface 3], in 全美宁阳第一届恳亲大会始末记 [Assembly of Ning Yeung People from Taishan in the U.S.], ed. Huang Fuling 黄福领 and Zhu Zhongji 朱仲缉 (Beijing: Ning Yeung Association 宁阳会馆, 1928), 34.

3. The porcelain tablet is collection of Li Jingyao 李镜尧, an amateur collector in Jiangmen, Guangdong.

4. Marlon K. Hom, *Songs of Gold Mountain: Cantonese Rhymes from San Francisco Chinatown* (Berkeley: University of California Press, 1987), 39. Translated into English and cited in Hom, Anon (Tan Bi'an), "Jinshan fu xing" [Songs of the wife of a Gold Mountain man], *Xinning zazhi* 1100 (January 1949): 68.

5. Hom, *Songs of Gold Mountain*, 49.

6. Evelyn Hu-Dehart, 何以为家——全球化时期华人的流散与播迁 *He yi wei jia: Quanqiuhua shiqi huaren de liusan yu boqian* [Finding Home in the Chinese Diaspora during the Age of Globalization], trans. Zhou Lin (Beijing: Zhejiang U. Press, 2015).

7. Xianfeng sannian shi'er yue Ting Zhuo, Ting Zao li qitie 咸丰三年十二月

廷倬、廷藻立讫帖 [A deed established by Ting Zhuo 廷倬 and Ting Zao 廷藻], collection of Li Jingyao 李镜尧, Jiangmen, Guangdong.

8. Historically, a tael was a unit of measure that varied in regions of China but when applied to silver most often was equivalent to 1.3 ounces. Thus, 120 taels would equal 156 ounces of silver—a not unsubstantial sum.

9. Tongzhi yuannian Yi Suo li rangtie 同治元年益所立让帖 [A transfer deed established by Yi Suo 益所 in the first reign year of Tongzhi 同治], collection of the Jiangmen Overseas Chinese Museum. The first reign year of Tongzhi was 1862.

10. Guan Ruyu qian yin dan 关如裕欠银单 [Guan Ruyu's loan receipt], March 12, 1897, collection of the Jiangmen Wuyi Overseas Chinese Museum.

11. Guan Dekuan gei Guan Tingjie de xin 关德宽给关廷杰的信 [Guan Dekuan's letter to Guan Tingjie], dated the twenty-fifth day of the third lunar month in 1888, collection of the Jiangmen Wuyi Overseas Chinese Museum.

12. "Muwu juqiu chijin ku" 木屋拘囚吃尽苦 [Suffering and imprisoned in a wooden house], Jinshan Geji 金山歌集, published by Daguan Shulin 大光书林 in the Gold Mountain 金山正埠, 1912: 14.

13. On the larger context of overseas wealth transfers and the practice of remittances, see Liu Jin, "Remittance Charges and the Change of Social Attitudes in the PRD Region," *Journal of Wuyi University,* 2011–2012, http://en.cnki.com.cn/Article_en/CJFDTotal-WYDS201102004.htm.

14. Yao Zengyin 姚曾癮, "Guangdong sheng de huaqiao huikuan" 广东省的华侨汇款 [Overseas Chinese remittances in Guangdong Province], *The Commercial Press,* 1943, 9. See also A. W. Loomis, "The Chinese Six Companies," *Overland Monthly,* September 1868, 221–227.

15. Guan Renzi zhi Guan Tingjie de xin 关壬子致关廷杰的信 [Guan Renzi's letter to Guan Tingjie], dated the twenty-first day of the fourth lunar month in 1883, collection of the Jiangmen Wuyi Overseas Chinese Museum.

16. Guan Renzi zhi Guan Tingjie de xin 关壬子致关廷杰的信 [Guan Renzi's letter to Guan Tingjie], dated the fourteenth day of the seventh lunar month in 1883, collection of the Jiangmen Wuyi Overseas Chinese Museum.

17. Guangxu sanshi nian Jiangmen kou Huanyang Maoyi Lunlue 光绪三十年江门口华洋贸易论略 [Jiangmen's overseas trade overview], in *Overseas Trade Handbook of the Customs in the Republic of China* (Taipei: National History Library, 1904), 96, 97.

18. Chaochang gei Guan Tingjie de xin 朝倡给关廷杰的信 [Chaochang's letter to Guan Tingjie], dated the second day of the fourth lunar month in 1883, collection of the Jiangmen Wuyi Overseas Chinese Museum.

19. Jin Ting 觐廷, *Duiyu Wen Gaohua buzhun huaren xinke daobu zhi ganyan (xugao)* [Comments on Vancouver's Ban on the Entry of the Chinese Immigrants (A Sequel)], *Xinning zazhi* 新宁杂志 15 (1914): 2.

20. Tan Mingfu Shenjin wangfei gaoshi 覃明府申禁妄费告示 [Tan Ming-fu's public notice on banning lavish spending], *Xinning Zazhi* 新宁杂志 1 (1909): 35.

Chapter 6

1. William F. Chew, *Nameless Builders of the Transcontinental* (Victoria, BC: Trafford Publishing, 2004).

2. W. H. Rhodes, *San Francisco Chronicle,* September 10, 1868, quoted in George Kraus, "Chinese Laborers and the Construction of the Central Pacific," *Utah Historical Quarterly* 37, no. 1 (1969): 51.

3. Barbara L. Voss, ed., "The Archaeology of Chinese Railroad Workers in North America," thematic issue, *Historical Archaeology* 49, no. 1 (2015).

4. Mary L. Maniery, Rebecca Allen, and Sarah Christine Heffner, *Finding Hidden Voices of the Chinese Railroad Workers: An Archaeological and Historical Journey,* Special Publications Series No. 13 (Germantown, MD: Society for Historical Archaeology, 2016).

5. Paul G. Chace and William S. Evans Jr., "Celestial Sojourners in the High Sierras: The Ethno-Archaeology of Chinese Railroad Workers (1865–1868)," *Historical Archaeology* 49, no. 1 (2015): 27–33.

6. R. Scott Baxter and Rebecca Allen, "The View from Summit Camp," *Historical Archaeology* 49, no. 1 (2015): 34–45; John Molenda, "Moral Discourse and Personhood in Overseas Chinese Contexts," *Historical Archaeology* 49, no. 1 (2015): 46–58.

7. Adrienne B. Anderson, "Ancillary Construction on Promontory Summit Utah: Those Domestic Structures Built by Railroad Workers," in *Forgotten Places and Things: Archaeological Perspectives on American History,* ed. Albert. E. Ward, 225–238 (Albuquerque, NM: Center for Anthropological Studies, 1983); Michael R. Polk, "Interpreting Chinese Worker Camps on the Transcontinental Railroad at Promontory Summit, Utah," *Historical Archaeology* 49, no. 1 (2015): 59–70; Michael R. Polk and Wendy Simmons Johnson, eds., *From Lampo Junction to Rozel: The Archaeological History of the Transcontinental Railroad across the Promontory Mountains, Utah,* GOSP Synthesis Report, Golden Spike National Historic Site, National Park Service and Central Pacific Railroad Grade, Area of Critical Environmental Concern, Utah Bureau of Land Management, 2012.

8. John Molenda, "Moral Discourse and Personhood in Overseas Chinese Contexts," *Historical Archaeology* 49, no. 1 (2015): 46–58.

9. Arnie L. Turner, *The History and Archaeology of Fenelon, a Historic Railroad Camp,* Archaeological Studies in the Cortez Mining District, Technical Report No. 8 (Reno, NV: US Bureau of Land Management, 1982).

10. Anan S. Raymond and Raymond E. Fike, *Rails East to Promontory: The Utah*

Stations (Salt Lake City: Utah State Office Bureau of Land Management, 1981; repr., Livingston, TX: Pioneer Enterprises, 1994).

11. Kenneth P. Cannon et al., *The Archaeology of Chinese Railroad Workers in Utah: Results of Surveys in Box Elder and Emery Counties,* USUAS Special Report No. 2, Utah State Project Report No. U15UJ0417b, report submitted to State of Utah, Department of Heritage and Arts, Salt Lake City, by USU Archaeological Services, Inc., Logan, UT, 2016.

12. A. Dudley Gardner, "The Chinese in Wyoming: Life in the Core and Peripheral Communities," in *Ethnic Oasis: The Chinese in the Black Hills—South Dakota History,* ed. Liping Zhu and Rose Estep (Pierre: South Dakota Historical Society Press, 2004), 86–96; A. Dudley Gardner, "Cores and Peripheries: Chinese Communities in Southwestern Wyoming, 1869–1922," *Wyoming Archaeologist* 49, no. 1 (2005): 19–39; A. Dudley Gardner, Barbara Clarke, and Lynn Harrell, *Final Report for the Aspen Section Camp 48UT660 and the Associated Union Pacific Railroad Grade 48UT668* (Rock Springs: Western Wyoming Community College, 2002); James W. MacNaughton, "A Historical Investigation of Changing Ethnicity and Consumption Patterns at the Union Pacific Railroad Section Camp of Peru (48SW3795): How Changing Ethnicity Can Be Interpreted in a Nineteenth Century Railroad Landscape" (master's thesis, Illinois State University, Normal, 2012).

13. Alton Briggs, "The Archaeology of 1882 Labor Camps on the Southern Pacific Railroad, Val Verde, Texas" (master's thesis, University of Texas at Austin, 1974).

14. Lyle M. Stone and Scott L. Fedick, *The Archaeology of Two Historic Homestead and Railroad Related Sites on the Southern Pacific Main Line Near Mobile, Maricopa County, AZ,* report prepared for Dibble and Associates, Phoenix, AZ, by Archaeological Resources Services, Inc., Tempe, AZ, 1990.

15. Gary Weisz, "Stepping Light: Revisiting the Construction Camps on the Lake Pend d'Oreille and Clark Fork Division of the Northern Pacific Railroad, 1879–1883," 3 vols. (unpublished manuscript on file at Idaho State Preservation Office, Boise, 2003); see also Christopher W. Merritt, "'The Coming Man from Canton': Chinese Experience in Montana (1862–1943)" (PhD diss., University of Montana, Missoula, 2010); Christopher W. Merritt, "The Continental Backwaters of Chinese Railroad Worker History and Archaeology: Perspectives from Montana and Utah" (paper presented at the Archaeology Network Workshop of the Chinese Railroad Workers in North America Project, Stanford University, Stanford, CA, October 10–12, 2013).

16. Keith Landreth, Keo Boreson, and Mary Condon, eds., *Archaeological Investigations at the Cabinet Landing Site (10BR413),* Eastern Washington University Reports in Archaeology and History, Report No. 100–45 (Cheney: Eastern Washington University, 1985).

17. Christopher W. Merritt, Gary Weisz, and Kelly J. Dixon, "'Verily the Road

Was Built with Chinaman's Bones': An Archaeology of Chinese Line Camps in Montana," *International Journal of Historical Archaeology* 16, no. 4 (2012): 666–695.

18. Rachel Stokeld and Mary Petrich-Guy, "Documenting Chinese Railroad Laborer Camps in Northern Idaho: A Professional/Amateur Collaboration" (paper presented at the 67th Annual Northwest Anthropological Conference, Bellingham, WA, 2014).

19. Kelly J. Dixon, "Historical Archaeologies of the American West," *Journal of Archaeological Research* 22, no. 3 (2014): 177–228.

20. David Eugene Wrobleski, "The Archaeology of Chinese Work Camps on the Virginia and Truckee Railroad" (master's thesis, University of Nevada, Reno, 1996).

21. Lynn Furnis and Mary L. Maniery, "An Archaeological Strategy for Chinese Workers' Camps in the West: Method and Case Study," *Historical Archaeology* 49, no. 1 (2015): 71–84.

22. Charlotte K. Sunseri, "Alliance Strategies in the Racialized Railroad Economies of the American West," *Historical Archaeology* 49, no. 1 (2015): 85–99.

23. Merritt, "The Continental Backwaters of Chinese Railroad Worker History and Archaeology."

24. Carl E. Conner and Nicole Darnell, *Archaeological Investigation of Site 5ME7351.1, Excelsior Train Station, Mesa County, Colorado,* prepared for the Colorado Historical Society by Dominquez Archaeological Research Group, Grand Junction, CO, 2012.

25. Timothy R. Urbaniak and Kelly J. Dixon, "Inscribed in Stone: Historic Inscriptions and the Cultural Heritage of Railroad Workers," *Historical Archaeology* 49, no. 1 (2015): 100–109.

26. Kevin B. Hallaran, Karen K. Swope, and Philip J. Wilke, *Historical and Archaeological Documentation of a Construction Camp ("China Camp") on the San Diego & Arizona Railway, Anza-Borrego Desert State Park, San Diego County, California,* prepared for California Department of Parks and Recreation, Sacramento, by Archaeological Research Unit, University of California, Riverside, 1989.

27. Marjorie Akin, James C. Bard, and Gary Weisz, "Asian Coins Recovered from Chinese Railroad Labor Camps: Evidence of Cultural Practices and Transnational Exchange," *Historical Archaeology* 49, no. 1 (2015): 110–121; Paul G. Chace, "Overseas Chinese Ceramics," in *The Changing Faces of Main Street: San Buenaventura Mission Plaza Project Archaeological Report, 1975,* ed. Roberta S. Greenwood (Ventura, CA: City of San Buenaventura Redevelopment Agency, 1976), 510–530; Patricia A. Etter, "The West Coast Chinese and Opium Smoking," in *Archaeological Perspectives on Ethnicity in America: Afro-American and Asian American Culture History,* ed. Robert L. Schuyler (Farmingdale, NY: Baywood Publishing, 1980), 97–101; William S. Evans, "Food and Fantasy: Material Culture of the Chinese in California and the West, circa 1850–1900," in *Archaeological Perspectives on Ethnicity*

in America: Afro-American and Asian American Culture History, ed. Robert L. Schuyler (Farmingdale, NY: Baywood Publishing, 1980), 89–96; Elyse Jolly, "Chinese Gaming in the Nineteenth-Century American West: An Ethnic and Cultural Reassessment" (master's thesis, University of Nevada, Reno, 2012); Ruth Ann Sando and David L. Felton, "Inventory Records of Ceramics and Opium from a Nineteenth Century Chinese Store in California," in *Hidden Heritage: Historical Archaeology of the Overseas Chinese,* ed. Priscilla Wegars (Amityville, NY: Baywood Publishing, 1993), 151–176.

28. Merritt, Weisz, and Dixon, "'Verily the Road Was Built with Chinaman's Bones'"; Sando and Felton, "Inventory Records"; Jerry Wylie and Richard E. Fike, "Chinese Opium Smoking Techniques and Paraphernalia," in *Hidden Heritage: Historical Archaeology of the Overseas Chinese,* ed. Priscilla Wegars (Amityville, NY: Baywood Publishing, 1993), 255–303.

29. Briggs, "The Archaeology of 1882 Labor Camps"; MacNaughton, "A Historical Investigation."

30. Barbara L. Voss, "The Historical Experience of Labor: Archaeological Contributions to Interdisciplinary Research on Chinese Railroad Workers," *Historical Archaeology* 49, no. 1 (2015): 4–23; Barbara L. Voss, "Towards a Transpacific Archaeology of the Modern World," *International Journal of Historical Archaeology* 20, no.1 (2016): 146–174.

Chapter 7

Acknowledgments: The field and laboratory research reported on in this essay was conducted by hundreds of archaeologists working throughout the US West over the past fifty years. I am deeply grateful to all the members of the Archaeology Network of the Chinese Railroad Workers in North America Project, who generously shared reports, site records, publications, photographs, and other documentation of this important scholarship. My thanks as well to Chinese Railroad Workers in North America Project codirectors Gordon Chang and Shelley Fisher Fishkin; their comments, as well as input from Hilton Obenzinger, Roland Hsu, Rebecca Allen, J. Ryan Kennedy, Sarah Heffner, Kelly Dixon, John Molenda, and anonymous reviewers, aided in finalizing this essay. The Stanford Archaeology Center generously hosted the October 2013 workshop on the archaeology of Chinese railroad workers. Support for the Archaeology Network of the Chinese Railroad Workers Project has been generously provided by the Chiang Ching-Kuo Foundation, Ming's Chinese Cuisine and Bar, and several Stanford University programs, including the Department of Anthropology, the Stanford Archaeology Center, the Department of History, the American Studies Program, International and Comparative Area Studies, and the Center for East Asian Studies.

1. C. W. Merritt, "The Continental Backwaters of Chinese Railroad Worker

History and Archaeology: Perspectives from Montana and Utah" (paper presented at the Archaeology Network Workshop of the Chinese Railroad Workers in North America Project, Stanford University, Stanford, CA, October 10–12, 2013).

2. J. Deetz, *In Small Things Forgotten* (New York: Doubleday, 1977).

3. W. S. J. Evans, "Food and Fantasy: Material Culture of the Chinese in California and the West, circa 1850–1900," in *Archaeological Perspectives on Ethnicity in America: Afro-American and Asian American Culture History,* ed. R. L. Schuyler (Farmingdale, NY: Baywood Publishing, 1980), 89–96; E. Sinn, *Power and Charity: A Chinese Merchant Elite in Colonial Hong Kong* (Hong Kong: Hong Kong University Press, 2003); E. Sinn, *Pacific Crossing: California Gold, Chinese Migration, and the Making of Hong Kong* (Hong Kong: Hong Kong University Press, 2013); P. C. F. S. Smith, *The Empress of China* (Philadelphia: Philadelphia Maritime Museum, 1984).

4. M. L. Maniery, R. Allen, and S. C. Heffner, *Finding Hidden Voices of the Chinese Railroad Workers: An Archaeological and Historical Journey*, Special Publications Series No. 13 (Germantown, MD: Society for Historical Archaeology, 2016), 6.

5. B. L. Voss, "Towards a Transpacific Archaeology of the Modern World," *International Journal of Historical Archaeology* 20, no. 1 (2016): 146–174.

6. R. S. Baxter and R. Allen, *National Register of Historic Places Evaluation and Damage Assessment for CA-PLA-2002/H (Summit Camp),* prepared by Past Forward, Inc., for Tahoe National Forest, United States Forest Service, 2008; R. S. Baxter and R. Allen, "The View from Summit Camp," *Historical Archaeology* 49, no. 1 (2015): 34–45; P. G. Chace, "Overseas Chinese Ceramics," in *The Changing Faces of Main Street: San Buenaventura Mission Plaza Project Archaeological Report, 1975,* ed. R. S. Greenwood (Ventura, CA: City of San Buenaventura Redevelopment Agency, 1976), 510–530; P. G. Chace, "Introductory Note to Chace and Evans' 1969 Presentation," *Historical Archaeology* 49, no. 1 (2015): 24–26; P. G. Chace, "The Twelve Donner Cantonese Railroad Workers Camps, and the Lack of Sub-Ethnic Archaeological Markers within a Dominated Export-Import Market" (paper presented at the Chinese Railroad Workers in North America Project Conference, Stanford University, 2016); P. G. Chace and W. S. Evans Jr., "Celestial Sojourners in the High Sierras: The Ethno-Archaeology of Chinese Railroad Workers (1865–1868)," *Historical Archaeology* 49, no. 1 (2015): 27–33; P. A. Etter, "The West Coast Chinese and Opium Smoking," in *Archaeological Perspectives on Ethnicity in America: Afro-American and Asian American Culture History,* ed. R. L. Schuyler (Farmingdale, NY: Baywood Publishing, 1980), 97–101; Evans, "Food and Fantasy"; J. Molenda, "Moral Discourse and Personhood in Overseas Chinese Contexts," *Historical Archaeology* 49, no. 1 (2015): 46–58.

7. For important exceptions, see K. B. Hallaran, K. K. Swope, and P. J. Wilke, *Historical and Archaeological Documentation of a Construction Camp ("China Camp")*

on the San Diego & Arizona Railway, Anza-Borrego Desert State Park, San Diego County, California, prepared for California Department of Parks and Recreation, Sacramento, by Archaeological Research Unit, University of California, Riverside, 1989; C. K. Sunseri, "Alliance Strategies in the Racialized Railroad Economies of the American West," *Historical Archaeology* 49, no. 1 (2015): 85–99; and T. Urbaniak and K. J. Dixon, "Inscribed in Stone: Historic Inscriptions and the Cultural Heritage of Railroad Workers," *Historical Archaeology* 49, no. 1 (2015): 100–109.

  8. Maniery, Allen, and Heffner, *Finding Hidden Voices*, 19–25.

  9. A. K. Briggs, "The Archaeology of 1882 Labor Camps on the Southern Pacific Railroad, Val Verde, Texas" (master's thesis, University of Texas at Austin, 1974), 197–204.

  10. L. Furnis and M. L. Maniery, "An Archaeological Strategy for Chinese Workers' Camps in the West: Method and Case Study," *Historical Archaeology* 49, no. 1 (2015): 71–84; C. L. Rogers, *Making Camp Chinese Style: The Archaeology of a V&T Railroad Graders' Camp, Carson City, Nevada*, ARS Project No. 865, prepared by Archaeological Research Services, Virginia City, NV, for Silver Oak Development Company, Carson City, NV, 1997; D. E. Wrobleski, "The Archaeology of Chinese Work Camps on the Virginia and Truckee Railroad" (master's thesis, University of Nevada Reno, Reno, 1996).

  11. See, for example, A. B. Anderson, "Ancillary Construction on Promontory Summit, Utah: Those Domestic Structures Built by Railroad Workers," in *Forgotten Places and Things: Archaeological Perspectives on American History,* ed. A. E. Ward (Albuquerque, NM: Center for Anthropological Studies, 1983), 225–238; Baxter and Allen, *National Register of Historic Places Evaluation,* 27–41, 46–48; M. R. Polk, "Interpreting Chinese Worker Camps on the Transcontinental Railroad at Promontory Summit, Utah," *Historical Archaeology* 49, no. 1 (2015): 64.

  12. Briggs, "The Archaeology of 1882 Labor Camps"; Maniery, Allen, and Heffner, *Finding Hidden Voices*, 89.

  13. D. E. Wrobleski, "The Archaeology of Chinese Work Camps on the Virginia and Truckee Railroad" (master's thesis, University of Nevada Reno, Reno, 1996); Furnis and Maniery, "An Archaeological Strategy," 71–84.

  14. Briggs, "The Archaeology of 1882 Labor Camps," 66–69; K. Landreth, K. Boreson, and M. Condon, eds., *Archaeological Investigations at the Cabinet Landing Site (10BR413)*, Reports in Archaeology and History No. 100–45 (Cheney: Eastern Washington University, 1985).

  15. Anderson, "Ancillary Construction on Promontory Summit"; Polk, "Interpreting Chinese Worker Camps"; M. R. Polk and W. Simmons Johnson, eds., *From Lampo Junction to Rozel: The Archaeological History of the Transcontinental Railroad across the Promontory Mountains, Utah,* GOSP Synthesis Report, Golden Spike National Historic Site, National Park Service and Central Pacific Railroad

Grade, Area of Critical Environmental Concern, Utah Bureau of Land Management, 2012.

16. E. Heath, "From Trail to Rail—the Story of the Beginning of the Southern Pacific," *Southern Pacific Bulletin* 15 (May 1927): 9–12; C. Nordhoff, *California: For Health, Pleasure, and Residence. A Book for Travellers and Settlers* (New York: Harper & Brothers, 1874): 189–194.

17. J. K. Yang and R. W. Hellmann, "A Second Look at Chinese Brown-Glazed Stoneware," in *Ceramic Identification in Historical Archaeology: The View from California, 1822–1940,* ed. R. Allen et al. (Germantown, MD: Society for Historical Archaeology, 2013), 215–227.

18. Polk, "Interpreting Chinese Worker Camps," 64.

19. Landreth, Boreson, and Condon, *Archaeological Investigations*; C. W. Merritt, G. Weisz, and K. J. Dixon, "'Verily the Road Was Built with Chinaman's Bones': An Archaeology of Chinese Line Camps in Montana," *International Journal of Historical Archaeology* 16, no. 4 (2012): 666–695; G. Weisz, "Stepping Light: Revisiting the Construction Camps on the Lake Pend d'Oreille and Clark Fork Division of the Northern Pacific Railroad, 1879–1883," 3 vols. (unpublished manuscript on file at Idaho State Preservation Office, Boise, 2003).

20. S. E. Ambrose, *Nothing Like It in the World: The Men Who Built the Transcontinental Railroad, 1863–1869* (New York: Simon & Schuster, 2000), 162; W. F. Chew, *Nameless Builders of the Transcontinental* (Victoria, BC: Trafford Publishing, 2004), 19; Molenda, "Moral Discourse and Personhood," 50.

21. Briggs, "The Archaeology of 1882 Labor Camps"; Furnis and Maniery, "An Archaeological Strategy"; Landreth, Boreson, and Condon, *Archaeological Investigations*; Polk, "Interpreting Chinese Worker Camps."

22. Furnis and Maniery, "An Archaeological Strategy," 78–80.

23. Maniery, Allen, and Heffner, *Finding Hidden Voices*, 89.

24. Chace and Evans, "Celestial Sojourners," 29; Merritt, Weisz, and Dixon, "'Verily the Road Was Built with Chinaman's Bones,'" 685.

25. R. P. Harrod and J. J. Crandall, "Rails Built of the Ancestors' Bones: The Bioarchaeology of the Overseas Chinese Experience," *Historical Archaeology* 49, no. 1 (2015): 148–161.

26. G. H. Chun, "Filling the Rice Bowl," in *Chinese in Chicago: 1870–1945,* ed. C. Ho and S. L. Moy (Mt. Pleasant, SC: Arcadia Publishing, 2005), 31.

27. P. P. Choy, "Interpreting 'Overseas Chinese' Ceramics Found on Historical Archaeology Sites: Manufacture, Marks, Classification, and Social Use," Society for Historical Archaeology Research Resources website, 2014, http://www.sha.org/index.php/view/page/chineseCeramics.

28. D. L. Felton, F. Lortie, and P. D. Schulz, *The Chinese Laundry on Second Street: Archaeological Investigations at the Woodland Opera House Site* (Sacramento:

Cultural Resource Management Unit, Resource Protection Division, State of California Department of Parks and Recreation, 1984); R. A. Sando and D. L. Felton, "Inventory Records of Ceramics and Opium from a Nineteenth Century Chinese Store in California," in *Hidden Heritage: Historical Archaeology of the Overseas Chinese*, ed. P. Wegars (Amityville, NY: Baywood Publishing, 1993), 151–176.

29. Rogers, *Making Camp Chinese Style.*

30. Briggs, "The Archaeology of 1882 Labor Camps."

31. Landreth, Boreson, and Condon, *Archaeological Investigations.*

32. Merritt, Weisz, and Dixon, "'Verily the Road Was Built with Chinaman's Bones,'" 687.

33. G. Michaels, "Peck-Marked Vessels from the San José Market Street Chinatown, a Study of Distribution and Significance," *International Journal of Historical Archaeology* 9, no. 2 (2005): 123–134.

34. Maniery, Allen, and Heffner, *Finding Hidden Voices*, 31.

35. Weisz, "Stepping Light."

36. Briggs, "The Archaeology of 1882 Labor Camps"; Furnis and Maniery, "An Archaeological Strategy"; Weisz, "Stepping Light."

37. M. K. Akin, "The Noncurrency Functions of Chinese *Wen* in America," *Historical Archaeology* 26, no. 2 (1992): 58–65; M. K. Akin, J. C. Bard, and G. Weisz, "Asian Coins Recovered from Chinese Railroad Labor Camps: Evidence of Cultural Practices and Transnational Exchange," *Historical Archaeology* 49, no. 1 (2015): 110–121; S. C. Heffner, "Exploring Health-Care Practices of Chinese Railroad Workers in North America," *Historical Archaeology* 49, no. 1 (2015): 134–147. See also Kennedy et al. in this volume.

38. Etter, "The West Coast Chinese and Opium Smoking"; J. Wylie and R. E. Fike, "Chinese Opium Smoking Techniques and Paraphernalia," in *Hidden Heritage: Historical Archaeology of the Overseas Chinese,* ed. P. Wegars (Amityville, NY: Baywood Publishing, 1993), 255–303.

39. Sinn, *Power and Charity.*

Chapter 8

Acknowledgments: I wholeheartedly thank Gordon Chang, Shelley Fisher Fishkin, Roland Hsu, Barbara Voss, and colleagues associated with Stanford's Chinese Railroad Workers in North America Project for their assistance and for the opportunity to present this material. I am grateful to researchers at Stanford's Spatial History Project for their pioneering work and am most thankful for feedback from colleagues who participated in the Sun Yat-sen University International Symposium on the North America Chinese Laborers and the Society of Guangdong Qiaoxiang in September 2014, with special thanks to Sue Fawn Chung. I thank the anonymous reviewers who provided comments on early drafts of this paper and am especially obliged to Rebecca Allen for dependable and priceless feedback, as well as for Rebecca Allen's and R. Scott Baxter's conscientious documentation of Summit Camp. Christopher Merritt took on a dissertation [and book] project that established an impressive foundation for investigations of Chinese cultural heritage in Montana. Gary Weisz had the foresight decades ago to document Chinese railroad sites in Idaho and Montana, and James Bard and Robert Weaver persevered in telling the story of Chinese laborers in northwestern North America. Thanks to Paul Chace and Bill Evans for sharing their early observations of the remains at Summit Camp, to Carrie Smith for serving as a steward to that site, and to Susan Lindström for her exemplary archaeological work in the region around and on Donner Summit. Doreen and Jim Stokes of Plains, Montana, kindly hosted a University of Montana class on their property so we could document one of the NPRR camps. Finally, I thank the Montana State Historic Preservation Office, the Montana State Historical Society, and Montana Rail Link, as well as students and colleagues from Montana State University–Billings and the University of Montana in Missoula.

1. Robert B. Marks, "'It Never Used to Snow': Climatic Variability and Harvest Yields in Late-Imperial South China, 1650–1850," in *Sediments of Time: Environment and Society in Chinese History*, ed. Mark Elvin and Liu Ts'ui-jung (Cambridge, UK: Cambridge University Press, 1998), 413.

2. Marks, "'It Never Used to Snow,'" 413; Lingling Ding et al., "Variations in Annual Winter Mean Temperature in South China since 1736," *Boreas: An International Journal of Quaternary Research* 45, no. 2 (October 2015): 252–259. See also Brian Fagan, *The Little Ice Age: How Climate Made History, 1300–1850* (New York: Basic Books, 2001), xiv–xvii, 3; Marcy Rockman, "Introduction: A L'Enfant Plan for Archaeology," in *Archaeology and Society: Its Relevance in the Modern World*, ed. Marcy Rockman and Joe Flatman (London: Springer, 2012), 8.

3. Mark McLaughlin, "Reign of the Sierra Storm King: Weather History of Donner Pass," *Journal of the Sierra College Natural History Museum* 2, no. 1 (2009), http://www.sierracollege.edu/ejournals/jscnhm/v2n1/stormking.html; Randall Osterhuber, "Climate Summary of Donner Summit, California, 1870–2001," *Journal of the Sierra College Natural History Museum* 2, no. 1 (2009), http://www.sierracol lege.edu/ejournals/jscnhm/v2n1/stormking.html.

4. *Donner Summit Snowfall and Snowpack, 1879–2011* (Soda Springs: University of California, Berkeley, Central Sierra Snow Laboratory, n.d.); McLaughlin, "Reign of the Sierra Storm King"; Osterhuber, "Climate Summary of Donner Summit."

5. McLaughlin, "Reign of the Sierra Storm King."

6. Just twenty years before, during the winter of 1846–1847, an overland group known as the Donner Party became snowbound with their horses, cattle, wagons, and families at elevations below and east of Donner Summit. Members of the Donner Party were trapped by the region's winter snows, and some of the survivors

resorted to starvation cannibalism; the dangerous pass and summit carry the place name *Donner*, reminding future travelers and residents of the foreboding power of the region's environmental conditions. See Mark McLaughlin, *The Donner Party: Weathering the Storm* (Carnelian Bay, CA: Mic Mac Media, 2007); McLaughlin, "Reign of the Sierra Storm King"; Kelly J. Dixon, Julie M. Schablitsky, and Shannon A. Novak, eds., *An Archaeology of Desperation: Exploring the Donner Party's Alder Creek Camp* (Norman: University of Oklahoma Press, 2011).

7. Barbara L. Voss and Rebecca Allen, "Overseas Chinese Archaeology: Historical Foundations, Current Reflections, and New Directions," *Historical Archaeology* 42, no. 3 (2008): 5–28; R. Scott Baxter and Rebecca Allen, "The View from Summit Camp," *Historical Archaeology* 49, no. 1 (2015): 34–45.

8. Baxter and Allen, "The View from Summit Camp," 35.

9. McLaughlin, "Reign of the Sierra Storm King."

10. Baxter and Allen, "The View from Summit Camp," 34, 35.

11. Baxter and Allen, "The View from Summit Camp," 35.

12. Baxter and Allen, "The View from Summit Camp," 39, 40.

13. Paul G. Chace and William S. Evans Jr., "Celestial Sojourners in the High Sierras: The Ethno-Archaeology of Chinese Railroad Workers (1865–1868)," *Historical Archaeology* 49, no. 1 (1969): 27–33 (presentation transcript published in 2015).

14. Baxter and Allen, "The View from Summit Camp," 41.

15. Chace and Evans, "Celestial Sojourners in the High Sierras"; Susan Lindström, "Letter Report to Greg Taylor and Levine Fircke, Re: Kinder Morgan Donner Summit Incident Release Site: Restoration Phase Preliminary Archaeological Metal Detection Survey, September 1, 2005" (manuscript, Tahoe National Forest, Truckee Ranger District, Truckee, CA); R. Scott Baxter and Rebecca Allen, *National Register of Historic Places Evaluation and Damage Assessment for CA-PLA-2002/H (Summit Camp),* prepared for Tahoe National Forest, Truckee Ranger District, Truckee, CA, 2008; Baxter and Allen, "The View from Summit Camp"; John Molenda, "Moral Discourse and Personhood in Overseas Chinese Contexts," *Historical Archaeology* 49, no. 1 (2015): 46–58.

16. Baxter and Allen, "The View from Summit Camp," 36, 37. See also Mary Maniery, Rebecca Allen, and Sarah C. Heffner, *Finding Hidden Voices of the Chinese Railroad Workers: An Archaeological and Historical Journey* (Germantown, MD: Society for Historical Archaeology, 2016), 18–21.

17. Baxter and Allen, "The View from Summit Camp," 37.

18. Kelly J. Dixon and Carrie E. Smith, "Rock Hearths and Rural Wood Camps in Jīn Shān/Gām Saan 金山: National Register of Historic Places Evaluations of 19th-Century Chinese Logging Operations at Heavenly Ski Resort in the Lake Tahoe Basin," in *Historical Archaeology of the American West*, ed. Margaret Purser and Mark Warner (Lincoln: University of Nebraska Press, 2017), 138–173.

19. Baxter and Allen, "The View from Summit Camp," 38.

20. Baxter and Allen, *National Register of Historic Places Evaluation and Damage Assessment for CA-PLA-2002/H (Summit Camp)*; Baxter and Allen, "The View from Summit Camp," 28–42.

21. For an indigenous, homeland-based perspective on the region's environment, see J. Nevers and P. Rucks, with contributions by L. Hicks, S. James, and M. Rakow, "Under Watchful Eyes: Washoe Narratives of the Donner Party," in *An Archaeology of Desperation: Exploring the Donner Party's Alder Creek Camp*, ed. K. J. Dixon, J. M. Schablitsky, and S. A. Novak (Norman: University of Oklahoma Press, 2011), 255–290.

22. See also Christopher W. Merritt, Gary Weisz, and Kelly J. Dixon, "'Verily the Road Was Built with Chinaman's Bones': An Archaeology of Chinese Line Camps in Montana," *International Journal of Historical Archaeology* 16 (2012): 666–695; and Baxter and Allen, "The View from Summit Camp."

23. Gary J. Weisz, "Stepping Light: Revisiting the Construction Camps on the Lake Pend d'Oreille and Clark Fork Division of the Northern Pacific Railroad, 1879–1883," vol. 3 (unpublished manuscript on file at Idaho State Historic Preservation Office, Boise, 2003). See also Merritt, Weisz, and Dixon, "'Verily the Road Was Built with Chinaman's Bones.'"

24. Sara A. Scott, "Indian Forts and Religious Icons: The Buffalo Road (*Qoq'aalx 'Iskit*) Trail before and after the Lewis and Clark Expedition," *International Journal of Historical Archaeology* 19, no. 2 (2015): 384–415.

25. Weisz, "Stepping Light," 83–87.

26. Louis T. Renz, *The History of the Northern Pacific Railroad* (Fairfield, WA: Ye Galleon Press, 1980), 95. See also Weisz, "Stepping Light," 83–87; Merritt, Weisz, and Dixon, "'Verily the Road Was Built with Chinaman's Bones,'" 682.

27. Baxter and Allen, *National Register of Historic Places Evaluation and Damage Assessment for CA-PLA-2002/H (Summit Camp)*; Baxter and Allen, "The View from Summit Camp," 42–45. See also Carrie E. Smith, and Kelly J. Dixon, *Determination of Eligibility for Inclusion in the National Register of Historic Places of 19 Historic Sites within the Heavenly Ski Resort, Douglas County, Nevada*, Report R2004-0519-00048, prepared for US Forest Service, Lake Tahoe Basin Management Unit, South Lake Tahoe and Heavenly Ski Resort, South Lake Tahoe, CA, 2005; and Dixon and Smith, "Rock Hearths and Rural Wood Camps."

28. Weisz, "Stepping Light," 89, 90.

29. K. Landreth, K. Boreson, and M. Condon, *Archaeological Investigations at the Cabinet Landing Site (10BR413), Bonner County, Idaho*, Eastern Washington University Reports in Archaeology and History, Report No. 100-45 (Cheney, WA: Eastern Washington University, 1985), 165.

30. Weisz, "Stepping Light."

31. Sue Fawn Chung, *Chinese in the Woods: Logging and Lumbering in the American West* (Champaign: University of Illinois Press, 2014).

32. Sue Fawn Chung, *The Chinese and Green Gold: Lumbering in the Sierras* (Sparks, NV: Humboldt-Toiyabe National Forest, 2003), www.fs.usda.gov/Internet/fse_documents/fsm9_026547.pdf.

33. Katrina Ryan, Montana Rail Link real estate supervisor, letter to Kelly J. Dixon, response to Temporary Occupancy Permit, August 17, 2018.

34. Barbara L. Voss, "Towards a Transpacific Archaeology of the Modern World," *International Journal of Historical Archaeology* 20, no. 1 (2016): 173.

35. Voss, "Towards a Transpacific Archaeology of the Modern World," 169.

36. Voss, "Towards a Transpacific Archaeology of the Modern World," 160. See also Marks, "'It Never Used to Snow,'" 412, 413, 444–446. See also Barbara Voss, "The Archaeology of Precarious Lives: Chinese Railroad Workers in Nineteenth-Century North America," *Current Anthropology* 59, no. 3 (2018): 287–313.

37. C. E. Orser Jr., "Twenty-First-Century Historical Archaeology," *Journal of Archaeological Research* 18, no. 2 (June 2010): 117.

38. Given the foundation created by Stanford's Spatial History Project's Western Railroad geodatabase, and given the potential of archaeological data that could be layered within that geodatabase, participants at the Chinese Railroad Workers in North America Project Archaeology Network Workshop held in October 2013 at the Stanford Archaeology Center concluded that one of the project's goals should be to develop a place-based database, or digital atlas, of historical, archaeological, architectural, and/or engineering sites associated with the cultural heritage of Chinese railroad workers.

39. Kelly J. Dixon, "Landscapes of Change: Culture, Nature, and Archaeological Heritage of Railroads in the American West," in 北美华工与广东侨乡社会 [Conference Proceedings, The North America Chinese Laborers and Guangdong Qiaoxiang Society] (Guangzhou, China: Sun Yat-sen University, 2016).

40. See Mary Ringhoff and Edward Stoner, *The River and the Railroad: An Archaeological History of Reno* (Reno: University of Nevada Press, 2011).

41. See, for example, Kerri S. Barile, "Race, the National Register, and Cultural Resource Management: Creating an Historic Context for Postbellum Sites," *Historical Archaeology* 38, no. 1 (2004): 92, 93; D. L. Hardesty, "Perspectives on Global-Change Archaeology," *American Anthropologist* 109 (2007): 1–7; Kent Lightfoot, *Indians, Missionaries, and Merchants: The Legacy of Colonial Encounters on the California Frontier* (Berkeley: University of California Press, 2005), 17.

42. N. B. Grimm et al., "Integrated Approaches to Long-term Studies of Urban Ecological Systems," in *Urban Ecology: An International Perspective on the Interaction between Humans and Nature*, ed. J. M. Marzluff et al. (London: Springer, 2008), 124.

43. See also P. B. deMenocal, "Cultural Responses to Climate Change during the

Late Holocene," *Science* 292 (2001): 672; and H. Locke and P. Deardon, "Rethinking Protected Areas and the New Paradigm," *Environmental Conservation* 32, no. 1 (2005): 1–10.

44. *Independent,* August 9, 1882, 3, cited in Merritt, Weisz, and Dixon, "'Verily the Road Was Built with Chinaman's Bones,'" 670.

45. C. E. Orser Jr., "Transnational Diaspora and Rights of Heritage," in *Cultural Heritage and Human Rights,* ed. Helaine Silverman and D. Fairchild Ruggles (New York: Springer, 2007), 92–105; Voss and Allen, "Overseas Chinese Archaeology"; Edward González-Tennant, "Creating a Diasporic Archaeology of Chinese Migration: Tentative Steps across Four Continents," *International Journal of Historical Archaeology* 15, no. 3 (2011): 509–532. See also Richard White, *Railroaded: The Transcontinentals and the Making of Modern America* (New York: W. W. Norton, 2011); and C. E. Orser Jr., "An Archaeology of Eurocentrism," *American Antiquity* 77, no. 4 (2012): 737–755.

Chapter 9

Acknowledgments: We would like to thank Gordon Chang and Shelley Fisher Fishkin for giving us the opportunity to be part of this volume and to participate in the Chinese Railroad Workers in North America Project at Stanford University. Barbara Voss first suggested this collaboration to investigate Chinese railroad workers' health and well-being, and Roland Hsu guided us through the publication process. Sue Fawn Chung provided historical context for the Chinese men buried in the Carlin cemetery. Prior collaborators and colleagues who analyzed the human skeletal remains from Carlin include Ryan Schmidt, Debra Martin, and Jennifer Thompson. Gary Weisz provided photographs and information on materials found at NPRR camps. Priscilla Wegars, Chris Merritt, Kenneth Cannon, and many others provided sources on health care artifacts recovered from Chinese railroad worker sites. Dudley Gardner and Martin Lammers provided faunal material and soil samples for macrobotanical analyses from the Aspen Section Camp.

1. George Kraus, *High Road to Promontory* (New York, Castle Books, 1969): 111, 217.

2. Thomas J. Csordas, "Introduction: The Body as Representation and Being in the World," in *Embodiment and Experience: The Existential Ground of Culture and Self,* ed. Thomas Csordas (Cambridge, UK: Cambridge University Press, 1994), 1–26; Linda Green, "Lived Lives and Social Suffering: Problems and Concerns in Medical Anthropology," *Medical Anthropology Quarterly, New Series* 12, no. 1 (1998): 3–7.

3. Benjamin N. Colby, "Well-Being: A Theoretical Program," *American Anthropologist* 89, no. 4 (1987): 879–895.

4. Stephen A. Mrozowski, Maria Franklin, and Leslie Hunt, "Archaeobotanical

Analysis and Interpretations of Enslaved Virginian Plant Use at Rich Neck Plantation (44WB52)," *American Antiquity* 73, no. 4 (2008): 703.

5. "Chinese Killed in Snow Slide onto Tracks," *Daily Alta California* (San Francisco), February 2, 1868, https://cdnc.ucr.edu/cgi-bin/cdnc.

6. John R. Gillis, *Tunnels of the Pacific Railroad* (New York: American Society of Civil Engineers, 1870): 158.

7. "Sandstorm," *Daily Alta California* (San Francisco), August 12, 1868, https://cdnc.ucr.edu/cgi-bin/cdnc.

8. "Statistics of California—1866," *Sacramento Daily Union*, January 1, 1867, https://cdnc.ucr.edu/cgi-bin/cdnc.

9. "Labor Riot at Sisson," *San Francisco Call*, August 11, 1896, https://cdnc.ucr.edu/cgi-bin/cdnc.

10. "Small-Pox on the Railroad," *Territorial Enterprise* (Virginia City, Nevada), January 5, 1869, https://cdnc.ucr.edu/cgi-bin/cdnc.

11. "Bones in Transit," *Sacramento Reporter*, June 30, 1870, https://cdnc.ucr.edu/cgi-bin/cdnc.

12. "Bones of Defunct Chinamen," *Sacramento Daily Union*, June 30, 1870, https://cdnc.ucr.edu/cgi-bin/cdnc.

13. Ryan P. Harrod and John J. Crandall, "Rails Built of the Ancestors' Bones: The Bioarchaeology of the Overseas Chinese Experience," *Historical Archaeology* 49, no. 1 (2015): 152.

14. Sue Fawn Chung, *In Pursuit of Gold: Chinese American Miners and Merchants in the American West* (Champaign: University of Illinois Press, 2011).

15. Russell R. Elliott and William D. Rowley, *History of Nevada,* 2nd ed., rev. (Lincoln: University of Nebraska Press, 1987), 114; David W. Toll, *The Complete Nevada Traveler: The Affectionate and Intimately Detailed Guidebook to the Most Interesting State in America* (Virginia City, NV: Gold Hill Publishing, 2002), 26; Shawn Hall, *Connecting the West: Historic Railroad Stops and Stage Stations of Elko County, Nevada* (Reno: University of Nevada Press, 2002), 92, 93.

16. Sue Fawn Chung, Fred P. Frampton, and Timothy W. Murphy, "Venerate These Bones: Chinese American Funerary and Burial Practices as Seen in Carlin, Elko County, Nevada," in *Chinese American Death Rituals: Respecting the Ancestors,* ed. Sue Fawn Chung and Priscilla Wegars (Lanham, MD: AltaMira Press, 2005), 107–146; Ryan W. Schmidt, "The Forgotten Chinese Cemetery of Carlin, Nevada: A Bioanthropological Assessment" (master's thesis, Department of Anthropology, University of Nevada, Las Vegas, 2006).

17. A. E. Perkins, "The Transcontinental Lines of the West," *Journal of Geography* 8, no. 5 (1910): 97–109.

18. Sue Fawn Chung, with the Nevada State Museum, *The Chinese in Nevada,* Images of America series (Charleston, SC: Arcadia Publishing, 2011), 50.

19. Chung, Frampton, and Murphy, "Venerate These Bones"; Douglas W. Owsley et al., *Preliminary Report: Osteology and Paleopathology of the Carlin Chinese Cemetery* (Washington, DC: National Museum of Natural History, Smithsonian Institution, 1997); Ryan P. Harrod, Jennifer L. Thompson, and Debra L. Martin, "Hard Labor and Hostile Encounters: What Human Remains Reveal about Institutional Violence and Chinese Immigrants Living in Carlin, Nevada (1885–1923)," *Historical Archaeology* 46, no. 4 (2013): 85–111; Harrod and Crandall, "Rails Built of the Ancestors' Bones"; Schmidt, "The Forgotten Chinese Cemetery of Carlin, Nevada"; Ryan W. Schmidt, "Perimortem Injury in a Chinese American Cemetery: Two Cases of Occupational Hazard or Interpersonal Violence," *Internet Journal of Biological Anthropology* 3, no. 2 (2009), doi: 10.5580/2939.

20. Chung, Frampton, and Murphy, "Venerate These Bones," 136, 137.

21. Harrod, Thompson, and Martin, "Hard Labor and Hostile Encounters."

22. Connie Yu, *Chinatown, San Jose, USA* (San Jose, CA: History San José and the Chinese Historical and Cultural Project, 2001), 4; Haiming Liu, "The Social Origins of Early Chinese Immigrants: A Revisionist Perspective," in *The Chinese in America: A History from Gold Mountain to the New Millennium,* ed. Susie Lan Cassel (Walnut Creek, CA: AltaMira Press, 2002), 29.

23. William M. Bowen, "Early Chinese Medicine in Southern California," *Gum Saan Journal* 17, no. 1 (June 1994): 5–6; Haiming Liu, "Chinese Herbalists in the United States," in *Chinese American Transnationalism: The Flow of People, Resources, and Ideas between China and America during the Exclusion Era,* ed. Sucheng Chan (Philadelphia: Temple University Press, 2006), 136–155.

24. Chung, Frampton, and Murphy, "Venerate These Bones," 125; Schmidt, "The Forgotten Chinese Cemetery of Carlin, Nevada."

25. Anne Charlton, "Medicinal Uses of Tobacco in History," *Journal of the Royal Society of Medicine* 97, no. 6 (2004): 292–296; John P. Hoffmann, "The Historical Shift in the Perception of Opiates: From Medicine to Social Menace," *Journal of Psychoactive Drugs* 22, no. 1 (1990): 53–62.

26. Zheng Yangwen, *The Social Life of Opium in China* (Cambridge University Press, 2005), 11–19.

27. Carol Benedict, *Golden-Silk Smoke: A History of Tobacco in China, 1550–2010* (Berkeley and Los Angeles: University of California Press, 2011), 108, 109.

28. Lu Gwei-djen and Joseph Needham, *Celestial Lancets: A History and Rationale of Acupuncture and Moxa* (London: RoutledgeCurzon, 1980), 170.

29. Daniel P. Reid, *Chinese Herbal Medicine* (Boston: Shambhala, 1993), 57.

30. Stephan Pálos, *The Chinese Art of Healing* (New York: Herder & Herder, 1971), 153; Reid, *Chinese Herbal Medicine,* 58.31. Ilkay Zihni Chirali, *Traditional Chinese Medicine: Cupping Therapy* (Edinburgh: Churchill Livingstone, 1999), 20–27, 32. Yi-Li Wu, "The Qing Period," in *Chinese Medicine and Healing. An Illustrated*

History, ed. T. J. Heinrichs and Linda L. Barnes (Cambridge, MA: Belknap Press of Harvard University Press, 2013), 166.

31. Wu, "The Qing Period"; Yi-Li Wu, *Reproducing Women: Medicine, Metaphor, and Childbirth in Late Imperial China* (Berkeley and Los Angeles: University of California Press, 2010).

32. Liu, "Chinese Herbalists in the United States," 139.

33. Frederick J. Simoons, *Food in China: A Cultural and Historical Inquiry* (Boca Raton, FL: CRC Press, 2001); Sarah Christine Heffner, "Exploring Healthcare Practices of the Lovelock Chinese: An Analysis and Interpretation of Medicinal Artifacts in the Lovelock Chinatown Collection," *Nevada Archaeologist* 26 (2013): 25–36; Sarah Christine Heffner, "Exploring Health-Care Practices of Chinese Railroad Workers in North America," *Historical Archaeology* 49, no. 1 (2015): 134–147.

34. Judith Farquhar, *Appetites: Food and Sex in Postsocialist China* (Durham, NC: Duke University Press, 2002), 63; Joerg Kastner, *Chinese Nutrition Therapy. Dietetics in Traditional Chinese Medicine (TCM)* (Stuttgart, Germany: Thieme, 2004), 21.

35. Eugene Newton Anderson, "Folk Nutritional Therapy in Modern China," in *Chinese Medicine and Healing: An Illustrated History,* ed. T. J. Heinrichs and Linda L. Barnes (Cambridge, MA: Belknap Press of Harvard University Press, 2013), 259, 260.

36. Simoons, *Food in China,* 15–18.

37. Johnny Kan, *Eight Immortal Flavors: Secrets of Cantonese Cookery from San Francisco's Chinatown* (San Francisco: California Living Books, 1980), 225–228.

38. Sucheng Chan, *Asian Americans: An Interpretive History* (New York: Twayne Publishers, 1991); Scott R. Baxter, "The Response of California's Chinese Populations to the Anti Chinese Movement," *Historical Archaeology* 42, no. 3 (2008): 29–36.

39. Jason Yaeger and Marcello A. Canuto, "Introducing an Archaeology of Communities," in *The Archaeology of Communities: A New World Perspective,* ed. Marcello A. Canuto and Jason Yaeger (London: Routledge, 2000), 1–15.

40. *On Gold Mountain,* Smithsonian Asia Pacific American Center online exhibit, accessed April 1, 2015. Exhibit is no longer available online.

41. Heffner, "Exploring Health-Care Practices of Chinese Railroad Workers in North America."

42. Michael Torbenson et al., "Lash's: A Bitter Medicine. Biochemical Analysis of an Historical Proprietary Medicine," *Historical Archaeology* 34, no. 2 (2000): 56.

43. Advertisement for Ballard Snow Liniment, *Amador Ledger* (Jackson, CA), April 30, 1909.

44. Richard E. Fike, *The Bottle Book: A Comprehensive Guide to Historic Embossed Medicine Bottles* (Caldwell, NJ: Blackburn Press, 2006), 147.

45. Roberta E. Bivins, *Alternative Medicine? A History* (New York: Oxford University Press, 2007), 89, 90.

46. Anan S. Raymond and Richard E. Fike, *Rails East to Promontory: The Utah Stations,* Bureau of Land Management Utah Resource Series no. 8 (Salt Lake City: Bureau of Land Management, 1981).

47. Carl-Hermann Hempen and Toni Fischer, *A Materia Medica for Chinese Medicine: Plants, Minerals and Animal Products* (Edinburgh: Churchill Livingstone, 2009): 60, 61.

48. Vivienne Lo, "Spirit of Stone: Technical Considerations in the Treatment of the Jade Body," *Bulletin of the School of Oriental and African Studies,* 65, no. 1 (2002): 114, 115; Pálos, *The Chinese Art of Healing,* 153.

49. Jeffrey G. Barlow and Christine Richardson, *China Doctor of John Day* (Hillsboro, OR: Binford & Mort, 1979), 67, 68.

50. Christopher H. Edson, "Excerpts from the Chinese in Eastern Oregon," in *Chinese on the American Frontier,* ed. Arif Dirlik and Malcom Yeung (Lanham, MD: Rowman & Littlefield, 2003) 94.

51. Kristine Madsen, "17th Century Chinese Coin" (manuscript on file, University of Idaho Chemistry Department, Moscow, 2015).

52. George Kraus, "Chinese Laborers and the Construction of the Central Pacific," *Utah Historical Quarterly* 37, no. 1 (1969): 46.

53. A. Dudley Gardner, "The Chinese in Wyoming: Life in the Core and Peripheral Communities," in *Ethnic Oasis: The Chinese in the Black Hills,* ed. Liping Zhu and Rose Estep Fosha (Pierre: South Dakota State Historical Society Press, 2004), 380–390; Kraus, "Chinese Laborers and the Construction of the Central Pacific"; Robert F. G. Spier, "Food Habits of Nineteenth-Century California Chinese (concluded)," *California Historical Quarterly* 37, no. 2 (1958): 129–136.

54. Charles Nordhoff, *California for Travellers and Settlers* (1873; repr., Berkeley, CA: Ten Speed Press, 1973), 190.

55. Alton Briggs, "The Archaeology of 1882 Labor Camps on the Southern Pacific Railroad, Val Verde County, Texas" (master's thesis, Department of Anthropology, University of Texas, Austin, 1974), 30, cited in Keith Landreth, Keo Boreson, and Mary Condon, *Archaeological Investigations at the Cabinet Landing Site (10BR413), Bonner County, Idaho,* Archaeological and Historical Services, Eastern Washington University Reports in Archaeology and History (Cheney: Eastern Washington University, 1985), 100–145.

56. "Life at Cabinet Landing," *Spokane Falls (WA) Chronicle,* July 25, 1882.

57. C. Lynn Rogers, *Making Camp Chinese Style: The Archaeology of a V&T Railroad Graders' Camp, Carson City, Nevada,* report prepared by Archaeological Research Services for Silver Oak Development Co. (Carson City, NV, 1997), 25.

58. J. Ryan Kennedy, "Zooarchaeology, Localization, and Chinese Railroad Workers in North America," *Historical Archaeology* 49, no. 1 (2015): 122–133.

59. David E. Wrobleski, "The Archaeology of Chinese Work Camps on the Virginia and Truckee Railroad" (master's thesis, Department of Anthropology, University of Nevada, Reno, 1996).

60. Rogers, *Making Camp Chinese Style.*

61. Landreth, Boreson, and Condon, *Archaeological Investigations at the Cabinet Landing Site.*

62. Charlotte K. Sunseri, "Food Politics of Alliance in a California Frontier Chinatown," *International Journal of Historical Archaeology* 19, no. 2 (2015): 416–431.

63. Sherri M. Gust, "Animal Bones from Historic Urban Chinese Sites: A Comparison of Sacramento, Woodland, Tucson, Ventura, and Lovelock," in *Hidden Heritage: Historical Archaeology of the Overseas Chinese,* ed. Priscilla Wegars (Amityville, NY: Baywood, 1993), 177–212; Shea C. Henry, "Ni Chi Le Ma, Have You Eaten Yet? Analysis of Foodways from Market Street Chinatown, San Jose, California" (master's thesis, Department of Anthropology, University of Idaho, 2012); Paul E. Langenwalter, "Mammals and Reptiles as Food and Medicine in Riverside's Chinatown," in *Wong Ho Leun: An American Chinatown,* vol. 2, ed. Great Basin Foundation (San Diego, CA: Great Basin Foundation, 1987), 53–106; Mary Praetzellis and Adrian Praetzellis, *Historical Archaeology of an Overseas Chinese Community in Sacramento, California,* report to US General Services Administration (Rohnert Park, CA: Anthropological Studies Center, Sonoma State University, 1997).

64. Gardner, "The Chinese in Wyoming."

65. Simoons, *Food in China,* 55, 305.

66. J. Ryan Kennedy, "*Fan* and *Cai*: Food, Identity, and Connections in the Market Street Chinatown" (Phd diss., Department of Anthropology, Indiana University, Bloomington, 2016).

67. See, for example, Meredith A. B. Ellis et al., "The Signature of Starvation: A Comparison of Bone Processing at a Chinese Encampment in Montana and the Donner Party Camp in California," *Historical Archaeology* 45, no. 2 (2011): 97–112.

68. Simoons, *Food in China,* 56, 57; Kennedy, "*Fan* and *Cai.*"

69. Nordhoff, *California for Travellers and Settlers,* 190; Briggs, "The Archaeology of 1882 Labor Camps," 30.

70. Kathryn Puseman, Linda Scott Cummings, and Chad Yost, *Macrofloral and Organic Residue (FTIR) Analysis of Sediment from Summit Camp (FS SITE 05-17-57-633),* Paleo Research Institute Technical Report 08-19, report prepared for Past Forward, Garden Valley, CA, 1998.

71. Landreth, Boreson, and Condon, *Archaeological Investigations at the Cabinet Landing Site,* 103.

72. Virginia S. Popper, *The Overseas Chinese Experience as Seen through Plants:*

Macrobotanical Analysis from the Market Street Chinatown, San Jose, California,
Technical Report no. 9 (Stanford, CA: Market Street Chinatown Archaeological
Project, Stanford University, 2014).

73. Landreth, Boreson, and Condon, *Archaeological Investigations at the Cabinet
Landing Site,* 101.

74. Virginia S. Popper, "Analysis of Macrobotanical Remains from Aspen Section
Camp, Wyoming," Technical Report, prepared for Western Wyoming Community
College, Rock Springs, 2016.

75. Gardner, "The Chinese in Wyoming," 382.

76. Linda Scott Cummings, Kathryn Puseman, and Thomas E. Moutoux,
*Pollen, Starch, Parasite, Macrofloral, and Protein Residue Analysis of Sediment from
the Evanston Chinatown Historic Archaeological Site, 48UT1749, Wyoming,* Paleo
Research Labs Technical Report 98-19, report prepared for Western Wyoming Community College, Rock Springs, 1998.

Chapter 10

Acknowledgments: I am grateful to the members of the Chinese Railroad Workers
in North America Project and to Madeline Hsu, Selia Tan, Charlie Egan, Loretta
Hee-Chorley, and the docents at Oroville and Weaverville temples for their insights
and suggestions on this project.

1. Madeline Hsu, *Dreaming of Gold, Dreaming of Home: Transnationalism and
Migration between the United States and South China, 1882–1943* (Stanford, CA:
Stanford University Press, 2000), 4, 5.

2. Stephan Feuchtwang, *Popular Religion in China: The Imperial Metaphor* (Richmond, Surrey, UK: Curzon Press, 2001), 27.

3. Yonghua Liu, *Confucian Rituals and Chinese Villagers: Ritual Changes and
Social Transformation in a Southeastern Chinese Community, 1368–1949* (Leiden,
the Netherlands: Brill, 2013), 18. Liu focuses on Sibao Township in Fujian Province.
According to Lynn Pan, this is one of "the two provinces which specialize in sending
people abroad" (the other being Guangdong). Lynn Pan, *Sons of the Yellow Emperor:
A History of the Chinese Diaspora* (New York: Kodansha International, 1994), 12, 13.
The rituals and religious practices of villagers in Fujian, as described by Liu, were
likely similar to those of villagers in Guangdong.

4. Liu, *Confucian Rituals,* 62–65.

5. Wendy L. Rouse, "'What We Didn't Understand': A History of Chinese Death
Ritual in China and California," in *Chinese American Death Rituals: Respecting the
Ancestors,* ed. Sue Fawn Chung and Priscilla Wegars (Lanham, MD: AltaMira Press,
2005), 26.

6. Rouse, "'What We Didn't Understand,'" 22, 23.

7. Chung and Wegars, *Chinese American Death Rituals,* 8.

8. Joseph A. Adler, *Chinese Religious Traditions* (Upper Saddle River, NJ: Prentice Hall, 2002), 13.

9. Jonathan H. X. Lee, *The Temple of Kwan Tai: California Historic Landmark No. 927. Celebrating Community and Diversity. Mendocino, California* (Mendocino, CA: Temple of Kwan Tai Inc., 2004), 28.

10. Adler, *Chinese Religious Traditions,* 103.

11. Feuchtwang, *Popular Religion in China,* 86.

12. Adler, *Chinese Religious Traditions,* 102, 103.

13. Feuchtwang, *Popular Religion in China,* 86.

14. Daniel Cleveland, "The Chinese in California," 1868–1869, M 72175–72177, Huntington Library, San Marino, CA, unnumbered draft chapter on "Missionary Labor among the Chinese in California," 12. I have sought to replicate the strikeouts and additions in the handwritten text through the use of [^] (for additions) and ~~strikeouts~~ (for strikeouts).

15. Cleveland, "The Chinese in California," 12, 13.

16. Cleveland, "The Chinese in California," chapter 11, "The Religion and Temples of the Chinese in California," 3.

17. Cleveland, "The Chinese in California," unnumbered draft chapter, "Missionary Labor," 13.

18. For background on Cleveland and his involvement with the San Diego and Gila Southern Pacific and Atlantic Railroad Company, as well as the Los Angeles and San Diego Railroad Company, see "Daniel Cleveland: San Diego Patron," *Journal of San Diego History, San Diego Historical Society Quarterly* 11, no. 1 (January 1965), https://www.sandiegohistory.org/journal/1965/january/cleveland-2/.

19. Lucy Cohen also describes how a group of Chinese railroad workers, on their way to work on the Houston and Texas Central in 1869, spoke with a Chinese resident of St. Louis who had come to California as an interpreter for an Episcopal missionary. Lucy Cohen, *The Chinese in the Post-Civil War South: A People without a History* (Baton Rouge: Louisiana State University Press, 1984), 86, 87.

20. Chen Chung, "Personal Recollections of Chen Chung," *The Occident,* January 1, 1870.

21. "Chinese Mission—Colportage," *The Occident,* December 1, 1869.

22. "A Chinese Editor in the Pulpit: The Rev. Mr. Chew of San Francisco Talks of China's Needs," *New York Times,* December 30, 1901.

23. Chuimei Ho and Bennet Bronson, *Three Chinese Temples in California: Marysville, Oroville, Weaverville* (Seattle: Chinese in Northwest America Research Committee, 2016), 10, 11.

24. Russell Conwell, "Letter from Russell. The Chinese in San Francisco. Their Celebration of New Year," *Boston Traveler,* March 2, 1870.

25. Conwell, "Letter from Russell."

26. Stereoscopic photograph and quotation are from Howard Goldbaum and Wendell Huffman, *Waiting for the Cars: Alfred A. Hart's Stereoscopic Views of the Central Pacific Railroad* (Carson City: Nevada State Railroad Museum, 2012).

27. Cleveland, "The Chinese in California," chapter 11, "The Religion and Temples of the Chinese in California," 32–34; see also smaller added-on pages, 1.

28. William Speer, *The Oldest and the Newest Empire: China and the United States* (San Francisco: H. H. Bancroft, 1870), 647, 648.

29. Speer, *The Oldest and the Newest Empire,* 670.

30. See Laurie Maffly-Kipp, "Engaging Habits and Besotted Idolatry: Viewing Chinese Religions in the American West," *Material Religion* 1, no. 1 (March 2005): 72–97.

31. Cleveland, "The Chinese in California," unnumbered chapter, "The Chinese in the Interior," 32, 33.

32. See Willie James Jennings, *The Christian Imagination: Theology and the Origins of Race* (New Haven, CT: Yale University Press, 2011).

33. Cleveland, "The Chinese in California," unnumbered chapter, "The Chinese in the Interior," 33.

34. "How Many Chinese workers Died Building the Transcontinental Railroad?" Chinese Railroad Workers in North America Project website, accessed October 2016, http://web.stanford.edu/group/chineserailroad/cgi-bin/wordpress/faqs/.

35. Augustus Ward Loomis, "Chinese 'Funeral Baked Meats,'" *Overland Monthly* 3, no. 1 (July 1869): 22.

36. Loomis, "Chinese 'Funeral Baked Meats,'" 22.

37. Loomis, "Chinese 'Funeral Baked Meats,'" 26.

38. Loomis, "Chinese 'Funeral Baked Meats,'" 29. Protestant missionaries also viewed Chinese religion through the lens of anti-Catholic sentiment; they defended the Chinese in a context in which Irish Catholic workingmen were claiming whiteness against the "heathen" Chinese. The anti-Chinese factions advocated a shared white Christian nation, whereas the Protestant missionaries initially envisioned a shared Protestant nation that might include converted Chinese as well as Native Americans and African Americans. See Joshua Paddison, *American Heathens: Religion, Race, and Reconstruction in California* (Berkeley: University of California Press, 2012).

39. Rouse, "'What We Didn't Understand,'" 37, 38.

40. "Bones in Transit," *Sacramento Reporter,* June 30, 1870. This article claimed that "about 20,000 pounds of bones" were being sent by train in order to be returned to China. See "How Many Chinese Workers Died Building the Transcontinental Railroad?" Chinese Railroad Workers in North America Project, accessed October 2016. http://web.stanford.edu/group/chineserailroad/cgi-bin/wordpress/faqs/. See also Hon-ming Yip, *The Tung Wah Coffin Home and Global Charity Network:*

Evidence and Findings from Archival Materials (Hong Kong: Joint Publishing , 2009).

41. Ho and Bronson, *Three Chinese Temples*, 43. The authors say that "several popular histories" date the "first Chinese temple in Oroville" to 1863.

42. Poster board in Fong Lee Room, Oroville Temple, California. From author's visit on August 25, 2016.

43. Stephen Magagnini, "Well-Preserved Chinese Temple in Oroville Recalls Gold Rush Era," *Sacramento Bee*, November 29, 2014, http://www.sacbee.com/entertainment/living/travel/article4171477.html.

44. Ho and Bronson, *Three Chinese Temples in California*, viii.

45. Other contemporaneous temples in California have survived as well, though, according to scholars, they are less intact. These include the Auburn Joss House, Cambria's Red House, and the Hanford Taoist Temple. See Lee, "Historic Temples in California," in *The Temple of Kwan Tai*, 39. The contents of the temples, including the deities, wall hangings, and altars, are also largely original, with the notable exception of the Guan Di painting in the Temple of Kwan Tai in Mendocino, California, a temporary replica of the original, which was "damaged during the restoration process" when a "gust of wind" damaged the original. Lee, *Temple of Kwan Tai*, 23.

46. Ho and Bronson, *Three Chinese Temples*, ix.

47. Ho and Bronson, *Three Chinese Temples*, 65–67. The authors also explain that the temple's name contained barely veiled reference to the Hong Shun Tong society, an anti-imperialist group.

48. Author's conversation with docent at Weaverville Temple, August 25, 2016.

49. Ho and Bronson, *Three Chinese Temples*, 68.

50. Lee, *The Temple of Kwan Tai*, 17. "Documented history of the temple dates back to 1883," but "oral history of George W. Hee, born in 1897 in Mendocino," dates the temple "back to 1854."

51. From author's conversation with Loretta Hee-Chorley at the Temple of Kwan Tai, August 28, 2016.

52. Ho and Bronson, *Three Chinese Temples*, 63.

53. Author's conversations with Weaverville docent and Loretta Hee-Chorley, August 25 and August 28, 2016.

54. Lee, *The Temple of Kwan Tai*, 9, 22.

55. Cited in Ho and Bronson, *Three Chinese Temples*, 73.

56. Ho and Bronson, *Three Chinese Temples*, 54. The Chan Room is known as such because "the Chans (or Chins or Chens) in America, like southern Chinese Chans elsewhere, have a particular reverence for him as a fellow clan member of the thirteenth century, Chen Zhong Zhen. His title, Suijing Bo, appears in almost all shrines of the Chan clan in America."

57. Ho and Bronson, *Three Chinese Temples*, 51.

58. Ho and Bronson, *Three Chinese Temples*, 2–7.

59. Ho and Bronson, *Three Chinese Temples*, 11.

60. See Thomas Tweed, *The American Encounter with Buddhism, 1844–1912: Victorian Culture and the Limits of Dissent* (Bloomington and Indianapolis: Indiana University Press, 1992).

61. Ho and Bronson, *Three Chinese Temples*, xi.

62. Author's conversation with Loretta Hee-Chorley, August 28, 2016.

Chapter 11

Acknowledgments: This chapter benefited from comments by Shelley Fisher Fishkin, Hilton Obenzinger, and Sue Fawn Chung. I offer special thanks to Gordon Chang and Shelley Fisher Fishkin for their remarkable leadership of the Chinese Railroad Workers in North America Project. Chang and Fishkin also serve with me as co-principal investigators of the international collaborative project Representing Chinese Railroad Workers, funded by the Chiang Ching-Kuo Foundation, Taiwan. Barbara Voss and the Archaeological Network of Chinese Railroad Workers in North America shared research findings and materials. Anna Szücs helped collect firsthand oral narratives from Native American tribes. Roland Hsu provided coordination across the Pacific. Yvonne Lin and Roy Wu also offered invaluable assistance for this essay.

1. See Stephen E. Ambrose, *Nothing Like It in the World: The Men Who Built the Transcontinental Railroad, 1863–1869* (New York: Touchstone, 2001); Art Chin and Doug Chin, *The Chinese in Washington State* (Seattle: OCA Greater Seattle, 2013); Mary Gaylord, *Eastern Washington's Past and Present: Chinese and Other Pioneers* (Washington, DC: US Forest Service, US Department of Agriculture, 1993); Lorraine Barker Hildebrand, *Straw Hats, Sandals, and Steel: The Chinese in Washington State* (Tacoma: Washington State American Revolution Bicentennial Commission, 1977); Daniel Liestman, "Horizontal Inter-Ethnic Relations: Chinese and American Indians in the 19th Century West," *Western Historical Quarterly* 30, no. 3 (1999): 327–349; Arnie Marchand, *The Way I Heard It: A Three Nation Reading Vacation* (Bloomington, IN: Xlibris, 2013); Robert H. Ruby and John A. Brown, *Half-Sun on the Columbia: A Biography of Chief Moses* (Norman: University of Oklahoma Press, 1965); Richard F. Steele, *An Illustrated History of Stevens, Ferry, Okanagan, and Chelan Counties* (Spokane, WA: Western Historical, 1904); John Hoyt Williams, *A Great and Shining Road: The Epic Story of the Transcontinental Railroad* (Lincoln: University of Nebraska Press, 1996); David Wilma, "Chelan County: Thumbnail History," *Historylink*, January 28, 2006, http://www.historylink.org/File/7624.

2. See "On This Day: May 29, 1869," New York Times Learning Network, accessed February 28, 2016, http://www.nytimes.com/learning/general/onthisday/harp/0529.html.

3. Jordan Hua, "'They Looked Askance': American Indians and Chinese in the

Nineteenth Century U.S. West" (honors thesis, Rutgers University, 2012), http:// history.rutgers.edu/docman-docs/undergraduate/honors-papers-2012/402-they -looked-askance-american-indians-and-chinese-in-the-nineteenth-century-u-s-west/ file, 10, 11.

4. David R. Roediger and Elizabeth D. Esch, *The Production of Difference: Race and the Management of Labor in U.S. History* (New York: Oxford University Press, 2012), 80.

5. See Samuel Bowles, *Our New West: Records of Travel between the Mississippi River and the Pacific Ocean* (Hartford, CT: Hartford Publishing, 1869); Sucheng Chan, *Asian Americans: An Interpretive History* (New York: Twayne, 1991); Concie Luna, "A Chinese Puzzle," *Lake Chelan Historical Society History Notes* 26 (2011): 8–11.

6. See Iris Chang, *The Chinese in America: A Narrative History* (New York: Viking, 2003), n.p.; C. M. Carpenter and K. Hyoejin Yoon, "Rethinking Alternative Contact in Native American and Chinese Encounters: Juxtaposition in Nine-teenth-Century US Newspapers," *College Literature* 41, no. 1 (2014): 7–42; Sue Fawn Chung, *In Pursuit of Gold: Chinese American Miners and Merchants in the American West* (Urbana: University of Illinois Press, 2011), 140; Ruthanne Lum McCunn, *Chinese American Portraits: Personal Histories, 1828–1988* (Seattle: University of Washington Press, 1996), 63; Ruth K. Billhimer, "Pawns of Fate: Chinese/Paiute Intercultural Marriages, 1860–1920, Walker River Reservation, Schurz, Nevada" (master's thesis, University of Nevada, Las Vegas, 1998); Elliott Young, *Alien Nation: Chinese Migration in the Americas from the Coolie Era through World War II* (Chapel Hill: University of North Carolina Press, 2014), 82, 224; Liestman, "Horizontal Inter-Ethnic Relations," 347; Charlotte K. Sunseri, "Alliance Strategies in the Racial-ized Railroad Economies of the American West," *Historical Archaeology* 49, no. 1 (2015): 95.

7. Ambrose, *Nothing Like It in the World,* 153.

8. McCunn, *Chinese American Portraits,* 63.

9. Chung, *In Pursuit of Gold,* 160.

10. Chung, *In Pursuit of Gold,* 140.

11. Kate B. Carter, comp., "The Early Chinese of Western United States," in Pioneer Heritage, Utah Division of State History, 17 vols. (Salt Lake City, 1958), 10: 464–469, quoted in Donald C. Conley, "The Pioneer Chinese of Utah," in *Chinese on the American Frontier,* ed. Arif Dirlik (Lanham, MD: Rowman & Littlefield, 2001), 291–306.

12. Carter, "The Early Chinese of Western United States," 10: 464–469.

13. George Kraus, "Chinese Laborers and the Construction of the Central Pacific," *Utah Historical Quarterly* 37, no. 1 (1969): 41. See also "Indian Workers on a Railroad," *Davenport (IA) Weekly Gazette,* August 8, 1883.

14. Kerry Brinkerhoff, "Native Americans and the Transcontinental Railroad," *Transcontinental* 1, no. 11 (2001): 8.

15. Kerry Brinkerhoff, "Chinese and the American Indian on the Transcontinental Railroad," *Gum Saan Journal* 22, no. 2 (1999): 9, 10. This story also appears in one of the oral histories that Connie Young Yu and Barre Fong, participants in the Chinese Railroad Workers in North America Project, have collected: Sandy Lee, interview with Connie Young Yu and Barre Fong, July 17, 2003, in Connie Young Yu and Barre Fong, "History from Descendants" (presentation, Conference of the Chinese Railroad Workers in North America Project at Stanford University, Stanford, CA, April 14–16, 2016).

16. Sunseri, "Alliance Strategies," 85.

17. Sunseri, "Alliance Strategies," 91.

18. Sunseri, "Alliance Strategies," 91.

19. *Daily Alta California* (San Francisco), November 1, 1852.

20. Sunseri, "Alliance Strategies," 94.

21. Barbara Voss offered insights on the concept of intimacy based on the evidence of the material life of the railroad workers in the "Representing Chinese Railroad Workers in North America" workshop (Academia Sinica, Taipei) on May 8, 2015, at which she delivered a keynote titled "The Archaeology of Chinese Railroad Workers in North America." Other ways of categorizing relations between Chinese and Native Americans may be found in Liestman, "Horizontal Inter-Ethnic Relations," 327–349.

22. Lisa Lowe, *The Intimacies of Four Continents* (Durham, NC: Duke University Press, 2015), 35.

23. Lowe, *The Intimacies of Four Continents*, 35.

24. Maxine Hong Kingston, *China Men* (New York: Knopf, 1980), 139; emphasis added.

25. Paul Yee, *A Superior Man* (Vancouver: Arsenal Pulp Press, 2015).

26. Homi Bhabha, *The Location of Culture* (1994; repr., London: Routledge, 2012), 53.

27. Yee, *A Superior Man*, 34.

28. Yee, *A Superior Man*, 52.

29. Walter (Walker River Paiute Tribe), interview by Edward C. Johnson, Walker River Tribal History Project: Oral History Interviews with Tribal Elders, March 1, 1974, 32.

30. Sunseri, "Alliance Strategies," 87.

31. Shelley Fisher Fishkin, in her essay "The Chinese as Railroad Builders after Promontory" in this volume, provides details on the role of Chinese laborers in the building of the nineteenth-century railway network in the United States. The chapter discusses rail lines mentioned here, including the Southern Pacific Railroad, the Virginia and Truckee Railroad, the Oregon Railway, and the Navigation Company.

32. Roediger and Esch, *The Production of Difference,* 15, 69.

33. Roediger and Esch, *The Production of Difference,* 71.

34. The project to examine relations between Native Americans and Chinese will continue to solicit and study oral histories and family narratives with assistance from tribal historian Misty Benner. For newspaper reports, see, for example, "An Indian Restaurant," *Walker Lake Bulletin* (Hawthorne, NV), May 16, 1883. An Indian agent was an official representative of the federal government to Native American tribes, especially those on reservations.

35. Sandy Lee, interview by Yu and Fong, July 17, 2013, in Connie Young Yu and Barre Fong, "History from Descendants" (presentation, Conference of the Chinese Railroad Workers in North America Project at Stanford University, Stanford, CA, April 14–16, 2016); Brinkerhoff, "Chinese and the American Indian on the Transcontinental Railroad," 9, 10.

36. Chung, *In Pursuit of Gold,* 140, 149, 164; Sue Fawn Chung, "Between Two Worlds: Ah Cum Kee (1876–1929) and Loy Lee Ford (1882–1921)," in *Ordinary Women, Extraordinary Lives: A History of Women in America,* ed. Kriste Lindenmeyer (Wilmington, DE: Scholarly Resources, 2000), 182; Sue Fawn Chung, "Their Changing World: Chinese Women of the Comstock," in *Women on the Comstock: The Making of a Mining Community,* ed. Ronald James and C. Elizabeth Raymond (Reno: University of Nevada Press, 1997), 223.

37. Kerry Brinkerhoff records a similar story that Native Americans told Chinese railroad workers: the desert has a huge lizard, instead of a snake, which can swallow an adult man. On hearing this, the Chinese were gone the next day. The crew's foreman had to chase down the workers and convince them that there were no dragons in the desert. Brinkerhoff, "Chinese and the American Indian," 10.

38. In 1868 the Central Pacific had a most unusual but major problem with its Chinese workforce. As Crocker wrote to Huntington, "The most tremendous yarns have been circulating among the Chinese. We have lost about 1,000 through fear of Indians out on the desert." It seemed that they had been told "there are Snakes fifty feet long that swallow Chinamen whole on the desert, and Indians 25 feet high that eat men and women for breakfast and hundreds of other equally ridiculous stories." Crocker solved the problem by sending twenty-two Chinese workers taken from different groups "up the Humbolt [*sic*] to see for themselves and they have just returned and things are more quiet since." Quoted in Ambrose, *Nothing Like It in the World,* 310.

39. Ambrose, *Nothing Like It in the World,* 310; Kraus, "Chinese Laborers and the Construction of the Central Pacific," 51, cited in Liestman, "Horizontal Inter-Ethnic Relations," 331; *Alta California* (San Francisco) June 20, 1868, cited in Kraus, "Chinese Laborers and the Construction of the Central Pacific," 51.

40. Liestman, "Horizontal Inter-Ethnic Relations," 331.

41. On the figure of snakes in Native American myths, see Karl Taube, *The Legendary Past: Aztec and Maya Myths* (London: British Museum Press, 1993); and Paula Gunn Allen, *The Sacred Hoop: Recovering the Feminine in American Indian Traditions* (1986; repr., Boston: Beacon Press, 1992), 127, 128.

42. Leslie Marmon Silko, "Notes on *Almanac of the Dead*," in *Yellow Woman and a Beauty of the Spirit: Essays on Native American Life Today* (New York: Simon & Schuster, 1996), 144.

43. Leslie Marmon Silko, *Gardens in the Dunes: A Novel* (New York: Simon & Schuster, 1999), 36.

44. Edna Jones, interview by Edward Johnson, February 7, 1974, Walker River Tribal History Project: Oral History Interviews with Tribal Elders, 10.

45. Silko opens her novel *Ceremony* with poetry that indicates an indigenous genesis of stories and power: "And in the belly of this story / The rituals and the ceremony / Are still growing." Leslie Marmon Silko, *Ceremony* (New York: Penguin, 1977), 2.

46. "A Trip from Mason Valley to Walker Lake," *Esmeralda Herald* (Aurora, NV), September 18, 1880.

47. "An Indian Restaurant," *Walker Lake Bulletin* (Hawthorne, NV), May 16, 1883.

48. 1861 Nevada Statutes, Walker River Paiute Tribal Archives, 93, 94, photocopies provided by Misty Benner, December 11, 2015.

49. "Bought a Chinese Girl," *Lyon County Times* (Dayton, NV), September 22, 1906.

50. Oral history interview, Cultural Resources Protection Program, Confederated Tribes of the Umatilla Indian Reservation, OHP-010.

51. Oral history interview, Cultural Resources Protection Program, Confederated Tribes of the Umatilla Indian Reservation, OHP-364.

52. Oral history interview, Cultural Resources Protection Program, Confederated Tribes of the Umatilla Indian Reservation, OHP-236.

53. Jacques Derrida, *Of Hospitality* (Stanford, CA: Stanford University Press, 2000), 55.

54. Donald Fixico, "Interview: Native Americans," *American Experience,* PBS website, accessed February 18, 2016, http://amextbg2.wgbhdigital.org/wgbh/americanexperience/features/interview/tcrr-interview/.

55. Kingston, *China Men,* 146.

Chapter 12

Acknowledgments: For critical feedback, I would like to thank Anthony H. Lee, Chelsea Rose, and especially Gordon Chang and Shelley Fisher Fishkin. I am also grateful to Teri Hessel for assistance in archival research.

1. Jonathan Crary, *Techniques of the Observer: On Vision and Modernity in the Nineteenth Century* (Cambridge, MA: MIT Press, 1992); Lynne Kirby, *Parallel Tracks: The Railroad and Silent Cinema* (Durham, NC: Duke University Press, 2014); Wolfgang Schivelbusch, *The Railway Journey: The Industrialization of Time and Space in the Nineteenth Century* (Berkeley: University of California Press, 2014).

2. Deirdre Murphy, "'Like Standing on the Edge of the World and Looking Away into Heaven': Picturing Chinese Labor and Industrial Velocity in the Gilded Age," *Common-Place*, April 2007, http://www.common-place-archives.org/vol-07/no-03/murphy/. See also Mary M. Cronin and William E. Huntzicker, "Popular Chinese Images and 'The Coming Man' of 1870: Racial Representations of Chinese," *Journalism History* 38, no. 2 (2012): 86–99.

3. For a discussion of these photographs and the production of a digital archive by Stanford University's Chinese Railroad Workers in North America Project, see Denise Khor, "Archives, Photography, and Historical Memory: Tracking the Chinese Railroad Workers in North America," *Southern California Quarterly* 98, no. 4 (Winter 2016): 429–456.

4. John C. Frémont, "Some General Results of a Winter Expedition across the Rocky Mountains, for Survey of a Route for a Railroad to the Pacific," December 27, 1854, http://umassboston.worldcat.org/title/col-fremonts-exploration-of-the-central-railroad-route-to-the-pacific/oclc/561998253.

5. Shawn Michelle Smith, *At the Edge of Sight: Photography and the Unseen* (Durham, NC: Duke University Press, 2013), 99–128. See also Robin Kelsey, *Archive Style: Photographs and Illustrations for U.S. Surveys, 1850–1890* (Berkeley: University of California Press, 2007).

6. For biographical accounts of Alfred A. Hart, see Glenn Willumson, "Alfred A. Hart: Photographer of the Transcontinental Railroad" (master's thesis, University of California, Davis, 1984); and Mead B. Kibbey and Peter E. Palmquist, *The Railroad Photographs of Alfred A. Hart, Artist* (Sacramento: California State Library Foundation, 1996).

7. As an homage to Hart's legacy, several contemporary artists rephotographed Hart's images of the transcontinental railroad (see the work of Jesse White and Art Clark). In addition, Li Ju, a present-day photographer and computer engineer based in Beijing, also rephotographed Hart's images in an effort to honor the Chinese railroad workers. His work was exhibited in Stanford University's Packard Electrical Engineering Building in 2015.

8. Glenn Willumson, *Iron Muse: Photographing the Transcontinental Railroad* (Berkeley: University of California Press, 2013).

9. Ginette Verstraete, "Railroading America: Towards a Material Study of the Nation," *Theory, Culture and Society* 19, no. 5 (2002): 145–159.

10. Leo Marx, *The Machine in the Garden: Technology and the Pastoral Ideal in America* (Oxford: Oxford University Press, 2000); Leo Marx, "The Railroad in the Landscape: An Iconological Reading of a Theme in American Art," *Prospects* 10 (1985): 77–117.

11. See John Kuo Wei Tchen, *New York before Chinatown: Orientalism and the Shaping of American Culture, 1776–1882* (Baltimore: Johns Hopkins University Press, 2001).

12. For a discussion of the political debates regarding the status of Chinese workers as "free" or "unfree" labor, see Moon-Ho Jung, *Coolies and Cane: Race, Labor, and Sugar in the Age of Emancipation* (Baltimore: Johns Hopkins University Press, 2006).

13. For a discussion of representations of Chinese railroad workers as emasculated, see Floyd Cheung, "Anxious and Ambivalent Representations: Nineteenth-Century Images of Chinese American Men," *Journal of American Culture* 30, no. 3 (2007): 293–309.

14. Alfred A. Hart, *The Traveler's Own Book* (Chicago: Horton & Leonard, 1870; repr. Chicago: Horton & Leonard, 1970). Most of the views in this book were scenic, and not a single image included a Chinese railroad worker. According to Peter Palmquist, it was unclear if Hart had support from the Central Pacific Railroad Company for this publication. See Peter Palmquist, "Alfred A. Hart and the Illustrated Traveler's Map of the Central Pacific Railroad," *Stereo World* 6, no. 6 (1980): 14–18.

15. In the fall of 1865, Chinese workers began constructing tunnels through the Sierra Nevada. The Central Pacific constructed fifteen tunnels in total, stretching from Cisco, California, to Lake Ridge, the eastern slope of the Sierra Nevada summit. John Gillis, an engineer who oversaw the construction of the Central Pacific, reported that Chinese laborers worked day and night in three shifts of eight hours each. Nitroglycerin was introduced in 1867 to expedite the construction, but it was unstable and caused numerous accidental explosions. The explosive material was used, according to Gillis, on the Tunnel 8 pictured in the Hart photograph. See John R. Gillis, "Tunnels of the Pacific Railroad," *Van Nostrand's Electric Engineering Magazine,* January 5, 1870, 418–423.

16. Willumson, *Iron Muse,* 70.

17. Bradley W. Richards and C. R. Savage, *The Savage View: Charles Savage, Pioneer Mormon Photographer* (Nevada City, CA: Carl Mautz Publishers, 1995).

18. Willumson, *Iron Muse,* 1–3; Michael W. Johnson, "Rendezvous at Promontory: A New Look at the Golden Spike Ceremony," *Utah Historical Quarterly* 72 (2004): 47–68.

19. J. D. B. Stillman, "The Last Tie," *Overland Monthly,* July 1869.

20. Stillman, "The Last Tie."

21. Edson T. Strobridge, "The Chinese at Promontory, Utah April 30–May 10,

1869 (An extract from the unfinished biography of James H. Strobridge)," Central Pacific Railroad History Museum, 2001, http://cprr.org/Museum/Chinese_at_Promontory_ETS.html.

22. Willumson, *Iron Muse,* 49, 50. See "Capt. Russell's Trip to California—Adventure among the Chinese—Goes to a Celestial Theatrical Entertainment," *Nunda* (NY) *News,* January 1, 1870.

23. Historian Ryan Dearinger notes that the closing speech at Promontory Summit by CPRR Superintendent James Campbell failed to acknowledge the Chinese workers. Other speakers, such as Judge Nathaniel Bennett, also left out the Chinese contribution. See Ryan Dearinger, *The Filth of Progress: Immigrants, Americans, and the Building of Canals and Railroads in the West* (Berkeley: University of California Press, 2015), 173, 201.

24. "The Last Rail," *Daily Alta California* (San Francisco), May 12, 1869.

25. "The Last Rail," *Daily Alta California* (San Francisco), May 12, 1869.

26. Barry A. Swackhamer, "J. B. Silvis, the Union Pacific's Nomadic Photographer," *Journal of the West* 33, no. 2 (1994), http://cprr.org/Museum/Silvis/.

27. For a description of the portrait, see Thomas Hill's self-published pamphlet, *The Last Spike, A Painting by Thomas Hill: Illustrating the Last Scene in the Building of the Overland Railroad. With a History of the Enterprise* (San Francisco: self-pub., January 1881).

28. Despite the undue prominence given to the Big Four (the founding executives of the CPRR: Leland Stanford, Collis P. Huntington, Mark Hopkins, and Charles Crocker) and the Central Pacific, Stanford disliked *The Last Spike* and refused to pay Hill his commission. See "Mystery of the 'Last Spike' Finally Solved," *New York Times,* November 27, 1910.

29. Before railroad financier Collis P. Huntington passed away, he gave the Central Pacific negatives made by Alfred Hart to Carleton Watkins. These negatives were printed under Watkins's own imprint and given the title "Watkins' Pacific Railroad" with no acknowledgment of Hart as the original photographer. In numerous archives and digitalized reproductions, Hart's timely and original photographs are miscredited to Watkins, who photographed the railroad route at a much later date and under vastly different circumstances. For a discussion of Watkins and Huntington, see Jennifer A. Watts, "The Photographer and the Railroad Man," *California History* 78, no. 3 (1999): 154–159.

Chapter 13

Acknowledgment: For their assistance in locating materials, I am obliged to Jean-Francis Clermont-Legros and Annick Foucrier. Note: Unless otherwise noted, all translations are by the author.

1. On the phenomenon of the French travel narrative of the United States, see

René Remond, *Les États-Unis devant l'opinion française, 1815–1852* [The United States in French Opinion, 1815–1852] (Paris: Armand Colin, 1962).

2. Frances Trollope, *Domestic Manners of the Americans* (1832; repr., New York: Oxford University Press, 2014); Charles Dickens, *American Notes for General Circulation* (1842; repr., London: Penguin Press, 2001); Harriet Martineau, *Society in America* (1837; repr., New York: Routledge, 1982); Michel Chevalier, *Society, Manners and Politics in the United States: Being a Series of Letters on North America* (Boston: Weeks, Jordan, 1839); Alexis de Tocqueville, *Democracy in America*, trans. Arthur Goldhammer (1835, 1840; repr., New York: Library of America, 2012); Friedrich Ratzel, *Sketches of Urban and Cultural Life in North America,* trans. Stewart Stehlin (New Brunswick, NJ: Rutgers University Press, 1988).

3. Jacques Portes, *Une fascination réticente: Les États-Unis dans l'opinion française, 1870–1914* [A Reluctant Fascination: The United States in French Opinion, 1870–1914] (Nancy, France: Presses Universitaires de Nancy, 1990). I found other narratives of Europeans who witnessed the building of the transcontinental railroad, but since these authors addressed the Chinese only in passing, I chose not to include them in my larger discussion. Consider, for example, this rather dehumanizing example: "The Chinese road workers swarm around us like ants. They are completing their work on the western side of the Sierra Nevada, and can't wait to concentrate on the [e]astern side, in order to advance toward the Great Salt Lake." V. A. Malte-Brun, ed., *Annales des voyages, de la géographie, de l'histoire et de l'archéologie* [Annals of Voyages, Geography, History, and Archeology], (Paris: Challamel, 1868), 118.

4. See, for example, F. Frédéric-Moreau, *Aux États-Unis: notes de voyage* [In the United States: Travel Notes] (Paris: Librairie Plon, 1888), 144–150; and Jules Huret, *En Amérique: de San Francisco au Canada* [In America: From San Francisco to Canada](Paris: Bibliothèque Charpentier, 1905), 76–84.

5. For this essay I limited myself to works written in French, and to a lesser extent German, because these are the foreign languages I speak best, and I selected works that were accessible in libraries or available on Gallica, the digital library of the Bibliothèque nationale de France (French National Library), www.bnf.fr.

6. Jacques Siegfried, *Seize mois autour du monde, 1867–1869, et particulièrement aux Indes, en Chine et au Japon* [Sixteen Months around the World, 1867–1869, and Particularly in the Indies, in China and in Japan] (Paris: J. Claye, 1869), 255, 256.

7. Siegfried, *Seize mois autour du monde.*

8. Wikipédia, s.v., "Ludovic de Beauvoir," accessed March 1, 2016, https://fr.wikipedia.org/wiki/Ludovic-de-Beauvoir. An interesting sidelight to the Count de Beauvoir's travels is that the novelist and philosopher Simone de Beauvoir, Beauvoir's grandniece, would later write narratives of her visits to both the United States and China, in the latter of which she mentioned her celebrated ancestor.

Simone de Beauvoir, *America Day by Day* (Berkeley: University of California Press, 2000); Simone de Beauvoir, *La longue marche* [The Long March] (Paris: Gallimard, 1957).

9. Ludovic de Beauvoir, *Voyages autour du monde: Australie, Java, Siam, Canton, Pékin, Yeddo, San Francisco* [Voyages around the World: Australia, Java, Siam, Canton, Peking, Yeddo, San Francisco] (Paris: Plon, 1878), 856, 858.

10. Beauvoir did not demonstrate the same level of respect toward Chinese immigrant laborers in Australia, whom he described in racist terms as "frightful jumping jacks," "yellow as tobacco juice," and "shrieking like cockatoos." Beauvoir further insisted that "They are smelly enough to scare off rats." Beauvoir, *Voyages*, vol. 1, 86, 110, cited in Marie Ramslade, "Impressions of a Young French Gentleman's 1866 Visit to the Australian Colonies," *Australian Studies* 2 (winter 2010): 10.

11. Edmond Cotteau, *Six mille lieues en soixante jours (Amérique du Nord): Extrait du bulletin de la Société des sciences historiques et naturelles de l'Yonne* [Six Thousand Leagues in Sixty Days (North America): Extract from the Bulletin of the Society of Historical and Natural Science of the Yonne] (Auxerre, France: Imprimerie G. Perriquet, 1877), 62, 63.

12. Guillaume Depping, "A travers le continent américain" [Across the American Continent], *Journal officiel de la République française,* October 16, 1876, 7528.

13. Hemmann Hoffmann, *Californien, Nevada und Mexico: Wanderungen eines Polytechnikers* [California, Nevada, and Mexico: Travels of a Polytechnician] (Basel, Switzerland: Hugo Richter, 1871), 210, 211. There was a second edition in 1874. I am obliged to Daniel Schaefer for his assistance with the English translations.

14. Hoffmann, *Californien, Nevada und Mexico,* 211, 212.

15. Hoffmann, *Californien, Nevada und Mexico,* 213.

16. Hoffmann, *Californien, Nevada und Mexico,* 213.

17. Hoffmann, *Californien, Nevada und Mexico,* 212.

18. "Émile Malézieux," Peintres & Sculpteurs website, accessed March 1, 2017, http://www.peintres-et-sculpteurs.com/biographie-384-malezieux-emile.html. See also M. Gariel, "Notice sur la vie et les travaux de M. Malézieux" [Notice on the Life and Work of Mr. Malézieux], *Annales des ponts et chaussées,* 1888, 514–570. Malézieux's anonymous source was likely the Central Pacific Railroad executive Charles Crocker, especially in light of similar comments elsewhere. See, for example, Baron Étienne Hulot, *De l'Atlantique au Pacifique à travers le Canada et le nord des États-Unis* [From the Atlantic to the Pacific across Canada and the Northern United States] (Paris: E. Plon, Nourrit, 1888), 324.

19. Émile Malézieux, *Travaux publics des États-Unis d'Amérique en 1870, rapport de mission, par M. Malézieux* [Public Works in the United States of America in 1870, Report of a Mission by Mr. Malézieux] (Paris: Dunod Éditeur, 1873), 207, 208.

20. Malézieux, *Travaux publics des États-Unis d'Amérique en 1870.*

21. "16 kilometers dans un jour" [Sixteen Kilometers in a Day], *Le Petit Journal,* May 11, 1870.

22. "16 kilometers dans un jour" [Sixteen Kilometers in a Day], *Le Petit Journal,* May 11, 1870.

23. "16 kilometers dans un jour" [Sixteen Kilometers in a Day], *Le Petit Journal,* May 11, 1870.

24. The question of foodways is especially pertinent to any discussion of the Chinese railroad workers. It is not a coincidence that at the turn of the twentieth century, many Chinese restaurants were opened by former railroad workers who had gained familiarity with mainstream American cooking through their experience. One of the staples of French Canadian cuisine is a version of shepherd's pie called "pâté chinois," so named because it was supposedly served to Chinese workers employed by the Canadian Pacific Railway to build the transcontinental line in the 1880s.

25. Wikipedia, s.v., "Rudolf Lindau (Schriftsteller)," accessed March 1, 2016, https://de.wikipedia.org/wiki/Rudolf_Lindau_%28Schriftsteller%29.

26. Lindau's account would be picked up soon after by the influential writer and geographer Louis-Laurent Simonin, whose unattributed account of the same events can be found in Louis-Laurent Simonin, *À travers les États-Unis, de l'Atlantique au Pacifique* [Across the United States, from the Atlantic to the Pacific] (Paris: Charpentier, 1875), 174.

27. The above-mentioned *Le Petit Journal* article notes only in passing the contribution of Chinese workers at the laying of the golden spike: "The ablest Chinese workers, who are excellent road workers, were selected to level the ground and finish the path that was to receive the last rails and ties." "16 kilometers dans un jour," *Le Petit Journal,* May 11, 1870, 1.

28. Rudolf Lindau, "Le chemin de fer du Pacifique à l'Atlantique" [From the Pacific to the Atlantic], *Revue des Deux Mondes,* November 1869, 15.

29. Joseph Alexander von Hübner, *Promenade autour du monde* [Stroll around the World], 5th ed. (1871; repr., Paris: Hachette, 1878), 168, 169. Hübner added a set of stylized illustrations.

Chapter 14

Acknowledgments: The author would like to thank Gordon Chang, Jeff Chang, Jennifer Duque, Evyn Le Espiritu, Neil Gotanda, Ramya Janandharan, Rachel Lim, Amy Lin, Michael Omi, Mihiri Tillakaratne, Gabriel Wolfenstein, Daniel Woo, and Jeffery Yamashita for their comments on earlier drafts of this essay.

1. David Saville Muzzey, *An American History* (Boston: Ginn, 1911).

2. For an example of an early textbook representation of Chinese immigrants, see Augusta Blanch Berard, *School History of the United States* (Philadelphia: Cowperthwait & Company, 1855), 214. For overviews of Chinese American history during

this period, see Sucheng Chan, *Asian Americans: An Interpretive History* (Boston: Twayne, 1991); Erica Lee, *The Making of Asian America: A History* (New York: Simon & Schuster, 2015); and Ronald Takaki, *Strangers from a Different Shore: A History of Asian Americans* (Boston: Little, Brown, 1989). For a more detailed look at Chinese immigration during this period, see Sucheng Chan, *This Bittersweet Soil: The Chinese in California Agriculture, 1860–1910* (Berkeley: University of California Press, 1986).

3. On the scholarly debate surrounding the issue of Chinese immigration, see Mary Roberts Coolidge, *Chinese Immigration* (New York: H. Holt, 1909); Stuart Creighton Miller, *The Unwelcome Immigrant: The American Image of the Chinese 1785–1882* (Berkeley: University of California Press, 1974); Alexander Saxton, *The Indispensable Enemy: Labor and the Anti-Chinese Movement in California* (Berkeley: University of California Press, 1975); and Andrew Gyory, *Closing the Gate: Race, Politics, and the Chinese Exclusion Act* (Chapel Hill: University of North Carolina Press, 1998).

4. M. E. Thalheimer, *The Eclectic History of the United States* (Cincinnati: Van Antwerp, Bragg, 1880), 341.

5. Alexander Johnston, *A History of the United States for Schools, with an Introductory History of the Discovery and English* (New York: Henry Holt, 1885), 391.

6. John Bach McMaster, *A School History of the United States* (New York: American, 1897), 443.

7. Horace Elisha Scudder, *A History of the United States of America* (Philadelphia: J. H. Butler, 1884), 424.

8. Charles Kendall Adams and William Trent, *A History of the United States* (Boston: Allyn & Bacon, 1903); Edward Eggleston, *A New Century History of the United States* (New York: American, 1904), 376–377.

9. Coolidge, *Chinese Immigration*. The bulk of Coolidge's discussion on railroad workers can be found on pages 52, 63, 64, and 349. On cigar makers, see pages 365–371; on boot makers, see pages 360–365.

10. A number of scholars have written about the role of coolies in both the popular and historical imaginations. See, for example, Moon-Ho Jung, *Coolies and Cane: Race, Labor, and Sugar in the Age of Emancipation* (Baltimore: Johns Hopkins University Press, 2006); and Robert G. Lee, *Orientals: Asian Americans in Popular Culture* (Philadelphia: Temple University Press, 1999).

11. Jung, *Coolies and Cane*, 5.

12. Frances FitzGerald, *America Revised: History Schoolbooks in the Twentieth Century* (Boston: Little, Brown, 1979), 59.

13. Muzzey, *An American History*, 516. The Burlingame Treaty allowed for the free emigration of citizens of China to the United States. It also ensured that Chinese in the United States were granted the same protections of travel and residence as those

granted to the most-favored nation. On the Burlingame Treaty, see Takaki, *Strangers from a Different Shore*, 114; Chan, *Asian Americans*, 54.

14. Muzzey, *An American History*, 513.

15. Lee, *Orientals*, 51–82.

16. Muzzey, *An American History*, 618, 619.

17. Mae Ngai, *Impossible Subjects: Illegal Aliens and the Making of Modern America* (Princeton, NJ: Princeton University Press, 2004), 37.

18. Joseph Moreau, *Schoolbook Nation: Conflicts over American History Textbooks from the Civil War to the Present* (Ann Arbor: University of Michigan Press, 2003), 175–177. Moreau also briefly discusses depictions of Chinese in American history textbooks. Moreau, 172–173.

19. David Saville Muzzey, *The American People* (Boston: Ginn, 1927), 449; David Saville Muzzey, *History of the American People* (Boston: Ginn, 1934), 449; David Saville Muzzey, *History of Our Country: A Textbook for High School Students* (Boston: Ginn, 1936), 483; David Saville Muzzey, *History of Our Country: A Textbook for High School Students* (Boston: Ginn, 1945), 483.

20. Muzzey, *History of Our Country* (1936), 456.

21. David Saville Muzzey, *Our Country's History* (Boston: Ginn, 1957), 342.

22. David Muzzey and Arthur Link, *Our American Republic* (Boston: Ginn, 1963), 353.

Chapter 15

Acknowledgments: I want to thank Shelley Fisher Fishkin and Gordon Chang for having gotten me involved in this wonderful and ambitious project from the beginning in 2012 to the present. I had been given so many great opportunities to interact with and learn from many leading historians and literary studies scholars in the United States, Canada, mainland China, and Taiwan. I also appreciate the hard work of Roland Hsu, who has read every version so meticulously. I should also acknowledge Xiao Fei, former dean of the School of Foreign Studies at Nanjing Forestry University, and Zhao Wenshu, dean of the Overseas College at Nanjing University, for their support of my research. I also want to thank my wife, Beixin Ni, who carefully checked my pinyin spelling in the essay.

1. S. Y. Teng, "Chinese Historiography in the Last Fifty Years," *Far Eastern Quarterly* 8, no. 2 (February 1949): 131–156. On p. 138, Teng writes: "The last Sino-Japanese war (1937–1945) dealt Chinese academic activities a severe blow. Academic work has been put back some ten or fifteen years as a result of the destruction of libraries, loss of good professors and students, and shortage of equipment and of the basic comforts necessary for mental activity."

2. Michel de Certeau, *The Practice of Everyday Life* (Berkeley: University of California Press, 1988), xi.

3. Paul Kennedy, *The Rise and Fall of Great Powers* (New York: Vintage Books, 1987), xv.

4. Teng, "Chinese Historiography," 155. In his discussion of the theory and practice of Chinese historiography in the first half of the twentieth century, Teng, a historian based at the University of Chicago, observed that Chinese historians during the past five decades had developed a more liberal-minded orientation and made a departure from their traditional conservative mentality.

5. *Encyclopaedia Britannica*, s.v. "Bandung Conference," accessed September 18, 2018, https://www.britannica.com/event/Bandung-Conference. Organized by Indonesia, Myanmar, Ceylon (Sri Lanka), India, and Pakistan, the Bandung Conference, also known as the Afro-Asian Conference, took place in Bandung, Indonesia, on April 18–24, 1955. Twenty-nine nation-states, representing more than half the world's population, discussed their frustration on issues varying from continuing Western colonialism, such as French interference in North Africa, to the Cold War tensions between the United States and the People's Republic of China. It was at this conference that the Chinese Premier Zhou Enlai advocated the five principles of peaceful coexistence as the foundation of China's foreign policy, which included mutual respect for each other's territorial integrity and sovereignty, mutual nonaggression, mutual noninterference in each other's internal affairs, equality and cooperation for mutual benefit, and peaceful coexistence.

6. See Ankit Panda, "Reflecting on China's Five Principles, 60 Years Later," *The Diplomat,* June 26, 2014, http://thediplomat.com/2014/06/reflecting-on-chinas-five-principles-60-years-later/.

7. Liu Danian, *Mei guo qin hua shi* [A History of U.S. Aggression against China], 2nd ed. (Beijing: Ren min chu ban she, 1954). According to Liu, there was another version of this book published in 1949.

8. Liu, *Mei guo qin hua shi,* 61–68.

9. This book was strongly criticized by Zeng Yanxiu, vice president of People's Press, for making claims without providing adequate historical evidence. The two had a critical debate in 1956. See "A Debate between Zeng Yanxiu and Liu Danian on *A History of US Aggression against China* [in Chinese]," Institute of Modern China Studies, Chinese Social Science Academy, accessed April 13, 2016, http://jds.cass.cn/Item/8135.aspx.

10. Liu, "Preface," *Mei guo qin hua shi,* 1, 2.

11. Zhang Renyu, *Mei di pai hua shi* [A History of US Imperialist Exclusion of the Chinese] (Beijing: Wen hua gong ying she, 1951).

12. Zhang, *Mei di pai hua shi,* 2, 3. This statement is historically inaccurate because the Chinese Exclusion Act replaced prohibitive fees with an outright ban on Chinese immigration to Canada with exceptions only for merchants, diplomats, students, and "special circumstances" cases in 1923.

13. Ding Zemin, *Mei guo pai hua shi* [A History of US Exclusion of the Chinese] (Beijing: Zhong hua shu ju, 1952).

14. See Mary Roberts Coolidge, *Chinese Immigration* (New York: Henry Holt, 1909). See also Hubert Howe Bancroft, *History of California: 1860–1890,* vol. 7 (San Francisco: History Company, 1890).

15. Baidu.com, s.v., "Ding Zemin," accessed January 15, 2016, http://baike.baidu .com/view/4912436.htm. Ding Zemin studied in the United States for two years and returned to China in 1949, before he could finish his doctoral work in history at the University of Washington in Seattle.

16. Qing Ruji, *Mei guo qin hua shi* [A History of US Aggression against China], 2 vols. (Beijing: San lian shu dian, 1952).

17. Qing, *Mei guo qin hua shi.* In his preface Qing claims that his work has drawn extensively from original historical documents based in the United States, ranging from the US presidents' directives to their cabinet members and US ambassadors' reports to the State Department, to autobiographies and memoirs published by major political figures in United States–China relations. He mentions the equal importance of Chinese archival sources, specifically *The Management of Barbarian Affairs from the Beginning to the End in the Qing Dynasty* (in Chinese), a collection of official documents compiled by the authorities of the Palace Museum in Beijing in the 1930s. According to S. Y. Teng, the documents, photolithographs of original compilations, were made under imperial auspices and presented to the emperor.

18. Shih-shan H. Ts'ai, "Chinese Immigration through Communist Chinese Eyes: An Introduction to the Historiography," *Pacific Historical Review* 43, no. 3 (August 1974): 395–408.

19. Qing, *Mei guo qin hua shi,* 519.

20. Zhu Shijia, *Mei guo po hai hua gong shi liao* [Historical Materials Concerning US Persecution of Chinese Laborers] (Beijing: Zhong hua shu ju, 1958).

21. Ts'ai, "Chinese Immigration," 408. Ts'ai, a historian based at the University of Arkansas, offered an assessment of the work of Zhu and Qing in 1974: "Chu Shih-chia's (Zhu Shijia) two books of selected archival materials are among the most important Sino-American historical documents prepared by any Chinese. Ch'ing Ju-chi's (Qing Ruji) lengthy work must also be ranked as a leading Sino-American diplomatic history in the Chinese language."

22. With a PhD in history from Columbia University and extensive research experience in archives, museums, and libraries in both China and the United States, Zhu Shijia obtained a position in the Asiatic Division of the Library of Congress in October 1939 and scrutinized all of the available Chinese-language material in the archives during his tenure there. He copied more than a thousand entries of United States–China diplomatic exchanges and other materials and donated them all to

the Chinese National Archives upon his return to China in 1950, at the invitation of Chen Hanseng, a prominent historian at Peking University, and after his resignation as an associate professor of history at the University of Washington in Seattle.

23. Zhu, *Mei guo po hai hua gong shi liao*, 22, 23.

24. A Ying, *Fan mei hua gong jin yue wen xue ji* [A Literary Anthology on Resistance to the US Exclusion of Chinese Laborers], vol. 5 of *Zhong guo jin dai fan qin lue wen xue ji* [Literary Collections of China's Modern Resistance to Foreign Aggressions] (Beijing: Zhong hua shu ju, 1960).

25. Wofoshanren, *Ku she hui* [Bitter Society] (Shanghai: Shanghai Tu shu zi liao she, 1905).

26. A Ying, *Fan mei hua gong jin yue wen xue ji*, 11.

27. Liang Qichao, *Xin da lu you ji* [Travel Writing on the New Continent] (Changsha, China: Yue lu shu she, 1985).

28. Lin Shu and Wei Yi, *Hei nu yu tian lu* [Documentation of a Black Slave's Appeal to Heaven] (1901; repr., Beijing: Shang wu yin shu guan, 1981). Harriet Beecher Stowe, *Uncle Tom's Cabin, or Life among the Lowly* (Boston: John P. Jewett & Company, 1852).

29. A Ying, *Fan mei hua gong jin yue wen xue ji*, 4.

30. His assertion that Chinese did not work for the Central Pacific Railroad after 1869 is erroneous, as Shelley Fisher Fishkin's chapter in this volume demonstrates.

31. Q. Edward Wang, "Encountering the World: China and Its Other(s) in Historical Narratives, 1949–89," *Journal of World History* 14, no. 3 (2003): 327–358.

32. *He Shang* [River Elegy], written and directed by Su Xiaokang, Wang Luxiang, and Xia Jun, six-part documentary, 1988.

33. See Arnold Toynbee, *A Study of History: Abridgement of Vols. 1–6*, abridgement by D. C. Somervell (Oxford: Oxford University Press, 1946). In his study of the rise and fall of twenty-six civilizations in world history, Toynbee concludes that their rises were mostly the result of successful responses to challenges under the guidance of a group of creative elite leaders.

34. Wang, "Encountering the World," 355.

35. See the eulogy, "The Life of Zhang Zhilian," *Chinese Studies in History* 43, no. 3 (Spring 2010): 107–110.

36. Ding Zemin, "Mei guo zhong yang tai ping yang tie lu de xing jian yu hua gong de ju da gong xian" [The Construction of America's Central Pacific Railroad and the Tremendous Contribution of Chinese Workers], *Shi xue ji kan* [Compilation of Historiography] 2 (1990): 47–54.

37. This pioneering book series 走向世界丛书 Zou xiang shi jie cong shu marked the beginning of what critics call "culture fever" and became one of the two most influential series in China during the 1980s. It included traveling writings and critical reflections upon Western cultures and societies written by Chinese diplomats and

scholars since the late nineteenth century. The editor of the book series was Zhong Shuhe. The series was published by Hunan People's Press from 1980 to 1983, but then moved its operation to Yuelu Press from 1985 to 1986. Accessed September 18, 2017, https://baike.baidu.com/item/走向世界丛书.

38. This book series 走向未来丛书 Zou xiang wei lai cong shu was published by Sichuan People's Press and became one of the two most popular series in China during the 1980s. The books encompass monographs written by young Chinese scholars and translate Western classics in sciences, social sciences, and the humanities. The editor in chief was Jin Guantao. Its associate editors and editorial advisers included the most influential scholars and public intellectuals of the time. It started in 1984 but was disrupted in 1988, partly because many of its associate editors and editorial advisers would be involved in the Tiananmen pro-democracy movement in June 1989. Accessed September 18, 2017, https://zh.wikipedia.org/wiki/走向未来丛书.

39. This book series focuses on the special topic of historical documents on Chinese workers going overseas. It consists of ten volumes, and some volumes also have subvolumes. Its editor in chief was Chen Hansheng, and the series was published by Zhong hua shu ju from 1980 to 1984.

40. Starting in 1990, this book series 世界华侨史丛书 Shi jie hua qiao shi cong shu specializes on the history of overseas Chinese around the world. It was published by Guangdong Higher Education Press and its editor in chief was Zhu Jieqin.

41. Chen Hansheng, preface, in *Zhong guo guan wen shu xuan ji* [Selection of Chinese Official Documents], ed. China's First National Archives and Lu Wendi, Chen Zexian, and Peng Jiali (Beijing: Zhong hua shu ju, 1985), 4–11, subvol. 1, vol. 1, of *Hua gong chu guo shi liao hui bian* [Collections of Historical Documents on Chinese Workers Going Overseas].

42. Chen, *Zhong guo guan wen shu xuan ji,* 13–15.

43. Chen, *Zhong guo guan wen shu xuan ji,* 19.

44. Lu Wendi, Peng Jiali, and Chen Zexian, eds., *Mei guo yue jia na da hua gong* [Chinese Laborers in the United States and Canada], vol. 7 in *Hua gong chu guo shi liao hui bian* [Collections of Historical Documents on Chinese Workers Going Overseas] (Beijing: Zhong hua shu ju, 1984).

45. George F. Seward, *Chinese Immigration in Its Social and Economic Aspects* (New York: Charles Scribner's Sons, 1881).

46. Gunther Paul Barth, *Bitter Strength: A History of the Chinese in the United States, 1850–1870* (Cambridge, MA: Harvard University Press, 1964).

47. Coolidge, *Chinese Immigration.*

48. Alexander Saxton, "The Army of Canton in the High Sierra," *Pacific Historical Review* 35, no. 2 (May 1966): 141–152.

49. Saxton, "The Army of Canton," 151. This quote has been used extensively and

appeared in almost all of the Chinese articles or history books related to the Chinese railroad workers written since the publication of the volumes.

50. Chan Koonchung, "Mei guo hua qiao xue lei jian shi" [A Brief Bloody History of Overseas Chinese in America], *Ming Pao Monthly* (October/November 1977): n.p.

51. For example, Huang Annian and Sheng Jianhong, two leading historians on the Chinese railroad workers in North America, made this mistake in their essays and books.

52. Yang Guobiao, Liu Hanbiao, and Yang Anyao, *Mei guo hua qiao shi* [A History of Overseas Chinese in the United States], in the series Shi jie hua qiao shi cong shu [The History of Overseas Chinese around the Globe], ed. Zhu Jieqin (Guang-zhou: Guang dong gao deng jiao yue chu ban she, 1989).

53. Li Chunhui and Yang Shengmao, *Mei zhou hua qiao hua ren shi* [A History of Overseas Chinese and Chinese Americans in the Americas] (Beijing: Dong fang chu ban she, 1990).

54. Li and Yang, *Mei zhou hua qiao hua ren shi,* 124. The 1,200 figure has been highly questioned. For example, according to one source, "The Chinese worker casualties due to construction accidents have likely been wildly exaggerated due to a single short Sacramento newspaper account claiming transportation of the bones of 1,200 dead which was contradicted by another newspaper article the same day reporting instead 50 dead (almost certainly including some who died in Nevada from smallpox)." "Corrections Regarding Chinese Workers," Central Pacific Railroad Photographic History Museum, accessed September 18, 2017, http://discussion.cprr .net/2010/05/corrections-regarding-chinese-workers.html.

55. Li and Yang, *Mei zhou hua qiao hua ren shi,* 125, 126.

56. Zhu Jieqin, "Shi jiu shi ji hou qi zhong guo ren zai mei guo kai fa zhong de zuo yong ji chu jing" [The Role and Predicament of the Chinese in the American Development in the Late Nineteenth Century], *Li shi yan jiu* [History Studies] 1 (1980): 93–111.

57. Ding Zemin, "Mei guo zhong yang tai ping yang tie lu de xue jian yu hua gong de ju da gong xian" [Construction of the American Central Pacific Railroad and the Tremendous Contribution of Chinese Workers], *Shi xue ji kan* [Collected Journal of Historical Studies] 2 (1990): 47–54.

58. See Kennedy, *The Rise and Fall of Great Powers,* xv.

59. *Da Guo Jiu Qi* [The Rise of the Great Powers], directed by Ren Xue'an, writ-ten by Chen Jin, narrated by Sun Zhanshan, CCTV-2, November 13 to December 24, 2006. See also Wang Jiafeng, Chen Yong, and Gao Dai, *Qiang Guo Zhi Jian* [The Lessons of Powerful Nations] (Beijing: Ren min chu ban she, 2007).

60. Huang Annian, *Mei guo de jue qi: 17–19 shi ji de mei guo* [The Rise of the

United States: The United States from the Seventeenth to the Nineteenth Century] (Beijing: Zhong guo she hui ke xue chu ban she, 1992).

61. Huang Annian, *Mei guo she hui jing ji shi lun* [The Socioeconomic History of the United States] (Taiyuan, China: Shan xi jiao yu chu ban she, 1993).

62. Huang Annian, "Zhong yang tai ping yang tie lu de jian cheng yu zai mei hua gong de gong xian" [The Completion of the Central Pacific Railroad and the Contribution of Chinese Workers in the United States], *He bei shi fan da xue xue bao* [Journal of Hebei Normal University] (Social Sciences) 22, no. 2 (1999): 97–112.

63. Huang Annian, "Hua gong jian she tai ping yang tie lu he mei guo de jue qi" [The Construction of the Central Pacific Railroad by Chinese Workers and the Rise of the United States], *li shi jiao xue wen ti* [Issues in History Teaching] 6 (2007): 39–41.

64. Huang Annian, "Zhao hui xing jian zhong yang tai ping yang tie lu hua gong li shi yin ji" [In Search of the Historical Footprints of the Chinese Workers Building the Central Pacific Railroad], *Zhong xue li shi jiao xue zhi nan* [Teaching References for High School History] 356 (2015): 10–13.

65. Huang Annian, *Dao ding, bu zai chen mo: jian she bei mei tie lu de hua gong* [Spikes, No Longer Silent: To the Chinese Workers Constructing North American Railroads] (Shenyang, China: Bai shan chu ban she, 2010).

66. Huang, *Dao ding, bu zai chen mo: jian she bei mei tie lu de hua gong.*

67. Huang Annian and Li Ju, *Chen mo dao ding de zu ji—ji nian hua gong jian she mei guo tie lu* [The Footprints of the Silent Spikes—In Memory of the Chinese Workers Who Constructed the American Railroads] (Beijing: Zhong guo tie dao chu ban she, 2015).

68. Huang, "Zhong yang tai ping yang tie lu de jian cheng yu zai mei hua gong de gong xian"; Xin Yi, *Zhong guo xue jie jiu tai ping yang tie lu hua gong yi ti xiang guan yan jiu cheng guo ping shu* [Summary and Evaluation of the Chinese Academic Scholarship on the Chinese Pacific Railroad Workers], *Zhong shan da xue yan jiu sheng xue kan* [Journal of Graduate Students at Sun Yat-sen University] (Social Sciences) 35, no. 3 (2014): 1–9, especially the discussion on page 4.

69. Sheng Jianhong, *Mei guo zhong yang tai ping yang tie lu jian she zhong de hua gong* [The Chinese Workers in the Construction of the United States' Central Pacific Railroad] (Shanghai: Zhong xi shu ju, 2010).

70. Huang, *Dao ding, bu zai chen mo: jian she bei mei tie lu de hua gong,* 43.

71. Xi Jinping, "Full Text of Xi Jinping's Speech on China–US Relations in Seattle," *Xinhua Net,* September 24, 2015. http://news.xinhuanet.com/english/2015 -09/24/c_134653326.htm.

Chapter 16

Acknowledgments: I am deeply grateful to Gordon Chang and Shelley Fisher

Fishkin for their outstanding leadership in initiating and promoting the Chinese Railroad Workers in North America Project. I would also like to thank Roland Hsu, Hilton Obenzinger, and Gabriel Wolfenstein for their kind assistance in so many ways. This paper is a partial result of the Extended Railroads: Literary and Cultural Representations of Chinese Railroad Workers in North America Project funded by the Ministry of Science and Technology of Taiwan, ROC (NSC/ MOST 102-2410-H-009-038-MY3).

1. Maxine Hong Kingston, *China Men* (New York: Vintage, 1989).

2. Shawn Hsu Wong, *Homebase* (1979; repr., New York: Plume, 1991).

3. Frank Chin, *The Chickencoop Chinaman/ The Year of the Dragon* (Seattle: Washington University Press, 1981); Kathleen Chang, *The Iron Moonhunter,* trans. Chiu-Chung Liao and Florence Lau (San Francisco: Children's Book Press, 1977).

In Act 2 of Chin's play *The Chickencoop Chinaman,* the protagonist, Tam, in his soliloquy reminisces about the legend of the Iron Moonhunter that his grandmother was always listening to while she was alive:

> And grandmaw heard thunder in the Sierra hundreds of miles away and listened for the Chinaman-known Iron Moonhunter, that train built by Chinamans who knew they'd never be given passes to ride the rails they laid. So of all American railroaders, only they sung no songs, told no jokes, drank no toasts to the ol' iron horse, but stole themselves some iron on the way, slowly stole up a pile of steel, children, and hid there in granite face of the Sierra and built themselves a wild engine to take them home. Every night, children, grandmaw listened in the kitchen, waiting, til the day she died. (31)

At the back of Chang's book the author writes that "*The Iron Moonhunter* is based on a legend that still circulates in Chinese America." Sau-ling Cynthia Wong in a footnote suggests that this "legend" may be invented by Chin. Sau-ling Cynthia Wong, *Reading Asian American Literature: From Necessity to Extravagance* (Princeton, NJ: Princeton University Press, 1993), 226.

4. Wong, *Homebase,* 95.

5. David Henry Hwang, *The Dance and the Railroad and Family Devotions: Two Plays* (New York: Dramatists Play Service, 1983).

6. Laurence Yep, *Dragon's Gate* (New York: Harper Trophy, 1993); Frank Chin, *Donald Duk* (Minneapolis: Coffee House, 1991).

7. François Jost defines *Bildung* as "the process by which a human being becomes a replica of his mentor, and is identified with him as the exemplary model." François Jost, "The Bildungsroman in Germany, England, and France," in *Introduction to Comparative Literature* (Indianapolis: Pegasus, 1974), 135.

8. Stephen Krensky's *The Iron Dragon Never Sleeps* also includes an interracial friendship between the white girl protagonist and a young Chinese tea boy, making the interracial plot appear to be a standard one for texts that feature young protagonists and are connected with the construction of the Central Pacific

Railroad. Stephen Krensky, *The Iron Dragon Never Sleeps* (New York: Yearling, 1995).

9. Yep, *Dragon's Gate*, 159.

10. The ten novels in the series Golden Mountain Chronicles are *The Serpent's Children*, set in 1849 (1984); *Mountain Light*, 1855 (1985); *Dragon's Gate*, 1867 (1993); *The Traitor*, 1885 (2003); *Dragonwings*, 1903 (1975); *Dragon Road*, 1939 (2007); *Child of the Owl*, 1960 (1977); *Sea Glass*, 1970 (1979); *Thief of Hearts*, 1995 (1995); and *Dragons of Silk*, 1835–2011 (2011).

11. Yep, *Dragon's Gate*, 5.

12. The Hakka people relocated from central China to Guangdong around the twelfth or thirteenth century during their second mass migration. To this day they are regarded as "guests" in the area. Mary S. Erbaugh, "The Secret History of the Hakkas: The Chinese Revolution as a Hakka Enterprise," *China Quarterly* 132 (1992): 946. The fourth and final mass migration of the Hakkas took place after the Taiping Rebellion (1850–1864) and Hakka–Bendi (local people) land wars. Erbaugh, "The Secret History of the Hakkas," 947. Otter's birth mother died in one of these wars. In the preface to *Dragon's Gate* Yep explains that in the mid-nineteenth century the local clans of Guangdong who took part in the Red Turban uprising sought revenge for the Manchu suppression and massacre by waging "a genocidal war against the ethnic group known as the Strangers because it is believed that the Strangers have provided information and aid to the Manchus. It is estimated that half of the three hundred thousand Strangers have died." Yep, *Dragon's Gate*, 2. Otter is orphaned in one of these interethnic conflicts.

13. Yep, *Dragon's Gate*, 8.

14. Yep, *Dragon's Gate*, 30.

15. Yep, *Dragon's Gate*, 72.

16. Jeffrey Santa Ana lists "happiness, optimism, comfort, anxiety, fear, ambivalence, and the emotion of remembering and forgetting Asian heritage and immigrant history" as emotions that "inform and shape the perception of Asian Americans as a racially different group." Jeffrey Santa Ana, *Racial Feelings: Asian America in a Capitalist Culture of Emotion* (Philadelphia: Temple University Press, 2015), 1. I would submit that estrangement is also one of the "racial feelings" that are constitutive to the Asian American cultural mindscape.

17. Yep, *Dragon's Gate*, 115.

18. Yep, *Dragon's Gate*, 42.

19. Yep, *Dragon's Gate*, 117.

20. Ronald Takaki, *Strangers from a Different Shore: A History of Asian Immigrants* (New York: Penguin, 1989), 84.

21. Yep, *Dragon's Gate*, 291.

22. Yep, *Dragon's Gate*, 240.

23. Yep, *Dragon's Gate*, 240.

24. Yep, *Dragon's Gate*, 241.

25. Yep, *Dragon's Gate*, 220.

26. The source of the whipping scene, which is mentioned in the afterword, is an article that appeared in the *Sacramento Union* on July 1, 1867, reporting how the strikers demanded "to deny the right of the overseers of the company to either whip or to restrain them from leaving the railroad when they desire to seek other employment." Yep, *Dragon's Gate*, 333.

27. Yep, *Dragon's Gate*, 194.

28. Yep, *Dragon's Gate*, 189.

29. Yep, *Dragon's Gate*, 164.

30. Yep, *Dragon's Gate*, 166.

31. Yep, *Dragon's Gate*, 49.

32. Yep, *Dragon's Gate*, 48.

33. Yep, *Dragon's Gate*, 274.

34. Chin, *Donald Duk*, 89.

35. Chin, *Donald Duk*, 90.

36. Chin, *Donald Duk*, 2.

37. Chin, *Donald Duk*, 2.

38. Chin, *Donald Duk*, 3.

39. Wenying Xu, "Masculinity, Food, and Appetite in Frank Chin's *Donald Duk* and 'The Eat and Run Midnight People,'" *Cultural Critique* 66 (2007): 81.

40. Yu-cheng Lee 李有成, 記憶 [Memory] (Taipei: Asian Culture, 2016), 80. Yu-cheng Lee argues that *Donald Duk* is a text that engages in a project of what Ngugi wa Thiong'o calls "decolonizing the mind." To carry out the project of decolonization, Lee claims, Frank Chin mobilizes a politics of memory to reconstruct Chinese American collective memory, to recollect an erased or silenced past of Chinese America, and to expose the fissures and gaps in official American history.

41. Lo Kuan-Chung, *Romance of the Three Kingdoms*, 2 vols., trans. C. H. Brewitt-Taylor (repr., North Clarendon, VT: Tuttle, 2002); Shi Naian, *The Water Margin: Outlaws of the Marsh*, trans. J. H. Jackson (repr., North Clarendon, VT: Tuttle, 2010).

42. Chin, *Donald Duk*, 118.

43. Chin, *Donald Duk*, 23, 25.

44. Chin, *Donald Duk*, 26.

45. Chin, *Donald Duk*, 29.

46. Other contemporary Chinatown characters in *Donald Duk* also travel back in time and have multiple identities; for example, Doong the tai chi master, who is also an opera musician and a flamenco guitarist in the narrative present, is selling kung fu brew in Donald's dream sequence. And the Frog Twins also appear in Donald's dream.

47. David L. Eng, *Racial Castration: Managing Masculinity in Asian America* (Durham, NC: Duke University Press, 2001), 70.

48. In *China Men* Maxine Hong Kingston writes about the importance of Kwan Kung, or Guan Goong, to the Chinese immigrants: he is "the God of War, also God of War and Literature.... Guan Goong, Grandfather Guan, our own ancestor of writers and fighters, of actors and gamblers, and avenging executioners who mete out justice. Our own kin. Not a distant relative but Grandfather." Kingston, *China Men*, 148. Kingston is making Guan Goong/Kwan Kung into a close family member while recognizing his godly status.

49. Chin, *Donald Duk*, 77.

50. Chin, *Donald Duk*, 78.

51. Chin, *Donald Duk*, 98.

52. Chin, *Donald Duk*, 97.

53. Chin, *Donald Duk*, 113.

54. Chin, *Donald Duk*, 114.

55. Chin, *Donald Duk*, 126.

56. Chin, *Donald Duk*, 105.

57. Chin has invented many fictional details about the railroad construction work. The story of the laurel crosstie is one of his inventions. According to Stephen E. Ambrose, James H. Strobridge and Samuel B. Reed laid the last laurel tie while a squad of Chinese placed one rail and an Irish squad from the Union Pacific did the other rail. Stephen E. Ambrose, *Nothing Like It in the World: The Men Who Built the Transcontinental Railroad, 1863–1869* (New York: Simon & Schuster, 2000). After the ceremony, the laurel tie was whittled to splinters by souvenir hunters. S. Y. Wu, a native of Kaiping who grew up with Gold Mountain stories, records another anecdote about the last crosstie that is related to interracial conflicts between the Chinese and Irish railroad workers. According to Wu, at the request of the Irish workers, the Chinese workers were banned from the golden spike ceremony. However, the last tie was mysteriously missing when Leland Stanford was ready to proceed with the ceremony. Four Chinese workers emerged from the crowd and laid the last crosstie. Wu describes this incident as an example of how the Chinese triumphed with their wits while being excluded by the whites. S. Y. Wu 吳尚鷹, 美國華僑百年紀實 [One Hundred Years of Chinese in the United States and Canada] (Hong Kong: Chia Low, 1954), 36.

58. Chin, *Donald Duk*, 151.

59. Chin, *Donald Duk*, 172. Lee Kuey is one the 108 outlaws in *The Water Margin*.

60. Yep, *Dragon's Gate*, 331.

61. Kingston, *China Men*, 133.

62. Yep, *Dragon's Gate*, 303.

63. Chin, *Donald Duk*, 138.

Chapter 17

Note: An asterisk (*) before a note indicates that the citations have been cut for length. More-complete references for this chapter may be found in Shelley Fisher Fishkin, "Bibliographic Essay for 'The Chinese as Railroad Workers after Promontory'" at the website of the Chinese Railroad Workers in North America Project at Stanford.

1.* "Pacific Coast Despatches," *Daily Alta California* (San Francisco), July 13, 1869, 1; "Chinese Labour in America," *Engineering: An Illustrated Weekly Journal* (London), May 28, 1869, 360.

2. "John Chinaman: How He Lives and What He Does—The Problem of Excellent Skilled Workmen," *Daily Constitutionalist* (Augusta, GA), July 18, 1869, 2.

3. "The Chinaman as Railroad Builder," *Idaho Statesman*, May 25, 1869, 3. The identical article ran in dozens of publications.

4.* Donald B. Robertson, *Encyclopedia of Western Railroad History,* vol. 2 (Dallas: Taylor Publishing, 1991), 37.

5.* Throughout this chapter I designate locations with the names by which they are known today.

6. Non-Chinese workers helped build many of these lines as well. Lines I cite as being built by the Chinese are those for which it is possible to document the role of a significant Chinese workforce in their construction.

7.* In addition to building the Central Pacific, Chinese laborers worked on several other railroads in the West before 1869, including the Central California Railroad in 1858, the San Jose–San Francisco line in 1860, and the East Side Railroad in Oregon in 1868. The survey presented here, however, is confined to railroads they built, rebuilt, and maintained between 1869 and 1889.

8.* "Lo! The Poor Indian! Where Are the Philanthropists?" *Crisis,* September 15, 1869, 265; Donald C. Conley, "The Pioneer Chinese of Utah" (master's thesis, Brigham Young University, 1976), Manuscript Archive, Special Collections, Paper 4616, 64, Brigham Young University Library.

9. *Colorado Families: A Territorial Heritage* (Denver: Colorado Genealogical Society, 1981), 116; John M. Monnett, "Sou, Chin Lin (1837–1894)," in *Encyclopedia of the Great Plains*, ed. David J. Wishart (Lincoln: University of Nebraska Press, 2004), http://plainshumanities.unl.edu/encyclopedia/doc/egp.asam.020.

10.* H. K. Wong, *Gum Sahn Yum—Gold Mountain Men* (Brisbane, CA: Fong Brothers Printing, 1987), 217.

11. *Rocky Mountain News* (Denver, CO), June 1, 1870, 4.

12. "Pacific Slope Brevities," *San Francisco Chronicle,* June 11, 1870, 1.

13.* "News of the Week," *Prairie Farmer* (Chicago), June 11, 1870, 184; "The West," *Cleveland Leader,* June 6, 1870, 1.

14.* Sue Fawn Chung, *Chinese in the Woods: Logging and Lumbering in the American West* (Urbana: University of Illinois Press, 2015), 157.

15.* Any rail line on which the Chinese worked is included in this list even if the line was not ultimately completed.

16. Alabama and Chattanooga Railroad: "The Chinese: The Coming Man Arrived," *Cincinnati Daily Gazette*, July 18 1870, 1; Bodie and Benton Railroad: Chung, *Chinese in the Woods*, 173; California and Oregon Railroad: *"California— Marysville," *Daily Alta California* (San Francisco), January 24, 1870, 1; California Central Narrow Gauge Railroad: *Russian River Flag* (Healdsburg, CA), May 29, 1873; California Pacific Railroad: *San Francisco Chronicle*, September 25, 1869, 2; California Southern Railroad (Atchison, Topeka & Santa Fe): Andrew Griego, "Rebuilding the California Southern Railroad: The Personal Account of a Chinese Labor Contractor, 1884," *Journal of San Diego History* 25, no. 4 (Fall 1979), https://www.sandiegohistory.org/journal/79fall/railroad.htm; Carson and Colorado Railroad: *Reno (NV) Gazette-Journal*, June 21, 1880, 2; Carson Tahoe Railroad: Chung, *Chinese in the Woods*, 163; Celilo and Wallula Railroad: *Seattle Post-Intelligencer*, February 18, 1880, 3; Cincinnati, Hamilton, and Dayton Railroad: *Indianapolis Sentinel*, July 9, 1873, 7; Clear Lake and San Francisco Railroad: *Napa Register*, October, 26, 1883, cited in Charlotte T. Miller, "Grapes, Queues and Quicksilver" (unpublished paper, Napa City-County Library, Napa, CA, 1966), 32; Coronado Railroad: *Joe Ditler, "Ode to the Coronado Train...," *Coronado (CA) Times*, June 11, 2014; Cuyamaca and Eastern Railroad (also known as the San Diego, Cuyamaca, and Eastern): "Another Railroad for Arizona," *Weekly Journal-Miner* (Prescott, AZ), January 16, 1889, 4; Denver and Rio Grande Western Railroad: Barbara Voss, "The Historical Experience of Labor: Archeological Contributions to Interdisciplinary Research on Chinese Railroad Workers," *Historical Archaeology* 49, no. 1 (2016): 4, and Christopher W. Merritt, "The Continental Backwaters of Chinese Railroad Worker History and Archaeology: Perspectives from Montana and Utah" (paper presented at the Archaeology Network Workshop of the Chinese Railroad Workers in North America Project, Stanford University, Stanford, CA, October 11, 2013); Denver Pacific Railroad: Monnett, "Sou, Chin Lin," and Rhonda Beck, *Union Station in Denver* (Mt. Pleasant, SC: Arcadia Publishing, 2016), chap. 3; East Side Railroad: *Daily Inter Ocean* (Chicago), August 21, 1869, 2; Echo and Park City Railroad: "Chinese Labor in Utah," *Silver Reef (UT) Miner*, June 10, 1882, 2, cited in Conley, "Pioneer Chinese of Utah," 30; Eureka and Palisade Railroad: Loren B. Chan, "The Chinese in Nevada: A Historical Survey, 1856–1970," *Nevada Historical Quarterly* 25 (Winter 1982): 283, and Gilbert H. Kneiss, *Bonanza Railroads* (Stanford, CA: Stanford University Press, 1941), 84, 85; Fremont, Elkhorn, and Missouri Valley Railroad: City of Deadwood, South Dakota, official home page, accessed July 11, 2016, http://www.cityofdeadwood.com/index.asp; Galveston, Harrisburg, and San Antonio Railroad: Marilyn

Dell Brady, *Asian Texans* (College Station: Texas A&M University Press, 2004), 12, and George C. Werner, "Galveston, Harrisburg and San Antonio Railway," *Handbook of Texas Online,* Texas State Historical Association website, accessed July 11, 2016, https://tshaonline.org/handbook/online/articles/eqg06; Great Northern Railway: *Kornel S. Chang, *Pacific Connections: The Making of U.S.–Canadian Borderlands* (Berkeley: University of California Press, 2012), 38, 39, and Willard G. Jue, "Chin Gee-Hee, Chinese Pioneer Entrepreneur in Seattle and Toishan," *Annals of the Chinese Historical Society of the Pacific Northwest* 1 (1983): 32–34; Houston and Texas Central Railroad: *Edward J. M. Rhoads, "The Chinese in Texas," *Southwestern Historical Quarterly* 81, no. 1 (July 1977): 3; Lake Valley Railroad: Chung, *Chinese in the Woods,* 164; Loma Prieta Railroad: Rick Hamman, *California Coastal Central Railways* (Boulder, CO: Pruett, 1980), 33–43, and Chung, *Chinese in the Woods,* 180; Long Island Railroad: *"Chinese Workers for Seventy Cents a Day," *New York Sun,* June 4, 1876, 1; Los Angeles and Independence Railroad: *Owyhee Daily Avalanche* (Silver City, ID), January 5, 1875, 2, and *New Orleans Times,* March 26, 1875, 8; Memphis and Selma Railroad: *Cincinnati Daily Enquirer,* June 30, 1871, 2; Mendocino Railroad: [Testimony of labor contractor on Mendocino Railroad], *Report of the Joint Special Committee to Investigate Chinese Immigration,* February 27, 1877, 44th Congress, 2nd Session, Senate Report No. 689 (Washington, DC: US Government Printing Office, 1877), 720; Midland Railroad: *"Coolies in New Jersey. Arrival of One Hundred and Fifty Chinamen at Pompton, N.J.—Three Hundred More on the Way—What the Contractors Pay for Their Services," *New York Times,* September 22, 1870, 3; Monterey and Salinas Valley Railroad: "The Monterey & Salinas Valley Railroad," Monterey County Historical Society website, accessed July 11, 2016, http://mchsmuseum.com/railroadm&sv.html; Napa and Lake Railroad: *St. Helena (CA) Star,* September 3, 1886, cited in Miller, "Grapes, Queues and Quicksilver," 32; Napa Valley Railroad: Mariam Hansen, "St. Helena's Chinese Heritage," June 2011, St. Helena (California) Historical Society website, http://shstory-oldsite.lyndabanks.net/wp-content/uploads/2011/12/Chinese-Heritage-of-St-Helena-by-Mariam-Hansen.pdf; Nevada-California-Oregon Railway: Chan, "Chinese in Nevada," 303, 304; Nevada County Narrow Gauge Railroad: Marvin Elliott Locke, "A History of the Nevada County Narrow Gauge Railroad" (master's thesis, University of California, Los Angeles, 1962), and *Nevada City (CA) Transcript,* February 18 and 27, 1875, and May 24, 1876, cited in Chung, *Chinese in the Woods,* 176; New Orleans, Mobile, and Texas Railroad: *"More Chinese," *Galveston (TX) Tri-weekly News,* June 22, 1870, 1; North Pacific Coast Railroad: *Sausalito Weekly Herald,* April 12, 1873, cited in Bruce MacGregor, *The Birth of California Narrow Gauge: A Regional Study of the Technology of Thomas and Martin Carter* (Stanford, CA: Stanford University Press, 2003), 89, 620n; Northern Pacific Railway: *Robert R. Swartout Jr., "Kwangtung to Big Sky: The Chinese Experience in Frontier Montana," in *Chinese on the American*

Frontier, ed. Arif Dirlik (Lanham, MD: Rowman & Littlefield, 2001), 370; Ohio
and Mississippi Rail Road: *Leavenworth (WI) Times,* July 22, 1869, 2; Oregon and
California Railroad: "Chinese Going to the Front," *Oregonian* (Portland), July 17,
1871, 3; Oregon Central Railroad: *Oregon Central Railroad Records, Online
Archive of California website, accessed April 25, 2017, http://www.oac.cdlib.org/fin
daid/ark:/13030/c8p55q8m/; Oregon Pacific Railroad (formerly Corvallis and
Yaquina Railroad): *Seattle Post-Intelligencer,* April 16, 1884, 1; Oregon Railway and
Navigation Company: *"Pacific Coast News," *Salt Lake Tribune*, September 24, 1881,
5; Pacific Coast Railway: Wong, *Gum Sahn Yum,* 7; Puyallup Railroad: *Seattle Post-
Intelligencer*, February 6, 1877, 3; Rutherford and Clear Lake Railroad: *Napa Register,*
October 26, 1883, and *St. Helena (CA) Star,* September 24, 1886, both cited in
Miller, "Grapes, Queues, and Quicksilver," 32, 33; San Diego and San Bernardino
Railroad: *"Work on the S. D. & S. B. R. R.," *San Diego Union*, November 26, 1872, 3;
San Francisco and North Pacific Railroad: "Chinese at Tiburon," *Daily Alta Califor-
nia* (San Francisco), February 4, 1886, 1; San Luis Railroad (also called the Port San
Luis Railroad): Wong, *Gum Sahn Yum,* 4, 6, 7; San Luis Obispo and Santa Maria
Valley Railroad: Wong, *Gum Sahn Yum,* 27; San Rafael and San Quentin Railroad:
American Traveller (Boston), September 11, 1869, 4; Santa Clara Valley Railroad:
MacGregor, *Birth of California Narrow Gauge,* 374; Santa Cruz Railroad: Susan Leh-
mann, "Transportation: Railroads and Streetcars," *Santa Cruz History,* Santa Cruz
Public Libraries/Local History website, accessed April 26, 2017, http://www.santa
cruzpl.org/history/articles/53/; Santa Cruz and Felton Railroad: Lehmann, "Trans-
portation"; Seattle and Walla Walla Railroad: *Seattle Post-Intelligencer*, September
15, 1876, 3; Selma and Gulf Railroad: "Arrival of 160 of Koopmanschap's Celestials in
St. Louis," *Cincinnati Daily Enquirer,* August 24, 1870, 5; Selma, Rome, and Dalton
Railroad: *Emporia (KS) Weekly News,* September 10, 1869, 4; Shenandoah Railroad:
Wheeling (WV) Register, March 30, 1880, 3; Sierra Valley and Mohawk Railroad:
*Timebook, Sierra Valley & Mohawk Railroad Collection, 1886–1887, California
State Railroad Museum; South Pacific Coast Railroad: *California Farmer and Journal of Useful Sciences,* November 22, 1877, 1; Southern Pacific Railroad: *"6000 Chi-
namen. How They Are Controlled by One Man. Judge, Jury, Executioner. Some Incidents of the Work of the Southern Pacific Railroad," *Philadelphia Times,* March 13,
1882, 15; Stockton and Copperopolis Railroad: Judith Marvin, Julia Costello, and
Salvatore Manna, "Stockton and Copperopolis Railroad," in *Angels Camp and Copperopolis* (Mt. Pleasant, SC: Arcadia Publishing, 2009), 115; Texas and Pacific Railway: *Dixon (IL) Sun,* January 8, 1873, 4; Thurston County Railroad: *Seattle Post-
Intelligencer*, September 6, 1877, 3; Utah and Pleasant Valley Railroad: Merritt, "The
Continental Backwaters," 3; Utah, Idaho, and Montana Railroad: *Clarence A.
Reeder, Jr., *The History of Utah's Railroads, 1869–1883,* chapter 6, UtahRails.net website, accessed April 26, 2017, http://utahrails.net/reeder/reeder-chap6.php, and

Brigham D. Madsen and Betty M. Madsen, "Corinne, The Fair: Gateway to Montana Mines," *Utah Historical Quarterly* 37, no. 1 (Winter 1969): 119, 120; Utah Northern Railroad: "The Utah Northern R.R.," *Helena (MT) Weekly Herald*, August 12, 1875, 2; Virginia and Truckee Railroad: *Chung, *Chinese in the Woods*, 40, 45, 170; Walla Walla and Columbia River Railroad: *"Walla Walla's Chinatown, 1860s–1950s— Once the Largest Chinese Community in Eastern Washington," Walla Walla 2020 website, accessed April 27, 2017, http://ww2020.net/historic-sites/chinatown/; West Side Railroad: *Oregon State Journal* (Eugene), July 5, 1879, 5; Western Pacific Railroad: *"Oakland Jottings," *San Francisco Chronicle*, June 3, 1870, 1, and "The Western Pacific Railroad," *San Francisco Bulletin* 13, no. 107 (August 1869): 3; Yosemite Mountain Sugar Pine Railroad: Chung, *Chinese in the Woods*, 175.

17.* To the best of my ability I have listed the lines by the names by which the railroads were known when the Chinese began working on them between 1869 and 1889.

18.* Thomas J. Noel, "All Hail the Denver Pacific: Denver's First Railroad," *Colorado Magazine* 50, no. 3 (Spring 1973): 91–116.

19.* Gilbert H. Kneiss, *The Virginia and Truckee Railway*, Hathi Trust Digital Collection (Boston: Railway and Locomotive Historical Society, 1938).

20.* "Olympia's Historic Chinese Community," http://olympiahistory.org/ olympias-historic-chinese-community-links, cited in Chung, *Chinese in the Woods*, 175.

21.* Edward J. M. Rhoads, "Chinese," *Handbook of Texas Online*, Texas State Historical Association website, accessed July 11, 2016, https://tshaonline.org/handbook/ online/articles/pjc01.

22. James B. Hedges, "The Colonization Work of the Northern Pacific Railroad," *Mississippi Valley Historical Review* 13, no. 3 (December 1926): 311–342; Swartout, "Kwangtung to Big Sky," 370–372; Carlos A. Schwantes, *The Pacific Northwest: An Interpretive History* (Lincoln: University of Nebraska Press, 1996), 177.

23.* *Santa Cruz County, California: Illustrations Descriptive of Its Scenery, Fine Residences, Public Buildings, Manufactories, Hotels, Farm Scenes, Business Houses, Schools, Churches, Mines, Mills, Etc., with Historical Sketch of the County* (San Francisco: W. W. Elliott & Co., 1879), 55, 70, 76; Chung, *Chinese in the Woods*, 153, 154, 160, 168, 173, 180; Hamman, *California Central Coast Railways*, 21–25, 41–45, 58–61; MacGregor, *Birth of California Narrow Gauge*, 7, 89, 98, 134, 135, 142, 143, 533–536, 544–555, 559; Richard Orsi, "Railroads in the History of California and the Far West: An Introduction," *California History* 70, no. 1 (Spring 1991): 2–11.

24.* "New York," *Hartford (CT) Daily Courant*, September 24, 1870, 3; *Trenton (NJ) State Gazette*, September 23, 1870, 2; "Chinese Laborers for the Midland Railroad," *New York Evangelist*, April 7, 1870, 8.

25.* "Coolies in New-Jersey," *New York Times*, September 22, 1870, 3.

26. "Coolies in New-Jersey," *New York Times,* September 22, 1870, 3.

27.* "Chinamen Working for Seventy Cents a Day," *New York Sun,* June 4, 1876, 1; Vincent F. Seyfried, *The Long Island Rail Road: A Comprehensive History. Part 1: South Side R. R. of L. I.* (self-pub., 1961), 62, 63. I am grateful to Long Island Railroad historian Carol Mills for having suggested that they were probably working on Long Island's Southern Railroad the year that the Long Island Railroad, the Flushing Railroad, the Central Railroad, and the South Side Railroad merged under the ownership of the Poppenhusen family.

28. MacGregor, *Birth of California Narrow Gauge,* 445, 446, 533.

29.* "The Heathen Chinese: The Experiment of the Cincinnati, Hamilton and Dayton Railroad with the Celestials," *Cincinnati Enquirer,* July 7, 1873, 5.

30. "Our Celestial Cousins," *Indianapolis Sentinel,* July 9, 1873, 7.

31.* *Saginaw (MI) News,* October 21, 1882, 4; *Elkhart (IN) Weekly Review,* October 19, 1882, 3.

32. "The Chinese in New York: How They Live and Make Money—Good Wages," *New York Times,* March 6, 1880.

33.* George Frederick Seward, *Chinese Immigration in Its Social and Economical Aspects* (New York: Charles Scribner's Sons, 1881), 108; Mary Roberts Coolidge, *Chinese Immigration* (1909; repr., New York: Arno Press, 1969), 367.

34. *Lake Village Times* (Laconia, NH), August 12, 1871, 4.

35. "Arrival of 160 of Koopmanschap's Celestials in St. Louis," *Cincinnati Daily Enquirer,* August 24, 1870, 5.

36. *Railroad Gazette,* September 10, 1870, quoted in Alton K. Briggs, "The Archaeology of 1882 Labor Camps on the Southern Pacific Railroad, Val Verde County, Texas" (master's thesis, University of Texas, Austin, 1974), 30.

37. *Railroad Gazette,* September 10, 1870.

38. "Business and Industrial Items," *Baltimore Sun,* September 28, 1878, suppl. 2.

39. "Sayings and Doings," *Harper's Bazaar,* October 16, 1869, 664.

40. "Chinese in West Virginia. Tunneling for the Chesapeake and Ohio Railroad," *New-York Daily Tribune,* July 28, 1870, 9.

41.* *Alexandria (VA) Gazette,* July 29, 1870, 2.

42.* *Richmond (VA) Whig,* September 16, 1870, 3.

43.* Charles Seymour to C. P. Huntington, August 20, 1870, Chesapeake and Ohio Railroad Company Papers, Western Reserve Historical Society, Cleveland, OH; "Chinese—Their Cost as Laborers—None on the Chesapeake and Ohio Railroad as Yet," *Richmond (VA) Whig,* September 16, 1870, 3.

44. Scott Reynolds Nelson, *Steel Drivin' Man—John Henry—the Untold Story of an American Legend* (New York: Oxford University Press, 2006).

45. Lucy M. Cohen, *Chinese in the Post–Civil War South: A People without a History* (Baton Rouge: LSU Press, 1984), 84, 85.

46. *St. Louis Democrat,* December 30, 1869, quoted in *Daily Alta California* (San Francisco), January 11, 1870; Cohen, *Chinese in the Post–Civil War South,* 85.

47. Charles Nordhoff, *California: For Health, Pleasure and Residence* (New York: Harper & Brothers, 1873), 190.

48. Griego, "Rebuilding the California Southern Railroad."

49. "The Flowery Kingdoms: Four Hundred and Sixty-Three Celestials in St. Louis," *National Aegis* (Worcester, MA), July 23, 1870, 2; "Arrival of 160 of Koopmanschap's Celestials in St. Louis," *Cincinnati Daily Enquirer,* August 24, 1870, 5.

50. See, for example, Alfred Hart, photo 313, *Chinese Camp, Brown's Station,* Chinese Railroad Workers in North America Project website, accessed April 27, 2017, http://web.stanford.edu/group/chineserailroad/cgi-bin/wordpress/977/.

51.* *New York Sun,* June 4, 1876; Voss, "The Historical Experience of Labor," 1, 12; John Molenda, "Aesthetically-Oriented Archaeology" (paper presented at the Archaeology Network Workshop of the Chinese Railroad Workers in North America Project, Stanford University, Stanford, CA, October 11, 2013); Briggs, "Archaeology," 53; Lynn Furnis and Mary L. Mainery, "An Archaeological Strategy for Chinese Workers' Camps in the West: Method and Case Study," *Historical Archaeology,* 49, no. 1 (2015): 75, 82; R. Scott Baxter and Rebecca Allen, "The View from Summit Camp," *Historical Archaeology,* 49, no. 1 (2015): 36–39.

52. Briggs, "Archaeology," 53.

53.* Briggs, "Archaeology," 83–88.

54. *Nevada State Journal* (Reno), August 17, 1883, 2.

55. Briggs, "Archaeology," 88–90.

56. *Pittsburgh (PA) Daily Commercial Appeal,* August 10, 1872, 2; *Inter Ocean* (Chicago), August 21, 1872, 1; *Daily Phoenix* (Columbia, SC), September 17, 1872, 3.

57. A correspondent who claimed to have employed the Chinese as laborers "in numbers from one to seventy-five or eighty at a time [during] a residence of sixteen years in California" notes that "they are an educated people," adding that "one who cannot read and write fluently, in their own language, is hard to find." *Morning Republican* (Little Rock, AR), September 11, 1869, 2. A similar comment—referring to the Chinese in China—appeared in the *Chicago Tribune,* where the paper's special correspondent writing from Omaha, Nebraska, on June 8, 1869, opined, "Every Chinaman can not only read and write, but understands something about the laws of his country." Aaron About, "The Chinese. Their Wealth, Education, and Civilization—Shall We Encourage Chinese Immigration?" *Chicago Tribune,* June 14, 1869, 2.

58. "Sayings and Doings," *Harper's Bazaar,* October 16, 1869, 664.

59. The *New York Post* story is cited in "Chinamen as Free Immigrants," *Massachusetts Spy* (Worcester), July 30, 1869, 2. He added, "Their friends at home have accurate knowledge of the country; and those who now make arrangements to cross the

Pacific in search of employment know where they are going and what to expect when they arrive in San Francisco. They could not be induced to go to Cuba or Peru."

60. "[The Chinese railroad builders] do not drink, fight, or strike." Nordhoff, *California: For Health, Pleasure and Residence,* 189.

61. "Pacific Coast Doings," *Hartford (CT) Daily Courant,* August 31, 1869, 3.

62. MacGregor, *Birth of California Narrow Gauge,* 97, 98.

63. "City Intelligence," *Sacramento Daily Union,* August 7, 1869, 5.

64. *Galveston (TX) Tri-weekly News,* September 2, 1870, quoted in Rhoads, "The Chinese in Texas," 6.

65. *Daily Rocky Mountain Gazette* (Helena, MT), December 19, 1871, 2.

66.* "Pacific Railroad Notes," *San Francisco Bulletin,* October 22, 1875, 1; *Santa Cruz* (CA) *Weekly Sentinel,* October 30, 1875, 2.

67. "Persons and Things," *New Haven (CT) Register,* May 16, 1881, 2.

68.* "A Chinese Strike," *Los Angeles Herald,* July 19, 1887, 1.

69. *San Bernardino (CA) Daily Courier,* July 24, 1887, 1.

70. Chung, *Chinese in the Woods,* 158. Chung cites the *San Francisco Bulletin,* July 5, 1867, noting that "After withholding food deliveries, the strike was settled on the old basis of thirty dollars per month with twelve-hour work days with the quiet understanding that their pay would be increased. A month later, they received thirty-five dollars for a twenty-six-day month, and the Chinese felt that they had helped James Strobridge 'save face' (an old Chinese concept) by delaying the raise and, in the traditional Confucian manner, accepting a compromise figure."

71. Chan, "Chinese in Nevada," 284.

72.* *Rocky Mountain News* (Denver), September 7, 1883, 2.

73. *Fresno (CA) Morning Republican,* July 11, 1889, 3.

74. "Items by Telegraph," *Jackson (MI) Citizen,* August 31, 1875, 7.

75. *St. Cloud (MN) Journal,* September 9, 1875, 2.

76. *Weekly Oregon Statesman* (Salem), August 19, 1870, 3.

77.* "A Tunnel Horror: Nearly Thirty Men Killed by an Explosion in San Francisco," *Cleveland Plain Dealer,* November 19, 1879, 2; MacGregor, *Birth of California Narrow Gauge,* 542–557.

78. "Washington Territory," *Oregonian* (Portland), March 11, 1881, 1.

79. "A Snow Slide. Eight Chinamen Buried Alive, Ten Barely Escape," *New Haven* (CT) *Register,* January 31, 1881, 1.

80. "General Intelligence," *New Hampshire Patriot and State Gazette* (Concord), December 14, 1882, 4.

81. *San Francisco Chronicle,* September 22, 1885, 8.

82.* "Attacks on the Chinese," *Cleveland Plain Dealer,* September 30, 1869, 1.

83. *Weekly Nonpareil* (Council Bluffs, IA), August 19, 1870, 3.

84. *Sacramento Daily Union,* November 17, 1870, 1.

85. *Columbus (GA) Daily Enquirer,* April 15, 1871, 2.

86. "The Chinese in California: Wanton Attack on Railroad Laborers," *New York Evening Post,* August 9, 1873, 4.

87.* Chung, *Chinese in the Woods,* 178.

88. Chan, "Chinese in Nevada," 284.

89. Chan, "Chinese in Nevada," 294.

90. "Murdered by Apaches," *New Southwest and Grant County Herald* (Silver City, NM), January 7, 1882, 3.

91. "News Notes," *Jackson City Patriot* (Jackson, MI), January 7, 1882, 1.

92. *Wilkes-Barre (PA) Times Leader,* September 28, 1885, 1.

93. *Charleston (SC) News and Courier,* September 4, 1885, 2.

94. *Charleston (SC) News and Courier,* September 4, 1885, 2.

95. Wallace A. Clay, interview by Donald C. Conley, December 2, 1974, in Donald C. Conley, "Pioneer Chinese of Utah," 45.

96. Wallace A. Clay, interview by Donald C. Conley, December 2, 1974, in Donald C. Conley, "Pioneer Chinese of Utah," 45.

97. Wong, *Gum Sahn Yum,* 98.

98. Wong, *Gum Sahn Yum,* 98. See also Jeanne Pfaelzer, *Driven Out: The Forgotten War against Chinese Americans* (Berkeley: University of California Press, 2008).

99. "Livermore Tunnel," *Sacramento Daily Union,* February 9, 1869, 3.

100.* "Railroad Items," *Daily Inter Ocean* (Chicago), June 14, 1869, 3.

101. "Western Pacific Railroad: Progress of the Work of Construction," *San Francisco Daily Morning Chronicle,* June 4, 1869, 1.

102.* "Western Pacific Railroad," *San Francisco Daily Morning Chronicle,* June 4, 1869, 1.

103. "Famed Tehachapi Loop Is an Engineering Marvel," *Tehachapi (CA) News,* May 17, 2016, http://www.tehachapinews.com/history-culture/2016/05/17/famed -tehachapi-loop-is-an-engineering-marvel.html.

104. "6000 CHINAMEN. How They Are Controlled by One Man. JUDGE, JURY, EXECUTIONER. Some Incidents of the Work of the Southern Pacific Railroad," *Philadelphia Times,* March 13, 1882, 15.

105. Remi Nadeau, *City Makers: The Story of Southern California's First Boom, 1868–1876* (Coronado del Mar, CA: Trans-Anglo Books, 1977), 124–131, 141–147; Thomas W. Chinn, Him Mark Lai, and Philip C. Choy, eds., *A History of the Chinese in California: A Syllabus* (San Francisco: Chinese Historical Society of America, 1969), 46.

106.* "Tearing Down the Mountain. How the Northern Pacific Railroad Is Driving the Iron Horse Through the Mountains," *Weekly Hawk-eye* (Burlington, IA), October 12, 1882, 4.

107. "Tearing Down the Mountain," *Weekly Hawk-eye* (Burlington, IA), October 12, 1882, 4.

108. Robert R. Swartout Jr., "Kwangtung to Big Sky," 371.

Chapter 18

Acknowledgments: This research was supported by the Social Sciences and Humanities Research Council of Canada. I would like to thank Gordon Chang and other participants in the Chinese Railroad Workers in North America Project for their comments on an earlier version of this essay.

1. The term *railway* in Canadian usage is slightly different from that in American English, but it is kept in reference to the transcontinental rail line in Canada.

2. The Chinese construction of the Canadian Pacific Railway is the major subject of the following sources: David Chuenyan Lai, *Canadian Steel, Chinese Grit: No Chinese Labour, No Railway* (n.p.: National Executive Council of the *Canadian Steel, Chinese Grit* Heritage Documentary, 1998); Julia Ningyu Li, ed., *Canadian Steel, Chinese Grit: A Tribute to the Chinese Who Worked on Canada's Railroads More Than a Century Ago*, trans. John Howard-Gibbon and Jan Walls (Toronto: Paxlink Communications, 2000); Lily Siewsan Chow, *Blood and Sweat over the Railway Tracks: Chinese Labourers Constructing the Canadian Pacific Railway, 1880–1885* (Vancouver, BC: Chinese Canadian Historical Society of British Columbia and Initiative for Student Teaching and Research in Chinese Canadian Studies, University of British Columbia, 2014). This subject has also been discussed in part or in passing by the following works: Li Donghai (David T. H. Lee), *Jianada Huaqiaoshi* [A history of Chinese in Canada] (Taipei: Zhonghua dadian bianyinhui, 1967), 123–156; Pierre Berton, *The Last Spike: The Great Railway, 1881–1885* (Toronto: McClelland & Stewart, 1971), 194–205; James Morton, *In the Sea of Sterile Mountains: The Chinese in British Columbia* (Vancouver, BC: J. J. Douglas, 1974), 79–142; Edgar Wickberg et al., *From China to Canada: A History of the Chinese Communities in Canada* (Toronto: McClelland & Stewart, 1982), 20–24; Patricia Roy, "A Choice between Evils: The Chinese and the Construction of the Canadian Pacific Railway in British Columbia," in *The CPR West*, ed. Hugh A. Dempsey (Vancouver, BC: Douglas & McIntyre, 1984), 13–34; Huang Kunzhang and Wu Jinping, *Jianada Huaqiao Huaren shi* [A history of Chinese sojourners and settlers in Canada] (Guangzhou: Guangdong gaodeng jiaoyu chubanshe, 2001), 36–43; Li Quan'en (David Lai), Ding Guo, and Jia Baoheng, *Jianada Huaqiao yiminshi* [History of Chinese migration to Canada] (Beijing: Renmin chubanshe, 2013), 28–44. For a conceptual analysis of the Chinese diaspora, see Zhongping Chen, "Building the Chinese Diaspora across Canada: Chinese Diasporic Discourse and the Case of Peterborough, Ontario," *Diaspora* 13, no. 2–3 (2004): 185–188, 195, 196, 205, 206.

3. Roy, "A Choice between Evils," 22–24; Patricia Roy, *A White Man's Province: British Columbia Politicians and Chinese and Japanese Immigrants, 1858–1914* (Vancouver, BC: University of British Columbia Press, 1989), 47.

4. Berton, *The Last Spike*, 185, 196; W. Kaye Lamb, *History of the Canadian Pacific Railway* (New York: Macmillan, 1977), 65.

5. *Inland Sentinel* (Emory, BC), August 12, 1880.

6. *Census of Canada, 1880–81* (Ottawa: Maclean, Roger & Co., 1882), vol. 1, 298, 405.

7. *British Columbian* (New Westminster, BC), June 3, 1882.

8. Li, *Jiananda Huaqiaoshi*, 127. The old-style spellings of the Lees' names are from historical documents.

9. *Li Wenzhuan gong jiasheng* [Genealogy of the revered Mr. Li Wenzhuang] (n.p., 1902), vol. 1, 12a; vol. 4, 38a, 39b, 42b, 57a. Taishan County was called Xinning County until 1914.

10. Li, *Jiananda Huaqiaoshi*, 127; Lai, *Canadian Steel, Chinese Grit*, 4, 28; David Chuenyan Lai, *Chinese Community Leadership: Case Study of Victoria in Canada* (Singapore: World Scientific Publishing, 2010), 18, 37, 38, 54, 55. Lun Chung & Co. also appeared as Lung Chong & Co. in historical documents.

11. The Lees' companies and their interrelations will be detailed in Zhongping Chen, "Chinese Labor Contractors and Laborers of the Canadian Pacific Railway in 1880–1885" (forthcoming).

12. *Inland Sentinel* (Yale, BC), December 21, 1882.

13. *Colonist* (Victoria, BC), May 23, 1885.

14. *British Columbian* (New Westminster, BC), April 1, 1882. The news report was reprinted from *Global* (Toronto), March 8, 1882.

15. *Report of the Royal Commission on Chinese Immigration: Report and Evidence* (Ottawa, 1885), 84; *Colonist* (Victoria, BC), March 25, 1951.

16. The best research on this subject is Roy, "A Choice between Evils," 23–33.

17. *Colonist* (Victoria, BC), April 13, 1880.

18. H. J. Cambie to J. M. R. Fairbairn, September 4, 1923, AM 1519, No. PAM 1923–22, "Canadian Pacific Railway Construction: Employment of Chinese [by] Andrew Onderdonk," City of Vancouver Archives.

19. *Colonist* (Victoria, BC), June 2, 1880.

20. *Sacramento Daily Union*, November 11, 1881. The newspaper report misspelled Ward's first name as "Dehanshaw."

21. Roy, "A Choice between Evils," 27.

22. *Report of the Royal Commission*, 84.

23. Roy, "A Choice between Evils," 32.

24. *Report of the Royal Commission*, 396, 398; Wickberg et al., *From China to Canada*, 22.

25. Li, Ding, and Jia, *Jianada Huaqiao yiminshi*, 33; Li, *Canadian Steel, Chinese Grit*, 172, 173, 186, 187; "Building the Canadian Pacific Railway," Library and Archives Canada, 2005, accessed February 18, 2016, https://www.collectionscanada.gc.ca/settlement/kids/021013-2031.3-e.html; Chow, *Blood and Sweat over the Railway Tracks*, 26, 27.

26. The figures on Chinese immigrants for 1881 to 1883 are from *Report of the Royal Commission*, 398; the number for 1884 is from *Colonist* (Victoria, BC), December 31, 1884.

27. *Standard* (Victoria, BC), May 28, 1880; *Colonist* (Victoria, BC), June 2 and 15, July 5, 10, and 11, 1880; May 31, June 7 and 23–25, July 1, 1885.

28. *Mainland Guardian* (New Westminster, BC), May 15, 1880, May 21, August 6 and 13, 1881.

29. Chen, "Chinese Labor Contractors and Laborers of the Canadian Pacific Railway in 1880–1885." A detailed statistical analysis of the Chinese immigrants and railroad workers in British Columbia during the CPR-building era will be included in this paper.

30. More detailed evidence will be presented in Chan, "Chinese Labor Contractors and Laborers of the Canadian Pacific Railway in 1880–1885."

31. Wickberg et al., *From China to Canada*, 22.

32. *Inland Sentinel* (Emory, BC), May 29, June 17, July 15, 1880, (Yale, BC) May 26, 1881; *Colonist* (Victoria, BC), December 11, 1881.

33. *British Columbian* (New Westminster, BC), June 3, 1882, September 22, 1883; *Colonist* (Victoria, BC), June 17, 1883, October 15, 1884; *Report of the Royal Commission*, 148.

34. *Inland Sentinel* (Yale, BC), July 6, 1882.

35. *Colonist* (Victoria, BC), October 15, 1884.

36. Berton, *The Last Spike*, 200; Wickberg et al., *From China to Canada*, 22; Li, *Canadian Steel, Chinese Grit*, 28, 29; Chow, *Blood and Sweat over the Railway Tracks*, 27, 28.

37. Wickberg et al., *From China to Canada*, 22. The book claims that "there appears to have been little organization among the Chinese railway workers" on the CPR line.

38. *Inland Sentinel* (Emory, BC), May 29, 1880.

39. *Inland Sentinel* (Emory, BC), May 29, June 10 and 17, July 15, 1880.

40. *British Columbian* (New Westminster, BC), May 17, 1882. This quotation is from Chief Engineer Edward G. Tilton of Onderdonk's company.

41. *Inland Sentinel* (Emory, BC), August 19, 1880.

42. *Inland Sentinel* (Emory, BC), August 26, 1880.

43. Leung Chik-wai (Liang Zhihuai), *Ye Chuntian xiansheng zhuanji* [Biography of Yip Sang] (Hong Kong, 1973), 5 (English section), 11 (Chinese section).

44. "The 1852 and 1881 Historical Censuses of Canada," Research Program in Historical Demography website, accessed February 18, 2016, http://www.prdh .umontreal.ca/census/en/main.aspx. The Chinese data were extracted from the 1881 Canadian census in Yale district (No. 189) by Patrick Frisby, the computing consultant at the University of Victoria. I thank Mr. Frisby and Dr. Eric Sager for their help with my research on the census data.

45. *Inland Sentinel* (Yale, BC), May 4, June 15, July 6, August 10, December 14, 1882.

46. *British Columbian* (New Westminster, BC), February 14 and 17, May 9, 1883. The articles indicate that other reports placed the number of Chinese victims of the first landslide as high as fifty.

47. *Inland Sentinel* (Yale, BC), December 21, 1882.

48. *Inland Sentinel* (Yale, BC), December 21, 1882.

49. *Inland Sentinel* (Yale, BC), November 30, 1882.

50. *Colonist* (Victoria, BC), April 3, 1883.

51. *British Columbian* (New Westminster, BC), January 24, 1883.

52. *Inland Sentinel* (Yale, BC), February 1, 1883.

53. *Inland Sentinel* (Yale, BC), February 15, March 1, 1883; *Colonist* (Victoria, BC), June 8, 1883.

54. *Inland Sentinel* (Yale, BC), March 1, 1883. The report and comments from this edition were reprinted in *British Columbian* (New Westminster, BC), March 7, 1883, and *Colonist* (Victoria, BC), March 8, 1883.

55. *Inland Sentinel* (Yale, BC), February 22, March 1 and 8, 1883, March 13, 1884; *Report of the Royal Commission*, 364.

56. Dian H. Murray and Qin Baoqi, *The Origins of the Tiandihui: The Chinese Triads in Legend and History* (Stanford, CA: Stanford University Press, 1994), 89–150; Sue Fawn Chung, "Between Two Worlds: The Zhigongtang in the United States, 1860–1949," in *Empire, Nation, and Beyond: Chinese History in Late Imperial and Modern Times, A Festschrift in Honor of Frederic Wakeman*, ed. Joseph W. Esherick, Wen-hsin Yeh, and Madeleine Zelin (Berkeley: Institute of East Asian Studies, University of California, 2006), 234.

57. *Daily Alta California* (San Francisco), January 5, 1854; *Daily California Chronicle* (San Francisco), January 30, 1854.

58. Bennet Bronson and Chuimei Ho, *Coming Home in Gold Brocade: Chinese in Early Northwest America* (Seattle: Chinese in Northwest America Research Committee, 2015), 125–26; Stanford M. Lyman, W. E. Willmott and Berching Ho, "Rules of A Chinese Secret Society in British Columbia," in *Bulletin of the School of Oriental and African Studies* 27, no. 3 (1964): 536; Liu Boji, *Meiguo Huaqiao shi* (A history of the Chinese in the United States of America) (Taibei: Xingzhengyuan qiaowu yuanweihui, 1976), 428–30; Yingying Chen, "In the Colony of Tang: Historical

Archaeology of Chinese Communities in the North Cariboo District, British Columbia, 1860s–1940s" (Ph.D. Diss., Simon Fraser University, 2002), 288–90.

59. Henry G. Langley, *The San Francisco Directory for the Year Commencing April 1879* (San Francisco: Francis, Valentine & Co., 1879), 932; Bronson and Ho, *Coming Home in Gold Brocade*, 125–126. A self-publication of the Chee Kong Tong (CKT) dates its origin in Canada to the founding of a Hongshun tang in 1863 by Chinese immigrants in Barkerville, a major gold mining town in the Cariboo Region. It also provides a list of CKT lodges in Victoria and nine other towns and cities in British Columbia, including three gold mining towns in the Cariboo Region, in 1877–1881. Such claims, however, lack confirming documentation; see Jian Jianping, *Zhongguo Homgmen zai Jianada* (The Chinese Freemasons in Canada) (Vancouver, BC: Zhongguo Hongmen Minzhidang zhu Jianada zongzhibu, 1989), 13.

60. *Inland Sentinel* (Yale, BC), August 30, 1883.

61. *Inland Sentinel* (Yale, BC), December 6, 1883.

62. G. Robin Hooper, *Gold, Stone Vaults, and Railways: An Archaeological Site Assessment in Old Yale Chinatown, British Columbia, 1994–1996* (Surrey, BC, 1996), 6, 7.

63. *Inland Sentinel* (Yale, BC), April 12, 1883.

64. *Inland Sentinel* (Yale, BC), November 30, 1882, April 24, 1884.

65. Jian, *Zhongguo Hongmen zai Jianada*, 13.

66. Morton, *In the Sea of Sterile Mountains*, 84; Lai, *Chinese Community Leadership*, 55; Chow, *Blood and Sweat over the Railway Tracks*, 73, 74.

67. *Colonist* (Victoria, BC), May 15 and 17, 1881; *Inland Sentinel* (Yale, BC), May 19, 1881.

68. *Inland Sentinel* (Yale, BC), May 19, 1881.

69. *Inland Sentinel* (Yale, BC), July 28, 1881.

70. *Mainland Guardian* (New Westminster, BC), May 21, July 30, 1881.

71. *Colonist* (Victoria, BC), July 3, July 17, 1881; W. Dewdney to British Columbia provincial secretary, November 2, 1882, in GR-526, Provincial Secretary, box 22, Correspondence Inward 1882, letter No. 374/82, British Columbia Archives, Victoria.

72. *Colonist* (Victoria, BC), August 9 and 16, 1881.

73. *Inland Sentinel* (Emory, BC), October 20, 1881.

74. *Dominion Pacific Herald* (New Westminster, BC), October 22, 1881.

75. *British Columbian* (New Westminster, BC), February 14, 1883.

76. Different reports about the event appeared in several English-language newspapers in British Columbia, but the *Inland Sentinel* (Yale, BC) published the most detailed report on May 17, 1883. Further details are taken from the Chinese testimonies at the court of assizes in Victoria on September 3, 1883; see *Colonist* (Victoria, BC), September 4, 1883.

77. *Colonist* (Victoria, BC), May 18, June 1 and 13, September 4, 1883.

78. Wong Hau-hon, "Reminiscences of an Old Chinese Railroad Worker," trans. Him Mark Lai, in *Chinese American Voices: From the Gold Rush to the Present,* ed. Judy Yung, Gordon H. Chang, and Him Mark Lai (Berkeley: University of California Press, 2006), 41. Wong worked on the CPR from 1882 to at least 1884. He provided the total number of labor gangs.

79. *Inland Sentinel* (Yale, BC), December 6, 1883. The report recorded Won Alexander Cumyow's name only as W. Cumyow. For his background, see Wickberg et al., *From China to Canada,* 14.

80. *Inland Sentinel* (Yale, BC), January 31, 1884.

81. See Berton, *The Last Spike,* 206–208. Pierre Berton discusses the financial crisis of Onderdonk's company around 1883 but attributes the solution of the crisis merely to the cost-cutting strategy of Michael Haney, who was hired to manage the railroad construction in March 1883.

82. Berton, *The Last Spike,* 206.

83. *Inland Sentinel* (Yale, BC), August 30, 1883; *Colonist* (Victoria, BC), December 6, 1883.

84. *Colonist* (Victoria, BC), June 8, 1883.

85. *Inland Sentinel* (Yale, BC), December 13, 1883.

86. *Colonist* (Victoria, BC), December 7, 1883.

87. *British Columbian* (New Westminster, BC), December 19, 1883, January 23, 1884.

88. *Inland Sentinel* (Yale, BC), January 17, 1884.

89. *Colonist* (Victoria, BC), January 18, 1884.

90. *Colonist* (Victoria, BC), January 10, October 15, 1884; *Inland Sentinel,* December 20, 1883.

91. *Inland Sentinel* (Yale, BC), March 20, 1884. The report was reprinted from the *Mainland Guardian* (New Westminster, BC).

92. *Inland Sentinel* (Yale, BC), December 13 and 20, 1883; *British Columbian* (New Westminster, BC), December 8 and 12, 1883, February 27, 1884; *Colonist* (Victoria, BC), January 1 and 5, 1884.

93. Lai, *Chinese Community Leadership,* 21, 22, 52–55, 240. Lai's book incorporates major sources and arguments of his previously published articles, which are listed in the bibliography of the cited work.

94. Lai, *Chinese Community Leadership,* 27–30. Lai's book includes a copy of the Chinese circular and a partial translation.

95. Donation Records to the CCBA, 1884–1885, No. 1977-084, Chinese Consolidated Benevolent Association fonds, box 5, folders 5 and 10, University of Victoria Archives, Victoria, BC.

96. *British Columbia Directory for 1884–85* (Victoria, BC: R. T. Williams, 1885), 85, 86, 166; "Petition of Chinese Residents of the City of Victoria, B.C. for an

Amendment of a Certain Act," 1894, RG6F, No. 1629, Library and Archives Canada, Ottawa.

97. *British Columbia Directory for 1884–85*, 85, 183; *Colonist* (Victoria, BC), March 18, 1882; "Leave Permits Issued by the Association to Chinese Residing in Thirty-Two Cities or Towns in B.C. [1884–1885]," No. 1977-084, Chinese Consolidated Benevolent Association fonds, box 2, folders 4–8, 11, 13, 14; box 3, folder 7; box 5, folders 7, 10, 11, University of Victoria Archives, Victoria, BC. On the books of leave permits issued by Kwong On Wo & Co., the names of Yale and Savona's Ferry were transliterated as Kezhe and Shenshi huali, respectively. Kwong On Wo & Co. in Kamloops was probably first founded as the "Chinese warehouse" of Onderdonk's railroad company in late 1884; see *Inland Sentinel* (Kamloops, BC), August 21, 1884. Until 1887 it advertised its "general merchandise and contractor's supplies," which may refer to its previous relations with the CPR's contractors; see *Inland Sentinel* (Kamloops, BC), February 19, 1887.

98. *Colonist* (Victoria, BC), April 1, 1884; *British Columbian* (New Westminster, BC), April 2, 1884; *Inland Sentinel* (Kamloops, BC), August 28, 1884.

99. *Colonist* (Victoria, BC), October 15, 1884.

100. Apart from in Roy, "A Choice Between Evils," this issue is discussed in John Murray Gibbon, *The Romantic History of the Canadian Pacific: The Northwest Passage of Today* (New York: Tudor Publishing, 1937), 281, 282.

101. *Port Moody Gazette*, April 5, 1884.

102. Berton, *The Last Spike*, 302–306; Gibbon, *The Romantic History of the Canadian Pacific*, 282.

103. *Colonist* (Victoria, BC), February 20, 1885.

104. *British Columbian* (New Westminster, BC), April 16 and 23, 1884.

105. Gibbon, *The Romantic History of the Canadian Pacific*, 295.

106. *Colonist* (Victoria, BC), September 5, October 2 and 3, 1885.

107. *Report of the Royal Commission*, 161, 366; *Colonist* (Victoria, BC), July 22, 1884; *Inland Sentinel*, May 22, 1884. In 1884 Huang Sic Chen indicated that $70 was needed for a trip between Hong Kong and British Columbia, see *Report of the Royal Commission*, 161.

108. *British Columbian* (New Westminster, BC), July 22, 1885.

109. *Colonist* (Victoria, BC), September 13, 1885.

110. Lieutenant Governor of British Columbia, "Chinese Discharged from the Canadian Pacific Railway Works in British Columbia, 30 Nov.–9 Dec. [1885]," RG6 A1, vol. 60, file 2235, Library and Archives Canada, Ottawa.

111. J. A. Chapleau, "Report to Council re. Destitute Condition of Certain Chinese Railway Labourers in British Columbia," February 10, 1886, in RG6 A1, vol. 60, file 2235, Library and Archives Canada, Ottawa.

112. Li, *Jianada Huaqiaoshi*, 132–135.

113. *Colonist* (Victoria, BC), January 22, 1886.

114. "Subscription book Kuang hsu 12th year [1886]," No. 1977-084, Chinese Consolidated Benevolent Association fonds, box 6, folder 4, University of Victoria Archives, Victoria, BC.

115. Sun Fang and Liu Xuhua, *Haiwai hongmen yu xinhai geming* [The Hong Fraternal Society overseas and the 1911 Revolution] (Beijing: Zhongguo zhigong chubanshe, 2011), 95–190.

Chapter 19

1. United States Bureau of the Census, *Ninth (1870) and Tenth (1880) Census of the United States,* State of Nevada, Washington, DC. (Hereafter, NV Census 1870 and 1880.)

2. See, for example, Erika Lee, *At America's Gates: Chinese Immigration during the Exclusion Era, 1882–1943* (Chapel Hill: University of North Carolina Press, 2003); and Charles McClain, ed., *Chinese Immigrants and American Law* (New York: Garland, 1994).

3. Daniel W. Levy, "Classical Lawyers and the Southern Pacific Railroad," *Western Legal History* 9, no. 2 (Summer/Fall 1996): 176–226.

4. John C. Hudson, "Towns of the Western Railroads," *Great Plains Quarterly* 2, no. 1 (1982): 41–54.

5. Robert Corbett, "Unionville, Nevada: Pioneer Mining Camp," *Nevada Historical Review* 2, no. 1 (1974): 7–26.

6. Nevada Historical Census (digital online database of Nevada's population, 1860–1920), https://library.unr.edu/census (modified from the original database by the Nevada State Historical Preservation Office). The Special 1875 Nevada State Census showed 290 Chinese in Humboldt County. Nevada State Legislature, *Appendix to the Journals of the Assembly and Senate, Seventh Session, 1875, Special Census of the Population.* (Hereafter, Nevada State Special Census, 1875.)

7. NV Census, 1870.

8. *Silver State* (Winnemucca, NV), December 5, 1878.

9. NV Census, 1870 and 1880. For example, in 1880 in Humboldt Township, railroad foreman Anton Frakes lived next door to six Chinese railroad workers.

10. James R. Chew, "Boyhood Days in Winnemucca, 1901–1910," *Nevada Historical Society* 4, no. 3 (September 1998): 206–209. The designation of "prostitute" or "harlot" was in support of the forthcoming 1875 Page Act aimed at prohibiting the immigration of Chinese women, all of whom, it was commonly believed, were prostitutes.

11. Pacific Railway Act, July 1, 1862, US Statutes at Large, vol. XII, 489ff; Heywood Fleisig, "The Central Pacific Railroad and the Railroad Land Controversy,"

Journal of Economic History 35, no. 3 (September 1975): 552–566; Nevada State
Legislature, "Report," 1915.

12. Elmer P. Rusco, "Riot in Unionville, Nevada: A Turning Point," in *The Chinese
in America: A History from Gold Mountain to the New Millennium,* ed. Susie Lan
Cassel (Walnut Creek, CA: AltaMira Press, 2001); and Elmer P. Rusco, "Chinese
Massacre of 1866," *Nevada Historical Society Quarterly* 45, no. 1 (2002): 3–30.

13. Humboldt Deed Index, 1883, Humboldt County Registrar's Office.

14. Beth Amity Au, "Home Means Nevada: The Chinese in Winnemucca,
Nevada, 1870–1950, a Narrative History" (master's thesis, University of California,
Los Angeles, 1993); Immigration and Naturalization Service, Chinese Partnership
Papers, RG 85, no. 13561/371, National Archives and Records Administration, San
Bruno, CA; Nevada State Census, 1870–1930.

15. *Silver State* (Winnemucca, NV), January 28, 1877.

16. Sue Fawn Chung, *Chinese in the Woods: Logging and Lumbering in the American West* (Urbana: University of Illinois Press, 2015), 66–70.

17. This is based on a survey of applications for duplicate certificates by cooks on
file in National Archives and Records Administration, San Bruno and Riverside.
See, for example, Soo Hoo Him, Box 4, #166, who earned $40 per month and Chew
Wing, Box 3, #102, who earned $35–40 per month. National Archives and Records
Administration Chinese Exclusion Files, Riverside.

18. *Silver State* (Winnemucca, NV), May 29, 1884.

19. Immigration and Naturalization Service, Record Group 85, file 12017/15290,
National Archives and Records Administration, San Bruno, CA. See also "Obituary:
Charley Chew Yee," *Nevada State Journal,* December 8, 1954, for the distribution of
Charley Chew Yee's estate.

20. Note that the family followed the traditional Chinese *ci* naming system. One
presumes that the man's name was Yee Chew but was reversed (last to first) by immigration officials.

21. William Chew's son, William F. Chew Jr., became interested in his family's
history and wrote *Nameless Builders of the Transcontinental* (Victoria, BC: Trafford,
2004).

22. Thomas was a soldier in the Chinese army, and when his colleaques spied one
of his brothers in an American military uniform, they mistakenly thought he was
Thomas and took him before the commanding officer. After much confusion and the
assistance of a translator, the situation was straightened out, and Thomas finally was
in contact with his birth family. The family tried for years to get a visa for him, but
this was not possible until after Nixon's normalization of relations with China.

23. Chew, "Boyhood Days in Winnemucca," 1998. Manuscript, located in the
Winnemucca Public Library and UNLV Special Collections, is dated 1981.

24. Au, "Home Means Nevada," 1993; Thomas Chinn, *Bridging the Pacific: San Francisco Chinatown and Its People* (San Francisco: Chinese Historical Society of America, 1989), 102; Jay P. Marden, "The History of Winnemucca" (unpublished manuscript, Humboldt County Library, Winnemucca, NV, 2005).

25. *Silver State* (Winnemucca, NV), May 24, 1890. Like most Chinese women of her era, Chew Fong Low did whatever job was necessary to make a living.

26. *Silver State* (Winnemucca, NV), July 8, 1913. See Madeline Hsu, *Dreaming of Gold, Dreaming of Home: Transnationalism and Migration between the United States and South China, 1882–1943* (Stanford, CA: Stanford University Press, 2000), for Chen's story.

27. Lucie Cheng and Liu Yuzun with Zheng Dehua, "Chinese Emigration, the Sunning Railway and the Development of Toisan," *Amerasia Journal* 9, no. 1 (1982): 59–74; *Copper Ore* (McGill, NV), July 21, 1913.

28. *Humboldt Star* (Winnemucca, NV), September 30, 1929, obituary.

29. In 1999 John Fong, a restaurant owner in Carlin, Nevada, told me that the Southern Pacific/Union Pacific continued a longtime practice of paying subsidies to his Chinese restaurant in order to have food service available for passengers and crew members twenty-four hours a day. This subsidy enabled him to operate his restaurant at a profit. Carlin was a major railroad repair and supply center.

30. Marden, "The History of Winnemucca," 2005. Jay P. Marden, who studied the local newspapers carefully, wrote about the first shipment of bones back to China:

> In March, 1870, the Chinese funeral car was working in Winnemucca on a siding near the present Bridge Street grade crossing preparing the deceased for their final trip home. Two car loads of bones, prepared and boxed in the most approved manner, and labeled with the appropriate Chinese characters, which gave the name, date of death, and tong to which they belonged, were shipped from Winnemucca to San Francisco at that time. From San Francisco the remains were shipped to China by boat.

31. On burial practices in nearby Carlin, Nevada, see Sue Fawn Chung, Fred P. Frampton, and Timothy Murphy, "Venerate These Bones: Chinese American Burial Practices as Seen in Carlin, Nevada," in *Chinese American Death Rituals,* ed. Sue Fawn Chung and Patricia Wegars (Walnut Creek, CA: AltaMira Press, 2005). Carlin is a major train center located west of Elko.

32. *Silver State* (Winnemucca, NV), February 17, 1888.

33. Shawn R. Hall, "A History of Elko, Nevada," *Northeastern Quarterly* 95, no. 3 (1995): 127. I am indebted to Shawn Hall, Anton Primeaux, Fred Frampton, and the staff of the Northeastern Nevada Museum for their assistance in this section on Elko and to the Forest Service, University of Nevada, Las Vegas, and Elko County Commission for grants that enabled me to search county records.

34. Hall, "A History of Elko, Nevada," 128.

35. Hall, "A History of Elko, Nevada," 138. The cook was not listed in the United States census.

36. Hall, "A History of Elko, Nevada," 146; Clarence I. Walther, "Ice Harvesting in Elko," *Northeastern Nevada Quarterly* 92, no. 1 (1992): 7–16.

37. On the disappearing railroad towns, see Hudson, "Towns of the Western Railroads," 1982.

38. NV Census, 1870.

39. Hall, "A History of Elko, Nevada," 129.

40. Nevada State Special Census, 1875.

41. The nine merchants were Car Sing, age thirty; Joy Loy, age forty; Hop Sing, age twenty-six; Sing Chung, age thirty-six; Lee King, age thirty-nine; Wun, age forty; Ah Tim, age thirty; Ah Sung, age thirty; and Ah Lung, age twenty-three. Ah Lung had a prosperous business and was probably connected to a firm in Hong Kong or Guangdong that supplied his products.

42. United States Census Manuscript, 1870 for Nevada, Elko County. The manuscript lists individuals, households, occupations, relationships, date of immigration, and other details not available in the summary census.

43. Immigration and Naturalization Service, Record Group 85, files 13561/224 and 9649/203, Box 49, National Archives and Records Administration, San Bruno, CA.

44. *Elko Daily Free Press,* March 6, 1961, and August 2, 1994.

45. Lester Mills, *Sagebrush Saga* (Springville, UT: Art City Publishing, 1956), 89.

46. *Elko Free Press,* May 3, 1902. China Sing does not appear in any census list.

47. Opie Rundle Burgess, "Quong Kee: Pioneer of Tombstone," *Arizona Highways* 25, no. 7 (July 1949): 14–16; Lawrence W. Cheek, "A Place Called Bisbee," *Arizona Highways* 65, no. 2 (February 1989): 4–11; Nevada State Census, 1870.

48. The Arizona Historical Society has photographs of Quong Kee in western dress, indicating that he adopted aspects of American culture early, and a photograph of his wife, who was European American.

49. Howard Hickson and Terry Hickson, "Elko General Hospital: The Beginnings and the End," *Northeastern Nevada Historical Society Quarterly* 1 (2007) 3, 4. Histories of Elko do not mention the Chinese hospital.

50. Elko Mortuary Records, 1870, Elko County Recorder's Office.

51. NV Census, 1870.

52. Anton Sohn, *The Healers of 19th Century Nevada: A Compendium of Medical Practitioners* (Reno: University of Nevada Press, 1997), 29.

53. *Elko Independent,* November 29, 1873.

54. Index to Marriage Records. Book 1, Elko Recorder's Office.

55. *Elko Free Press,* February 16, 1917.

56. Charles Paul Keyser, "Reminiscences of Elko—circa 1890," manuscript 4-6-30, dated October 1958, Northeastern Nevada Museum, Elko, NV.

57. Chung and Wegars, 2005; James William Hefferon, "Bad Eye: Last of the Central Pacific Chinese Workers Left in Elko, Nevada," 1986, originally online but withdrawn due to its derogatory comments; copy available from the Asian American Comparative Collection, University of Idaho.

58. In 1981 the Chinese Historical Society of America and the Republic of China, with support from the state of Nevada, dedicated an elaborate marble marker with the inscription in Chinese and English in the James C. Lillard Railroad Park in Sparks, Nevada, honoring the Chinese CPRR workers and Nevada's Chinese population.

Chapter 20

Acknowledgments: The author would like to thank Wingston Chan, a great-grandson of Chin Gee Hee, for his many contributions to this essay. He was generous in offering his time, his memories, and his personal research on the family history. I would also like to thank Gordon H. Chang for his comments and the American Council of Learned Societies and the Harry Frank Guggenheim Foundation for financial support.

1. William F. Chew, *Nameless Builders of the Transcontinental Railroad* (Victoria, BC: Trafford, 2004); Annian Huang, ed., *The Silent Spikes: Chinese Laborers and the Construction of North American Railroads,* trans. Zhang Juguo (Beijing: China Intercontinental Press, 2006).

2. Kornel Chang, *Pacific Connections: The Making of the U.S.-Canadian Borderland* (Berkeley: University of California Press, 2012), 36; Judy Yung, Gordon H. Chang, and Him Mark Lai, *Chinese American Voices: From the Gold Rush to the Present* (Berkeley: University of California Press, 2006), 125; "China Willing to Have Road," *San Francisco Call,* July 29, 1905; "Recent Reports Unsatisfactory," *San Francisco Call,* August 13, 1905; "Secures Millions to Build Road," *San Francisco Call,* April 7, 1907; Willard Jue, "Biographic Sketch," Willard Jue Papers, Chin Gee Hee Subgroup, box 1, folder 9, University of Washington Special Collections, Seattle, 1–6.

3. Madeline Yuan-yin Hsu, *Dreaming of Gold, Dreaming of Home: Transnationalism and Migration between the United States and South China, 1882–1943* (Stanford, CA: Stanford University Press, 2000), 156; Todd Stevens, "Brokers between Worlds: Chinese, Merchants, and Legal Culture in the Pacific Northwest, 1852–1925" (PhD diss., Princeton University, 2003, ProQuest Dissertations, UMI 305309871), 31; Jue, "Biographic Sketch," 1.

4. Wingston Chan, personal communication, November 16, 2015; Jue "Biographic Sketch," 1.

5. Wingston Chan, personal communication, September 15, November 16, 2015;

Mae Ngai, "Chinese Gold Miners and the 'Chinese Question' in Nineteenth-Century California and Victoria," *Journal of American History* 101, no. 4 (2015): 1087; Erika Lee, *The Making of Asian America: A History* (New York: Simon & Schuster, 2015), 64; Yong Chen, *Chinese in San Francisco, 1850–1943: A Transpacific Community* (Stanford, CA: Stanford University Press, 2000), 2–44; Shih-Shah Henry Tsai, *The Chinese Experience in America* (Bloomington: Indiana University Press, 1986), 34, 35.

6. Gunther Paul Barth, *Bitter Strength: A History of the Chinese in the United States, 1850–1870* (Cambridge, MA: Harvard University Press, 1974), 66–69; Theresa A. Sparks, *China Gold* (Fresno, CA: Academy Library Guild, 1954), 25; Wingston Chan, personal communication, November 16, 2015.

7. Huie Kin, *Reminiscences* (Peingpin, China: San Yu Press, 1932), 3–22; see also Stevens, "Brokers between Worlds," 22.

8. Tsai, *The Chinese Experience in America*, 10; Kin, *Reminiscences*, 25.

9. Lorraine Baker Hildebrand, *Straw Hats, Sandals, and Steel: The Chinese in Washington State* (Seattle: Washington State American Revolution Bicentennial Commission, 1977), 23.

10. Stevens, "Brokers between Worlds," 22; "In the Matter of the Application of Chin Gee Hee," March 26, 1905, Chin Gee Hee, Immigration Case File, ca. 1900–1920, box 9, no. 139–157, Chinese Exclusion Case File, RG85, National Archives, Pacific Alaska Region, Seattle, 1. (Hereafter cited as CGH Case File.)

11. US Census Bureau, North San Juan, Nevada County, California, Records of the Bureau of the Census, 1880, Record Group 29, National Archives, Washington, DC, NARA microfilm publication T9, roll 70; Chin Gee Hee, "Account and Letterbook," Willard Jue Papers, Chin Gee Hee Subgroup, box 1, folder 12, University of Washington Special Collections, Seattle, 158.

12. "In the Matter of the Application of Chin Gee Hee," March 26, 1905, CGH Case File, 2.

13. Erika Lee, *At America's Gate: Chinese Immigration during the Exclusion Era, 1882–1943* (Chapel Hill: University of North Carolina Press, 2005), 175; Kornel Chang, "Transpacific Borderlands and Boundaries: Race, Migration and State Formation in the North American Pacific Rim, 1882–1917" (PhD diss., University of Chicago, 2007, ProQuest Dissertations, UMI 3272988), 116.

14. Robert Edward Wynne, *Reaction to the Chinese in the Pacific Northwest and British Columbia, 1850–1910* (New York: Arno Press, 1978), 42.

15. Robert E. Ficken and Charles Pierce LeWarne, *Washington: A Centennial History* (Seattle: University of Washington Press, 1988), 180. This description was written nine years after Chin left the mill.

16. Robert E. Ficken, *Washington Territory* (Pullman: Washington State University Press, 2002), 128.

17. Chin Gee Hee, "Account and Letterbook," 158–162.

18. Wynne, *Reaction to the Chinese,* 42; US Census Bureau, Seattle, King, Washington Territory, 1880, microfilm, roll: 1396; Family History Film: 1255396, Enumeration District: 0071880, *1880 United States Federal Census.*

19. Stevens, "Brokers between Worlds," 23.

20. Stevens, "Brokers between Worlds," 27.

21. US Census Bureau, Seattle, King County, Washington Territory, Records of the Bureau of the Census, 1880, Record Group 29, National Archives, Washington, DC, NARA microfilm publication T9, roll 1396; Doug Chin, "How and Why the Chinese Associations Developed," *International Examiner,* January 20, 1982, 10, 11.

22. Chin, "Account and Letterbook," 4–22.

23. Hsu, *Dreaming of Gold,* 159.

24. Chin, "Account and Letterbook," 159–161.

25. Chin, "Account and Letterbook," 159–161.

26. Chin, "Account and Letterbook," 162.

27. Chang, *Pacific Connections,* 38; A. L. Blake to A. W. Bash, July 11, 1883, San Juan Subport, US Custom Service, RG 36, National Archives Pacific Alaska Region, Seattle.

28. Mae Ngai, *The Lucky Ones: One Family and the Extraordinary Invention of Chinese America* (Boston: Houghton Mifflin Harcourt, 2010), 224. On the distinction between Chinese restriction and exclusion, see Beth Lew-Williams, *The Chinese Must Go: Violence, Exclusion, and the Making of the Alien in America* (Cambridge, Mass: Harvard University Press, 2018).

29. A. L. Blake to A. W. Bash, July 11, 1883, San Juan Subport, US Customs Service, RG 36, National Archives Pacific Alaska Region, Seattle; "Tried to Bribe Dr. Gardner," *San Francisco Call,* September 22, 1897.

30. Adam McKeown, "Ritualization of Regulation: The Enforcement of Chinese Exclusion in the United States and China," *The American Historical Review* 108, no. 2 (April 2003): 377–403.

31. "In the Matter of the Application of Chin Gee Hee," March 26, 1905, CGH Case File; Passenger and Crew Lists of Vessels Arriving at Seattle, Washington, Records of the Immigration and Naturalization Service, 1787–2004, Record Group 85, National Archives, Washington, DC, NARA Microfilm Publication M1383.

32. "Recent Reports Unsatisfactory," *San Francisco Call,* August 13, 1905.

33. Doug Chin, "How and Why the Chinese Associations Developed," *International Examiner,* January 20, 1982, 10, 11.

34. "Tried to Bribe Dr. Gardner," *San Francisco Call,* September 22, 1897.

35. Chin Gee Hee, "Account and Letterbook," n.p.

36. Owyang Ming to Thomas Bayard, November 5, 1885, Notes from the Chinese Legation in the United States to the Department of State, 1863–1906, microfilm, vol.

1, no. 98, RG39, M98, Pacific Regional Branch of the National Archives, San Bruno, CA.

37. "In the District Court Holding Terms at Seattle," November 4, 1885, *Territory v. Chin Gee Hee,* King County, Case No. 4694, Puget Sound Regional Archives, Bellevue, WA.

38. "The Victory Is Ours," *Seattle Daily Call,* November 5, 1885; Wynne, *Reaction to the Chinese,* 220.

39. Wynne, *Reaction to the Chinese,* 237.

40. Jules Alexander Karlin, "The Anti-Chinese Outbreaks in Seattle, 1885–1886," *Pacific Northwest Quarterly* 39, no. 2 (1948): 103–129.

41. Karlin, "The Anti-Chinese Outbreaks in Seattle," 113.

42. Edward Wood, "In the Matter of Chinese Quarters at Coal Creek," in Watson Squire to Thomas Bayard (and enclosed documents), July 17, 1886, Miscellaneous Letters of the Department of State 1789–1906, M179, microfilm, roll 707, General Records of the Department of State, RG59, National Archives and Records Administration, Washington, DC; Ouyang Ming to Chinese Consul at San Francisco, October 20, 1885, part 2, item 9, in Zhu Shijia, *Meiguo pohai hua gong shiliao* [Historical Materials Concerning America's Persecution of Chinese Laborers] (Beijing: Zhonghua shuju, 1958), 80–81.

43. Yen Hoon Chang to Thomas Bayard, March 2, 1888, *Papers Relating to the Foreign Relations of the United States, Part 1* (Washington, DC: US Government Printing Office, 1889), 389, 390; Zhang Yinhuan (Cheng Yen Hoon), *Sanzhou riji* [Diary of the Three Continents] (Jingdu: Yuedong xinguan, 1896).

44. Chang Yen Hoon to Thomas Bayard, May 4, 1886, Notes from the Chinese Legation in the United States to the Department of State, 1863–1906, microfilm, vol. 2, no. 98, RG39, M98, Pacific Regional Branch of the National Archives, San Bruno, CA.

45. Chang Yen Hoon to Thomas Bayard, February 7, 1887, Notes from the Chinese Legation in the United States to the Department of State, 1863–1906, microfilm, vol. 2, no. 98, RG39, M98, Pacific Regional Branch of the National Archives, San Bruno, CA.

46. [Historian] Herbert Hunt to Secretary of the Treasury William Gibbs McAdoo, May 20, 1916, box 1, file 3d, "Chinese in Tacoma," Washington Historical Society, Tacoma, WA. The indemnity paid to the Chinese government totaled $276,619.75, but this sum was meant to redress "all losses and injuries sustained by Chinese subjects within the United States at the hands of residents thereof," not just the riots in Washington Territory in 1885 and 1886.

47. Jue, "Biographical Sketch," 3.

48. Two historians wrote to the Chinese and US governments attempting to discover what happened to this money, but neither found any indication that it reached

the Chinese merchants. See Hunt to McAdoo, May 20, 1916, box 1, file 3d, "Chinese in Tacoma," Washington Historical Society, Tacoma, WA; T. L. Tsui to Jules Karlin, March 19, 1951, box 1, file 3d, "Chinese in Tacoma," Washington Historical Society, Tacoma, WA.

49. Chang, *Pacific Connections,* 35, 36; "In the Matter of the Application of Chin Gee Hee," March 26, 1905, CGH Case File, 6.

50. Chin, "Account and Letterbook," 192.

51. Lucie Cheng, Liu Yuzun, and Zheng Dehua, "Chinese Emigration, the Sunning Railway and the Development of Toisan," *Amerasia* 9, no. 1 (1982): 59–74; Hsu, *Dreaming of Gold,* 156, 166; Yung, Chang, and Lai, *Chinese American Voices,* 125–128; Chin, "Account and Letterbook," 231–232.

52. Hsu, *Dreaming of Gold,* 157; Shelley Sang-Hee Lee, *Claiming the Oriental Gateway: Prewar Seattle and Japanese America* (Philadelphia: Temple University Press, 2011), 27, 28; Cheng, Yuzun, and Dehua, "Chinese Emigration, the Sunning Railway and the Development of Toisan," 59–74.

53. Cheng, Yuzun, and Dehua, "Chinese Emigration, the Sunning Railway and the Development of Toisan," 59–74; Hsu, *Dreaming of Gold,* 156–175; Yung, Chang, and Lai, *Chinese American Voices,* 125–128.

54. Jue, "Biographical Sketch," 6.

Chapter 21

1. From conversations that the author has had with Chinese Americans over the years.

2. Stanford Historical Photograph Collection (SC1071), series 2, box 3, sf14853, Special Collections, Green Library, Stanford University; William Speer, *The Oldest and Newest Empire: China and the United States* (Hartford, CT: S. S. Scranton and Co., 1870), 527, 528. The main biographies of Stanford contain only brief mention of his relationship to the Chinese. See, for example, George T. Clark, *Leland Stanford: War Governor of California, Railroad Builder and Founder of Stanford University* (Stanford, CA: Stanford University Press, 1931); and Norman E. Tutorow, *The Governor: The Life and Legacy of Leland Stanford,* 2 vols. (Spokane, WA: Arthur H. Clark Co., 2004).

3. Leland Stanford, "Inaugural Address," The Governers Gallery, January 10, 1862, accessed September 13, 2017, http://governors.library.ca.gov/addresses/08-Stanford .html.

4. Leonard L. Richards, *The California Gold Rush and the Coming of the Civil War* (New York: Knopf, 2007), 175. In office Stanford elaborated on these views. See "Letter from Governor Stanford," *Sacramento Daily Union,* April 12, 1862; and "Governor's Message, January 7, 1863," *Sacramento Daily Union,* January 8, 1863.

5. William Hoy, "Moy Jin Mun—Pioneer," *Chinese Digest,* May 15, 1936, 10, 11, 14;

Wilson Chu, "The Chinese Railroad Men," *N.Y.C. Chinatown Reunion Newsletter*, May 11, 2006; and Thomas W. Chinn, *Bridging the Pacific: San Francisco Chinatown and Its People* (San Francisco: Chinese Historical Society of America, 1989), 71–74.

6. Stephen Magagnini, "Chinese Transformed 'Gold Mountain'—Few Struck It Rich, but Their Work Left an Indelible Mark," *Sacramento Bee*, January 18, 1998; Julie A. Cain, "The Chinese and the Stanfords: Immigration Rhetoric in Nineteenth-Century California" (master's thesis, California State University, East Bay, June 2011, 29–32); and "Dr. Yee Fung Cheung," *Journal of Sierra Nevada History and Biography* 5 (Winter 2013): 1. The author thanks Julie Cain for generously sharing her research and insights. The author also thanks the great-grandsons of Yee Fung Cheung, Herbert and Franklin Yee, who shared extensive family memorabilia with him. These materials can be found at the Chinese Railroad Workers in North America Project at Stanford, in the Yee Family Scrapbooks.

7. George Kraus, "Chinese Laborers and the Construction of the Central Pacific," *Utah Historical Quarterly* 37, no. 1 (Winter 1969): 41–57; Leland Stanford, "Statement Made to the President of the United States, and Secretary of the Interior, of the Progress of the Work," October 10, 1865 (Sacramento, CA: H. S. Crocker & Co., 1865); "Leland Stanford Report to Stockholders, July 13, 1865," *Sacramento Daily Union*, July 14, 1865.

8. Oscar Lewis, *The Big Four: The Story of Huntington, Stanford, Hopkins, and Crocker, and of the Building of the Central Pacific* (New York: Knopf, 1938), 69–71.

9. Leland Stanford, "To the Stockholders of the Central Pacific Railroad Company, July 13, 1865," *Railroad Record*, August 24, 1865, 323, 324.

10. Stanford, "Statement Made to the President of the United States," October 10, 1865.

11. Stanford to Crocker, n.d., cited in John Hoyt Williams, *A Great and Shining Road: The Epic Story of the Transcontinental Railroad* (Lincoln: University of Nebraska Press, 1988) 304, n. 159.

12. E. B. Crocker to Collis Huntington, September 12, 1867, and Huntington to Crocker, October 3, 1867, Letters from Collis P. Huntington to Mark Hopkins, Leland Stanford, Charles Crocker, E. B. Crocker, Charles F. Crocker, and D. D. Cotton [*sic*], from August 20, 1867, to [March 31, 1876], 192908, Huntington Library.

13. Cain, "The Chinese and the Stanfords," 47–51; Kraus, "Chinese Laborers," 47–57; Gerald M. Best, "Rendezvous at Promontory: The 'Jupiter' and No. 119"; and J. N. Bowman, "Driving the Last Spike at Promontory," *Utah Historical Quarterly* 37, no. 1 (Winter 1969): 69–75, 76–101.

14. "The China Mail Line," *Sacramento Daily Union*, January 3, 1867.

15. "The Summit Deserted—a Scramble for Relics" and "Honors to John Chinaman," *San Francisco News Letter and California Advertiser*, May 15, 1869.

16. Barbara Voss, message to author et al., "Research note," n.d. [2016], in author's possession; Cain, "The Chinese and the Stanfords," 65–81; Norman E. Tutorow, *The Governor* 516; *Memorial Addresses Upon the Life and Character of Leland Stanford*, US 53d Congress (Washington, DC: US Government Printing Office, 1894), 15.

17. Bertha Berner, *Mrs. Leland Stanford: An Intimate Account* (Stanford, CA: Stanford University Press, 1934), 92.

18. Berner, *Mrs. Leland Stanford*, 16; Christopher Lowman, "'Our First Chinese': Social Interaction and Potential Archaeological Remains of Chinese Communities at Stanford University," *SCA Proceedings* 27 (2013): 188–192.

19. Berner, *Mrs. Leland Stanford*, 36, 38.

20. Site Report, LUEP-FCF-SHARP5140, October 21, 1998, included in email from Laura Jones to Gordon Chang, October 8, 2016.

21. Denis Kearney, "Appeal from California: The Chinese Invasion," *Indianapolis Times*, February 28, 1878; and Scott Zesch, *The Chinatown War: Chinese Los Angeles and the Massacre of 1871* (New York: Oxford University Press, 2012).

22. *Evening Bulletin* (Philadelphia), November 5, 1877; "The Mob Spirit Threatens," *Sacramento Daily Union*, November 5, 1877.

23. Stanford to H. H. Ellis, n.d., folder 1877, Stanford Papers, Special Collections, Green Library, Stanford University.

24. Denis Kearney, "Kearney at Faneuil Hall," n.d., *Speeches of Dennis [sic] Kearney Labor Champion* (New York: Jesse Haney & Co., 1878), 7.

25. "A Tourist in the Far West: A Month on the Pacific Coast," *New York Times*, February 9, 1878.

26. *Sacramento Daily Union*, March 11, 1878; *Los Angeles Herald*, March 14, 1878; *Daily Alta* (San Francisco), May 8, 1878, and May 10, 1878.

27. *Sacramento Daily Union*, May 13, 1886; Tutorow, *The Governor*, 516, 517. See also newspaper clipping, June 1, 1887, Stanford Family Scrapbooks, 1865–1894, SC0033F, box 6, 58, Special Collections, Green Library, Stanford University; Stanford Interviewed, n.d., n.p., clipping, n.d., n.p., "Gov. Stanford's Reply," n.d., n.p., "The Vina Ranch," *Record Union* (?), July 3, 1886, Stanford Family Scrapbooks, box 32/C, 5, 6, 12, 19. In the late 1880s, other newspapers carried articles that described Stanford's support for anti-Chinese immigration efforts. See, for example, "Senator Stanford's Views," n.d., n.p., Stanford Family Scrapbooks, box 10, 8; "The Uses of Wealth: Senator Stanford's Views—An Office Goes Begging," *Morning Call*, May 6, 1886; Stanford Family Scrapbooks, box 10, 40; "Woman's Labor League," n.d., n.p. The scrapbooks are a multivolume collection of primarily newspaper clippings compiled by the Stanford University Library early in the twentieth century. Many of the clippings are not accompanied by a full citation. The organization of the clippings and volumes is roughly chronological but also haphazard.

28. Tutorow, *The Governor*, 839.

29. Cain, "The Chinese and the Stanfords," 170–176. See also "The Uses of Wealth: Senator Stanford's Views—An Office Goes Begging," n.d., n.p.; "Peaceful California," *Morning Call* (San Francisco), May 6, 1886; and "Woman's Labor League," n.d., n.p., Stanford Family Scrapbooks, box 10, 40, 44, 70, 73; "Senators and Celestials," n.d., n.p.; and clippings, n.d., n.p., Stanford Family Scrapbooks, box 16, 13.

30. *The Tribune*, April 11, 1888, Stanford Family Scrapbooks, boxes 18, 19.

31. "Stanford's Views," *Sacramento Daily Union*, January 16, 1889.

32. Tutorow, *The Governor*, 839.

33. "Stanford Million," *Chicago Journal*, February 1893, Stanford Family Scrapbooks, box 3, 91.

34. "Favors the Chinese," *San Francisco Chronicle*, May 1893; and "Defending the Chinese," *Hartford Post*, May 1893, newspaper clippings, Stanford Family Scrapbooks, box 3, 112.

35. *Columbus Despatch*, May 1893, and *San Francisco Argus*, May 1893, newspaper clippings, Stanford Family Scrapbooks, box 3, 112, 119. See also clippings in scrapbook box 3: *New York Christian Adventure* (?), September 1893, 163; "The Terrors of Immigration," 162; "Chinese in the United States," n.d., 133; "Senator Stanford's Shovel," January 1893, 144; and "Washington Letter: Our Chinese Brethren," *Philadelphia Observer*, May 1893, 127.

36. "Favors the Chinese: Senator Stanford against Restriction," *San Francisco Chronicle*, May 1893, Stanford Family Scrapbooks, box 3, 113.

37. "Honor to Senator Stanford," *Washington Post*, May 1893, clipping in Stanford Family Scrapbooks, box 3, 119. See also Cain, "The Chinese and the Stanfords," 180, 181.

38. "Chinese Flags at Half-Mast," *San Francisco Morning Call*, June 26, 1893, quoted in Cain, "The Chinese and the Stanfords," v, 182, 183; and "China Flag," Stanford Family Scrapbooks, box 4, 36.

39. "As Leland Stanford Sees It," *New York World,* April 1888, Stanford Family Scrapbooks, 14, 70.

40. Stanford to Cornelius Cole, February 9, 1867, quoted in Margaret Holt Mudgett, "The Political Career of Leland Stanford" (master's thesis, Department of History, University of Southern California, January 9, 1933, 76), Special Collections, Green Library, Stanford University.

41. "The China Mail Line," *Sacramento Daily Union*, January 3, 1867.

42. Cain, "The Chinese and the Stanfords," 71–83, 98–110.

43. Cain, "The Chinese and the Stanfords," 143–149. The resort location is now the site of the United States Naval Postgraduate School. Fire destroyed the original hotel.

44. Charles Hodges, "Reminiscences of Stanford University and Its Founders," Charles Hodges Papers, 2499, Stanford University Archives, p. 2; Cain, "The Chinese and the Stanfords," 112–118.

45. "Celebrities at Home: Leland Stanford of California," *Times and Gazette,* June 25, 1887, Stanford Family Scrapbooks, box 14, 35, 36; "The Stanford Museum," *Chicago Mail,* May 16, 1887, Stanford Family Scrapbooks, box 14, 38.

46. Cain, "The Chinese and the Stanfords," 119–122; Ethel Ingalls, "Mrs. Leland Stanford," *Ladies' Home Journal,* February 1892, 3; *Washington Post,* February 1892, Stanford Family Scrapbooks, box 3, 14; and clipping, n.d., n.p., Stanford Family Scrapbooks, 11, 51.

47. Cain, "The Chinese and the Stanfords," 124–132.

48. The affidavit is reproduced in Cain, "The Chinese and the Stanfords," 93; Cecilia Tsu, *Garden of the World: Asian Immigrants and the Making of Agriculture in California's Santa Clara Valley* (New York: Oxford University Press, 2013), 230nn81, 82.

49. Cain, "The Chinese and the Stanfords," 96, 97, 189–191; Robert W. P. Cutler, *The Mysterious Death of Jane Stanford* (Palo Alto, CA: Stanford University Press, 2003), 28, 29.

50. Kong H. Chow, interview, 1969, quoted in Kenneth Chow, "The History of the Chinese in Santa Clara County," in *Chinese Argonauts: An Anthology of the Chinese Contributions to the Historical Development of Santa Clara County,* ed. Gloria Sun Hom (San Mateo, CA: California History Center, 1971), 1–17.

51. Connie Young Yu, letter to author, June 8, 2016; Connie Young Yu email message to author, June 5, 2017, that includes a photo of a 1965 diary page of her mother's that describes the close relationship of the Stanfords with local Chinese.

52. Cain, "The Chinese and the Stanfords," 133–138.

53. Ah Wing, eyewitness account, San Francisco Earthquake and Fire Collection, 1906–1979, SC 206, box 1, folder 21 and 22, Special Collections, Green Library, Stanford University, with revised translation January 2006 and additional translation provided by Keren He, December 30, 2012.

54. Fei Xiaotong, quoted in R. David Arkush and Leo O. Lee, *Land without Ghosts: Chinese Impressions of America from the Mid-Nineteenth Century to the Present* (Berkeley: University of California Press, 1989), 175–181; Gordon H. Chang, "China and the Pursuit of America's Destiny: Nineteenth-Century Imagining and Why Immigration Restriction Took So Long," *Journal of Asian American Studies* 15, no. 2 (June 2012): 145–169.

Glossary

Pinyin	Characters	Notes
dà yīng yuán	大鹰元	Mexican dollars
diāo lóu	碉樓	defensive *diaolou* towers
gōng sī	公司	company
gōng suǒ	公所	family associations
guān dì / guān gōng	关帝/关公	Guan Di/Guan Gong
guān yīn	观音	bodhisattva
guān yǔ / guān yún cháng	关羽/关云长	Guan Yu/Yunchang
huá qiáo	华侨	overseas Chinese
jīn shān	金山	Gold Mountain
jīn shān bó	金山伯	Gold Mountain elderly uncle
jīn shān ér	金山儿	Gold Mountain son
jīn shān kè	金山客	Gold Mountain guest
jīn shān nán	金山男	Gold Mountain man
jīn shān nǚ	金山女	Gold Mountain daughter
jīn shān pó	金山婆	Gold Mountain elderly aunt
jiù jīn shān	旧金山	Old Gold Mountain (San Francisco)
kè jiā	客家	the Hakka people
liǎng	两	Chinese unit of weight

Pinyin	Characters	Notes
lú	庐	Western-style mansions based on the local 3-room, 2-corridor house form
qiáo huì	侨汇	overseas remittance
qiáo xiāng	侨乡	overseas Chinese hometown
ràng tiě	让帖	money-lending deed
shuāng xǐ	双喜	double happiness/double joy
sì yì	四邑	Sze Yap, four former counties of Taishan
táng	堂	secret societies/fraternal brotherhoods/or a branch of a clan
tiān hòu / mā zǔ	天后/妈祖	Empress of Heaven/sea goddess Mazu (*Mazu* means "Maternal Ancestor")
wǔ yì mù yú diào	五邑 木鱼调	"Wooden Fish" folk song
xìn	信	family letters
xīn níng / tái shān	新宁/台山	county in Guangdong Province
xīn níng tiě lù	新宁铁路	Xinning Railroad
yín	银	Chinese unit of currency
yín huì	银会	Chinese money-lending associations
yín xìn	银信	remittance letters
zè zhǐ	仄纸	bank draft
zhì gōng táng	致公堂	Chee Kong Tong benevolent association, or Chinese Freemason association
zhōng huá huì guǎn (zhōng huá gōng suǒ)	中华会馆 (中华公所)	Chinese Consolidated Benevolent Association/Chinese Six Companies
zhōng xī rì bào	中西日報	China West Daily
zǔ fù	祖父	paternal grandfather

Works Cited

Books

Adams, Charles Kendall, and William Trent. *A History of the United States.* Boston: Allyn & Bacon, 1903.

Adler, Joseph A. *Chinese Religious Traditions.* Upper Saddle River, NJ: Prentice Hall, 2002.

Allen, Paula Gunn. *The Sacred Hoop: Recovering the Feminine in American Indian Traditions.* Boston: Beacon Press, 1986.

Ambrose, Stephen E. *Nothing Like It in the World: The Men Who Built the Transcontinental Railroad, 1863–1869.* New York: Touchstone, 2001. First published 2000 by Simon & Schuster.

Anderson, Adrienne B. "Ancillary Construction on Promontory Summit Utah: Those Domestic Structures Built by Railroad Workers." In *Forgotten Places and Things: Archaeological Perspectives on American History.* Edited by Albert E. Ward, 225–238. Albuquerque, NM: Center for Anthropological Studies, 1983.

Anderson, Eugene Newton. "Folk Nutritional Therapy in Modern China." In *Chinese Medicine and Healing. An Illustrated History.* Edited by T. J. Heinrichs and Linda L. Barnes, 259–263. Cambridge, MA: Belknap Press of Harvard University Press, 2013.

Arkush, R. David, and Leo O. Lee. *Land without Ghosts: Chinese Impressions of America from the Mid-Nineteenth Century to the Present.* Berkeley: University of California Press, 1989.

Bain, David Haward. *Empire Express: Building the First Transcontinental Railroad.* New York: Penguin Books, 2000.

Bancroft, Hubert Howe. *History of California: 1860–1890.* San Francisco: History Company, 1890.

Barlow, Jeffrey G., and Christine Richardson. *China Doctor of John Day.* Hillsboro, OR: Binford & Mort, 1979.

Barth, Gunther Paul. *Bitter Strength: A History of the Chinese in the United States, 1850–1870.* Cambridge, MA: Harvard University Press, 1964.

Beauvoir, Ludovic de. *Voyages autour du monde: Australie, Java, Siam, Canton, Pékin, Yeddo, San Francisco.* Paris: Plon, 1878.

Beauvoir, Simone de. *La longue marche.* Paris: Gallimard, 1957.

Beck, Rhonda. *Union Station in Denver.* Mt. Pleasant, SC: Arcadia Publishing, 2016.

Benedict, Carol. *Golden-Silk Smoke: A History of Tobacco in China, 1550–2010.* Berkeley: University of California Press, 2011.

Berner, Bertha. *Mrs. Leland Stanford: An Intimate Account.* Stanford, CA: Stanford University Press, 1934.

Berton, Pierre. *The Last Spike: The Great Railway, 1881–1885.* Toronto: McClelland & Stewart, 1971.

Bhabha, Homi. *The Location of Culture.* London: Routledge, 1994.

Bing, Zhu, and Wang Hongcai. *Basic Theories of Traditional Chinese Medicine.* London: Singing Dragon, 2010.

Bingham, A. Walker. *The Snake-Oil Syndrome: Patent Medicine Advertising.* Hanover, MA: Christopher Publishing House, 1994.

"Biographical Sketch." In *Memorial Addresses on the Life and Character of Leland Stanford.* Washington, DC: US Government Printing Office, 1894.

Bivins, Roberta E. *Alternative Medicine? A History.* New York: Oxford University Press, 2007.

Bourdieu, Pierre. *Outline of a Theory of Practice.* Cambridge: Cambridge University Press, 1977.

Bowles, Samuel. *Our New West: Records of Travel between the Mississippi River and the Pacific Ocean.* Hartford, CT: Hartford Publishing, 1869.

Brady, Marilyn Dell. *Asian Texans.* College Station: Texas A&M University Press, 2004.

British Columbia Directory for 1884–85. Victoria, BC: R. T. Williams, 1885.

Bronson, Bennet, and Chuimei Ho. *Coming Home in Gold Brocade: Chinese in Early Northwest America.* Seattle: Chinese in Northwest America Research Committee, 2015.

Census of Canada, 1880–81. Ottawa: Maclean, Roger & Co., 1882.

Central Sierra Snow Laboratory. *Donner Summit Snowfall and Snowpack, 1879–2011.* Soda Springs: University of California at Berkeley, n.d.

Certeau, Michel de. *The Practice of Everyday Life.* Berkeley: University of California Press, 1988.

Chan, Sucheng. *Asian Americans: An Interpretive History.* Boston: Twayne, 1991.

———. *This Bittersweet Soil: The Chinese in California Agriculture, 1860–1910.* Berkeley: University of California Press, 1986.

Chang, Gordon H. *Fateful Ties: A History of America's Preoccupation with China.* Cambridge, MA: Harvard University Press, 2015.

Chang, Iris. *The Chinese in America: A Narrative History.* New York: Viking, 2003.

Chang, K. C. Introduction to *Food in Chinese Culture: Anthropological and Historical Perspectives.* Edited by K. C. Chang. New Haven, CT: Yale University Press, 1977.

Chang, Kathleen. *The Iron Moonhunter.* Translated by Chiu-Chung Liao and Florence Lau. San Francisco: Children's Book Press, 1977.

Chang, Kornel S. *Pacific Connections: The Making of U.S.–Canadian Borderlands.* Berkeley: University of California Press, 2012.

Chen Hansheng 陈翰笙编, ed. *Huagong chuguo shiliao huibian* 华工出国史料汇编 [Collection of the Historical Materials about the Overseas Chinese Laborers]. Beijing: Zhonghua shuju 中华书局, 1984.

———. Preface to *Zhong guo guan wen shu xuan ji* [Selection of Chinese Official Documents]. Edited by China's First National Archives and Lu Wendi, Chen Zexian, and Peng Jiali, 4–11. Beijing: Zhong hua shu ju, 1985.

Chen, Yong. *Chinese in San Francisco, 1850–1943: A Transpacific Community.* Stanford, CA: Stanford University Press, 2000.

Chen Yuanzhu 陈元柱编, ed. *Taishan geyao ji* 台山歌谣集 [Taishan Ballads]. Guangzhou: Guoli Zhongshan daxue yuyan lishixue yanjiusuo 国立中山大学言语历史学研究所, 1929.

Chevalier, Michel. *Society, Manners and Politics in the United States: Being a Series of Letters on North America.* Boston: Weeks, Jordan, 1839.

Chew, William F. *Nameless Builders of the Transcontinental Railway: The Chinese Workers of the Central Pacific Railroad.* Bloomington, IN: Trafford, 2003.

Chin, Art, and Doug Chin. *The Chinese in Washington State.* Seattle: OCA Greater Seattle, 2013.

Chin, Frank. *The Chickencoop Chinaman and The Year of the Dragon.* Seattle: Washington University Press, 1981.

———. *Donald Duk.* Minneapolis: Coffee House, 1991.

Ching-Hwang Yen. "Chinese Coolie Emigration, 1845–74." In *Routledge Handbook of the Chinese Diaspora.* Edited by Tan Chee-Beng. London: Routledge, 2013.

Chinn, Thomas. *Bridging the Pacific: San Francisco Chinatown and Its People.* San Francisco: Chinese Historical Society of America, 1989.

Chinn, Thomas W., Him Mark Lai, and Philip C. Choy, eds. *A History of the Chinese in California: A Syllabus.* San Francisco: Chinese Historical Society of America, 1969.

Chirali, Ilkay Zihni. *Traditional Chinese Medicine: Cupping Therapy*. Edinburgh: Churchill Livingstone, 1999.

Chow, Kenneth. "The History of the Chinese in Santa Clara County." In *Chinese Argonauts: An Anthology of the Chinese Contributions to the Historical Development of Santa Clara County*. Edited by Gloria Sun Hom, 1–17. San Mateo, CA: California History Center, 1971.

Chow, Lily Siewsan. *Blood and Sweat over the Railway Tracks: Chinese Labourers Constructing the Canadian Pacific Railway, 1880–1885*. Vancouver, BC: Chinese Canadian Historical Society of British Columbia and Initiative for Student Teaching and Research in Chinese Canadian Studies, University of British Columbia, 2014.

Chun, Grace Hong. "Filling the Rice Bowl." In *Chinese in Chicago: 1870–1945*. Edited by Chuimei Ho and Soo Lon Moy, 31–56. Mt. Pleasant, SC: Arcadia Publishing, 2005.

Chung, Sue Fawn. "Between Two Worlds: Ah Cum Kee (1876–1929) and Loy Lee Ford (1882–1921)." In *Ordinary Women, Extraordinary Lives: A History of Women in America*. Edited by Kriste Lindenmeyer, 179–195. Wilmington, DE: Scholarly Resources, 2000.

———. "Between Two Worlds: The Zhigongtang in the United States, 1860–1949." In *Empire, Nation, and Beyond: Chinese History in Late Imperial and Modern Times, A Festschrift in Honor of Frederic Wakeman*. Edited by Joseph W. Esherick, Wen-hsin Yeh, and Madeleine Zelin. Berkeley: Institute of East Asian Studies, University of California, 2006.

———. *Chinese in the Woods: Logging and Lumbering in the American West*. Urbana: University of Illinois Press, 2015.

———. *In Pursuit of Gold: Chinese American Miners and Merchants in the American West*. Urbana: University of Illinois Press, 2011.

———. "Their Changing World: Chinese Women of the Comstock." In *Women on the Comstock: The Making of a Mining Community*. Edited by Ronald James and C. Elizabeth Raymond, 203–228. Reno: University of Nevada Press, 1997.

———. "The Zhigontang in the United States, 1860–1949." In *Empire, Nation, and Beyond: Chinese History in Late Imperial and Modern Times*. Edited by Wen-hsin Yeh and Joseph Esherick. 231–249. Berkeley: University of California Press, 2006.

Chung, Sue Fawn, Fred P. Frampton, and Timothy Murphy. "Venerate These Bones: Chinese American Burial Practices as Seen in Carlin, Nevada." In *Chinese American Death Rituals*. Edited by Sue Fawn Chung and Patricia Wegars. Walnut Creek, CA: AltaMira Press, 2005.

Chung, Sue Fawn, with the Nevada State Museum. *The Chinese in Nevada*. Images of America Series. Charleston, SC: Arcadia Publishing, 2011.

Clark, George T. *Leland Stanford: War Governor of California, Railroad Builder and Founder of Stanford University.* Stanford, CA: Stanford University Press, 1931.

Cohen, Lucy M. *Chinese in the Post–Civil War South: A People without a History.* Baton Rouge: Louisiana State University Press, 1984.

Colorado Genealogical Society. *Colorado Families: A Territorial Heritage.* Denver: Colorado Genealogical Society, 1981.

Conley, Donald C. "The Pioneer Chinese of Utah." In *Chinese on the American Frontier.* Edited by Arif Dirlik, 291–306. Lanham, MD: Rowman & Littlefield, 2001.

Conway, Russell H. *Why and How. Why the Chinese Emigrate, and the Means They Adopt for the Purpose of Reaching America.* Boston: Lee & Shepard, 1871.

Coolidge, Mary Roberts. *Chinese Immigration.* New York: Henry Holt, 1909. Reprint, New York: Arno Press, 1969.

Cotteau, Edmond. *Six mille lieues en soixante jours (Amérique du Nord)* [Six Thousand Places in Sixty Days (North America)]. Auxerre, France: Imprimerie G. Perriquet, 1876.

Crary, Jonathan. *Techniques of the Observer: On Vision and Modernity in the Nineteenth Century.* Cambridge, MA: MIT Press, 1992.

Csordas, Thomas J. "Introduction: The Body as Representation and Being in the World." In *Embodiment and Experience: The Existential Ground of Culture and Self.* Edited by Thomas Csordas, 1–26. Cambridge: Cambridge University Press, 1994.

Cutler, Robert W. P. *The Mysterious Death of Jane Stanford.* Stanford, CA: Stanford University Press, 2003.

David, Jules, ed. *American Diplomatic and Public Papers: The United States and China.* Series 1, vol. 17: "The Coolie Trade and Chinese Emigration." Wilmington, DE: Scholarly Resources, 1973.

Dearinger, Ryan. *The Filth of Progress: Immigrants, Americans, and the Building of Canals and in the West.* Berkeley: University of California Press, 2015.

Deetz, James. *In Small Things Forgotten.* New York: Doubleday, 1977.

Derrida, Jacques. *Of Hospitality.* Stanford, CA: Stanford University Press, 2000.

Ding Zemin. *Mei guo pai hua shi* [A History of U.S. Exclusion of the Chinese]. Beijing: Zhong hua shu ju, 1952.

Dixon, Kelly J., Julie M. Schablitsky, and Shannon A. Novak, eds. *An Archaeology of Desperation: Exploring the Donner Party's Alder Creek Camp.* Norman: University of Oklahoma Press, 2011.

Dixon, Kelly J., and Carrie E. Smith. "Rock Hearths and Rural Wood Camps in Jīn Shān/Gām Saan 金山: National Register of Historic Places Evaluations of 19th-Century Chinese Logging Operations at Heavenly Ski Resort in the Lake Tahoe Basin." In *Historical Archaeology of the American West.* Edited by Margaret Purser and Mark Warner. Lincoln: University of Nebraska Press, 2017.

Dobres, Marcia-Anne. "Technology's Links and Chaines [*sic*]: The Processual Unfolding of Technique and Technician." In *The Social Dynamics of Technology: Practice, Politics, and Worldviews*. Edited by Marcia-Anne Dobres and Christopher R. Hoffman, 124–145. Washington, DC: Smithsonian Institution Press, 1999.

"Economy and Politics." In *Kaiping xian zhi* 开平县志 [Kaiping County Annals]. Edited by Kaiping shi difang zhi banggongshi 开平市地方志办公室. Vol. 13. Beijing: Zhonghua shuju 中华书局, 2002.

Eggleston, Edward. *A New Century History of the United States*. New York: American, 1904.

Elliott, Russell R., and William D. Rowley. *History of Nevada*. 2d ed., rev. Lincoln: University of Nebraska Press, 1987.

Eng, David L. *Racial Castration: Managing Masculinity in Asian America*. Durham, NC: Duke University Press, 2001.

Etter, Patricia A. "The West Coast Chinese and Opium Smoking." In *Archaeological Perspectives on Ethnicity in America: Afro-American and Asian American Culture History*. Edited by Robert L. Schuyler, 97–101. Farmingdale, NY: Baywood Publishing, 1980.

Evans, William S. "Food and Fantasy: Material Culture of the Chinese in California and the West, circa 1850–1900." In *Archaeological Perspectives on Ethnicity in America: Afro-American and Asian American Culture History*. Edited by Robert L. Schuyler, 89–96. Farmingdale, NY: Baywood Publishing, 1980.

Fagan, Brian. *The Little Ice Age: How Climate Made History 1300–1850*. New York: Basic Books, 2001.

Fan, Warner J. W. *A Manual of Chinese Herbal Medicine: Principles and Practice for Easy Reference*. Boston: Shambhala, 1996.

Farquhar, Judith. *Appetites: Food and Sex in Postsocialist China*. Durham, NC: Duke University Press, 2002.

Faure, David. *The Structure of Chinese Rural Society: Lineage and Village in the Eastern New Territories, Hong Kong*. Hong Kong: Oxford University Press, 1986.

Feuchtwang, Stephan. *Popular Religion in China: The Imperial Metaphor*. Richmond, UK: Curzon Press, 2001.

Ficken, Robert E., and Charles Pierce LeWarne. *Washington: A Centennial History*. Seattle: University of Washington Press, 1988.

Fike, Richard E. *The Bottle Book: A Comprehensive Guide to Historic Embossed Medicine Bottles*. Caldwell, NJ: Blackburn Press, 2006.

Fishkin, Shelley Fisher, ed. *The Mark Twain Anthology: Great Writers on His Life and Work*. New York: Library of America, 2010.

FitzGerald, Frances. *America Revised: History Schoolbooks in the Twentieth Century*. Boston: Little, Brown, 1979.

Foucrier, Annick. *Le rêve californien. Migrants français sur la côte Pacifique, XVIIIe–XXe siècles* [The California Dream: French Migrants on the Pacific Coast, Eighteenth to Twentieth Centuries]. Paris: Belin, Collection Cultures Américaines, 1999.

Frédéric-Moreau, F. *Aux États-Unis: notes de voyage* [In the United States: Travel Notes]. Paris: Librairie Plon, 1888.

Fu Yunlong 傅云龙. *Youli Guba tujing erjuan* 游历古巴图经二 卷. [Traveling through Cuba, 2 vols] China, 1889.

Gardner, A. Dudley. "The Chinese in Wyoming: Life in the Core and Peripheral Communities." In *Ethnic Oasis: The Chinese in the Black Hills—South Dakota History*. Edited by Liping Zhu and Rose Estep. Pierre: South Dakota Historical Society Press, 2004.

Gaylord, Mary. *Eastern Washington's Past and Present: Chinese and Other Pioneers.* Washington, DC: US Forest Service, US Department of Agriculture, 1993.

Gibbon, John Murray. *The Romantic History of the Canadian Pacific: The Northwest Passage of Today.* New York: Tudor Publishing, 1937.

Gillis, John R. *Tunnels of the Pacific Railroad.* New York: American Society of Civil Engineers, 1870.

Goldbaum, Howard, and Wendell Huffman. *Waiting for the Cars: Alfred A. Hart's Stereoscopic Views of the Central Pacific Railroad.* Carson City: Nevada State Railroad Museum, 2012.

Grimm, N. B., J. M. Grove, S. T. A. Pickett, and C. L. Redman. "Integrated Approaches to Long-term Studies of Urban Ecological Systems." In *Urban Ecology: An International Perspective on the Interaction between Humans and Nature.* Edited by J. M. Marzluff et al., 123–141. London: Springer, 2008.

Griswold, Wesley S. *A Work of Giants: Building the First Transcontinental Railroad.* New York: McGraw-Hill, 1962.

Guangxu sanshi nian Jiangmen kou Huanyang Maoyi Lunlue 光绪三十年江门口 华洋贸易论略 [Jiangmen's Overseas Trade Overview]. In *Overseas Trade Handbook of the Customs in the Republic of China.* Taipei: National History Library, 1904.

Gust, Sherri M. "Animal Bones from Historic Urban Chinese Sites: A Comparison of Sacramento, Woodland, Tucson, Ventura, and Lovelock." In *Hidden Heritage: Historical Archaeology of the Overseas Chinese.* Edited by Priscilla Wegars, 177–212. Amityville, NY: Baywood, 1993.

Gyory, Andrew. *Closing the Gate: Race, Politics, and the Chinese Exclusion Act.* Chapel Hill: University of North Carolina Press, 1998.

Hall, Shawn. *Connecting the West: Historic Railroad Stops and Stage Stations of Elko County, Nevada.* Reno: University of Nevada Press, 2002.

Hamman, Rick. *California Coastal Central Railways.* Boulder, CO: Pruett, 1980.

Hart, Alfred A. *The Traveler's Own Book*. Chicago: Horton & Leonard, 1970. First published 1870 by Horton & Leonard.

Hastorf, Christine. "The *Habitus* of Cooking Practices in Neolithic Çatalhöyük: What Was the Place of the Cook?" In *The Menial Art of Cooking*. Edited by Sarah R. Graff and Enrique Rodriguez-Alegria, 65–86. Boulder: University Press of Colorado, 2012.

Hempen, Carl-Hermann, and Toni Fischer. *A Materia Medica for Chinese Medicine: Plants, Minerals and Animal Products*. Edinburgh: Churchill Livingstone, 2009.

Hildebrand, Lorraine Barker. *Straw Hats, Sandals, and Steel: The Chinese in Washington State*. Tacoma: Washington State American Revolution Bicentennial Commission, 1977.

Hill, Thomas. *The Last Spike, a Painting by Thomas Hill: Illustrating the Last Scene in the Building of the Overland Railroad. With a History of the Enterprise*. San Francisco, January 1881.

Ho, Chuimei, and Bennet Bronson. *Three Chinese Temples in California: Marysville, Oroville, Weaverville*. Seattle: Chinese in Northwest America Research Committee (CINARC), 2016.

Hobsbawm, Eric. *The Age of Capital: 1848–1875*. New York: Vintage, 1996.

Hoffmann, Hemmann. *Californien, Nevada und Mexico: Wanderungen eines Polytechnikers* [California, Nevada and Mexico: Walks of a Polytechnician]. Basel, Switzerland: Hugo Richter, 1871.

Hom, Marlon K. *Songs of Gold Mountain: Cantonese Rhymes from San Francisco Chinatown*. Berkeley: University of California Press, 1987.

Hooper, G. Robin. *Gold, Stone Vaults, and Railways: An Archaeological Site Assessment in Old Yale Chinatown, British Columbia, 1994–1996*. Surrey, BC, 1996.

Hsu, Madeline. *Dreaming of Gold, Dreaming of Home: Transnationalism and Migration between the United States and South China, 1882–1943*. Stanford, CA: Stanford University Press, 2000.

Hu-Dehart, Evelyn. *Studying the Chinese Diaspora and the Caribbean: Huagong and Huashang in Latin America and the Caribbean*. Translated by Zhou Lin. Hangzhou, China: Zhejiang University Press, 2016.

Hu Shiu-ying. *Food Plants of China*. Hong Kong: Chinese University Press, 2005.

Huang Annian. *Mei guo de jue qi: 17-19 shi ji de mei guo* [The Rise of the United States: The United States from the Seventeenth to the Nineteenth Century]. Beijing: Zhong guo she hui ke xue chu ban she, 1992.

——, ed. *The Silent Spikes: Chinese Laborers and the Construction of North American Railroads*. Translated by Zhang Juguo. Beijing: China Intercontinental Press, 2006.

——. *Mei guo she hui jing ji shi lun* [The Socioeconomic History of the United States]. Taiyuan, China: Shan xi jiao yu chu ban she, 1993.

———. *Dao ding, bu zai chen mo: jian she bei mei tie lu de hua gong* [Spikes, No Longer Silent: To the Chinese Workers Constructing North American Railroads]. Shenyang, China: Bai shan chu ban she, 2010.

Huang Annian and Li Ju. *Chen mo dao ding de zu ji—ji nian hua gong jian she mei guo tie lu* [The Footprints of the Silent Spikes—In Memory of the Chinese Workers Who Constructed the American Railroads]. Beijing: Zhong guo tie dao chu ban she, 2015.

Huang Kunzhang and Wu Jinping. *Jianada Huaqiao Huaren shi* [A History of Chinese Sojourners and Settlers in Canada]. Guangzhou: Guangdong gaodeng jiaoyu chubanshe, 2001.

Hübner, Joseph Alexander von. *Promenade autour du monde* [Walk around the World]. 5th ed. Paris: Hachette, 1878. First published 1871.

Hulot, Étienne. *De l'Atlantique au Pacifique à travers le Canada et le nord des États-Unis* [From the Atlantic to the Pacific across Canada and the Northern United States]. Paris: E. Plon, Nourrit, 1888.

Huret, Jules. *En Amérique: de San Francisco au Canada* [In America: From San Francisco to Canada]. Paris: Bibliothèque Charpentier, 1905.

Hwang, David Henry. *The Dance and the Railroad and Family Devotions: Two Plays.* New York: Dramatists Play Service, 1983.

Jennings, Willie James. *The Christian Imagination: Theology and the Origins of Race.* New Haven, CT: Yale University Press, 2011.

Jian Jianping. *Zhongguo Hongmen zai Jianada* [The Chinese Freemasons in Canada]. Vancouver, BC: Zhongguo Hongmen Minzhidang zhu Jianada zongzhibu, 1989.

Jinshan po zi tan 金山婆自叹 [The Sighs of Gold Mountain Wives]. Guangzhou: Huaxing shuju 华兴书局, n.d.

Johnston, Alexander. *A History of the United States for Schools, with an Introductory History of the Discovery and English.* New York: Henry Holt, 1885.

Jost, François. "The Bildungsroman in Germany, England, and France." In *Introduction to Comparative Literature,* 134–150. Indianapolis: Pegasus, 1974.

Jung, Moon-Ho. *Coolies and Cane: Race, Labor, and Sugar in the Age of Emancipation.* Baltimore: Johns Hopkins University Press, 2006.

Kan, Johnny. *Eight Immortal Flavors: Secrets of Cantonese Cookery from San Francisco's Chinatown.* San Francisco: California Living Books, 1980.

Kastner, Joerg. *Chinese Nutrition Therapy. Dietetics in Traditional Chinese Medicine (TCM).* Stuttgart, Germany: Thieme, 2004.

Kearney, Denis. "Kearney at Faneuil Hall." In *Speeches of Dennis* [sic] *Kearney, Labor Champion.* New York: Jesse Haney & Co., 1878.

Kelsey, Robin. *Archive Style: Photographs and Illustrations for U.S. Surveys, 1850–1890.* Berkeley: University of California Press, 2007.

Kennedy, Paul. *The Rise and Fall of Great Powers.* New York: Vintage Books, 1987.

Kibbey, Mead B., and Peter E. Palmquist. *The Railroad Photographs of Alfred A. Hart, Artist.* Sacramento: California State Library Foundation, 1996.

Kingston, Maxine Hong. *China Men.* New York: Vintage, 1989. First published 1980 by Knopf.

Kirby, Lynne. *Parallel Tracks: The Railroad and Silent Cinema.* Durham, NC: Duke University Press, 2014.

Kneiss, Gilbert H. *Bonanza Railroads.* Stanford, CA: Stanford University Press, 1941.

———. *The Virginia and Truckee Railway.* Hathi Trust Digital Collection. Boston: Railway and Locomotive Historical Society, 1938.

Krause, Keith. "War, Violence and the State." In *Securing Peace in a Globalized World.* Edited by Michael Brzoska and Axel Krohn, 183–202. London: Palgrave Macmillan, 2009.

Krensky, Stephen. *The Iron Dragon Never Sleeps.* New York: Yearling, 1995.

Kuhn, Philip A. *Chinese among Others: Emigration in Modern Times.* Lanham, MD: Rowman & Littlefield, 2008.

Lai, David Chuenyan. *Canadian Steel, Chinese Grit: No Chinese Labour, No Railway.* National Executive Council of the *Canadian Steel, Chinese Grit* Heritage Documentary, 1998.

———. *Chinese Community Leadership: Case Study of Victoria in Canada.* Singapore: World Scientific Publishing, 2010.

Lai, Him Mark. *Becoming Chinese American: A History of Communities and Institutions.* Walnut Creek, CA: AltaMira Press, 2004.

Lamb, W. Kaye. *History of the Canadian Pacific Railway.* New York: Macmillan, 1977.

Langenwalter, Paul E. "Mammals and Reptiles as Food and Medicine in Riverside's Chinatown." In *An American Chinatown.* Vol. 2. Edited by Wong Ho Leun, 53–106. San Diego, CA: Great Basin Foundation, 1987.

Langley, Henry G. *The San Francisco Directory for the Year Commencing April 1879.* San Francisco: Francis, Valentine & Co., 1879.

Lary, Diana. *Chinese Migrations: The Movement of People, Goods, and Ideas over Four Millennia.* Lanham, MD: Rowman & Littlefield, 2012.

Lee, Erika. *At America's Gates: Chinese Immigration during the Exclusion Era, 1882–1943.* Chapel Hill: University of North Carolina Press, 2003.

———. *The Making of Asian America: A History.* New York: Simon & Schuster, 2015.

Lee, Jonathan H. X. *The Temple of Kwan Tai: California Historic Landmark No. 927. Celebrating Community and Diversity. Mendocino, California.* Mendocino, CA: Temple of Kwan Tai, 2004.

Lee, Robert G. *Orientals: Asian Americans in Popular Culture.* Philadelphia: Temple University Press, 1999.

Lee, Shelley San-Hee. *Claiming the Oriental Gateway: Prewar Seattle and Japanese America*. Philadelphia: Temple University Press, 2011.

Lemonnier, Léon. *La ruée vers l'or en Californie* [The California Gold Rush]. Paris: Gallimard, 1944.

Leung Chik-wai (Liang Zhihuai). *Ye Chuntian xiansheng zhuanji* [Biography of Yip Sang]. Hong Kong, 1973.

Lewis, Oscar. *The Big Four: The Story of Huntington, Stanford, Hopkins, and Crocker, and of the Building of the Central Pacific*. New York: Knopf, 1938.

Li, Julia Ningyu, ed. *Canadian Steel, Chinese Grit: A Tribute to the Chinese Who Worked on Canada's Railroads More Than a Century Ago* Translated by John Howard-Gibbon and Jan Walls. Toronto: Paxlink Communications, 2000.

Li Chunhui and Yang Shengmao. *Mei zhou hua qiao hua ren shi* [A History of Overseas Chinese and Chinese Americans in the Americas]. Beijing: Dong fang chu ban she, 1990.

Li Donghai (David T. H. Lee). *Jianada Huaqiaoshi* [A History of Chinese in Canada]. Taipei: Zhonghua dadian bianyinhui, 1967.

Li Quan'en (David Lai), Ding Guo, and Jia Baoheng. *Jianada Huaqiao yiminshi* [History of Chinese Migration to Canada]. Beijing: Renmin chubanshe, 2013.

Liang Qichao. *Xin da lu you ji* [Travel Writing on the New Continent]. Changsha, China: Yue lu shu she, 1985.

Lightfoot, Kent. *Indians, Missionaries, and Merchants: The Legacy of Colonial Encounters on the California Frontier*. Berkeley: University of California Press, 2005.

Lim Tong Kwee. *Edible Medicinal and Non-Medicinal Plants*. Vol. 1, *Fruits*. New York: Springer, 2012.

Limerick, Patricia Nelson. *Legacy of Conquest: The Unbroken Past of the American West*. New York: Norton, 1987.

Lin Shu and Wei Yi. *Hei nu yu tian lu* [Documentation of a Black Slave's Appeal to Heaven]. Beijing: Shang wu yin shu guan, 1981. First printed in 1901.

Liping Zhu. *The Road to Chinese Exclusion: The Denver Riot, 1880 Election, and Rise of the West*. Lawrence: University of Kansas Press, 2013.

Liu Boji. *The History of Overseas Chinese in America*. Taipei: Dawn Cultural Enterprise, 1983.

———. *Meiguo Huaqiao shi* [A History of the Chinese in the United States of America]. Taipei: Xingzhengyuan qiaowu yuanweihui, 1976.

Liu Danian. *Mei guo qin hua shi* [A History of US Aggression against China]. 2d ed. Beijing: Ren min chu ban she, 1954.

Liu Haiming. "Chinese Herbalists in the United States." In *Chinese American Transnationalism: The Flow of People, Resources, and Ideas between China and America during the Exclusion Era.* Edited by Sucheng Chan, 136–155. Philadelphia: Temple University Press, 2006.

———. "The Social Origins of Early Chinese Immigrants: A Revisionist Perspective." In *The Chinese in America: A History from Gold Mountain to the New Millennium.* Edited by Susie Lan Cassel, 21–36. Walnut Creek, CA: AltaMira Press, 2002.

Liu Yonghua. *Confucian Rituals and Chinese Villagers: Ritual Changes and Social Transformation in a Southeastern Chinese Community, 1368–1949.* Leiden, the Netherlands: Brill, 2013.

Lo Kuan-Chung. *Romance of the Three Kingdoms.* 2 vols. Translated by C. H. Brewitt-Taylor. Reprint, North Clarendon, VT: Tuttle, 2002.

Lowe, Lisa. *The Intimacies of Four Continents.* Durham, NC: Duke University Press, 2015.

Lu Gwei-djen and Joseph Needham. *Celestial Lancets: A History and Rationale of Acupuncture and Moxa.* London: RoutledgeCurzon, 1980.

Lu, Henry C. *Chinese Natural Cures: Traditional Methods for Remedies and Prevention.* New York: Black Dog & Leventhal, 1994.

Lu Wendi, Peng Jiali, and Chen Zexian, eds. *Mei guo yue jia na da hua gong* [Chinese Laborers in the United States and Canada]. In Hua gong chu guo shi liao hui bian [Collections of Historical Documents on Chinese Workers Going Overseas], vol. 7. Edited by Chen Hansheng. Beijing: Zhong hua shu ju, 1984.

MacGregor, Bruce. *The Birth of California Narrow Gauge: A Regional Study of the Technology of Thomas and Martin Carter.* Stanford, CA: Stanford University Press, 2003.

Maciocia, G. *The Foundations of Chinese Medicine. A Comprehensive Text for Acupuncturists and Herbalists.* Edinburgh: Churchill Livingstone, 1989.

Malézieux, Émile. *Travaux publics des États-Unis d'Amérique en 1870, rapport de mission, par M. Malézieux* [Public Works of the United States of America in 1870: Mission Report by Mr. Malézieux]. Paris: Dunod Éditeur, 1873.

Malte-Brun, V. A., ed. *Annales des voyages, de la géographie, de l'histoire et de l'archéologie* [Annals of Travel, Geography, History, and Archaeology]. Paris: Challamet, 1868.

Maniery, Mary L., Rebecca Allen, and Sarah Christine Heffner. *Finding Hidden Voices of the Chinese Railroad Workers: An Archaeological and Historical Journey.* Special Publications Series No. 13. Germantown, MD: Society for Historical Archaeology, 2016.

Marchand, Arnie. *The Way I Heard It: A Three Nation Reading Vacation.* Bloomington, IN: Xlibris, 2013.

Marks, Robert B. "'It Never Used to Snow': Climatic Variability and Harvest Yields in Late-Imperial South China, 1650–1850." In *Sediments of Time: Environment and Society in Chinese History*. Edited by Mark Elvin and Liu Ts'ui-jung, 411–446. Cambridge: Cambridge University Press, 1998.

Martin, Debra L., Ryan P. Harrod, and Ventura R. Pérez. *Bioarchaeology: An Integrated Approach to Working with Human Remains*. New York: Springer, 2013.

Marvin, Judith, Julia Costello, and Salvatore Manna. "Stockton and Copperopolis Railroad." In *Angels Camp and Copperopolis*. Mt. Pleasant, SC: Arcadia Publishing, 2009.

Marx, Leo. *The Machine in the Garden: Technology and the Pastoral Ideal in America*. Oxford: Oxford University Press, 2000.

McClain, Charles, ed. *Chinese Immigrants and American Law*. New York: Garland, 1994.

McCunn, Ruthanne Lum. *Chinese American Portraits: Personal Histories, 1828–1988*. Seattle: University of Washington Press, 1996.

McMaster, John Bach. *A School History of the United States*. New York: American, 1897.

Miller, Stuart Creighton. *The Unwelcome Immigrant: The American Image of the Chinese 1785–1882*. Berkeley: University of California Press, 1974.

Mills, Lester. *Sagebrush Saga*. Springville, UT: Art City Publishing, 1956.

Monnett, John M. "Sou, Chin Lin (1837–1894)." In *Encyclopedia of the Great Plains*. Edited by David J. Wishart. Lincoln: University of Nebraska Press, 2004. http://plainshumanities.unl.edu/encyclopedia/doc/egp.asam.020.

Moreau, Joseph. *Schoolbook Nation: Conflicts over American History Textbooks from the Civil War to the Present*. Ann Arbor: University of Michigan Press, 2003.

Morton, James. *In the Sea of Sterile Mountains: The Chinese in British Columbia*. Vancouver, BC: J. J. Douglas, 1974.

Murray, Dian H., and Qin Baoqi. *The Origins of the Tiandihui: The Chinese Triads in Legend and History*. Stanford, CA: Stanford University Press, 1994.

Muwu juqiu chijin ku 木屋拘囚吃尽苦 [Suffering and Imprisoned in a Wooden House]. In Jinshan Geji 金山歌集. *Daguan Shulin* 大光书林 *in the Gold Mountain* 金山正埠, 1912.

Muzzey, David Saville. *An American History*. Boston: Ginn, 1911.

———. *History of Our Country: A Textbook for High School Students*. Boston: Ginn, 1936, 1945.

———. *History of the American People*. Boston: Ginn, 1934.

———. *Our Country's History*. Boston: Ginn, 1957.

Muzzey, David, and Arthur Link. *Our American Republic*. Boston: Ginn, 1963.

Nadeau, Remi. *City Makers: The Story of Southern California's First Boom, 1868–1876*. Coronado del Mar, CA: Trans-Anglo Books, 1977.

Naef, Weston, and Christine Hult-Lewis. *Carleton Watkins: The Complete Mammoth Photographs*. Los Angeles: J. Paul Getty Museum, 2011.

Nelson, Scott Reynolds. *Steel Drivin' Man—John Henry—the Untold Story of an American Legend*. New York: Oxford University Press, 2006.

Nevers, J., and P. Rucks, with contributions by L. Hicks, S. James, and M. Rakow. "Under Watchful Eyes: Washoe Narratives of the Donner Party." In *An Archaeology of Desperation: Exploring the Donner Party's Alder Creek Camp*. Edited by K. J. Dixon, J. M. Schablitsky, and S. A. Novak, 255–290. Norman: University of Oklahoma Press, 2011.

Ngai, Mae. *Impossible Subjects: Illegal Aliens and the Making of Modern America*. Princeton, NJ: Princeton University Press, 2004.

———. *The Lucky Ones: One Family and the Extraordinary Invention of Chinese America*. Boston: Houghton Mifflin Harcourt, 2010.

Nordhoff, Charles. *California: For Health, Pleasure and Residence*. New York: Harper & Brothers, 1873.

———. *California for Travellers and Settlers*. Berkeley, CA: Ten Speed Press, 1973. Originally published in 1873 by Harper & Brothers.

Olsen, Gilbert, and Richard Floyd. "The San Jose Railroad and Crocker's Pets." In *Chinese Argonauts: An Anthology of the Chinese Contributions to the Historical Development of Santa Clara County*. Edited by Gloria Sun Hom. Los Altos Hills, CA: Foothill Community College District/California History Center, 1971.

Orser, C. E. Jr. "Transnational Diaspora and Rights of Heritage." In *Cultural Heritage and Human Rights*. Edited by H. Silverman and D. Ruggles, 92–105. New York: Springer, 2007.

Ortner, Sherry B. *Anthropology and Social Theory: Culture, Power, and the Acting Subject*. Durham, NC: Duke University Press, 2006.

Owsley, Douglas W., Kari Bruwelheide, Juliet Brundige, David Hunt, Chip Clark, and Rebecca Redmond. *Preliminary Report: Osteology and Paleopathology of the Carlin Chinese Cemetery*. Washington, DC: National Museum of Natural History, Smithsonian Institution, 1997.

Paddison, Joshua. *American Heathens: Religion, Race, and Reconstruction in California*. Berkeley: Published for the Huntington–USC Institute on California and the West by the University of California Press; San Marino, CA: Huntington Library, 2012.

Pálos, Stephan. *The Chinese Art of Healing*. New York: Herder & Herder, 1971.

Pan, Lynn. *Sons of the Yellow Emperor: A History of the Chinese Diaspora*. Reprint, New York: Kodansha International, 1994.

Patterson, Edna, Louise A. Ulph, and Victor Goodwin. *Nevada's Northeast Frontier*. Reno: University of Nevada Press, 1991.

Pfaelzer, Jeanne. *Driven Out: The Forgotten War against Chinese Americans*. Berkeley: University of California Press, 2008.

Plotz, John. *Portable Property: Victorian Culture on the Move*. Princeton, NJ: Princeton University Press, 2009.

Portes, Jacques. *Une fascination réticente: Les États-Unis dans l'opinion française, 1870–1914* [A Reluctant Fascination: The United States in the Opinion of the French, 1870–1914]. Nancy, France: Presses Universitaires de Nancy, 1990.

Qing Ruji. *Mei guo qin hua shi* [A History of U.S. Aggression against China]. 2 vols. Beijing: San lian shu dian, 1952.

Ratzel, Friedrich. *Sketches of Urban and Cultural Life in North America*. Translated by Stewart Stehlin. New Brunswick, NJ: Rutgers University Press, 1988.

Raymond, Anan S., and Raymond E. Fike. *Rails East to Promontory: The Utah Stations*. Salt Lake City: Utah State Office Bureau of Land Management, 1981. Reprint, Livingston, TX: Pioneer Enterprises, 1994.

Reid, Daniel P. *Chinese Herbal Medicine*. Boston: Shambhala, 1993.

Remond, René. *Les États-Unis devant l'opinion française, 1815–1852* [The United States in Front of French Public Opinion]. Paris: Armand Colin, 1962.

Renz, Louis T. *The History of the Northern Pacific Railroad*. Fairfield, WA: Ye Galleon Press, 1980.

Richards, Bradley W., and C. R. Savage. *The Savage View: Charles Savage, Pioneer Mormon Photographer*. Nevada City, CA: Carl Mautz Publishers, 1995.

Richards, Leonard L. *The California Gold Rush and the Coming of the Civil War*. New York: Knopf, 2007.

Ringhoff, Mary, and Edward Stoner. *The River and the Railroad: An Archaeological History of Reno*. Reno: University of Nevada Press, 2011.

Robertson, Donald B. *Encyclopedia of Western Railroad History*. Vol. 2. Dallas: Taylor Publishing, 1991.

Rockman, Marcy. "Introduction: A L'Enfant Plan for Archaeology." In *Archaeology and Society: Its Relevance in the Modern World*. Edited by M. Rockman and J. Flatman, 1–20. London: Springer, 2012.

Roediger, David R., and Elizabeth D. Esch. *The Production of Difference: Race and the Management of Labor in U.S. History*. New York: Oxford University Press, 2012.

Ross, Douglas E. "Overseas Chinese Archaeology." In *Encyclopedia of Global Archaeology*. Edited by C. Smith, 5675–5686. New York: Springer, 2013.

Ross, James. *From Wisconsin to California and Return, As Reported for the "Wisconsin State Journal."* Madison, WI: Ross, James, 1869.

Rouse, Wendy L. "'What We Didn't Understand': A History of Chinese Death Ritual in China and California." In *Chinese American Death Rituals: Respecting the Ancestors*. Edited by Sue Fawn Chung and Priscilla Wegars. Lanham, MD: AltaMira Press, 2005.

Roy, Patricia. "A Choice between Evils: The Chinese and the Construction of the

Canadian Pacific Railway in British Columbia." In *The CPR West*. Edited by Hugh A. Dempsey, 13–34. Vancouver, BC: Douglas & McIntyre, 1984.

———. *A White Man's Province: British Columbia Politicians and Chinese and Japanese Immigrants, 1858–1914*. Vancouver, BC: University of British Columbia Press, 1989.

Ruby, Robert H., and John A. Brown. *Half-Sun on the Columbia: A Biography of Chief Moses*. Norman: University of Oklahoma Press, 1965.

Rusco, Elmer P. "Riot in Unionville, Nevada: A Turning Point." In *The Chinese in America: A History from Gold Mountain to the New Millennium*. Edited by Susie Lan Cassel. Walnut Creek, CA: AltaMira Press, 2001.

Sabin, Edwin L. *Building the Pacific Railway*. Philadelphia: J. B. Lippincott, 1919.

Sando, Ruth Ann, and David L. Felton. "Inventory Records of Ceramics and Opium from a Nineteenth Century Chinese Store in California." In *Hidden Heritage: Historical Archaeology of the Overseas Chinese*. Edited by Priscilla Wegars, 151–176. Amityville, NY: Baywood Publishing, 1993.

Santa Ana, Jeffrey. *Racial Feelings: Asian American in a Capitalist Culture of Emotion*. Philadelphia: Temple University Press, 2015.

Santa Cruz County, California: Illustrations Descriptive of Its Scenery, Fine Residences, Public Buildings, Manufactories, Hotels, Farm Scenes, Business Houses, Schools, Churches, Mines, Mills, Etc., with Historical Sketch of the County. San Francisco: W. W. Elliott & Co., 1879.

Saxton, Alexander. *The Indispensible Enemy: Labor and the Anti-Chinese Movement in California*. Berkeley: University of California Press, 1975.

Schieldrop, Edgar B. *The Railway: Conquest of Space and Time*. London: Hutchinson, 1939.

Schivelbusch, Wolfgang. *The Railway Journey: The Industrialization of Time and Space in the Nineteenth Century*. Berkeley: University of California Press, 2014. First published 1979 by Urizen Books.

Schuyler, Robert L. "Asian American Culture History: Introduction." In *Archaeological Perspectives on Ethnicity in America: Afro-American and Asian American Culture History*. Edited by Robert L. Schuyler, 87, 88. Farmingdale, NY: Baywood Publishing, 1980.

Schwantes, Carlos A. *The Pacific Northwest: An Interpretive History*. Lincoln: University of Nebraska Press, 1996.

Schweitzer, Sophia V., and Bennet Hymer. *Big Island Journey*. Honolulu, HI: Mutual Publishing, 2009.

Scudder, Horace Elisha. *A History of the United States of America*. Philadelphia: J. H. Butler, 1884.

Seward, George Frederick. *Chinese Immigration in Its Social and Economical Aspects*. New York: Charles Scribner's Sons, 1881.

Seyfried, Vincent F. *The Long Island Rail Road: A Comprehensive History. Part 1: South Side R. R. of L. I.* Self-published, 1961.

Sheng Jianhong, *Mei guo zhong yang tai ping yang tie lu jian she zhong de hua gong* [The Chinese Workers in the Construction of the United States' Central Pacific Railroad]. Shanghai: Zhong xi shu ju, 2010.

Shi, John, Xingqian Ye, Bo Jiang, Ying Ma, Donghong Liu, and Sophia Jun Xie. "Traditional Medicinal Wines." In *Nutraceutical Science and Technology, No. 10.* Edited by John Shi, Chi-Tang Ho and Fereidoon Shabidi, 417–430. Boca Raton, FL: CRC Press, 2010.

Shi Naian. *The Water Margin: Outlaws of the Marsh.* Translated by J. H. Jackson. Reprint, North Clarendon, VT: Tuttle, 2010.

Siegfried, Jacques. *Seize mois autour du monde, 1867–1869, et particulièrement aux Indes, en Chine et au Japon* [Sixteen Months around the World, 1867–1869, and Especially in India, China, and Japan]. Paris: J. Claye, 1869.

Silko, Leslie Marmon. *Ceremony.* New York: Penguin, 1977.

———. *Gardens in the Dunes: A Novel.* New York: Simon & Schuster, 1999.

———. "Notes on *Almanac of the Dead.*" In *Yellow Woman and a Beauty of the Spirit: Essays on Native American Life Today,* 135–145. New York: Simon & Schuster, 1996.

Simonin, Louis-Laurent. *À travers les États-Unis, de l'Atlantique au Pacifique* [Across the United States, from the Atlantic to the Pacific]. Paris: Charpentier, 1875.

Simoons, Frederick J. *Food in China: A Cultural and Historical Inquiry.* Boca Raton, FL: CRC Press, 1991.

Sinn, Elizabeth. *Pacific Crossing: California Gold, Chinese Migration, and the Making of Hong Kong.* Hong Kong: Hong Kong University Press, 2013.

———. *Power and Charity: A Chinese Merchant Elite in Colonial Hong Kong.* Hong Kong: Hong Kong University Press, 2003.

Siu, Lok C. D. *Memories of a Future Home: Diasporic Citizenship of Chinese in Panama.* Stanford, CA: Stanford University Press, 2005.

Smith, Philip Chadwick Foster. *The Empress of China.* Philadelphia: Philadelphia Maritime Museum, 1984.

Smith, Shawn Michelle. *At the Edge of Sight: Photography and the Unseen.* Durham, NC: Duke University Press, 2013.

Sohn, Anton. *The Healers of 19th Century Nevada: A Compendium of Medical Practitioners.* Reno: University of Nevada Press, 1997.

Sparks, Theresa A. *China Gold.* Fresno, CA: Academy Library Guild, 1954.

Speer, William. *The Oldest and the Newest Empire: China and the United States.* San Francisco: H. H. Bancroft & Co., 1870.

Stanford, Leland. "Statement Made to the President of the United States, and Secretary of the Interior, of the Progress of the Work." Sacramento, CA: H. S. Crocker & Co., 1865.

Staski, Edward. "Asian American Studies in Historical Archaeology." In *International Handbook of Historical Archaeology*. Edited by Teresita Majewski and David Gaimster, 347–359. New York: Springer, 2009.

———. "The Overseas Chinese in El Paso: Changing Goals, Changing Realities." In *Hidden Heritage: Historical Archaeology of the Overseas Chinese*. Edited by Priscilla Wegars, 125–149. Amityville, NY: Baywood Publishing, 1993.

Steele, Richard F. *An Illustrated History of Stevens, Ferry, Okanagan, and Chelan Counties*. Spokane, WA: Western Historical, 1904.

Stewart, Watt. *Chinese Bondage in Peru: A History of the Chinese Coolie in Peru, 1849–1874*. Durham, NC: Duke University Press, 1951.

———. *Henry Meiggs: Yankee Pizarro*. Durham, NC: Duke University Press, 1946.

Stowe, Harriet Beecher. *Uncle Tom's Cabin, or Life Among the Lowly*. Boston: John P. Jewett & Company, 1852.

Sun Fang and Liu Xuhua. *Haiwai hongmen yu xinhai geming* [The Hong Fraternal Society Overseas and the 1911 Revolution]. Beijing: Zhongguo zhigong chubanshe, 2011.

Sutton, Mark Q., and B. S. Arkush. *Archaeological Laboratory Methods: An Introduction*. Dubuque, IA: Kendall/Hunt Publishing, 1996.

Swartout, Robert R. Jr. "Kwangtung to Big Sky: The Chinese Experience in Frontier Montana." In *Chinese on the American Frontier*. Edited by Arif Dirlik. Lanham, MD: Rowman & Littlefield, 2001.

Takaki, Ronald. *Strangers from a Different Shore: A History of Asian Immigrants*. New York: Penguin, 1989.

Tan Biao 谭镖, ed. *Xinhui xiangtu zhi* 新会乡土志 [Xinhui Local Annals]. Vol. 9. Guangzhou: Yuedong bianyi gongzi 粤东编译公司, 1908.

Tan Qianchu 谭乾初. *Guba Zazhi* 古巴杂记. China, 1887.

Taube, Karl. *The Legendary Past: Aztec and Maya Myths*. London: British Museum Press, 1993.

Tchen, John Kuo Wei. *New York before Chinatown: Orientalism and the Shaping of American Culture, 1776–1882*. Baltimore: Johns Hopkins University Press, 2001.

Thalheimer, M. E. *The Eclectic History of the United States*. Cincinnati: Van Antwerp, Bragg, 1880.

Tocqueville, Alexis de. *Democracy in America*. Translated by Arthur Goldhammer. New York: Library of America, 2012.

Todd, John. *The Sunset Land; or, The Great Pacific Slope*. Boston: Lee & Shepard, 1870.

Toll, David W. *The Complete Nevada Traveler: The Affectionate and Intimately*

Detailed Guidebook to the Most Interesting State in America. Virginia City, NV: Gold Hill Publishing, 2002.

Toynbee, Arnold. *A Study of History: Abridgement of Vols. I–VI.* Abridgement by D. C. Somervell. Oxford: Oxford University Press, 1946.

Trouillot, Michel-Rolph. *Global Transformations: Anthropology and the Modern World.* New York: Palgrave Macmillan, 2003.

Tsai, Shih-Shah Henry. *The Chinese Experience in America.* Bloomington: Indiana University Press, 1986.

Tsu, Cecilia. *Garden of the World: Asian Immigrants and the Making of Agriculture in California's Santa Clara Valley.* New York: Oxford University Press, 2013.

Tupin, Pierre. *Recueil de documents historiques sur la ruée vers l'or en Californie, 1848–1854—vue par la presse française* [Collection of Historical Documents on the California Gold Rush, 1848–1854—Seen by the French Press]. Paris: P. Tupin, 1998.

Tutorow, Norman E. *The Governor: The Life and Legacy of Leland Stanford.* 2 vols. Spokane, WA: Arthur H. Clark Co., 2004.

Tweed, Thomas. *The American Encounter with Buddhism, 1844–1912: Victorian Culture and the Limits of Dissent.* Bloomington: Indiana University Press, 1992.

US 53d Congress. *Memorial Addresses upon the Life and Character of Leland Stanford.* Washington, DC: US Government Printing Office, 1894.

Van Dyke, Paul. *The Canton Trade: Life and Enterprise on the China Coast, 1700–1845.* Hong Kong: Hong Kong University Press, 2005.

———. *Merchants of Canton and Macao.* Hong Kong: Hong Kong University Press, 2011.

Wakeman, Frederic. *Stranger at the Gate: Social Disorder in South China, 1839–1861.* Berkeley: University of California Press, 1966.

Wegars, Priscilla., ed. *Hidden Heritage: Historical Archaeology of the Overseas Chinese.* Amityville, NY: Baywood Publishing, 1993.

Wei Ningyang kenqin dahui zhici 为宁阳恳亲大会致辞 [A Speech in Assembly of Ning Yeung People]. In 建议筹建台山男女免费义学 [A Proposal to Open a Free Private School in Taishan]. Edited by Huang Fuling 黄福领 and Zhu Zhongji 朱仲缉. Ning Yeung Association 宁阳会馆, 1928.

White, Richard. *Railroaded: The Transcontinentals and the Making of Modern America.* New York: W. W. Norton, 2011.

Whitney, Asa. *A Project for a Railroad to the Pacific.* New York: George W. Wood, 1849.

Wickberg, Edgar, ed. *From China to Canada: A History of the Chinese Communities in Canada.* Toronto: McClelland & Stewart, 1982.

Williams, John Hoyt. *A Great and Shining Road: The Epic Story of the Transcontinental Railroad.* Lincoln: University of Nebraska Press, 1996.

Willumson, Glenn. *Iron Muse: Photographing the Transcontinental Railroad.* Berkeley: University of California Press, 2013.

Wofoshanren. *Ku she hui* [Bitter Society]. Shanghai: Shanghai Tu shu zi liao she, 1905.

Wong, H. K. *Gum Sahn Yum—Gold Mountain Men.* Brisbane, CA: Fong Brothers Printing, 1987.

Wong Hau-hon. "Reminiscences of an Old Chinese Railroad Worker." Translated by Him Mark Lai. In *Chinese American Voices: From the Gold Rush to the Present.* Edited by Judy Yung, Gordon H. Chang, and Him Mark Lai. Berkeley: University of California Press, 2006.

Wong, Sau-ling Cynthia. *Reading Asian American Literature: From Necessity to Extravagance.* Princeton, NJ: Princeton University Press, 1993.

Wong, Shawn Hsu. *Homebase.* Reprint, New York: Plume, 1991.

Wu, S. Y. 吳尚鷹. 美國華僑百年紀實 [One Hundred Years of Chinese in the United States and Canada]. Hong Kong: Chia Low, 1954.

Wu, Tingfang. *America through the Spectacles of an Oriental Diplomat.* New York: Frederick A. Stokes, 1914.

Wu, Yi-Li. "The Qing Period." In *Chinese Medicine and Healing. An Illustrated History.* Edited by T. J. Heinrichs and Linda L. Barnes, 161–204. Cambridge, MA: Belknap Press of Harvard University Press, 2013.

———. *Reproducing Women: Medicine, Metaphor, and Childbirth in Late Imperial China.* Berkeley: University of California Press, 2010.

Wylie, Jerry, and Richard E. Fike. "Chinese Opium Smoking Techniques and Paraphernalia." In *Hidden Heritage: Historical Archaeology of the Overseas Chinese.* Edited by Priscilla Wegars, 255–303. Amityville, NY: Baywood Publishing, 1993.

Yaeger, Jason, and Marcello A. Canuto. "Introducing an Archaeology of Communities." In *The Archaeology of Communities: A New World Perspective.* Edited by Marcello A. Canuto and Jason Yaeger, 1–15. London: Routledge, 2000.

Yang Guobiao, Liu Hanbiao, and Yang Anyao. *Mei guo hua qiao shi* [A History of Overseas Chinese in the United States]. Guangzhou: Guang dong gao deng jiao yue chu ban she, 1989.

Yang, Jeannie K., and Ray W. Hellmann. "A Second Look at Chinese Brown-Glazed Stoneware." In *Ceramic Identification in Hisorical Archaeology: The View from California, 1822–1940.* Edited by Rebecca Allen, Julia E. Huddleson, Kimberly J. Wooten, and Glenn J. Farris, 215–227. Germantown, MD: Society for Historical Archaeology, 2013.

Yee, Paul. *A Superior Man.* Vancouver: Arsenal Pulp Press, 2015.

Yep, Laurence. *Dragon's Gate.* New York: Harper Trophy, 1993.

Ying, A. *Fan mei hua gong jin yue wen xue ji* [A Literary Anthology on Resistance to the US Exclusion of Chinese Laborers] In *Zhong guo jin dai fan qin lue wen xue ji* [Literary Collections of China's Modern Resistance to Foreign Aggressions]. Beijing: Zhong hua shu ju, 1960.

Yip, Hon-ming. *The Tung Wah Coffin Home and Global Charity Network: Evidence and Findings from Archival Materials.* Hong Kong: Joint Publishing (HK), 2009.

Young, Elliott. *Alien Nation: Chinese Migration in the Americas from the Coolie Era through World War II.* Chapel Hill: University of North Carolina Press, 2014.

Yu Baiyun 余白云, ed. *Jinshan geji* 金山歌集 [Ballads of Gold Mountain]. San Francisco: Daguang shulin yinhang 大光书林印行, n.d.

Yu, Connie. *Chinatown, San Jose, USA.* San Jose, CA: History San José and the Chinese Historical and Cultural Project, 2001.

Yu-cheng Lee 李有成. 記憶 [Memory]. Taipei: Asian Culture, 2016.

Yun, Lisa. *The Coolie Speaks: Chinese Indentured Laborers and African Slaves in Cuba.* Philadelphia: Temple University Press, 2008.

Yung, Judy, Gordon H. Chang, and Him Mark Lai. *Chinese American Voices: From the Gold Rush to the Present.* Berkeley: University of California Press, 2006.

Zesch, Scott. *The Chinatown War: Chinese Los Angeles and the Massacre of 1871.* New York: Oxford University Press, 2012.

Zhang Qichen 张启琛, ed. *Hukou* 户口 [Households]. In *Kaiping xian xiangtu zhi* 开平县乡土志 [Kaiping Local Records]. Kaiping, China, 1909.

Zhang Renyu. *Mei di pai hua shi* [A History of US Imperialist Exclusion of the Chinese]. Beijing: Wen hua gong ying she, 1951.

Zhang Xie 张燮. *Dong Xi Yang Kao* 东西洋考 [Investigation of East and West Oceans]. Taipei, 1962. First published 1618.

Zhongguo minjian wenxue jicheng Guangdong juan Taishan xian ziliao ji 中国民间文学集成广东卷台山县资料集 [Guangdong Taishan Data Set of the Chinese Folklore Collections]. Taishan, China: Taishan xian minjian wenxue jicheng bianwei hui 台山县民间文学集成编委会, 1987.

Zhu Shijia. *Mei guo po hai hua gong shi liao* [Historical Materials Concerning US Persecution of Chinese Laborers]. Beijing: Zhong hua shu ju, 1958.

Zhu Zhongji 朱仲绲. "Xuyan san" 序言三 [Preface 3]. In 全美宁阳第一届恳亲大会始末记 [The Historical Record of the First Family Reunion Assembly of Ning Yeung People from Taishan in the US]. Edited by Huang Fuling 黄福领 and Zhu Zhongji 朱仲绲. Ning Yeung Association, 宁阳会馆, 1928.

Zolberg, Aristide R. "The Great Wall against China: Responses to the First Immigration Crisis, 1885–1925." In *Migration, Migration History, History: Old Paradigms and New Perspectives.* Edited by Jan Lucassen and Leo Lucassen, 291–316. Bern, Switzerland: Peter Lang, 1999.

Journals and Magazines

Akin, Marjorie Kleiger. "The Noncurrency Functions of Chinese *Wen* in America." *Historical Archaeology* 26, no. 2 (1992): 58–65.

Akin, Marjorie, James C. Bard, and Gary Weisz. "Asian Coins Recovered from Chinese Railroad Labor Camps: Evidence of Cultural Practices and Transnational Exchange." *Historical Archaeology* 49, no. 1 (2015): 110–121.

Barile, Kerri S. "Race, the National Register, and Cultural Resource Management: Creating an Historic Context for Postbellum Sites." *Historical Archaeology* 38, no. 1 (2004): 90–100.

Baxter, R. Scott. "The Response of California's Chinese Populations to the Anti-Chinese Movement." *Historical Archaeology* 42, no. 3 (2008): 29–36.

Baxter, R. Scott, and Rebecca Allen. "The View from Summit Camp." *Historical Archaeology* 49, no. 1 (2015): 34–45.

Best, Gerald M. "Rendezvous at Promontory: The 'Jupiter' and No. 119." *Utah Historical Quarterly* 37, no. 1 (Winter 1969): 69–75.

Bowen, William M. "Early Chinese Medicine in Southern California." *Gum Saan Journal*, no. 1 (June 1994): 5–6.

Bowman, J. N. "Driving the Last Spike at Promontory." *Utah Historical Quarterly* 37, no. 1 (Winter 1969): 76–101.

Brinkerhoff, Kerry. "Chinese and the American Indian on the Transcontinental Railroad." *Gum Saan Journal* 22, no. 2 (1999): 9, 10.

———. "Native Americans and the Transcontinental Railroad." *Transcontinental* 1, no. 11 (2001): 8.

Burgess, Opie Rundle. "Quong Kee: Pioneer of Tombstone." *Arizona Highways* 25, no. 7 (July 1949): 14–16.

Carpenter, C. M., and K. Hyoejin Yoon. "Rethinking Alternative Contact in Native American and Chinese Encounters: Juxtaposition in Nineteenth-Century US Newspapers." *College Literature* 41, no. 1 (2014): 7–42.

Carter, Greg Lee. "Social Demography of the Chinese in Nevada, 1870–1880." *Nevada Historical Quarterly* 18 (Summer 1975): 72–89.

Chace, Paul G. "Introductory Note to Chace and Evans's 1969 Presentation." *Historical Archaeology* 49, no. 1 (2015): 24–26.

Chace, Paul G., and William S. Evans, Jr. 1969. "Celestial Sojourners in the High Sierras: The Ethno-Archaeology of Chinese Railroad Workers (1865–1868)." *Historical Archaeology* 49, no. 1 (2015): 27–33.

Chace, Paul G., and William S. Evans Jr. "Celestial Sojourners in the High Sierras: The Ethno-Archaeology of Chinese Railroad Workers (1865–1868)." *Historical Archaeology* 49, no. 1 (2015): 27–33.

Chan Koonchung. "Mei guo hua qiao xue lei jian shi" [A Brief Bloody History of

Overseas Chinese in America]. *Ming Pao Monthly* (October/November 1977): n.p.

Chan, Loren B. "The Chinese in Nevada: A Historical Survey, 1856–1970." *Nevada Historical Quarterly* 25 (Winter 1982): 266–314.

Chang, Gordon H. "China and the Pursuit of America's Destiny: Nineteenth-Century Imagining and Why Immigration Restriction Took So Long." *Journal of Asian American Studies* 15, no. 2 (June 2012): 145–169.

Charlton, Anne. "Medicinal Uses of Tobacco in History." *Journal of the Royal Society of Medicine* 97, no. 6 (2004): 292–296.

Cheek, Lawrence W. "A Place Called Bisbee." *Arizona Highways* 65, no. 2 (February 1989): 4–11.

Chen Chung. "Personal Recollections of Chen Chung." *The Occident.* January 1, 1870.

Chen, Yong. "The Internal Origins of Chinese Emigration to California Reconsidered." *Western Historical Quarterly* 28, no. 4 (Winter 1997): 532–535.

Cheng, Lucie, and Liu Yuzun with Zheng Dehua. "Chinese Emigration, the Sunning Railway and the Development of Toisan." *Amerasia Journal* 9, no. 1 (1982): 59–74.

Cheong Kee Cheok. "Chinese Overseas Remittances to China: The Perspective from South-East Asia." *Journal of Contemporary Asia* 43, no. 1 (2013): 75–101.

Cheung, Floyd. "Anxious and Ambivalent Representations: Nineteenth-Century Images of Chinese American Men." *Journal of American Culture* 30, no. 3 (2007): 293–309.

Chew, James R. "Boyhood Days in Winnemucca, 1901–1910." *Nevada Historical Society* 4, no. 3 (September 1998): 206–209.

"China and the Indies—Our 'Manifest Destiny' in the East." *DeBow's Review* 15 (December 1853): 541–571.

"The Chinaman as a Railroad Builder." *Scientific American.* July 31, 1869: 75.

"Chinese Labour in America." *Engineering: An Illustrated Weekly Journal* (London). May 28, 1869, 360.

"Chinese Mission—Colportage." *The Occident.* December 1, 1869.

Cohen, Lucy M. "The Chinese of the Panama Railroad: Preliminary Notes on the Migrants of 1854 Who 'Failed.'" *Ethnohistory* 18 no. 4 (Autumn 1971): 309–320.

Colby, Benjamin N. "Well-Being: A Theoretical Program." *American Anthropologist* 89, no. 4 (1987): 879–895.

Corbett, Robert. "Unionville, Nevada: Pioneer Mining Camp." *Nevada Historical Review* 2, no. 1 (1974): 7–26.

Cronin, Mary M., and William E. Huntzicker. "Popular Chinese Images and 'The Coming Man' of 1870: Racial Representations of Chinese." *Journalism History* 38, no. 2 (2012): 86–99.

Dalglish, Christopher. "Archaeology and Landscape Ethics." *World Archaeology* 44, no. 3 (2012): 327–341.

"Daniel Cleveland: San Diego Patron." *Journal of San Diego History, San Diego Historical Society Quarterly* 11, no. 1 (January 1965). https://www.sandiegohistory .org/journal/1965/january/cleveland-2/.

deMenocal, P. B. "Cultural Responses to Climate Change During the Late Holocene." *Science* 292 (2001): 667–673.

Depping, Guillaume. "A travers le continent américain" [Across the American Continent]. *Journal officiel de la République française,* October 16, 1876, 7528.

DeVarenne, Alexandra Kichenik. "Goji Farm USA Brings Superfruit to Sonoma County." *Edible* 29 (Spring 2016): 67–70.

Dillon, Sidney. "Historic Moments: Driving the Last Spike of the Union Pacific." *Scribner's* 12, September 1892, 253–259.

Ding Zemin. "Mei guo zhong yang tai ping yang tie lu de xing jian yu hua gong de ju da gong xian" [The Construction of America's Central Pacific Railroad and the Tremendous Contribution of Chinese Workers]. *Shi xue ji kan* [Compilation of Historiography] 2 (1990): 47–54.

Dixon, Kelly J. "Historical Archaeologies in the American West." *Journal of Archaeological Research* 22, no. 3 (2014): 177–228.

Douglas, Mary. "Deciphering a Meal." *Daedalus* 101, no. 1 (1972): 61–81.

"Dr. Yee Fung Cheung." *Journal of Sierra Nevada History and Biography* 5 (Winter 2013): 1.

Duruz, Jean. "Floating Food: Eating 'Asia' in Kitchens of the Diaspora." *Emotion, Space and Society* 3 (2010): 45–49.

Ellis, Meredith A. B., Christopher W. Merritt, Shannon A. Novak, and Kelly J. Dixon. "The Signature of Starvation: A Comparison of Bone Processing at a Chinese Encampment in Montana and the Donner Party Camp in California." *Historical Archaeology* 45, no. 2 (2011): 97–112.

Erbaugh, Mary S. "The Secret History of the Hakkas: The Chinese Revolution as a Hakka Enterprise." *China Quarterly* 132 (1992): 937–968.

Fleisig, Heywood. "The Central Pacific Railroad and the Railroad Land Controversy." *Journal of Economic History* 35, no. 3 (September 1975): 552–566.

Furnis, Lynn, and Mary L. Mainery. "An Archaeological Strategy for Chinese Workers' Camps in the West: Method and Case Study." *Historical Archaeology* 49, no. 1 (2015): 71–84.

Gardner, A. Dudley. "Cores and Peripheries: Chinese Communities in Southwestern Wyoming, 1869–1922." *Wyoming Archaeologist* 49, no. 1 (2005): 19–39.

Gariel, M. "Notice sur la vie et les travaux de M. Malézieux" [Record of the Life and Works of Mr. Malézieux]. *Annales des ponts et chaussées* (1888): 514–570.

George, Henry. "What the Railroad Will Bring Us." *Overland Monthly* 1, no. 4 (October 1868).

Gillis, John R. "Tunnels of the Pacific Railroad." *Van Nostrand's Electric Engineering Magazine,* January 5, 1870, 418–423.

González-Tennant, Edward. "Creating a Diasporic Archaeology of Chinese Migration: Tentative Steps across Four Continents." *International Journal of Historical Archaeology* 15 (2011): 509–532.

Green, Linda. "Lived Lives and Social Suffering: Problems and Concerns in Medical Anthropology." *Medical Anthropology Quarterly,* n.s., 12, no. 1 (1998): 3–7.

Griego, Andrew. "Rebuilding the California Southern Railroad: The Personal Account of a Chinese Labor Contractor, 1884." *Journal of San Diego History* 25, no. 4 (Fall 1979). https://www.sandiegohistory.org/journal/79fall/railroad.htm.

Hall, Shawn R. "A History of Elko, Nevada." *Northeastern Quarterly* 95, no. 3 (1995).

Hardesty, D. L. "Perspectives on Global-Change Archaeology." *American Anthropologist* 109 (2007): 1–7.

Hardesty, Donald L. "Comments on 'Historical Archaeology Adrift?' Response to Charles E. Cleland's 'Historical Archaeology Adrift?'" *Historical Archaeology* 35, no. 2 (2001): 23–24.

Harrod, Ryan P., and John J. Crandall. "Rails Built of the Ancestors' Bones: The Bioarchaeology of the Overseas Chinese Experience." *Historical Archaeology* 49, no. 1 (2015): 148–161.

Harrod, Ryan P., Jennifer L. Thompson, and Debra L. Martin. "Hard Labor and Hostile Encounters: What Human Remains Reveal about Institutional Violence and Chinese Immigrants Living in Carlin, Nevada (1885–1923)." *Historical Archaeology* 46, no. 4 (2013): 85–111.

Heath, Earle. "From Trail to Rail—The Story of the Beginning of the Southern Pacific." *Southern Pacific Bulletin* 15 (May 1927): 9–12.

Hedges, James B. "The Colonization Work of the Northern Pacific Railroad." *Mississippi Valley Historical Review* 13, no. 3 (December 1926): 311–342.

Heffner, Sarah C. "Exploring Health-Care Practices of Chinese Railroad Workers in North America." *Historical Archaeology* 49, no. 1 (2015): 134–147.

———. "Exploring Healthcare Practices of the Lovelock Chinese: An Analysis and Interpretation of Medicinal Artifacts in the Lovelock Chinatown Collection." *Nevada Archaeologist* 26 (2013): 25–36.

Hickson, Howard, and Terry Hickson. "Elko General Hospital: The Beginnings and the End." *Northeastern Nevada Historical Society Quarterly* 1 (2007).

Hoffmann, John P. "The Historical Shift in the Perception of Opiates: From Medicine to Social Menace." *Journal of Psychoactive Drugs* 22, no, 1 (1990): 53–62.

"How Our Chinamen Are Employed." *Overland Monthly* 2, no. 3 (March 1869): 231.

Huang Annian. "Zhong yang tai ping yang tie lu de jian cheng yu zai mei hua gong de gong xian" [The Completion of Central Pacific Railroad and the Contribution of Chinese Workers in the United States]. *He bei shi fan da xue xue bao* [Journal of Hebei Normal University] (Social Sciences) 22, no. 2 (1999): 97–112.

———. "Hua gong jian she tai ping yang tie lu he mei guo de jue qi" [The Construction of the Central Pacific Railroad by Chinese Workers and the Rise of the United States]. *li shi jiao xue wen ti* [Issues in History Teaching] 6 (2007): 39–41.

———. "Zhao hui xing jian zhong yang tai ping yang tie lu hua gong li shi yin ji" [In Search of the Historical Footprints of the Chinese Workers Building the Central Pacific Railroad]. *Zhong xue li shi jiao xue zhi nan* [Teaching References for High School History] 356 (2015): 10–13.

Hudson, John C. "Towns of the Western Railroads." *Great Plains Quarterly* 2, no. 1 (1982): 41–54.

Ingalls, Ethel. "Mrs. Leland Stanford." *Ladies' Home Journal.* February 1892, 3.

Jin Ting 覲廷. *Duiyu Wen Gaohua buzhun huaren xinke daobu zhi ganyan (xugao)* [Comments on Vancouver's Ban on the Entry of the Chinese Immigrants (A Sequel)]. *Xinning zazhi* 新宁杂志 15 (1914): 2.

Johnson, Michael W. "Rendezvous at Promontory: A New Look at the Golden Spike Ceremony." *Utah Historical Quarterly* 72 (2004): 47–68.

Jue, Willard G. "Chin Gee-Hee, Chinese Pioneer Entrepreneur in Seattle and Toishan." *Annals of the Chinese Historical Society of the Pacific Northwest* 1 (1983): 31–38.

Karlin, Jules Alexander. "The Anti-Chinese Outbreak in Tacoma, 1885." *Pacific Historical Review* 23, no. 3 (1954): 271–283.

Kennedy, J. Ryan. "Zooarchaeology, Localization, and Chinese Railroad Workers in North America." *Historical Archaeology* 49, no. 1 (2015): 122–133.

Khor, Denise. "Archives, Photography, and Historical Memory: Tracking the Chinese Railroad Workers in North America." *Southern California Quarterly* 98, no. 4 (Winter 2016).

Kowal, Emma, Wendy Gunthorpe, and Ross S. Bailie. "Measuring Emotional and Social Well Being in Aboriginal and Torres Strait Islander Populations: An Analysis of a Negative Life Events Scale." *International Journal for Equity in Health* 6, no. 18 (2007). doi: 10.1186/1475-9276-6-18.

Kraus, George. "Chinese Laborers and the Construction of the Central Pacific." *Utah Historical Quarterly* 37, no. 1 (Winter 1969): 41–57.

Lake, Holly. "Construction of the CPRR: Chinese Immigrant Contribution." *Northeastern Nevada Historical Society Quarterly* 4 (1994): 188–199.

Levy, Daniel W. "Classical Lawyers and the Southern Pacific Railroad." *Western Legal History* 9, no. 2 (Summer/Fall 1996): 176–226.

Liestman, Daniel. "Horizontal Inter-Ethnic Relations: Chinese and America Indians in the 19th Century West." *Western Historical Quarterly* 30, no. 3 (1999): 327–349.

"The Life of Zhang Zhilian." *Chinese Studies in History* 43, no. 3 (Spring 2010): 107–110.

Lindau, Rudolf. "Du pacifique à l'atlantique" [From Pacific to Atlantic]. *Revue des Deux Mondes,* November 1869, 15.

Lingling Ding, Ge Quansheng, Zheng Jingyun, and Hao Zhixin. "Variations in Annual Winter Mean Temperature in South China since 1736." *Boreas: An International Journal of Quaternary Research* 45, no. 2 (October 2015): 252–259.

Liu Jin. "Remittance Charges and the Change of Social Attitudes in the PRD Region." *Journal of Wuyi University,* 2011–2012. http://en.cnki.com.cn/Article_en/CJFDTotal-WYDS201102004.htm.

"Lo! The Poor Indian! Where Are the Philanthropists?" *Crisis,* September 15, 1869, 265.

Lo, Vivienne. "Spirit of Stone: Technical Considerations in the Treatment of the Jade Body." *Bulletin of the School of Oriental and African Studies* 65, no. 1 (2002): 99–128.

Locke, H., and P. Deardon. "Rethinking Protected Areas and the New Paradigm." *Environmental Conservation* 32, no. 1 (2015): 1–10.

Loomis, A. W. "The Chinese Six Companies." *Overland Monthly,* September 1868, 221–227.

Loomis, Augustus Ward. "Chinese 'Funeral Baked Meats.'" *Overland Monthly* 3, no. 1 (July 1869): 22.

Lowman, Chris. "'Our First Chinese': Social Interaction and Potential Archaeological Remains of Chinese Communities at Stanford University." *SCA Proceedings* 27 (2013): 188–192.

Luna, Concie. "A Chinese Puzzle." *Lake Chelan Historical Society History Notes* 26 (2011): 8–11.

Lyman, Stanford M., W. E. Willmott Lyman, and Berching Ho. "Rules of a Chinese Secret Society in British Columbia." *Bulletin of the School of Oriental and African Studies* 27, no. 3 (1964): 536.

Madsen, Brigham D., and Betty M. Madsen. "Corinne, The Fair: Gateway to Montana Mines." *Utah Historical Quarterly* 37, no. 1 (Winter 1969): 102–123.

Maffly-Kipp, Laurie. "Engaging Habits and Besotted Idolatry: Viewing Chinese Religions in the American West." *Material Religion* 1, no. 1 (March 2005): 72–97.

Maniery, Mary L. "The Archaeology of Asian Immigrants: Thirty-Five Years in the Making." *SAA Archaeological Record* 4, no. 5 (2004): 10–13.

Marx, Leo. "The Railroad in the Landscape: An Iconological Reading of a Theme in American Art." *Prospects* 10 (1985): 77–117.

McLaughlin, Mark. "Reign of the Sierra Storm King: Weather History of Donner Pass." *Journal of the Sierra College Natural History Museum* 2, no. 1 (2009). http://www.sierracollege.edu/ejournals/jscnhm/v2n1/stormking.html.

Merritt, Christopher W., Gary Weisz, and Kelly J. Dixon. "'Verily the Road Was Built with Chinaman's Bones': An Archaeology of Chinese Line Camps in Montana." *International Journal of Historical Archaeology* 16, no. 4 (2012): 666–695.

Michaels, Gina. "Peck-Marked Vessels from the San José Market Street Chinatown, a Study of Distribution and Significance." *International Journal of Historical Archaeology* 9, no. 2 (2005): 123–134.

Molenda, John. "Moral Discourse and Personhood in Overseas Chinese Contexts." *Historical Archaeology* 49, no. 1 (2015): 46–58.

Mrozowski, Stephen A., Maria Franklin, and Leslie Hunt. "Archaeobotanical Analysis and Interpretations of Enslaved Virginian Plant Use at Rich Neck Plantation (44WB52)." *American Antiquity* 73, no. 4 (2008): 699–728.

Ngai, Mae. "Chinese Gold Miners and the 'Chinese Question' in Nineteenth-Century California and Victoria." *Journal of American History* 101, no. 4 (2015): 1082–1105.

Noel, Thomas J. "All Hail the Denver Pacific: Denver's First Railroad." *Colorado Magazine* 50, no. 3 (Spring 1973): 91–116.

Orser, C. E. Jr. "An Archaeology of Eurocentrism." *American Antiquity* 77 (2012): 737–755.

———. "Twenty-First-Century Historical Archaeology." *Journal of Archaeological Research* 18 (2010): 111–150.

Orsi, Richard. "Railroads in the History of California and the Far West: An Introduction." *California History* 70, no. 1 (Spring 1991): 2–11.

Osterhuber, Randall. "Climate Summary of Donner Summit, California 1870–2001." *Journal of the Sierra College Natural History Museum* 2, no. 1 (2009). http://www.sierracollege.edu/ejournals/jscnhm/v2n1/stormking.html.

Palmquist, Peter. "Alfred A. Hart and the Illustrated Traveler's Map of the Central Pacific Railroad." *Stereo World* 6, no. 6 (1980): 14–18.

Panda, Ankit. "Reflecting on China's Five Principles, 60 Years Later." *The Diplomat*, June 26, 2014. http://thediplomat.com/2014/06/reflecting-on-chinas-five-principles-60-years-later/.

Perkins, A. E. "The Transcontinental Lines of the West." *Journal of Geography* 8, no. 5 (1910): 97–109.

Polk, Michael R. "Interpreting Chinese Worker Camps on the Transcontinental Railroad at Promontory Summit, Utah." *Historical Archaeology* 49, no. 1 (2015): 59–70.

Qi Yuan 启元. Tangmei xuexiao shilve 唐美学校史略 [A Brief History of Taimei's Schools]. *Tangmei Jikan* 唐美季刊 1 (1935): 1.

Ramslade, Marie. "Impressions of a Young French Gentleman's 1866 Visit to the Australian Colonies." *Australian Studies* 2 (2010): 10.

Rhoads, Edward J. M. "The Chinese in Texas." *Southwestern Historical Quarterly* 81, no. 1 (July 1977): 1–36.

Rusco, Elmer P. "Chinese Massacre of 1866." *Nevada Historical Society Quarterly* 45, no. 1 (2002): 3–30.

Saxton, Alexander. "The Army of Canton in the High Sierra." *Pacific Historical Review* 35, no. 2 (May 1966): 141–152.

Schmidt, Ryan W. "Perimortem Injury in a Chinese American Cemetery: Two Cases of Occupational Hazard or Interpersonal Violence." *Internet Journal of Biological Anthropology* 3, no. 2 (2009). doi: 10.5580/2939.

Scott, Sara A. "Indian Forts and Religious Icons: The Buffalo Road (*Qoq'aalx 'Iskit*) Trail before and after the Lewis and Clark Expedition." *International Journal of Historical Archaeology* 19, no. 2 (2015): 384–415.

Sohoni, Deborah. "Unsuitable Suitors: Anti-miscegenation Laws, Naturalization Laws, and the Construction of Asian Identities." *Law and Society Review* 41, no. 3 (2007).

Spier, Robert F. G. "Food Habits of Nineteenth-Century California Chinese (concluded)." *California Historical Quarterly* 37, no. 2 (June 1958): 129–136.

Sunseri, Charlotte K. "Alliance Strategies in the Racialized Railroad Economies of the American West." *Historical Archaeology* 49, no. 1 (2015): 85–99.

———. "Food Politics of Alliance in a California Frontier Chinatown." *International Journal of Historical Archaeology* 19, no. 2 (2015): 416–431.

Swackhamer, Barry A. "J. B. Silvis, the Union Pacific's Nomadic Photographer." *Journal of the West* 33, no. 2 (1994). http://cprr.org/Museum/Silvis/.

"Tan Mingfu Shenjin wangfei gaoshi" 覃明府申禁妄费告示 [Tan Mingfu's Public Notice on Banning Sumptuous Spending]. *Xinning Zazhi* 新宁杂志 1 (1909): 35.

Teng, S. Y. "Chinese Historiography in the Last Fifty Years." *Far Eastern Quarterly* 8, no. 2 (February 1949): 131–156.

Torbenson, Michael, Robert H. Kelly, Jonathon Erlen, Lorna Cropcho, Michael Moraca, Bonnie Beiler, K. N. Rao, and Mohamen Virji. "Lash's: A Bitter Medicine. Biochemical Analysis of an Historical Proprietary Medicine." *Historical Archaeology* 34, no. 2 (2000): 56–64.

Ts'ai, Shih-shan H. "Chinese Immigration through Communist Chinese Eyes: An Introduction to the Historiography." *Pacific Historical Review* 43, no. 3 (August 1974): 395–408.

Urbaniak, Timothy R., and Kelly J. Dixon. "Inscribed in Stone: Historic Inscriptions and the Cultural Heritage of Railroad Workers." *Historical Archaeology* 49, no. 1 (2015): 100–109.

Verstraete, Ginette. "Railroading America: Towards a Material Study of the Nation." *Theory, Culture and Society* 19, no. 5 (2002): 145–159.

Voss, Barbara L., ed. "The Archaeology of Chinese Railroad Workers in North America." Thematic issue of *Historical Archaeology* 49, no. 1 (2015).

———. "The Historical Experience of Labor: Archaeological Contributions to Interdisciplinary Research on Chinese Railroad Workers." *Historical Archaeology* 49, no. 1 (2016): 4–23.

———. "Towards a Transpacific Archaeology of the Modern World." *International Journal of Historical Archaeology* 20, no. 1 (2016): 146–174.

Voss, Barbara L., and B. Williams, eds. "Overseas Chinese Archaeology." *Historical Archaeology* 42, no. 3 (2008): 1–193.

Voss, Barbara L., and Rebecca Allen. "Overseas Chinese Archaeology: Historical Foundations, Current Reflections, and New Directions." *Historical Archaeology* 42, no. 3 (2008): 5–28.

Walther, Clarence I. "Ice Harvesting in Elko." *Northeastern Nevada Quarterly* 92, no. 1 (1992): 7–16.

Wang, Q. Edward. "Encountering the World: China and Its Other(s) in Historical Narratives, 1949–89." *Journal of World History* 14, no. 3 (2003): 327–358.

Watts, Jennifer A. "The Photographer and the Railroad Man." *California History* 78, no. 3 (1999): 154–159.

Wegars, Priscilla. "Who's Been Workin' on the Railroad? An Examination of the Construction, Distribution, and Ethnic Origins of Domed Rock Ovens on Railroad-Related Sites." *Historical Archaeology* 25, no. 1 (1991): 37–65.

Wenying Xu. "Masculinity, Food, and Appetite in Frank Chin's *Donald Duk* and 'The Eat and Run Midnight People.'" *Cultural Critique* 66 (2007): 78–103.

Xin Yi. "Zhong guo xue jie jiu tai ping yang tie lu hua gong yi ti xiang guan yan jiu cheng guo ping shu" [Summary and Evaluation of the Chinese Academic Scholarship on the Chinese Pacific Railroad Workers]. *Zhong shan da xue yan jiu sheng xue kan* [Journal of Graduate Students at Sun Yat-sen University] (Social Sciences) 35, no. 3 (2014): 1–9.

Zhongping Chen. "Building the Chinese Diaspora across Canada: Chinese Diasporic Discourse and the Case of Peterborough, Ontario." *Diaspora* 13, no. 2–3 (2004): 185–188, 195, 196, 205, 206.

Zhu Jieqin, "Shi jiu shi ji hou qi zhong guo ren zai mei guo kai fa zhong de zuo yong ji chu jing" [The Role and Predicament of the Chinese in the American Development in the Late Nineteenth Century]. *Li shi yan jiu* [History Studies] 1 (1980): 93–111.

Newspapers and Newsletters

"16 kilometres dans un jour" [Sixteen Kilometers in One Day]. *Le Petit Journal.* May 11, 1870.

"6000 CHINAMEN. How They Are Controlled by One Man. JUDGE, JURY,

EXECUTIONER. Some Incidents of the Work of the Southern Pacific Railroad." *Philadelphia Times.* March 13, 1882.

About, Aaron. "The Chinese. Their Wealth, Education, and Civilization—Shall We Encourage Chinese Immigration?" *Chicago Tribune.* June 14, 1869.

"Another Railroad for Arizona." *Weekly Journal-Miner* (Prescott, AZ). January 16, 1889.

"Arrival of 160 of Koopmanschap's Celestials in St. Louis." *Cincinnati Daily Enquirer.* August 24, 1870.

"Attacks on the Chinese." *Cleveland Plain Dealer.* September 30, 1869.

"Bones in Transit." *Sacramento Reporter.* June 30, 1870. https://cdnc.ucr.edu/cgi-bin/cdnc.

"Bones of Defunct Chinamen." *Sacramento Daily Union.* June 30, 1870. https://cdnc.ucr.edu/cgi-bin/cdnc.

"Bought a Chinese Girl." *Lyon County Times* (Dayton, NV). September 22, 1906.

"The China Mail Line." *Sacramento Daily Union.* January 3, 1867.

"The Chinaman as Railroad Builder." *Idaho Statesman* (Boise). May 25, 1869.

"Chinamen as Free Immigrants." *Massachusetts Spy* (Worcester). July 30, 1869.

"Chinamen Working for Seventy Cents a Day." *New York Sun.* June 4, 1876.

"The Chinese." *Commercial Advertiser* (New York). July 6, 1869.

"The Chinese: The Coming Man Arrived." *Cincinnati Daily Gazette.* July 18, 1870.

"Chinese at Tiburon." *Daily Alta California* (San Francisco). February 4, 1886.

"A Chinese Editor in the Pulpit: The Rev. Mr. Chew of San Francisco Talks of China's Needs." *New York Times.* December 30, 1901.

"Chinese Flags at Half-Mast." *San Francisco Morning Call.* June 26, 1893.

"Chinese Going to the Front." *Oregonian* (Portland). July 17, 1871.

"The Chinese in California: Wanton Attack on Railroad Laborers." *New York Evening Post.* August 9, 1873.

"The Chinese in New York: How They Live and Make Money—Good Wages." *New York Times.* March 6, 1880.

"Chinese in West Virginia. Tunneling for the Chesapeake and Ohio Railroad." *New-York Daily Tribune.* July 28, 1870.

"Chinese Killed in Snow Slide onto Tracks." *Daily Alta California* (San Francisco). February 2, 1868. http://www.lasvegassun.com/news/1999/dec/30/a-century-turns/.

"Chinese Labor in Utah." *Silver Reef (UT) Miner.* June 10, 1882.

"Chinese—Their Cost as Laborers—None on the Chesapeake and Ohio Railroad as Yet." *Richmond (VA) Whig.* September 16, 1870.

"Chinese Workers for Seventy Cents a Day." *New York Sun.* June 4, 1876.

Chu, Wilson. "The Chinese Railroad Men." *N.Y.C. Chinatown Reunion Newsletter.* May 11, 2006.

"Coolies in New-Jersey. Arrival of One Hundred and Fifty Chinamen at Pompton, N.J.—Three Hundred More on the Way—What the Contractors Pay for Their Services." *New York Times.* September 22, 1870.

Ditler, Joe. "Ode to the Coronado Train...." *Coronado (CA) Times.* June 11, 2014.

"Famed Tehachapi Loop Is an Engineering Marvel." *Tehachapi (CA) News.* May 17, 2016. http://www.tehachapinews.com/history-culture/2016/05/17/famed-teha chapi-loop-is-an-engineering-marvel.html.

"The Flowery Kingdoms: Four Hundred and Sixty-Three Celestials in St. Louis." *National Aegis* (Worcester, MA). July 23, 1870.

"Governor's Message, January 7, 1863." *Sacramento Daily Union.* January 8, 1863.

"The Heathen Chinese: The Experiment of the Cincinnati, Hamilton and Dayton Railroad with the Celestials." *Cincinnati Enquirer.* July 7, 1873.

"Honors to John Chinaman." *San Francisco News Letter and California Advertiser.* May 15, 1869.

Hoy, William. "Moy Jin Mun—Pioneer." *Chinese Digest.* May 15, 1936.

"An Indian Restaurant." *Walker Lake Bulletin* (Hawthorne, NV). May 16, 1883.

"Indian Workers on a Railroad." *Davenport (IA) Weekly Gazette.* August 8, 1883.

"John Chinaman: How He Lives and What He Does—The Problem of Excellent Skilled Workmen." *Daily Constitutionalist* (Augusta, GA). July 18, 1869.

Kearney, Denis. "Appeal from California: The Chinese Invasion." *Indianapolis Times.* February 28, 1878.

"The Last Rail." *Daily Alta California* (San Francisco), May 12, 1869.

"Leland Stanford Report to Stockholders, July 13, 1865." *Sacramento Daily Union.* July 14, 1865.

"Letter from Governor Stanford." *Sacramento Daily Union.* April 12, 1862.

"Livermore Tunnel." *Sacramento Daily Union.* February 9, 1869.

Magagnini, Stephen. "Chinese Transformed 'Gold Mountain'—Few Struck It Rich, but Their Work Left an Indelible Mark." *Sacramento Bee.* January 18, 1998.

———. "Well-Preserved Chinese Temple in Oroville Recalls Gold Rush Era." *Sacramento Bee.* November 29, 2014. http://www.sacbee.com/entertainment/living/travel/article4171477.html.

"The Mob Spirit Threatens." *Sacramento Daily Union.* November 5, 1877.

"More Chinese." *Galveston (TX) Tri-weekly News.* June 22, 1870.

"Murdered by Apaches." *New Southwest and Grant County Herald* (Silver City, NM). January 7, 1882.

"Mystery of the 'Last Spike' Finally Solved." *New York Times.* November 27, 1910.

"Our Celestial Cousins." *Indianapolis Sentinel.* July 9, 1873.

"Pacific Coast Despatches." *Daily Alta California* (San Francisco). July 13, 1869.

"Pacific Railroad Affairs." *Daily Alta California* (San Francisco). June 19, 1868. http://www.lasvegassun.com/news/1999/dec/30/a-century-turns/.

"Peaceful California." *Morning Call* (San Francisco). May 6, 1886.

"Sandstorm." *Daily Alta California* (San Francisco). August 12, 1868. http://www
.lasvegassun.com/news/1999/dec/30/a-century-turns/.

"Small-Pox on the Railroad." *Territorial Enterprise* (Virginia City, NV). January 5,
1869. http://www.lasvegassun.com/news/1999/dec/30/a-century-turns/.

"A Snow Slide. Eight Chinamen Buried Alive, Ten Barely Escape." *New Haven (CT)
Register.* January 31, 1881.

Stanford, Leland. "To the Stockholders of the Central Pacific Railroad Company,
July 13, 1865." *Railroad Record.* August 24 1865.

"The Stanford Museum." *Chicago Mail.* May 16, 1887.

"Stanford's Views." *Sacramento Daily Union.* January 16, 1889.

"Statistics of California—1866." *Sacramento Daily Union,* January 1, 1867. http://
www.lasvegassun.com/news/1999/dec/30/a-century-turns/.

Stillman, J. D. B. "The Last Tie." *Overland Monthly.* July 1869.

"The Summit Deserted—a Scramble for Relics." *San Francisco News Letter and California Advertiser.* May 15, 1869.

"Tearing Down the Mountain. How the Northern Pacific Railroad Is Driving the
Iron Horse through the Mountains." *Weekly Hawk-eye* (Burlington, IA). October
12, 1882.

"A Tourist in the Far West: A Month on the Pacific Coast." *New York Times.* February 9, 1878.

"Transcontinental Railroad Postscript." *San Francisco News Letter and California
Advertiser.* May 15, 1869.

"A Trip from Mason Valley to Walker Lake." *Esmeralda Herald* (Aurora, NV). September 18, 1880.

"A Tunnel Horror: Nearly Thirty Men Killed by an Explosion in San Francisco."
Cleveland Plain Dealer. November 19, 1879.

"The Uses of Wealth: Senator Stanford's Views—An Office Goes Begging." *Morning
Call* (San Francisco). May 6, 1886.

"The Utah Northern R.R." *Helena (MT) Weekly Herald.* August 12, 1875.

"The Western Pacific Railroad." *San Francisco Bulletin* 13, no. 107 (August 1869): 3.

"Western Pacific Railroad: Progress of the Work of Construction." *San Francisco
Daily Morning Chronicle.* June 4, 1869.

"Work on the S. D. & S. B. R. R." *San Diego Union.* November 26, 1872.

Reports, Papers, and Interviews

Baxter, R. Scott, and Rebecca Allen. *National Register of Historic Places Evaluation
and Damage Assessment for CA-PLA-2002/H (Summit Camp).* Prepared by Past
Forward, Inc., for Tahoe National Forest, United States Forest Service, 2008.

California Department of Transportation (Caltrans). *Work Camps: Historic Context and Archaeological Research Design.* Prepared by HARD Work Camps Team and Caltrans Staff for the California Department of Transportation, Sacramento, 2013.

Cannon, Kenneth P., Houston L. Martin, Jonathan M. Peart, Molly Boeka Cannon, John Blong, Paul Santarone, Kathy Selmon, and Kassidy Price. *The Archaeology of Chinese Railroad Workers in Utah: Results of Surveys in Box Elder and Emery Counties.* USUAS Special Report No. 2, Utah State Project Report No. U15UJ0417b. Report submitted to State of Utah, Department of Heritage and Arts, Salt Lake City, by USU Archaeological Services, Inc., Logan, UT, 2016.

Chace, Paul G. "Overseas Chinese Ceramics." In *The Changing Faces of Main Street: San Buenaventura Mission Plaza Project Archaeological Report, 1975.* Edited by Roberta S. Greenwood, 510–530. Ventura, CA: City of San Buenaventura Redevelopment Agency, 1976.

Chung, Sue Fawn. "The Chinese and Green Gold: Lumbering in the Sierras." Unpublished report for the Humboldt-Toiyabe National Forest, 2003. www.fs .usda.gov/Internet/FSE_DOCUMENTS/fsm9_026547.pdf.

Conner, Carl E., and Nicole Darnell. *Archaeological Investigation of Site 5ME7351.1, Excelsior Train Station, Mesa County, Colorado.* Report prepared for the Colorado Historical Society by Dominquez Archaeological Research Group, Grand Junction, CO, 2012.

Cummings, Linda Scott, Kathryn Puseman, and Thomas E. Moutoux. *Pollen, Starch, Parasite, Macrofloral, and Protein Residue Analysis of Sediment from the Evanston Chinatown Historic Archaeological Site, 48UT1749, Wyoming.* Paleo Research Labs Technical Report 98-19. Report prepared for Western Wyoming Community College, Rock Springs, 1998.

Felton, David L., Frank Lortie, and Peter D. Schulz. *The Chinese Laundry on Second Street: Archaeological Investigations at the Woodland Opera House Site.* Sacramento: Cultural Resource Management Unit, Resource Protection Division, State of California Department of Parks and Recreation, 1984.

Frémont, John C. "Some General Results of a Winter Expedition across the Rocky Mountains, for Survey of a Route for a Railroad to the Pacific." December 27, 1854. http://umassboston.worldcat.org/title/col-fremonts-exploration-of-the -central-railroad-route-to-the-pacific/oclc/561998253.

Gardner, A. Dudley, Barbara Clarke, and Lynn Harrell. *Final Report for the Aspen Section Camp 48UT660 and the Associated Union Pacific Railroad Grade 48UT668.* Prepared for Wyoming Bureau of Land Management by Western Wyoming Community College, Rock Springs, 2002.

Hallaran, Kevin B., Karen K. Swope, and Philip J. Wilke. *Historical and Archaeological Documentation of a Construction Camp ("China Camp") on the San Diego & Arizona Railway, Anza-Borrego Desert State Park, San Diego County, California.*

Report prepared for California Department of Parks and Recreation, Sacramento, by Archaeological Research Unit, University of California, Riverside, CA, 1989.

Jones, Edna. Interview by Edward Johnson, February 7, 1974. Walker River Tribal History Project: Oral History Interviews with Tribal Elders.

Landreth, K., K. Boreson, and M. Condon. *Archaeological Investigations at the Cabinet Landing Site (10BR413), Bonner County, Idaho.* Eastern Washington University Reports in Archaeology and History. Report Number 100-45. Cheney, WA, 1985.

Lindström, Susan. "Letter Report to Greg Taylor and Levine Fircke, Re: Kinder Morgan Donner Summit Incident Release Site: Restoration Phase Preliminary Archaeological Metal Detection Survey, 1 September." Tahoe National Forest, Truckee Ranger District, Truckee, CA, 2005.

Polk, Michael R., and Wendy Simmons Johnson, eds. *From Lampo Junction to Rozel: The Archaeological History of the Transcontinental Railroad across the Promontory Mountains, Utah.* GOSP Synthesis Report. Golden Spike National Historic Site, National Park Service and Central Pacific Railroad Grade, Area of Critical Environmental Concern, Utah Bureau of Land Management, 2012.

Popper, Virginia S. *Analysis of Macrobotanical Remains from Aspen Section Camp, Wyoming.* Paleo Research Labs Technical Report. Prepared for Western Wyoming Community College, Rock Springs, 2016.

———. *The Overseas Chinese Experience as Seen through Plants: Macrobotanical Analysis from the Market Street Chinatown, San Jose, California.* Technical Report no. 9. Market Street Chinatown Archaeological Project, Stanford University, Stanford, CA, 2014.

Praetzellis, Mary, and Adrian Praetzellis. *Historical Archaeology of an Overseas Chinese Community in Sacramento, California.* Report to US General Services Administration. Report prepared by Anthropological Studies Center, Sonoma State University, Rohnert Park, CA, 1997.

Puseman, Kathryn, Linda Scott Cummings, and Chad Yost. *Macrofloral and Organic Residue (FTIR) Analysis of Sediment from Summit Camp (FS SITE 05-17-57-633).* Paleo Research Institute Technical Report 08-19. Report prepared for Past Forward, Garden Valley, CA, 1998.

Raymond, Anan S., and Richard E. Fike. *Rails East to Promontory: The Utah Stations.* Bureau of Land Management Utah Resource Series no. 8. Bureau of Land Management, Salt Lake City, UT, 1981.

Report of the Joint Special Committee to Investigate Chinese Immigration. Sen. Rpt. 689, 44th Cong., 2d sess. Washington, DC, 1877.

Rogers, C. Lynn. *Making Camp Chinese Style: The Archaeology of a V&T Railroad Graders' Camp, Carson City, Nevada.* ARS Project No. 865. Report prepared by

Archaeological Research Services, Virginia City, NV, for Silver Oak Development Company, Carson City, NV, 1997.

Royal Commission on Chinese Immigration. *Report of the Royal Commission on Chinese Immigration: Report and Evidence.* Ottawa: Author, 1885.

Smith, Carrie E., and Kelly J. Dixon. *Determination of Eligibility for Inclusion in the National Register of Historic Places of 19 Historic Sites within the Heavenly Ski Resort, Douglas County, Nevada.* Report R2004-0519-00048 prepared for US Forest Service, Lake Tahoe Basin Management Unit, South Lake Tahoe and Heavenly Ski Resort, South Lake Tahoe, CA, 2005.

Stone, Lyle M., and Scott L. Fedick. *The Archaeology of Two Historic Homestead and Railroad Related Sites on the Southern Pacific Main Line Near Mobile, Maricopa County, AZ.* Report prepared for Dibble and Associates, Phoenix, AZ, by Archaeological Resources Services, Inc., Tempe, AZ, 1990.

Turner, Arnie. L. *The History and Archaeology of Fenelon, a Historic Railroad Camp.* Archaeological Studies in the Cortez Mining District, Technical Report No. 8. Reno, NV: US Bureau of Land Management, 1982.

Walter (Walker River Paiute Tribe). Interview by Edward C. Johnson. March 1, 1974. Walker River Tribal History Project: Oral History Interviews with Tribal Elders.

Zier, Charles D. *Archaeological Data Recovery Associated with the Mt. Hope Project, Eureka County, Nevada.* Cultural Resource Series No. 8. Reno, NV: US Bureau of Land Management, 1985.

Dissertations, Theses, and Manuscripts

Au, Beth Amity. "Home Means Nevada: The Chinese in Winnemucca, Nevada, 1870–1950, a Narrative History." Master's thesis, University of California, Los Angeles, 1993.

Billhimer, Ruth K. "Pawns of Fate: Chinese/Paiute Intercultural Marriages, 1860–1920, Walker River Reservation, Schurz, Nevada." Master's thesis, University of Nevada, Las Vegas, 1998.

Briggs, Alton K. "The Archaeology of 1882 Labor Camps on the Southern Pacific Railroad, Val Verde County, Texas." Master's thesis, University of Texas, Austin, 1974.

Cain, Julie A. "The Chinese and the Stanfords: Immigration Rhetoric in Nineteenth-Century California." Master's thesis, California State University, East Bay, June 2011.

Chang, Kornel. "Transpacific Borderlands and Boundaries: Race, Migration and State Formation in the North American Pacific Rim, 1882–1917." PhD diss., University of Chicago, 2007.

Cleveland, Daniel. "The Chinese in California." Unpublished manuscript. Mss. HM 72175–72177. Huntington Library, San Marino, CA.

Conley, Donald C. "The Pioneer Chinese of Utah." Master's thesis, Brigham Young University, 1976. Paper 4616, Manuscript Archive, Special Collections, Brigham Young University Library.

Gilcrest, Evelyn. "Alford Ranch [Eastern Oregon] Interlude." Unpublished manuscript. Bancroft Library, University of California at Berkeley, n.d.

Henry, Shea C. "Ni Chi Le Ma, Have You Eaten Yet? Analysis of Foodways from Market Street Chinatown, San Jose, California." Master's thesis, Department of Anthropology, University of Idaho, Moscow, 2012.

Hua, Jordan. "'They Looked Askance': American Indians and Chinese in the Nineteenth Century U.S. West." Honors thesis, Rutgers University, 2012. http://history.rutgers.edu/docman-docs/undergraduate/honors-papers-2012/402-they-looked-askance-american-indians-and-chinese-in-the-nineteenth-century-u-s-west/file.

Jolly, Elyse. "Chinese Gaming in the Nineteenth-Century American West: An Ethnic and Cultural Reassessment." Master's thesis, University of Nevada, Reno, 2012.

Kennedy, J. Ryan. "*Fan* and *Tsai:* Food, Identity, and Connections in the Market Street Chinatown." PhD diss., Department of Anthropology, Indiana University, Bloomington, 2016.

Keyser, Charles Paul. "Reminiscences of Elko—circa 1890." Unpublished manuscript 4-6-30. Northeastern Nevada Museum, Elko, 1958.

Locke, Marvin Elliott. "A History of the Nevada County Narrow Gauge Railroad." Master's thesis, University of California, Los Angeles, 1962.

MacNaughton, James W. "A Historical Investigation of Changing Ethnicity and Consumption Patterns at the Union Pacific Railroad Section Camp of Peru (48SW3795): How Changing Ethnicity Can Be Interpreted in a Nineteenth Century Railroad Landscape." Master's thesis, Illinois State University, Normal, 2012.

Madsen, Kristine. "17th Century Chinese Coin." Unpublished manuscript on file at University of Idaho Chemistry Department, Moscow, 2015.

Marden, Jay P. "The History of Winnemucca." Unpublished manuscript. Humboldt County Library, Winnemucca, NV, 2005.

Merritt, Christopher W. "'The Coming Man from Canton': Chinese Experience in Montana (1862–1943)." PhD diss., University of Montana, Missoula, 2010.

Miller, Charlotte T. "Grapes, Queues and Quicksilver." Unpublished manuscript. Napa City-County Library, Napa, CA, 1966.

Mudgett, Margaret Holt. "The Political Career of Leland Stanford." Master's thesis, Department of History, University of Southern California, January 1933. Special Collections, Green Library, Stanford University, Stanford, CA.

Schmidt, Ryan W. "The Forgotten Chinese Cemetery of Carlin, Nevada: A Bioanthropological Assessment." Master's thesis, Department of Anthropology, University of Nevada, Las Vegas, 2006.

Stevens, Todd. "Brokers between Worlds: Chinese, Merchants and Legal Culture in the Pacific Northwest, 1852–1925." PhD diss., Princeton University, Princeton, NJ, 2003.

Weisz, Gary. "Chinese Comparative Collection, Archaeology of the Overseas Chinese (A Pictorial Essay)." Vols. 1 and 2. Unpublished manuscript on file at Idaho State Preservation Office, Boise, 2014.

———. "Stepping Light: Revisiting the Construction Camps on the Lake Pend d'Oreille and Clark Fork Division of the Northern Pacific Railroad, 1879–1883." 3 vols. Unpublished manuscript on file at Idaho State Preservation Office, Boise, 2003.

Willumson, Glenn. "Alfred A. Hart: Photographer of the Transcontinental Railroad." Master's thesis, University of California, Davis, 1984.

Wrobleski, David Eugene. "The Archaeology of Chinese Work Camps on the Virginia and Truckee Railroad." Master's thesis, University of Nevada, Reno, 1996.

Wynne, Robert Edward. "Reaction to the Chinese in the Pacific Northwest and British Columbia, 1850–1910." PhD diss., University of Washington, Seattle, 1964.

Yingying Chen. "In the Colony of Tang: Historical Archaeology of Chinese Communities in the North Cariboo District, British Columbia, 1860s–1940s." PhD diss., Simon Fraser University, Burnaby, BC, 2002.

Conferences, Workshops, and Symposia

Chace, Paul G. "The Twelve Donner Cantonese Railroad Workers Camps, and the Lack of Sub-Ethnic Archaeological Markers within a Dominated Export-Import Market." Paper presented at the Chinese Railroad Workers in North America Project 2016 Conference, Stanford University, 2016.

Chace, Paul G., and William S. Evans Jr. "Celestial Sojourners in the High Sierras: The Ethno-Archaeology of Chinese Railroad Workers." Paper presented at the Annual Meeting of the Society for Historical Archaeology, Tucson, AZ, 1969.

Folch, Dolors. "Crime and Punishment: Ming Criminal Justice as Seen in Sixteenth-Century Spanish Sources." Paper presented at the World History Association Meeting, Beijing, July 9, 2011.

Hu-DeHart, Evelyn. "From Plantation to Chinatown: Hakka–Punti Relations in Cuba." Paper presented at the Changing Hakka Culture and Society Workshop, Hakka Research Department of Jiaying University, Meixian, Guangdong, China, May 7–9, 2014.

Merritt, Christopher W. "The Continental Backwaters of Chinese Railroad Worker

History and Archaeology: Perspectives from Montana and Utah." Paper presented at the Archaeology Network Workshop of the Chinese Railroad Workers in North America Project, Stanford University, Stanford, CA, October 11, 2013.

Molenda, John. "Aesthetically Oriented Archaeology." Paper presented at the Archaeology Network Workshop of the Chinese Railroad Workers in North America Project, Stanford University. Stanford, CA, October 11, 2013.

Stokeld, Rachel, and Mary Petrich-Guy. "Documenting Chinese Railroad Laborer Camps in Northern Idaho: A Professional/Amateur Collaboration." Paper presented at the 67th Annual Northwest Anthropological Conference, Bellingham, WA, 2014.

Voss, Barbara. "The Archaeology of Chinese Railroad Workers in North America." Paper presented at the Representing Chinese Railroad Workers in North America Workshop, Academia Sinica, Taipei, May 8, 2015.

Yu, Connie Young, and Barre Fong. "History from Descendants." Paper presented at the Conference of the Chinese Railroad Workers in North America Project at Stanford University, Stanford, CA, April 14–16, 2016.

Films and Videos

Su Xiaokang, Wang Luxiang, and Xia Jun, dir. *He Shang* [River Elegy]. Six-part documentary. 1988.

Online Sources

"The 1852 and 1881 Historical Censuses of Canada." Research Program in Historical Demography website. Accessed February 18, 2016. http://www.prdh.umontreal .ca/census/en/main.aspx.

"Bandung Conference," accessed September 18, 2018. https://www.britannica.com/ event/Bandung-Conference.

Chinese Historical Society of America. "Work of Giants." Online exhibit. Accessed September 13, 2013. www.chsa.org/exhibits/online-exhibits/work-of-giants.

Chinese in Northwest America Research Committee website. "Death: Dying, Funerals and Cemeteries in North America." Accessed October 26, 2015. http://www .cinarc.org/Death-2.html.

Chinese Railroad Workers in North America Project website. Accessed April 27, 2017. http://web.stanford.edu/group/chineserailroad/cgi-bin/wordpress/977/.

Choy, Philip P. "Interpreting 'Overseas Chinese' Ceramics Found on Historical Archaeology Sites: Manufacture, Marks, Classification, and Social Use." Society for Historical Archaeology Research Resources website. 2014. https://sha.org/ resources/chinese-ceramics/.

City of Deadwood, South Dakota, official website. Accessed July 11, 2016. http:// www.cityofdeadwood.com/index.asp.

Encyclopaedia Britannica, s.v. Baidu.com, s.v., "Ding Zemin," accessed January 15, 2016, http://baike.baidu.com/view/4912436.htm.

Fixico, Donald. "Interview: Native Americans." *American Experience* PBS website. Accessed February 18, 2016. http://amextbg2.wgbhdigital.org/wgbh/american experience/features/interview/tcrr-interview/.

Hansen, Mariam. "St. Helena's Chinese Heritage." June 2011. St. Helena Historical Society (California) website. Accessed April 26, 2017. http://shstory-oldsite .lyndabanks.net/wp-content/uploads/2011/12/Chinese-Heritage-of-St-Helena -by-Mariam-Hansen.pdf.

Institute of Modern China Studies, Chinese Social Science Academy. "A Debate between Zeng Yanxiu and Liu Danian on *A History of U.S. Aggression against China*" (in Chinese). Accessed April 13, 2016. http://jds.cass.cn/Item/8135.aspx.

Lehmann, Susan. "Transportation: Railroads and Streetcars." *Santa Cruz History*. Santa Cruz Public Libraries/Local History website. Accessed April 26, 2017. http://www.santacruzpl.org/history/articles/53/.

Library and Archives Canada. "Building the Canadian Pacific Railway." 2005. https://www.collectionscanada.gc.ca/settlement/kids/021013-2031.3-e.html.

Monterey County Historical Society website. "The Monterey & Salinas Valley Railroad." Accessed July 11, 2016. http://mchsmuseum.com/railroadm&sv.html.

Murphy, Deirdre. "'Like Standing on the Edge of the World and Looking Away into Heaven': Picturing Chinese Labor and Industrial Velocity in the Gilded Age." *Common-Place*. April 2007. http://www.common-place-archives.org/vol-07/ no-03/murphy/.

Nevada State Historic Preservation Office. Online database of Nevada's population, 1860–1920. Accessed April 20, 2107. https://library.unr.edu/census.

New York Times Learning Network. "On This Day: May 29, 1869." Accessed February 28, 2016. http://www.nytimes.com/learning/general/onthisday/harp/0529.html.

Olympia Historical Society website. "Olympia's Historic Chinese Community." Accessed April 27, 2017. http://olympiahistory.org/olympias-historic-chinese -community-links.

Peintres & Sculpteurs website. "Émile Malézieux." http://www.peintres-et-sculp teurs.com/biographie-384-malezieux-emile.html.

Reeder, Clarence A. Jr. *The History of Utah's Railroads, 1869–1883*. UtahRails.net website. Accessed April 26, 2017. http://utahrails.net/reeder/reeder-chap6.php.

Rhoads, Edward J. M. "Chinese." *Handbook of Texas Online*. Texas State Historical Association website. Accessed July 11, 2016. https://tshaonline.org/handbook/ online/articles/pjc01.

Stanford, Leland. "Inaugural Address." January 10, 1862. http://governors.library.ca .gov/addresses/08-Stanford.html.

Strobridge, Edson T. "The Chinese at Promontory, Utah April 30–May 10, 1869 (An

Extract from the Unfinished Biography of James H. Strobridge)." Accessed March 18, 2016. http://cprr.org/Museum/Chinese_at_Promontory_ETS.html.

Walla Walla 2020 website. "Walla Walla's Chinatown, 1860s–1950s—Once the Largest Chinese Community in Eastern Washington." Accessed April 27, 2017. http://ww2020.net/historic-sites/chinatown/.

Werner, George C. "Galveston, Harrisburg and San Antonio Railway." *Handbook of Texas Online.* Texas State Historical Association website. Accessed July 11, 2016. https://tshaonline.org/handbook/online/articles/eqg06.

Wilma, David. "Chelan County: Thumbnail History." *Historylink.* January 28, 2006. http://www.historylink.org/File/7624.

Xi Jinping. "Full Text of Xi Jinping's Speech on China–U.S. Relations in Seattle." *Xinhua Net.* September 24, 2015. http://news.xinhuanet.com/english/2015-09/24/c_134653326.htm.

Archives and Other Collections

"The Bank Intends to Set Up Offices in Honolulu: Investigative Report" (in Chinese), 1947–1948. Guangdong Bank Archives, no. 41, cat. no. 3, vol. 289, Guangdong Provincial Archives.

"The Bank Permits Guangdong Foreign Nationals to Open Branches" (in Chinese), 1947. Guangdong Bank Archives, no. 41, cat. no. 3, vol. 284, Guangdong Provincial Archives.

Chin Gee Hee. Immigration Case File, Box 9, No. 139-157, Chinese Exclusion Case File, RG85, ca. 1900–1920. National Archives, Pacific Alaska Region, Seattle.

Chinese Consolidated Benevolent Association fonds. University of Victoria Archives, Victoria, BC.

"Chinese in Tacoma." Box 1, file 3d. Washington Historical Society, Tacoma, WA.

Crocker, E. B., to Collis P. Huntington, June 27, 1867, and Mark Hopkins to Collis P. Huntington, June 27, 1867. Collis P. Huntington Papers, 1856–1904, microfilm, Stanford University Libraries.

Cultural Resources Protection Program. Confederated Tribes of the Umatilla Indian Reservation.

"Guangdong Uncovered a Theft Involving Compatriots' Postal Letters from Home, Impersonators Stealing Paper Money in Case after Case." Guangdong Provincial Archives, Post Office Archives, no. 29, cat. no. 2, vol. 367, 1949.

Hodges, Charles. "Reminiscences of Stanford University and Its Founders." Charles Hodges Papers, 1891–1929, no. 2499, SC0389, Stanford University Archives.

Huntington, Collis P., to Mark Hopkins, Leland Stanford, Charles Crocker, E. B. Crocker, Charles F. Crocker, and D. D. Cotton [*sic*], from August 20, 1867, to March 31, 1876. Huntington Library, San Marino, CA.

"Inspector Liang Chun's Investigation of Xinchang, Jiangmen Post Office. On

Improving the Central Jurisdiction and Countryside Postal Situation. Report 1948" (in Chinese), 1948. Post Office Archives, no. 29, vol. 229, Guangdong Provincial Archives.

Jue, Willard Papers. Chin Gee Hee Subgroup. University of Washington Special Collections, Seattle.

Oregon Central Railroad Records. Online Archive of California website. Accessed April 25, 2017. http://www.oac.cdlib.org/findaid/ark:/13030/c8p55q8m/.

Overseas Chinese letters, loan receipts, transfer deeds. Jiangmen Wuyi Overseas Chinese Museum.

"Overseas Compatriots' and Relatives' Addresses; Domestic Survey, Import and Export Statistics; Overseas Postal" (in Chinese), 1948. Post Office Archives, no. 29, cat. no. 2, vol. 372, Guangdong Provincial Archives.

Owyang Ming. November 5, 1885. Notes from the Chinese Legation in the United States to the Department of State, 1863–1906, microfilm, vol. 2, no. 98, RG39, M98. Pacific Regional Branch of the National Archives, San Bruno, CA.

[San Francisco] Earthquake (1906) Collection. Special Collections, Green Library, Stanford University.

Seymour, Charles, to C. P. Huntington, August 20, 1870. Chesapeake and Ohio Railroad Company Papers. Western Reserve Historical Society, Cleveland.

Stanford Family Scrapbooks, 1865–1894 (SC033). Special Collections, Green Library, Stanford University.

Stanford Historical Photograph Collection (SC1071). Special Collections, Green Library, Stanford University.

Stanford Papers. Special Collections, Green Library, Stanford University.

Timebook. Sierra Valley & Mohawk Railroad Collection, 1886–1887. California State Railroad Museum, Sacramento.

List of Contributors

GORDON H. CHANG is professor of history at Stanford University and the Olive H. Palmer Professor of Humanities. Among his books are *Friends and Enemies: The United States, China, and the Soviet Union, 1948–1972*; *Morning Glory, Evening Shadow: The Wartime Writing of Yamato Ichihashi, 1942–1945*; and *Fateful Times: A History of America's Preoccupation with China*. He has published many essays on America-China interactions during the Cold War, and on Asian American history. He is the editor of *Asian Americans and Politics: Perspectives, Experiences, Prospects*, coeditor of *Chinese American Voices: From the Gold Rush to the Present*, and coeditor of *Asian American Art: A History, 1850–1970*. He has been a fellow of the Guggenheim Foundation, the American Council of Learned Societies, and, three times, the Stanford Humanities Center.

ZHONGPING CHEN is professor of Chinese history and the history of the global Chinese diaspora at the University of Victoria. He has published dozens of journal articles and four books in Chinese and English, including *Modern China's Network Revolution: Chambers of Commerce and Sociopolitical Change in the Early Twentieth Century*. His most recent publication is an edited volume of conference proceedings (in Chinese), *Toward a Multicultural Global History: Zheng He's Maritime Voyages (1405–1433) and China's Relations with the Indian Ocean World*. He is currently working on a new book entitled "The Rise, Reform and Revolution of the Transpacific Chinese Diaspora, 1878–1918."

SUE FAWN CHUNG taught for thirty-nine years at the University of Nevada, Las Vegas, and became professor emerita in 2014. Born and raised in Los Angeles, she has a long-standing interest in Chinese American history and wrote her University of California, Los Angeles senior honors thesis on the Chinese American Citizens Alliance. She received her master's from Harvard and her doctorate from the University of California, Berkeley. She has worked with community leaders in recognizing the efforts of Chinese railroad workers in the dedication of commemorative plaques in places such as Cape Horn near Colfax, California, and Sparks, Nevada. She is the author of two recent books, *In Pursuit of Gold: Chinese Miners and Merchants in the American West* (2011) and *The Chinese in the Woods: Logging and Lumbering in the American West* (2015).

JOHN J. CRANDALL, a bioarchaeologist and ethnohistorian, is a PhD candidate at the University of Nevada, Las Vegas. His research interests include inequality, the body, and ethnic violence in the American West and the precontact Americas. He is the coeditor of *Tracing Childhood: Bioarchaeological Investigations of Early Lives in Antiquity* and has coedited special issues of the *Cambridge Archaeological Journal* and *International Journal of Paleopathology*.

KELLY J. DIXON is an archaeologist and professor of anthropology at the University of Montana. Her research and publications include case studies of archaeological sites that date from the past several centuries, and those that include sites and landscapes indicative of overseas Chinese contributions to the history of the American West. Dixon's recent research emphasizes the ways in which archaeological investigations of the modern world can help democratize the histories of people who have been marginalized in mainstream presentations of the past.

PIN-CHIA FENG is chair and professor in the Department of Foreign Languages and Literatures at National Chiao Tung University (NCTU); research fellow at the Institute of European and American Studies, Academia Sinica (joint appointment); and adjunct distinguished professor at Chung Hua University. Currently, she is also the director of NCTU's Asian American Studies Research Center. Her monograph *Diasporic Representations: Reading Chinese American Women's Fiction* received Academia Sinica's Scholarly Monograph Award in the Humanities and Social Sciences (2012). Feng earned her PhD in English from the University of Wisconsin–Madison (1994). She writes on issues of gender, race, and representation in films, as well as on Asian American, African American, and Afro-Caribbean literature.

SHELLEY FISHER FISHKIN is the Joseph S. Atha Professor of Humanities, a professor of English, and the director of American Studies at Stanford University. She is the author, editor, or coeditor of forty-seven books and has published more than one hundred articles, essays, and reviews. Many of her books and articles have focused on issues of race and racism in America and on recovering previously silenced voices from the past. Her books have won two Outstanding Academic Title awards from *Choice*. She holds a PhD in American studies from Yale, is past president of the American Studies Association, and is a founding editor of the *Journal of Transnational American Studies*.

KATHRYN GIN LUM is an assistant professor of religious studies, in collaboration with the Center for Comparative Studies in Race and Ethnicity, and history (by courtesy), at Stanford University. She is the author of *Damned Nation: Hell in America from the Revolution to Reconstruction* (2014) and coeditor, with Paul Harvey, of *The Oxford Handbook of Religion and Race in American History* (2018). She is currently working on a book tentatively titled "The Heathen World and America's Humanitarian Impulse."

WILLIAM GOW is a San Francisco–based historian, filmmaker, and educator. Currently a doctoral candidate in ethnic studies, Gow's dissertation is tentatively titled "Performing Chinatown: Hollywood Cinema, Tourism, and the Making of a Los Angeles Community, 1931–1949." His project developed out of the time he spent serving as a volunteer public historian and board member with the Chinese Historical Society of Southern California (CHSSC), a community-based nonprofit in Los Angeles Chinatown. His written work on Chinese American genealogical research, community history, and documentary filmmaking has appeared in *Amerasia Journal, Chinese America: History and Perspective,* and the CHSSC's *Gum Saan Journal.*

RYAN P. HARROD is an assistant professor of anthropology at the University of Alaska Anchorage. He has coauthored and coedited several books, including *The Bioarchaeology of Climate Change and Violence* (coauthored with Debra Martin, 2014), *Bioarchaeology: An Integrated Approach to Working with Human Remains* (coauthored with Debra Martin and Ventura Perez, 2013), and *The Bioarchaeology of Violence* (coedited with Debra Martin and Ventura Perez, 2012). He serves on editorial boards for the book series Bioarchaeology and Social Theory at Springer Press, and for the journals *International Journal of Osteoarchaeology*, *Landscapes of Violence*, and *Alaska Natives Studies*.

SARAH HEFFNER, PhD, is a senior historical archaeologist at PAR Environmental Services, Inc., in Sacramento, California. She has published six papers and a book and has given presentations at more than fifteen state, regional, and national anthropological and archaeological conferences. Her research interests are diverse and include historical archaeology and material culture studies, overseas Chinese, collections research, and oral history.

ROLAND HSU is the author and editor of multiple works on migration, social and political integration, and ethnic identity. His edited books include *Ethnic Europe: Mobility, Identity, and Conflict in a Globalized World* (2010) and *Migration and Integration: New Models for Mobility and Coexistence* (2016). His pieces on migration and geopolitics have appeared in scholarly collections and journals of contemporary affairs, including *Le Monde Diplomatique*. Hsu is the director of research of the Chinese Railroad Workers in North America Project at Stanford. He earned his PhD at the University of Chicago and was assistant professor of history at the University of Idaho.

HSINYA HUANG is provost for academic affairs and faculty advancement and professor of American and comparative literature at National Sun Yat-sen University, Taiwan. She is the author or editor of books and articles, published in Taiwan and abroad, on Native American and indigenous literatures, ecocriticism, and postcolonial and ethnic studies. These works include *(De)Colonizing the Body: Disease, Empire, and (Alter)Native Medicine in Contemporary Native American Women's Writings* (2004); *Huikan beimei yuanzhumin wenxue: duoyuan wenhua de shengsi* (Native North American Literatures: Reflections on Multiculturalism, 2009), the first Chinese essay collection on Native North American literature; *Aspects of Transnational and Indigenous Cultures* (2014); and *Ocean and Literature* (2016). She edited the English translation of *The History of Taiwanese Indigenous Literatures* and is currently editing *Ocean and Ecology in the Trans-Pacific Context*.

EVELYN HU-DEHART is professor of history, American studies, and ethnic studies at Brown University, where she was also the director of the Center for the Study of Race and Ethnicity in America from 2002 to 2014. In 2014–2015 she directed the Consortium for Advanced Study Abroad in Havana, Cuba.

Born in China, she arrived in the United States as a child refugee, grew up in Palo Alto, attended Stanford University, and received her PhD in Latin America/Caribbean history from the University of Texas at Austin. She is the author and editor of more than ten books and sixty articles in English, Spanish, and Chinese. Her body of work has focused on two main topics: indigenous peoples of the United States–Mexico borderlands and the Chinese diaspora in Latin America and the Caribbean.

J. RYAN KENNEDY is a zooarchaeologist who has studied animal bones from both urban (Market Street Chinatown) and rural (Aspen Section Camp) Chinese immigrant archaeological sites. His research explores how Chinese immigrants localized their food practices to life in North America and how food practices linked Chinese immigrant communities to other peoples and places via the trade of food items such as salt fish. He is currently a visiting scholar at Tulane University.

DENISE KHOR is an assistant professor of American studies at the University of Massachusetts Boston (UMB), where she specializes in Asian American history and the history of film, photography, and media. Prior to her arrival at UMB, she held an Ethnicity, Race, and Migration postdoctoral fellowship in the Department of Film and Media Studies at Yale University. She is also the former research director of Stanford University's Chinese Railroad Workers in North America Project. Her first book project (currently in progress), "Pacific Theater: Movie-Going and Migration in Asian America 1907 to 1950," explores the historical experiences of Japanese and Japanese Americans at the cinema during the first half of the twentieth century.

BETH LEW-WILLIAMS is an assistant professor of history at Princeton University. She is a historian of race and migration in the United States, specializing in the study of Asian Americans. She is the author of *The Chinese Must Go: Racial Violence and the Making of the Alien in America* (2018). Lew-Williams earned her AB from Brown University and PhD in history from Stanford University. She has held fellowships from the Harry Frank Guggenheim Foundation, the Andrew W. Mellon Foundation, and the American Council of Learned Societies.

LIU JIN is professor of history at Guangdong Qiaoxiang Cultural Research Center at Wuyi University in China. His research currently focuses on *qiaoxiang* documental materials, including remittance letters, account books, bills, contracts, confession papers, and *qiaokan*. His recent publications include *Taishan Yinxin, Wuyi Yinxin*, and *Yinxin and the Wuyi Qiaoxiang Society* (in Chinese). He is the editor of *Selected Archival Materials on Overseas Remittance in Jiangmen City* and *Comparing, Referencing, and Looking Forward: Research on International Migration Letters* (in Chinese).

HILTON OBENZINGER is a critic, poet, novelist, and historian, as well as the recipient of the American Book Award. He is the author of *American Palestine: Melville, Twain, and the Holy Land Mania; Cannibal Eliot and the Lost Histories of San Francisco; New York on Fire*; and other books, as well as articles in scholarly journals on American Holy Land travel, the history of California, Mark Twain, Herman Melville, and American cultural interactions with the Middle East. Among his most recent books is the autobiographical novel *Busy Dying*. He has taught writing and American studies at Stanford University and is currently the associate director of the Chinese Railroad Workers in North America Project.

VIRGINIA POPPER is an archaeologist who specializes in paleoethnobotany. She is a research associate at the Fiske Center for Archaeological Research, University of Massachusetts Boston, and a visiting scientist at the Center for Materials Research in Archaeology and Ethnology, Massachusetts Institute of Technology. Her research includes investigations of foodways at historic sites in California (such as Market Street Chinatown, San Bernardino Chinatown, the Rancho Mission Vieja de la Purisima, and the Presidio of San Francisco) and at the Jacksonville Chinese Quarter Site in Oregon.

GREG ROBINSON is a professor of history at the Université du Québec à Montréal. He is a specialist in North American ethnic studies and US political history, and his books include *By Order of the President* (2001), which uncovers President Franklin Roosevelt's central involvement in the wartime confinement of 120,000 Japanese Americans, and *A Tragedy of Democracy* (2009), which studies Japanese American and Japanese Canadian confinement in a transnational context and was the winner of the 2009 American Association for the Advancement of Science history book award. His book *After Camp* (2012), which centers on postwar resettlement, was the winner of the Caroline Bancroft History Prize.

YUAN SHU is an associate professor of English and comparative literature and director of the Asian Studies Program at Texas Tech University. He has published articles in journals varying from *Cultural Critique* to *MELUS,* from *College Literature* to *Amerasia Journal.* He has coedited two essay volumes, *American Studies as Transnational Practice: Turning toward the Pacific* (with Donald E. Pease, 2015) and *Oceanic Archives and Transnational American Studies* (with Otto Heim and Kendall Johnson). His manuscript "Empire and Geopolitics: Technology, Transpacific Movements, and Chinese American Writing" is under review at a university press.

BARBARA L. VOSS is an associate professor of anthropology at Stanford University. Her current research projects include the Market Street Chinatown Archaeology Project in San Jose, California (principal investigator); the interdisciplinary Chinese Railroad Workers of North America Project (director of archaeology); and Research Cooperation on Home Cultures of Nineteenth-Century Overseas Chinese (coprincipal investigator, with Dr. Jinhua [Selia] Tan). Voss's publications include *Archaeologies of Sexuality* (coedited with Robert A. Schmidt, 2000), *The Archaeology of Ethnogenesis* (2008), *The Archaeology of Colonialism: Intimate Encounters and Sexual Effects* (coedited with Eleanor Casella, 2012), and two thematic issues of the journal *Historical Archaeology,* The Archaeology of Chinese Immigrant and Chinese American Communities (coedited with Bryn Williams, 2008) and The Archaeology of Chinese Railroad Workers in North America (2015).

YUAN DING is a professor of history and the director of the East Asian Studies Center of Sun Yat-sen University, Guangzhou, China. He is the executive director of the Guangdong Overseas Chinese Historical Society, vice president of the Guangdong Overseas Chinese Study Association, executive director of the China Southeast Asian Studies Association, and associate editor in chief of the Guangdong Overseas Chinese History Project. The project utilizes historical materials of Guangdong Chinese immigrants to conduct a systematic and comprehensive survey of social and economic development, assimilation, and contribution of these immigrants to their migrated countries. His publications include *Overseas Chinese Affairs and Negotiations between China and Foreign Countries in the Late Qing Dynasty* and *Study on Modern Overseas Affairs Policy* (in Chinese).

ZHANG GUOXIONG is the director of the Guangdong Qiaoxiang Cultural Research Center and a professor at Wuyi University in China. He has long been engaged in researching the history of overseas Chinese, *qiaoxiang* culture, and world heritage studies. His major works include the coauthored *Wuyi Overseas Chinese History, Research on Kaiping Diaolou and Villages, Chikan Town, Liang Xi Village* (in Chinese); and *Taishan Confession Papers* (in Chinese), as well as the edited collection *Research on Chinese Qiaoxiang* (in Chinese).

Index

Page numbers followed by *t* indicate a table and those followed by *f* indicate a figure.